D1035348

ECONOMICS
IN OUR TIMES

WEST'S COMMITMENT TO THE ENVIRONMENT

In 1906, West Publishing Company began recycling materials left over from the production of books. This began a tradition of efficient and responsible use of resources. Today, up to 95 percent of our legal books and 70 percent of our college and school texts are printed on recycled, acid-free stock. West also recycles nearly 22 million pounds of scrap paper annually—the equivalent of 181,717 trees. Since the 1960s, West has devised ways to capture and recycle waste inks, solvents, oils, and vapors created in the printing process. We also recycle plastics of all kinds, wood, glass, corrugated cardboard, and batteries, and have eliminated the use of Styrofoam book packaging. We at West are proud of the longevity and the scope of our commitment to the environment.

Production, Prepress, Printing, and Binding by West Publishing Company.

COPYRIGHT © 1995 By WEST PUBLISHING COMPANY

610 Opperman Drive
P.O. Box 64526
St. Paul, MN 55164-0526

Library of Congress Cataloging-in-Publication Data

Arnold, Roger A.
    Economics / Roger A. Arnold.
        p.   cm.
    Includes index.
    ISBN 0-314-02901-X (student edition)
    1. Economics.   I. Title.
HB171.5.A695   1995
330—dc20
                              93-32249
                              ∞ CIP

Printed with **Printwise**
Environmentally Advanced Water Washable Ink

ART: Precision Graphics
COMPOSITION: American Composition & Graphics, Inc.

Acknowledgments

Cover Images: © Comstock, Inc., Tom Grill; © Tom Van Sant/Geosphere Project, Santa Monica/Science Photo Library, Photo Researchers, Inc.;

Chapter 1
1 © Seth Resnick, 1994; 3 © F. Hibon, Sygma; 5 (left and right) © David Young-Wolff, PhotoEdit; 8 © Tom Van Sant/Geosphere Project, Santa Monica/Science Photo Library, Photo Researchers, Inc.; 10 AP/Wide World Photos; 11 (left and right) © Mary Kate Denny, PhotoEdit; 18 (top left) © Mike J. Howell, The Picture Cube; (top right) © Billy E. Barnes, PhotoEdit; (bottom left) © Kevin Horan, Stock, Boston, Inc.; (bottom right) © Courtesy of Next Computers; 19 Wide World Photos, Inc.; 24 © Michael Newman, PhotoEdit;

Chapter 2
31 © John Coletti, Stock, Boston, Inc.; 33 (top) © Michael Newman, PhotoEdit; (bottom left) © Mark Richards, PhotoEdit; (bottom right) Courtesy of Apple Computers, Inc.; 36 © Bettmann Archives; 38 (left) © Alan Singer, CBS Inc.; (right) © Eddie Adams, Sygma; 40 John Coletti, The Picture Cube; 41 © Amanda Merulla, Stock, Boston, Inc.; 43 © Bettmann Archives; 45 (left) © Bill Nation, Sygma; (right) © E. Pitchal, Sygma;

Chapter 3
59 Tony Freeman, PhotoEdit; 64 © David Young-Wolff, PhotoEdit; 67 © Focus on Sports; 71 © Tony Freeman, PhotoEdit; 72 Courtesy of Sonia Melara, CommuniQue World Marketing, Inc.; 80 © P. Perrin, Sygma; 81 © Bob Daemmrich, Stock, Boston, Inc.;

Chapter 4
91 © Robert Brenner, PhotoEdit; 95 © Pat & Tom Leeson, Photo Researchers, Inc.; 98 © Carolyn Hine, The Picture Cube; 99 © Brown Brothers; 101 © AP/Wide World Photos, inc.; 104 © Gilles Mingason, Gamma Liaison; 105 Tony Freeman, PhotoEdit; 109 © Tampa Tribune, Sygma;

Chapter 5
114 © Mazzaschi, Stock, Boston, Inc.; 117 © Gerald Ranginan, Sygma; 118 © Patrick Forestier, Sygma; 128 Bart Richmond; 132 © J.P. Laffont, Sygma; 136 © Paul Conklin, PhotoEdit; 138 © Darryl Estrine;

Chapter 6
147 © Ken Lax, Photo Researchers, Inc.; 149 © J. P. Laffont, Sygma; 150 Courtesy of the Schomburg Center for Research in Black Culture, The New York Public Library; 152 © Charles Nelan, The New York Herald, Brown Brothers; 153 © Frank Siteman, The Picture Cube; 154 © Brown Brothers; 155 © Brown Brothers; 161 © Michael Newman, PhotoEdit;

ECONOMICS
IN OUR TIMES

ROGER A. ARNOLD
California State University San Marcos

WEST PUBLISHING COMPANY
MINNEAPOLIS/ST. PAUL   NEW YORK   LOS ANGELES   SAN FRANCISCO

ABOUT THE AUTHOR

Professor Roger Arnold is first and foremost an economics educator, having taught a variety of economics courses at several major universities. He has also served for many years as Director for a Center for Economic Education. He currently teaches at California State University in San Marcos, California, where he is Chairperson of the Economics Department.

Professor Arnold received his Bachelor of Social Science degree from the University of Birmingham, England, and his Master's and Doctorate degrees from Virginia Polytechnic Institute and State University. He completed his Ph.D. dissertation under Nobel Laureate James M. Buchanan.

Professor Arnold is an experienced teacher, researcher, and writer. He has written numerous successful textbooks, as well as articles and columns for *The Wall Street Journal* and other respected publications.

DEDICATION
To Walter V. Arnold, my father, in loving memory

EDITORIAL REVIEW BOARD

PREFACE

There are many different reasons and ways to write a book. I wanted to write a book that would capture the excitement and relevance of economics in today's world. To accomplish this goal, I knew that it would be necessary to help you, the reader, both understand and also feel what economics is all about. Both the mind and the heart are valid parts of the total learning experience.

There has never been a more exciting time to write a book about economics than now. Economics plays a large role in Russia, China, and Eastern European countries as they move from one economic system to another. International economic agreements are on the front page of newspapers all over the world, and often lead stories about economic issues are on the TV nightly news. Increasingly, the condition of the economy influences choices about who is elected to public office.

Not only is economics involved in world events, it also largely influences our daily lives. It touches our livelihoods, our hopes, and our dreams. Interest rates may sound like a rather dry topic to some. However, when we realize that interest rates determine whether people can afford to buy a house, it becomes central to life. The unemployment rate is a statistic, a number. But its importance looms large if we realize how it affects people's incomes, their self-esteem, their families, and more. Looked at in this way the unemployment rate takes on a human dimension. We can see how economics and people's lives are intertwined.

This is an economics book—no doubt about it. But below the surface, is a story about people. People buying and selling goods, people working and hiring other people to work at jobs, people starting families and building houses, people farming, and people working to make their lives better. In short, it is a book about us and our everyday lives.

Customarily, economics is presented in one of two ways. One way is to present economics as a series of topics such as unemployment, inflation, interest rates, trade deficits, budget deficits, prices, costs, and more. A second way presents economics as a way of thinking. For the most part, throughout this book I have taken this second approach.

What is the economic way of thinking? In general, the economic way of thinking refers to the way economists view, interpret, and analyze the world. Consider an analogy from the field of architecture. Suppose you see a skyscraper in New York City. With your untrained eye you see only a building that rises high into the sky. Architects see much more. They see a certain form and style, the strength and integrity of the design, the way the geometric shapes have come together to create an atmosphere and a mood. Architects see things others cannot. So it is with economists. In a grocery store you may see shelves of food. Economists see more. They see buyers and sellers having come together to determine what goods will be produced and at what prices the goods will be sold. Economists see cost and production, buyers and sellers trying to make themselves better off, profit and loss. Economists see the process that results in the shelves of food in much the same way that architects see the process that creates the skyscraper.

As you read this book, I hope you will come to understand that economics is more than just a series of topics. It can be the lens which provides a clearer, more exciting image of our lives and the world in our times.

CONTENTS IN BRIEF

CONTENTS

CONTENTS

CONTENTS

The Economy of the United States 252

CONTENTS

UNIT 4
The Global Economy 396

UNIT
5

Consumer Economics 470

CONTENTS

The Resource Center R-1

LIST OF FEATURES

CASE STUDIES

DEVELOPING ECONOMIC SKILLS

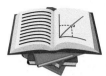

ANALYZING PRIMARY SOURCES

ECONOMIC FOCUSES

CONSUMER ECONOMIC DECISIONS

ECONOMICS AND PEOPLE

Exhibits, Graphs, Tables, and Maps

Exhibits, Graphs, Tables, and Maps

ECONOMICS
IN OUR TIMES

Introduction to Economics

Economics in Today's World

INTRODUCTION

Why learn economics? An economist would readily answer: economics is an interesting subject, a rewarding subject, and a subject that provides insights into the way the world works.

These claims are true, but they could be made about many other subjects. Is there any more urgent reason to study economics? Just look around you, and you'll see why it is important to learn this subject.

■ Economics is on the minds of the president of the United States and the members of the U.S. Congress.

■ Economics is on the minds of the nation's business and union leaders.

■ Economics is on the mind of the person buying a house, the person buying a car, the person starting a new business.

■ Economics is on the mind of the high-school student looking for a summer job.

Doesn't it make sense to learn about something that is so important to so many people, including yourself?

открытие ресторана
31 января 1990 г.

McDonald's

1. Explain how economists think.
2. Define *scarcity* and explain how it affects your daily life.
3. Explain why everybody has to make choices.
4. Define *opportunity cost* and explain how it relates to your everyday actions.
5. Identify the four resources that are used to produce goods.
6. Discuss the three economic questions that every society must answer.
7. Discuss the major differences between free enterprise and socialism.

KEY TERMS

Capital	Land
Economic Plan	Macroeconomics
Economic System	Microeconomics
Economics	Mixed Economy
Entrepreneurship	Opportunity Cost
Free Enterprise	Resource
Global Economy	Scarcity
Income	Socialism
Distribution	Tangible
Intangible	Utility
Labor	Want

SECTION 1   THINKING LIKE AN ECONOMIST

You may be wondering if economics is like any subject you have studied before—such as government, social studies, or history. The answer is yes, in that some of the topics you studied in these courses are topics you will study in your economics course. You will be familiar with other topics discussed in economics from your daily life. For example, economics deals with people who buy products, people who work, people who make choices, and so on. These are things that you do: you buy products, you work (perhaps at a job or at doing your homework), and you make countless choices.

What is different about economics is not so much *what* is studied but *how* it is studied. Through your study of economics, you will acquire new *tools*, *concepts*, and *ways of thinking*. You will then use these tools, concepts, and ways of thinking to analyze many topics with which you are already familiar. In this section, we focus on *how economists think*.

As you read, keep these key questions in mind:

- How do economists think about the world?
- What is opportunity cost?
- How does macroeconomics differ from microeconomics?

Thinking in Terms of Costs and Benefits

According to an economist, there are costs and benefits to almost everything we do. For example, an economist would ask: What are the costs and benefits of learning economics? Next, she would want to know whether the benefits were greater or less than the costs. According to the economist, if the benefits are greater than the costs, then it is worthwhile to learn economics; but if the costs are greater than the benefits, it isn't. So in order to decide whether it is worthwhile to learn economics, we have to know what the costs and benefits of learning economics will likely be.

In economics, the cost of anything—learning economics, driving a car, or buying a house—is the most highly valued opportunity or alternative you forfeit, or give up, when you make a choice. For example, let's consider something that we already know you have chosen to do. A few minutes ago, you chose to read this chapter. What is the *cost* of reading this chapter? An economist would say that the cost is what you would be doing if you weren't reading it. For example, suppose you would be watching television. In short, this is the most highly valued opportunity or alternative you gave up to read this chapter. It follows that watching television is the cost (to you) of reading this chapter.

Many people think of the word *cost* as meaning *money*. For instance, in thinking about the cost of reading this chapter, you may at first have thought of a cost like $5, $10, or $15. In economics, though, cost means something different. As we have just seen, it means the *opportunity* you forfeit, or give up, when you choose to do something. Because the word *opportunity* is very important here, economists often use the term **opportunity cost** instead of simply *cost*.

Let's rephrase our original question: What are the *benefits* and *opportunity costs* of learning economics? The opportunity costs are different for different people, since what one person gives up to learn economics is not always what someone else gives up. For example, if Maria didn't learn economics, perhaps she would learn chemistry. If Dave didn't learn economics, perhaps he would learn history. Finally, if Bob didn't learn economics, perhaps he would not learn anything at all; perhaps he would just take it easy.

What are the benefits of learning economics? The biggest benefit is gaining the ability to see things going on in the world that you cannot see now. This brings us to the next topic in our consideration of how economists think.

▲ What is the opportunity cost of the young woman working at the computer? If, instead of working at the computer, she were playing soccer, then playing soccer would be the opportunity cost of her working at the computer.

Thinking in Terms of What Would Have Been

Most people have the ability to think in terms of what was (the past), what is (the present), and what will be (the future). Economists think in these terms, too; then they add at least one more—thinking in terms of *what would have been*.

Suppose the federal government builds a new interstate highway system. It hires thousands of people to work on the project. The newspapers in the towns the interstate highway passes through report on all the increased job activity. It looks as if there are more people working on road construction and no fewer people working at anything else. It also appears that there are more highways and nothing less of anything else (no fewer cameras, computers, cars, and so on). We might conclude

that we have gained the benefits of more jobs and highways without paying an opportunity cost.

However, we need to remind ourselves that someone had to pay for the new interstate highway system—namely, the taxpayers. What did the taxpayers give up by paying their taxes? They gave up the opportunity to buy more clothes, computers, books, and so on. We now begin to think in terms of all the products that would have been produced and consumed had the highway not been built. And if, say, more clothes would have been produced had the highway not been built, it follows that more

MINI GLOSSARY

Opportunity Cost The most highly valued opportunity or alternative forfeited or given up when a choice is made.

Noneconomic way of thinking	Economic way of thinking
There is one more interstate highway system in the world and nothing less of anything else.	There is one more interstate highway system in the world and less of some other things.

◀ **EXHIBIT 1-1. The Noneconomic and Economic Way of Thinking About a New Interstate Highway System.** The person who thinks like an economist understands that there is one more interstate highway system and less of some other things. The person who does not think like an economist mistakenly thinks that there is one more interstate highway system and nothing less of anything else.

people would have worked in the clothing industry. So we begin to think in terms of all the people that would have worked in the clothing industry had the highway not been built. In short, we begin to think in terms of *what would have been*. It is important to be able to think in terms of what would have been, because only then do we know the opportunity costs for what is. (See Exhibit 1-1.)

QUESTION: *Because the new interstate highway system was built, people had to give up the opportunity to buy as many clothes, computers, books, and so on. The costs of the interstate highway system seem high. Does it follow that it would have been better if the federal government hadn't built the new interstate highway system?*

ANSWER: *Not necessarily. Remember, an economist thinks in terms of costs and benefits—not costs only. The things that "would have been" (had the interstate highway system not been built) relate to the costs of the highway system. It is still possible for the benefits of building the new interstate highway system to be greater than the costs. In short, it does not necessarily follow that*

things would have been better if the federal government hadn't built the interstate highway system.

Thinking in Terms of Unintended Effects

Has anything turned out differently from what you intended? No doubt you can provide numerous examples. Economists think in terms of unintended effects. Suppose, for example, that on an average day a shoe store sells 100 pairs of shoes at an average price of $40 a pair. On an average day, then, it earns $4,000 (100 pairs of shoes × $40 = $4,000). One day the store owner decides to raise the price of shoes from an average of $40 to $50. What does he intend or expect the effect of this action to be? He probably expects to increase his earnings from $4,000 a day to some greater amount. Perhaps he intends to increase his earnings to $5,000 (100 pairs of shoes × $50 = $5,000). But this may not occur. At a higher price, it is very likely that the shoe store owner will sell fewer pairs of shoes. Let's suppose that at a price of $50 a pair, the shoe store owner sells an average of 70 pairs of shoes a day. What are his average daily earnings now? They are $3,500 (since 70 pairs of shoes $\times$ $50 = $3,500). The shoe store owner did not intend for things to turn out this way. He intended to increase his earnings by raising the price of shoes. The decrease in his earnings is an unintended effect of his actions.

Consider another example to illustrate the idea of unintended effects. Suppose there are two nations, the United States and Japan. Currently, people in the United States are buying some goods produced in Japan (such as Japanese cars), and people in Japan are buying some goods produced in the United States (such as U.S. computers). Then, things change: the Japanese government decides to place a $200 tax (or tariff) on every U.S. computer sold in Japan. (A tax on foreign goods imported into a nation is called a *tariff*.) In short, any person in Japan who buys a U.S. computer will have to pay $200 more than he or she would have paid without the tax (tariff). Why might the Japanese government do this? It may want Japanese computers to outsell U.S. computers; it may want to generate higher profits and greater employment in the Japanese computer industry. To accomplish these goals, it deliberately makes U.S. computers more expensive than Japanese computers, by way of placing the tariff on U.S. computers. This ends up hurting U.S. computer companies because they sell fewer computers.

The United States could decide to retaliate, or return like for like. Suppose the U.S. government places a tariff on Japanese cars sold in the United States. This will make Japanese cars more expensive in the United States and fewer will be sold. This action will hurt Japanese car companies.

What we have is this: Japan initially takes an action—placing a tariff on U.S. computers sold in Japan—in the hopes of getting the Japanese people to buy more Japanese computers and fewer U.S. computers. This is the intended effect of the action. Furthermore, let's say that the intended effect is realized: the Japanese people actually do buy more Japanese computers and fewer U.S. computers.

But there is an unintended effect, too. It is the U.S. placing a tariff on Japanese cars, which ends up hurting Japanese car companies. When the Japanese placed a tariff on U.S. computers, they did not intend for the United States to retaliate and place a tariff on Japanese cars. This was an unintended effect of their actions.

Do unintended effects matter? Yes, they do, since they are part of the whole picture. Economists think in terms of the full effects of any action—both intended and unintended.

Thinking in Terms of a Global Economy

Many economists think in terms of a **global economy**, an economy in which economic actions taken anywhere in the world may affect your standard of living. To illustrate, economists often talk loosely about an economy being healthy or sick. When an economy is "healthy," people are buying and selling goods, factories are being built, most people who want to work are working, and so on. When an economy is "sick," people are not buying or selling as much, factories are not being built, and people who want to work are unemployed.

Now suppose that the Japanese, German, Mexican, and Canadian economies are sick. The people in these nations are not buying as much as they would buy if their economies were healthy. Some of the things they are no longer buying are things produced in other countries, such as the United States. Because Americans are not selling as many products in Japan, Germany, Mexico, and Canada, they do not earn as much income. Some U.S. workers may even lose their jobs because the businesses they work for are not selling as much to people in other nations. In turn, the U.S. economy may become a little sick. No doubt Americans do not want the economic illness

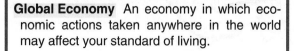

MINI GLOSSARY

Global Economy An economy in which economic actions taken anywhere in the world may affect your standard of living.

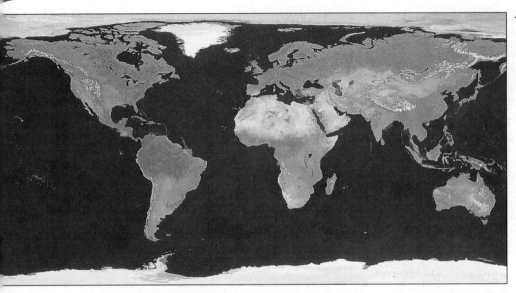

◀ Many economists think in terms of the global economy, in which economic actions taken anywhere in the world may affect your standard of living.

of other nations to come to the United States, in much the same way you might not want to catch a cold from the person sitting next to you in class. But wishing will not make it so. Just like real colds, economic "colds" are often contagious.

Fortunately, economic health can be contagious, too. If the Japanese, German, Mexican, and Canadian economies get well, and the people in these nations start to buy more goods, they may end up buying more U.S. goods, thus helping U.S. businesses and American workers.

Thinking in Terms of the Small and the Big

Economics is divided into two branches—**microeconomics** and **macroeconomics**. In *micro*economics, economists look at the small picture. They study the behavior and choices of relatively small economic units, such as the individual or a single business firm. In *macro*economics, economists look at the big picture. They study behavior and choices as they relate to the entire economy. For example, in microeconomics, an economist would study and discuss the unemployment that exists in a particular industry, such as the car indus-

try; in macroeconomics, an economist would study and discuss the unemployment that exists in the nation. In microeconomics, an economist would study the buying behavior of consumers in regard to a single product, such as computers; in macroeconomics, an economist would study the buying behavior of consumers in regard to all goods. We might say that the tools of macroeconomics are telescopes, while the tools of microeconomics are microscopes. Macroeconomics stands back from the trees in order to see the forest. Microeconomics gets up close and examines the tree itself, its bark, its branches, and the soil in which it grows.

QUESTION: *Does someone have to be a trained economist to think like an economist? For example, might some people think in terms of unintended effects, the global economy, or the small and the big without ever having taken an economics course?*

ANSWER: *A person may "think like an economist" without ever having taken a course in economics, much as a person may have a beautiful singing voice without ever having taken a singing lesson. However, taking economics courses increases the probability that a person will come to think like an economist.*

LEARNING CHECK

1. According to economists, there are costs and benefits to almost everything we do. Identify the costs and benefits of each of the following: going to the dentist for a checkup, doing your homework, getting an extra hour of sleep.
2. You are currently answering the questions in this learning check. What would you be doing if you weren't answering these questions? How does your answer relate to the concept of opportunity cost?
3. James is earning $5 an hour working after school for the Davis Bakery. Suppose the U.S. Congress passes a law stating that no business can pay any employee less than $6 an hour. What might be an unintended effect of the legislation?
4. What is the difference between microeconomics and macroeconomics?

SECTION 2   SCARCITY, CHOICE, AND OPPORTUNITY COST

Three important concepts in economics are scarcity, choice, and opportunity cost, about which you already know something. In this section, we discuss scarcity and choice, and then we relate these two concepts to opportunity cost.

As you read, keep these key questions in mind:

- What is *scarcity*?
- How is *choice* related to scarcity?
- How is *opportunity cost* related to choice?
- Is there a difference between zero *price* and zero *cost*?

What is Scarcity?

People have **wants**. But they do not want just anything. They want things that they expect will give them **utility** or satisfaction. For example, people may want cars, houses, clothes, food, money to give to their favorite charities, more and deeper friendships, better health, and countless other things. You will notice that some things that people want are **tangible** and some things are **intangible**. Something is tangible if it can be felt or touched. For example, a computer is tangible. It is possible to touch a computer. Something is intangible if it cannot be felt or touched. For example, a deep friendship is intangible.

Wants cannot be satisfied by wishing it so. Nanette may want a computer, but she is not going to get a computer by simply wishing for one. It takes **resources** to produce a computer and it takes money to buy one.

 ## MINI GLOSSARY

Microeconomics The branch of economics that deals with human behavior and choices as they relate to relatively small units—the individual, the business firm, a single market.

Macroeconomics The branch of economics that deals with human behavior and choices as they relate to the entire economy.

Wants Things that we desire to have.

Utility A synonym for this word is satisfaction.

Tangible Able to be felt by touch. For example, a book is tangible: you can touch and feel it.

Intangible Not able to be felt by touch. For example, an economics lecture is intangible.

Resources Anything that is used to produce goods or services. For example, a person's labor may be used to produce computers, TV sets, and much more, and therefore a person's labor is a resource. Resources fall into four categories: land, labor, capital, and entrepreneurship.

CASE STUDY

Economics in the U.S. Senate

Imagine that you are listening in on three U.S. senators having a discussion.

"Our first priority must be education," says the senator from Florida. "Everything must take second place to spending more money on education."

"I disagree," says the senator from South Carolina. "First we must rebuild our inner cities, and then later we will put more money into education."

"You are both misguided," says the senator from California. "What we need to do first is to take better care of the unfortunate among us: the old, the sick, and the poor."

Sound familiar? It should. Words to this effect are spoken daily in the U.S. Congress, in state legislatures, on nightly news programs, and in our own homes. The sentiments expressed by these words are so commonplace that we rarely take notice of them anymore. People disagree—that is the way life is, you may say.

Notice, though, that the disagreements concern choices. The senator from Florida *chooses* education over other things. The senator from South Carolina *chooses* to rebuild the inner cities. The senator from California *chooses* to help the poor. The senators are involved in a political tug-of-war because not all of them can get what they want. More resources for education mean fewer resources for helping the poor. Why? The answer, in one word, is scarcity. As we have seen, when there are not enough resources to satisfy all our wants, we have to *choose* which wants will be satisfied and which wants will go unsatisfied.

Will the debate over choices continue forever? Will people (like the three senators) continue to argue about what should be done with the limited resources? The answer is yes. The reason is that scarcity isn't going to disappear. Our wants will always be greater than the resources available to satisfy them. And since scarcity isn't going to disappear, neither will the need to make choices disappear. Scarcity is here to stay, and so is the need to choose.

---

1. Give examples of some economic choices the principal of your school has to make. (Hint: Perhaps more money for library books means less money for athletic equipment. What else?)
2. Give examples of some economic choices you have made in the last two weeks.
3. Can you think of anyone who doesn't have to make choices? Explain your answer.

▲ Some things that people want are tangible, and some things are intangible. This young man wants food (tangible) and friendship (intangible).

Here is the problem we find in life, and it is an economic problem: People's wants are unlimited, while the resources available to satisfy these wants are limited. Stated differently, people's wants are greater than the resources available to satisfy their wants. This condition—people's wants are greater than the resources available to satisfy their wants—is called **scarcity**. Scarcity is a fact of life, much as the law of gravity is a fact of life.

You may be wondering if people really do have unlimited wants. For example, you may know someone whom you think has only a few wants (some food, a place to sleep, a few clothes, and that's all). You may have this opinion because you believe that people want only tangible goods (such as cars and houses). Once such needs have been met, we often assume there are no other wants. But people want other things, too. They want love, friendship, peace in the world, a cleaner environment, more leisure time, and so on. If we take into account all the things that people may want—all the things from which people can possibly derive utility or satisfaction—it is likely that their wants

will be unlimited. There is a stark contrast between unlimited wants and limited resources.

Because of Scarcity, Choices Have to Be Made

Wants are unlimited, resources are limited—scarcity exists. Because scarcity exists, choices have to be made. After all, if there are not enough resources to satisfy all our wants (yours, mine, and everybody else's), we have to choose which wants

MINI GLOSSARY

Scarcity The condition in which our wants are greater than the resources available to satisfy all those wants. Everyone, and every society, faces the basic problem of scarcity. There is scarcity in the United States, Russia, France, Argentina, and every other country in the world.

ECONOMIC FOCUS

ecause scarcity exists—because people's wants are greater than the resources available to satisfy those wants—people must make choices. Does the same hold for governments, too? Does scarcity exist for governments; do governments have to make choices? The answer is yes.

Let's look at the process. State governments raise funds principally through taxation. For example, you pay a state sales tax when you buy a product at a store. If the state sales tax is 5 percent, and you buy a product for $50, you pay $2.50 ($50 × 0.05 = $2.50) in state sales taxes in addition to the $50 price. Once the state government has the tax revenues, it has to decide how to spend them.

▼ **EXHIBIT S-1-1a.** How States Spend Their Money, 1991 ($ millions).

(1) STATE	(2) TOTAL STATE SPENDING	(3) EDUCATION	(4) HIGHWAYS	(5) PUBLIC WELFARE	(6) HEALTH AND HOSPITALS	(7) NATURAL RESOURCES	(8) ADMINIS-TRATION	(9) OTHER
Alabama	$8,855.5	$3,508.8	$679.3	$1,356.9	$1,048.7	$152.6	$237.6	$1,871.6
Alaska	4,941.0	1,098.0	501.8	434.9	173.8	242.5	220.8	2,269.2
Arizona	7,872.0	2,807.2	1,094.0	1034.4	357.4	126.8	274.6	2,177.6
Arkansas	4,649.2	1,840.8	459.4	953.5	294.0	103.7	115.7	882.1
California	85,639.9	27,217.8	3,888.8	18,990.7	5,805.6	1,659.5	2,439.1	25,638.4
Colorado	6,992.3	2,653.8	670.7	1,131.9	384.5	127.6	268.1	1,755.7
Connecticut	11,114.7	2,334.6	1,019.0	2,068.7	1,029.7	73.4	379.7	5,348.7
Delaware	2,318.0	758.2	257.3	256.8	147.4	28.9	111.4	758.0
Florida	25,167.8	9,096.9	1,778.8	4,556.1	594.6	690.5	953.3	7,497.6
Georgia	13,286.3	5,199.4	1,019.8	2,672.8	1,013.5	256.1	211.4	2,913.3
Hawaii	4,510.0	1,368.8	276.6	478.0	369.7	109.5	221.2	1,686.2
Idaho	2,305.1	862.4	278.5	285.2	87.2	88.3	66.6	636.9
Illinois	24,619.2	7,206.2	2,375.8	4,860.2	1,530.2	278.1	648.2	7,720.5
Indiana	11,547.5	4,404.5	1,044.2	2,271.7	763.2	138.1	253.7	2,672.1
Iowa	6,819.8	2,581.1	866.7	1,171.2	576.0	164.6	233.5	1,226.7
Kansas	5,134.2	1,945.4	633.2	825.1	422.3	149.6	201.3	957.3
Kentucky	9,047.8	3,039.6	826.1	1,936.7	473.1	210.8	312.9	2,248.6
Louisiana	10,537.2	3,464.8	842.5	1,831.8	997.5	235.8	220.0	2,944.8
Maine	3,514.6	960.8	286.9	877.7	178.0	75.6	112.9	1,022.7
Maryland	12,576.3	3,353.6	1,187.0	2,107.8	895.9	228.1	444.2	4,359.7
Massachusetts	20,348.9	3,299.5	699.0	5,784.7	1,603.0	146.3	761.0	8,055.4
Michigan	24,036.6	6,948.1	1,436.7	5,125.2	2,377.2	254.1	536.0	7,359.3
Minnesota	12,730.4	4,501.1	1,011.7	2,375.4	893.2	273.6	359.2	3,316.2
Mississippi	5,171.3	1,902.4	496.2	868.4	374.8	127.6	99.1	1,302.8
Missouri	9,254.2	3,454.0	902.6	1,771.7	715.1	195.7	258.2	1,956.9

SOURCE: *Facts and Figures On Government Finance, 1993* (Washington, D.C.: Tax Foundation, 1993).

SCARCITY, CHOICE, AND STATE SPENDING

Exhibit S-1-1a shows how states chose to spend their money in 1991. For example, look at the case of Alabama, the first state in our exhibit. From column 2 we learn that in 1991 this state spent a total of $8,855.5 million. Of this total, it *chose* to spend $3,508.8 million on education, as column 3 shows us. Column 4 shows us that Alabama chose to spend $679.3 million on highways, and in column 5 we see that it chose to spend $1,356.9 million on public welfare.

We can look at states' choices in a different way, too. Exhibit S-1-1b lists the dollar amounts spent on public education per pupil in each of the 50 states. For example, you will notice that New Jersey chose to spend $9,159 per pupil in 1991, whereas New York chose to spend $8,500 per pupil. This is similar to one person choosing to spend $600 of a limited budget each year on clothes, and another person choosing to spend $500 on clothes.

▼ **EXHIBIT S-1-1a (continued).**

(1) STATE	(2) TOTAL STATE SPENDING	(3) EDUCATION	(4) HIGHWAYS	(5) PUBLIC WELFARE	(6) HEALTH AND HOSPITALS	(7) NATURAL RESOURCES	(8) ADMINIS- TRATION	(9) OTHER
Montana	2,384.3	752.8	272.2	331.1	114.5	116.6	76.9	720.2
Nebraska	3,266.2	1,161.2	434.9	594.4	326.0	107.9	79.6	562.2
Nevada	3,435.5	997.7	242.5	262.5	105.2	49.6	118.8	1,659.2
New Hampshire	2,135.2	404.3	175.3	398.3	142.7	28.8	100.4	885.4
New Jersey	23,250.5	5,830.3	1,372.1	4,185.7	1,313.2	169.8	664.7	9,714.7
New Mexico	4,526.8	1,777.9	364.4	537.5	371.5	81.0	163.4	1231.1
New York	64,320.9	14,580.5	2,569.1	17,015.3	5,352.5	352.6	2,261.1	22,189.8
North Carolina	15,036.2	6,258.1	1,389.9	2,361.9	1,085.0	286.6	405.4	3,249.3
North Dakota	1,792.8	622.6	196.4	255.8	93.1	74.6	41.4	508.9
Ohio	27,790.8	8,008.5	2,046.7	5,712.1	1,751.4	242.3	655.6	9,374.2
Oklahoma	7,266.8	2,597.0	778.6	1,263.3	546.3	101.2	246.4	1,734.0
Oregon	7,248.9	1,891.9	783.9	1,144.1	573.9	195.0	298.0	2,362.1
Pennsylvania	29,525.9	6,892.2	2,362.7	6,115.1	1,846.7	386.6	748.1	11,174.5
Rhode Island	3,465.3	724.9	194.4	651.3	254.6	28.4	129.6	1,482.1
South Carolina	8,970.3	3,021.8	510.9	1,538.1	917.4	145.0	182.5	2,654.6
South Dakota	1,416.5	409.0	209.3	212.1	92.2	58.6	47.7	387.6
Tennessee	9,237.8	3,074.1	1,060.6	1,977.5	703.5	110.9	218.3	2,092.9
Texas	29,525.9	12,310.3	2,612.4	5,393.4	2,115.6	386.5	575.0	6,132.7
Utah	4,108.3	1,804.5	300.3	533.6	329.5	87.6	136.4	916.4
Vermont	1,735.9	540.1	169.8	345.5	64.4	60.1	69.1	486.9
Virginia	13,351.9	4,868.3	1,696.9	1,814.4	1,312.5	172.3	494.6	2,992.9
Washington	15,666.0	5,748.5	1,104.7	2,451.8	988.6	487.5	327.3	4,557.6
West Virginia	4,740.5	1,721.0	500.9	708.2	188.0	109.8	133.2	1,379.4
Wisconsin	12,488.4	3,948.3	829.1	2,480.4	729.4	205.6	269.8	4,025.8
Wyoming	1,813.1	535.7	324.7	152.1	100.7	73.5	71.1	555.3

u.S. ECONOMIC FOCUS (continued)

▼ **EXHIBIT S-1-1b.** Spending on Public Education, Per Pupil, 1991.

STATE	$	STATE	$	STATE	$
1. New Jersey	$9,159	18. Michigan	$5,257	35. Missouri	$4,415
2. New York	8,500	19. Wyoming	5,255	36. Kentucky	4,390
3. Connecticut	7,914	20. Montana	5,184	37. Nebraska	4,381
4. Alaska	7,887	21. Florida	5,154	38. South Carolina	4,327
5. Rhode Island	6,989	22. Illinois	5,062	39. Texas	4,238
6. Pennsylvania	6,534	23. Indiana	5,051	40. Arizona	4,231
7. Massachusetts	6,351	24. West Virginia	5,046	41. Louisiana	4,012
8. Maryland	6,184	25. Washington	5,045	42. Oklahoma	3,742
9. Delaware	6,016	26. Kansas	5,009	43. South Dakota	3,730
10. Wisconsin	5,946	27. Hawaii	5,008	44. Tennessee	3,707
11. Maine	5,894	28. Georgia	4,860	45. North Dakota	3,685
12. Vermont	5,740	29. Iowa	4,839	46. Alabama	3,648
13. Ohio	5,639	30. California	4,826	47. Arkansas	3,334
14. New Hampshire	5,504	31. Colorado	4,809	48. Mississippi	3,322
15. Virginia	5,360	32. North Carolina	4,802	49. Idaho	3,200
16. Oregon	5,291	33. Nevada	4,564	50. Utah	2,993
17. Minnesota	5,260	34. New Mexico	4,446		

SOURCE: *Almanac of the 50 States* (Palo Alto, CA.: Information Publications, 1993).

Finally, the choices a state makes can be interpreted differently depending on the data being considered. To illustrate, we see from Exhibit S-1-1b that New York spent more on public education per pupil ($8,500) than Maine ($5,894). Consequently, there may be a tendency to conclude that New York values education more than Maine. But consider the data from Exhibit S-1-1a. Here we learn that, of the $64,320.9 million New York spent in 1991, $14,580.5 million went for education. In other words, approximately 22.7 percent ($14,580.5 million ÷ $64,320.9 million = 0.227 and 0.227 × 100 = 22.7 percent) of New York's total spending went for education. In 1991, Maine spent a total of $3,514.6 million; $960.8 million went for education. In short, approximately 27.3 percent ($960.8 million ÷ $3,514.6 million = 0.273 and 0.273 × 100 = 27.3 percent) of Maine's total spending

went for education. One might interpret things differently according to whether one looks at education spending on a percentage basis or on a dollars-per-pupil basis. For example, one might conclude that Maine values education more than New York does because the state of Maine allocated a larger percentage of its total spending to education than did New York.

1. What percentage of your state's total spending went for education in 1991? for highways? for public welfare?
2. Brittany chooses to spend $300 a year seeing movies, and Jack chooses to spend $200. Does it follow that Brittany values seeing movies more than Jack values seeing movies? Explain your answer.

(of the unlimited number of wants we have) we will satisfy. On an individual basis, it is similar to having a limited income. Barbara earns $1,000 a month. She wants a new outfit, 10 new books, a trip to Hawaii, a new car, and many other things. The problem is that she can't have everything she wants given her income. She has to make choices. Is it going to be the new outfit, or the 10 new books?

Consider the choices a society has to make because scarcity exists. If you listen to what different groups of people in the United States say you will perhaps hear: more health care for the poor, more police protection, more schools, and a cleaner environment. As we know, these wants are not realized simply by the asking. It takes resources to bring these things about. The problem, though, is that even if we could satisfy all the wants we have listed here, there would be more later. In other words, even if we were to provide more health care to the poor, hire more police officers, build more schools, and clean up the environment, there would be other things to do, too. There will always be more wants. But there will never be enough resources to satisfy our unlimited wants. We must choose how we are going to use our limited resources. We must choose which wants we will try to satisfy, and which wants will be left unsatisfied.

if he hadn't purchased the computer? If he would have spent the $3,000 on a big-screen television set, then he has given up the big-screen television set to get the computer. The big-screen television set is the opportunity cost of the computer.

QUESTION: *Suppose Rachel spends $10,000 on a new car. If she hadn't spent the $10,000 on a car, she could have done any of the following:*

- *Purchased $10,000 worth of clothes.*
- *Spent the $10,000 traveling.*
- *Given the $10,000 to charity.*
- *Used the $10,000 to make a down payment on a house.*

Since she could have done any of these things, aren't all of these things the opportunity cost of buying the car?

ANSWER: *No. It is necessary to differentiate between what Rachel could have done and what she would have done. Opportunity cost refers to what Rachel would do if she didn't buy the car. If she would spend the $10,000 traveling around the world, then traveling—and only traveling—is what she actually gives up by buying the new car.*

From Choices to Opportunity Costs

Every time a person makes a choice—such as choosing to buy a sweater instead of two compact discs—he incurs an opportunity cost. As stated earlier, in economics, the most valued opportunity or alternative you give up (or forfeit) to do something is that something's opportunity cost. Thus, in this example, the opportunity cost of choosing to buy a sweater is two compact discs.

Consider another example. Suppose Lionel spends $3,000 to buy a computer. What is the opportunity cost of the computer? Lionel must ask himself, what would he have done with the $3,000

The Link between Scarcity, Choice, and Opportunity Cost

We know that because scarcity exists, choices have to be made. That is, because our wants are greater than the resources available to satisfy our wants, we must *choose* which of our wants will be satisfied and which will remain unsatisfied. Now we add something to this: because choices have to be made, opportunity costs will be incurred. Why? Because every time we make a choice we give up the opportunity to do something else—that is, we incur an opportunity cost. Think of these three important economic concepts—scarcity, choice, and opportunity cost—as chained together. For a quick review, see Exhibit 1-2.

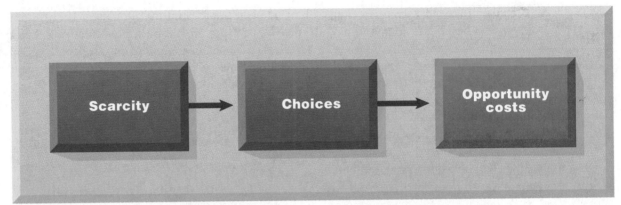

▲ **EXHIBIT 1-2. The Link between Scarcity, Choices, and Opportunity Costs.** Because scarcity exists, people must make choices. When people make choices, they incur opportunity costs. Since people make choices and incur opportunity costs every day, they also face the fact of scarcity every day.

QUESTION: *Suppose Roberto buys a ticket to an upcoming music concert and, at the last minute, decides not to go. He gives the ticket to Brad, asking for nothing in return. If Brad goes to the concert, couldn't we say that his going to the concert comes with no (or zero) opportunity cost? After all, he hasn't had to give up any money to go to the concert.*

ANSWER: *No. Brad gives up something, if not money, to attend the concert. He gives up the time that he could be using in alternative ways. He gets into his car, drives 10 miles, stands in line, watches the concert for 90 minutes, walks back to his car, and drives home. He could be doing something else in the time it takes him to do all this. The point is a simple one. There is a* difference between *zero price (Brad paid nothing for the ticket; it was given to him) and* zero opportunity cost.

A Definition of Economics

So far, you have learned about three important economic concepts—scarcity, choice, and opportunity cost—and know something of the economic way of thinking. Now that you have started to think about economics, it's time for a formal definition of the term. **Economics** is the science that studies the choices of people trying to satisfy their wants in a world of scarcity.

 LEARNING CHECK

1. What is utility?
2. Because scarcity exists, individuals must make choices. Explain why.
3. Give an example to illustrate that a person may incur an opportunity cost without paying anyone any money.
4. Is the opportunity cost of attending high school the same for all high-school students? Explain why or why not.

SECTION 3 RESOURCES

Scarcity is the condition in which our wants are greater than the resources available to satisfy those wants. In economics, a synonym for *resources* is *factors of production*. Resources, or factors of production, are what people use to produce goods. For example, wood and a machine are resources that may be used to produce a desk. Economists place resources in four broad categories: *land, labor, capital*, and *entrepreneurship*.

As you read, keep these key questions in mind:

- What is *land*?
- What is *labor*?
- What is *capital*?
- What is *entrepreneurship*?

Land

When the word **land** is mentioned, you may get a picture of an acre of ground in your mind's eye. The resource land is more. It is all the natural resources found in nature—such things as water, minerals, undeveloped land (for example, the thousands of miles of desert in Nevada and California), animals, forests, and so on.

Labor

Labor refers to the physical and mental talents that people contribute to the production of goods and services. For example, a person working in a factory is considered to be the resource labor. A TV weatherperson telling you what the weather will be like tomorrow is considered to be the resource labor.

Capital

In economics, **capital** refers to produced goods that can be used as resources for further produc-

tion. Such things as machinery, tools, computers, trucks, buildings, and factories are all considered to be capital. Each is used to produce some other good.

Entrepreneurship

If someone asked you to point to the resource land, you might point to a forest. If someone asked you to point to the resource labor, you might point to yourself. If someone asked you to point to capital, you might point to a computer. But what would you point to if someone asked you to point to **entrepreneurship**? This resource is not so easy to identify.

Entrepreneurship refers to the special talent that some people have for searching out and taking advantage of new business opportunities, and developing new products and new ways of doing things. For example, Steven Jobs, one of the developers of the first personal computer, exhibited entrepre-

MINI GLOSSARY

Economics The science that studies the choices of people trying to satisfy their wants in a world of scarcity.

Land All the natural resources found in nature. An acre of land, mineral deposits, and water in a stream are all considered land.

Labor The physical and mental talents that people contribute to the production of goods and services.

Capital Produced goods that can be used as resources for further production. Such things as factories, machines, and farm tractors are capital.

Entrepreneurship The special talent that some people have for searching out and taking advantage of new business opportunities and for developing new products and new ways of doing things.

Land

Labor

Capital

Entrepreneurship: Steven Jobs, cofounder of Apple Computer, Inc.

▲ Here we show the four resources: land, labor, capital, and entrepreneurship.

neurship. He saw a use for the personal computer and developed it, and hundreds of thousands of customers purchased his product—the Apple computer.

QUESTION: *Since only people can exhibit entrepreneurship, why isn't entrepreneurship considered a kind of labor? In short, why aren't there only three resources: land, labor, and capital?*

ANSWER: *Economists consider entrepreneurship sufficiently different from the ordinary talents of people to deserve its own category. Consider this explanation. Both an apple and a squash are nonmeats, but we don't put them into the same category. An apple is a fruit, and a squash is a vegetable. Obviously they are different enough to be placed in different categories. The ordinary mental and physical talents of people are considered labor. The special talents that are directed toward searching out and taking advantage of new business opportunities and so on are considered entrepreneurship.*

Reginald F. Lewis

Reginald F. Lewis, who died in 1993, was considered the most prominent African American entrepreneur of his generation. Lewis went to college at Virginia State University and earned a degree in economics. After college, he attended Harvard Law School and graduated in 1968. For the next two years, Lewis worked as an attorney for the New York law firm of Paul, Weiss, Rifkind, Wharton & Garrison. In 1973, he started his own law practice, Lewis & Clarkson.

In 1983, Lewis started to concentrate on buying and selling companies. The first company he purchased was McCall Pattern Company, a sewing business. At the time he made the purchase, McCall Pattern Company was struggling to stay alive. Lewis instituted some changes, cut costs, and turned the company into a healthy enterprise. In 1987, Lewis sold McCall Pattern for $90 million, earning $50 million for himself in the deal.

Lewis next turned his attention to a much bigger company, Beatrice International Foods Company, a distributor of ice cream, snacks, and other foods. He bought the company for $985 million. Under Lewis, Beatrice became the first and only African American-owned company to earn $1 billion a year.

Lewis, who built a fortune estimated at $400 million, was a person who enjoyed giving to worthwhile causes. For example, he gave millions of dollars to educational institutions, such as Harvard Law School, Howard University, and Virginia State University.

Among the things for which Lewis is remembered are his enterprising ways and hard work. He said that he wanted to be judged by his performance, and he refused to accept race as either a crutch or a barrier to his success. Reginald Lewis stands as a shining example to all men and women that hard work, enterprising ways, and an imagination can lead to success.

1. In what subject did Reginald Lewis receive a degree from Virginia State University?
2. What law school did Reginald Lewis attend?
3. What company did Reginald Lewis purchase in 1983?
4. According to what criterion did Reginald Lewis want to be judged?

The Monetary Payments to Resources

When someone wants to use resources to produce a good—such as a house or a car—that person has to pay for the resources. This fact implies that we can link monetary, or money, payments to the resources that are used to produce goods. Pay-ment to a land resource is called *rent*; payment to labor is called *wages*; payment to capital is called *interest*; and payment to entrepreneurship is called *profits*. Stated differently, land earns rent, labor earns wages, capital earns interest, and entrepreneurship earns profits.

Suppose you want to build a house. You hire some workers (labor), you buy some tools (capital), and you buy a lot (land). You have to make monetary payments for each of the resources you buy. Let's say you pay $24,000 in total for the workers you hire (this figure includes what you pay yourself as a worker, too). You pay $10,000 for the tools you buy and $25,000 for the lot you buy. These dollar figures represent the earnings from the resources of labor, capital, and land. If we add these figures, we get a total of $59,000 ($24,000 + $10,000 + $25,000 = $59,000). Now let's suppose that you sell the house to someone for $70,000. The difference between the cost of the house and the sales price of the house is $11,000, and this $11,000 is profit ($70,000 −

$59,000 = $11,000). Profit is the payment to the resource entrepreneurship.

Notice what we can do with this example. We can take the sales price of the house ($70,000) and break it up into the payments to different resources: $24,000 to labor, $10,000 to capital, $25,000 to land, and $11,000 to entrepreneurship. Looking at things this way, we notice that the price that a consumer pays for a good purchased is more than simply the money that the seller receives. Included in it are the monetary payments to different resources, or factors of production.

 ## LEARNING CHECK

Identify the following resources. Write "Ld" for land, "Lb" for labor, "C" for capital, and "E" for entrepreneurship.

1. Francis's work as a secretary
2. Iron ore
3. A farm tractor
4. A computer used to write a book
5. A comedian telling jokes on a television show
6. A singer singing at an outdoor concert

7. Your teacher teaching you economics
8. Someone inventing a new product
9. Crude oil
10. Oil-drilling equipment

SECTION 4 THREE ECONOMIC QUESTIONS EVERY SOCIETY MUST ANSWER

Each nation in the world has something fundamental in common with all the other nations: each has to decide how to answer three economic questions. We examine these three questions in this section.

As you read, keep these key questions in mind:

■ What are the three economic questions that every society must answer?
■ What is an economic system?
■ What are the major differences between free enterprise and socialism?
■ What is a mixed economy?

Three Economic Questions

The first economic question that every society has to answer is, **What goods will be produced**? We know that because of scarcity, no nation can produce every good it wants in the quantity it would like. More of one good (say, television sets) leaves fewer resources to produce other goods (such as cars). No matter what society we are talking about—the U.S. society, the Chinese society, or the Brazilian society—each society has to decide what goods will be produced.

Once it has been decided which goods will be produced, the next question every society has to answer is, **How will the goods be produced**? For example, will farmers using modern tractors produce food, or will farmers using primitive tools produce it? Will the food be produced on private farms, where production decisions are made by individual farmers, or will it be produced on collective farms, where production decisions are made by people in the government?

The third question to be answered is, **For whom will the goods be produced**? Will anyone who is able and willing to pay the prices for the goods be able to obtain them, or will government decide who will have the goods?

The way in which a society answers these three economic questions defines its **economic system**. Stated differently, it is the function of an economic system to answer these three economic questions. There are two major economic systems. The first is **free enterprise**. Sometimes free enterprise is called *capitalism* or a *market economy*. Throughout this book, we will mainly use the term *free enterprise*, but occasionally we will speak of a capitalist economic system or a market economy. The other major economic system is **socialism**. Just as free enterprise is sometimes referred to as a market economy, socialism is sometimes loosely referred to as a *command economy*. To be more accurate, a command economy is a particular type of socialist economic system, which we will discuss in some detail in Chapter

18. In this chapter, we discuss the broad outlines of free enterprise and socialism.

Major Differences between Free Enterprise and Socialism

Let's look at the major differences between free enterprise and socialism in a few areas.

Resources. Resources are used to produce goods and services. In a free-enterprise economic system, these resources are owned by private individuals. In a socialist economic system, the government owns many of the resources.

Government's Role in the Economy. In a free-enterprise economic system, government has a small role to play in the economy. It does not decide what goods and services will be produced, or how they will be produced, or the like. Under socialism, government may decide what goods and services will be produced, how they will be produced, and so on.

Economic Plans. Under socialism, government decision makers may write an **economic plan** that specifies the direction economic activities are to take

THINKING LIKE AN ECONOMIST

Some people look at nations and see differences. *For example, people speak French in France and English in the United States. The crime rate is higher in the United States than it is in England. The economist looks at nations and sees* similarities. *For example, the United States has to decide what goods will be produced and so do China, Russia, Germany, Mexico, and Egypt.*

MINI GLOSSARY

Economic System The way in which a society decides what goods to produce, how to produce them, and for whom goods will be produced.

Free Enterprise An economic system in which individuals (not government) own most, if not all, the resources and control their use. Government plays a very small role in the economy.

Socialism An economic system in which government owns and controls many of the resources. Government plays a major role in the economy.

Economic Plan A government program specifying economic activities, such as what goods are to be produced and what prices will be charged.

in the next five to ten years. For example, their plan may state that over the next five years, the nation's economy will produce more manufactured goods (such as cars and trucks) and fewer agricultural goods (such as wheat and corn). There would be no such plan in a free-enterprise economic system.

The Income Distribution.   **Income distribution** refers to how all the income earned in a country is divided among different groups of income earners. In the United States in the early 1990s, for example, the top one-fifth of income earners earned 44.3 percent of the total income, and the bottom one-fifth of income earners earned 4.6 percent of the total income. In a free-enterprise economic system, the government pays little attention to the equality or inequality of income distribution. In a socialist economic system, much greater attention is paid to the income distribution. Government decision makers under socialism are much more likely to use government's powers to redistribute income—usually directing it away from society's high-income earners.

Controlling Prices.   In a free-enterprise economic system, prices are allowed to fluctuate—that is, to go up and down. Government does not attempt to control prices. In a socialist economic system, government decision makers do control prices, although not all socialist systems control prices to the same extent. For example, government decision makers may think that the price of bread is too high at $2 a loaf and thus order that no one be allowed to buy or sell bread for more than $1.50 a loaf. Or they may feel that wage rates for unskilled labor are too low at $4 an hour and thus order that no one be allowed to "buy" or "sell" unskilled labor for less than $6 an hour. We will discuss arguments that have arisen about these and other matters in later chapters.

Economic Systems and Reality

In reality, a nation's economic system may contain some ingredients of free enterprise and some ingredients of socialism. For example, the United States is considered to have a free-enterprise economic system. After all, most of the resources are owned by private individuals, and there are no economic plans to speak of. But the U.S. government plays a larger role in the economy than it would play in a pure free-enterprise system, and some prices are controlled. Thus, while the United States is considered a free-enterprise nation, it has a few features of socialism.

A similar point can be made for other nations. For example, China is considered to be a socialist economic nation. In China, many resources are owned by government, economic plans are customary, and some prices are controlled. But in some areas, China has recently been experimenting with free-enterprise practices. To say that China is 100 percent socialist would therefore be incorrect.

Sometimes, economies that have features of both free enterprise and socialism are called **mixed economies**. If we were to adopt this terminology, then we would have to say that both the U.S. economy and the Chinese economy were mixed economies. In a sense, though, to call both nations mixed economies is misleading. It makes both nations sound alike, but they are not. The United States has much more free enterprise than China, and China has much more socialism than the United States; the economies of these two nations are quite different. It is clearer to refer to the United States as a free-enterprise nation and to China as principally a socialist nation, while noting that there are some socialist practices in the United States and some free-enterprise practices in China.

Perhaps it is best to look at the two radically different economic systems—free enterprise and socialism—as occupying opposite ends of an economic spectrum, as illustrated in Exhibit 1-3. Nations' economies lie along this economic spectrum, some closer to the free-enterprise end and some closer to the socialist end.

QUESTION: *Suppose seven nations are identified as being free-enterprise, or market, economies. Does it follow that the seven nations are free-enterprise, or market, economies to the same degree?*

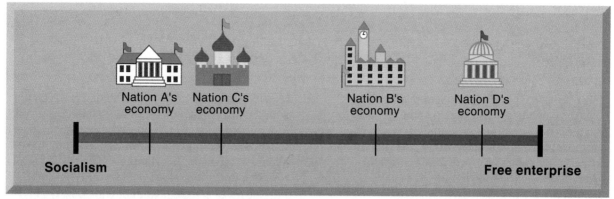

▲ **EXHIBIT 1-3. A Spectrum of Economic Systems.** There are two major and radically different economic systems: pure free enterprise and pure socialism. Here, these two economic systems lie at opposite ends of a spectrum. Most nations' economies fall somewhere between socialism and free enterprise on this spectrum, although an economy is usually closer to one end than the other. For example, Nation D's economy is more nearly a free-enterprise system and less a socialist system than Nation B's economy.

ANSWER: *No. To understand, consider an analogy: class grades. Suppose Mary gets an 89 on a test and Bianca gets an 81. Both of them receive a B for a grade, and thus both are B students. We can't really say which student is more of a B student, but we can say that Mary, who is a B student, is a little closer to being an A student than Bianca, who is also a B student. Similarly, we might say that Country X, which is considered a free-enterprise country, has more elements of free enterprise in its economy than* *Country Y, which is also considered a free-enterprise country.*

MINI GLOSSARY

Income Distribution The way all the income earned in a country is divided among different groups of income earners.
Mixed Economy An economy that has features of both free enterprise and socialism.

 LEARNING CHECK

1. What are the three economic questions that every society must answer?
2. What is the difference between free enterprise and socialism when it comes to the ownership of most resources?
3. "The economy of the United States is a pure free-enterprise economy." Do you agree or disagree? Explain your answer.
4. If most economies of the world are mixed economies, does it follow that most economies of the world are the same? Explain your answer.

DEVELOPING ECONOMIC SKILLS

Illustrating Ideas with Graphs

A picture is worth a thousand words. It is with this familiar saying in mind that economists construct their graphs. A few lines, some curves, and much can be said. In this section, we examine a few of the graphs commonly used in economics.

Pie Charts (or Pie Graphs)

A pie chart is a convenient way to represent the parts of something that, added together, equal the whole. Suppose we consider a typical 24-hour weekday for Danny Chien. On a typical weekday, Danny spends 8 hours sleeping, 6 hours in school, 2 hours at football practice, 2 hours doing homework, 1 hour watching television, and 5 hours doing nothing (we'll call it "hanging out"). It is easy to represent the breakdown of a typical weekday for Danny in pie chart form, as in Exhibit 1-4.

As you will notice, pie charts give you a quick visual message that shows rough percentage breakdowns and relative relationships. For

▼ **EXHIBIT 1-4. A Pie Chart.** The pie chart represents the breakdown of Danny Chien's activities during a typical 24-hour weekday. For example, it is easy to see that Danny spends the same amount of time at football practice as he spends doing his homework and twice as much time doing homework as watching television.

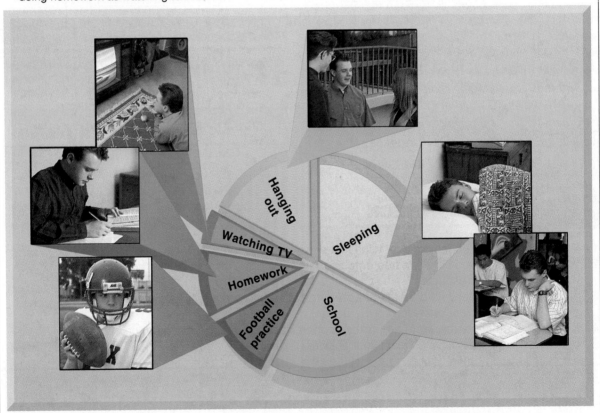

DEVELOPING ECONOMIC SKILLS (continued)

example, in Exhibit 1-4, it is easy to see that Danny spends much of his time sleeping (the "sleeping" slice of the pie is the largest slice). He spends the same amount of time at football practice as doing his homework and twice as much time doing his homework as watching television.

Bar Graphs

The bar graph is another visual aid that economists use to convey relationships. For example, suppose we wanted to represent the projected population of various states at the beginning of the year 2000, as in Exhibit 1-5. Among the many relationships shown, we can see that Texas is projected to have a slightly

greater population than New York, and California is expected to have more people than either of those two states.

Line Graphs

Sometimes information is best and most easily displayed in a line graph. Line graphs are particularly useful to illustrate changes in a factor over some time period. For example, suppose we want to illustrate the variations in average points per game for a high school basketball team in recent years. As you can see from part a of Exhibit 1-6, the basketball team was on a roller coaster during the years 1980–1993. It seems that the team's performance was not consistent from one year to the next.

▼ **EXHIBIT 1-5. A Bar Graph.** The bar graph illustrates the projected population figures for eight states in the year 2000.

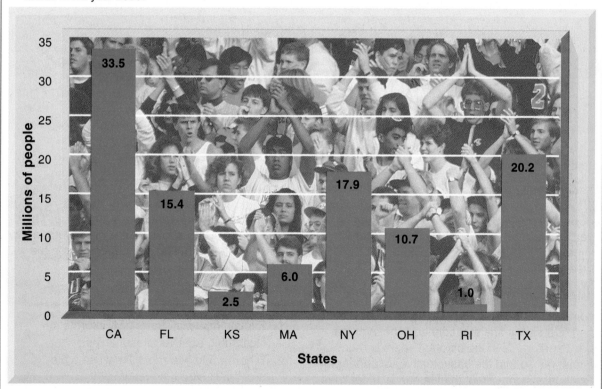

SOURCE: U.S. Bureau of the Census, *Statistical Abstract of the United States: 1990.*

DEVELOPING ECONOMIC SKILLS (continued)

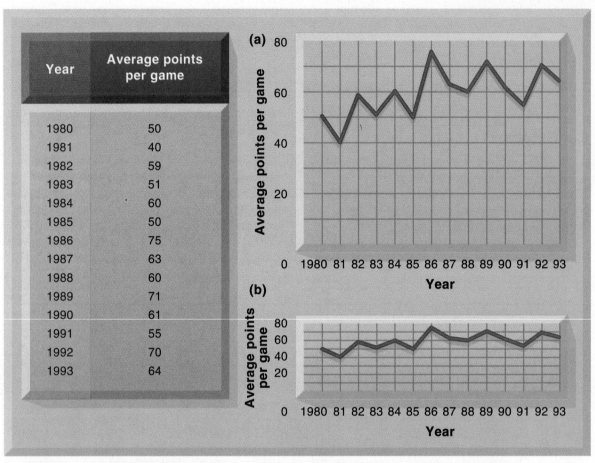

Year	Average points per game
1980	50
1981	40
1982	59
1983	51
1984	60
1985	50
1986	75
1987	63
1988	60
1989	71
1990	61
1991	55
1992	70
1993	64

▲ **EXHIBIT 1-6. Two Line Graphs Plot the Same Data.** Part *a* shows the average points per game for a high school basketball team over several years. The variation—ups and downs—from year to year is sharp and pronounced. Part *b* shows the same data, but the variation in performance appears to be less, because the measurement scale has been changed.

But suppose we take the data presented in part *a* of Exhibit 1-6 and show it in another way in part *b*. This time, we use a different measurement scale on the vertical axis. With this scale, the distance between 20 and 40 points, and the distance between 40 and 60 points, and so on are less than the distances in part *a*. Now the line that connects the average points per game in the different years is much straighter, so that the basketball team appears much less inconsistent than in part *a*. In fact, we could choose a scale that would allow us to end up with something close to a straight line. The point is this: Data shown in line graph form may convey different messages depending on the measurement scale used.

1. Explain how pie charts give information illustrating relative relationships.
2. When would you most likely use a pie chart to illustrate something?
3. When are line graphs most useful?

CHAPTER 1 REVIEW

CHAPTER SUMMARY

1. Economists think in terms of (a) costs and benefits, (b) what would have been, (c) unintended effects, (d) a global economy, and (e) the small (*micro*economics) and the big (*macro*economics), among other things.
2. Scarcity is the condition in which our wants are greater than the resources available to satisfy those wants.
3. Scarcity is the basic economic problem that everybody faces.
4. Because scarcity exists, choices have to be made.
5. Every time a choice is made, an opportunity cost is incurred.
6. Opportunity cost is the most highly valued opportunity or alternative given up when a choice is made.
7. Economics is the science that studies the choices of people trying to satisfy their wants in a world of scarcity.
8. Resources, which are used to produce goods, fall into one of four categories: land, labor, capital, and entrepreneurship.
9. Land refers to all the natural resources found in nature. The payment to land is called *rent*.
10. Labor refers to the physical and mental talents that people contribute to the production process. The payment to labor is called *wages*.
11. Capital refers to produced goods that can be used as resources for further production. The payment to capital is called *interest*.
12. Entrepreneurship refers to the special talent that some people have for searching out and taking advantage of new business opportunities and for developing new products and new ways of doing things. The payment to entrepreneurship is called *profits*.
13. Every society must answer three economic questions: What goods will be produced? How will the goods be produced? For whom will the goods be produced?
14. The way in which a society answers the three economic questions defines its economic system. The two major economic systems are free enterprise and socialism.
15. In reality, most nations' economies are neither purely free-enterprise nor purely socialist systems. Instead, they have features of both free enterprise and socialism and are sometimes referred to as mixed economies.

BUILD YOUR ECONOMIC VOCABULARY

Match the word with the correct definition, example, or statement.

1. economics
2. scarcity
3. opportunity cost
4. zero opportunity cost
5. macroeconomics
6. satisfaction
7. choice
8. zero price

a. no dollars or cents are charged for a good
b. what you give up to do what you are doing
c. a consequence of scarcity
d. the science that studies the choices of people trying to satisfy their wants in a world characterized by scarcity
e. utility
f. wants greater than resources
g. exists when someone doesn't give up anything in choosing to do something else
h. the big picture

CHAPTER 1 REVIEW
(continued)

REVIEW QUESTIONS

1. Why is it preferable to think in terms of costs and benefits rather than to think in terms of benefits only?

2. Suppose there is a high cost to building more schools in your city or town. Does it necessarily follow that the schools should not be built? Explain your answer.

3. Suppose apples are currently selling for 25 cents each. Someone says that apple sellers can't make a decent living if they sell their apples so cheaply. He says there should be a law stating that no one can sell an apple for less than 50 cents. He intends for the law to raise the income of apple sellers. What might be an unintended effect of this law? Explain your answer.

4. What is the difference between microeconomics and macroeconomics?

5. Economists commonly use the word *utility*. For example, an economist might say that Jim receives greater utility from reading a good book than watching a good movie on television. What is a synonym for the word *utility*?

6. What is scarcity?

7. Explain this statement: Because scarcity exists, choices must be made.

8. If you attend a public high school, there is no admission price or tuition. Does it follow then that there is no opportunity cost to your attending school? Explain your answer.

9. How does entrepreneurship differ from labor?

10. What is an economic system? What are the two major economic systems in the world today?

11. List three ways in which free enterprise and socialism are different.

12. Why might it be better to refer to the U.S. economy as a free-enterprise economy and the Chinese economy as a socialist economy than to refer to both as mixed economies, even though both economies have both free-enterprise and socialist elements?

13. Define the following words: (a) global economy, (b) opportunity cost, (c) scarcity, (d) free enterprise, (e) socialism.

SHARPEN YOUR CRITICAL THINKING SKILLS

1. "Because we have to make choices, there is scarcity." What is wrong with this statement?

2. The person who developed *Music Television* (MTV) said that today's younger generation particularly enjoys two things: (1) television and (2) music, especially rock music. His idea was to combine the two—television and music—and so MTV was born. Would you say he was exhibiting entrepreneurship? Explain your answer.

3. What are the costs and benefits of attending college? (Hint: Think of costs in terms of opportunity costs.)

SHARPEN YOUR CRITICAL THINKING SKILLS (continued)

4. Read your local newspaper for a week looking for stories with economic errors. Write a paragraph or more about at least two stories, making certain to point out the errors. For example, you may read an editorial implying that some-thing that has zero price has no opportunity cost. You may read a report that assumes people do not have to make choices.

ACTIVITIES AND PROJECTS

1. Suppose a generous person gives $1,000 to your economics class and says that the class is free to spend the money any way it chooses. As a class, discuss how to spend the money. Then, write a one-page paper identifying what the economic concepts of scarcity, choice, and opportunity cost had to do with the class discussion.

ECONOMIC DICTIONARY

Capital (Pg. 17)
Economic Plan (Pg. 21)
Economic System (Pg. 21)
Economics (Pg. 16)
Entrepreneurship (Pg. 17)
Free Enterprise (Pg. 21)
Global Economy (Pg. 7)
Income Distribution (Pg. 22)
Intangible (Pg. 9)
Labor (Pg. 17)
Land (Pg. 17)

Macroeconomics (Pg. 8)
Microeconomics (Pg. 8)
Mixed Economy (Pg. 22)
Opportunity Cost (Pg. 4)
Resource (Pg. 9)
Scarcity (Pg. 11)
Socialism (Pg. 21)
Tangible (Pg. 9)
Utility (Pg. 9)
Want (Pg. 9)

CHAPTER

2

Our Free-Enterprise System: Markets, Ethics, and Entrepreneurs

INTRODUCTION

Today, many of us take life's conveniences for granted—such things as being able to wash clothes in a washer, listen to music in a car, turn on the television set and be entertained, or work on a computer at school. Largely, things like these that make our lives more pleasant and easier were developed in free-enterprise economies. In this chapter, we take a close look at the free-enterprise system. We consider what it is, how it operates, the roles government and entrepreneurs play in it, and its ethical basis.

AFTER YOU STUDY THIS CHAPTER, YOU WILL BE ABLE TO:

1. Discuss how the free-enterprise economic system answers the three economic questions.
2. List and discuss the five major features of free enterprise.
3. Identify the role that profit and loss play in a free-enterprise economy.
4. Discuss the relationship of free enterprise to the U.S. Constitution, the Declaration of Independence, and the Bill of Rights.
5. Identify the role of government in a free-enterprise economy.
6. Identify important economic relationships by using the diagram that shows the circular flow of economic activity.

KEY TERMS

Circular Flow of Economic Activity
Contract
Entrepreneur
Ethics
Free Rider
Household
Incentive

Loss
Private Good
Private Property
Public Good
Public Property
Profit
Total Cost
Total Revenue

The last chapter stated that the *way* in which a society answers the three economic questions—What will be produced? How will it be produced? For whom will it be produced?—defines its economic system. This section discusses how the free-enterprise economic system answers these questions.

As you read, keep these key questions in mind:

- What goods will be produced in a free-enterprise economy?
- Who decides how goods will be produced in a free-enterprise economy?
- For whom will goods be produced in a free-enterprise economy?
- What are five major features of free enterprise?

Free Enterprise and the Three Economic Questions

First, let's look briefly at how the three economic questions are answered in a free-enterprise economy.

What goods will be produced? In a free-enterprise economy, business firms are free to choose which goods they will produce. They exercise their freedom of choice by producing those goods or products they predict consumers will be willing and able to buy at a price and quantity that will earn profits for the company. For example, suppose consumers are willing and able to buy goods A, B, and C at a price and quantity that earns profits for business firms, but they are either unwilling or unable to buy goods D, E, and F at a price and quantity that will result in profits. Business firms will produce goods A, B, and C, and they will not produce D, E, and F.

How will these goods be produced? The individuals who own and manage the business firms will decide how the goods will be produced. For example, if the owners and managers of an automobile company want to use robots to produce

cars, then they will purchase the robots and produce cars with them. If a company prefers that its secretaries use typewriters instead of personal computers, then typewriters will be used at this company.

For whom will the goods be produced? In a free-enterprise economy, goods are produced for those people who are *willing* and *able* to buy them. Notice that it takes both willingness *and* ability to make a purchase. A person has the ability to buy a $20,000 car if that person has $20,000 to spend. But if the person is unwilling to spend $20,000 for the car, the car will not be purchased. There is also no purchase if a person has the willingness to buy something but is unable to do so. For example, Shelly may be willing to spend $2,000 to buy a computer but may currently be unable to do so because she doesn't have the money.

Five Features of Free Enterprise

Five major features or characteristics define free enterprise. They are private property, choice, voluntary exchange, competition, and incentives.

Private Property. Any good—such as a car, a house, a factory, or a piece of machinery—that is owned by an individual or a business is referred to as **private property**. Any good that is owned by the government—such as the Statue of Liberty—is referred to as **public property**. Under free enterprise, individuals and businesses have the right to own property. Furthermore, they may own as much property as they are willing and able to purchase, and they may sell whatever property they own.

Choice. Choice is a key element of free enterprise. Workers have the right to choose what work they will do and for whom they will work. Businesses have the right to choose the products they

◀ These pictures relate to the three economic questions every society has to answer. Can you tell which picture goes with which question?

will produce and offer for sale. Buyers have the right to choose the products they will buy.

Voluntary Exchange.   In free enterprise, individuals have the right to make exchanges or trades they believe will make them better off. For example, suppose Stephanie has $10 and Michael has a book. They trade. We conclude that Stephanie believes she is better off having the book than the $10 and Michael believes he is better off having the

MINI GLOSSARY

Private Property Any good that is owned by an individual or a business. For example, suppose John, an individual living in Anywhere, USA, owns his own car. It follows that his car is his private property.

Public Property Any good that is owned by government.

$10 than the book. Individuals make themselves better off by entering into exchanges—by trading what they value less for what they value more.

Competition.   Under free enterprise, individuals are free to compete with others. Suppose you live in a town with five bakeries. You think that you would like to open up a bakery and compete for customers with the five bakeries that now exist. In a free-enterprise system, there is no person or law to stop you from doing this.

As a consumer living in a free-enterprise system, you are likely to benefit from the competition between sellers. First, you are likely to have a bigger selection of products from which to choose. Second, sellers will compete with each other for your dollars by increasing the quality of the goods they sell, offering lower prices, providing better service, and so on. Of course, a consumer living in a free-enterprise system may still have a justified consumer complaint. The point here is that a free-enterprise system usually provides major advantages to the consumer. It may also have some disadvantages, which may or may not be present in other economic systems. We will examine consumer economic issues in a later chapter.

As a worker in a free-enterprise economy, you may benefit in another way. The competition between employers for your labor services will often result in your earning a higher wage or income than if there were no competition. For example, suppose you are a baker working for one of the five bakeries referred to earlier. A person opens up another bakery in town and tries to get you to come to work for her. How might she get you to quit your present job and come to work for her? Perhaps by offering you a higher income than you are currently earning.

Economic Incentives.   An **incentive** is something that encourages or motivates a person toward action. Under free enterprise, money acts as an incentive to produce. If you produce goods and services that people are willing and able to buy, you receive money in return. Adam Smith, often considered the father of modern economics, understood the usefulness of economic (or monetary) incentives in a free-enterprise economy when he said:

"It is not from the benevolence of the butcher, the brewer, or the baker, that we expect our dinner, but from their regard to their own interest."[1]

In other words, the butcher, the brewer, and the baker are interested in making themselves better off—they want to earn an income that they can use to purchase what they want. It is the desire for an *income* that strongly motivates them to produce for others.

Their desire to make themselves better off also has positive effects for others. Before they can obtain an income, they must provide something of worth to others. This is the essence of a free-enterprise economic system: Someone (the butcher, the brewer, or the baker) can get what he or she wants (more income) by offering to sell something that others want to buy.

---

1.   Adam Smith, *An Inquiry into the Nature and Causes of the Wealth of Nations*, vol. 1 (Chicago: University of Chicago Press, 1976), p. 18.

 # LEARNING CHECK

1. How is the question "For whom are goods produced?" answered in a free-enterprise economy?
2. What is the difference between private property and public property?
3. Under free enterprise, everyone has the right to own property. Does it follow that everyone will own property? Why or why not?
4. How does voluntary exchange benefit a person?
5. What advantages do consumers get from the competition between sellers that exists in a free-enterprise economy?

We have seen how a free-enterprise system answers the three economic questions and we have briefly discussed the five major features of free enterprise. In this section, we turn to the role of profits and losses in a free-enterprise economy.

As you read, keep these key questions in mind:

■ What roles do profits and losses play in a free-enterprise economy?
■ What do profits, losses, and resources have to do with each other?

Profits in a Free-Enterprise Economy

Suppose it costs $2,000 for a computer company to produce a computer and the company sells the computer for $3,500. The company earns $1,500 ($3,500 − $2,000 = $1,500) in *profit*. **Profit** is the amount of money left over after all the costs of production have been paid.

We can also look at profit in terms of total revenue and total cost. **Total revenue** is the price of a good, times the number of units of the good sold. For example, suppose you sell radios. The price of each one is $50. On Monday, you sell five radios. The total revenue for Monday is $250 ($50 × 5 = $250).

Total cost is the average cost (or expense) of a good, times the number of units of the good sold. Suppose the average cost of the five radios you sell is $30 per radio. The total cost is $150 ($30 × 5 = $150).

For the five radios, the difference between total revenue ($250) and total cost ($150) is $100 ($250 − $150 = $100). This $100 is profit. Notice that there is profit any time total revenue is greater than total cost. When the reverse holds—when total cost is greater than total revenue—there is a **loss**. For example, suppose a clothing store has a total revenue of $150,000 for the year but also has total costs of $200,000 for the year. If we subtract the store's costs from its revenues, we get −$50,000 ($150,000 − $200,000 = negative (−) $50,000). This is a loss for the year.

At any time in a free-enterprise economy, some business firms are earning profits and some firms are taking losses. Profits and losses are (1) signals to the firms actually earning the profits or taking the losses and (2) signals to other firms standing on the sidelines.

Let's illustrate these two points with an example. Suppose NBC television network puts on a comedy show on Thursday night that earns high ratings. Because companies will pay more to advertise on a high-rated show, the show creates high profits for NBC. CBS network puts on a crime show on Thursday night that receives low ratings and losses. With respect to the two shows, NBC earns profits and CBS takes losses. What are NBC and CBS likely to do now?

NBC is likely to do nothing but stand firm. The comedy show is earning high ratings, and the network is earning high profits. The public has spoken: it likes NBC's show, and so NBC will continue to run the show.

CBS, on the other hand, will probably cancel its crime show. The public has spoken: it doesn't like CBS's show, and so CBS will probably end up

---

MINI GLOSSARY

Incentive Something that encourages or motivates a person toward an action.

Profit The amount of money left over after all the costs of production have been paid. Profit exists whenever total revenue is greater than total cost.

Total Revenue Price of a good, times the number of units of the good sold.

Total Cost Average cost (or expense) of a good, times the number of units of the good sold.

Loss The amount of money by which total cost exceeds total revenue.

ECONOMICS AND PEOPLE

Adam Smith

Adam Smith, considered by many to be the father of modern economics, was born in Kircaldy, on the east coast of Scotland, on June 5, 1723, and died on July 17, 1790. Smith studied at both Glasgow University in Scotland and Oxford University in England.

1776: The Declaration of Independence and *The Wealth of Nations*

In 1776, the year the Declaration of Independence was signed, Smith published his famous work *An Inquiry into the Nature and Causes of the Wealth of Nations*. Today, most economists simply call this book *The Wealth of Nations*. Many of this country's founding fathers were familiar with Smith's book. For example, Thomas Jefferson, in a letter dated June 14, 1807, recommended it highly. He said in that letter, "If your views of political inquiry go further, to the subjects of money and commerce, Smith's *Wealth of Nations* is the best book to be read." [a]

Voluntary Exchange

Smith argued that both parties to a voluntary exchange must benefit, or they will not enter into the exchange. For Smith, this principle was equally true for two people living in the same country or for two people living in different countries. For example, when a person living in New York City buys something from a person in Los Angeles, both persons benefit. And when an American buys something from a German, both the American and the German benefit. Smith was definitely in favor of free international trade. He wanted people in different countries to be able to trade with each other without any government prohibitions. In today's world, there are certain government barriers to international trade called quotas and tariffs. A *tariff* is a tax on foreign goods imported into a country; a *quota* is a restriction on the number of foreign goods that can be sold in the country.

Smith was pro–free enterprise (which is different from being pro-business) Some people believe that if you favor a free-enterprise economy, you must favor everything that businesspersons do. This is incorrect. At times, businesspersons may want to hamper the free-enterprise economy. For example, suppose an American automobile manufacturer wants government to restrict the number of new foreign cars that enter the country to be sold. The manufacturer may want to do this to lessen competition. Is this act consistent with a free-enterprise economy? Not at all. Here, then, is an example in which a businessperson's interests are contrary to the interests of consumers in the free-enterprise economy. Smith recognized that businesspersons may sometimes want to hamper the free-enterprise economy so that they can benefit at someone else's expense. He said:

"People of the same trade seldom meet together, even for merriment and diversion, but the conversation ends in a conspiracy against the public, or in some contrivance to raise prices." [b]

Minimal Government

Smith was an advocate of minimal government. In his view, government existed to

a.   Thomas Jefferson, *Writings* (New York, The Library of America, 1984), p. 1176.

b.   Adam Smith, *An Inquiry into the Nature and Causes of the Wealth of Nations*, vol. 1 (Chicago: University of Chicago Press, 1976), p. 144.

provide goods that the free-enterprise economy did not provide, or did not provide in the quantities desired by the public. According to Smith, government should be involved in providing national defense, a court system, roads, and education. Beyond this, he believed that there was not much government should or could do without creating problems.

What Can Free Enterprise and Limited Government Produce?

Recall that Smith's most famous work was titled *An Inquiry into the Nature and Causes of the Wealth of Nations*. In other words, in this work Smith was interested in what exactly *causes* nations to be wealthy. We might put it this way today: Why are some nations wealthier than others? Why is the standard of living (the level of material goods and comforts a person

enjoys) of some people in some nations higher than the standard of living of other people in other nations? Smith's answer was that free enterprise and limited government caused nations to be wealthy. If Smith were a physician called in to diagnose a sick economy, he would call for a big dose of free enterprise coupled with limited government. For Smith, that's the medicine that would get the patient-nation healthier in time.

1. Explain how being pro–free enterprise is different from being pro-business.
2. According to Smith, what should government do?
3. What is the title of Smith's famous book?
4. What did Smith say about voluntary exchange?

---

taking the show off the air. It might replace the crime show with a comedy, because NBC has already shown that a comedy does better than a crime show.

Now consider the third major network, ABC. So far, it has been on the sidelines watching what has been happening to NBC and CBS on Thursday night. ABC is currently thinking about developing a new program. Will what has happened to NBC and CBS influence ABC's decision as to what type of program it will develop? Most likely it will. ABC will be more likely to develop a comedy than a crime show.

Let's step back from our example for a minute and see what has happened.

- First, the people at home decide what they want to watch on television.
- Second, many more people watch the NBC show than the CBS show. The NBC show has high ratings, and the CBS show has low ratings.

- Third, companies pay more to advertise on high-rated shows than low-rated shows, so NBC earns profits on its Thursday show whereas CBS takes losses.
- Fourth, NBC realizes it has a winning show, so it keeps the comedy show on the air. CBS realizes it has a losing show, so it takes the crime show off the air.
- Fifth, ABC, on the sidelines, decides to copy NBC instead of CBS.

At this point, stop and think about what is happening to resources. You will recall that resources consist of land, labor, capital, and entrepreneurship. When CBS decides to take its crime show off the air and replace it with, perhaps, a comedy show, what is happening to the resources that were previously used to produce the crime show?

An economist would say the resources are being *reallocated*—the resources are being moved from one place to another, or they are being used

▲ Two late-night talk shows were at war in 1993. David Letterman's show received high ratings; Chevy Chase's show was canceled because of low ratings. The resources used to produce Chevy Chase's show were released to be used for other things.

differently. The resources used to produce the crime show—the people who worked on the show, the cameras used to film the show, the accountants who kept the books—will probably be used to work on a comedy show instead of a crime show. Simply put, *resources flow toward profit; resources flow away from losses*. Think of it this way: Profit is like a big magnet—it *pulls* resources toward it. Loss is like a big wind—it pushes resources away.

QUESTION: *Suppose CBS and ABC copy NBC's success and put a comedy show on the air. Will CBS and ABC then earn as much profit from their comedy shows as NBC currently earns from its comedy show?*

ANSWER: *Not necessarily. Profit is never guaranteed in a free-enterprise system. CBS and ABC may develop unpopular comedy shows (not every comedy show is a winner) and not earn any profits at all. However, if CBS and ABC do develop popular comedy shows, the increased competition most likely will cut into NBC's profits. To summarize: (1) profit is never guaranteed in a free-enterprise system, and (2) competition from other firms usually reduces the profits of those firms currently earning profits.*

Profits: A Photo or a Video?

A photo shows you what happens at *one instant in time*—at the second the photo was taken. A video shows you what happens *over time*.

To think like an economist, you must learn to think in terms of videos, not photos. To illustrate, consider profits. If you take a photo of a business firm at one instant in time, you may see it earning profits. You may conclude that it always did, does now, and always will earn profits. But if you turn on the video camcorder, you may see profits being earned, and then you may see other firms trying to take some of the profits away through competition, and then you may see resources flowing toward the profit. With the camcorder running, you see much more of the story of profits than you see in a photo.

LEARNING CHECK

1. Define *total revenue*.
2. Define *total cost*.
3. Explain how profits and losses affect where resources will be used.
4. If a business is currently earning high profits producing lamps, what are other firms that observe this likely to do? Explain your answer.

SECTION 3 — THE ETHICS OF THE FREE-ENTERPRISE SYSTEM

There is little doubt that free enterprise gives us the ability to produce goods and services in vast quantities. In the words of Adam Smith, it can create *the wealth of nations*. This is considered one of the major benefits of free enterprise. But is free enterprise an ethical economic system? In other words, is it a moral or good system? We consider the **ethics** of free enterprise in this section.

As you read, keep these key questions in mind:

■ What are some of the qualities or characteristics of an ethical economic system?
■ What are some of the freedoms in free enterprise?

Ethics and Free Enterprise

It is not unusual to evaluate a person as being ethical or not. Can we do the same thing for an economic system? For example, is the free-enterprise system an ethical economic system?

Another way of approaching this question is to ask: What characteristics or qualities would the free-enterprise system need in order to be an ethical system? What goals would it need to meet? Here is what the supporters of free enterprise say.

First, they state that an economic system must allow individuals to choose their own occupations or professions. An ethical system, they say, does not force people to do jobs or tasks that they would rather not do. On this count, the supporters of free enterprise argue that it is an ethical system.

Under free enterprise, no one is forced to work at a job he or she does not want. A person is free to choose what to do. Although all workers may at times grumble about their jobs, this is not evidence that they would choose to do something else or that they are being forced to do their jobs. The ethical consideration concerns whether or not a person is being forced by someone to do the job.

Second, to be ethical, an economic system must produce the goods and services preferred by both the majority and the minority. Here, again, the supporters of free enterprise argue that it is an ethical system. Under free enterprise, if the majority of the people want to buy cars that are light colored and medium sized, with AM-FM radios, then this is the kind of cars that manufacturers will produce. (After all, they do not want to produce goods that consumers are not willing to buy.) But if a minority of people want big cars instead of medium-sized cars, then it is likely that some big cars will be produced, too. And if a different minority want small cars, some small cars will probably be produced.

Think of free enterprise at work in the restaurant business. In most American cities of moderate size, there are many different types of restaurants—restaurants that serve home cookery, fast

MINI GLOSSARY

Ethics Relates to principles of right and wrong, morality and immorality, good and bad.

food, Italian food, health food, and so on. The point is that, under free enterprise, a wide variety of goods and services is available because free enterprise has responded both to the majority and to minorities.

Third, an ethical economic system must reward (or punish) producers according to how well (or poorly) they respond to the preferences of the buying public. Free enterprise certainly does do this. Sellers that continue to give consumers what they want to buy in terms of (1) type of good, (2) quality of good, and (3) price of good will earn profits and stay in business. Those that do not end up taking losses and going out of business.

Fourth, the proponents of free enterprise argue that no economic system can be ethical if it limits people's freedom. In free enterprise, they say, people have numerous freedoms: the freedom to work where they want to work, the freedom to start their own businesses if they want, the freedom to acquire property, the freedom to buy and sell the goods they want to buy and sell, and even the freedom to fail.

Let's consider the freedom to fail. Suppose Harris Jackson takes his entire savings and opens up a

▼ The supporters of free enterprise say that, under free enterprise, individuals have the right to choose their professions or occupations.

shoe store. Six months later, Harris shuts down his business and declares bankruptcy. His problem: very few people wanted to buy shoes from him. Can this happen in a free-enterprise system? It can, and it does, every day in the United States.

Implicit in free enterprise is the freedom to spend our money as we choose, and sometimes this freedom results in other people's failing in business. Individuals must accept the consequences of their decisions. Free enterprise does not offer any guaranteed outcomes; rather, it offers freedom.

QUESTION: *What use is the freedom to start your own business in a free-enterprise economy if you don't have the money to start the business? Simply put, there is a difference between having the* freedom *to do something and having the* ability *to do it. Without the ability, the freedom seems useless. Comment on this problem.*

ANSWER: *Neither of the two major economic systems—free enterprise or socialism—can provide people with the* ability *to do anything, such as write a great novel, run the four-minute mile, or be a successful entrepreneur. But economic systems may or may not give the individuals the* opportunity *to realize their potential. The supporters of free enterprise argue that free enterprise does provide people with the* opportunity, *or freedom, to start a business if they have the ability.*

In addition, they argue that free enterprise gives individuals the opportunity to strengthen and develop their abilities. Suppose a person doesn't currently have the money or the knowledge to open up her own business; suppose she is currently working at a relatively low-wage job. Is she destined never to start her own business? Not necessarily. Perhaps she can today begin doing those things that are necessary to start her own business in the future. These may include working hard in her current job, saving some money, attending school to learn about the business she wants to start, obtaining a business loan, and so on. The economic history of the United States, under free enterprise, is full of stories of people who were poor and uneducated (and in many cases didn't know the English language), yet went on to start their own businesses and become economically successful.

CASE STUDY

Russia Moves Toward Free Enterprise

The Soviet Union, once a nation composed of 15 republics, just as the United States is now a nation composed of 50 states, had a strong socialist economic system. In the late 1980s and early 1990s, the Soviet Union experienced immense economic and political pressures. Because of these pressures the nation was dissolved in December 1991. Russia, once a Soviet republic, but now an independent country, began to move away from a socialist economy and toward a free-enterprise system. As a result of this move, some people lost their jobs.

▲ A typical day in the former Soviet Union: A long line of people wait to buy shoes.

Before we reach any conclusions about why people lost their jobs, let's back up and look at some things more closely. When Russia had strictly a socialist or command economy, government officials decided what goods would be produced, what prices these goods would sell for, and so on. These officials were ordering factory managers to produce some goods that very few Russians wanted to buy. At the same time, some goods that the Russian people wanted to buy were not being produced. To illustrate, suppose the Russian people want to buy 2,000 toasters and 4,000 radios at certain prices. The Russian government officials do not know this (how would they know?). They order factory managers to produce 5,000 toasters and only 200 radios. As far as the Russian consumer is concerned, too many toasters have been produced (5,000 − 2,000 = 3,000 units too many) and too few radios have been produced (4,000 − 200 = 3,800 units too few).

The same problem—too much of one thing and too little of something else—was multiplied many thousands of times over in the Russian socialist economy. The move toward free enterprise was made to get some balance between what people wanted to buy and what was produced. But it is easy to see that as a change like this takes place, some people will lose their jobs. For instance, in our example, some of the people making toasters will lose their jobs.

Elena Alyoshechkina, who lives in Nizhny Novgorod, Russia, lost her job.[a] The business she worked for was sold to a private citizen. This private citizen wanted to produce something other than what the business had been producing—

---

a.   Elena's story was reported in "Russians Face New Threat: The Pink Slip," *Wall Street Journal*, June 8, 1992, p. A6.

CASE STUDY (continued)

buttons—and so he fired some workers. Free enterprise had brought a new freedom to Russia—the freedom to fire employees.

Certainly the story of Elena is a sad one. But let's consider it in light of the fundamental issue of scarcity, discussed in Chapter 1. Scarcity tells us that our wants are greater than the resources—such as land, labor, and capital—available to satisfy those wants. Thus, it is better to use what resources we have to produce goods that people want to buy than to use the resources to produce goods that people do not want to buy. In fact, producing goods that no one wants to buy is a waste of resources.

In the short run, then, Elena loses her job, and we are sad for her. But Elena's services were wasted if she was producing something that people did not want to buy in the quantities she and others were producing it. (Might there have been too many buttons being produced?) Elena lost her job as the result of Russia's moving from an economy in which official decisions ruled to one where buyers' preferences ruled. In the long run, it is likely that Elena will find another job—a job where she is producing or selling a good that people want to buy.

1. When Russia had a strictly socialist economy, how did producers or factory managers decide how much of a particular good to produce?
2. "Elena's work services were wasted if she was busy producing more of a particular good than people wanted to buy." Do you agree or disagree? Explain your answer.

Economic Principles and the Constitution, the Bill of Rights, and the Declaration of Independence

The Constitution, the Bill of Rights, and the Declaration of Independence hold a special place in the hearts and minds of most Americans. It can also be argued that these three documents have a special significance to free enterprise. Specifically, each document has "free-enterprise economic principles" contained within it.

Remember that private property, choice, and competition are important features of free enterprise and that freedom captures the essence of what free enterprise is all about. It is not difficult to find evidence that the Constitution, the Bill of Rights, and the Declaration of Independence are also about private property, choice, competition, and freedom, among other things.

In the Bill of Rights, for example, it is noted that "private property [shall not] be taken for public use, without just compensation." In other words, if the government wants, say, the land you own in order to put in a road, it cannot simply take that land from you. It must justly compensate, or pay, you for that land. This fact shows the high regard in which private property is held in the Bill of Rights.

In the Declaration of Independence, the signers listed many complaints against the king of Great Britain, George III. One was that the king had prevented the 13 colonies from "trad[ing] with all parts of the world." Surely the signers of the Declaration of Independence were angry at being denied the freedom to choose with whom they would trade. They were angry at King George III for not allowing them to practice free trade—which is an essential ingredient of free enterprise—with the rest of the world.

▶ The United States has a long history of being a free-enterprise country. Free-enterprise elements are found in the Constitution, the Bill of Rights, and the Declaration of Independence.

Article 1, Section 8, of the Constitution of the United States says that "no tax or duty shall be laid on articles exported from any State." In this provision, we see that the Constitution favors preserving competition. If states had been allowed the right to impose a tax on each other's goods, competition within each state would have been lessened. For example, suppose the people in North Carolina and Virginia produce shoes. Furthermore, suppose the North Carolina government imposes a tax on all shoes imported into North Carolina from Virginia. This would make the shoes produced in Virginia more expensive in North Carolina and thus less competitive there than the shoes produced in North Carolina. To preserve competition—an important feature of free enterprise—it was important to deny states the right to tax each other's goods.

Economic Rights and Responsibilities in a Free-Enterprise Economy

People have certain rights in a free-enterprise economy, but rights rarely come without responsibilities. What are the responsibilities of persons in a free-enterprise economy?

Many people argue that the right to voluntary exchange comes with the responsibility of giving the other person involved in the exchange accurate information about what is being exchanged. For example, suppose Steve wants to exchange (sell) his 12-year-old house for the $130,000 that Roberto is willing and able to pay for it. In a free-enterprise economic system, Steve and Roberto have the economic right to complete this exchange, but Steve also has the responsibility to tell Roberto the particulars about the house. For example, if the house has faulty plumbing, Steve should tell Roberto this fact. If the house has termites, then Steve must tell Roberto this, too. In other words, Steve has the responsibility of truthfully relating to Roberto the facts about the product that Roberto is considering buying. This is a matter of simple fairness or justice.

Consider another economic right in a free-enterprise economy—the right to private property. What responsibility is associated with this right? It is the responsibility of using one's property only for legal purposes. Stated differently, it is a responsibility to respect and abide by the law. For example, suppose Isabella owns a car. She certainly has the right to use that car to drive to and from work, go on vacations, pick up friends at school, and so on, but she also has the responsibility of obeying the speed limit and driving carefully.

Finally, consider the economic right to compete in a free-enterprise system. The responsibility attached to this right is to compete in a truthful, legitimate manner. For example, if both Mario and Yolanda own pizzerias in town, and are thus in competition with each other, both Mario and Yolanda have the responsibility to be truthful about the other's business. For example, Mario should not lie to his customers and tell them Yolanda's pizzeria was cited by the government health examiner for having insects in the kitchen when this is not true. Yolanda must not lie and say that Mario uses less cheese in his pizzas than in fact he does use.

LEARNING CHECK

1. "Under free enterprise, only the majority of people may buy the goods they have a preference for; the minority will always end up buying those goods they would prefer not to buy." Do you agree or disagree? Explain your answer.
2. "Free enterprise guarantees economic success." Do you agree or disagree? Explain your answer.
3. Explain what responsibility goes with each of the following rights: (a) the right to voluntary exchange, (b) the right to private property, (c) the right to compete.

SECTION 4 ENTREPRENEURS

Within a free-enterprise economy, there are **entrepreneurs**. What does an entrepreneur do? Chapter 1 discussed *entrepreneurship* as one of the four broad categories of resources that an economy can make use of. An entrepreneur, then, is a person that exhibits entrepreneurship. That is, an entrepreneur is a person who has that special talent for searching out and taking advantage of new business opportunities and developing new products and new ways of doing things. In this section, we examine the role of the entrepreneur in a free-enterprise economy.

As you read, keep these key questions in mind:

■ What is an entrepreneur?
■ How does an entrepreneur help you?

It Is Not Easy to Be an Entrepreneur

To get some idea of what it is like to be an entrepreneur, let's try to place ourselves in the shoes of one. Our definition of an entrepreneur says he or she does any or all of three things: (1) searches out and takes advantage of new business opportunities, (2) develops new products, or (3) develops new ways of doing things.

With respect to the first task—searching out and taking advantage of new business opportunities—let's first ask ourselves how we would go about searching out new business opportunities. There is no book in the library which will give you

▲ Entrepreneurs change our lives through the development of new products.

a personalized answer. There is no book on *Your New Business Opportunities* with a specific blueprint for you. And even if there were, by the time the book was published and found its way into the library, the business opportunities listed in it would no longer be new. Most people, when confronted with the task of finding a new business opportunity, end up scratching their heads. The fact is, most people are not entrepreneurs. Entrepreneurs are a tiny minority of the population.

Think about the second task—developing new products. What new product can we think of developing? We are accustomed to thinking in terms of products that already exist—televisions, computers, cars, VCRs, and so on. It is not easy to think of a new product, especially one that has a high potential for sales. For example, here is a product: a simple gadget that you attach to the top of your book as you are reading. When you finish reading a page, you simply say, "Turn page," and the gadget turns to the next page. Is this an idea for a new product? Yes. But we are not sure that many people would want to buy this product. After all, turning the pages of a book is not a major difficulty for most people.

Think about the third task—developing new ways of doing things. First, ask yourself, What

"things" would we want to do differently? This, in itself, is a hard question to answer. The next question is, How would we do these things differently?

The discussion so far should give you some idea of the types of obstacles, problems, and questions the entrepreneur has to overcome, solve, and answer. Now, let's consider another issue. If an entrepreneur comes up with an idea for a new product, develops and produces it, and then offers it for sale, how are we made better off?

Think of entrepreneurs who have done this in the past and how you were helped. For example, think again about Steven Jobs, one of the developers of the personal computer. Was your life affected in a good or a bad way as a result of his entrepreneurship? Most of us would say that we were affected positively by the introduction of the personal computer. What about the entrepreneur

MINI GLOSSARY

Entrepreneur A person who has that special talent for searching out and taking advantage of new business opportunities, and developing new products and new ways of doing things.

ANALYZING PRIMARY SOURCES

The Wealth of Nations, by Adam Smith

Each field of study has its major books. One of the major books in economics is An Inquiry into the Nature and Causes of the Wealth of Nations *(usually simply called* The Wealth of Nations*), by Adam Smith, published in 1776. Among other things, Smith discusses the important role the division of labor plays in increasing the wealth of a people.*

The division of labor *refers to a system in which the job to be done is broken down into smaller tasks, and each worker (or a group of workers) performs only one of these tasks. For example, in an automobile factory, some people only bolt doors, whereas others only paint cars. In your school, probably some teachers teach only mathematics whereas others teach only history. In the automobile factory, and in the school, there is a division of labor.*

Read what Smith has to say about the division of labor in a pin factory. (Don't forget that Smith was writing in the 18th century.)

"The effects of the division of labour, in the general business of society, will be more easily understood, by considering in what manner it operates in some particular manufactures . . . .

To take an example, therefore, from a very trifling manufacture; but one in which the division of labour has been very often taken notice of, the trade of the pin-maker; a workman not educated to this business (which the division of labour has rendered a distinct trade), nor acquainted with the use of the machinery employed in it (to the invention of which the same division of labor has probably given occasion), could scarce, perhaps, with his utmost industry, make one pin in a day, and certainly could not make twenty. But in the way in which this business is now carried on, not only the whole work is a peculiar trade, but it is divided into a number of branches, of which the greater part are likewise peculiar trades. One

man draws out the wire, another straights it, a third cuts it, a fourth points it, a fifth grinds it at the top for receiving the head; to make the head requires two or three distinct operations; to put it on, is a peculiar business, to whiten the pins is another; it is even a trade by itself to put them into the paper; and the important business of making a pin is, in this manner, divided into about eighteen distinct operations, which, in some manufactories, are all performed by distinct hands, though in others the same man will sometimes perform two or three of them. I have seen a small manufactory of this kind where ten men only were employed, and where some of them consequently performed two or three distinct operations. But though they were very poor, and therefore but indifferently accommodated with the necessary machinery, they could, when they exerted themselves, make among them about twelve pounds of pins in a day. There are in a pound upwards of four thousand pins in a middling size. Those ten persons, therefore, could make among them upwards of forty-eight thousand pins in a day. Each person, therefore, making a tenth part of forty-eight thousand pins, might be considered as making four thousand eight hundred pins in a day. [a] **"**

---

1. According to Smith, producing a pin can be broken down into how many operations?
2. According to Smith, how many pins could 10 persons make in a day if each person specialized in a particular task?
3. Summarize the main idea of the passage.
4. List two settings in which the division of labor operates.

---

a.   Adam Smith, *An Inquiry into the Nature and Causes of the Wealth of Nations*, vol. 1 (Chicago: University of Chicago Press, 1976), pp. 7–9.

who first developed the compact disc, the felt-tip pen, or the quartz digital watch? Most of us would say that the development of these products affected our lives in a positive way. The entrepreneur, it would seem, plays an important role in society. He or she takes the risks to develop new products or new ways of doing things, and the public benefits from this risk taking. From a consumer's point of view, more entrepreneurs in a society likely means more choices of goods and services in that society.

Finally, an entrepreneur has an ethical responsibility to people. He or she has the responsibility to put forth a safe product or service, one that consumers can benefit from and will not harm them in any way. Also, the entrepreneur has the responsibility to deal honestly with people. For example, it is unethical to falsely advertise a new product, to claim that it can do certain things that it cannot do.

LEARNING CHECK

1. What does an entrepreneur do?
2. How might an entrepreneur's risk-taking activities benefit society?

SECTION 5 THE ROLE OF GOVERNMENT IN A FREE-ENTERPRISE ECONOMY

Advocates of free enterprise usually say that government should play a limited role in the economy. According to them, government should be limited to (1) enforcing contracts and (2) providing public goods.

As you read about government's role in a free-enterprise or market economy, keep these key questions in mind:

- What would happen if government did not enforce contracts?
- What is a public good?
- In a free-enterprise economy, why won't individuals produce public goods for sale?

Government as Enforcer of Contracts

Think of what life would be like in a nation without government—no city government, no state government, no federal government. Suppose you own a construction company and regularly purchase supplies from people. On Tuesday, you

enter into a **contract** with a person. You agree to pay him $1,000 today if he delivers a shipment of wood to you on Friday. Friday comes and there is no wood. Saturday, no wood. Sunday, no wood. On Monday you call the person who was supposed to deliver the wood to ask what has happened. The person says that he has no intention of delivering the wood to you. "But you took my $1,000. That is theft," you say. The person just laughs at you and hangs up the phone.

What do you do now? You can't turn to the police, because police services are part of government, and there is no government.

You can't take the person to court, because the court system is a part of government, and there is no government.

You can see that there is a need for some institution to enforce contracts. Government is such an

MINI GLOSSARY

Contract An agreement between two or more people to do something.

institution. In our society today, government stands ready to punish persons who break their contracts.

Who is better off and who is worse off with government standing ready to enforce contracts? Just about everybody is better off. Only the contract breakers are worse off, because they can no longer break their contracts without at least the threat of punishment.

Could the free-enterprise system function without government there to enforce contracts? Most economists believe that it could function, but not nearly as well as it does now. Instead, it would be severely crippled.

Their argument is this. Without government to enforce contracts, the risk of going into business would be too great for many people. (Would you go into business if you knew people could break their contracts with you and not be punished?) Only a few people would assume the high risks of producing television sets, houses, cars, computers, and so on. The economy would be much smaller. For some economists, a free-enterprise system will be a large, thriving economy when government acts to enforce contracts and a small, sluggish economy when it does not.

Government as Provider of Public Goods

In addition to enforcing contracts, government provides **public goods** . A public good is a good or product that, once produced and provided to one person, gives benefits to more than one person. More importantly, *it is a good whose benefits cannot be denied to anyone.* For example, national defense—which consists of airplanes, tanks, bombs, ships, security systems, missiles, and so on—is a public good. Once U.S. national defense is produced, no one living in the United States can be denied its benefits—namely, protection. It is impossible to protect a person living in New York and not also protect a person living in Los Angeles. It is impossible to protect a person living in Detroit, Michigan, and not also protect a person

living in Kalamazoo, Michigan. The benefits of national defense are there to be consumed by all.

A dam is another commonly cited example of a public good. Suppose 125 persons in a certain area occasionally have their land flooded. The government decides to build a dam so that flooding will no longer be a problem. Once the dam is built and properly working, its benefits cannot be denied to any person. It is impossible for Jones to receive the benefits and Smith be denied the same benefits.

Now contrast a public good with a **private good** . A private good is a good or product whose benefits can be denied to people. There are hundreds of examples of private goods: computers, cars, clothes, and shoes are only a few. Consider a pair of jeans. Once the jeans are produced and purchased by you, the jeans cannot be worn (at the same time) by anyone else. The jeans are yours. You, and you alone, reap their benefits.

Economists contend that in a free-enterprise economy, people will be willing to produce private goods, but no one will want to produce public goods. Why? Because once a public good is produced, no one will need to buy it. Again, why? Because the benefits of public goods cannot be denied to anyone. People will not pay for the benefits of a good that cannot be denied to them if they don't pay.

To illustrate, suppose a private company builds a dam to stop the flooding on people's land. After the dam is built, representatives of the company go to the people and ask them if they want to buy the dam's services (flood prevention). Each person says, "The dam is already in place and I am benefiting from it. Why should I pay for benefits I am already receiving?" Economists have a name for

---

MINI GLOSSARY

Public Good A good or product whose benefits cannot be denied to anyone. National defense is a public good.

Private Good A good or product whose benefits can be denied to a person other than the owner. A car is a private good.

CONSUMER ECONOMIC DECISIONS

Guidelines for a Wise Consumer

anette, 16, attends high school in Columbus, Ohio. Her days are filled with going to school, attending band practice, doing her homework, talking to her friends, going shopping, working part-time, and watching television. Recently, she has noticed that she has been buying more of the goods she sees advertised on television. Consequently, she has been spending more of her part-time earnings and saving less. Nanette wishes she weren't so attracted to the goods she sees advertised on television. She admits she has become a compulsive buyer. This is a person who feels driven to buy things. She wants to change. But how does she go about changing?

Guidelines for Becoming a Wise Consumer

Becoming a wise consumer requires us to think before we buy; it requires us to follow some basic rules. As buyers, keep the following rules and thoughts in mind:

1. *Think of the opportunity cost of what you plan to buy.* Suppose your friend has recently purchased a new style of coat. You think the coat looks good on him, and you want to buy one for yourself. Before you do, ask yourself: What can't I buy or do if I spend the money to buy the coat? In other words, you want to know the opportunity cost of buying the coat. You want to know what you will give up, or forfeit, if you buy it. You may give up the opportunity to buy some shirts, or add to your savings account, or at-

tend as many movies. In the end, you have to ask yourself if the coat is worth what you would give up to buy it. Thinking in terms of opportunity cost helps us to think in terms of the reality of things.

2. *Ask yourself if there are substitutes for what you plan to buy.* Ramona's friend Alicia has recently purchased an Apple computer. Ramona is seriously thinking of buying an Apple computer as well, but she has not yet saved enough money to do so. Before Ramona buys an Apple, she should consider whether there are any substitutes for the Apple that may serve her better and be cheaper. What about an IBM computer? Or a Zenith computer? Too often, buyers rush to buy a particular product without considering the many substitutes that may exist for it. Considering the substitutes opens the door to a wider range of choice, where price, quality, and other things can be more fully considered.

3. *Don't be persuaded to buy something based on a flashy commercial jingle.* In a free-enterprise economy, where there is stiff competition between sellers to sell their products, flashy ads and jingles are used to get buyers' attention. There is, at times, a tendency for buyers to respond to the ads or jingles by buying the products. It is important to realize, though, that flashy ads and jingles rarely inform us about the quality and price of the product under consideration. If quality and price matter to you, then it is important to go beyond the ad and jingle and become informed on these matters.

Making CONSUMER ECONOMIC DECISIONS (continued)

4. *Keep in mind your long-run goals.* Bryan, 16, has a long-run goal of buying a car. He currently attends high school in Arlington, Virginia, and works part-time as a stockboy at a building-supplies store after school and on weekends.

During the course of a week, Bryan sees many things that he would like to buy—new clothes, new CDs, and so on. If he buys these things, it will become harder for him to accomplish his long-run goal of buying a car. Bryan has to make a choice: buy more of what he wants now, and decrease the probability of buying a car, or buy less of what he wants now, and increase the probability of buying a car.

Should long-run goals *always* take precedence over short-run goals? If so, then aren't we always living for the future and never for the present? There is no absolute right or wrong here. It's not that long-run goals should always take precedence over short-run goals or that short-run goals should always take precedence over long-run goals. It's simply that *sometimes* a person's short-run goals conflict with his or her long-run goals and he or she should be aware of this. If Bryan, in our example, is not aware that his short-run goal of buying clothes and CDs is at odds with his being able to buy a car, then he will probably end up not buying a car as soon. At a future date, he may regret having spent too much in the present and not keeping an eye on the future.

---

1. Think of a time when you purchased something priced at more than $15 and failed to consider one or more of the four consumer guidelines. Would you still have made the purchase had you considered the guidelines? Explain why or why not.

---

persons who receive the benefits of a good without paying for it. They are called **free riders**.

When it comes to a public good, then, people know they cannot usually get others to voluntarily pay for it, so they decide not to produce it. (Looking back, we can see that the private company in our example would probably not have built the dam in the first place.)

Contrast public goods with private goods. Every day, people produce private goods—cars, television sets, radios, copying machines, sunglasses, and so on. They do so because they can withhold the benefits of these goods *until* people pay for them. A car salesperson says to a customer, "Would you like to buy this new car?" If the customer wants the car, there is no way she can receive the benefits of the car without paying for it. The rule is: Pay first, and then the car is yours. There are no free riders when it comes to private goods, because there is no way to receive the benefits of the good without paying for it.

To summarize, it can be said that in a purely free-enterprise economy, people will produce private goods, but they will not produce public goods. They will not produce public goods because of the *free-rider problem*: there is no incentive to pay for the public goods once they are produced.

People still want public goods, though. National defense and dams are useful goods that people desire to have. Who or what will produce these goods? The answer is government. Government will provide public goods and pay for them with taxes. Many economists argue that government *should* provide public goods, because no one else will. In fact, the framers of the U.S. Constitution recognized the legitimate role of government in providing public goods, such as national defense. Here is the preamble to the Constitution:

> We, the People of the United States, in Order to form a more perfect Union, establish Justice, insure domestic Tranquility, *provide for the common defence*, promote the general Welfare, and secure the Blessings of Liberty to ourselves and our Posterity, do ordain and establish this Constitution for the United States of America. (Emphasis added)

QUESTION: *How do people communicate to government what public goods, and how much of these goods, it should provide?*

ANSWER: *In the U.S. system of government, one way people communicate what public goods, and how much of these goods, they want is through the political process. U.S. citizens have the right to vote, and they can influence what government does through the ballot box. For example, suppose the majority of the people want the U.S. government to provide less national defense instead of more national defense. They will likely vote for politicians who voice this same preference and vote against politicians who do not share their preference. Americans also have the right to lobby their elected representatives directly, by writing letters or talking to their elected representatives in person.*

LEARNING CHECK

1. Identify each of the following as a public or a private good: (a) a pair of shoes, (b) sunshine, (c) a pen, (d) a pizza, and (e) national defense.
2. Explain why a free-enterprise economy is larger when government enforces contracts than when it does not.
3. Why won't a private business firm produce a public good?
4. How are public goods paid for?

SECTION 6 | **THE CIRCULAR FLOW OF ECONOMIC ACTIVITY: A PICTURE IS WORTH A THOUSAND WORDS**

We have examined the free-enterprise system in some detail in this chapter. We end with a picture of it—one that shows the routes of economic activity in the economy. The picture represents the *circular flow of economic activity*.

As you read, keep the following key question in mind:

■ In an economy, what are the economic relationships between (a) businesses and households, (b) government and households, (c) government and business, (d) households and foreign economies, and (e) foreigners and the U.S. economy?

The Circular Flow

Look at Exhibit 2-1. It is a picture of the **circular flow of economic activity**. At first sight, it simply

MINI GLOSSARY
Free Rider A person who receives the benefits of a good without paying for it.
Circular Flow of Economic Activity Shows the economic relationships that exist between different economic groups in the economy.

looks like a picture with lines going every which way. But those lines tell a story.

1. It is customary to think of the U.S. economy as composed of businesses, government, and **households**. In the exhibit, businesses, government, and households are identified in green.
2. There is an economic relationship between businesses and households. Businesses sell goods and services to households (light blue arrow) for which households make monetary payments (dark blue arrow). For example, a consumer buys a sofa from a furniture company.
3. There is another economic relationship between businesses and households. Individuals in households sell resources (such as their labor services) to business firms (red arrow). In return, businesses pay individuals for these resources (light green arrow). For example, a business pays a worker a day's wage.
4. Both businesses and households have a certain economic relationship with government. Households pay taxes to the government (orange arrow) and in return receive certain goods and services (purple arrow). For example, government provides individuals with roads, schools, and national defense. The same kind of relationship holds between businesses and government. Businesses pay taxes to government (grey arrow), and government provides certain goods and services to businesses (brown arrow).

If we step back from Exhibit 2-1 and look at it as a whole, rather than focusing on any of its parts, we will see a representation of the economic activity that goes on in the U.S. economy. One thing in particular is important to notice—the relationships between different economic agents. For example, there is a relationship between:

- Businesses and households—*Households sell resources to businesses, and businesses pay for these resources. Also, businesses sell goods and services to households, and households pay for these goods and services.*

- Government and households—*Households pay taxes to government, and government provides goods and services to households.*
- Government and businesses—*Businesses pay taxes to government, and government provides goods and services to businesses.*

Why Is the Circular-Flow Diagram Useful?

Suppose you are watching the news one night on television. An economist who works for the president of the United States is stating that the president is seriously considering raising people's taxes. Look at Exhibit 2-1 and ask yourself which arrow is going to be affected by this action. It is the orange arrow labeled "Households pay taxes," which goes from households to government. If all other things remain the same, this arrow is going to grow larger, because there will be more tax dollars flowing through it.

Next, ask yourself this question: If there are more tax dollars flowing through the orange arrow from households to government, are there going to be any fewer dollars flowing through some other arrow? The answer is yes—the blue arrow that moves from households to businesses. In other words, because households pay more of their income in taxes, they will have less of their income to buy television sets, cars, computers, and so on. (In turn, the government will have more money to spend on public goods and services, for example.)

In conclusion, the circular-flow diagram allows us to see how a change in one thing in the economy—such as taxes—will lead to a change somewhere else in the economy—such as in the amount households spend on goods and services produced by businesses.

MINI GLOSSARY

Household An economic unit of one person or more that sells resources and buys goods and services.

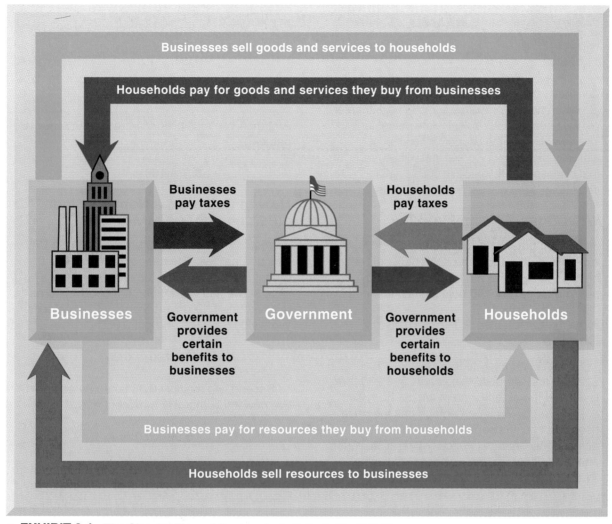

The Circular Flow of Economic Activity in the U.S. Economy.

Businesses sell goods and services to households

Households pay for goods and services they buy from businesses

Businesses pay taxes

Households pay taxes

Businesses

Government provides certain benefits to businesses

Government

Government provides certain benefits to households

Households

Businesses pay for resources they buy from households

Households sell resources to businesses

▲ **EXHIBIT 2-1.** The Circular Flow of Economic Activity in the U.S. Economy.

 LEARNING CHECK

1. According to the circular flow of economic activity, in what economic activities is government engaged? (Look at Exhibit 2-1 to help you answer the question.)

2. According to the circular flow of economic activity, in what economic activities are households engaged?

3. According to the circular flow of economic activity, in what economic activities are businesses engaged?

4. Businesses both buy and sell goods or products. For example, a car company might buy tires, carpet, and radios to install in the cars that it sells. Pick a company. Then identify two goods that it buys and one good that it sells. (Warning: Be sure that you identify a good that a company buys and not a resource. For example, the car company in our example might buy the labor of thousands of workers, but labor is not a good, it is a resource.)

DEVELOPING ECONOMIC SKILLS

Calculating Percentages

In their work, economists often have to calculate percentages. For example, in the next chapter, we will have occasion to calculate percentages when we discuss the economic concept of elasticity of demand. So that you will be ready for that discussion, the specifics of calculating percentages are discussed in this feature.

What Does *Percent* Mean?

Percent means *per one hundred*. For example, if Frank says he scored 87 percent on his biology test, this means he received 87 points out of every 100 points he could obtain.

How to Calculate a Percentage Change

Suppose the price of a car last year was $12,000 and the price this year is $13,200. We know that the actual price of the car has risen by $1,200. But by what percentage has the price risen? To find this percentage, we take the *actual dollar change in price* (which is $1,200) and divide it by *last year's price* (which was $12,000). This gives us the number 0.1.

$$\$1,200 \div \$12,000 = 0.1$$

We multiply 0.1, which is called the quotient, by 100 to convert it into percentage terms.

$$0.1 \times 100 = 10\%$$

We conclude that the car's price has risen by 10 percent.

How to Calculate One Number as a Percentage of Another Number

What percentage is 10 of 100? Perhaps you know the answer right away. It is 10 percent. How did you calculate the percentage? You divided 10 by 100, like this:

$$10 \div 100 = 0.1$$

And then you multiplied 0.1 times 100 to get 10 percent.

$$0.1 \times 100 = 10\%$$

How to Calculate a Number When a Percentage Is Known

Yesterday the temperature in New York City was 50 degrees. The temperature today is 6 percent higher. What is today's temperature?

First, we find what 6 percent of 50 is. To do this, we need to convert 6 percent to decimals. We divide 6 by 100 and get 0.06.

$$6 \div 100 = 0.06$$

Second, we multiply 0.06 times 50 and get 3. We now know that 3 is 6 percent of 50.

$$0.06 \times 50 = 3$$

Third, since we know that today's temperature in New York is 6 percent higher than yesterday's temperature, we add 3 to 50 to find today's temperature—53 degrees.

$$3 + 50 = 53$$

---

1. The price of a famous painting was $10,000 in 1989. The price of the same painting was $30,000 in 1993. What is the percentage increase in price between 1989 and 1993?
2. 40 is what percentage of 120?
3. Smith earned $45,000 last year. This year he earned 10 percent more than last year. What did he earn this year?

CHAPTER 2 REVIEW

CHAPTER SUMMARY

1. In a free-enterprise economy, business firms are free to choose which goods they will produce. They exercise their freedom of choice by producing those goods they predict consumers will be willing and able to buy at a price and quantity that will earn profits.

2. In a free-enterprise economy, the individuals who own and manage the business firms decide how the goods will be produced.

3. In a free-enterprise economy, goods are produced for those people who are willing and able to buy them.

4. The major features that define free enterprise are: (a) private property, (b) choice, (c) voluntary exchange, (d) competition, and (e) economic, or monetary, incentives.

5. Profit exists when total revenue is greater than total cost.

6. Loss exists when total cost is greater than total revenue.

7. Resources flow toward profits; resources flow away from losses.

8. Adam Smith, who many economists consider the father of modern economics and a supporter of free enterprise, said that businesspersons may sometimes want to hamper the free-enterprise economy in order to benefit at someone else's expense.

9. The supporters of free enterprise believe that an ethical economic system would (a) allow individuals to choose their own occupations or professions, (b) produce the goods and services preferred by both the majority and the minority, (c) reward (or punish) producers according to how well (or poorly) they respond to the preferences of the buying public, and (d) permit people numerous freedoms. The supporters of free enterprise believe that it satisfies all four conditions and is therefore an ethical economic system.

10. An entrepreneur is a person who has that special talent for searching out and taking advantage of new business opportunities, and developing new products and new ways of doing things.

11. Supporters of a free-enterprise economy contend that government is needed to enforce contracts and provide public goods.

12. Individuals in a free-enterprise economy will not produce public goods because of the problem of free riders: no one will pay for the goods once they are produced.

13. The circular flow of economic activity shows the economic relationships between economic agents, such as households, businesses, and government.

BUILD YOUR ECONOMIC VOCABULARY

Match the word with the correct definition, example, or statement.

1. free rider
2. private good
3. public good
4. contract
5. total revenue
6. incentive

a. price times number of units sold
b. an agreement between two or more people to do something
c. benefits of the good cannot be denied to anyone
d. receives the benefits but does not pay anything
e. benefits of the good can be denied to a person
f. encourages or motivates a person toward action

CHAPTER 2 REVIEW
(continued)

REVIEW QUESTIONS

1. How is the question "How will goods be produced?" answered in a free-enterprise economy?
2. Explain how voluntary exchange can make individuals better off.
3. Calculate the profit or loss in each of the following situations (TR stands for total revenue and TC stands for total cost):

   a. TR = $400, TC = $322
   b. TR = $4,323, TC = $4,555
   c. TR = $576, TC = $890
   d. TR = $899,765, TC = $456,897

   Be sure to put a minus (−) in front of a loss figure.
4. Company Z produces men's clothes. For the last 18 months, the company has been taking a loss. What is the loss "saying" to Company Z? Stated differently, what message should be coming through loud and clear to Company Z?
5. An economist would say that profit attracts resources. What does this mean? You may want to give an example to illustrate your point.
6. What was Adam Smith's position on the role of government?
7. According to supporters of free enterprise, what should government do? Why should it do these things?
8. Is education a private or a public good? Explain your answer.
9. What are the five major features of a free-enterprise economy?
10. According to the supporters of free enterprise, what are the four characteristics of an ethical economic system?
11. Define the following terms: *household, profit, total revenue, total cost, entrepreneur, free rider*.
12. What does the circular-flow diagram (such as in Exhibit 2-1) show and how is it useful?

SHARPEN YOUR CRITICAL THINKING SKILLS

1. Here is a short debate between two people, Turner and Carlin. First, read the debate carefully. Then, write an essay supporting the person you think makes the stronger points. It is important for you to address *why* you think one person's points are stronger than the other's.

   Turner: Taxation is theft. The government should not be involved in taxing people.

   Carlin: The government has to tax people in order to raise the funds to pay for public goods.

   Turner: If people wanted the public goods, they would gladly pay for them. The fact that they have to be forced—through the tax sys-tem—to pay for them must mean that they do not want the goods.

   Carlin: There is a special problem here. People may want the public goods but not be willing to pay for them on a voluntary basis.

   Turner: Who are you to decide what people do and do not want? Why not simply make these judgments based on people's behavior? If they really want something, they will purchase it. If they don't really want something, they won't purchase it. Let people's behavior be your guide to what it is the people want.

SHARPEN YOUR CRITICAL THINKING SKILLS (continued)

Carlin: Again, it is not that easy. People may want national defense, for example, but not be willing to pay for it because it is a public good. The government already provides national defense, and its benefits cannot be denied to anyone.

Turner: So what? Air cannot be denied to anyone, but we don't tax people to breathe it, do we?

Carlin: No we don't, but air is provided free by nature. National defense is not provided free. We must pay for it if we want it.

Turner: Ah-hah, you just said "we must pay for it if we want it." The key word there was "if." The fact that we are forced to pay for it,

through the tax system, leads me to believe that we don't want it. I never have to be forced to do something I want to do. I am only forced to do things I don't want to do.

Carlin: I still say that taxation is necessary because, without it, we wouldn't have certain public goods.

Turner: And I still say that if we really wanted the public goods, we would be willing to pay for them on a voluntary basis. We don't need taxes to get us what we don't want.

2. When discussing profit, why should an economist think in terms of "videos" rather than "photos"?

ACTIVITIES AND PROJECTS

1. When it comes to the topic of free enterprise, there is often debate. For example, some people see numerous benefits in the free-enterprise economic system, and others do not. Some people will say that free enterprise is an ethical economic system, that it maximizes personal freedom, that it produces numerous goods for consumers to buy, and so on. Others will argue that free enterprise doesn't take care of the poor in its midst, that it cares more about profits than people, that it is an economic system which promotes competition instead of cooperation, and so on. In Chapter 1, we stated that economists often think of things in terms of benefits and costs. In groups of five persons, discuss the benefits and costs of free enterprise, as you see them.

ECONOMIC DICTIONARY

Circular Flow of Economic Activity (Pg. 51)
Contract (Pg. 47)
Entrepreneur (Pg. 44)
Ethics (Pg. 39)
Free Rider (Pg. 50)
Household (Pg. 52)
Incentive (Pg. 34)
Loss (Pg. 35)

Private Good (Pg. 48)
Private Property (Pg. 32)
Profit (Pg. 35)
Public Good (Pg. 48)
Public Property (Pg. 32)
Total Cost (Pg. 35)
Total Revenue (Pg. 35)

CHAPTER 3

Demand and Supply

What do you see in a grocery store? People buying and selling groceries. What do you see in a clothing store in a shopping mall? People buying and selling clothes. Almost everywhere you turn, someone is buying and selling something. We take a close-up look at buying and selling in this chapter.

You may think that buying is buying and selling is selling. What more is there to it? For one thing, there are *laws*—not laws like the one that sets the speed limit at 55 miles per hour, or the one that says you will be punished if you steal something, but laws similar to the law of gravity. The law of gravity informs us of what will happen if we hold a pencil in our hands and drop it. It will fall to the floor. Similarly, there is a law that specifies what a buyer will do if price drops. There is also a law that specifies what a seller will do if price drops. We can't really understand these two important everyday activities until we understand the laws that they obey.

AFTER YOU STUDY THIS CHAPTER, YOU WILL BE ABLE TO:

1. State the law of demand.
2. Draw a demand curve.
3. List and discuss the factors that can change demand.
4. Discuss the concept of elasticity of demand.
5. Explain the difference between (a) elastic, (b) inelastic, and (c) unit-elastic demand.
6. Explain why a price rise sometimes results in an increase in total revenue and sometimes results in a decrease in total revenue.
7. State the law of supply.
8. Explain why some supply curves are upward sloping and others are vertical.
9. List and discuss the factors that can change supply.

KEY TERMS

Advancement in Technology
Complement
Demand
Demand Curve
Demand Schedule
Direct Relationship
Elastic Demand
Elasticity of Demand
Elastic Supply
Elasticity of Supply
Good
Inelastic Demand
Inelastic Supply
Inferior Good
Inverse Relationship
Law of Demand

Law of Diminishing Marginal Utility
Law of Supply
Market
Neutral Good
Normal Good
Per-unit Cost
Quantity Demanded
Quantity Supplied
Quota
Service
Substitute
Supply
Supply Curve
Supply Schedule
Technology
Unit-Elastic Demand
Unit-Elastic Supply

SECTION 1 DEMAND

Economists study **markets**. A market is any place where people come together to buy and sell goods or services. A **good** is a tangible item that gives a person utility or satisfaction. For example, apples, computers, and shoes are goods for most people. A **service** is an intangible item that gives a person utility or satisfaction. For example, a history lecture is a service for most people.

We need both a buyer and a seller before we have a market. Economists put it this way: There is a buying side and a selling side to every market. In economics, the buying side is relevant to what is called *demand*, and the selling side is relevant to what is called *supply*. In this section, we discuss demand.

As you read, keep these key questions in mind:

- What is demand?
- Why do price and quantity demanded move in opposite directions?
- What is the difference between a demand schedule and a demand curve?

What Is Demand?

The word **demand** has a specific meaning in economics. It refers to the *willingness and ability* of buyers to purchase a good or service. Remember from Chapter 2 that *willingness to purchase* means that a person wants or desires a good; *ability to purchase* means that the person has the

money to pay for the good. Both willingness and ability must be present for demand to exist. For example, Cruz may be willing to buy a car but unable to pay the price. Thus, there is no demand. Tanya may be unwilling to buy the car but be able to pay the price. Still, there is no demand.

The Law of Demand: You Already Know What It Says

Suppose the average price of a compact disc rises from $10 to $15. Will individuals want to buy more or fewer compact discs at the higher price? Most people would say, fewer. Now suppose the average price of a compact disc falls from $10 to $5. Will individuals want to buy more or fewer compact discs at the lower price? Most people would say, more. If you answered the questions the way most people would, you instinctively understand the **law of demand**, which says that *as the price of a good increases, the quantity demanded of the good decreases, and as the price of a good decreases, the quantity demanded of the good increases.* In other words, when price goes up, quantity demanded goes down; and when price goes down, quantity demanded goes up. We can show this relationship in symbols:

$$P\uparrow \quad Q_d\downarrow$$
$$P\downarrow \quad Q_d\uparrow$$

where P = price, and Q_d = quantity demanded.

What Is Quantity Demanded?

Quantity demanded refers to the number of units of a good purchased at a specific price. For example, let's say that a consumer will purchase four oranges when oranges are priced at $1 apiece.

THINKING LIKE AN ECONOMIST

Bill says, *"The more money people have, the more expensive the cars they will buy."* He is not *thinking like an economist.* An economist knows that having the ability to buy something does not necessarily mean having the willingness to buy it.

Four is the quantity demanded at the specific price of $1 each. If the consumer will purchase five oranges when oranges are 75 cents apiece, then five is the quantity demanded at the specific price of 75 cents each.

QUESTION: *Is there a difference between* demand *and* quantity demanded*? These terms sound similar.*

ANSWER: *Yes, there is a difference between* demand *and* quantity demanded. *Again, demand refers to the willingness and ability of buyers to purchase a good or service. For example, we might say Karen has a demand for popcorn. This means she has both the willingness and ability to purchase popcorn. In other words, Karen is going to buy popcorn. The term* quantity demanded *refers to how much popcorn Karen buys at a specific price. For example, suppose the price of popcorn is a dollar a bag and Karen buys two bags. Therefore, two bags of popcorn is the quantity of popcorn demanded at a dollar a bag. An easy way to remember the difference between demand and quantity demanded is that quantity demanded is always given as a number. In our example it was the number "two"—as in two bags of popcorn.*

Why Do Price and Quantity Demanded Move in Opposite Directions?

We know that the law of demand says that price and quantity demanded move in opposite directions. But why is this the case? According to economists, it is because of the **law of diminishing marginal utility**. The law of diminishing marginal utility states that as a person consumes additional units of a good, eventually the utility or satisfaction gained from each additional unit of the good decreases. For example, you may receive more utility (satisfaction) from eating your first hamburger at lunch than your second and, if you continue on, more utility from your second hamburger than your third.

What does this have to do with the law of demand? Economists state that the more utility (satisfaction) you receive from a unit of a good, the higher price you are willing to pay for it; and the less utility you receive from a unit of a good, the lower price you are willing to pay for it. Since, according to the law of diminishing marginal utility, individuals eventually obtain less utility or satisfaction from additional units of a good (such as hamburgers), then it follows that they will only buy larger quantities of a good at lower prices. And this is the law of demand.

A Demand Schedule

Suppose you were asked to represent the law of demand in numbers. How would you do this?

Let's recall what the law of demand says. It says that as price goes up, quantity demanded goes down; and as price goes down, quantity demanded

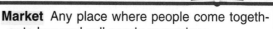

MINI GLOSSARY

Market Any place where people come together to buy and sell goods or services.

Good A tangible item that gives a person utility or satisfaction. Sometimes a *good* is referred to as a *product*.

Service An intangible item that gives a person utility or satisfaction.

Demand The willingness and ability of buyers to purchase a good or service.

Law of Demand Law stating that as the price of a good increases, the quantity demanded of the good decreases, and as the price of a good decreases, the quantity demanded of the good increases.

Quantity Demanded The number of units of a good purchased at a specific price.

Law of Diminishing Marginal Utility Law stating that as a person consumes additional units of a good, eventually the utility gained from each additional unit of the good decreases.

goes up. This up-down relationship is called an **inverse relationship**.

Exhibit 3-1a shows a two-column chart that numerically represents the inverse relationship between price and quantity demanded.

Looking at Exhibit 3-1a, we see that as we move down the Price column, price falls (from $4 to $3 to $2 to $1). As this happens, quantity demanded rises (from 1 to 2 to 3 to 4). A numerical chart such as this one that illustrates the law of demand is called a **demand schedule**.

A Demand Curve

Suppose you were asked to illustrate the law of demand in picture form. How would you do this?

The simple way is to plot the data in the demand schedule. Exhibit 3-1b shows how the price-quantity combinations in Exhibit 3-1a are plotted.

The first price-quantity combination, consisting of a price of $4 and a quantity demanded of 1, is labeled point A in part b. The second price-quantity combination, consisting of a price of $3 and a quantity demanded of 2, is labeled point B. The same process continues for points C and D.

If we connect all four points, from A to D, we have a line that slopes downward from left to right. This line is called a **demand curve**.[1] A demand curve is the graphical representation of the law of demand.

_____

1. Although points A–D lie along a straight *line*, many economists loosely refer to it as a demand *curve*. Don't let this confuse you. The standard practice in economics is to call the graphical representation of the relationship between price and quantity demanded a demand *curve* whether it is a curve or a straight line.

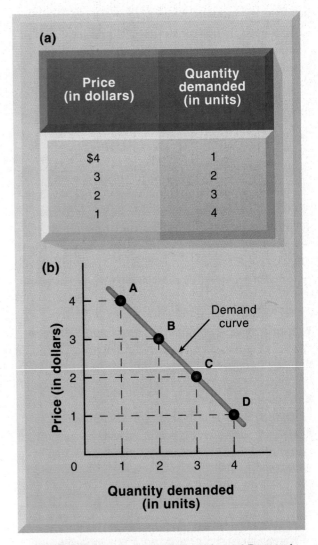

▲ **EXHIBIT 3-1. Demand Schedule and Demand Curve.** Part *a*: A demand schedule for a good. Notice that as price decreases, quantity demanded increases. Part *b*: Plotting the four combinations of price and quantity demanded from part *a* and connecting the points gives us a demand curve. Price, on the vertical axis, represents price per unit of a good. Quantity demanded, on the horizontal axis, always applies to a specific time period (a week, a month, a year, and so on).

 LEARNING CHECK

1. Is demand relevant to buying or to selling?
2. Elizabeth is willing to purchase a computer, but she does not have enough money to do so. Is it appropriate to say that Elizabeth demands the computer? Why or why not?
3. Define *quantity demanded*.

LEARNING CHECK—continued

4. State the law of demand in words; next, numerically illustrate the law of demand; finally, graphically illustrate the law of demand.
5. Of what is a demand curve the graphical representation?

SECTION 2 | **FACTORS THAT CAN CAUSE THE DEMAND CURVE TO SHIFT**

In this section, we examine factors that can shift a demand curve to the left and to the right. These factors include income, preferences, and prices of related goods. First, however, we discuss what it means when a demand curve shifts to the left or to the right.

As you read, keep these key questions in mind:

■ What does it mean when a demand curve shifts to the right?
■ What does it mean when a demand curve shifts to the left?
■ What is a normal good? an inferior good? a neutral good?
■ What are substitutes? complements?

What Does It Mean When the Demand Curve Shifts?

Look at the demand curve labeled original demand curve, or D_1, in Exhibit 3-2. Suppose that

this demand curve represents the current demand for orange juice. A week passes, and the demand curve for orange juice shifts to the right, to D_2. We can see what it means for the demand curve to shift to the right by focusing our attention on key points in Exhibit 3-2.

First, look at point A on D_1, the original demand curve. This point represents 400 quarts of orange juice purchased at $1 per quart. Now look at point B on D_2, the new demand curve. Point B represents the same price as before, $1 per quart,

▼ **EXHIBIT 3-2.** **Shifts in a Demand Curve.**
Moving from D_1 (original demand curve) to D_2 represents a rightward shift in the demand curve. Demand has increased. Moving from D_1 to D_3 represents a leftward shift in the demand curve. Demand has decreased.

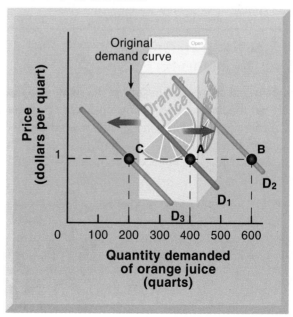

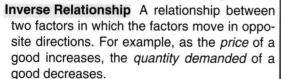
MINI GLOSSARY

Inverse Relationship A relationship between two factors in which the factors move in opposite directions. For example, as the *price* of a good increases, the *quantity demanded* of a good decreases.
Demand Schedule A table showing quantities of a good demanded at varying prices.
Demand Curve The graphical representation of the law of demand. It is a graph showing the amount of a good buyers are willing and able to buy at various prices.

but a greater quantity demanded, 600 quarts. What does a rightward shift in a demand curve, such as the shift from D_1 to D_2, mean? *It means that buyers are willing and able to purchase more of a good* at the original price and at all other prices. Demand has increased.

To identify what a shift to the left in a demand curve means, focus on points A and C in Exhibit 3-2. Again, looking at point A on D_1, we see that at a price of $1 per quart, 400 quarts of orange juice are purchased. Now look at point C on D_3. D_3 represents the demand curve after it has shifted to the left. At $1 per quart, buyers are now willing and able to purchase only 200 quarts. What does a leftward shift in a demand curve mean? *It means that buyers are willing and able to purchase less of a good* at the original price and at all other prices. Demand has decreased.

QUESTION: *Does a shift rightward in the demand curve represent an increase in demand and a shift leftward represent a decrease in demand?*

ANSWER: *Yes. When the demand for a good increases, the demand curve for that good shifts rightward. When the demand for a good decreases, the demand curve for that good shifts leftward.*

▲ This person is buying a compact disc (CD). For him, CDs are a normal good: if his income increases, he buys more CDs. Do you know anyone for whom CDs are a neutral good? an inferior good?

What Factors Cause Demand Curves to Shift?

Demand curves do not shift to the right or to the left without cause. Something must change for a demand curve to shift. Changes in several factors can cause demand curves to shift. These factors include income, preferences, and prices of related goods.

Income. As a person's income rises, he or she can buy more of any particular good. But remember that having the *ability* to buy more of a good does not necessarily mean having the *willingness* to buy more. For example, Andrew may receive an increase in his income and thus have a greater

ability to buy jeans, but he may not be willing to buy more jeans.

If a person receives an increase in income and, as a result, buys more of a certain good, that good is called a **normal good**. For example, suppose Quentin currently earns $1,000 a month and buys three CDs a month at a price of $12 each. If his income rises to $1,200 a month, and he buys four CDs a month at a price of $12 each, then CDs are a normal good for Quentin. Quentin's demand curve for CDs shifts to the right.

MINI GLOSSARY

Normal Good A good the demand for which rises as income rises and falls as income falls.

CONSUMER ECONOMIC DECISIONS

Advertising and You

Advertising is all around us. The most common way of advertising is through the newspaper. For example, in 1992, 23.4 percent of all advertising expenditures in the United States went for newspaper advertisements. The next-largest form of advertising is television advertising, where, in 1992, 22.4 percent of all advertising expenditures were directed. Direct mail accounted for 19.3 percent; advertising in the yellow pages accounted for 7.1 percent; and magazine advertising captured 5.3 percent of all advertising expenditures in 1992.

Advertising is big business. For example, in 1992, $131.7 billion was spent on advertising in the United States. The company that spent the most money on advertising that year was the company of Procter and Gamble, which spent approximately $1.2 billion to advertise many soaps and detergents. The three major U.S. automakers, General Motors, Ford, and Chrysler, were all among the top 10 advertisers in 1992. General Motors spent $947 million in advertising that year. Ford spent $601 million, and Chrysler spent $567 million.

Why do companies advertise? Mostly, they advertise in the hopes of increasing the demand for the goods and services they sell. For example, when a company such as Ford Motor Company advertises cars on television, it hopes that more people will want to buy its cars. Instead of, say, 90,000 people wanting to purchase a Taurus (a car manufactured by Ford), it hopes the number will jump to 100,000 or more. Of course, the result may not turn out this way. Not all advertisements are successful. For example,

many years ago Ford came out with a car, the Edsel, which was well advertised. It was a major flop; the Edsel didn't sell well at all.

Some of the critics of advertising say that slick advertising can create a demand for a product. In other words, a company develops a product that few people initially want to buy. Then it has the product shown on TV, in a movie, or being used by a sports celebrity, or a beautiful person in an exotic setting. Supposedly, these advertising tactics make the consumer want to buy the product—perhaps to be like the

▲ Car companies tend to be big advertisers. Here is an ad for the Ford Taurus.

celebrity who endorsed it, or to be like the beautiful person in the exotic setting.

Some economists take issue with this account. They argue that it is in the best interest of a company to develop a product the customer wants to buy; if this is done, less money has to be spent on advertising. For example, it would probably take little advertising money to sell a cure for the common cold. There is probably already a huge demand for such a product. Word of mouth about such a product would be likely to spread quickly.

Economists also point to the fact that many business firms spend millions of dollars each year trying to figure out what products consumers will buy. Along these lines, McDonald's might come up with a new sandwich. Instead of immediately advertising the new product on television, it will be sold in a few limited markets. For example, the sandwich might only be offered for sale in St. Louis, Missouri, and Seattle, Washington. If the people in these cities like the new sandwich, McDonald's might test it out in a few more cities. Finally, when McDonald's is reasonably sure that it has a product people want to buy, the sandwich will be advertised on national television. If McDonald's could sell anything just by advertising, why would the company go to all the trouble and expense, some economists ask, to develop a product and first test it out in limited markets?

Is there anything you should watch out for when it comes to advertising? Here are a few things:

1. *Some ads may be misleading.* For example, a car company once advertised by claiming to have sold more small cars than any other car company in the world. What was not mentioned was what was meant by a small car. If a company defines a small car as one that is only a certain weight (not one pound heavier or lighter), with a specific size wheelbase (not one inch more or less), and so on, then it is possible to count only the small cars the company itself sells. Obviously it will sell more small cars than any other company in the world. The claim is technically correct, given the company's definition of a small car, but such a claim is misleading.

Similarly, some grocery store chains will advertise that they have checked their prices on commonly purchased items against those of their competitors, and that they have come up with lower prices overall. Critics point out that almost every week some grocery store runs a sale on certain items. Suppose a grocery store chooses to compare its prices with those of its competitors on the week it is running a sale on many items. For that week, its prices may be lower than the competitors' prices, but the question remains whether that week is representative of all weeks in the year.

2. *Bait-and-switch advertising.* Bait-and-switch advertising is illegal. It occurs when a seller advertises a product or service at a very low price (bait), and then when the buyer offers to buy the product, the seller tries to get him or her to purchase a more expensive item (switch). For example, suppose you see a CD player advertised for a low price in the newspaper. You go to the store which advertised the item. You ask to see the CD player; a salesclerk tells you that the item is

Making CONSUMER ECONOMIC DECISIONS (continued)

out of stock and that he will have to back-order the item. He says it will take about six weeks for it to come in. Then he suggests that you look at a different CD player, since the one you want to buy isn't really that good anyway.

3. *Advertising and celebrities.* Many companies will hire celebrities to advertise their products. For example, a famous sports figure might advertise a sports shoe, tennis racket, or baseball mitt; a movie star might advertise a credit card; a TV star might advertise a car. Advertisers often say that it is important to hire a celebrity to advertise a product because, with so many ads in the media, something has to be done to get peo-

▲ Sometimes a company will hire celebrities to advertise its products.

ple's attention. Your favorite movie star advertising a product on television is more likely to get your attention than someone you don't know. Critics argue that this type of advertising sometimes gets in the way of our good sense.

4. *Advertising and Psychology.* Some people suggest that advertisers sometimes play on the emotions of potential buyers. Advertisers may want to imply in their ads that, if you want to be smarter, better looking, more confident, or anything else along these lines, you need to buy their products. A certain pair of jeans might make you look better and thus have more friends, for example. Does this kind of thing happen in advertising? Most people think so; what is debated is how effective it is.

---

1. Watch one hour of television, listen to one hour of radio, look through one entire newspaper, or look through one entire magazine, and write a short description of each commercial or advertisement you see or hear. For example, give the name of the product that is being advertised, what is being said, the pictures or images that are being shown or talked about, and so on. In any or all of the ads, identify anything you consider to be misleading or deceptive advertising.

2. Identify the last 10 items that you have purchased. Did advertising play a role in any of these purchases? If so, explain how advertising affected the purchase.

If a person receives an increase in income and, as a result, buys less of a certain good, that good is called an **inferior good**. For example, suppose Richard is currently earning $800 a month and buys five hot dogs a month at $1 each. If his income rises to $900 a month, and he buys four hot dogs a month at $1 each, then hot dogs are an inferior good for Richard. Richard's demand curve for hot dogs shifts to the left.

Finally, if a person receives an increase in income and buys neither more nor less of a good, that good is called a **neutral good**. For example, if Yvonne receives a pay raise, and buys neither more nor less toothpaste as a result, toothpaste is a neutral good for Yvonne. Yvonne's demand curve for toothpaste does not shift.

Preferences.   People's preferences affect how much of a good they buy. A change in preferences in favor of a good shifts the demand curve to the right. A change in preferences away from a good shifts the demand curve to the left. For example, if people begin to favor spy novels and buy more of them than they did before, the demand curve for spy novels shifts to the right.

Prices of Related Goods.   The demand for a good is affected by the prices of related goods. There are two types of related goods, **substitutes** and **complements**.

With substitutes, the demand for one good moves in the same direction as the price of the other good. For example, for many people, coffee is a substitute for tea. Thus, if the price of coffee increases, the demand for tea also increases as people substitute tea for the higher-priced coffee. This means tea's demand curve shifts to the right, as shown in Exhibit 3-3b. Other examples of substitutes include corn chips and potato chips, Chrysler cars and Toyota cars, and two brands of margarine.

Two goods are complements if they are consumed together. For example, tennis rackets and tennis balls are used together to play tennis. With complementary goods, the demand for one moves in the opposite direction as the price of the other.

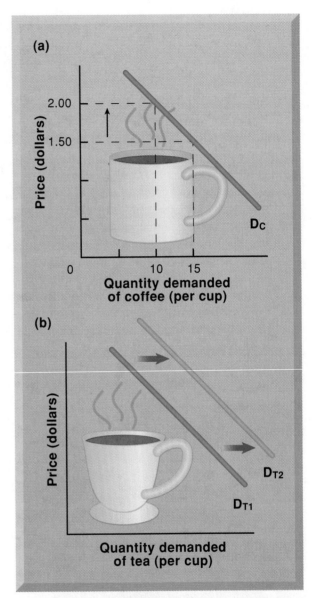

▲ **EXHIBIT 3-3**. **Increased Demand for Tea after a Rise in the Price of Coffee**. The price of coffee per cup increases from $1.50 to $2.00 in part *a*. This causes the demand for tea to shift to the right, as shown in part *b*. Since the *price of coffee* and the *demand for tea* move in the same direction (both increase), coffee and tea are substitutes.

For example, as the price of tennis rackets rises, the demand for tennis balls falls. Other examples of complements (or complementary goods) include cars and tires, shirts and trousers, light bulbs and lamps, and golf clubs and golf balls.

✓ LEARNING CHECK

1. Vernon buys more books as a result of an increase in his income. What kind of good are books for Vernon?
2. Sharon buys fewer pencils even though her income has increased. What kind of good are pencils for Sharon?
3. Nissan cars and Chevrolet cars are substitutes. If the price of Chevrolets rises, what happens to the demand for Nissans?
4. People's preferences move in favor of apples. As a result, does the demand curve for apples shift to the right or to the left?
5. If the demand for a good increases, does the demand curve shift to the right or to the left?

SECTION 3	ELASTICITY OF DEMAND

There are two goods, apples and bread. Both goods rise in price by 10 percent. But whereas the quantity demanded of apples falls by 30 percent, the quantity demanded of bread falls by a mere 1 percent. To describe the difference between these two goods, economists use the concept of elasticity of demand, which we examine in this section. Elasticity of demand describes the responsiveness of quantity demanded to a change in price.

As you read, keep these key questions in mind:

■ What is elasticity of demand?
■ How do we compute elasticity of demand?
■ What does it mean to say that the demand for a product is elastic? inelastic? unit elastic?
■ What factors can change the elasticity of demand?
■ Does a rise in price for a good necessarily bring about a higher total revenue?

What Is Elasticity of Demand?

The law of demand states that price and quantity demanded move in opposite directions. When price increases, quantity demanded decreases; and when price decreases, quantity demanded increases. What the law of demand does not tell us is *how much* quantity demanded decreases as price increases and *how much* quantity demanded increases as price decreases. This is where elasticity of demand comes into play. **Elasticity of demand** measures the relationship between the percentage

---

MINI GLOSSARY

Inferior Good A good the demand for which falls as income rises and rises as income falls.
Neutral Good A good the demand for which remains unchanged as income rises or falls.
Substitutes Similar goods. With substitutes, the price of one and the demand for the other move in the same directions.
Complements Goods that are consumed jointly. With complements, the price of one and the demand for the other move in opposite directions.
Elasticity of Demand The relationship between the percentage change in quantity demanded and the percentage change in price.

change in quantity demanded and the percentage change in price. We can look at this as a ratio.

$$\text{Elasticity of demand} = \frac{\text{Percentage change in quantity demanded}}{\text{Percentage change in price}}$$

In the preceding equation, you will notice that there is a numerator (percentage change in quantity demanded) and a denominator (percentage change in price). **Elastic demand** exists when the quantity demanded changes by a greater percentage than the percentage change of price—that is, when the numerator changes by more than the denominator. For example, suppose the price of light bulbs increases by 10 percent, and the quantity demanded of light bulbs decreases by 30 percent. The numerator (30 percent) would have changed by more than the denominator (10 percent). The demand for light bulbs is elastic.

Inelastic demand exists when the quantity demanded changes by a smaller percentage than the percentage change of price—that is, when the numerator changes by less than the denominator. For example, suppose the price of salt increases by 10 percent, and the quantity of salt demanded decreases by 2 percent. The numerator (2 percent) would have changed by less than the denominator (10 percent). The demand for salt is inelastic.

Finally, **unit-elastic demand** exists when the quantity demanded changes by the same percentage as the percentage change of price—that is, when the numerator changes by the same percentage as the denominator. For example, suppose the price of picture frames increases by 10 percent and the quantity of picture frames demanded decreases 10 percent. The numerator (10 percent) would have changed by the same percentage as the denominator (10 percent). The demand for picture frames is unit elastic.

Exhibit 3-4 reviews the descriptions of elastic, inelastic, and unit-elastic demand.

Determinants of Elasticity

The demand for some goods is inelastic, while the demand for others is elastic. Why the differ-

◄ **EXHIBIT 3-4**. Elasticity of Demand.

If demand is	That means
1. Elastic	Quantity demanded changes by a larger percentage than price. For example, if price rises by 10 percent, quantity demanded falls by, say, 15 percent.
2. Inelastic	Quantity demanded changes by a smaller percentage than price. For example, if price rises by 10 percent, quantity demanded falls by, say, 5 percent.
3. Unit elastic	Quantity demanded changes by the same percentage as price. For example, if price rises by 10 percent, quantity demanded falls by 10 percent.

ence? Here we examine four factors that affect the elasticity of demand: the number of substitutes available, luxuries versus necessities, the percentage of income spent on the good, and time.

Number of Substitutes. The demand for goods with many substitutes is likely to be elastic; the demand for goods with zero or very few substitutes is likely to be inelastic. Consider two goods, heart medicine and bread. There are relatively few substitutes for heart medicine. Many people must have the medicine to stay well. One would imagine that even if the price of heart medicine went up by 50, 100, or 150 percent, quantity demanded would not fall by much.

In contrast, a particular brand of bread has many substitutes. If the price of Brand X rises, a person can turn to Brand Y, Brand Z, or some other brand. We would expect that if the price of any one brand rises, the quantity demanded for that brand will fall off greatly, because people have other brands to turn to.

Luxuries versus Necessities. As a term used in everyday language, luxury goods (luxuries) are goods that a person feels he or she does not need in order to survive. For example, a $40,000 car would be a luxury good for most people. Necessary goods (necessities) are goods that a person feels he or she needs to survive. For example, the heart medicine we talked about earlier may be a necessity for some people. Food is a necessity. Generally speaking, if the price of a necessity— such as food—increases, people cannot cut back very much on the quantity, demanded. (They need a certain amount of food to live.) However, if the price of a luxury good increases, people are more able to cut back on the quantity of it demanded. Between the two types of goods—luxury goods and necessities—the demand for necessities is more likely to be inelastic.

Percentage of Income Spent on the Good. Claire Rossi has a monthly income of $2,000. Of this amount, she spends $20 on paper and $400 on dinners at restaurants. In percentage terms, she spends 1 percent of her monthly income on paper

▲ The demand for medicine is likely to be inelastic. Even when medicine prices rise, it is sometimes difficult to cut back on the amount purchased and consumed.

($20 ÷ $2,000 = .01 or 1 percent) and 20 percent of her monthly income on dinners at restaurants ($400 ÷ $2,000 = .20 or 20 percent).

Suppose the price of paper and the price of dinners at restaurants double. What will Claire be more likely to change, the quantity demanded of paper or the quantity demanded of dinners at restaurants? The answer is the *quantity demanded of dinners at restaurants*. The reason is that she will feel this price change more strongly, because

MINI GLOSSARY
Elastic Demand When demand is elastic, the percentage change in quantity demanded is greater than the percentage change in price.
Inelastic Demand When demand is inelastic, the percentage change in quantity demanded is less than the percentage change in price.
Unit-Elastic Demand When demand is unit elastic, the percentage change in quantity demanded is the same as the percentage change in price.

ECONOMICS AND PEOPLE

Sonia Melara

Sonia Melara grew up in El Salvador and came to the United States when she was 15 years old. She was trained as a social worker, and from 1982 to 1984 she served as the National Director of Leadership Programs of the Mexican-American Legal Defense and Education Fund.

Sonia Melara is now an entrepreneur. Important to entrepreneurship is detecting a demand for a product or service that doesn't exist and then supplying that product or service yourself. This is what Sonia Melara has done.

In 1984, she founded the *Hispanic Yellow Pages*, which serves the San Francisco area. Today, the publication has a staff of 100 persons, covers 16 territories, and has a circulation of over a million. The market that Sonia Melara tapped consisted of (1) people who read only Spanish, (2) people who are bilingual (which means they can speak two languages) but prefer to read in Spanish, and (3) people who politically and culturally identify themselves as Hispanic and choose to use the *Hispanic Yellow Pages* to reinforce their identities.

Sonia Melara also helped to establish *Mensajero*, a Spanish-language publication that serves northern California and provides

Hispanics with news from their home countries.

In 1990, Sonia Melara founded a new company called CommuniQue World Marketing, Inc. This business firm provides planning and marketing services to companies that want to reach ethnic markets. She came up with the idea for this company because she noticed that many older, more established U.S. firms did not have the knowledge to sell their products in ethnic markets. The company has been said to be a bridge between cultures.

1. Sonia Melara started three business enterprises: *Hispanic Yellow Pages*, *Mensajero*, and CommuniQue World Marketing, Inc. In each case, identify the product or service that was being demanded but was not being (sufficiently) supplied.
2. Some people say that owning your own business shows only self-interest and has nothing at all to do with serving your community. Do you agree or disagree, given your reading of Sonia Melara's story? Explain your answer.

SOURCE: Joline Godfrey, *Our Wildest Dreams*, (New York: Harper Business, 1992).

it affects a larger percentage of her income. Claire may shrug off a doubling in the price of paper, on which she spends only one percent of her income, but she is less likely to shrug off a doubling in the price of dinners at restaurants, on which she spends 20 percent. In short, buyers are more responsive to price changes in goods on which they spend a larger percentage of their income. It follows that the demand for goods on which consumers spend a small percentage of their income (like paper for Claire) is more likely to be inelastic than the demand for goods on which consumers spend a large percentage of their income (like dinners at restaurants for Claire).

Time.   As time passes, buyers have greater opportunities to change quantity demanded in response to a price change. If the price of electricity went up today, and you knew about it, you probably would not change your consumption of electricity much today. By three months from today, you would probably have changed it much more. As time passes, you have more chances to change your consumption by finding substitutes (natural gas), changing your lifestyle (buying more blankets and turning down the thermostat at night), and so on. We conclude that the less time you have to respond to a price change, the more likely it is that your demand for a good is going to be inelastic.

Elasticity and Total Revenue: Why Does Elasticity Matter?

What does it matter if the demand for a particular good is elastic? Isn't this just a fact of life that people should accept—much as they accept the weather, the fact that the sun rises in the morning and sets at night, and so on?

Elasticity matters (especially to business firms and other sellers) because it relates to total revenue. Remember that total revenue is the price of a good, times the quantity sold. For example, if Javier sells 100 basketballs at $20 each, his total revenue is $2,000 ($20 × 100 = $2,000).

Suppose the demand for Javier's basketballs is elastic. He raises the price of his basketballs to $22 each; this is a 10 percent increase in price (2 ÷ 20 = .10 or 10 percent). The law of demand states that quantity demanded will fall. Since the demand for the basketballs is elastic, the percentage change in quantity demanded must fall by more than the percentage rise in price—specifically, by more than 10 percent. Suppose the quantity demanded falls from 100 to 75. This is a 25 percent reduction (25 ÷ 100 = .25 or 25 percent).

What is Javier's total revenue at the new price and quantity demanded? It is $1,650. We get this dollar amount by multiplying the new price ($22) by the number of balls sold (75) ($22 × 75 =

$1,650). Compare this with $2,000, the total revenue when the price was $20.

We have learned an important lesson—namely, that a rise in price does not always bring about a rise in total revenue. For Javier, a higher price brought about a lower total revenue. This is because the demand for his good, basketballs, is elastic.

Have you ever thought that sellers always prefer higher prices to lower prices? You might have assumed that sellers are better off selling their goods and services at higher rather than lower prices. An understanding of demand elasticity tells us this is not so. In fact, whenever demand is elastic, a rise in price brings about a lower total revenue.

QUESTION: *Isn't a seller sometimes better off selling his or her goods at a higher price than at a lower price?*

ANSWER: *Yes, sometimes this is the case. Specifically, it is the case when the demand for the good or service is* inelastic. *Again consider the example of Javier. This time, suppose that the demand for his basketballs is inelastic instead of elastic. This means that when price changes, quantity demanded will change by a lesser percentage. Again suppose there is a 10 percent increase in price, from $20 to $22 (2 ÷ 20 = .10 or 10 percent). Quantity demanded falls, as before, but not by 25 percent. Suppose it falls from 100 to 95, which is a 5 percent reduction (5 ÷ 100 = .05 or 5 percent). Total revenue for Javier at the new price ($22) and the new quantity demanded (95) is $2,090 ($22 × 95 = $2,090). This is $90 more than when the price was $20 and the quantity demanded was 100 ($2,090 − $2,000 = $90). The lesson: When demand is inelastic, a rise in price will bring about an increase in total revenue.*

FOLLOW-UP QUESTION: *We now know that (1) when demand is elastic, a rise in price brings about a lower total revenue, and (2) when demand is inelastic, a rise in price brings about a higher total revenue. In both cases, we have dealt with a rise in price. What about a fall in price? Is* it ever possible to get a higher total revenue by lowering price?

ANSWER: *Yes. If demand is elastic, a lower price brings about a higher total revenue. Suppose Javier lowers the price from $20 to $18; this is a 10 percent reduction in price (2 ÷ 20 = .10 or 10 percent). We know from the law of demand that when price falls, quantity demanded rises. We also know that when demand is elastic, the change in quantity demanded is greater than the change in price. Quantity demanded must therefore rise in this example by more than 10 percent. Suppose quantity demanded rises by 20*

percent, from 100 basketballs sold to 120 (20 ÷ 100 = .20 or 20 percent). What is the new total revenue? It is $2,160, which we obtain by multiplying the new price ($18) by the new quantity demanded (120) ($18 × 120 = $2,160). Lesson learned: When demand is elastic, a fall in price can bring about a higher total revenue.

Here is an exercise for you to complete. Determine what happens to total revenue if price falls and demand is inelastic. Then determine what happens to total revenue if price falls or rises and demand is unit elastic. Check your answers by looking at Exhibit 3-5.

▼ **EXHIBIT 3-5**. Relationship of Elasticity of Demand and Total Revenue.

Type of demand	Change in price	Change in total revenue	
Elastic	↑ ↓	↓ ↑	Notice that price and total revenue move in opposite directions if demand is elastic.
Inelastic	↑ ↓	↑ ↓	Notice that price and total revenue move in the same direction if demand is inelastic.
Unit elastic	↑ ↓	No change No change	

LEARNING CHECK

1. Which changes by a larger percentage—quantity demanded or price—if demand is inelastic?
2. Which changes by a larger percentage—quantity demanded or price—if demand is elastic?
3. Explain why sellers are not always better off selling their goods at higher prices.
4. If demand is elastic, how will a rise in price affect total revenue?
5. If demand is inelastic, how will a rise in price affect total revenue?
6. Price rises by 20 percent, and quantity demanded falls by 10 percent. Is demand elastic, inelastic, or unit elastic?

SECTION 4 SUPPLY

This section defines supply, states the law of supply, and derives both a supply schedule and a supply curve.

As you read, keep these key questions in mind:

- What is supply?
- Are all supply curves upward sloping?
- What is the difference between a supply schedule and a supply curve?

What Is Supply?

Like the word *demand*, the word **supply** has a specific meaning in economics. It refers to the willingness and ability of sellers to produce and offer to sell a good or service.

It is important to keep in mind that there is no supply of a good or service, and a person is not a seller, unless there is both *willingness* and *ability* to produce and sell. When we speak of *willingness to produce and sell*, we mean that the person wants or desires to produce and sell the good. When we speak of *ability to produce and sell*, we mean that the person is capable of producing and selling the good. For example, if Jackie is willing to produce and offer to sell a chair but is unable to

do so, there is no supply. If Masako is able to produce and offer to sell a chair but is unwilling to do so, there is still no supply.

The Law of Supply

Suppose you are a supplier, or producer, of TV sets, and the price of the sets rises from $300 to $400. Would you want to supply more or fewer TV sets at the higher price? Most people would say, more. If you did, you instinctively understand the **law of supply**, which holds that *as the price of a good increases, the quantity supplied of the good increases, and as the price of a good decreases, the quantity supplied of the good decreases.* In

MINI GLOSSARY

Supply The willingness and ability of sellers to produce and offer to sell a good or service.

Law of Supply Law stating that as the price of a good increases, the quantity supplied of the good increases, and as the price of a good decreases, the quantity supplied of the good decreases.

other words, price and quantity supplied move in the same direction. That is, they have a **direct relationship**. We can write the law of supply in symbols:

$$P\uparrow \quad Q_s\uparrow$$
$$P\downarrow \quad Q_s\downarrow$$

where P = price and Q_s = quantity supplied.

What Is Quantity Supplied?

Quantity supplied refers to the number of units of a good produced and offered for sale at a specific price. For example, let's say that a seller will produce and offer five hamburgers for sale when the price is $2 each. Five is the quantity supplied at this price. If the seller will produce and offer six hamburgers for sale when the price is $2.50 each, then six is the quantity supplied at this price.

A Supply Schedule

We can represent the law of supply in numbers, just as we did with the law of demand. The law of supply states that as price rises, quantity supplied rises. The chart in Exhibit 3-6a shows just such a relationship. As the price goes up from $1, to $2, to $3, to $4, the quantity supplied goes up from 10, to 20, to 30, to 40. A numerical chart like this that illustrates the law of supply is called a **supply schedule**.

A Supply Curve

We can also illustrate the law of supply in graphical form. We can do this by plotting the data in the supply schedule, as in Exhibit 3-6b. Point A is the first price-quantity combination from the supply schedule, consisting of a price of $1 and a quantity supplied of 10. Point B represents a price of $2 and a quantity supplied of 20; Point C, a price of $3 and a quantity supplied of 30; and Point D, a price of $4 and a quantity supplied of 40.

(a)

Price (dollars)	Quantity supplied (units)
$1	10
2	20
3	30
4	40

(b)

▲ **EXHIBIT 3-6. Supply Schedule and Supply Curve**. Part *a*: A supply schedule for a good. Notice that as price increases, quantity supplied increases. Part *b*: Plotting the four combinations of price and quantity supplied from part *a* and connecting the points gives us a supply curve.

Connecting points A–D gives us a line that slopes upward from left to right. This line is called a **supply curve**.[2] The upward-sloping supply curve in Exhibit 3-6b is the graphical representation of the law of supply.

_____

2. Again, although points A–D lie along a *line*, many economists loosely refer to it as a supply *curve*.

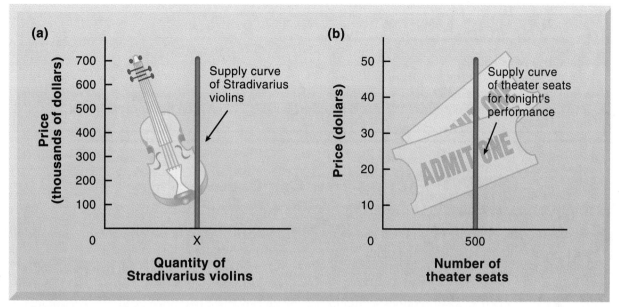

▲ **EXHIBIT 3-7. Supply Curves When No More Can Be Produced and When There is Not Time to Produce More.** The supply curve is not upward sloping when additional units cannot be produced or when there is no time to produce additional units. In these cases, the supply curve is vertical. In part *a*, the letter X at the base of the supply curve represents the quantity of Stradivarius violins that currently exist in the world.

QUESTION: *Consider a good such as Stradivarius violins. These violins were made by Antonio Stradivari over 200 years ago. It is impossible for an additional Stradivarius violin to be produced today, because Stradivari has been dead since 1737. No matter how high the price goes, the quantity supplied cannot increase to more than the total number of Stradivarius violins that currently exist. Does this mean the supply curve of Stradivarius violins is not upward sloping but instead is vertical, as shown in Exhibit 3-7a?*

ANSWER: *The supply curve for Stradivarius violins is not upward sloping. It is vertical at the quantity that exists in the world.*

This is an important point: The law of supply, which holds that as price rises, quantity supplied rises, does not hold for all goods and over all time periods. First, it does not hold for goods that cannot be produced any longer, such as Stradivarius violins. Second, it does not hold when there is no time to produce more units of a good.

For example, a theater in St. Louis, Missouri, is

sold out for tonight's play. Even if ticket prices were to increase from $30 to $40, there would be no additional seats in the theater tonight. There is no time to enlarge the theater and add more seats. For tonight's performance, the supply curve of theater seats is vertical, as illustrated in Exhibit 3-7b.

MINI GLOSSARY

Direct Relationship A relationship between two factors in which the factors move in the same direction. For example, as one rises, the other rises, too.

Quantity Supplied The number of units of a good produced and offered for sale at a specific price.

Supply Schedule A numerical chart that illustrates the law of supply.

Supply Curve A graph showing the amount of a good sellers are willing and able to sell at various prices. Only the upward-sloping supply curve is a graphical representation of the law of supply.

LEARNING CHECK

1. State the law of supply.
2. Graphically represent the law of supply.
3. What is a supply schedule?
4. You are drawing a supply curve. What is on the vertical axis? What is on the horizontal axis?

SECTION 5 FACTORS THAT CAN CAUSE THE SUPPLY CURVE TO SHIFT

In this section, we consider factors that can shift a supply curve to the left and to the right. These factors include resource prices, technology, taxes, and quotas.

As you read, keep these key questions in mind:

- What does it mean when a supply curve shifts to the right?
- What does it mean when a supply curve shifts to the left?
- What factors cause sellers to supply more or less of a good?

What Does It Mean When the Supply Curve Shifts?

Look at the supply curve labeled original supply curve, or S_1, in Exhibit 3-8. We'll say that this supply curve represents the current supply of personal computers. Three months pass, and the supply curve shifts to the right, to S_2. What does this mean? We can see by looking at Exhibit 3-8.

Look first at point A on S_1, the original supply curve. This point represents 4,000 computers supplied at $1,000 per computer. Now look at point B on S_2, the new supply curve. Point B represents the same price as before, $1,000 per computer. But now the quantity supplied of computers is 6,000. What does a rightward shift in the supply curve, such as the shift from S_1 to S_2, mean? *It means that sellers are willing and able to produce and offer to*

sell more of a good at the original price and at all other prices. Supply has increased.

What about a shift to the left in a supply curve? Start again at point A on S_1, where 4,000 computers are supplied at a price of $1,000 per computer. Now suppose the supply curve shifts leftward to S_3. At $1,000 per computer, sellers are now willing to supply only 2,000 computers. What does a leftward shift in a supply curve mean? *It means that sellers are willing and able to produce and offer to sell less of a good at the original price and at all other prices.* Supply has decreased.

QUESTION: *Does a shift rightward in the supply curve represent an increase in supply and a shift leftward represent a decrease in supply?*

ANSWER: *Yes. When the supply of a good increases, the supply curve for that good shifts rightward. When the supply of a good decreases, the supply curve for that good shifts leftward.*

What Factors Cause Supply Curves to Shift?

Supply curves do not shift to the right or to the left without cause, any more than demand curves do. Something must change to cause this to happen. Changes in resource prices, technology, taxes, and quotas can cause supply curves to shift.

Resource Prices. Chapter 1 identified four resources, or factors of production: land, labor, capi-

▶ **EXHIBIT 3-8. Shifts in a Supply Curve**. Moving from S₁ (the original supply curve) to S₂ represents a rightward shift in the supply curve. Supply has increased. Moving from S₁ to S₃ represents a leftward shift in the supply curve. Supply has decreased.

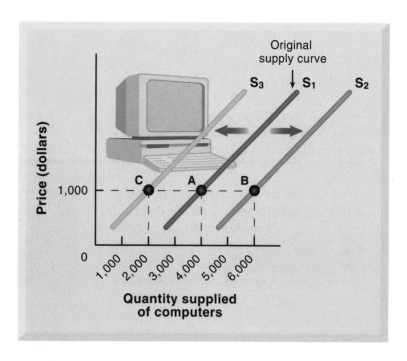

tal, and entrepreneurship. For now, concentrate on land, labor, and capital. These resources are used to produce goods and services. When resource prices fall, sellers are willing and able to produce and offer to sell more of the good (the supply curve shifts to the right). Why? Because it is cheaper to make the good. When resource prices rise, sellers are willing and able to produce and offer to sell less of a good (the supply curve shifts to the left). Why? Because it is more expensive to make the good.

For example, suppose the wage rate rises for employees working for a car manufacturer, while everything else remains the same. As a result, the car manufacturer will produce and offer to sell fewer cars—the supply curve shifts leftward.

Technology. **Technology** is the body of skills and knowledge relevant to the use of resources in production. For example, the technology of farming today is much different from that of 200 years ago. Today, tractors, pesticides, and special fertilizers are used in farming; 200 years ago, they were not used.

An **advancement in technology** refers to the ability to produce more output with a fixed amount of resources. Again, consider farming. With the use

of fertilizers and pesticides, farmers can produce much more output on an acre of land than farmers could many years ago. This advancement in technology, in turn, lowers the **per-unit costs**, or average cost, of production for farmers. Farmers respond to lower per-unit costs by being willing and able to produce and offer to sell more output. In other words, the supply curve shifts to the right.

Taxes. Some taxes increase per-unit costs. Suppose a shoe manufacturer must pay a $2 tax for each pair of shoes it produces. This "extra cost" of

---

MINI GLOSSARY

Technology The body of skills and knowledge concerning the use of resources in production.
Advancement in Technology The ability to produce more output with a fixed amount of resources.
Per-Unit Cost The average cost of a good. For example, if $400,000 is spent to produce 100 cars, the average, or per-unit, cost is $4,000 ($400,000 ÷ 100 = $4,000).

doing business causes the manufacturer to supply less output. (This is similar to the price of a resource rising, thus making it more expensive, and less profitable, for the producer to manufacture the good. As a result, the producer has less output.) The supply curve shifts to the left. If the tax is eliminated, the supply curve will shift rightward to its original position.

Quotas.   **Quotas** are restrictions on the number of units of a foreign-produced good (or import) that can enter a country. For example, suppose Japanese producers are currently sending, and want to continue to send, 100,000 cars to the United States each year. Now suppose the U.S. government imposes a quota on Japanese cars, say, at 80,000 a year. This means that no more than 80,000 Japanese cars can be imported into the United States. A quota causes supply to be less, and so the supply curve shifts to the left. The elimination of the quota causes the supply curve to shift rightward to its original position.

▲ Given a quota on foreign cars, the supply of cars in the United States is less than it would be otherwise.

Elasticity of Supply

Earlier in this chapter we discussed elasticity of demand. There is **elasticity of supply**, too. Elasticity of supply measures the relationship between the percentage change in quantity supplied and the percentage change in price. We can look at this as a ratio.

$$\text{Elasticity of supply} = \frac{\text{Percentage change in quantity supplied}}{\text{Percentage change in price}}$$

Looking at the preceding equation, you will notice that there is a numerator (percentage change in quantity supplied) and a denominator (percentage change in price). **Elastic supply** exists when the quantity supplied changes by a greater percentage than the percentage of price does—that is, when the numerator changes by more than the denominator. For example, suppose the price of light

bulbs increases by 10 percent, and the quantity supplied of light bulbs increases by 20 percent. The numerator (20 percent) would have changed by more than the denominator (10 percent). The supply of light bulbs is elastic.

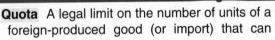

MINI GLOSSARY

Quota A legal limit on the number of units of a foreign-produced good (or import) that can enter a country.

Elasticity of Supply The relationship between the percentage change in quantity supplied and the percentage change in price.

Elastic Supply When supply is elastic, the percentage change in quantity supplied is greater than the percentage change in price.

CASE STUDY

Can You Get Better Grades Than You Have Been Getting?

Students often have some idea of the grades they are capable of obtaining. They also often believe that the level of grades they have been getting will not change. For example, a student may believe that he is a B student and that he will always be a B student. But an economist wouldn't necessarily agree. An economist would suggest that a student (who has not yet reached his or her potential) will get

higher grades in some settings than others. Let's look at this idea in terms of a supply curve.

As you know, an upward-sloping supply curve tells us that a seller will produce and offer to sell more units of a good at a higher price than at a lower price. (If you need to refresh your memory on this, see Exhibit 3-6). If this is so, will students "produce" higher grades the more they are "paid" to do so?

Of course, students in a classroom are not paid money by the teacher to get high grades. The teacher doesn't stand in front of the class and say, "I will pay $10 to anyone who gets an A on the test, $7 to anyone who gets a B," and so on.

But just suppose students *were* paid. Suppose, for example, that Lacy has always received a C on her history tests. Two days before the next history test, someone tells Lacy she will receive $1,000 if she gets an A on the test. The chance to receive $1,000 gets Lacy excited. She thinks of all the things she can buy with $1,000. Now stop right here. Do you think Lacy is going to do better than usual on the upcoming history test? If your answer

is yes, then you believe that Lacy has not previously done as well as she could in history and that she will get higher grades the more she is offered to get high grades.

What about you? Would you force your mind to work harder and more thoroughly and to grab for more information if you were offered $1,000 than if you were offered nothing? To find out if you can obtain higher grades than you are currently—and to learn a little economics, too—consider conducting the following experiment. First, identify something you want and can provide to yourself—say, a movie that has recently come out that you greatly want to see. Second, promise yourself that you will not go to the movie (or rent the video months later) if you do not bring up your average on the next English, history, or economics test. Then, when the time comes to study for the test, notice if you are concentrating more, working harder, and so on. If you are, you're likely to pull up your average. If you do, and if the test wasn't easier than usual and nothing else was different, then you will have learned something about yourself. You will have learned that you can get higher grades by providing yourself with the incentive to do so.

---

1. A student says, "I've always been a C student, I'm currently a C student, and I'll always be a C student." What might the student be overlooking?

THINKING LIKE AN ECONOMIST

The story of the C student illustrates the way in which economists think about things. For an economist, performance is often tied to incentives. If you offer a person an incentive—say, an incentive to work harder—then you will usually get more hard work than if you do not offer the incentive. Some noneconomists may disagree. They may think that hard work, or the grades a person receives, are unrelated to the incentives one is offered to work hard or to get good grades.

Inelastic supply exists when the quantity supplied changes by a smaller percentage than price—that is, when the numerator changes by less than the denominator. Finally, **unit-elastic supply** exists when the quantity supplied changes by the same percentage as price—that is, when the numerator changes by the same percentage as the denominator.

The Responsibilities of Buyers and Sellers

In this chapter we have discussed the activities of both buyers (demanders, or consumers) and sellers (suppliers, or producers). Both buyers and sellers should behave in a responsible and ethical way. For example, suppose a buyer is thinking about buying a used car from someone. She has the re-

sponsibility to become informed about the car (ask questions) and to make sure the car is in working order. She should not simply accept what the seller (of the car) says without question or evidence. Once she has agreed to purchase the car, she has the ethical responsibility to pay the seller the agreed-upon price. For example, some transactions are made with checks. If the buyer of the car pays for the car by check, she has the ethical responsibility to make sure the funds to pay for the car are in her checking account. It is unethical, and illegal, to write a check for an amount you do not have in your checking account.

The seller has certain responsibilities, too. He has the responsibility to inform the buyer about the good he is thinking about purchasing. The used-car seller should inform the car buyer about the condition of the car. For example, if the car begins to shake when it is going 50 miles an hour, then the seller has the responsibility to tell this to the buyer. He also has the responsibility of selling the buyer a safe product. For example, if he knows the tires on the car are worn and ready to burst, he has the responsibility of replacing the tires before he sells the car.

MINI GLOSSARY

Inelastic Supply When supply is inelastic, the percentage change in quantity supplied is less than the percentage change in price.

Unit-Elastic Supply When supply is unit elastic, the percentage change in quantity supplied is the same as the percentage change in price.

LEARNING CHECK

1. What happens to the supply curve as a result of a fall in the price of resources?

2. What happens to the supply curve as a result of a quota?

3. What happens to the supply curve as a result of an advancement in technology?

4. What happens to the supply curve as a result of furniture producers' having to pay a $40 tax for each piece of furniture they produce?

5. If the supply of a good decreases, does the supply curve shift to the right or to the left?

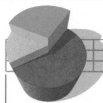

DEVELOPING ECONOMIC SKILLS

Working with Supply and Demand Curves

We have introduced both a demand curve and a supply curve in this chapter. In the next chapter, we will put supply and demand together (in one diagram) and talk about a market. But before we do this, it is important to make sure you have the details of demand and supply curves firmly down. Here are a few points to keep in mind.

A demand curve tells us the relationship between what is on the vertical axis (price) and what is on the horizontal axis (quantity demanded).

Think of a demand curve as saying something to you. What does it say? If you look at Exhibit 3-9a, you can almost "hear" what it has to say. Notice that there are two axes: a vertical axis, on which we have written "Price," and a horizontal axis, on which we have written "Quantity demanded." The demand curve has something to "say" about these two factors. It says as price decreases, say, from $10 to $5 in the exhibit, quantity demanded increases from 100 units to

170 units. And when price increases, quantity demanded decreases. In other words, the demand curve tells us the relationship between price and quantity demanded. When one increases, the other decreases. That is what the demand curve is saying.

A supply curve tells us the relationship between what is on the vertical axis (price) and what is on the horizontal axis (quantity supplied).

Not to be outdone, the supply curve has something to say, too. Look at Exhibit 3-9b. Again, notice that there are two axes: a vertical axis, on which we have written "Price," and a horizontal axis, on which we have written "Quantity supplied." The supply curve says that as price increases, say, from $2 to $4 in the exhibit, quantity supplied increases, from 110 units to 170 units. In other words, the supply curve tells us the relationship between price and quantity supplied. When one increases, the other also increases.

▼ **EXHIBIT 3-9. Sample Supply and Demand Curves.**

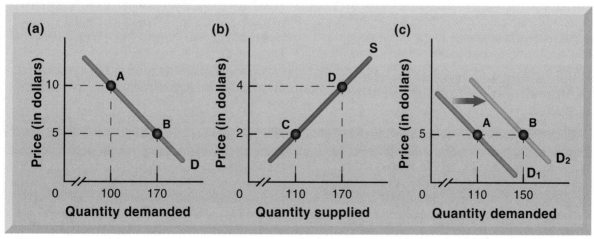

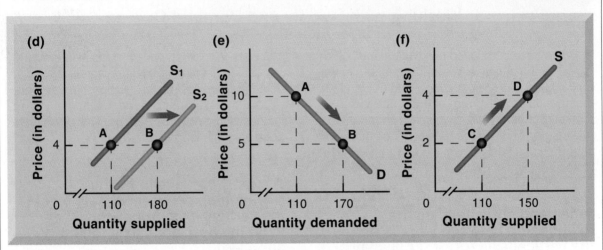

▲ EXHIBIT 3-9. Sample Supply and Demand Curves (continued).

When a demand curve shifts, it tells us something new about quantity demanded.

Suppose a demand curve shifts to the right, from D_1 to the new curve D_2 in Exhibit 3-9c. What do demand curves "tell" us when this happens? They tell us something new about quantity demanded. The exhibit tells us that at the price of $5, buyers (demanders) now are willing and able to buy 150 units (of the good or service) instead of 110 units. In other words, when a demand curve shifts to the right it says: Buyers want to buy more at each and every price. Ask yourself what a demand curve "says" if it shifts to the left. Although we have not drawn it here, it says: Buyers want to buy less than before at each and every price.

When a supply curve shifts, it tells us something new about quantity supplied.

Suppose a supply curve shifts to the right, from S_1 to the new curve S_2 in Exhibit 3-9d. What do supply curves "tell" us when they do this? They tell us something new about quantity supplied. The exhibit tells us that at a price of $4, sellers (suppliers) now are willing and able to produce and offer to sell 180 units (of the good

or service) instead of 110 units. In other words, when a supply curve shifts to the right it says: Sellers want to produce and sell more at each and every price. Ask yourself what the supply curve "says" if it shifts to the left. Although we have not drawn it here, it says: Sellers want to produce and sell less than before at each price.

There is a difference between a shift in a demand curve, and a movement along a demand curve.

You already know what a shift in a demand curve looks like. For example, there is a picture of this in Exhibit 3-9c. When a demand curve shifts, you should think of it as simply getting up and moving to a different spot in the two-dimensional diagram. This is what the demand curve did in Exhibit 3-9c. It got up from its position at D_1, and moved to a new position, at D_2. As you learned in this chapter, there are a number of factors that can shift a demand curve: changes in income, preferences, and prices of related goods.

A movement along a demand curve is altogether different from a shift in a demand curve. We have illustrated a movement along a demand curve in Exhibit 3-9e. A movement

DEVELOPING ECONOMIC SKILLS (continued)

along a demand curve is illustrated visually by the arrow between points A and B on the demand curve in Exhibit 3-9e. What we see there is a movement from one point (A) on the demand curve to another point (B) on the demand curve. What can cause this movement? Answer: A change in price. Notice in the exhibit that when the price is $10, the quantity demanded is 110 units, and we are at point A. But when the price changes to $5, the quantity demanded increases to 170 units, and we are now at point B. Remember this: A movement along a demand curve is caused by a change in price.

A shift in a demand curve occurs when the entire demand curve gets up and moves to another spot, as in Exhibit 3-9c. This can be caused by changes in income, preferences, or the prices of related goods. On the other hand, a movement along a demand curve occurs when we move from one point on a given demand curve to another point on the same demand curve. This is illustrated in Exhibit 3-9e. A movement along a demand curve is caused by a change in price.

There is a difference between a shift in a supply curve and a movement along a supply curve.

We have illustrated a shift in a supply curve in Exhibit 3-9d. A shift in a supply curve can be seen when the supply curve simply gets up and moves to a different spot in the two-dimensional diagram. As you learned in this chapter, a shift in a supply curve can be caused by different factors, such as changes in resource prices, technology, taxes, and quotas.

A movement along a supply curve is altogether different from a shift in a supply curve. We have illustrated a movement along a supply curve in Exhibit 3-9f. A movement along a supply curve is illustrated visually by the arrow between points C and D on the supply curve in Exhibit 3-9f. What we see there is a movement from one point (C) on the supply curve to another point (D) on the supply curve. What can cause this movement? Answer: A change in price. Notice in the exhibit when the price is $2, the quantity supplied is 110 units, and we are at point C. But when the price changes to $4, the quantity supplied increases to 150 units, and we are now at point D. Remember this: A movement along a supply curve is caused by a change in price.

---

1. In Exhibit 3-9, which panel (a–f) shows a shift in a demand curve?
2. In Exhibit 3-9, which panel shows a shift in a supply curve?
3. In Exhibit 3-9, which panel shows a movement along a supply curve?
4. What does a shift in a demand curve tell us?
5. What does a shift in a supply curve tell us?
6. What does a demand curve tell us?
7. What does a supply curve tell us?
8. What can cause a movement along a supply curve? Can the same thing cause a shift in a supply curve? Explain your answer.
9. What can cause a movement along a demand curve? Can the same thing cause a shift in a demand curve? Explain your answer.

CHAPTER 3 REVIEW

CHAPTER SUMMARY

1. There are two sides to a market, a buying side and a selling side. The buying side represents demand; the selling side represents supply.

2. The law of demand holds that as the price of a good increases, the quantity demanded of the good decreases, and as the price of a good decreases, the quantity demanded of the good increases.

3. Quantity demanded refers to the number of units of a good purchased at a specific price. For example, we might say that quantity demanded is 100 units at a price of $1 each.

4. The law of diminishing marginal utility states that as a person consumes additional units of a good, eventually the utility gained from each additional unit of the good decreases.

5. A demand schedule is a numerical chart that illustrates the law of demand. (See Exhibit 3-1a.)

6. A demand curve is the graphical representation of the law of demand. (See Exhibit 3-1b.)

7. When a demand curve shifts to the right, it means that buyers are willing and able to purchase more of a good at every price.

8. When a demand curve shifts to the left, it means that buyers are willing and able to purchase less of a good at every price.

9. Changes in income, preferences, and prices of related goods can cause demand curves to shift.

10. If an increase in income prompts an increase in the demand for a good, that good is a normal good. If an increase in income prompts a decrease in the demand for a good, that good is an inferior good. If an increase in income does not change the demand for a good, that good is a neutral good.

11. A change in preferences in favor of a good shifts the demand curve to the right. A change in preferences away from the good shifts the demand curve to the left.

12. Two goods are substitutes if they satisfy similar needs or desires. With substitute goods, the demand for one and the price of the other move in the same directions. For example, if goods X and Y are substitutes, then the demand for good X *increases* as the price of good Y *increases*.

13. Two goods are complements if they are consumed jointly. With complementary goods, the demand for one moves in the opposite direction as the price of the other. For example, if goods C and D are complements, then the demand for good C *decreases* as the price of good D *increases*.

14. Elasticity of demand deals with the relationship between the percentage change in quantity demanded and the percentage change in price.

15. When demand is elastic, quantity demanded changes by a larger percentage than price.

16. When demand is inelastic, quantity demanded changes by a smaller percentage than price.

17. When demand is unit elastic, quantity demanded changes by the same percentage as price.

18. If demand is elastic, price and total revenue move in opposite directions. If demand is inelastic, price and total revenue move in the same direction. If demand is unit elastic, a change in price does not change total revenue. (See Exhibit 3-5.)

19. The law of supply holds that as the price of a good increases, the quantity supplied of the good increases, and as the price of a good decreases, the quantity supplied of the good decreases.

20. A supply schedule is a numerical chart that illustrates the law of supply. (See Exhibit 3-6a.)

21. An upward-sloping supply curve illustrates the law of supply. (See Exhibit 3-6b.)

CHAPTER SUMMARY (continued)

22. The law of supply does not hold for all goods and over all time periods. It does not hold for goods that cannot be produced any longer, and it does not hold when there is no time to produce more units of a good.

23. Elasticity of supply deals with the relationship between the percentage change in quantity supplied and the percentage change in price.

24. A leftward shift in a supply curve means that sellers are willing and able to produce and offer to sell less of a good.

25. Changes in resource prices, technology, taxes, and quotas can cause supply curves to shift.

26. When resource prices fall, the supply curve shifts to the right. When resource prices rise, the supply curve shifts to the left.

27. An advancement in technology lowers per-unit costs of production and shifts the supply curve to the right.

28. Some taxes increase per-unit costs, causing the supply curve to shift to the left. The elimination of the taxes causes the supply curve to shift to the right to its original position.

29. A quota causes the supply curve to shift to the left. The elimination of the quota causes the supply curve to shift to the right to its original position.

BUILD YOUR ECONOMIC VOCABULARY

Match the word with the correct definition, example, or statement.

1. law of demand

2. law of diminishing marginal utility

3. quantity supplied

4. unit elastic

5. increase in resource prices

6. normal good

7. substitutes

a. percentage change in quantity demanded equals percentage change in price

b. eventually the utility of additional unit decreases

c. price of good A moves in same direction as demand for good B

d. price and quantity demanded move in opposite directions

e. income rises, demand for good rises

f. will end up shifting supply curve to the left

g. specific number of units of a good produced and offered for sale at a specific price

REVIEW QUESTIONS

1. Express the law of demand in (a) words, (b) symbols, and (c) graphical form.

2. "The law of diminishing marginal utility holds that a person receives greater utility from consuming the first two units of a good than from the first unit only." Is this statement true or false? Explain your answer.

3. Write out a demand schedule for four different combinations of price and quantity demanded.

4. Margarine and butter are substitutes. What

CHAPTER 3 REVIEW
(continued)

REVIEW QUESTIONS (continued)

happens to the demand for margarine as the price of butter rises?

5. Explain what happens to the demand curve for apples as a consequence of each of the following:
   a. More people begin to prefer apples to oranges.
   b. The price of peaches rises (peaches are a substitute for apples).
   c. People's income rises (apples are a normal good).

6. "Sellers always prefer higher to lower prices." Do you agree or disagree with this statement? Explain your answer.

7. What is the difference between inelastic demand and elastic demand?

8. Explain how the law of diminishing marginal utility is related to the law of demand.

9. What is the difference between a demand schedule and a demand curve?

10. What does it mean when a demand curve shifts to the right? to the left?

11. In each of the following cases, identify whether the demand for the good is elastic, inelastic, or unit elastic:
   a. The price of apples rises 10 percent as the quantity demanded of apples falls 20 percent.
   b. The price of cars falls 5 percent as the quantity demanded of cars rises 10 percent.
   c. The price of computers falls 10 percent as the quantity demanded of computers rises 10 percent.

12. Define each of the following:
   a. elastic demand
   b. inelastic demand
   c. unit-elastic demand

13. State whether total revenue rises or falls in each of the following situations:
   a. Demand is elastic and price increases.
   b. Demand is inelastic and price decreases.
   c. Demand is elastic and price decreases.
   d. Demand is inelastic and price increases.

14. Express the law of supply in (a) words, (b) symbols, and (c) graphical form.

15. Miriam is willing to produce and offer to sell plastic cups. Is Miriam a supplier of plastic cups? Why or why not?

16. Are all supply curves upward sloping? Why or why not?

17. Write out a supply schedule for four different combinations of price and quantity supplied.

18. Identify whether the supply curve for each of the following would be vertical or upward sloping:
   a. desks in your classroom, at this moment
   b. seats at a football stadium, at this moment
   c. television sets, over time
   d. Apple computers, over time
   e. Picasso paintings (Hint: Picasso is dead.)

19. What does it mean when a supply curve shifts to the right? to the left?

20. Between the price of $10 and $15, supply is inelastic. What does this mean?

21. What is the difference between a supply schedule and a supply curve?

22. Explain what happens to the supply curve of television sets as a consequence of each of the following:
   a. Resource prices fall.
   b. There is a technological advancement in the television industry.
   c. A tax is placed on the production of television sets.

23. The price of a computer in 1992 was $2,000. The price of the same computer in 1993 was $1,500. By what percentage did price fall between 1992 and 1993?

24. What is the difference between a shift in a supply curve and a movement along a supply curve?

SHARPEN YOUR CRITICAL THINKING SKILLS

1. Suppose you are a producer and seller of a new brand of cosmetics. You want to begin advertising your product in magazines and on television. All other things being the same, you prefer the demand for your product to be inelastic. This is because if demand is inelastic, you can (up to some point) raise price and increase total revenue, too. What "message" should your advertising convey to the buying public with respect to substitute products? Think up an ad campaign for this new product.

2. Suppose you are in business producing and selling pens. How would you go about determining whether the demand for your product is inelastic, elastic, or unit elastic?

3. "The price of apples fell, and the demand curve for apples shifted to the right." Identify the economic error in this statement. Next, write the statement so that it is correct. (Hint: Is there a difference between *demand*, in terms of the law of demand or a demand curve, and *quantity demanded*?)

ACTIVITIES AND PROJECTS

1. In groups of five persons, read through newspapers and magazines to find at least three examples of the law of demand and at least two examples of the law of supply. For example, you may read that a construction company has built homes that it can't sell. Finally, it lowers the price of the homes, and sales pick up. This shows that people buy more units of a good at lower prices than at higher prices. Here, then, is an example of the law of demand.

ECONOMIC DICTIONARY

Advancement in Technology (Pg. 79)
Complement (Pg. 68)
Demand (Pg. 60)
Demand Curve (Pg. 62)
Demand Schedule (Pg. 62)
Direct Relationship (Pg. 76)
Elastic Demand (Pg. 70)
Elastic Supply (Pg. 80)
Elasticity of Demand (Pg. 69)
Elasticity of Supply (Pg. 80)
Good (Pg. 60)
Inelastic Demand (Pg. 70)
Inelastic Supply (Pg. 82)
Inferior Good (Pg. 68)
Inverse Relationship (Pg. 62)
Law of Demand (Pg. 60)
Law of Diminishing Marginal Utility (Pg. 61)

Law of Supply (Pg. 75)
Market (Pg. 60)
Neutral Good (Pg. 68)
Normal Good (Pg. 64)
Per-Unit Costs (Pg. 79)
Quantity Demanded (Pg. 60)
Quantity Supplied (Pg. 76)
Quotas (Pg. 80)
Service (Pg. 60)
Substitute (Pg. 68)
Supply (Pg. 75)
Supply Curve (Pg. 76)
Supply Schedule (Pg. 76)
Technology (Pg.79)
Unit-Elastic Demand (Pg. 70)
Unit-Elastic Supply (Pg. 82)

Determining Prices

INTRODUCTION

You might pay $10 for a new book and $25 for a new shirt. Did you ever wonder how these prices came to be? Does someone simply decide that $10 will be the price of a new book? Why not $9 or $11? This chapter explains why not.

Think of something else. Suppose one day you go to the store, as you have many times before. This time, though, there are no prices on the merchandise. Confused, you take an item to the manager and ask, "How much is this?" The manager tells you that at this store prices are no longer used. "No prices!" you exclaim. "Then how do I know what I can and cannot buy?" What would a world without prices be like? This chapter explores this and other questions.

AFTER YOU STUDY THIS CHAPTER, YOU WILL BE ABLE TO:

1. Explain how supply and demand work together to determine price.
2. Explain what happens to price when there is a surplus.
3. Explain what happens to price when there is a shortage.
4. Explain why, in a world of scarcity, there is a need for a rationing device.
5. Explain how price rations resources and goods.

KEY TERMS

Equilibrium	Inventory
Equilibrium Price	Rationing Device
Equilibrium Quantity	Shortage
	Surplus

The English economist Alfred Marshall (1842–1924) compared supply and demand to the two blades of a pair of scissors. It is impossible to say which blade does the actual cutting. In the same way, it is impossible to say whether demand or supply is responsible for the market price we observe. The fact is, price is determined by both sides of the market.

As you read, keep these key questions in mind:

■ How do supply and demand together determine price?
■ What happens to price if there is a surplus in the market?
■ What happens to price if there is a shortage in the market?

Supply and Demand at Work at an Auction

Supply and demand work together to determine price. To see exactly how this happens, think of yourself at an auction where bushels of corn are bought and sold. This auction may be different from those you have heard about or seen before. At this auction, price will be allowed to go up and down in response to supply and demand.

Suppose for now that the supply curve for corn is vertical, as in Exhibit 4-1. It cuts the horizontal axis at 40,000 bushels of corn. This means that no more and no fewer than 40,000 bushels of corn will be auctioned off. The demand curve for corn is downward sloping. Furthermore, suppose in our auction each potential buyer of corn is sitting in front of a computer that registers the number of bushels he or she wants to buy. For example, if Nancy Berkeley wants to buy 5,000 bushels of corn, she simply types the number 5,000 into her computer.

The auction begins. (Follow along in Exhibit 4-1 as you read about what is happening at the auction.) The auctioneer calls out the price:

■ $6. The potential buyers think for a second, and then each registers the number of bushels he or she wants to buy at that price. The total is 20,000, which is the quantity demanded of corn at $6 per bushel. The quantity supplied, though, is 40,000. In economics, when quantity supplied is greater than quantity demanded, a **surplus** exists. At a price of $6 per bushel, the surplus equals 20,000 bushels (which is the difference between the quantity supplied and the

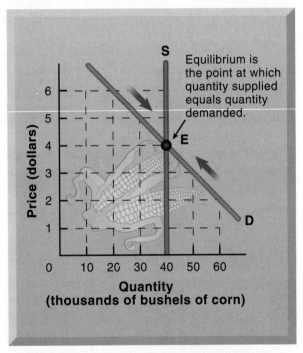

Equilibrium is the point at which quantity supplied equals quantity demanded.

▲ **EXHIBIT 4-1. Supply and Demand at Work at an Auction.** The auctioneer calls out different prices, and buyers record how much they are willing and able to buy. At prices $6 and $5, quantity supplied is greater than quantity demanded—there is a surplus. At prices $2 and $3, quantity demanded is greater than quantity supplied—there is a shortage. Only at a price of $4 is the quantity demanded equal to the quantity supplied—there is neither a surplus nor a shortage. (By the way, the supply curve is vertical at 40,000 bushels of corn because we have assumed that no more and no fewer than 40,000 bushels of corn will be auctioned off.)

quantity demanded; 40,000 − 20,000 = 20,000). The auctioneer, realizing that 20,000 bushels of corn will go unsold at this price, decides to lower the price per bushel to:

- $5. The quantity demanded increases to 30,000 bushels, but still the quantity supplied of corn at this price is greater than the quantity demanded. There is still a surplus of corn—specifically, 10,000 bushels (40,000 − 30,000 = 10,000). The auctioneer lowers the price again, this time to:

- $2. At this price, the quantity demanded jumps to 60,000 bushels and is greater than the quantity supplied. When quantity demanded is greater than quantity supplied, a **shortage** is said to exist. The auctioneer, realizing that he can't sell 60,000 bushels of corn, because this quantity doesn't exist, decides to raise the price to:

- $3. At this price, quantity demanded falls to 50,000 bushels but is still greater than quantity supplied. A shortage still exists, although it is smaller than the shortage that existed at $2 per bushel. The auctioneer raises the price to:

- $4. At the price of $4, the quantity demanded is 40,000 and the quantity supplied is 40,000. The auction stops. The 40,000 bushels of corn are bought and sold at $4. The corn market is said to be in **equilibrium**. A market is in equilibrium when the quantity demanded of a good equals the quantity supplied. The quantity 40,000 bushels of corn is referred to as the **equilibrium quantity**, and $4 is referred to as the **equilibrium price**.

Moving to Equilibrium: What Happens to Price When There Is a Surplus or a Shortage?

What did the auctioneer do when the price was $6 and there was a surplus of corn? He lowered the price. What did the auctioneer do when the price was $2 and there was a shortage? He raised the price. The behavior of the auctioneer can be summarized this way: If a surplus exists, lower price; if

a shortage exists, raise price. This is how the auctioneer moved the corn market into equilibrium.

Not all markets have auctioneers. (When was the last time you saw an auctioneer in the grocery store?) But many markets act *as if* an auctioneer were calling out higher and lower prices until equilibrium price is reached. In many real-world markets, prices fall when there is a surplus and rise when there is a shortage. Why?

Why Does Price Fall When There Is a Surplus? With a surplus, suppliers will not be able to sell all they had hoped to sell. As a result, their **inventories** grow beyond the level they normally hold. Storing extra goods can be costly and inefficient; thus, sellers will want to reduce their inventories. Some will lower prices to do so; some will cut back on producing output; others will do a lit-

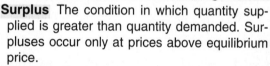

MINI GLOSSARY

Surplus The condition in which quantity supplied is greater than quantity demanded. Surpluses occur only at prices above equilibrium price.

Shortage The condition in which quantity demanded is greater than quantity supplied. Shortages occur only at prices below equilibrium price.

Equilibrium The condition of being at rest or balanced. Equilibrium in a market exists when the quantity of a good that buyers are willing and able to buy is equal to the quantity of the good that sellers are willing and able to produce and offer for sale (that is, quantity demanded equals quantity supplied). Graphically, equilibrium in a market is shown as the intersection point of the supply and demand curves.

Equilibrium Quantity The quantity of a good that is bought and sold in a market that is in equilibrium.

Equilibrium Price The price at which a good is bought and sold in a market that is in equilibrium.

Inventory The stock of goods that a business or store has on hand.

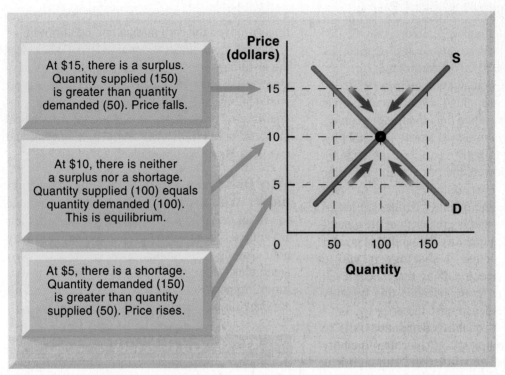

At $15, there is a surplus. Quantity supplied (150) is greater than quantity demanded (50). Price falls.

At $10, there is neither a surplus nor a shortage. Quantity supplied (100) equals quantity demanded (100). This is equilibrium.

At $5, there is a shortage. Quantity demanded (150) is greater than quantity supplied (50). Price rises.

▲ **EXHIBIT 4-2. Moving to Equilibrium.** If there is a surplus—as there is at a price of $15—price and quantity of output fall. If there is a shortage—as there is at a price of $5—price and quantity of output rise. At $10, there is neither a surplus nor a shortage. Consequently, there is no change in price or quantity of output.

tle of both. As shown in Exhibit 4-2, there is a tendency for price and output to fall until equilibrium is achieved.

Why Does Price Rise When There Is a Shortage?   With a shortage, buyers will not be able to buy all they had hoped to buy. Some buyers will offer to pay a higher price to get sellers to sell to them instead of to other buyers. The higher prices will get suppliers to start producing more output. Thus, there is a tendency for price and output to rise until equilibrium is achieved (see Exhibit 4-2).

QUESTION: *In Exhibit 4-2, how do we determine quantity demanded and quantity supplied of the good at the various prices?*

ANSWER: *Let's determine the quantity demanded and the quantity supplied at a price of $15 in*

Exhibit 4-2. To find the quantity demanded, we start at the price of $15 on the vertical axis and follow the dotted horizontal line over to the demand curve (D). Then we follow the dotted vertical line downward to the horizontal (or quantity) axis. The number we see here is 50. This means that the quantity demanded is 50 at $15.

To find the quantity supplied at $15, we start again at the price of $15 on the vertical axis and follow the dotted horizontal line over to the supply curve (S). Then we follow the dotted vertical line downward to the horizontal axis. The number we see here is 150. This means that the quantity supplied is 150 at $15.

Is there a surplus or a shortage at $15? Since the quantity supplied (150) is greater than the quantity demanded (50), there is a surplus. What happens to price if a surplus exists? It falls.

CASE STUDY

The Spotted Owl and Timber Prices

We begin with the facts. First, the federal government and many state governments have laws that protect spotted owls. For example, timber companies cannot cut trees in the area in which the spotted owl lives. Second, Weyerhaeuser Company is a major forest-products company that is involved in cutting millions of acres of timberland.

On the surface, we might think that Weyerhaeuser would not like the laws that protect the spotted owl, since these laws prevent it from cutting some of its own timberland. Weyerhaeuser says it has restricted logging on 320,000 acres of its land in order to comply with federal and state rules protecting the spotted owl.

But this is only part of the story. The rest involves land the federal government owns. On federally-owned land, loggers are permitted to cut timber where there are no spotted owls. However, the federal government has put logging restrictions on 5 million acres of the land it owns in the Pacific Northwest where there are spotted owls.

What do laws that protect the spotted owl, and thus prevent timber companies from cutting down some forests, do to the supply of timber? The supply of timber diminishes, which causes the supply curve to shift to the left from where it would otherwise be. And if the supply curve for a good shifts left, and demand remains the same, price rises.

(See Exhibit 4-3d.) Conclusion: Laws that protect the spotted owl drive up the price of timber.

Again we return to Weyerhaeuser. On the one hand, Weyerhaeuser is hurt by the laws that protect the spotted owl, because it cannot cut down the trees on some of its land. But on the other hand, these laws drive the price of timber up, enabling Weyerhaeuser to sell its timber for a higher price.

In 1992, Weyerhaeuser was helped more by the higher prices of timber than it was hurt by not being able to cut down trees on some of its land. In short, the laws protecting the spotted owl helped Weyerhaeuser's profits more than they hurt them. The *Wall Street Journal* reported that "owl-driven profits enabled the company to earn $86.6 million in the first quarter, up 81 percent from a year earlier."[a]

---

1. The story of the spotted owl and Weyerhaeuser can be told in a diagram with a horizontal and a vertical axis. Draw it. (Hint: Place "Quantity of Timber" on the horizontal axis and "Price" on the vertical axis. Also, in your diagram, you will have two supply curves. Think of what each represents.)

---

a. "Owls, of All Things, Help Weyerhaeuser Cash In on Timber," *Wall Street Journal*, June 24, 1992, p. 1.

Changes in Equilibrium Price

So far, we have established that equilibrium price is determined by both supply and demand. In Exhibit 4-2, the equilibrium price is $10. What would have to happen in order for the equilibrium price to change? Either supply or demand would have to change. Let's consider demand first.

Demand Changes and Equilibrium Price Changes. Exhibit 4-3a shows the demand for

and supply of television sets. The original demand curve is D_1, the supply curve is S_1, equilibrium is at point 1, and the equilibrium price is $300. Now suppose the demand for television sets increases. (Recall from Chapter 3 the factors that can shift the demand curve for a good: income, preferences, and prices of related goods.) The demand curve shifts to the right from D_1 to D_2. D_2 is now the relevant demand curve. At $300 per television, the quantity demanded (using the new demand curve, D_2) is 300,000, and the quantity supplied (using the one and only supply curve, S_1) is 200,000.

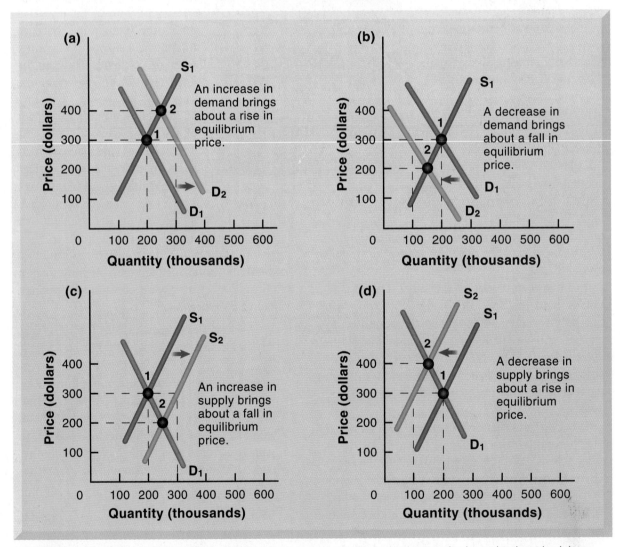

▲ **EXHIBIT 4-3. Changes in Equilibrium Price.** A change in equilibrium price can be brought about by (a) an increase in demand, (b) a decrease in demand, (c) an increase in supply, or (d) a decrease in supply.

Since quantity demanded is greater than quantity supplied, a shortage exists in the television market. What happens? Price begins to rise. As it does, the television market moves to point 2, where it is in equilibrium again. The new equilibrium price is $400. We conclude that an increase in the demand for a good will increase price, all other things remaining the same.

Now suppose the demand for television sets decreases (see Exhibit 4-3b). The demand curve shifts to the left from D_1 to D_2. At $300, the quantity demanded (using the new demand curve, D_2) is 100,000, and the quantity supplied (again using S_1) is 200,000. Since quantity supplied is greater than quantity demanded, a surplus exists. What happens? Price begins to fall. As it does, the television market moves to point 2, where it is in equilibrium again. The new equilibrium price is $200. We conclude that a decrease in the demand for a good will decrease price, all other things remaining the same.

Supply Changes and Equilibrium Price Changes. Exhibit 4-3c shows the demand for and supply of television sets. The demand curve is D_1, the original supply curve is S_1, equilibrium is at point 1, and the equilibrium price is $300. Now

suppose the supply of television sets increases (Recall from Chapter 3 the factors that can shift the supply curve for a good: resource prices, technology, taxes, and quotas.) The supply curve shifts to the right from S_1 to S_2. At $300, the quantity supplied (using the new supply curve, S_2) is 300,000, and the quantity demanded (using D_1) is 200,000. Since quantity supplied is greater than quantity demanded, a surplus exists in the television market. Price begins to fall, and the television market moves to point 2, where it is in equilibrium again. The new equilibrium price is $200. We conclude that an increase in the supply of a good will decrease price, all other things remaining the same.

Now suppose the supply of television sets decreases, as in Exhibit 4-3d. The supply curve shifts leftward from S_1 to S_2. At $300, the quantity supplied (using S_2) is 100,000, and the quantity demanded (using D_1) is 200,000. Since quantity demanded is greater than quantity supplied, a shortage exists in the television market. Price begins to rise, and the television market moves to point 2, where it is again in equilibrium. The new equilibrium price is $400. We conclude that a decrease in the supply of a good will increase price, all other things remaining the same.

 LEARNING CHECK

1. Define *surplus*.
2. Define *shortage*.
3. If demand increases and supply is constant, what happens to equilibrium price?
4. If supply increases and demand is constant, what happens to equilibrium price?

SECTION 2 PRICE AS A RATIONING DEVICE

We know how price is determined—by the forces of supply and demand. But what are the functions of price? *What does price do?* Price acts as a rationing device. We discuss this function of price next.

As you read, keep these key questions in mind:

■ What is a rationing device?
■ What are some other rationing devices besides price?

Rationing Devices in a World of Scarcity

Wants are unlimited; resources are limited. In short, scarcity exists. Furthermore, because resources are limited, and since the production of goods requires resources, goods are also limited. Consequently, a **rationing device** is needed to determine who gets what of the available limited resources and goods. Price acts as a rationing device. It rations scarce resources to those persons who pay the price for the resources. It rations scarce goods to those persons who pay the price for the goods. It is as simple as this: Pay the price, and the resources or goods are yours. Don't pay the price, and they aren't.

Resources and goods need not be rationed by price. They could be rationed by political favor, physical appearance, favoritism, brute force, or on a first-come, first-served basis, to name only a few possibilities. All these means could be used to decide who gets what. Therefore all could be rationing devices.

▲ Outside this shop in Moscow, people wait to buy bread and other goods. This is an example of goods being rationed by price and on a first-come-first-served basis.

What would a world where brute force was used as a rationing device look like? In this world, if you wanted something you did not produce yourself—such as food, or clothes, or maybe even a house—you would have to physically take it from someone else. Jonathan wants a radio; he notices that Robert has a radio; he hits Robert over the head and takes the radio. Jonathan gets what he wants not by paying the price but through sheer brute force. The strongest persons most willing to use their muscle to get what they wanted would rule. How would you fare in this world?

Is It Fair to Use Price as a Rationing Device?

Using price as a rationing device is often criticized because it discriminates against the poor. And there is no doubt about it. If you are poor, you can't buy as many goods and services as you can if you are rich. Does this mean that, in the United States, price should be replaced with some other rationing device? Some people say yes; some people say no. What would you say, and why?

To help you reach an answer, consider the following. Suppose you and everyone else were magically transported to a place—we'll call it the Land-of-Know-Nothing—where you have no idea of what you look like, who your parents are, how smart you are, how old you are, whether you are rich, poor, or somewhere in between, or anything else about yourself.[1] In short, you "know nothing" about yourself.

What you and others do know, though, is that scarcity exists in the real world and that there has to be some way of dealing with it. This means

---

MINI GLOSSARY

Rationing Device A means for deciding who gets what of available goods and resources.

---

1. The setting described here was first proposed by John Rawls, a philosopher, in his book *A Theory of Justice*. He called the setting the *original position*.

Alfred Marshall (1842–1924)

Alfred Marshall was born in Bermondsey, a London suburb, on July 26, 1842. He died at his home in Cambridge, England, on July 13, 1924, at the age of 81. William Marshall, Alfred Marshall's father, was a strict disciplinarian who pushed his son to the point of mental and physical exhaustion. Alfred Marshall refused a classics scholarship at Oxford University and instead studied mathematics at Cambridge University. Marshall taught at both Oxford and Cambridge. In July 1877, he married his former student, Mary Paley.

Supply and Demand

Marshall's book, *Principles of Economics*, has had a major impact on the economics profession. Often referred to as the bible of British economics, it introduced many economic concepts that are still used today. Marshall discussed supply and demand in terms of a pair of scissors. He said that just as the two blades of a pair of scissors are equally important in cutting, so are supply and demand equally important in determining price. Here is what he said:

We might as reasonably dispute whether it is the upper or the under [lower] blade of a pair of scissors that cuts a piece of paper, as whether value [price] is governed by utility [demand] or cost of production [supply]. It is true that when one blade is held still, and the cutting is effected by moving the other, we may say with careless brevity that the cutting is done by the second; but the statement is not strictly accurate, and is to be excused only so long as it claims to be merely a popular and not strictly scientific account of what happens.[a]

Elasticity of Demand

Marshall was the first person to define the concept of elasticity of demand, though others had come close to a definition. (This concept was discussed earlier in Chapter 3.)

The Issue of Poverty

Marshall was greatly concerned with social issues, especially poverty, which he believed was at the root of many social problems. He hoped that the study of economics would enable him to better understand the causes of poverty and to find a solution to it.

---

1. In your own words, explain what Marshall is saying in the quoted passage cited here. It begins, "We might as reasonably dispute. . . "
2. What did Marshall study at Cambridge University?

---

a. Alfred Marshall, *Principles of Economics*, 8th ed. (London: Macmillan, 1920), p. 348.

---

there has to be some rationing device, some means of deciding who gets what of the available resources and goods.

In this setting, where you know nothing about yourself, you have to decide which rationing device you want to use when you are transported back to the real world. Once the decision has been made, you will return to the real world, where you will find out who you are, who your parents are, how much money you have, and so on.

What rationing device would you choose?

You could turn out to be very rich, and so price might be the best rationing device to choose. But, then, you could turn out to be very poor. Price wouldn't be as good a rationing device for you under this condition.

You could choose a particular ethnic background as a rationing device, say, Chinese. But suppose you turned out to be something other than Chinese?

You could choose intelligence, as measured by an IQ test. The higher you scored on the IQ test, the more resources and goods would be available to you. But suppose you turned out to score low?

It is not an easy decision to make, but still it must be made. How would you decide?

QUESTION: *Why not use* need *as a rationing device?*

ANSWER: *There are some problems here. First, who would determine need? Would Republicans argue that they should determine need and Democrats argue that they should? Second, what is it that people really need? We might agree that all people need a certain amount of food, water, clothing, and shelter. But what else? Do people*

need television sets, VCRs, cars, trips to Aspen, Colorado, in the winter, and so forth? Third, if need were the rationing device, would there be an incentive to work? With price as the rationing device, people have to produce goods and services to earn the income necessary to buy goods. If they could obtain these goods and services without working—by simply expressing a "need"—would anything be produced? Would anyone actually work under such a system?

THINKING LIKE AN ECONOMIST

A *key question for the economist is,* What are the alternatives? *This is evident in the discussion of price as a rationing device. An economist is not content to sit and listen to a person say that he or she dislikes price as a rationing device. The economist quickly thinks, "If not price as a rationing device, then what?"*

LEARNING CHECK

1. What is a rationing device?
2. List three rationing devices besides price.
3. What does price ration?

SECTION 3   SUPPLY AND DEMAND IN ACTION

The violin teacher can show you how to play the violin, but unless you do it yourself, you will never learn. It is similar with supply and demand. You know what supply is, what demand is, and how price is determined. But as yet, you have not seen supply and demand at work in real-world situations. We'll take care of that in this section.

As you read, keep these key questions in mind:

■ What do earthquakes in California have to do with the price of bottled water?

■ How are candy bar prices different from real estate prices?

Why There Are Long Lines for Some Rock Concerts

Suppose tickets for a rock concert go on sale at 8 A.M. on Saturday. When the ticket booth opens, there is a long line of people waiting to buy tickets. The average person has to wait an hour to buy

▲ Long lines of people waiting to buy a good or service usually indicate that shortage exists in the market. Prices may soon rise.

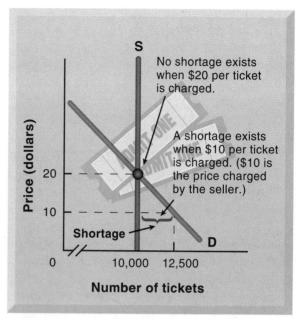

▲ **EXHIBIT 4-4. Rock Concert Ticket Price.** In our example, the seller of rock concert tickets sells 10,000 tickets at a price of $10 each. At this price, there is a shortage. The seller has charged *too low a price*. A price of $20 per ticket would have achieved equilibrium in the market. Question: Do you know why the supply curve is vertical at 10,000 seats in this graph? Because this is the total number of seats in the auditorium. Even if a higher price is offered per ticket, no additional seats will be forthcoming.

a ticket. Some people don't get to buy tickets at all, since the tickets sell out before they get to the ticket booth.

Why is there a long line of people waiting to buy tickets to the rock concert, when there is not a long line of people waiting to buy food at the grocery store, TVs at the electronics store, and so on? Also, why are some of the people waiting to buy tickets to the rock concert turned away, when no one who wants to buy bread is turned away at the grocery store, and no one who wants to buy a TV set is turned away at the electronics store? The market for the rock concert tickets (at least in this instance) must differ somehow. But how?

Return to the long line of people waiting to buy concert tickets. Some of these people were turned away. Translate this observation into economics. What does it mean, in economic terms, when some people go away without being able to buy what they came to buy? It means that quantity demanded exceeds quantity supplied. It means there is a *shortage* in the market.

We learned earlier that if there is a shortage in a market, price will rise. Eventually, it will rise to its equilibrium level. The problem in our rock concert example, though, is that the tickets were bought and sold *before* the seller realized there was a shortage of tickets. In hindsight, the seller now knows that the price charged for the tickets was *too low*. This pricing caused a shortage. If the seller had charged the equilibrium price, there would have been no shortage, no long lines, and no one being turned away without a ticket.

As shown in Exhibit 4-4, the seller charged $10 a ticket. At this price, quantity demanded (12,500) was greater than quantity supplied (10,000). If the price had been $20 a ticket, quantity supplied (10,000) would have equaled quantity demanded (10,000), and there would have been no shortage.

ECONOMIC FOCUS

The price of a house is less in Montana than in California. In 1990, the median price of a house in Montana was $56,600; in California, it was $195,500. (The *median* price is the *middle* price. Suppose there are only three houses located on Elm Street. The prices of the three houses, going from the lowest to the highest, are $78,000, $82,000, and $84,000. If we arrange house prices from lowest to highest, as we did, the median price is always the middle price—or $82,000 in our example.[a] So, when we say that the median price of a house in Montana is $56,600, it follows that half of all houses in Montana are priced below $56,600, and half of all houses are priced above $56,600.)

Why is the median price of a house higher in California than in Montana? The answer is, because the demand for and supply of houses in California is different than it is in Montana. Specifically, the demand for houses in California is *higher* than in Montana, relative to the supply of houses.

To understand this, ask yourself what happens to the price of any good if the demand for it increases relative to its supply. As we learned in this chapter, price does increase. The price of houses is higher in California than in Montana because the demand for houses is higher (has increased more) relative to the supply of houses.

Why is the demand for houses relative to the supply of houses higher in California than in Montana? As we learned in Chapter 3, there are

three factors that can cause a shift in a demand curve: changes in income, preferences, and the prices of related goods (substitutes and complements). For example, a change in preferences in favor of a good increases the demand for that good and shifts the demand curve for that good to the right. In turn, this causes price to increase. Perhaps the demand for houses in California is higher than in Montana relative to the supply of houses because many more people have a stronger *preference* for living in California rather than Montana. The reasons why more people may prefer to live in California rather than Montana can be varied. Some people may prefer the climate in California to the climate in Montana. For others, California has a wider variety of job opportunities than Montana.

In Exhibit S-4-1 we list the median price of a house in each of the 50 states. Be careful not to conclude that because the median price of a house in your state is, say, $100,000 that the median price of a house in every city in your state is $100,000. Just as the median price of a house can be different among states, it can be different among cities in a given state, too. For example, we mentioned that the median price of a house in California in 1990 was $195,500. In some cities in California, such as San Bernardino, the median price was lower; it was $132,000. In other cities in California, such as Los Angeles, the median price was higher; it was $212,200.

It is interesting to ask what might cause the median price of a house in one city in a state to be higher or lower than the median price of a house in another city in the same state. Our general answer, again, is that the demand for houses relative to the supply of houses is higher in one city than in the other. But, still again, we wonder

---

a. Suppose there had been four houses on Elm Street instead of three. Their prices were $78,000, $82,000, $83,000, and $84,000, arranged from lowest to highest. What would be the middle or median price? This would be the average price of the two prices in the middle. These two prices are $82,000 and $83,000; ($82,000 + $83,000 = $165,000 and $165,000 ÷ 2 = $82,500). $82,500 is the median price.

HOUSE PRICES ACROSS THE STATES

▼ **EXHIBIT S-4-1. Median Price of a House In Each of the 50 States.**

STATE	$	STATE	$	STATE	$
Hawaii	$245,300	Colorado	$82,700	Louisiana	$58,500
California	195,500	Arizona	80,100	Tennessee	58,400
Connecticut	177,800	Florida	77,100	Idaho	58,200
Massachusetts	162,800	Minnesota	74,000	Montana	56,600
New Jersey	162,300	Georgia	71,300	Indiana	53,900
Rhode Island	133,500	New Mexico	70,100	Alabama	53,700
New York	131,600	Pennsylvania	69,700	Kansas	52,200
New Hampshire	129,400	Utah	68,900	North Dakota	50,800
Maryland	116,500	Oregon	67,100	Nebraska	50,400
Delaware	100,100	North Carolina	65,800	Kentucky	50,200
Nevada	95,700	Ohio	63,500	Oklahoma	48,100
Vermont	95,500	Wisconsin	62,500	West Virginia	47,900
Alaska	94,400	Wyoming	61,600	Arkansas	46,300
Washington	93,400	South Carolina	61,100	Iowa	45,900
Virginia	91,000	Michigan	60,600	Mississippi	45,600
Maine	87,400	Missouri	59,800	South Dakota	45,200
Illinois	83,800	Texas	59,600		

SOURCE: U.S. Bureau of the Census, *Statistical Abstract of the United States: 1993,* 113th Edition. Data are for 1990.

why this is the case. The difference in the prices of a house in San Bernardino and a house in Los Angeles cannot be attributable to a difference in climate (as perhaps would be the case with California and Montana) because the two cities are located only about 80 miles apart.

Some economists have suggested that the difference has to do with people generally preferring to live near their work. Since there are more business firms in Los Angeles than in San Bernardino, and thus more people who have jobs there, more people would prefer to live in Los Angeles than in San Bernardino.

---

1. House prices tend to be higher in densely populated cities than in sparsely populated cities. Explain why.

2. In 1991, the median price of a house in San Antonio, Texas, was $64,900; the median price of a house in Hartford, Connecticut, was $148,200. The price difference was $83,300 ($148,200 − $64,900 = $83,300). One year later, in 1992, the median price of a house in San Antonio had increased to $70,400 and the median price of a house in Hartford had decreased to $141,100. The price difference was then $70,700 ($141,100 − $70,400 = $70,700). As the price difference between the houses in the two cities became smaller, were the supply and demand of houses in the two cities becoming more similar or dissimilar? Explain your answer.

QUESTION: *Why didn't the seller charge the higher equilibrium price, instead of a price that was too low?*

ANSWER: *The seller might have charged the equilibrium price had he or she known it. Think back to the auctioneer example. Did the auctioneer call out the equilibrium price at the start of the auction? No. He called out $6, which was too high a price. There was a surplus at that price. Later, he called out $2, which was too low a price. There was a shortage at that price. It was only through trial and error that the auctioneer finally hit upon the equilibrium price. The seller of the rock concert tickets didn't have the luxury of trial and error.*

Earthquakes in California and Bottled Water Prices

On January 17, 1994, a strong earthquake hit the San Fernando Valley in California. Over fifty persons were killed, and there was much physical destruction. People who lived in the San Fernando Valley noticed that within hours after the earth-quake, the price of bottled water in the stores had increased by about 400 to 500 percent. A bottle of water that had cost 90 cents before the earthquake was selling for approximately $4 shortly after the earthquake. Why the sharp increase in price?

We know that price is determined by supply and demand. Had the earthquake done anything to affect either the supply or the demand for water? Yes, it probably affected both. The earthquake had broken water pipes and thus interrupted the flow of water to some people's houses and apartments. In short, the supply of water had fallen. This, by itself, would be enough to raise price. But price was probably also pushed up because of an increase in demand. For example, probably people's fear of less water being available in the near future changed their preferences for water in the present: they wanted to buy much more of it in the present so that they would not be without it in the future.

Candy Bars, Bread, and Real Estate Prices

In general, no matter where you go in the United States, the price of a candy bar (pick your fa-

◄ Immediately after the January 17, 1994, earthquake in California, there was a shortage of clean water to drink. This led to higher prices for bottled water.

CONSUMER ECONOMIC DECISIONS

Obtaining Important Consumer Information

A well-respected dictionary says that information includes facts gathered in any way, as by reading, observation, or hearsay. John Naisbitt, a best-selling nonfiction author, writes, "We now produce information the way we used to mass-produce cars." Richard Wurman, another nonfiction author, writes, "A weekday edition of the *New York Times* [newspaper] contains more information than the average person was likely to come across in a lifetime in 17th-century England." An increasingly larger percentage of the American labor force is now employed gathering, categorizing, and processing information. Today, you can obtain information on almost anything you can imagine. The problem, though, is knowing *where to find* the information.

As a student, you know how important information is. You need information in order to do well in school. You get most of this information from your teachers and from your textbooks.

As a consumer, you will need plenty of information. For example, suppose you are thinking about buying a car. Do you know the safety record of the car you are thinking about buying? Do you know if its needs for maintenance are high or low? Suppose you buy a product and then have trouble with it. You take it back to the store that sold it to you, but the store will not return your money. What do you do then? To whom do you turn? Or suppose you buy a product and it causes you bodily injury? To whom do you report it? This section points out some of the places you can go for the information that will help you get answers to these and other questions.

▲ A good source for useful consumer information is *Consumer Reports*.

Consumers Union and *Consumer Reports*

Consumers Union is a nonprofit corporation organized to provide consumers with information on consumer goods and services. Its major publication, *Consumer Reports*, is published monthly and is full of useful information for consumers. It regularly reports on and rates a host of different consumer goods according to such things as price, quality, and safety. Reading *Consumer Reports* is a must if you are thinking about buying a car. The car edition usually comes out in April. You will probably

Making CONSUMER ECONOMIC DECISIONS (continued)

find a copy of *Consumer Reports* in your school or town library or at a well-stocked magazine stand. The telephone number for Consumers Union and *Consumer Reports* is 914-378-2000.

Consumer Information Center

The federal government publishes numerous free-of-charge publications on consumer issues. These publications can be ordered through the Consumer Information Center (CIC), which is a federal government agency. Write to:

Consumer Information Center
Pueblo, Colorado 81009

The CIC quarterly publishes a major catalog, *Consumer Information Catalog*, which lists over 200 government publications on a wide range of consumer topics, such as electronic products, buying a used car, ways to lower your auto insurance costs, diet and nutrition, mental illness, home mortgages, tips for energy savers, life insurance, and more. The telephone number for the CIC is 719-948-3334, but it prefers written requests.

Federal Information Center

The Federal Information Center (FIC) is a federal agency whose basic responsibility is to help consumers find information or locate the appropriate agency to help them with their problems. The FIC answers a wide range of questions, not only those that relate to consumer issues. You can locate the nearest Federal Information Center by looking in the telephone book under "U.S. Government" or by calling the toll-free number, 800-726-4995.

Better Business Bureaus

Better Business Bureaus (BBBs) are non-profit organizations sponsored by local businesses. BBBs offer a variety of consumer education programs, provide information on companies, handle consumer inquiries, settle complaints, and maintain records of consumer satisfaction or dissatisfaction with individual companies. If you are thinking of buying a product from a company in your town, it is a good idea to check with the local BBB to find out about any consumer complaints it might have received about the company. Your local BBB is listed in the telephone directory.

Magazines and Other Publications

There are numerous specialty consumer magazines that report on and rate various consumer items, such as camping equipment, computers, boats, cars, and financial investments. A good library will carry most of these magazines.

Consumer Protection Offices

State and city governments have consumer protection offices. You may find one located in the governor's office, state attorney general's office, or mayor's office. These offices help to resolve consumer complaints, furnish information on helpful publications, and provide other consumer services. The consumer protection

Making CONSUMER ECONOMIC DECISIONS (continued)

office in your city or state is listed in the telephone book.

Consumer Product Safety Commission

The Consumer Product Safety Commission (CPSC) is a federal government agency whose basic responsibility is to protect consumers against injuries associated with consumer products. It also conducts consumer education and information programs. The CPSC operates a toll-free hotline that consumers can call to report a product-related injury or possible product defect or to request information on product safety. The toll-free number is 800-638-2772.

---

1. Here are some questions that a consumer might ask. After each question, answer by writing whom the consumer should call, what publication he or she should consult, or the like. Here is a sample:

Question: I want to know whether or not the car I am thinking about buying has a good safety record. Where do I go to find out?
Answer: Consult the April edition of *Consumer Reports*. This publication reports on and rates various makes of automobiles as to quality, price, and safety.

a. Question: I am getting ready to buy some athletic equipment from a company. I want to know if there are any consumer complaints about this company. Whom do I call?

b. Question: I want to become more informed on issues that interest consumers. Where might I obtain some written information?

c. Question: I bought a product today that I think might be dangerous. I want people to know about this so that they won't get hurt. To whom do I report this?

d. Question: I bought four tires the other day and had them put on my car. A week later, one of the tires blew out. I went back to the store and complained, but I didn't get anywhere. I have already registered a complaint with the Better Business Bureau. I want my complaint resolved. To whom do I turn?

e. Question: I have a question that I think someone in the federal government can answer, but I am not sure which agency I should call. How do I find out to whom I should direct my question?

---

vorite brand) is the same. A candy bar in Toledo, Ohio, is the same price as a candy bar in Miami, Florida. The same holds, to a large degree, for a loaf of bread.

Now consider real estate prices—in particular, the price of a house in San Francisco and the price of a similar house in a similar neighborhood in Louisville, Kentucky. The house in San Francisco will sell for approximately two to three times the price of the house in Louisville. Why the large difference? Why, when it comes to candy bars and bread, does a good sell for approximately the same price no matter where it is purchased in the United States, whereas a house purchased in San Francisco is so much more expensive than a similar house in Louisville?

Supply and demand give us the answer. Consider the case of the candy bar. There is a demand for, and a supply of, candy bars in both City A and City B. Let's say the price of a candy bar is higher in City A because the demand for candy bars is higher in City A.

Suppose that the price of a candy bar is a dollar in City A and 50 cents in City B. Given the price difference, the suppliers of candy bars would prefer to sell more of their product in City A than in City B. As a result, the supply of candy bars shifts to the right in City A and to the left in City B. Since the supply of candy bars has increased in City A, the price of a candy bar will decrease (say, from a dollar to 75 cents); and since the supply of candy bars has decreased in City B, the price of a candy bar will increase (say, from 50 cents to 75 cents). Only when the prices of candy bars are the same in the two cities would suppliers no longer have an incentive to rearrange the supply of candy bars in the two cities. The same analysis holds for the price of bread in two cities. We conclude that when suppliers can shift supply from one location to another, price will tend to be uniform for products.[2]

Now consider houses in different cities. As stated earlier, housing prices are much higher in San Francisco than in Louisville. This is because in San Francisco the demand for houses is higher, relative to the supply of houses, than it is in Louisville. If houses were candy bars or bread, suppliers would shift supply from Louisville to San Francisco. But, of course, houses are not similar to candy bars or bread in this regard. Houses are built on land, and the price of the land is part of the price of the houses. Naturally, suppliers cannot pick up an acre of land in Louisville and move it to San Francisco.

We conclude that where the supply of a good cannot be moved in response to a difference in price between cities, prices for this good are likely to remain different in these cities.

---

2. For simplicity, our analysis does not take into account transportation costs. In reality, prices of candy bars and bread are still the same everywhere, having adjusted for transportation costs.

✔ LEARNING CHECK

1. Suppose a seller charges a price for his product that is below equilibrium price. Why would someone do this?
2. Why aren't housing prices the same across the country?
3. Suppose the price of carpet is higher in Los Angeles than in New York City. How will this affect the behavior of carpet suppliers?

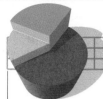

DEVELOPING ECONOMIC SKILLS

Understanding What Price Tells Us

Price is commonly thought of as a number with a dollar sign in front of it—such as $30. In this chapter, it is this, and more. It acts as a rationing device. It also affects behavior. For example, when the price of a good rises, people buy fewer units of the good. In short, a change in price affects people's *buying* behavior. It also affects sellers' *supplying behavior*: as price rises, sellers supply more units of a good; as price falls, they supply fewer units.

Besides being a rationing device and affecting behavior, price serves as a transmitter of information. To illustrate, consider the following set of events. On Saturday, Noelle walks into a local grocery store and purchases a half-gallon of orange juice for $2.50. On Sunday, unknown to her, a cold spell hits Florida and wipes out one-quarter of the orange crop. The cold spell shifts the supply curve of oranges to the left and leads to a rise in the price of oranges. Higher orange prices, in turn, shift the supply curve of orange juice to the left and drive up the price of orange juice. Next Saturday, Noelle returns to the grocery store and notices that the price of a half-gallon of orange juice is $3.50 instead of what it was last week, $2.50. She decides to buy a quart of orange juice for $1.75 instead of a half-gallon for $3.50. (Her demand curve for orange juice is downward sloping: she buys less at higher prices rather than at lower prices.)

What kind of information does price transmit? By moving up and down, it transmits information on the *relative scarcity* of a good. The higher price for orange juice is saying (once we translate its message into English): "There has been a cold spell in Florida resulting in less orange juice. The gap between people's wants for orange juice and the amount of orange juice available to satisfy those wants has widened."

Notice, too, that while Noelle's direct response to the higher price of orange juice is to cut back on her consumption (remember price

▲ If a cold snap hits Florida orange groves, the supply of oranges and orange juice will decrease. In time, the prices of oranges and orange juice will increase.

affects behavior), she indirectly responds to the information of the increased relative scarcity of orange juice—even without being aware of Florida weather conditions.

---

1. The supply of some good increases; consequently, the price of the good decreases. What information is price transmitting about the relative scarcity of the good?
2. The demand for some good rises; consequently, the price of the good rises. What information is price transmitting about the relative scarcity of the good?

CHAPTER 4 REVIEW

CHAPTER SUMMARY

1. Supply and demand work together to determine price. Both sides of the market are equally important in the determination of price.

2. A surplus exists when the quantity supplied of a good is greater than the quantity demanded. A surplus occurs at a price *above* equilibrium price.

3. A shortage exists when the quantity demanded of a good is greater than the quantity supplied. A shortage occurs at a price *below* equilibrium price.

4. Equilibrium price is the price at which the quantity supplied of a good equals the quantity demanded.

5. If demand increases and supply remains the same, equilibrium price increases. If demand decreases and supply remains the same, equilibrium price decreases.

6. If supply increases and demand remains the same, equilibrium price decreases. If supply decreases and demand remains the same, equilibrium price increases.

7. Price acts as a rationing device. It rations scarce resources and goods to those persons who pay the price for the resources and goods.

8. If price is not chosen or is not permitted to serve as a rationing device, something else must. As long as there is scarcity, and people's wants are greater than the resources available to satisfy those wants, something needs to serve as a rationing device.

BUILD YOUR ECONOMIC VOCABULARY

Match the word with the correct definition, example, or statement.

1. shortage
2. surplus
3. equilibrium price
4. equilibrium
5. brute force
6. price

a. a commonly used rationing device in the United States

b. a rationing device that is not commonly used today in the United States

c. exists when quantity demanded is greater than quantity supplied

d. exists when quantity supplied is greater than quantity demanded

e. the price that exists in the market when the quantity supplied of a good equals the quantity demanded

f. the market setting in which the quantity supplied of a good equals the quantity demanded

REVIEW QUESTIONS

1. Explain why price falls if there is a surplus.
2. Explain why price rises if there is a shortage.
3. Look at the prices listed in Exhibit 4-1. At what prices is there a surplus? What is the equilibrium price and what is the equilibrium quantity in the exhibit?

REVIEW QUESTIONS (continued)

4. a. Which way does the demand curve shift when demand decreases?

b. Which way does the supply curve shift when supply decreases?

5. Using diagrams, present the following situations. In each case, label the horizontal axis "Quantity" and the vertical axis "Price." Label the first, or original, equilibrium point with the number 1 and the second, or new, equilibrium point with the number 2. Label original demand and supply curves as D_1 and S_1 and new demand and supply curves as D_2 and S_2. (For a review, see how this is done in Exhibit 4-3.)

a. Demand increases, and supply remains the same.

b. Demand decreases, and supply remains the same.

c. Supply increases, and demand remains the same.

d. Supply decreases, and demand remains the same.

6. List three rationing devices besides price.

7. What is the argument against using need as a rationing device?

8. "All markets at all points in time are necessarily in equilibrium." Do you agree or disagree? Explain your answer.

9. What might we see when a market is experiencing a shortage? (Hint: It is not enough to say that quantity demanded is greater than quantity supplied, since this is simply a definition of *shortage*. You must identify a tangible event that is evidence of a shortage.)

10. Pens and pencils sell for about the same price in every city in the country, but houses do not. Why?

SHARPEN YOUR CRITICAL THINKING SKILLS

1. "The price of houses is higher this year than three years ago. It must be because the supply of houses is less this year than three years ago." What, if anything, is wrong with this statement?

2. Is it possible for scarcity to exist when the quantity supplied of a good equals the quantity demanded of a good? Explain your answer.

ACTIVITIES AND PROJECTS

1. As a class, discuss the following: Is it fair to use price as a rationing device?

2. Find a newspaper or magazine article that describes an example of either a change in demand, or a change in supply, that changes price.

ECONOMIC DICTIONARY

Equilibrium (Pg. 93)
Equilibrium Price (Pg. 93)
Equilibrium Quantity (Pg. 93)
Inventory (Pg. 93)
Rationing Device (Pg. 98)
Shortage (Pg. 93)
Surplus (Pg. 92)

Business,
The Marketplace, and
Economic Decisions

Business Decisions: Costs, Revenues, and Profits

INTRODUCTION

When you buy groceries, you buy them from a business firm. When you buy clothes, you buy them from a business firm. If you have a job, it is probably with a business firm. Almost every day of your life, you come into contact with business firms.

Yet few of us know much about business firms. For many of us, business firms are simply there, much as the sun is there. In this chapter, we examine some of the features of business firms.

SECTION 1 TYPES OF BUSINESS FIRMS

Ways in which **business firms** differ include: what they produce, how many people they employ, what their revenues and their costs are, where they are located, and so on. Many of the differences between firms are minor, but some are not. One major difference is how a firm is legally categorized. Business firms commonly fall into one of three legal categories: sole proprietorships, partnerships, and corporations. One major role of all businesses, no matter which category they fit into, is to produce goods and services that consumers demand.

As you read, keep these key questions in mind:

- What is a sole proprietorship?
- What is a partnership?
- What is a corporation?
- What is unlimited liability?
- What is limited liability?

Sole Proprietorships

A **sole proprietorship** is a business that is (a) owned by one individual, (b) who makes all business decisions, (c) receives all the profits or takes all the losses of the firm, and (d) is legally responsible for the debts of the firm. Many family farms are sole proprietorships, as are many barbershops, restaurants, carpet-cleaning services, and so on. Sole proprietorships in the United States outnumber partnerships and corporations combined. In the early 1990s, nearly three out of every four firms are sole proprietorships. In contrast, sole proprietorships account for a relatively small percentage of total business revenues—approximately 6.1 percent. Corporations account for the largest percentage of total business revenues—approximately 89 percent.

Advantages of Sole Proprietorships. There are certain advantages to sole proprietorships.

1. **Sole proprietorships are easy to form and to dissolve.** To start a sole proprietorship, you need only meet certain broadly defined government regulations. For some firms, these include health and zoning regulations. For example, if you are starting a restaurant, you must be sure that the restaurant is clean (a health regulation) and that it is located in an area where restaurants are permitted (a zoning regulation). Also, you need to register the name of the business with local government officials. To dissolve a sole proprietorship, one need only stop doing business.

2. **All decision-making power resides with the sole proprietor.** If you are the owner of a sole proprietorship, you alone can make all the business decisions. There are no stockholders or partners to consult when you are deciding whether to expand your business, buy more supplies, advertise on the radio, and so on. Decisions can be made quickly and easily, since only one person counts—the sole proprietor.

3. **The profit of the firm is taxed only once.** There are different types of taxes in the United States. For example, there are sales taxes, property taxes, corporate income taxes, and personal income taxes. If you are the owner of a sole proprietorship, the profit you earn is counted as your income, and only **personal income taxes** apply to it. Proprietorships do not pay **corporate income taxes**. As you will see, neither do partnerships. Only corporations pay corporate income taxes.

Disadvantages of Sole Proprietorships. Sole proprietorships have disadvantages, too.

1. **The sole proprietor faces unlimited liability**. *Liability* is a legal term that has to do with the responsibility to pay debts. Saying that the sole proprietor has **unlimited liability** means that his or her personal assets may be used to pay off the debts of the firm. For example, suppose

▶ This sandwich shop is owned by a sole proprietor. A sole proprietor makes all business decisions—such as whether a six-foot-long sandwich will be made or not.

Jones opens his own cookie shop in the shopping mall. A year passes, and Jones is taking a loss on the business. He is also in debt to his suppliers—the person from whom he buys flour, the person from whom he rents the shop, and so on. Since Jones has unlimited liability, his personal assets—such as his car and his house—may have to be sold to pay off his business debts.

2. **Sole proprietorships have limited ability to raise funds for business expansion.** Sole proprietorships do not find borrowing funds easy, because lenders are not eager to lend funds to business firms whose success depends on one person. The sole proprietor's sources of money are often limited to his or her own personal funds and the funds of close friends and family members.

3. **Sole proprietorships usually end with the death of the proprietor; they have limited life.** When the owner of a proprietorship dies, the business "dies" as well. From the point of view of the business community and the firm's employees, this is a disadvantage. Employees

usually like to work for firms that offer some permanency and the possibility of moving upward.

MINI GLOSSARY

Business Firm An organization that uses resources to produce goods and services, which are sold to consumers, other firms, or the government.

Sole Proprietorship A business that is owned by one individual, who makes all business decisions, receives all the profits or takes all the losses of the firm, and is legally responsible for the debts of the firm.

Personal Income Tax A tax paid on a person's income.

Corporate Income Tax A tax paid on a corporation's profits.

Unlimited Liability The legal responsibility of a sole proprietor of a business or a partner in a business to pay any money owed by the business. The proprietor's or partner's personal assets may be used to pay these debts.

Partnerships

A **partnership** is a business that is (a) owned by two or more co-owners called partners, (b) who share any profits the business earns, and (c) are legally responsible for any debts incurred by the firm. Simply put, you may think of a partnership as a proprietorship with more than one owner. Partnerships include such businesses as some medical offices, law offices, and advertising agencies.

Advantages of Partnerships. The advantages of partnerships include the following.

1. **In a partnership, the benefits of specialization can be realized.** If, for example, one partner in an advertising agency is better at public relations and another is better at artwork, each can work at the tasks for which he or she is best suited. The ad agency then has a better chance of succeeding than if only one person ran it.

2. **The profit of the partnership is the income of the partners, and only personal income taxes apply to it.** The owners of a partnership, like the owner of a sole proprietorship, only pay personal income taxes. Corporate income taxes do not apply to them.

Disadvantages of Partnerships. The disadvantages of partnerships include the following.

1. **Partners' liability is unlimited.** Partners face unlimited liability, just as sole proprietors do. But in a way, it is even more of a disadvantage in a partnership than it is in a sole proprietorship. In a sole proprietorship, the proprietor incurs his or her own debts and is solely responsible for them. In a partnership, one partner might incur the debts, but all partners are responsible for them. For example, if partner Matson incurs a debt by buying an expensive piece of medical equipment without the permission of partners Bradbury and Chan, that is too bad for partners Bradbury and Chan. They are still legally responsible for the debts incurred by Matson, their partner.

2. **Decision making in a partnership can be complicated and frustrating.** Suppose that Smithies, a partner in our fictional law firm, wants to move the partnership in one direction, to specialize in corporate law, and Yankelovich wants to move it in another direction, to specialize in family law. Who makes the decision in this tug-of-war? Possibly no one will make the decision, and things will stay as they are,

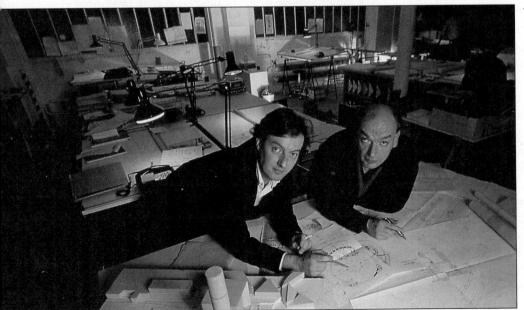

◄ These two men are partners in an architectural firm. One of the disadvantages of a partnership is that each partner is responsible for the business debts incurred by the other partners.

which may not be a good thing for the growth of the partnership.

QUESTION: *Isn't there such a thing as a limited partnership that avoids some of the problems of unlimited liability?*

ANSWER: *Yes, in a **limited partnership**, there are usually **general partners** and **limited partners**. General partners have unlimited liability, but limited partners do not. The limited partner's liability is restricted to the amount he or she has invested in the firm. For example, if limited partner Rodriguez has invested $10,000 in the firm, then she cannot lose more than this $10,000. Usually, limited partners do not participate in the management of the firm, nor do they enter into contracts on behalf of the firm.*

Corporations

A **corporation** is (a) a legal entity that can conduct business in its own name in the same way that an individual does and (b) that is owned by its **stockholders**. Stockholders are people who buy shares of **stock**. A share of stock represents a claim on the **assets** of the corporation. (Assets are anything of value to which the firm has legal claim.) A share of stock gives the purchaser a share of the ownership of the corporation.

What does it mean when we say that a corporation is a legal entity that can conduct business in its own name? It means that, for purposes of the law, a corporation is a living, breathing entity (like an individual), even though in reality a corporation is not a living thing. Let's say that 1,000 people want to form a corporation and call it XYZ Corporation. The law treats XYZ Corporation as if it were a person. What this means in practice can be seen through an example. Suppose XYZ Corporation has a debt of $3 million. It has only $1 million with which to pay the debt. Legally, can the remainder of the debt ($2 million) be obtained from the owners (stockholders) of the corporation? The answer is no. It is the corporation which owes the money, not the owners of the corporation. The owners of

the corporation have *limited liability*. For your information, Exhibit 5-1 lists the top 10 U.S. corporations in terms of revenues.

Advantages of Corporations. The advantages of corporations include the following.

1. **The owners of the corporation, the stockholders, are not personally liable for the debts of the corporation; they have limited liability.** To say that the stockholders have **limited liability** means that they cannot be sued for the corporation's failure to pay its

MINI GLOSSARY

Partnership A business that is owned by two or more co-owners called partners, who share any profits the business earns and are legally responsible for any debts incurred by the firm.
Limited Partnership A partnership made up of general partners and limited partners. The general partners manage the business and have unlimited liability; the limited partners do not manage the business and have limited liability.
General Partner In a limited partnership, a partner who is responsible for the management of the firm and who has unlimited liability.
Limited Partner In a limited partnership, a partner who cannot participate in the management of the firm and who has limited liability.
Corporation A legal entity that can conduct business in its own name in the same way that an individual does. Ownership of the corporation resides with the stockholders.
Stockholder A person who owns shares of stock in a corporation. The stockholders of a corporation are the owners of the corporation.
Stock A claim on the assets of a corporation that gives the purchaser a share of the ownership of the corporation.
Asset Anything of value to which the firm has legal claim.
Limited Liability A condition in which an owner of a business firm can only lose the amount invested (in the firm) by him or her. Stockholders of a corporation have limited liability.

Rank	Company	Revenues (dollars)
1	General Motors	$132,774,000,000
2	Exxon	103,547,000,000
3	Ford Motor	100,785,000,000
4	IBM	65,096,000,000
5	General Electric	62,202,000,000
6	Mobil	57,389,000,000
7	Philip Morris	50,157,000,000
8	E.I. Du Pont deNemours	37,643,000,000
9	Chevron	37,464,000,000
10	Texaco	37,130,000,000

◀ **EXHIBIT 5-1. The Top 10.** The exhibit shows the top 10 U.S. firms in terms of revenues for 1992.

SOURCE: "The *Fortune 500* Largest Industrial Corporations," *Fortune,* April 19, 1993, p. 184–85. FORTUNE 500, ©1993 Time Inc. All rights reserved.

debts. They are not personally responsible for these debts. For example, if Turner is a stockholder in Corporation X, and Corporation X cannot pay off its creditors, Turner does not have to sell her personal assets (her house, car, and so on) to pay the debts of the corporation. She can only lose her investment and nothing more. For example, if she bought 50 shares of stock in the corporation at a price of $10 each, her investment is $500. She may never see this $500 again, but she will lose no more than this.

2. **Corporations continue to exist even if one or more owners of the corporation sell their shares or die.** This is because the corporation itself is a legal entity. Its existence does not depend on the existence of its owners.

3. **Corporations are usually able to raise large sums of money by selling stock.** Because of limited liability, people are more willing to invest in a corporation than in other business forms. The price of a share of stock may be small, so many more people can afford an investment. Furthermore, they can invest as much or as little as they want. For example, a person may buy either 10 or 1,000 shares of stock in a corporation. In addition, because corporations can sell bonds and issue stock, they have ways of raising money that do not exist for propri-

etorships or partnerships. We look at bonds and stocks in more detail later in the chapter.

Disadvantages of Corporations. The disadvantages of corporations include the following.

1. **Corporations are subject to double taxation.** To illustrate, suppose Corporation XYZ earns $3 million profit this year. This amount is subject to the corporate income tax. If the corporate income tax rate is 25 percent, then $750,000 is paid in taxes ($3,000,000 × .25 = $750,000), and $2.25 million remains for **dividends** and other uses ($3,000,000 − $750,000 = $2,250,000 or $2.25 million). Dividends are shares of the corporation's profits distributed to stockholders.

Suppose that half of the $2.25 million is distributed to stockholders as dividends. This is considered income for the stockholders and is taxed at personal income tax rates. In short, the $3 million profit was subject to both the corporate income tax and the personal income tax— two taxes, or *double taxation*. Contrast this situation with the profit earned by a proprietorship. A proprietorship that earns $3 million in profit is only subject to one tax, the personal income tax.

Type of business firm	Examples	Advantages	Disadvantages
Sole Proprietorship	1. Local barbershop 2. Many restaurants 3. Family farm 4. Carpet-cleaning service	1. Easy to form and to dissolve. 2. All decision-making power resides with the sole proprietor. 3. Profit is taxed only once.	1. Proprietor faces unlimited liability. 2. Limited ability to raise funds for business expansion. 3. Usually ends with retirement or death of proprietor.
Partnership	1. Some medical offices 2. Some law offices 3. Some advertising agencies	1. Benefits of specialization can be realized. 2. Profit is taxed only once.	1. Partners face unlimited liability (one partner can incur a debt and all partners are legally responsible for payment of the debt). 2. Decision making can be complex and frustrating.
Corporation	1. IBM 2. AT&T 3. General Motors	1. Owners (stockholders) have limited liability. 2. Corporation continues if owners sell their shares of stock or die. 3. Usually able to raise large sums of money.	1. Double taxation. 2. Corporations are complicated to set up.

▲ **EXHIBIT 5-2. Advantages and Disadvantages of Different Types of Business Firms**.

2. Corporations are complicated to set up. Corporations are more difficult to organize than sole proprietorships and partnerships. We discuss this in the next section.

For your information, Exhibit 5-2 summarizes the advantages and disadvantages of corporations and compares them with the advantages and disadvantages of proprietorships and partnerships.

How to Form a Corporation

Forming a corporation is a fairly complicated procedure. Here are a few key points related to the formation of a corporation.

1. Promoters and the prospectus—Promoters are those persons that take the first steps to form the corporation. One of their tasks is to issue a *prospectus*, which is a document that contains information and facts about the new corporation, especially those that relate to its financial operations. A promoter often gives the prospectus to those persons he or she believes would be interested in purchasing stock in the corporation.

2. Articles of incorporation—A document called the *articles of incorporation* gives basic information about the future corporation, such as its name, the purpose for which it is being organized, and so on. This document must be filled out and submitted to the appropriate state officials in the state in which the corporation will be registered. A filing fee must also be paid. The persons who complete these tasks are called *incorporators*.

MINI GLOSSARY

Dividend A share of the profits of a corporation distributed to stockholders.

3. **Corporate charter**—If the articles of incorporation are approved by state officials, the state grants the new corporation a *corporate charter*. This entitles the corporation to conduct business.

4. **Organizational meeting**—Once the corporate charter has been obtained, the first organizational meeting of the corporation takes place. At this meeting, the board of directors of the corporation is chosen, corporate bylaws are passed, and so on.

The Corporate Structure

As a group, the stockholders are the most important persons in a corporation. They are its owners. They elect the members of the board of directors. Voting for the board of directors is usually an annual event, with each stockholder having the right to cast as many votes as he or she has shares of stock. For example, a person with one share of stock has one vote, whereas a person with 10,000 shares of stock has 10,000 votes.

The board of directors is an important decision-making body in the corporation. It determines corporate policies and goals. For example, it decides what products the corporation will produce and sell, what percentage of the profits of the firm will go to stockholders (as stock dividends), and what percentage will go for modernization and expansion. Also, the board of directors chooses the corporation's top officers. These persons include the president, one or more vice presidents, the secretary, and the treasurer. The corporation's top officers carry out the day-to-day operations of the corporation. In order to do this, they often appoint other vice presidents and department heads. Department heads supervise all other employees in their departments. Exhibit 5-3 shows this structure.

Financing Corporate Activity

Corporations have options for raising money that do not exist for proprietorships and partnerships. All firms, whether proprietorships, partnerships, or corporations, can raise money by borrowing from banks and other lending institutions. Corporations, however, have two other avenues. They can *sell bonds* (sometimes referred to as *issuing debt*), and they can *issue* (or *sell*) *additional shares of stock*.

Bonds and Stocks. Think of a **bond** as a piece of paper on which is written a promise to pay—simply an IOU. For example, when General Motors Corporation issues a bond, it is promising to pay a certain amount of money at a certain time.

Here is the process at work:

1. Quentin buys a bond issued by General Motors in 1990. We'll say he paid $10,000 for it. The $10,000 is now in the possession of General Motors (it might use the money to help build a new plant) and the bond (a piece of paper) is in the possession of Quentin.

2. The bond that Quentin has in his hands has a few things written on it. For one thing, it has a dollar figure written on it. This dollar figure is called the **face value** (or **par value**) of the bond. We'll say it is $10,000. There is also a percentage written on the bond. This percentage is called the **coupon rate** of the bond. For Quentin's bond, we'll say the coupon rate is 10

MINI GLOSSARY

Board of Directors An important decision-making body in a corporation. It decides corporate policies and goals, among other things.

Bylaws Internal rules of the corporation.

Bond A statement of debt issued by a corporation. The corporation promises to pay a certain sum of money at maturity and also to pay periodic fixed sums until that date.

Face Value (Par Value) Dollar amount specified on a bond.

Coupon Rate A percentage of the face value of a bond that is paid out regularly (usually quarterly or annually) to the holder of the bond.

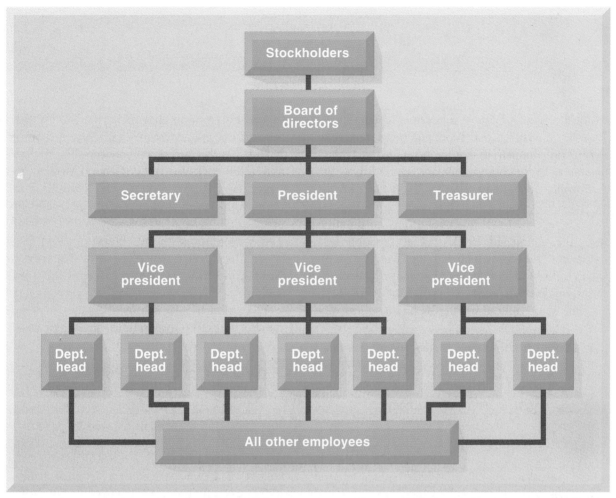

▲ **EXHIBIT 5-3. Structure of a Typical Corporation.** Stockholders occupy the top position in a corporation. They elect the board of directors, which, in turn, chooses the corporation's top officers (the president and others). Vice presidents answer to the president, department heads answer to vice presidents, and all other employees either directly or indirectly answer to department heads.

percent. Finally, there is a *maturity date* written on the bond. This is the date the bond *matures*, or is paid off by General Motors. We'll say this date is 1999.

3. The bond is a legal promise that General Motors has made to Quentin. The promise has two parts. First, General Motors has promised to pay the face value of the bond at the maturity date. Second, it has promised to pay the coupon rate, times the face value of the bond, each year until the maturity date. The coupon rate is 10 percent and the face value of the

bond is $10,000; 10 percent of $10,000 is $1,000 ($10,000 × 0.10 = $1,000), so Quentin receives $1,000 in 1991 and in each year through 1999. (This $1,000 is called the annual coupon payment.) In 1999, Quentin receives not only $1,000 but also the face value of the bond, $10,000, since 1999 is the maturity date of the bond. He receives $11,000 ($1,000 + $10,000 = $11,000) in 1999.

Now, instead of selling bonds, General Motors could have issued stock to raise money. Remember that a share is a claim on the assets

ECONOMIC FOCUS

Each year, *Fortune* magazine, which reports on business and economic news, ranks the top 500 (industrial) corporations in the United States. These corporations are referred to as the *Fortune 500*. To be number 1 on the *Fortune 500* list, a corporation has to have the largest sales revenue (total revenue) of any corporation in the nation. In 1992, that corporation was General Motors, which has its headquarters in Detroit, Michigan. Its total revenue was $132 billion; in other words, General Motors, in 1992, sold $132 billion worth of products (mostly cars).

The corporation that earns the largest total revenue doesn't necessarily earn the largest profit. Profit is the difference between total revenue and total cost. In 1992, General Motors, the largest corporation in the United States in terms of its total revenue, actually did not earn any profit at all. Instead, it took a loss of $23 billion. The corporation with the biggest profit in 1992 was Phillip Morris, which has its headquarters in New York City. It earned a profit of $4.93 billion.

In Exhibit S-5-1a, we list the states in which the *Fortune 500* corporations have their head-

▼ **EXHIBIT S-5-1a. Cities, States, and the *Fortune 500*.**

STATE	NUMBER OF FORTUNE 500 CORPORATIONS	LARGEST FORTUNE 500 CORPORATION	INDUSTRY OF THE LARGEST FORTUNE 500 CORPORATION
New York	53	IBM	Computers, Office Equipment
Illinois	47	Amoco	Petroleum Refining
California	44	Chevron	Petroleum Refining
Ohio	36	Procter & Gamble	Soaps, Cosmetics
Texas	36	Exxon	Petroleum Refining
Pennsylvania	29	USX	Petroleum Refining
Connecticut	27	General Electric	Electronics, Electrical Equipment
New Jersey	25	Johnson & Johnson	Pharmaceuticals
Michigan	21	General Motors	Motor Vehicles and Parts
Minnesota	18	Minnesota Mining and Manufacturing	Scientific, Photographic, and Control Equipment
Massachusetts	15	Digital Equipment	Computers, Office Equipment
Missouri	15	McDonnell Douglas	Aerospace
Virginia	13	Mobil	Petroleum Refining
Wisconsin	13	Johnson Controls	Scientific, Photographic, and Control Equipment
Indiana	12	Eli Lilly	Pharmaceuticals
Georgia	11	Coca-Cola	Beverages
North Carolina	8	Collins & Aikman Group	Textiles
Florida	7	W. R. Grace	Chemicals
Colorado	6	Total Petroleum	Petroleum Refining
Alabama	5	Intergraph	Computers, Office Equipment

SOURCE: *Fortune* magazine, April 19, 1993. FORTUNE 500, © 1993 Time Inc. All rights reserved.

CITIES, STATES, AND THE FORTUNE 500 CORPORATIONS

quarters. We also specify the single largest *Fortune 500* corporation in each state, and what industry it is in. In economics, the words *industry* and *market* often mean the same thing. For example, to say that a company like IBM is in the computer and office equipment industry is the same as saying that it is in the computer and office equipment market. Specifically, it is a supplier or seller in that market.

The state with more *Fortune 500* corporations than any other state is New York, with a total of 53. Next is Illinois with 47, followed by California with 44, and Ohio and Texas with 36 each. In

fact, 216 of the *Fortune 500* corporations are located in these five states.

In Exhibit S-5-1*b*, we list the top 10 cities for *Fortune 500* corporations in different years. For example, in 1992, 35 *Fortune 500* corporations were located in New York City, 21 were located in Chicago, and 13 were located in Houston. It is interesting to note that although New York is still the top city in the nation for *Fortune 500* corporations, the number of corporations that have made New York their home has been dropping over the years. For example, in 1967, 139 *Fortune 500* corporations had their headquarters

STATE	NUMBER OF FORTUNE 500 CORPORATIONS	LARGEST FORTUNE 500 CORPORATION	INDUSTRY OF THE LARGEST FORTUNE 500 CORPORATION
Washington	5	Boeing	Aerospace
Arkansas	4	Tyson Foods	Food
Iowa	4	Maytag	Electronics, Electrical Equipment
Louisiana	4	McDermott	Metal Products
Maryland	4	Martin Marietta	Aerospace
Nebraska	4	Conagra	Food
Oklahoma	4	Phillips Petroleum	Petroleum Refining
Oregon	4	Wilamette Industries	Forest and Paper Products
Rhode Island	4	Textron	Aerospace
South Carolina	4	Springs Industries	Textiles
District of Columbia	3	Washington Post	Publishing, Printing
Arizona	2	Phelps Dodge	Metals
Delaware	2	E. I. Du Pont deNemours	Chemicals
Kansas	2	Doskocil	Food
Kentucky	2	Ashland Oil	Petroleum Refining
New Hampshire	2	Tyco Laboratories	Metal Products
Idaho	1	Boise Cascade	Forest and Paper Products
South Dakota	1	Gateway 2000	Computers, Office Equipment
Tennessee	1	Arcadian	Chemicals
Utah	1	Thiokol	Aerospace
West Virginia	1	Weirton Steel	Metals

The following states have no *Fortune 500* corporation headquarters in their states: Alaska, Hawaii, Maine, Mississippi, Montana, Nevada, New Mexico, North Dakota, Vermont, and Wyoming.

U.S. ECONOMIC FOCUS (continued)

CITY	1992	1987	1982	1967
New York	35	51	66	139
Chicago	21	24	27	39
Houston	13	12	11	2
Cleveland	12	12	11	18
Dallas	12	11	12	5
St. Louis	10	10	9	10
Stamford, Conn.	9	10	12	2
Minneapolis	8	10	7	8
Pittsburgh	8	13	16	18
Los Angeles	7	9	11	4

▲ **EXHIBIT S-5-1b. Top Ten Cities and the *Fortune 500*.**

in New York, but in 1982 the number had dropped to 66. Five years later, in 1987, the number was down to 51. And in the five years from 1987 to 1992, the number dropped to 35. The same downward trend is evident in Chicago and Pittsburgh. Los Angeles is different: in 1992 the city had more *Fortune 500* corporations than it did in 1967, but the number of *Fortune 500* corporations in Los Angeles steadily declined from 1982, when there were 11, to 1987, when there were nine, to 1992, when there were seven.

Two cities in which the trend has gone the other way are Houston and Dallas. For example, in 1967 in Dallas, five *Fortune 500* corporations were located there, but in 1992 there were 12. In Houston in 1967, there were two *Fortune 500* corporations, but by 1992 there were 13.

The move away from cities such as New York, Chicago, and Pittsburgh to cities such as Dallas and Houston reflects what has been happening in the U.S. economy as a whole. While economic activity in the nation was once heavily concentrated in places in the northeastern states (such as New York and Pennsylvania) and the northern midwestern states (such as Illinois, Ohio, and Michigan), today we are seeing less concentration and greater evenness in economic activity across the nation.

1. In 1992, Exxon was the second-largest *Fortune 500* corporation in the United States; it earned the second-largest total revenue, approximately $103 billion. It was also the second-most profitable corporation in the United States, earning $4.77 billion in profit. Does it always follow that the more total revenue a firm earns, the more profit it earns? Explain your answer.

2. Identify the state in which each of the following corporations is located: General Electric, Chevron, General Motors, Coca-Cola, Boeing, and Ashland Oil.

of the corporation that gives the purchaser a share of the ownership of the corporation. Whereas the buyer of a corporate bond is *lending* funds to the corporation, the buyer of a share of stock is acquiring an *ownership right* in the corporation. Simply put, if you buy a bond from a corporation, you are a lender, not an owner. If you buy shares of stock in a corporation, you are an owner, not a lender.

QUESTION: *Does the stockholder receive yearly payments from the corporation as Quentin, who purchased a bond, did?*

ANSWER: *The corporation is under no legal obligation to pay stockholders. Bond purchasers, remember, have lent money to the corporation. The corporation must repay these loans, along with extra payments (such as the $1,000 Quentin received each year), to the bond purchasers for the use of their money. But stockholders have not lent funds to the corporation. Instead, they have bought a part of the corporation. If the corporation does well, the value of their stock will rise, and they will be able to sell it at a price higher than the price they paid for it. On the other hand, if the corporation does poorly, the value of their stock will fall, and they will most likely have to sell it for less than the purchase price.*

Other Business Organizations: Cooperatives and Franchises

Sole proprietorships, partnerships, and corporations aren't the only types of business organization—they are simply the most common. This section describes two other types of business organization: the *cooperative* and the *franchise*.

Cooperatives. A **cooperative**, or co-op, is a business that provides services to its members and is not run for profit. Usually, a cooperative is formed when a group of persons (the members) want to pool their resources to gain some benefit that they, as individuals, could not otherwise obtain. For example, sellers often offer reduced

prices to buyers who purchase in bulk. Individual consumers can take advantage of these reduced prices by forming a *consumer cooperative*. Consumer cooperatives buy large quantities of consumer items (food, home appliances, and so on) at reduced prices and then pass the savings on to their members through lower prices.

Franchises. Franchises are a form of business organization that has become more common in the last 25 years. A **franchise** is a contract by which a firm (usually a corporation) lets a person or group use its name and sell its goods or services. In return, the person or group must make certain payments and meet certain requirements. For example, McDonald's Corporation offers franchises. Individuals can buy the right to use McDonald's name and to sell its products (Big Macs, McChicken sandwiches, and so on), as long as they meet certain requirements. The corporation, or parent company, is called the **franchiser**. It is the entity that offers the franchise. The person or group that buys the franchise is called the **franchisee**. A few well-known franchises are McDonald's, Burger King, Wendy's, Pizza Hut, Domino's Pizza, Taco Bell, Dunkin' Donuts, and ComputerLand.

The franchise agreement works this way: (1) The franchisee pays an initial fee (the average

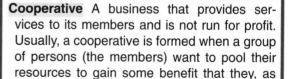

MINI GLOSSARY

Cooperative A business that provides services to its members and is not run for profit. Usually, a cooperative is formed when a group of persons (the members) want to pool their resources to gain some benefit that they, as individuals, could not otherwise obtain.

Franchise A contract by which a firm (usually a corporation) lets a person or group use its name and sell its goods in exchange for certain payments being made and certain requirements being met.

Franchiser The entity that offers a franchise.

Franchisee The person or group that buys a franchise.

◀ McDonald's is one of the most successful franchises in history. Its franchises have the advantages of McDonald's well-known name and many hours of television advertising.

initial fee for a McDonald's franchise is approximately $65,000). (2) The franchisee often pays a royalty, or percentage of the profits, to the franchiser for a period of years. (3) The franchisee usually agrees to meet certain quality standards decided on by the franchiser. (For example, all McDonald's franchises cook Big Macs for the same length of time.) In return, the franchisee receives from the franchiser: (1) the right to use the parent company name, (2) the right to sell a certain product, (3) financial assistance, (4) assistance in training employees and personnel, and (5) national advertising.

Franchises offer several advantages to franchisees. For many franchisees, the national advertising is especially important. Consider how many hours of national TV advertising McDonald's annually buys. This advertising benefits its franchisees from Maine to California. Furthermore, with a well-established company such as McDonald's or Burger King, the franchisee buys a business that has been proved successful. For example, consider the risk of starting your own restaurant compared with the risk of opening a McDonald's or a Burger King. The U.S. Department of Commerce reports

that the failure rate is about 12 times higher for independently owned businesses than for franchises.

Of course, franchise business arrangements aren't always smooth sailing. Sometimes, the franchiser fails to provide the financial and training support the franchisee expects, and occasionally the franchisee doesn't provide the quality of service and product that the franchiser expects.

Are franchises the wave of the future? We don't know for sure. What we do know is that, in the last 25 years, they have proved to be a very successful form of business organization.

The Small Business Administration

A small business firm usually has a much smaller operation (fewer employees, less revenue) than a large corporation. The fact is, some people think that the small business firm is at a disadvantage compared with a large corporation. For example, the small business firm might not have the money or the management expertise that a large

CONSUMER ECONOMIC DECISIONS

How to Buy and Sell Stocks and Bonds

The day may come when you want to buy stocks or bonds. Where would you go to do this? Most people go to a stocks and bonds brokerage firm. Some of the bigger full-service brokerage firms include Merrill Lynch, Dean Witter Reynolds, Paine Webber, and Prudential Bache. A few of the major discount brokerage firms include Charles Schwab, Quick and Reilly, Fidelity Brokerage, and Kennedy, Cabot & Company. The telephone numbers for these companies and many more are listed in the yellow pages of many telephone books.

Let's listen in as a fictional character, Denise Stewart, telephones a stocks and bonds brokerage firm.

Receptionist at the brokerage firm: Hello, this is Adams and Baker. Can I help you?

Denise: Yes, I want to talk to someone about possibly opening an account with your firm and purchasing some stocks and bonds.

Receptionist: Just one moment and I will connect you to one of our account executives. [An account executive is sometimes referred to as a stockbroker.]

Account executive: Hello, this is Elizabeth Sullivan. May I help you?

Denise: Hi, my name is Denise Stewart. I want some information on how I would go about buying and selling stocks and bonds.

Elizabeth: Do you currently have an account with another brokerage firm?

Denise: No. To tell you the truth, I don't know how someone goes about setting up an account.

Elizabeth: Well, it is really very simple. If you were to open up an account with Adams and Baker, I would simply need to get your Social Security number, phone number, and home address. Sometimes we require that you place into the account the dollar amount of the stock or bond purchase you wish to make before we do the buying on your behalf.

Denise: Okay. Well, suppose I wanted to buy 100 shares of Exxon stock. How do I go about buying it?

Elizabeth: Well, I see from my computer that Exxon is currently selling for $60 a share. This comes to $6,000 plus the brokerage firm's commission.

Denise: How much is the commission?

Elizabeth: On 100 shares, it is 2 percent of the total dollar amount. So it is 2 percent of $6,000, or $120. [Commission rates vary among brokerage firms. For example, they are lower at discount brokers than full-service brokers. Of course, there are some services a full-service broker provides that a discount broker does not. Commission rates also vary with the number of shares purchased. For example, usually the rate is higher when fewer shares of stock are purchased.]

Denise: So, if I want to make this purchase, I need to send a check to your firm for $6,120. Is that right?

Elizabeth: Yes, that's right.

Denise: Will you send me the shares of stock after you purchase them for me?

Elizabeth: We could do that, but usually we simply keep them in our office for you. Most people don't like to take physical possession of the stock. It is up to you, though.

Making CONSUMER ECONOMIC DECISIONS (continued)

Denise: I see. Well, all right, I would like to make the purchase. I'll bring the check down to your office today.

Elizabeth: I'll be looking forward to meeting you when you come by.

Denise: Oh, by the way, when I want to sell the stock, how do I do this?

Elizabeth: Just give me a telephone call and I'll have it done. In the meantime, you can check the newspaper daily to see at what price your stock is selling.

Denise: Yes, I'll do that.

Elizabeth: By the way, Denise, our research staff here at Adams and Baker usually has some good tips for stocks to buy. Should I give you a call when I learn of them? [A full-service brokerage usually has a research staff; a discount brokerage does not.]

Denise: Please do. Goodbye.

Elizabeth: Goodbye.

Here are some things to keep in mind if you call an account executive and ask about opening an account.

1. *Deal with someone with whom you feel comfortable.* Account executives come with different personalities, as do doctors, lawyers, and plumbers. Choose to deal with an account executive to whom you can easily speak. Many people choose their account executives through word of mouth. For example, a friend may say that his account executive is considerate, knowledgeable, and easy to be around, and so you may choose to deal with the same person.

2. *Ask questions.* It is natural sometimes not to ask questions because you feel the questions are somehow too basic or dumb. There are no "too basic" or "dumb" questions. Ask your account executive any question you want to ask about stocks, bonds, and your account. If, by chance, your account executive makes you feel dumb for asking the question, or makes you feel you are wasting his or her time, then you know what you have to do—get another account executive.

3. *Don't feel that you have to buy or sell stock every day, week, or month.* When people first open an account at a stocks and bonds brokerage firm, they sometimes are so excited that they want to trade (buy or sell stock) on a daily, weekly, or monthly basis. A wise investor does not trade because it is exciting. He or she trades when it makes economic sense to trade.

---

1. What is an account executive?
2. A person buys 100 shares of stock priced at $49 a share. The commission rate is 1 percent. How much does the person pay in commission?
3. Do people who buy shares of stock usually take physical possession of them?
4. What are two differences between a full-service brokerage firm and a discount brokerage firm?

corporation has. This could put the small business firm at a competitive disadvantage.

Congress set out to protect small businesses in 1953 by passing the Small Business Act. This act set up the Small Business Administration (SBA). The SBA's job is to assist small businesses. For example, the SBA often directly lends money to people who want to start a new small business or expand an old one. Similarly, it guarantees loans that a small business might obtain from a bank. (When the SBA guarantees a loan, it makes it easier for the owner of a small business to obtain a loan from a bank.) It also provides loans to small businesses that have been damaged by natural di-

sasters, such as hurricanes or earthquakes. Furthermore, the SBA has set up programs to promote economic opportunities for minority groups. For example, it makes special loans to handicapped individuals, and it makes sure that women have equal access to all its services.

If you are thinking of starting your own small business, it would be in your best interest to contact the Small Business Administration and find out what assistance—financial and otherwise—is available to you. You will usually find the SBA listed in the telephone book under "United States Government."

LEARNING CHECK

1. What does it mean to say that corporations face double taxation?
2. What is a limited partnership?
3. Which type of business organization is the most numerous in the United States?
4. Which type of business organization accounts for the largest share of total business revenues?
5. Why might a person want a franchise instead of an independently owned business of his or her own?
6. Do you think the initial fee for all franchises (McDonald's, Burger King, Wendy's, ComputerLand, and so on) is the same? Why or why not? (Hint: Think in terms of supply and demand.)
7. If the face value of a bond is $10,000, and the coupon rate is 5 percent, what is the annual (yearly) payment to the bondholder?

SECTION 2 COSTS

Suppose you are in the business of producing cars. Do you know offhand how many cars you would produce? Would it be 1,000, or 2,000, or 100,000? How would you go about determining the "right" quantity to produce? You may have a feeling that you shouldn't produce "too few" or "too many," but how would you know what "too few" and "too many" were? To begin to answer these questions, we need to look more closely at costs and revenues. We begin with costs.

As you read, keep these key questions in mind:

■ What are fixed costs? variable costs?
■ What do total costs equal?
■ How do we compute average fixed cost? average variable cost? average total cost? marginal cost?

Fixed and Variable Costs

All businesses have costs, but not all costs are the same. For example, suppose Barbara Harris

CASE STUDY

U.S. Business in the Global Economy

H ere are some statistics that show how U.S. firms and workers compare to foreign firms and workers in other countries.[a]

1. In the United States, it takes an average of 25.1 hours to make a car; in Japan, it takes an average of 16.8 hours.
2. In the United States, an average worker produces $39 worth of product value in an hour. In Canada, an average worker produces $37 worth of value per hour; in France, $33; in Germany, $32; and in Japan, $28.30.
3. The average workweek is 38.9 hours in the United States, 46.8 hours in Japan, 39.9 hours in Germany, 38 hours in Canada, and 34.9 hours in New Zealand.
4. In the United States, the average salary of the president of a corporation is $543,000. In Canada, it is $360,350; in Japan, it is $352,500.
5. Most U.S. business firms are involved in providing services, not in manufacturing products. For example, only 20 percent of all U.S. businesses are involved in manufacturing.
6. Of every 1,000 persons working in the United States, 746 persons have a high-school diploma or more. In Japan, 878 persons out of every 1,000 persons working have a high-school diploma or more.

7. In the United States, only 2.9 percent of the work force are farmers. In Turkey, farmers make up 50 percent of the work force; in Germany, 3.7 percent; in Italy, 9.3 percent. The United States has witnessed a 76 percent decline in the number of farmers over the past 50 years.
8. In the United States, 68.1 percent of all women of working age are employed outside the home. In Germany, it is 54.8 percent; in Japan, 59.3 percent; and in Spain, 39.9 percent.
9. In the United States, the average worker is absent from work 7.1 days a year; in Germany, 19.2 days; in Italy, 17.9 days; and in Japan, 4.3 days.

---

1. Overall, do U.S. workers produce more or less product value in an hour than Japanese workers? Explain your answer.
2. What percentage of U.S. businesses are involved in producing services?

---

a. Data from *Where We Stand* By Michael Wolff and the World Research Team. Copyright © 1992 By Michael Wolff and Company Inc. Used by permission of Bantam Books a division of Bantam Doubleday Dell Publishing Group, Inc.

owns a business that produces a certain kind of toy. In her business, Harris needs a plant, or factory, in which the toy can be produced. She also needs insurance, employees, machines, certain materials for producing the toy (such as plastic, rubber, and so on), paper, pens, typewriters, electricity, and much more. Consider one of the many things Harris needs—a plant. Currently, she rents a plant from Terry Adams. The rental contract specifies that Harris agrees to pay Adams $2,000 rent each month for 12 months.

But what if Harris doesn't want to rent the plant after she has paid only 3 months' rent? Must she pay rent for the remaining 9 months? Given the contract that Harris and Adams have entered into, the answer is yes. In other words, no matter whether Harris produces 1 toy, 1,000 toys, 10,000 toys (or even zero toys) in the plant each month, still she has the legal obligation to pay rent of $2,000 a month for 12 months.

Costs, or expenses, that are the same no matter how many units of a good are produced are called **fixed costs**. The $2,000 rent is a fixed cost for Harris for a period of 12 months.

Now suppose Harris employs 10 workers and pays each $50 a day. Her labor cost per day is $500 ($50 per worker × 10 workers = $500). One day, she gets a special order for many hundreds of toys. In order to meet the order, she hires 5 additional workers at $50 per day. As a result, her labor cost rises by $250 (5 × $50 = $250) to a total of $750 ($500 + $250 = $750). Notice that the *increase* in labor cost goes along with an *increase* in the number of toys being produced. Costs, or expenses, that vary, or change, with the number of units of a good produced are called **variable costs**.

If we add fixed costs to variable costs, we have **total costs**.

Total costs = Fixed costs + Variable costs[1]

Suppose we want to compute total costs for a month. If fixed costs are $2,000 for the month and

variable costs are $750 for the month, then total costs are $2,750 for the month ($2,000 + $750 = $2,750).

Average Costs

Suppose a teacher gives a test to five students. The grades are as follows: 80, 90, 100, 60, and 75. The total number of points—the sum of the individual grades—is 405. To find the average grade, we divide the total, 405, by the number of students, 5. This gives us 81. The average grade on the test is 81.

Suppose we wanted to find the average of each of the three costs just described: fixed cost, variable cost, and total cost. How would we go about it? To find **average fixed cost** (AFC), we would simply divide fixed costs by the number of units produced (or quantity of output).

$$\text{Average fixed cost (AFC)} = \frac{FC}{Q}$$

Here, FC = fixed costs and Q = quantity of output. For example, suppose Harris produces 1,000 toys and her fixed cost is $2,000. The average fixed cost is $2 ($2,000 ÷ 1,000 = $2).

Similarly, we would find **average variable cost** (AVC) by dividing variable costs by quantity of output.

$$\text{Average variable cost (AVC)} = \frac{VC}{Q}$$

MINI GLOSSARY

Fixed Cost Cost, or expense, that is the same no matter how many units of a good are produced.

Variable Cost Cost, or expense, that changes with the number of units of a good produced.

Total Cost The sum of fixed costs plus variable costs.

Average Fixed Cost Fixed cost divided by quantity of output.

Average Variable Cost Variable cost divided by quantity of output.

---

1. Total cost is defined differently here than it was in Chapter 2. Do not be confused. It can be defined two ways.

Type of cost	Description	Example
Fixed Cost (FC)	Cost, or expense, that does not change as output changes	A firm's monthly rent is a fixed cost.
Variable Cost (VC)	Cost, or expense, that changes as output changes	The amount a firm spends on employee's wages is usually a variable cost.
Total Cost (TC)	Fixed costs plus variable costs (FC + VC)	If fixed costs equal $2,000, and variable costs equal $4,000, then total cost equals $6,000.
Average Fixed Cost (AFC)	Fixed costs divided by quantity of output $\left(\dfrac{FC}{Q}\right)$	If fixed costs equal $2,000, and quantity equals 1,000 units, then average fixed cost equals $2.
Average Variable Cost (AVC)	Variable costs divided by quantity of output $\left(\dfrac{VC}{Q}\right)$	If variable costs equal $4,000, and quantity equals 1,000 units, then average variable cost equals $4.
Average Total Cost (ATC)	Total cost divided by quantity of output $\left(\dfrac{TC}{Q}\right)$	If total cost equals $6,000, and quantity equals 1,000 units, then average total cost equals $6.
Marginal Cost (MC)	Change in total cost divided by change in quantity of output $\left(\dfrac{\triangle TC}{\triangle Q}\right)$	If total cost equals $6,000, when quantity equals 1,000 units, and total cost equals $6,008, when quantity equals 1,001 units, then marginal cost equals $8.

▲ **EXHIBIT 5-4. Seven Cost Concepts**.

Here, VC = variable costs and Q = quantity of output. For example, if variable cost is $4,000 and quantity of output is 1,000 toys, then average variable cost is $4 ($4,000 ÷ 1,000 = $4).

Finally, we would find **average total cost** (ATC) by dividing total cost by quantity of output.

$$\text{Average total cost (ATC)} = \frac{TC}{Q}$$

Here, TC = total cost and Q = quantity of output. For example, if total cost is $6,000 and 1,000 toys are produced, then average total cost is $6 ($6,000 ÷ 1,000 = $6).

Marginal Cost: A Very Important Cost Concept

Suppose that Harris currently produces 1,000 toys and total cost is $6,000. Harris then decides to produce an *additional* unit of the toy; in other words, she produces one more toy. As a result, total cost rises from $6,000 to $6,008. What is the *change* in total cost that results from this *change* in output? It is $8. That is, total cost went from $6,000 to $6,008 when output went from 1,000 units to 1,001 units.

The change in total cost that results from producing an additional unit of output is called

marginal cost . In other words, *marginal cost is the additional cost of producing an additional unit of a good*. In our example, marginal cost is $8. When you think about marginal cost, focus on the word *change*. Marginal cost describes a *change* in one thing—total cost—caused by a *change* in something else—quantity of output.

In economics, the triangle symbol ($\triangle$) means "change in."

$$\triangle \text{ means "change in."}$$

So when we write:

$$\text{Marginal cost (MC)} = \frac{\triangle TC}{\triangle Q}$$

we mean "marginal cost equals the change in total cost divided by the change in quantity of output." Let's place the numbers from our example in this equation. $\triangle TC$, the change in total cost, is $8 ($6,008 − $6,000 = $8). $\triangle Q$, the change in quantity produced, is 1 (1,001 − 1,000 = 1).

$$\text{Marginal cost (MC)} = \$8 \div 1$$
$$= \$8$$

Eight dollars is the marginal cost.

Exhibit 5-4 reviews the seven cost concepts discussed in this chapter so far.

LEARNING CHECK

1. Give an example of a fixed cost.
2. Give an example of a variable cost.
3. Total costs are $3,000, and fixed costs are $1,200. What do variable costs equal?
4. Define *marginal cost*.

 **3** REVENUES AND DECIDING HOW MUCH TO PRODUCE

Now that we have examined costs, we turn to a discussion of revenues. Then we look at costs and revenues together to determine how much of a good a firm will produce.

As you read, keep these key questions in mind:

■ What is total revenue?
■ What is marginal revenue?
■ Why does a business firm compare marginal revenue (MR) with marginal cost (MC) when deciding how many units of a good to produce?

Total Revenue and Marginal Revenue

In Chapter 2, total revenue was defined as the price of a good, times the quantity sold. For exam-

ple, if the price of a book is $5 and 100 are sold, then total revenue is $500 ($5 × 100 = $500). With this in mind, consider the following: (1) Harris sells each toy for a price of $10. (2) Harris currently sells 1,000 toys. (3) This means that Harris's total revenue is $10,000 ($10 × 1,000 = $10,000). Question: If Harris sells one more toy

MINI GLOSSARY

Average Total Cost Total cost divided by quantity of output.
Marginal Cost The change in total cost that results from producing an additional unit of output.

for $10, what is the change in total revenue that results from the change in output sold?

To answer this question, we first calculate what total revenue is when Harris sells 1,001 instead of 1,000 toys. It is $10,010 ($10, the price, times 1,001, the quantity sold; $10 × 1,001 = 10,010). We conclude that total revenue changes from $10,000 to $10,010 when an additional toy is sold. In other words, there is a change in total revenue of $10 ($10,010 − $10,000 = $10).

The change in total revenue that results from selling an additional unit of output is **marginal revenue**. In other words, *marginal revenue is the additional revenue from selling an additional unit of a good*. In our example, $10 is marginal revenue. We can write it this way:

$$\text{Marginal revenue (MR)} = \frac{\triangle \text{TR}}{\triangle \text{Q}}$$

Marginal revenue equals the change in total revenue divided by the change in the quantity of output sold.

Deciding How Much to Produce

Firms compare *marginal revenue* with *marginal cost* when deciding how much output to produce and sell. The process amounts to common sense. As long as marginal revenue is greater than, or equal, to marginal cost, the firm wants to produce an additional unit of output. The firm does not want to produce an additional unit of output when marginal cost is greater than marginal revenue.

To illustrate, consider Exhibit 5-5. There are four columns. Column 1 tells us which unit of the good we are discussing. Column 2 tells us the marginal revenue for that particular unit. Column 3 tells us the marginal cost for that unit. Column 4 notes whether the firm would produce the unit of the good under consideration.

For the first unit of the good, marginal revenue is $5 and marginal cost is $2. This means that the added revenue from selling the first unit of the

▲ A tractor company produces the quantity of tractors for which marginal revenue equals marginal cost.

good is greater than the added cost of producing the first unit of the good. Obviously, under these circumstances, the firm would want to produce and sell the first unit of the good.

What about the second unit? The firm also wants to produce and sell the second unit, since again the added revenue from producing and selling this unit of the good is greater than the added cost of producing it. The same holds for the third unit of the good. For the fourth unit, marginal revenue equals marginal cost, and the firm is impartial between producing and selling the good and not producing and selling it. Customarily, economists assume that the firm produces the unit of the good for which marginal revenue equals marginal cost. Finally, for the fifth unit of the good, marginal cost is greater than marginal revenue. The firm does not want to produce and sell this unit. We

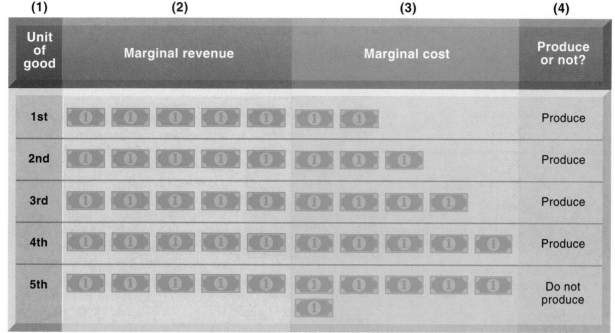

(1)	(2)	(3)	(4)
Unit of good	Marginal revenue	Marginal cost	Produce or not?
1st	① ① ① ① ① ① ①		Produce
2nd	① ① ① ① ①	① ① ①	Produce
3rd	① ① ① ① ①	① ① ① ①	Produce
4th	① ① ① ① ①	① ① ① ① ①	Produce
5th	① ① ① ① ①	① ① ① ① ① ①	Do not produce

▲ **EXHIBIT 5-5. What Quantity of Output Does the Firm Produce?** The firm continues to produce output as long as marginal revenue is greater than or equal to marginal cost. It does not produce those units of the good for which marginal cost is greater than marginal revenue. In the exhibit, the firm produces the first unit through the fourth unit of the good, but not the fifth unit.

conclude that the firm will produce only four units of the good.

QUESTION: *Wouldn't it be better for a firm simply to produce and sell whatever quantity of goods customers would buy? For example, if a firm could sell 13,000 cars, but no more, then why wouldn't it simply produce and sell 13,000 cars? In other words, why wouldn't firms produce and sell every car that someone is willing to buy?*

ANSWER: *A firm doesn't do this because it incurs costs in producing goods, and sometimes the costs of producing a particular unit of a good are greater than what the firm hopes to earn by selling the good. Suppose, in our example, that the firm could sell the 13,000th car for no more than $11,000 but that it would cost the firm $14,000 to produce the car. Should it produce and sell the car? Definitely not. Remember, a firm concerns itself not only with how many dollars*

come into the firm but also with how many dollars go out.

Profit, Marginal Revenue, and Marginal Cost

So far, we know that a firm will produce and sell an additional unit of a good if marginal revenue is greater than, or equal to, marginal cost, but that it won't produce and sell an additional unit of a good if marginal cost is greater than marginal

---

MINI GLOSSARY

Marginal Revenue The change in total revenue that results from selling an additional unit of output.

Howard Schultz

If you have ever read the book *Moby Dick*, you may recall the name of the first mate—Starbuck. That is the name of a coffee company that was started in 1971 by three young entrepreneurs. The three owners started out selling whole-bean coffee in the Pike Place Market in Seattle, Washington. By 1982, they owned five stores, a small roasting facility, and a wholesale business selling coffee to local restaurants. In 1982, the owners asked Howard Schultz, who was 29 years old and living and working in New York, to manage retail sales and marketing for the company. Schultz said yes, packed up, and moved to Seattle.

A year later, Schultz was visiting Italy. In Italy he noticed people sitting at coffee bars sipping their coffee and talking. He wondered whether Americans, too, would like to sit in relaxing coffee bars, sipping good coffee and talking with their friends. Schultz returned to the United States and tried to convince his bosses to turn Starbucks into a chain of coffee bars. They did not like the idea. Schultz then began to approach potential investors. Within a year, he had raised $1.7 million, and by April 1986, he had opened his first coffee bar. A year later, Schultz offered to buy Starbucks from his old bosses. They ended up selling him the company for about $4 million.

Schultz's success in the coffee business has been quite remarkable. Starbucks has become one of the fastest-growing businesses in North America. By April 1993, the company had 185 retail outlets and was opening one store a week. In 1992, its sales were about $93 million. Sales are projected to reach $1 billion by the end of the decade.

The road to success was not an easy one for Schultz. The new Starbucks company lost money in each of the first three years of operation. Schultz said that he "cried a lot. But we had tremendous conviction that this was the way to build a company and that the losses were going to end."[a]

It is interesting to note that Howard Schultz attributes some of his success as an entrepreneur to a book called *Jacob's Journey*, by Noah benShea. Here is a quote from that work: "Strength is not the absence of weakness but how we wrestle with our weakness."

---

1. What was the original idea that eventually led to Schultz's success?
2. What do you think it means to say, "Strength is not the absence of weakness but how we wrestle with our weakness?"

---

a. First appeared in SUCCESS April 1993. Written by Ingrid Abramovitch. Reprinted with permission of SUCCESS Magazine. Copyright © 1993 by Hal Holdings Corporation.

---

revenue. This has everything to do with the objective of business firms, which is to maximize profit. To illustrate, as stated in Chapter 2, profit exists when total revenue is greater than total cost. For example, if total revenue is $400,000, and total cost is $320,000, then profit is $80,000 ($400,000 − $320,000 = $80,000).

The firm wants profit to be as large as possible; it wants to maximize profit. One way to do this is to make sure it produces and sells an additional unit of a good as long as doing so adds more to total revenue than to total cost. For example, again suppose that for a business firm total revenue is $400,000, total cost is $320,000, and profit is

$80,000. Now suppose it produces and sells an additional unit of a good. The additional revenue from selling this unit of the good—the marginal revenue, in other words—is $40, and the additional cost of producing this unit of the good—the marginal cost, in other words—is $10. In turn, total revenue will rise to $400,040 ($400,000 + $40 = $400,040), and total cost will rise to $320,010 ($320,000 + $10 = $320,010). What will happen to profit? It will increase to $80,030 ($400,040 − $320,010 = $80,030). We conclude that whenever the firm produces and sells an additional unit of a good and marginal revenue is greater than marginal cost, it is adding more to its total revenue than to its total cost, and therefore it is maximizing profit.

The Law of Diminishing Returns and Whether or Not an Additional Worker Should Be Hired

A business firm has to make numerous decisions. As we have already shown, it has to decide what quantity of output to produce. For example, does it produce 100 units, 1,000 units, or 10,000 units? The answer is that it produces the quantity of output at which marginal revenue (MR) equals marginal cost (MC).

Another decision a business firm has to make is whether or not it should hire an additional worker. For example, suppose it currently has 10 workers. Should it hire one more? If so, and the number of workers increases to 11, should it hire still one more worker?

Here is how economists tell us to proceed. First, we need to know about the **law of diminishing returns**. This law states that if we add additional units of a resource (such as labor) to another resource (such as capital) that is in fixed supply, eventually the additional output produced (as a result of hiring an additional worker) will decrease. To illustrate, look at Exhibit 5-6. Reading across the first row, we see that when there are zero workers, there is no output. Now let's add a work-

THINKING LIKE AN ECONOMIST

The analysis we have just undertaken—comparing marginal revenue (MR) with marginal cost (MC) in order to determine how many units of a good a firm will produce—is typical of the type of thinking used in economics. It is thinking in terms of benefits and costs.

We can think of marginal revenue as the additional benefits of selling another unit of a good and marginal costs as the additional costs of producing another unit of a good. The firm simply compares these benefits and costs. If the additional benefits are greater than or equal to the additional costs, then the firm will produce the additional unit of the good. If the additional costs are greater than the additional benefits, then the firm won't produce an additional unit of the good.

er. We see that quantity of output (shown in the second column) is 5 units. In the third column we show the additional output produced as a result of hiring an additional worker. Since output is zero with no workers and 5 units with one worker, we conclude that hiring an additional (the first) worker increased output by 5 units.

Now let's add a second worker. When we do this, the quantity of output (shown in column 2) increases to 11 units. How much did output increase as a result of an additional (the second) worker? The answer is 6 units (11 − 5 = 6), as shown in column 3. If we add a third worker, out-

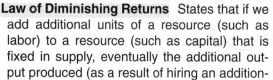

MINI GLOSSARY

Law of Diminishing Returns States that if we add additional units of a resource (such as labor) to a resource (such as capital) that is fixed in supply, eventually the additional output produced (as a result of hiring an additional worker) will decrease.

(1) Workers	(2) Quantity of output produced each day	(3) Additional output produced (each day) as a result of hiring an additional worker	
0	0 units	0 units	
1	5	5 (5 − 0 = 5)	
2	11	6 (11 − 5 = 6)	Diminishing returns set in with the addition of the fourth worker.
3	18	7 (18 − 11 = 7)	
4	23	5 (23 − 18 = 5)	
5	26	3 (26 − 23 = 3)	

▲ **EXHIBIT 5-6. Illustrating the Law of Diminishing Returns.**

put rises to 18 units, and the additional output produced as a result of the hiring of an additional (the third) worker is 7 units (18 − 11 = 7), as shown in column 3.

Before we go on, notice what has been happening in column 3: the numbers have been increasing. We started with zero, then we went up to 5, then 6, then 7. But notice what happens when we add a fourth worker. Output increases to 23 units, but the additional output produced as a result of hiring an additional (the fourth) worker is 5 units. This is less than the additional output produced as a result of adding the next-to-last (the third) worker. Here it was 7 units. What we are observing here is the law of diminishing returns at work. Remember, we said that the law of diminishing returns states that eventually the additional output produced (as a result of hiring an additional worker) will decrease. This is exactly what has happened here. We added another worker (the fourth

worker) and the additional output (shown in column 3) decreased from 7 to 5 units. In short, diminishing returns set in with the addition of the fourth worker.

Do you think the firm should have hired a fourth worker? The answer is, it depends. Specifically, it depends on the cost and benefit of hiring a fourth worker. The benefit of hiring a fourth worker is that output rises by 5 units. Suppose that the firm can sell these 5 units for $30 each, for a total of $150 ($30 × 5 = $150). What the firm has to do now is to compare this $150 with the cost of hiring a fourth worker. Suppose the firm has to pay this fourth worker $70. It would seem, then, that it is worth hiring a fourth worker. In other words, because of the fourth worker, 5 additional units of output are produced, which can be sold for $150, but the firm only has to pay the worker $70. The firm is better off by $80 by hiring the fourth worker ($150 − $70 = $80).

 LEARNING CHECK

1. Price is $15.43, and quantity sold is 499. What does total revenue equal?
2. At a quantity of 120 units, total revenue is $4,390; and at a quantity of 121 units, total revenue is $4,420. What does marginal revenue equal?
3. Why might a firm want to hire an additional worker even though diminishing returns set in with that worker?

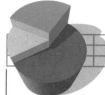

DEVELOPING ECONOMIC SKILLS

Reading the Financial Pages

If you look in almost any newspaper, you will see a few pages that report on stock and bond activity. Monday through Friday, many millions of people are buying and selling stocks and bonds. In this feature, we discuss how to make sense of the stock and bond activity reported in the newspaper. We start with stocks, and then turn to bonds.

Reading the Stock Market Page in the Newspaper

In Exhibit 5-7*a* we show the key elements of one line of the stock market page in a newspaper. Here is the meaning of the number or words in each column 1–9.

Column 1: This is the highest price per share paid for this stock in the last 52-week (one-year) period. The price was $65.25. (The ¼ in the number 65¼ refers to ¼ of a dollar. In fact, all fractions in Exhibit 5-7*a* are fractions of a dollar.)

Column 2: This is the lowest price per share paid for this stock in the last 52-week (one year) period. The price was $22.00.

Column 3: This is the abbreviation of the name of the company that issues the stock. The company here is Apple Computer.

Column 4: This is the last annual dividend per share of stock. When companies earn profits, they may issue a share of the profits to the stockholders. This is called a dividend. The last annual dividend per share of Apple Computer stock was 48 cents. This means if a person owns, say, 1,000 shares of Apple Computer stock, she would receive $480 as a dividend payment (1,000 shares × $0.48 = $480).

Column 5: This is the number of shares traded (in hundreds) on a particular day. The data in this exhibit are for November 12, 1993. On this day, 1,282,700 shares of Apple Computer stock were traded (bought and sold).

Column 6: This is the highest dollar price per share of stock that was paid on November 12, 1993. Here it was $32.

Column 7: This is the lowest dollar price per share of stock that was paid on November 12, 1993. Here it was $30.50.

Column 8: This was the closing price per share of stock on November 12, 1993. In short, when trading (buying and selling) of Apple Computer stock ended on November 12, 1993, the price per share was $31.75.

Column 9: This compares the closing price given in column 8 with the closing price of the day before (November 11). A plus sign (+) indicates the closing price is higher than the previous day's; a minus sign (−) means the closing price is lower than the previous day's. Here we have +⅜. This means the closing price on November 12 was 37.5 cents higher (⅜ of $1.00 is 37.5 cents) than it was on November 11.

◄ **EXHIBIT 5-7*a*.** Reading the Stock Market Page.

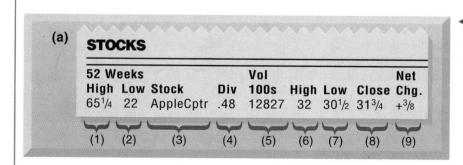

DEVELOPING ECONOMIC SKILLS (continued)

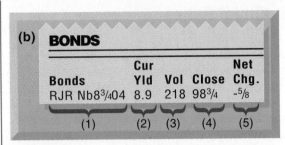

(b) BONDS

Bonds	Cur Yld	Vol	Close	Net Chg.
RJR Nb8¾04	8.9	218	98¾	-⅝
(1)	(2)	(3)	(4)	(5)

▲ **EXHIBIT 5-7b. Reading the Bond Market Page.**

Reading the Bond Market Page in the Newspaper

In Exhibit 5-7b we show the key elements of one line of the bond market page in a newspaper. Here is the meaning of the number or words in each column 1–5.

Column 1: The letters here (RJR Nb) are an abbreviation of the name of the company that issues the bond. The company here is RJR Nabisco. Next, you see the number 8¾. This is the coupon rate of the bond. (Most corporate bonds have a $1,000 face value.) Finally, there is the number 04. This indicates when the bond matures: the year 2004. If the number had been 98, this means the bond would mature in 1998. It is understood that the first two digits of the number in this spot are always 19 or 20.

Column 2: This is the current yield, which is 8.9 percent. This means that if the bond is purchased today at the closing price (see column 4), it will provide a yield of 8.9 percent. Let's be clear: the yield is different than the coupon rate. We discussed the coupon rate earlier in this chapter. It is the percentage written on the bond itself. The coupon rate equals the annual coupon payment divided by the face value of the bond. For example, if the annual coupon payment is $100 and the face value of the bond is $1,000, the coupon rate is 10 percent ($100 ÷ $1,000 = 0.10, and 0.10 × 100 = 10 percent). The yield equals the annual coupon payment divided by the price paid for the bond. For example, let's say the annual coupon

payment is $100, as we did before. And again we'll say the face value of the bond is $1,000. But suppose a person didn't pay $1,000 for this bond; instead, a person paid $900. In this case, the yield would be 11.1 percent ($100 ÷ $900 = 0.11, and 0.11 × 100 = 11 percent).

Column 3: This is the dollar volume for this bond for this particular day. The data here are for December 27, 1993. This means $218,000 worth of this particular bond (issued by RJR Nabisco) were traded on this day. (Always add three zeros and a dollar sign to the number listed in the newspaper.)

Column 4: This is the closing price for this company's bonds on this day, December 27, 1993. It was $987.50. You may be wondering how we got this dollar amount from the number 98¾. When it comes to corporate bonds, we simply multiply the closing price (that we read in the newspaper) by 10. In other words, we would multiply $98.75 (which is 98¾ in dollar terms) times 10 to get $987.50 ($98.75 × 10 = $987.50).

Column 5: This is the net change in the price of the bond from the previous day. The fraction here is -⅝. We first convert this to dollars and cents. Five-eighths of a dollar is 62.50 cents ($1.00 × ⅝ = $0.625). Then we multiply this by 10. This gives us $6.25 ($0.625 × 10 = $6.25). Since we were dealing with a negative fraction, it follows that the price of this bond was $6.25 lower on December 27, 1993 than it was on the previous day this bond was bought and sold.

---

1. The dividend listed in the newspaper is 0.56 for a particular stock. Jane has 500 shares of this stock. What is her total dividend payment?
2. The closing price for a particular bond reads "97¾." What is this in dollars and cents?

CHAPTER 5 REVIEW

CHAPTER SUMMARY

1. Three major forms of business organizations are sole proprietorships, partnerships, and corporations.

2. The owner of a sole proprietorship has unlimited liability, as do the regular partners in a partnership. The owners of a corporation (the stockholders) have limited liability.

3. The owner of a sole proprietorship and the partners in a partnership must pay personal income taxes on the profits of their businesses. The corporation is subject to the corporate income tax, and the owners of the corporation must pay personal income taxes on dividends paid to them.

4. The corporation sells bonds and issues stock to raise money.

5. A person who buys a bond issued by a corporation is a lender to the corporation; he or she is not an owner of the corporation. A person who buys shares of stock in a corporation is an owner of the corporation.

6. A franchise is a contract by which a firm lets a person or a group of persons use its name and sell its goods or services in exchange for certain payments being made and certain requirements being met.

7. Costs, or expenses, that are the same no matter how many units of a good are produced are called fixed costs. Costs, or expenses, that vary, or change, with the number of units of a good produced are called variable costs. Fixed costs plus variable costs equal total costs.

8. Average fixed cost equals fixed costs divided by quantity of output (the number of units of a good produced). For example, if fixed costs are $400 and quantity of output is 100, then the average fixed cost is $4 ($400 ÷ 100 = $4).

9. Average variable cost equals variable costs divided by quantity of output. For example, if variable costs are $600 and quantity of output is 100 units, then the average variable cost is $6 ($600 ÷ 100 = $6).

10. Average total cost equals total cost divided by quantity of output. For example, if total cost is $1,000 and quantity of output is 100, then the average total cost is $10 ($1,000 ÷ 100 = $10).

11. Marginal cost is the change in total cost that results from a change in quantity of output. In other words, marginal cost is the additional cost of producing an additional unit of a good. For example, if it costs an additional $5 to produce an additional unit of a good, then $5 is the marginal cost.

12. Total revenue is the price of a good, times the quantity sold. For example, if the price for a bag of cookies is $3 and 1,000 bags are sold, then total revenue is $3,000 ($3 × 1,000 = $3,000).

13. Marginal revenue is the change in total revenue that results from a change in quantity of output. In other words, marginal revenue is the additional revenue from selling an additional unit of a good. For example, if the revenue gained from selling an additional unit of a good is $7, then $7 is the marginal revenue.

14. Business firms will continue to produce a good as long as marginal revenue is greater than or equal to marginal cost.

15. The objective of a business firm is to maximize profit.

CHAPTER 5 REVIEW (continued)

BUILD YOUR ECONOMIC VOCABULARY

Match the word with the correct definition, example, or statement.

1. fixed cost
2. board of directors
3. corporation
4. marginal revenue
5. partnership
6. stockholder
7. total cost

a. one of the owners of the corporation
b. form of business organization in which owners have limited liability
c. form of business organization in which owners have unlimited liability
d. chosen by the stockholders of the firm
e. does not change as business firm produces more units of a good
f. fixed cost plus variable cost
g. additional revenue gained from selling an additional unit of a good

REVIEW QUESTIONS

1. List and explain two major differences between a corporation and a partnership.
2. Some people say that corporations are taxed twice. What does this mean? (To what taxes are we referring?)
3. Suppose a bond has a $10,000 face value and a coupon rate of 8 percent. What is the dollar amount of each annual coupon payment?
4. What is the relationship between a bondholder and the firm that issued the bond? What is the relationship between a stockholder and the firm that issued the stock?
5. Describe the structure of a typical corporation.
6. How does a cooperative differ from a corporation?
7. Give an example of a fixed cost and an example of a variable cost. In general, what is the difference between fixed and variable costs?
8. Calculate the marginal cost for the additional unit in each of the following cases. (TC = total cost and Q = quantity of output.)
   a. Q = 100, TC = $4,322; Q = 101, TC = $4,376

   b. Q = 210, TC = $5,687; Q = 211, TC = $5,699
   c. Q = 547, TC = $10,009; Q = 548; TC = $10,123
9. In your own words, explain why a firm continues to produce those units of a good for which marginal revenue is greater than marginal cost.
10. As a business firm produces more units of a good, would we expect average fixed cost to rise or fall? Explain your answer.
11. How does a firm go about deciding what quantity of a good to produce?
12. A firm will produce and sell units of a good if marginal revenue is greater than marginal cost. Does this have anything to do with the firm's objective to maximize profit? Explain your answer.
13. Calculate the average total cost in each of the following cases. (TC = total cost and Q = quantity of output.)
    a. Q = 120, TC = $3,400
    b. Q = 200, TC = $4,560
    c. Q = 150, TC = $1,500

SHARPEN YOUR CRITICAL THINKING SKILLS

1. Not all franchise agreements are identical. For example, when Dairy Queen first entered into franchise agreements, it did not require franchisees to handle all the Dairy Queen products (some carried hamburgers and some did not). In contrast, McDonald's franchise agreements do require its franchisees to handle all the McDonald's products. If you were the owner of a company that granted franchises, what kind of franchise agreement would you want, and why?

2. "As quantity of output rises, average fixed cost rises." What is wrong with this statement?

ACTIVITIES AND PROJECTS

1. If a person buys 100 shares of stock at $22 a share on Monday and sells all 100 shares on Friday at $24 a share, he has benefited monetarily. In short, there is little doubt that an individual can benefit from buying and selling shares of stock. We wonder: Is there any bene- fit to society from individuals buying and selling stock? In other words, because some people buy and sell stock, is society better off than it would be if there were no stocks to buy and sell? As a class, discuss this question.

ECONOMIC DICTIONARY

Assets (Pg. 119)
Average Fixed Cost (Pg. 133)
Average Total Cost (Pg. 134)
Average Variable Cost (Pg. 133)
Board of Directors (Pg. 122)
Bond (Pg. 122)
Business Firm (Pg. 116)
Bylaws (Pg. 122)
Cooperative (Pg. 127)
Corporate Income Tax (Pg. 116)
Corporation (Pg. 119)
Coupon Rate (Pg. 122)
Dividend (Pg. 120)
Face Value (Par Value) (Pg. 122)
Fixed Cost (Pg. 133)
Franchise (Pg. 127)
Franchisee (Pg. 127)

Franchiser (Pg. 127)
General Partner (Pg. 119)
Law of Diminishing Returns (Pg. 139)
Limited Liability (Pg. 119)
Limited Partner (Pg. 119)
Limited Partnership (Pg. 118)
Marginal Cost (Pg. 135)
Marginal Revenue (Pg. 136)
Partnership (Pg. 118)
Personal Income Tax (Pg. 116)
Sole Proprietorship (Pg. 116)
Stock (Pg. 119)
Stockholder (Pg. 119)
Total Cost (Pg. 133)
Unlimited Liability (Pg. 116)
Variable Cost (Pg. 133)

Competition and Markets

INTRODUCTION

Not all business firms face the same degree of competition. For example, a shoe company may face more competition from other shoe companies than, say, a cable TV company faces from other cable TV companies. The degree of competition a firm faces, and the amount of control it has over price, defines its market structure. In this chapter, we consider four market structures: perfect competition, monopoly, monopolistic competition, and oligopoly. As a consumer, you will buy goods from businesses in each of these four market structures.

1. List and discuss the characteristics of perfect competition, monopoly, monopolistic competition, and oligopoly.
2. Discuss the advantages and disadvantages of patents.
3. Explain the difference between a government monopoly and a market monopoly.
4. Explain why monopolistic competitors and oligopolists advertise and perfect competitors do not.
5. Identify the legal barriers to entry into a market.

KEY TERMS

Barrier to Entry
Monopolistic
    Competition
Monopoly
Natural Monopoly

Oligopoly
Perfect
    Competition
Public Franchise

W e first consider perfect competition. Firms that find themselves in a perfectly competitive market experience a great degree of competition.

As you read, keep these key questions in mind:

- What are the characteristics of perfect competition?
- What are some examples of perfectly competitive markets?
- What does it mean to say that a firm has no control over price?

The Characteristics of Perfect Competition

Four conditions characterize **perfect competition**.

1. **There are many buyers and many sellers**. In a perfectly competitive market, there are many buyers and many sellers for the good under consideration. For example, in the wheat market, there are many people who buy wheat, and there are also many people (wheat farmers) who sell wheat.
2. **All firms sell identical goods**. There is no difference (as far as the buyer is concerned) between the goods one firm sells and those other firms sell. For example, the buyer may look upon Farmer Jones's wheat as identical to Farmer Smith's wheat.
3. **Buyers and sellers have all relevant information about prices, product quality, sources of supply, and so on**. All buyers and sellers in the perfectly competitive market know everything that is relevant to them about buying and selling. For example, Farmer Jones knows who else is selling wheat, the price at which the wheat is being sold, the quality of the wheat, and so on.
4. **There is easy entry into the market and easy exit out of the market**. Any seller who wants to enter a perfectly competitive market can do

so—nothing prevents this. There are no government regulations or laws that prohibit it. Also, any time a seller wants to leave (exit) the market, he or she can do so.

What Do We Conclude from the Four Conditions? Sellers Have No Control Over Price

Given the four characteristics of a perfectly competitive market, we conclude that the sellers have *no control over price*. This means each seller can only sell his or her good at the equilibrium price as determined by the forces of supply and demand (described in Chapter 4).

To illustrate, consider Farmer Smith, a seller in the perfectly competitive wheat market. Farmer Smith wakes up in the morning, turns on the radio to listen to the morning wheat report, and hears that wheat is selling for $3.57 a bushel. This is the equilibrium price for wheat as determined in the wheat market by the forces of supply and demand. Farmer Smith must sell his wheat for this price— not one penny more.

If he tries to sell his wheat for even a penny more, buyers will know it. After all, buyers have all information relevant to buying and selling (according to condition 3). And certainly Farmer Smith's attempt to sell his wheat for one penny more is a piece of information relevant to buying and selling. Consequently, buyers will buy wheat from other sellers (according to condition 1, there are many sellers to buy from), and this wheat is identical (according to condition 2) to Farmer Smith's wheat.

QUESTION: *If a firm does not have control over price, does this mean that it cannot sell its good for one penny more than equilibrium price, as determined by the forces of supply and demand?*

ANSWER: *Yes. For example, suppose the equilibrium price is $10 for some good. If Firm A has*

▶ Agricultural markets are considered to be perfectly competitive. This means that the sellers in these markets have no control over price: each seller can only sell his or her good at the equilibrium price as determined by the forces of supply and demand.

no control over price, it cannot sell any of its good for more than $10. It may be selling 10,000 units of the good at $10 each, but it won't be able to sell even one unit at $10.01. Another way of saying that a firm has no control over price is to say it takes *the equilibrium price and sells only at this price. It is a price-taker, in short. Firm A takes the price of $10, and sells all it has at this price, because it cannot sell any units of its good at any higher price.*

A firm that has some control over price can sell some of its good at different prices. For example, at $8 per unit, it might sell 100 units, and if it raises its price to $9, it might sell 95 units.

that is very similar to what is sold by the other sellers. In other words, all widgets are much alike, although they are not identical. Next, buyers and sellers have a lot of information that is relevant to the market, but they certainly don't have *all* information. Finally, there is relatively easy entry into and exit from the market. Is the widget market an example of a perfectly competitive market?

Most people would say no, because the widget market does not precisely meet the four characteristics of perfect competition. For example, the widget market has *few* sellers, whereas in a perfectly competitive market, there are *many* sellers.

But we ought not to put too much emphasis on the specific characteristics of the perfectly com-

Even Though a Market Does Not Meet Every Condition of Perfect Competition, Its Sellers Still May Have No Control over Price

Suppose there is a fictional market called the *widget market*. In this market, there are many buyers and only a few sellers. Each seller sells a good

MINI GLOSSARY

Perfect Competition A market structure in which (1) there are many buyers and many sellers, (2) all firms sell identical goods, (3) buyers and sellers have all relevant information about buying and selling activities, and (4) there is easy entry into the market and easy exit out of the market.

Madam C. J. Walker

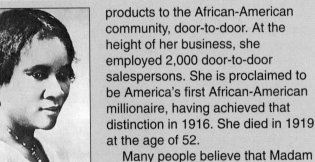

Madam C. J. Walker was born in Delta, Louisiana, in 1867. Like most African Americans then, she worked as a laborer, working 14-hour days as a washerwoman for wealthy whites in St. Louis. She had gone to St. Louis after her husband was murdered by a lynch mob.

Walker noticed that the environment she worked in—hot steam, vapors, fumes, and harsh soaps—took a toll on her hair and skin. For instance, her hair was beginning to fall out. She also noticed that the white employers she worked for had creams, lotions, and ointments to keep their skin and hair in good condition.

One night, according to Walker, she had a dream in which a man came to her and told her what to mix together to help her hair. Some of these ingredients were available only in Africa. She sent for them and prepared the hair remedy. After she applied it to her own head, her hair began to grow back. She gave some of the remedy to her friends, and it worked for them too.

Walker quit working as a washerwoman and began to develop and sell her skin and hair products to the African-American community, door-to-door. At the height of her business, she employed 2,000 door-to-door salespersons. She is proclaimed to be America's first African-American millionaire, having achieved that distinction in 1916. She died in 1919 at the age of 52.

Many people believe that Madam C. J. Walker blazed the way for door-to-door sales of cosmetics. Avon Products and Mary Kay Cosmetics are two companies that tread the path Walker once trod.

---

1. Was Madam C. J. Walker selling her skin and hair products in a perfectly competitive market?
2. How do you think the skin and hair products market has changed since Walker was selling her products?

---

petitive market. Instead, we ought to ask whether widget sellers have any control over price.

If the answer is that they do not have any control over price, then we must conclude that even though the widget market does not precisely meet all four characteristics of perfect competition, sellers within the widget market *act as if the widget market is perfectly competitive*. For economists, if a market *acts as if* it is perfectly competitive, then it is considered to be perfectly competitive.

Two real-world examples of perfectly competitive markets are agricultural markets and the stock market. The wheat market, which we touched on earlier, is an agricultural market. Let's turn to the stock market.

Suppose Ahmad has 100 shares of stock. One day he decides to sell all 100 shares. At what price does he sell the shares? He must sell them at the equilibrium price. This price is quoted on the stock market page of the newspaper. He can't sell his 100 shares for one penny more per share. Why? Because buyers would simply purchase the stock from someone else at the lower price. Ahmad has no control over the price at which he sells his stock.

QUESTION: *To determine whether a market (like the wheat, widget, or stock market) is perfectly competitive, it seems that all we need to know is whether sellers have control over price. If they do not have control over price, then the market is perfectly competitive. If they do have control over price, then the market is not perfectly competitive. Why, then, do we bother with the four character-* *istics of a perfectly competitive market? We don't seem to be using them to determine whether a market is perfectly competitive.*

ANSWER: *We need to consider these characteristics because many more times than not, in markets that do have the characteristics (or nearly do), sellers have no control over price.*

 # LEARNING CHECK

1. What does it mean to say that there is easy entry into the market and easy exit out of the market?
2. "A seller in a perfectly competitive market has some control over price." Do you agree or disagree? Explain your answer.
3. Does a market have to precisely meet all four characteristics of a perfectly competitive market before it is labeled as one? Explain your answer.
4. What question do we try to answer when deciding whether a market is perfectly competitive?
5. What are the four characteristics of a perfectly competitive market?

SECTION 2 — MONOPOLY

Next, we turn to the opposite of the perfectly competitive market. We turn to monopoly. In a monopoly market, there is very little, if any, competition.

As you read, keep these key questions in mind:

■ What are the characteristics of monopoly?
■ What are examples of barriers to entry?
■ Do monopolists ever face competition?

The Characteristics of Monopoly

Three conditions characterize **monopoly** .

1. There is one seller. Contrast this with the perfectly competitive market, where there are many sellers.

2. The single seller sells a product for which there are no close substitutes. Because there are no close substitutes for its product, the single seller—or the monopolist—faces little, if any, competition.

3. There are extremely high barriers to entry, which means that entry into the market is extremely difficult. In a perfectly competitive market, it is easy for a firm to enter the market. In a monopoly market, it is very hard, if not

MINI GLOSSARY

Monopoly A market structure in which (1) there is a single seller, (2) the seller sells a product for which there are no close substitutes, and (3) there are extremely high barriers to entry.

impossible, to enter the market. There are extremely high **barriers to entry** that keep new firms out. We consider the nature of these barriers shortly.

Monopolists Have Control over Price

A monopolist has control over price. This means it can raise its price and still sell some of its product.

Remember, though, that demand curves are downward sloping, and even though the monopolist can sell some of its product at a higher price, it can't sell as much of its product at a higher price as it can sell at a lower price. After all, according to the law of demand, price and quantity demanded move in opposite directions. This tells us that there is an *upper limit* on how high a price the monopolist can charge and still sell some of its product. At some high price, quantity demanded becomes zero.

Barriers to Entry

Suppose the XYZ Company is a monopolist. It is currently charging a relatively high price for its product and earning large profits. Why don't other businesses enter the market and produce the same product as the XYZ Company? The answer is that, as noted, there are high barriers to entry into a monopoly market. These high barriers include (1) legal barriers, (2) a monopolist's extremely low average total costs, and (3) a monopolist's exclusive ownership of a scarce resource.

1. **Legal barriers**. Legal barriers include public franchises, patents, and copyrights. A **public franchise** is a right granted to a firm by government that permits the firm to provide a particular good or service and excludes all others from doing so. This eliminates potential competition by law. For example, in many towns, there is only one public utility company. This company has been given the exclusive right to

"New York's Octopus."

▲ The common perception of a monopolist is of a firm that has you at its mercy.

produce and sell, say, electricity. If an organization other than the designated company were to start producing and selling electricity, it would be breaking the law.

In the United States, a *patent* is granted to the inventor of a product or process for a period of 17 years. During this time, the patent holder is shielded from competitors. No one else can legally produce and sell the patented product or process. Some people argue that patents are necessary in order to encourage innovation. They say that few persons would waste their time and money trying to invent a new product if their competitors could immediately copy the product and sell it.

Copyrights give authors or originators of literary or artistic productions the right to publish, print, or sell their intellectual productions for a period of time. For example, consider books. Either the author of a book holds a copyright to the work, or the company that published the book holds the copyright. West Publishing Company, for example, holds the copyright to this book. That means West Publishing Company essentially owns the book. Anyone else who copies large sections of the book and tries to sell it is breaking the law.

2. **Extremely low average total cost (low per-unit cost).** Chapter 5 discussed different kinds of costs. One was average total cost, which is total cost divided by quantity of output. This is also called per-unit cost. For example, if total cost is $1,000 and quantity of output is 1,000 units, then average total cost is $1 per unit ($1,000 ÷ 1,000 = $1).

   In some industries, a firm has an average total cost that is extremely low. In fact, it is so low that no other firm can compete with this firm. To see why, let's consider the relationship of average total cost and price. A business will earn a per-unit profit when it sells its product for a price that is higher than its average total cost. For example, if its average total cost is $5 per unit and it sells its product for $7 per unit, it receives a profit of $2 per unit.

   Now, some companies may have such a low average total cost that they can lower price to a very low level and still earn a profit. This may put competitors out of business. For example, suppose 17 companies are currently competing to sell a good. One of the companies, however, has a much lower average total cost than the others. Say Company A's average total cost is $5, whereas the other companies' average total cost is $8. This puts Company A in a good position. It can sell its good for, say, $6, earn a $1 profit on each unit sold, and make it impossible for the other companies to compete with it. The other companies cannot compete at a price of $6, since if they sold their goods at this price they would take a loss of $2 per unit. In the end, Company A, the company with the lowest average total cost, is the only seller of the good. A company that ends up the only seller of a good because of its low average total cost is called a **natural monopoly**.

3. **Exclusive ownership of a scarce resource.** It takes oranges to produce orange juice. Suppose one firm owned all the oranges. This firm

▲ In many towns, there is only one public utility company that has been granted the right to provide some good or service.

would be considered a monopoly firm. The classic example of a monopolist that controls a resource is the Aluminum Company of America (Alcoa). For a long time, this company controlled almost all sources of bauxite (the main source of aluminum) in the United States. This made Alcoa the sole producer of aluminum in the country from the late 19th century until the 1940s.

MINI GLOSSARY

Barriers to Entry Anything that prohibits a firm from entering a market.

Public Franchise A right granted to a firm by government that permits the firm to provide a particular good or service and excludes all others from doing so.

Natural Monopoly The condition in which one firm has such a low average total cost (per-unit cost) that only it can survive in the market.

ANALYZING PRIMARY SOURCES

Robert Fulton and the Steamboat

This chapter distinguished between a government monopoly and a market monopoly. U.S. economic history is full of examples in which businesspersons tried to use government to prevent other persons from competing with them. In short, it is full of examples of people's attempts to get government to award them a monopoly position. One such person was Robert Fulton (1765–1815), inventor, engineer, and designer of the first commercially successful U.S. steamboat. Gary Walton has written about this episode in American history. Read his words:[a]

"**W**ith one steamboat plying the Hudson River, and an absolute monopoly already granted him by New York for all steam navigation within the state, Fulton and his partner, Robert Livingston, schemed to win exclusive control over all steam navigation throughout the

---

a. Excerpted from: *Second Thoughts: Myths and Morals of U.S. Economic History*, edited by Donald M. McCloskey. Copyright © 1993 by Oxford University Press, Inc. Reprinted by permission.

entire trans-Appalachian West, a natural highway network of approximately forty-five rivers extending over 16,000 miles. To lock up so vast an area, they diligently petitioned the main states and territorial assemblies along the trunk rivers, boasting of the benefits to the areas served, but claiming that their federal patent was of too short a duration to cover expected startup costs. Fulton and Livingston thus sought twenty years of exclusive control for building and operating one steamboat, plus an additional five years for a second boat and another five years for a third.

This petition was relentlessly fought by William Thornton, a spirited public servant who served as superintendent of the U.S. Patent Office. In a letter-writing campaign to the petitioned states and territories, Thornton pointed out that exclusive monopoly privileges based on state patents were expressly forbidden after 1789 by the Constitution of the United States. . . . Thornton's campaign succeeded in most states. . . . Kentucky's legislative committee rejected Fulton and Livingston's petition, warning: 'It would be dangerous and impolitic to invest a man or set of

◀ In the early 1800s, Robert Fulton and Robert Livingston tried to gain a monopoly position for their steamboat business.

ANALYZING PRIMARY SOURCES (continued)

▲ Robert Fulton (1765–1815)

men with the sole power of . . . controlling or directing the most considerable part of the commerce of the country for so great a period.'

Fulton and Livingston, however, were not to be deterred, and they recognized there was really only one essential territory to control: the 'Crescent City' of New Orleans, gateway between the valleys of the Mississippi and Ohio. Approval by the legislative assembly of the Territory of New Orleans, known as the State of Louisiana after 1812, could give them the control they sought. One vital, political victory was all they needed.

To this end, a close friend of Fulton's came into contact with W. C. C. Clairborne, governor of the Territory of Orleans, and in 1810 invited him steamboating in the West. Like most Westerners, Clairborne had harbored doubts on the technical feasibility of steam power against mighty western currents, but such doubts were eliminated after several days of partying with Fulton and Livingston. Clairborne duly agreed to sponsor their petition, and to personally present it to the legislative assembly, which granted exclusive steam navigation rights to Fulton and Livingston in April 1811. The monopoly was to last eighteen years.

The response was hostile throughout the West, especially in towns along the Ohio River. The Ohio and Kentucky legislatures passed resolutions denouncing the monopoly grant and urging congressional intervention. Mass meetings and broadsheet editorials called for 'the annihilation of the swindling patent rights' that had allowed Fulton to lock the gateway to the West. . . .

Meanwhile, a group of 'Westerners' near Pittsburgh quickly entered the business. Fulton and Livingston's most feared interloper was the mechanic and inventor Henry Shreve, whose vessels performed extremely well, thanks to his clever innovations and skillful adaptations to western river conditions. Legal skirmishes to halt Shreve and the other interlopers began in 1815, when one of Shreve's steamboats arrived in New Orleans; his vessel was seized and then released on bail, but other ships were impounded. . . .

Shreve's boats were built of lighter wood with broad, shallow hulls for lighter draft, and were propelled by more powerful engines; to avoid snags and river debris, the paddle wheels were placed at the stern rather than the side. Of course, Fulton and Livingston eventually could have adopted Shreve's designs as did others. Their first line of business, however, was to win the court battle at New Orleans because as long as they had the Louisiana monopoly they could exclude superior competition and control business to and from the interior [of the country]. Despite an 1816 State Supreme Court ruling that the steamboat monopoly was unconstitutional, local politics remained in their favor. Although their exclusive privileges were detested throughout other western states, the Louisiana legislature rejected an 1817 petition to abolish their monopoly.

During these years of legal entanglements Fulton and Livingston died, but their heirs continued the court battle against Shreve. After the case was dismissed by the Louisiana State Supreme Court, Edward Livingston renewed legal proceedings in the U.S. District Court of Louisiana on behalf of his brother's and Fulton's estates. Despite an alleged bribe to Shreve from

Livingston to instruct his lawyers to throw the case, Shreve remained undeterred. The Federal District Court ruled that since both the plaintiffs and the defendant were citizens of states other than Louisiana, it had no jurisdiction over the case. Anticipating a fairly sure loss at the only tribunal left—the Supreme Court in Washington, D.C.—the heirs abandoned the fight. Consequently, open competition on the western rivers was assured by the end of 1817, when sixteen steamboats were running between Louisville and New Orleans; two years later there were fifty-nine steamboats plying the trunk rivers.

The gain to the West and the entire nation from free entry and open competition on the rivers was immense. Because the steamboat monopoly was broken, freight rates fell faster and reached lower levels than would have prevailed otherwise. Also, on account of competition, freight shipments grew faster and reached higher levels, and steamboats contributed to the early nineteenth-century transportation revolution. If Fulton's monopoly had been protected, the West would have been populated and developed, of course, but at a slower pace; the impact of another dozen years of monopoly at New Orleans would not have been trivial. . . .

History students and enthusiasts will find at least two familiar lessons in the story of Fulton's Folly. First is the observation that it is very difficult to establish or sustain a monopoly without government patents, licensing, tariffs, or regulation to keep out competition. Once Fulton and Livingston lost legal protection they were overwhelmed by competitive forces, and no single owner or group of owners could stem the tide of new entrants who were soon beating down freight rates. A multitude of suppliers responded, as if led by an invisible hand, to build and operate more and more boats at lower and lower costs. No central planning was involved here, just a wide-open competitive fray.

The second lesson is that open markets generate a multitude of productivity advances, large and small, that stimulate trade and lower the costs of goods and services. Because of competition in the steamboat business, consumers received more goods at lower retail prices, and producers sold their farm goods and other merchandise in greater volume at higher wholesale prices. . . .

Thanks to the U. S. Constitution, state-chartered monopolies of the type envisioned by Fulton and Livingston have seldom succeeded for long in the United States. Americans' distaste for monopoly has a long and historically rich tradition; the American Revolution was sharply spurred by colonial reactions to the granting of a monopoly in tea to the English East India Company in 1773. Nevertheless, the quest for monopoly is an eternal force that begs for heroes to fight against it and sustain the progress of competition. The heroes in Fulton's Folly are William Thornton, Henry Shreve, and all the little guys who added to progress through competition. Each generation, it is hoped, will energize like-minded citizens to combat the temptations of exclusive control."

1. Many people believe that businesspersons favor a free market and competition and that government officials and the courts favor government intervention and regulation. Does the story of Fulton and Livingston support this view or offer evidence against it? Explain your answer.
2. Do you think it was ethically right for Fulton and Livingston to push for monopoly rights to control steam navigation in and out of New Orleans? Do you see a tradeoff here between earning profits and doing what is ethically right? Explain your answer.

Government Monopoly and Market Monopoly

As we have seen, sometimes high barriers to entry exist because competition is legally prohibited, and sometimes they exist for other reasons. Where high barriers take the form of public franchises, patents, or copyrights, competition is legally prohibited. In contrast, where high barriers take the form of one firm's low average total cost or exclusive ownership of a resource, competition is not legally prohibited. In these cases, there is no law to keep rival firms from entering the market and competing, even though they may choose not to do so.

Some economists use the term *government monopoly* to refer to monopolies that are legally protected from competition. They use the term *market monopoly* to refer to monopolies that are not legally protected from competition. These terms do not mean that one type of monopoly is better or worse than the other. They simply remind us that some sellers in the real world are legally protected from competition and some are not.

 # LEARNING CHECK

1. What are the three characteristics of a monopoly market?
2. What is a natural monopoly?
3. Give an example of a legal barrier to entry.
4. What is the difference between a government monopoly and a market monopoly?

SECTION 3 MONOPOLISTIC COMPETITION

Between perfect competition at one extreme and monopoly at the other, there are two types of markets. One is monopolistic competition, and the other is oligopoly. This section discusses monopolistic competition.

As you read, keep these key questions in mind:

- What are the characteristics of monopolistic competition?
- What are some examples of monopolistic competition?
- Do monopolistic competitors have any control over price?

The Characteristics of Monopolistic Competition

Three conditions characterize **monopolistic competition**.

1. **There are many buyers and many sellers**. This is one of the characteristics of perfect competition, too. Because it is, it might seem that monopolistic competitive firms, like perfectly competitive firms, have no control over price. This is untrue, though. It is untrue because of the following additional characteristic.
2. **Firms produce and sell slightly differentiated products**. In a perfectly competitive market, all firms produce and sell identical products. In

 ### MINI GLOSSARY

Monopolistic Competition A market structure in which (1) there are many buyers and many sellers, (2) sellers produce and sell slightly differentiated products, and (3) there is easy entry into and easy exit from the market.

ECONOMIC FOCUS

Firms that sell goods in monopolistic competitive markets are called monopolistic competitors. A few examples include supermarkets, department stores, and gasoline service stations. In Exhibit S-6-1, we have listed the number of each of these specific types of monopolistic competitive firms for each of the 50 states.

Earlier in this chapter we said that monopolistic markets are characterized by having many buyers. Certainly supermarkets, department stores, and gasoline service stations have many buyers for what they sell. Monopolistic competition is also characterized by having many sellers. The large numbers of supermarkets,

▼ **EXHIBIT S-6-1.** Supermarkets, Department Stores, and More.

STATE	NUMBER OF SUPER-MARKETS	NUMBER OF DEPARTMENT STORES	NUMBER OF GASOLINE SERVICE STATIONS	STATE	NUMBER OF SUPER-MARKETS	NUMBER OF DEPARTMENT STORES	NUMBER OF GASOLINE SERVICE STATIONS
Alabama	4,867	3,479	1,830	Montana	1,287	426	465
Alaska	1,209	432	236	Nebraska	1,888	1,139	1,023
Arizona	6,169	2,246	1,769	Nevada	2,057	989	636
Arkansas	3,268	1,885	1,191	New Hampshire	2,206	875	563
California	40,600	17,747	13,916	New Jersey	12,876	5,262	3,852
Colorado	5,217	2,521	1,704	New Mexico	2,000	845	735
Connecticut	4,809	2,221	1,809	New York	24,345	10,099	6,154
Delaware	1,022	547	346	North Carolina	9,039	3,586	3,215
Florida	19,836	10,291	6,837	North Dakota	806	503	479
Georgia	8,795	4,751	3,500	Ohio	13,943	8,673	6,690
Hawaii	2,043	1,224	655	Oklahoma	4,382	2,088	1,398
Idaho	1,444	482	509	Oregon	4,312	2,226	1,566
Illinois	13,536	8,879	6,446	Pennsylvania	16,468	7,838	5,322
Indiana	6,543	4,089	3,574	Rhode Island	1,188	597	470
Iowa	3,986	2,041	1,907	South Carolina	5,085	1,988	1,899
Kansas	3,393	1,910	1,510	South Dakota	921	406	527
Kentucky	4,802	2,684	1,954	Tennessee	5,797	3,788	2,562
Louisiana	7,094	3,040	1,943	Texas	26,667	12,533	8,567
Maine	2,177	610	663	Utah	2,353	1,031	808
Maryland	6,579	3,470	2,405	Vermont	947	212	304
Massachusetts	9,144	4,174	2,993	Virginia	9,244	4,047	3,298
Michigan	10,397	8,879	5,671	Washington	8,116	3,082	2,552
Minnesota	5,909	3,656	2,973	West Virginia	2,295	1,021	787
Mississippi	2,959	1,459	922	Wisconsin	5,947	3,572	3,299
Missouri	6,603	4,406	3,393	Wyoming	604	226	311

SOURCE: U.S. Bureau of the Census, *Statistical Abstract of the United States:* 1993, 113th edition.

SUPERMARKETS, DEPARTMENT STORES, AND MORE

department stores, and gasoline service stations in Exhibit S-6-1 are evidence of this.

Further, monopolistic competition is characteristically made up of firms selling slightly differentiated products. This is largely true in the case of department stores. Is it also true for supermarkets and gasoline service stations? One gasoline service station may sell exactly the same kind of gasoline as another (for example, Exxon gas is sold at many different stations), but not all gasoline service stations provide the same kind of service if you want to get your car fixed. Similarly, 100 supermarkets may all sell a particular kind of bread, soft drink, or potato chips, but not all supermarkets offer the same shopping experience. Finally, in monopolistic competitive markets entry and exit are easy. This is the case for supermarkets, department stores, and gasoline service stations.

We also mention later in this chapter that monopolistic competitive firms will tend to advertise. Monopolistic competitive firms compete with each other not only through their advertisements, but also through their locations. Have you ever seen four gasoline service stations at one intersection? Have you ever seen department stores within a short walking distance of each other at a shopping mall? Have you ever seen one supermarket directly across the street

from another supermarket? There is an explanation for the concentration of similar types of firms. We explain in Exhibit S-6-2.

In Part *a*, there are two gasoline service stations, A and B. Station A is located at the far left end of the street, and Station B is located at the far right end. The cars in the exhibit represent buyers of the products that the two stations sell. There are 28 cars, or 28 buyers. We will assume that each buyer will buy from the station that is located closer to him or her. Those buyers in the dark purple cars will buy from Station A, while those buyers in the light purple cars will buy from Station B. Each station ends up with 14 customers.

Now suppose we add a little magic to things. We are going to let both of the gasoline stations change their locations at no cost. In other words, if Station A wants to move away from the far left end of the street, it can do so with a snap of its owner's fingers. Look at part *b* (on page 160) Station A has moved away from the far left end of the street and toward the middle of the street. As a result, it picks up customers. Now there are 16 buyers closer to Station A, and only 12 buyers closer to Station B.

Station B notices it has lost some customers. The owner of Station B snaps her fingers and changes her location, as seen in part *c*. Conse-

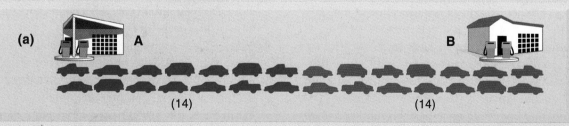

(a) A B

(14) (14)

▲ EXHIBIT S-6-2

U.S. ECONOMIC FOCUS (continued)

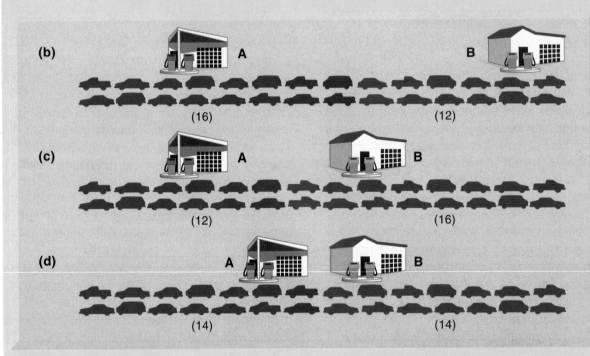

▲ **EXHIBIT S-6-2 (continued).**

quently, Station B increases the number of its customers to 16, and Station A is left with 12 customers.

Finally, Station A makes one last move, as seen in part *d*. Now the two stations, A and B, are next to each other. Each station serves 14 customers. It is unlikely for either station to want to move from its present location in part *d*, because a move away from its present location could only make things worse, not better. For example, if Station A were to move back to its location in part *c*, it would lose customers. Similarly, if Station B were to move back toward the far right end of the street, it would lose customers. It is likely that both stations will stay right where they are: next door to each other.

What holds for gasoline service stations holds for supermarkets and department stores, too. The competition for customers draws them close to each other.

─────────────────────

1. In many cities across the nation, car dealerships are located near each other. Explain why. Do you think car dealerships are monopolistic competitive firms?

2. Find out the population of your state. (You may want to ask the librarian in your school library what book or books will have this information.) Next, compute the number of supermarkets per 10,000 persons in your state. Do the same for department stores and gasoline service stations.

a monopoly, there is only one firm, and it produces a unique product—one for which there are no close substitutes. In a monopolistic competitive market, there are many firms, each producing a product that is slightly different from the other firms' products. For example, McDonald's hamburgers and Burger King's hamburgers are slightly differentiated products.

3. **There is easy entry into and exit from the market**. Monopolistic competition resembles perfect competition in this respect. There are no barriers to entry or exit, legal or otherwise.

Many Monopolistic Competitors Would Rather Be Monopolists

Suppose you own a business that is considered a monopolistic competitive firm. Your business is one of many sellers, you sell a product slightly differentiated from the products of your competitors, and there is easy entry into and exit from the industry. Would you rather your business were a monopolist firm instead? Wouldn't it be better for you to be the only seller of a product than to be one of many sellers?

Most business owners would say yes, it is better to be a monopolist firm than to be a monopolistic competitive firm. This being the case, we ought to consider *how* monopolistic competitors may go about trying to become monopolists.

One suggested way is through advertising. If a monopolistic competitor can, through advertising, persuade the buying public that her product is more than simply *slightly differentiated* from those of her competitors, she stands a better chance of becoming a monopolist.

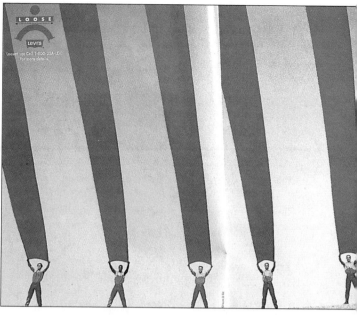

▲ Companies sometimes try to distinguish their products through advertising. Shown here is a Levi's® ad.

Consider an example. Many firms produce men's and women's jeans. To many people, the jeans produced by these firms look very much alike. How, then, does any one of the firms differentiate its product from the pack?

It could add a "designer label" to the jeans to suggest that the jeans are unique—that they are the only Levi's® jeans, or Girbaud jeans, or the like. Or through advertising, it could try to persuade the buying public that its jeans are "the" jeans worn by the most famous, best-looking people living and vacationing in the most exciting places in the world. Whether or not the advertising is successful in meeting its objective is an issue with which we are not concerned here. The point is that through advertising, firms sometimes try to differentiate their products from their competitors' products.

 LEARNING CHECK

1. In what ways is monopolistic competition like perfect competition?
2. Give two examples of a monopolistic competitive market.
3. "Monopolistic competitors have some control over price." Do you agree or disagree? Explain.

Finally, we turn to the fourth market structure, oligopoly.

As you read, keep these key questions in mind:

- What are the characteristics of oligopoly?
- What are some examples of oligopoly?
- Do oligopolists have any control over price?
- Why do oligopolists advertise?

The Characteristics of Oligopoly

Three conditions characterize **oligopoly**.

1. **There are few sellers**. In an oligopolistic market, there are only a few sellers. Each seller is aware that its actions affect the other sellers and that the actions of the other sellers affect it. For example, General Motors and Ford Motor Company are considered oligopolists. Economists assume that General Motors and Ford know that what each does influences what the other does. For example, General Motors knows that if it comes out with a new, sporty car and lowers prices on its existing cars, Ford may follow suit.

2. **Firms produce and sell either identical or slightly differentiated products**. Steel is a homogeneous or identical product produced in an oligopolistic market. Every firm's steel is the same as every other firm's steel. Cars are a slightly differentiated product produced in an oligopolistic market. Ford's cars are slightly different from General Motors' cars.

3. **There are significant barriers to entry, which means that entry into the market is difficult**. Low average total costs (or per-unit costs) are perhaps the most significant barrier to entry in oligopoly, but patents and exclusive control over an essential resource also act as barriers to entry here.

   Because oligopolists sometimes produce slightly differentiated products, and because entry into the market is difficult, oligopolists have some control over price (but not as much as monopolists do). For review, Exhibit 6-1 summarizes the characteristics of the four market structures discussed in this chapter.

How Do We Know Which Industries Are Oligopolistic?

Economists determine whether a market is oligopolistic by looking at the percentage of sales accounted for by the top four firms in the industry. If only a few firms account for a large percentage of sales, then the market is considered oligopolistic. For example, suppose there are 10 firms in an industry and the total revenue of the industry is $100 million. Further, suppose the four firms with the highest sales generate $80 million in revenue. This means that the top four firms account for 80 percent of total revenues in the industry (since $80 million is 80 percent of $100 million). In other words, the industry is dominated by the top four firms. It is an example of an oligopolistic market.

Now consider a real-world example. The American automobile industry is largely made up of General Motors, Ford Motor Company, and Chrysler Corporation. Together, these three firms account for about 90 percent of American-made cars sold in the United States.

Other examples of oligopolistic markets include industries that produce cigarettes, tires and inner tubes, cereal breakfast foods, farm machinery, telephone and telegraph services, and soap and detergents.

Oligopoly and Competition

Some people believe that because a firm is an oligopolist, it doesn't face much competition (especially since such a firm is likely to be very large). This is not necessarily correct, though.

Market structure	Number of sellers	Type of product	Barriers to entry	Control over price	Examples of products and services sold in this type of market
Perfect Competition	Many	Identical	None	None	Wheat, corn, stocks
Monopoly	One	Unique	Extremely high	Considerable amount	Water, electricity, delivery of first-class mail
Monopolistic Competition	Many	Slightly differentiated	None	Yes, but not as much as in monopoly	Clothing, meals at restaurants
Oligopoly	Few	Identical or slightly differentiated	Significantly high	Yes, but not as much as in monopoly	Cars, cereal

▲ **EXHIBIT 6-1.** Characteristics of Market Structures.

THINKING LIKE AN ECONOMIST

In Chapter 1, we stated that economists think in terms of a global economy. Our discussion of oligopoly makes this point in an indirect way. For example, if we were to look only at the major U.S. manufacturers of cars—General Motors, Ford Motor Company, and Chrysler—we might conclude that they face little competition since there are merely three of them. But, of course, reality is much different; we need to look beyond the borders of the United States. The three U.S. companies face a lot of competition once we look at things on a global scale. Cars are manufactured in Japan, Germany, Italy, and other nations, too, and all these cars compete with those produced in the U.S. When it comes to matters of economics, the global perspective turns out to be increasingly central to our lives.

Ford Motor Company, for example, faces stiff competition from General Motors and Chrysler, two American companies. If we look at the world market for cars, there is even more competition for Ford. It faces extremely stiff competition from Japanese car companies such as Toyota, Nissan, Honda, and Mitsubishi. Oligopoly and stiff competition often do go together.

Oligopoly and Advertising

Like the monopolistic competitor, the oligopolist is often motivated to become a monopolist. One way for an oligopolist firm to do this is to try to differentiate its product from its competitors'

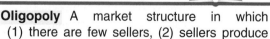

MINI GLOSSARY

Oligopoly A market structure in which (1) there are few sellers, (2) sellers produce and sell either identical or slightly differentiated products, and (3) there are significant barriers to entry.

products as much as it can. It hopes that the buying public will see its product as unique. General Motors, for example, has done this somewhat successfully with one of its cars, the Corvette. For many people, there is only one sporty car, and it is the Corvette. Oligopolist firms often try to differentiate their products—make their products seem more nearly unique—through advertising. Many of the advertisements on television are for goods produced by oligopolist firms. Breakfast cereal companies, car companies, detergent companies—all of which are oligopolists—advertise heavily on television.

LEARNING CHECK

1. What are the characteristics of oligopoly?
2. Give two examples of oligopoly.
3. "Oligopolist firms in the same industry [in the same country] never face competition from each other, only from foreign producers." Do you agree or disagree? Explain your answer.

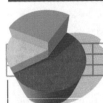

DEVELOPING ECONOMIC SKILLS

The Economics Paper: Finding A Topic

Suppose your economics teacher gives you the assignment of writing an essay on a topic of your choice. What topic would you choose? How would you go about researching it? How would you write it? These are some of the important questions we will answer as we discuss how to write a research paper, beginning in this chapter and continuing through Chapter 9.

In this chapter, we discuss how to find an economics topic to research and write about. In Chapter 7, we explain how to research your topic. In Chapter 8, we discuss how to write the paper. Finally, in Chapter 9, we discuss how to rewrite the paper.

Before you start to look for a topic, take a moment to think about the purpose of the essay and your intended audience. Is your assignment to report the factual information that you have learned about your topic or to express an opinion and develop an argument that will support your case? Who is going to read your essay? Your choice of topic might be very different if you are writing for a school newspaper than if you are writing for your teacher. A few minutes spent thinking about your purpose and your intended audience will help as you set about looking for a topic.

There are a number of ways to find a topic. One way is to make a list, as you read, of questions that you would like answered. For example, you have been reading about a number of topics in this book, such as supply and demand, opportunity costs, the free-enterprise system, prices, scarcity, business firms, profit, and so on. Go back to one of these topics that you found interesting and, as you reread the pages, write down a question every two or three paragraphs. For example, you might read about business firms, as you did in the last chapter. Here are some of the questions that might come to mind: (1) Why do some business firms earn higher profits than others? (2) What determines where business firms will locate? (3) Do U.S. business firms face much competition from foreign business firms? (4) Do business firms do things differently today than, say, 20

DEVELOPING ECONOMIC SKILLS (continued)

years ago? It is important to find questions that *you* find interesting. After all, you're the one who will be spending the time to research and write the essay. Besides, if you aren't interested in the topic of your essay, do you really think someone reading it will find it interesting?

At this stage, you should not be concerned with whether your questions make sense. You should simply write down the questions that come to mind. Free yourself to ask anything you want. Then, once you have written down a few questions, go back to see if any of them contains a topic to write about. For example, look at question 3. There is a topic contained in this question. It is "U.S. Businesses and Foreign Competition." This then could be the title of your economics paper.

When looking for a topic, should you limit your reading just to economics textbooks? The answer is "no." Economics topics can be found in news and business magazines (such as *Time, Newsweek, Forbes,* and *Fortune*), in newspapers, encyclopedias, and elsewhere.

Perhaps you have trouble coming up with questions as you read. What do you do then? Newspaper reporters often think in terms of the following questions: Who? What? Where? When? How? Why? For example, suppose a news reporter must write a story about a fire. She might begin by trying to get answers to the series of who—what—where—when—how—why questions. For example, she might ask *who* reported the fire? *What* damage has been done? *Where* did the fire start? *When* was the fire reported? *How* did the fire get so large? *Why* did the fire fighters have trouble getting the blaze under control?

This method of asking who—what—where—when—how—why is effective in economics, too. It helps to remind us to ask questions that we might not ordinarily ask. For example, returning to the topic of business firms, you might ask: *What* is the world's largest business firm? *What* does it produce? *Where* is it located? *How* did it become so large?

It is unlikely that all six questions (Who? What? Where? When? How? Why?) will be reasonable questions to ask about all economics topics. But you will find that many of these questions will often serve as a useful prompt to start you on your way to finding a good essay topic.

A common mistake that many students make is to choose a topic that is too broad. For example, after reading this chapter a student might consider writing about the topic "Competition." That is an enormous topic about which many people have written entire books! You couldn't begin to address that question within the scope of a brief paper and an attempt to do this could be very frustrating. In choosing an appropriate topic for your paper, try to narrow the question down to one that you can realistically expect to answer by the time you have finished and that you can complete in time to meet your assignment deadline.

Remember that selecting a topic is one of the most important aspects of writing an essay. Make sure you take the time to think about for whom you are writing, the purpose of the essay, and what is expected. Write down a lot of questions about an area that interests you and, chances are, one of these questions will contain a topic that you will want to write about. Taking the time to select an appropriate topic will pay off.

1. Go back through this chapter and, for each numbered section, write three or four questions that you would like to have answered. Remember, free up your mind to ask any question that is interesting to you.
2. For every set of these questions, choose one question to rewrite in the form of a title for an economics paper. Follow the example that we developed in this feature. The question, "Do U.S. businesses firms face much competition from foreign firms?" became "U.S. Businesses and Foreign Competition."

CHAPTER 6 REVIEW

CHAPTER SUMMARY

1. A perfectly competitive market has four characteristics: (1) There are many buyers and many sellers. (2) All firms sell identical goods. (3) Buyers and sellers have all relevant information about prices, product quality, sources of supply, and so on. (4) There is easy entry into the market and easy exit out of the market. Certain agricultural markets and the stock market are examples of perfectly competitive markets. Perfect competitors have no control over price.

2. A monopoly market has three characteristics: (1) There is one seller. (2) The single seller sells a product for which there are no close substitutes. (3) There are extremely high barriers to entry, which means that entry into the market is extremely difficult. Monopolies have a great deal of control over price.

3. For a monopoly market, high barriers to entry consist of legal barriers (which include franchises, patents, and copyrights), the monopolist's extremely low average total costs (low per-unit costs), and the monopolist's exclusive ownership of a scarce resource.

4. Some economists use the term *government monopoly* to refer to monopolies that are legally protected from competition and the term *market monopoly* to refer to monopolies that are not legally protected from competition.

5. A monopolistic competitive market has three characteristics: (1) There are many buyers and many sellers. (2) Firms produce and sell slightly differentiated products. (3) There is easy entry into and exit from the market. Monopolistic competitors have some control over price, but not as much as monopolists. Examples of firms in monopolistic competitive markets include retail clothing stores and restaurants.

6. An oligopolistic market has three characteristics: (1) There are few sellers. (2) Firms produce and sell either identical or slightly differentiated products. (3) There are significant barriers to entry, which means that entry into the market is difficult. Oligopolists have some control over price, but not as much as monopolists. Examples of oligopolistic markets include industries that produce cigarettes, tires and inner tubes, and cereal breakfast foods.

BUILD YOUR ECONOMIC VOCABULARY

Match the word with the correct definition, example, or statement.

1. government monopoly
2. copyright
3. perfect competition
4. monopolist
5. monopolistic competition
6. oligopoly
7. patent

a. effective for 17 years
b. a market in which firms have no control over price
c. single seller of a good
d. many sellers and slightly differentiated products
e. few sellers and identical or slightly differentiated products
f. legally protected from competition
g. like a patent, but for authors or publishers

REVIEW QUESTIONS

1. One characteristic of a perfectly competitive market is easy entry into and exit out of the market. What does this mean?

2. What does it mean to say that a perfectly competitive firm has no control over price?

3. Why doesn't a wheat farmer, say Farmer Jones, advertise her wheat on television?

4. List the three characteristics of a monopoly market.

5. Explain how a natural monopoly can outcompete its competitors.

6. What is a public franchise?

7. What is the difference between a government monopoly and a market monopoly?

8. What is one way to determine which industries are oligopolistic?

9. List the characteristics of a monopolistic competitive market.

10. List the characteristics of an oligopolistic market.

11. Many oligopolists and monopolistic competitive firms try to become monopolists, although they aren't usually successful. What is their objective in trying?

SHARPEN YOUR CRITICAL THINKING SKILLS

1. Occasionally, U.S. producers of a good try to influence Congress to prevent foreign producers from selling their goods in the United States. (By the way, foreign producers also lobby their governments to prohibit U.S. goods from coming into their countries.) For example, suppose the U.S. producers of computer chips convince the Congress to pass a law that prohibits any foreign producer of computer chips from selling its chips in the United States. Would this law be a barrier to entry? Why or why not? Would the law give U.S. producers more or less control over price than they had without the law?

2. "Since the monopolist produces a unique product, it can charge any price it wants. No price is too high." What's wrong with this statement?

ACTIVITIES AND PROJECTS

1. In groups of five persons, debate the issue of patents. Some people think there should be no patents. Patents, they say, simply keep prices high. Other people say that without patents, companies wouldn't invest the time and money to develop new products. What do you think? Explain your answer.

ECONOMIC DICTIONARY

Barrier to Entry (Pg. 152)   **Natural Monopoly** (Pg. 153)   **Public Franchise** (Pg. 152)
Monopolistic Competition (Pg. 157)   **Oligopoly** (Pg. 162)
Monopoly (Pg. 151)   **Perfect Competition** (Pg. 148)

CHAPTER 7

The Labor Force

INTRODUCTION

Every day in this country, millions of persons go to work. They work as cab drivers, computer programmers, attorneys, salespersons, construction workers, and accountants, among other things. These persons are part of the civilian labor force. One day soon, you will be part of the labor force, if you are not already. When that day arrives, you may give little thought to the particulars of the labor market in which you find yourself. But as you will learn in this chapter, the particulars of the labor market will have much to do with how high, or how low, your income turns out to be.

1. Explain why some persons earn higher wages than others.
2. Describe the employment effects of the minimum wage law in the labor market.
3. Describe how labor unions try to affect the demand for and supply of their labor.
4. Explain how labor unions affect union and nonunion wages.
5. Discuss the major economic forces currently affecting the workplace.
6. Explain the difference between the employment rate and the unemployment rate.

KEY TERMS

Closed Shop
Downsizing
Employment Rate
Global
 Competition
Labor Union
Minimum Wage
 Law

Right-to-Work Law
Strike
Taft-Hartley Act
Unemployment
 Rate
Union Shop
Wage Rate

SECTION 1 WHAT DETERMINES WAGES?

Why do some people earn higher wages or incomes than other persons? A baseball player may earn a million dollars a year, whereas a secretary earns much less, as do computer programmers, truck drivers, and many others. Who or what determines what people earn as workers in the labor force? In a competitive labor market, the answer is simple: supply and demand.

As you read, keep these key questions in mind:

- What does the demand curve for labor look like?
- What does the supply curve of labor look like?
- Why do wage rates differ?

Supply and Demand in the Labor Market

In Chapter 3, you learned about supply and demand. That chapter discussed goods or products—such things as apples, cars, and houses. Labor is not a product, it is a *resource*, or *factor of production*. However, supply and demand can also be used to analyze how the price of a resource or factor of production is determined.

We start with the fundamentals. There are people who *demand* labor (these people are usually referred to as *employers*) and people who *supply* labor (these people are usually referred to as *employees*). It follows, then, that there is a *demand curve* for labor and a *supply curve* of labor. The price of labor is called the **wage rate**.

What does the demand curve for labor look like? It is downward sloping, as shown in Exhibit 7-1*a*. A downward-sloping demand curve implies that employers will be willing and able to hire more people at lower wage rates than at higher wage rates. For example, employers are willing and able to hire more workers if the wage rate is $7 per hour than if the wage rate is $10 per hour.

What does the supply curve of labor look like? It is upward sloping, as shown in Exhibit 7-1*b*. An upward-sloping supply curve implies that more people will be willing and able to work at higher wage rates than at lower wage rates. For example, more people are willing and able to work if the wage rate is $10 per hour than if the wage rate is $7 an hour.

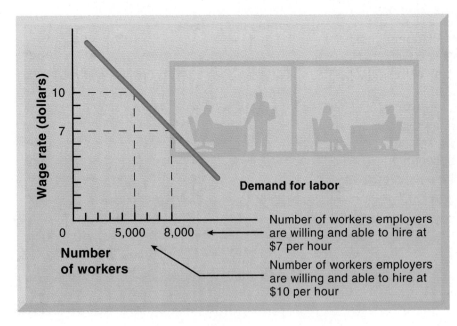

Number of workers

Number of workers employers are willing and able to hire at $7 per hour

Number of workers employers are willing and able to hire at $10 per hour

◄ **EXHIBIT 7-1***a*. **The Demand for Labor.** The demand curve for labor is downward sloping; employers are willing and able to hire more persons at lower wage rates than at higher wage rates.

▶ **EXHIBIT 7-1***b*. **The Supply of Labor.** The supply curve for labor is upward sloping; more persons are willing and able to work at higher wage rates than at lower wage rates.

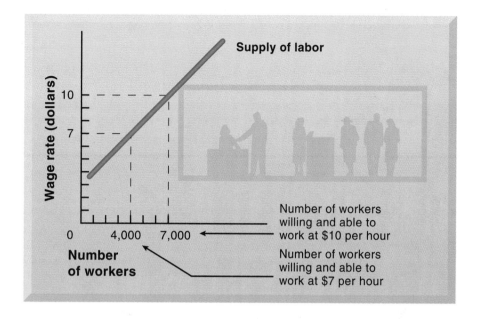

How the Equilibrium Wage Rate Is Established.

Recall from Chapter 4 the definition of the *equilibrium price*. It is the price at which the quantity demanded of a good equals the quantity supplied. For example, suppose $14 is the equilibrium price of compact discs. That means that at this price, the number of compact discs sellers are willing and able to sell equals the number of compact discs buyers are willing and able to buy.

Similarly, in the labor market, the *equilibrium wage rate* is the wage at which the quantity demanded of labor equals the quantity supplied of labor. Stated differently, it is the wage rate at which the number of persons employers are willing and able to hire is the same as the number of persons who are willing and able to be hired.

With this in mind, consider Exhibit 7-2*a*. You see here that when the wage rate is $9, the number of people who are willing and able to work (7,000) is greater than the number of people employers are willing and able to hire (3,000). It follows that $9 is not the equilibrium wage rate. At $9, there is a surplus of labor. In Chapter 4, you learned that when there is a surplus of a good, its price falls. Things are similar in a competitive labor market. When there is a surplus of labor, the wage rate falls.

▲ These people are waiting to apply for different jobs. They represent part of the supply side of the labor market.

MINI GLOSSARY

Wage Rate The price of labor.

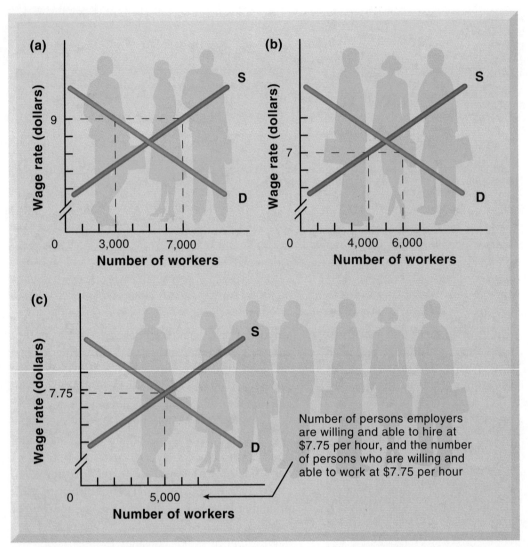

▲ **EXHIBIT 7-2.** **Finding the Equilibrium Wage Rate.** Part *a*: At $9 per hour, the number of persons willing and able to work (7,000) is greater than the number employers are willing and able to hire (3,000). We conclude that $9 is not the equilibrium wage rate. Part *b*: At $7 per hour, the number of persons employers are willing and able to hire (6,000) is greater than the number willing and able to work (4,000). We conclude that $7 is not the equilibrium wage rate. Part *c*: At $7.75 per hour, the number of persons willing and able to work (5,000) is the same as the number employers are willing and able to hire (5,000). We conclude that $7.75 *is* the equilibrium wage rate.

Now consider Exhibit 7-2*b*. The wage rate is $7, and the number of people employers are willing and able to hire (6,000) is greater than the number of people who are willing and able to work (4,000). It follows that $7 is not the equilibrium wage rate. At $7, there is a shortage of labor. When there is a shortage of labor, the wage rate rises.

In Exhibit 7-2*c*, the wage rate is $7.75, and the number of people employers are willing and able to hire (5,000) equals the number of people who are willing and able to work (5,000). We conclude that $7.75 is the equilibrium wage rate. There is no tendency for the wage rate to rise or fall. (Why? Because there is no shortage or surplus of labor.)

In General, Why Wage Rates Differ

Our discussion of supply and demand helps us to understand why some people earn higher wages than others. First, suppose that the demand for every type of labor is the same. For example, the demand for accountants is the same as the demand for construction workers, and so on. Now suppose you learn that the equilibrium wage rate for accountants is higher than the wage rate for construction workers. If demand for the two types of labor is the same, how would we account for the difference in wage rates? Obviously, the supply of accountants and the supply of construction workers must not be the same. If accountants earn more than construction workers, it must be because the supply of accountants is less than the supply of construction workers. We conclude that *wage rates can differ because supply conditions for different types of labor are not the same.*

Now, suppose instead that supply conditions for different types of labor *are* the same. For example, the supply of bank tellers is the same as the supply of car mechanics. If car mechanics earn more than bank tellers, what would explain the difference? Obviously, the demand for bank tellers and car mechanics must not be the same. We conclude that *wage rates can differ because demand conditions for different types of labor are not the same.*

We can combine these two conclusions and state that, in general, *wage rates may differ because the demand conditions for different types of labor are not the same or because the supply conditions for different types of labor are not the same.*

The Demand for a Good and Wage Rates

John lives in Detroit and works in a factory helping to produce cars. Suppose the demand for cars decreases. (See Exhibit 7-3a.) What do you think will happen?

The process works this way: If the demand for cars decreases, then car companies do not need to hire as many people to produce cars, so the demand for workers decreases. (See Exhibit 7-3b.) As the demand for workers decreases and the supply stays constant, the wage rate decreases.

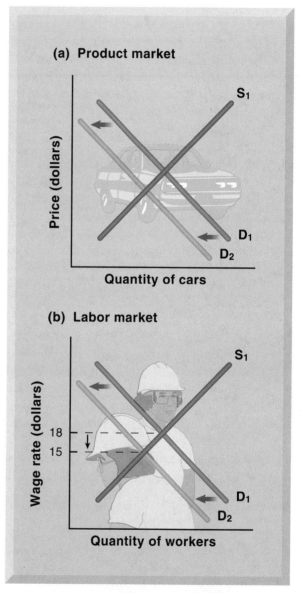

▲ **EXHIBIT 7-3**. **The Demand for Cars, the Demand for the Workers Who Produce the Cars, and Their Wage Rates.** The demand for cars affects the demand for the workers who produce the cars and their wages. Part *a*: The demand for cars falls. As a result, car companies do not need as many workers. Part *b*: The demand for car workers falls. As a result of this, wage rates fall from $18 to $15 per hour.

ECONOMIC FOCUS

Workers in different states do not earn the same wage rate. In Exhibit S-7-1 we list the average hourly wage (average wage rate) of production workers in each of the 50 states in 1992. Notice that the average wage rate in Michigan for a production worker is $14.81, the highest of any state. The average wage rate in South Dakota is $8.84, the lowest of any state. The production worker in Michigan gets an average of $5.97 an hour more than the production worker in South Dakota. In an eight-hour day, this difference adds up to $47.76 ($5.97 × 8 = $47.76). In a five-day workweek, the difference adds up to $238.80 ($47.76 × 5 = $238.80).

Why does a production worker in Michigan earn more than a production worker in South Dakota? There may be a number of reasons. First, we need to be careful about what we mean by a production worker. Michigan is known for its automobile industry; many of the production workers in Michigan are automobile workers. This is not the case in South Dakota. Suppose production workers in South Dakota mainly consist of agricultural machinery workers. In this chapter we said that the demand for a person's labor is dependent upon the demand for the product the worker helps to produce; if the demand for cars is greater than the demand for agricultural machinery, then the demand for auto workers will be greater than the demand for agricultural machinery workers, all other things remaining the same. Consequently, wage rates for auto workers will be higher than wage rates for agricultural machinery workers. In conclusion, one reason that a production worker in Michigan may earn more than a production worker in South Dakota is that the Michigan worker's product may be in greater demand than the South Dakota worker's product.

Another way to make this point is to look at another group of workers. Suppose writers in North Carolina earn an average of $30,000 a year and writers in Florida earn an average of $75,000 a year. Someone may say that this is unfair. But suppose the writers in Florida are mainly writing advertising copy and the writers in North Carolina are mainly writing novels. The demand for advertising copy may be greater than the demand for novels, and this fact is reflected in the earnings of writers in the two states.

Now let's make things harder for ourselves. Let's suppose that workers in two states are producing the same product, but that the production workers in one state are earning a higher wage rate than the production workers in the other state. For example, the production workers in Massachusetts, earning $12.15 an hour, are producing the same product (with the same tools) as the production workers in Mississippi earning $8.90 an hour. In a situation like this, we may wonder why some of the workers in Mississippi don't simply move to Massachusetts and earn the higher wage rate.

One reason this doesn't happen may be because many of the workers in Mississippi were born and raised in Mississippi, and they would prefer to live and work there, earning less, than to live and work in Massachusetts, earning more. A typical production worker in Mississippi may prefer to earn $8.90 an hour and have his friends and family nearby than to move to Massachusetts and earn $12.15 an hour and not have any friends and family nearby. (Of course, with time he would make friends in Massachusetts, but the

WAGES ACROSS THE STATES

▲ **EXHIBIT S-7-1**. The Average Hourly Wage (Wage Rate) of Production Workers by State.

STATE	AVERAGE HOURLY WAGE	STATE	AVERAGE HOURLY WAGE
Michigan	$14.81	Oklahoma	$11.39
Washington	13.58	Colorado	11.31
Ohio	13.53	Kentucky	11.28
Indiana	12.82	Missouri	11.23
New Jersey	12.59	Montana	11.23
Maryland	12.50	New Hampshire	11.22
Connecticut	12.47	Utah	11.09
Delaware	12.34	Wyoming	11.08
Louisiana	12.21	Arizona	10.98
California	12.19	Texas	10.92
Massachusetts	12.15	Alaska	10.75
West Virginia	12.12	Virginia	10.71
Oregon	11.98	Nebraska	10.22
Iowa	11.93	Tennessee	10.12
Minnesota	11.92	Alabama	10.00
Pennsylvania	11.86	Rhode Island	9.92
Wisconsin	11.86	Georgia	9.86
Illinois	11.85	New Mexico	9.70
New York	11.72	Florida	9.61
Hawaii	11.61	North Dakota	9.61
Kansas	11.61	North Carolina	9.50
Nevada	11.55	South Carolina	9.48
Vermont	11.52	Arkansas	9.05
Idaho	11.42	Mississippi	8.90
Maine	11.40	South Dakota	8.84

SOURCE: U.S. Bureau of the Census, *Statistical Abstract of the United States: 1993,* 113th edition. Data are for 1992.

U.S. ECONOMIC FOCUS (continued)

time it takes him to do this may not be worth the higher wage rate.)

There may be another reason, too. In Chapter 4, we listed the median price of a house in each of the 50 states. The median price of a house in Massachusetts was $162,800; the median price of a house in Mississippi was $45,600. The worker in Mississippi may be attracted to the higher wage rate in Massachusetts, but also be attracted to the lower house prices in Mississippi. It may be that he is more attracted by the lower house prices in Mississippi than the higher wage rates in Massachusetts, thus choosing to stay in Mississippi. Stated differently, he may wonder what is the use of a higher wage rate in Massachusetts if he will have to end up spending more to buy the same style and size of house he could buy in Mississippi for less.

In both the example of the friends and family and the example of the lower house prices in Mississippi, we identified something that compensated the production workers in Mississippi for earning less than their counterparts in Massachusetts. When economists see a difference in wage rates paid to workers in different states, they don't naturally jump to the conclusion that something is very unfair. Often, they realize that there is something that is gained in the lower-wage-rate location to compensate for the higher wage rate in the other location.

To see this from a different perspective, let's change our example. Suppose now that not only do workers in Mississippi produce the same product as the workers in Massachusetts, but suppose everything—yes, everything!—in the two states is identical except for the fact that the wage rate is higher in Massachusetts. We wonder how long it will stay higher with everything the same.

Under these conditions, workers in Mississippi would move to Massachusetts. (Why not? Massachusetts is the same as Mississippi, remember: same friends and family, same house prices, same everything.) As workers from Mississippi move to Massachusetts, the supply of production workers in Massachusetts increases and the supply of production workers in Mississippi decreases. Consequently, the wage rate decreases (from $12.15) in Massachusetts and the wage rate increases (from $8.90) in Mississippi. Workers in Mississippi will continue to move to Massachusetts until there is no reason to move. And this will only occur when the wage rate in the two states is the same.

1. Looking at Exhibit S-7-1, you will notice that the wage rate for production workers in Hawaii is the same as the wage rate in Kansas. Does this mean that Hawaii is identical to Kansas? Explain your answer. (Hint: The fact that a calculator and a radio are each $30 doesn't mean they are the same product.)

2. Schoolteachers in Alaska are usually paid a higher salary than schoolteachers in any of the remaining 49 states. What do you think is the reason?

We conclude that the demand for cars (or any good) and the wage rates of the employees who produce cars (or any good) decrease and increase together. For example, as the demand for cars decreases, the wages of the employees who produce cars decrease.

Government and Wages

The **minimum wage law** sets a *wage floor*—that is, a level below which wages rates are not allowed to fall. The law, passed during the Great Depression of the 1930s, initially established a minimum wage of 25 cents an hour. In April 1991, the minimum wage was set at $4.25 an hour. This meant that employers could not legally pay their employees less than $4.25 an hour.

Who or what determines what the minimum wage will be—whether it will be $4.25 or $3.25 or $5.25? The answer is, the Congress of the United States.

Earlier, you read that supply and demand determine wage rates. Now it appears that the Congress of the United States determines a particular wage—the minimum wage. What is going on? It is simple. Supply and demand are not always *allowed* to determine wages.

To illustrate, suppose that in a particular labor market the equilibrium wage rate is $3.10 an hour. In other words, the demand for and the supply of labor intersect at a wage rate of $3.10. Congress then argues that a wage rate of $3.10 an hour is too low. It orders employers to pay employees at least $4.25 an hour. This rate is then the minimum wage. It becomes unlawful to pay an employee less than this hourly wage.

QUESTION: *If the equilibrium wage rate (in some subset of the labor market) was $3.10 an hour, wouldn't Congress be justified in raising the wage rate to some higher level? Isn't $3.10 an hour just too low?*

ANSWER: *In economics, we are not as interested in what government is justified in doing as we are in the effects of what government does. Economists ask, "What are the effects of government's setting the minimum wage rate above the equilibrium wage rate?" For example, do you think employers will hire as many workers at the minimum wage rate of $4.25 as they would at the equilibrium wage rate of $3.10? The answer is no. Remember, the demand curve for labor is downward sloping. This means that as the wage rate falls, employers will hire more workers; and as the wage rate rises, employers will hire fewer workers. We conclude that a minimum wage rate that is set by Congress above the equilibrium wage rate will result in employers being willing and able to hire fewer workers.*

MINI GLOSSARY

Minimum Wage Law A federal law that specifies the lowest hourly wage rate that can be paid to workers.

 ## LEARNING CHECK

1. "Everyone who works receives a wage that has been determined by supply and demand." Do you agree or disagree? Explain your answer.
2. Why do wage rates differ between competitive labor markets?
3. Suppose the supply of all types of labor is the same. Does it follow that wage rates for all types of labor will be the same? Explain your answer.
4. Explain how the minimum wage law can put some people out of work.
5. Specify the relationship between the demand for radios and the wage rate of the workers who produce radios.

In 1991, approximately 16 percent of the work force in the United States belonged to a labor union. This amounted to approximately 16 million workers. A **labor union** is an organization that seeks to increase the wages and improve the working conditions of its members. This section discusses the practices and effects of labor unions.

As you read, keep these key questions in mind:

- How might labor unions affect the demand for and supply of union labor?
- What is a union shop?
- What is the purpose of a strike?

Some Practices of Labor Unions

One objective of a labor union, at times, is to obtain higher pay for its members. This means it must direct its activities to increasing the demand for its labor, or decreasing the supply of its labor, or both. First, we consider labor union practices aimed at increasing demand.

The Demand for Union Labor. As stated earlier, if the demand for a good decreases, then the demand for the labor that produces the good decreases, too. For example, if the demand for cars decreases, then the demand decreases for the workers that produce cars. If the demand for cars increases, of course, the demand increases for the workers that produce cars.

With that in mind, suppose you are a union worker in the American automobile industry, centered in Detroit, Michigan. Would you want the demand for American-made cars to increase, stay constant, or decrease? Obviously, you would want the demand for American-made cars to increase, because you know that if it increases, the demand for your labor increases, too. And as the demand for your labor increases, your wage rate increases, all other things remaining the same.

What might your labor union do to try to get the demand to increase for the product it produces? It might launch an advertising campaign urging people to purchase only union-produced goods. For example, in recent years, television commercials have been shown urging people to "look for the union label"—in other words, buy union-made goods. Also, when American union workers are in competition with workers in other countries (as, for example, American car workers are in competition with Japanese car workers), they may urge people to buy goods "made in the U.S.A."—another union slogan in recent years.

Unions also know that if they can increase the productivity of their membership, employers will have a greater demand for their workers. Productivity relates to how much output labor can produce. For example, if Jones can produce more radios per hour than Smith, we would say that Jones is more productive than Smith. Firms have a higher demand for more productive workers. Because of this, some unions provide training programs for new entrants. The training programs are meant to increase the productivity of workers.

The Supply of Union Labor. Now let's turn to union activities involving supply. Suppose you work as a truck driver. Would you prefer to be one of 1,000 truck drivers in the United States, or one of 10,000 truck drivers? Your answer probably is "one of 1,000." You know that if the supply of truck drivers is less, then your wage rate will be higher, all other things remaining the same.

Some critics of labor unions charge that labor unions do, at times, try to control the supply of labor. In the past, some unions tried to do this through their support for **closed shops**. A closed shop is an organization that hires only union members. For example, what if, in the construction industry in a certain area, many companies were closed shops? In order for a person to work for these companies, he or she would first have to join the labor union. The labor union, in turn, might hold down the number of workers that could join (and thus work in the construction industry) in order to keep the supply of construction workers low and keep wage rates high. The union could perhaps do this by limiting membership, or by requiring long training periods. Today, the closed shop is illegal. It was prohibited by the **Taft-Hartley Act**, passed by the U.S. Congress in 1947.

The **union shop**, however, is legal in many states. A union shop does not require individuals to be union members in order to be hired, but it does require employees to join the union within a certain period of time after being hired. Labor unions favor union shops, because if everyone working in a particular trade or industry has to become a member of the union within a certain period of time, the labor union gains greater control over the supply of labor. For example, consider the **strike**, a work stoppage called by union members to put pressure on an employer. It is easier for the union to call a strike if everyone in a particular trade or industry is a member of the union.

Today, 21 states have passed **right-to-work laws**, which make it illegal to require union membership for purposes of employment. In short, in states with right-to-work laws, the union shop is illegal. Exhibit 7-4 lists the states that have passed right-to-work laws.

MINI GLOSSARY

Labor Union An organization that seeks to increase the wages and improve the working conditions of its members.

Closed Shop An organization that hires only union members.

Taft-Hartley Act An act, passed in 1947 by the U.S. Congress, which gave states the right to pass right-to-work laws. These right-to-work laws prohibit employers from establishing union membership as a condition of employment.

Union Shop An organization that requires employees to join the union within a certain period after being hired.

Strike A work stoppage called by members of a union to place pressure on an employer.

Right-to-Work Law A state law that prohibits the practice of requiring employees to join a union in order to work.

States that have right-to-work laws

▲ **EXHIBIT 7-4. States That Have Right-to-Work Laws.** In the 21 states that have right-to-work laws, the union shop is illegal.

CASE STUDY

A Brief History of the Labor Movement

National unionism began to emerge in the United States after the Civil War. This discussion begins at that point.

The Knights of Labor

In 1869, a union organization called the Knights of Labor was organized. Seventeen years later, in 1886, its membership totaled approximately 800,000. The Knights of Labor welcomed anyone who worked for a living—farmers, skilled workers, and unskilled workers—with a few exceptions, such as liquor dealers. The Knights of Labor called for higher wages and an eight-hour working day.

On May 4, 1886, approximately 100,000 members of the Knights of Labor demonstrated in front of the McCormick Harvester Works in Haymarket Square in Chicago. Some people tossed a bomb into the crowd, and a riot erupted in which several people were killed. Public sentiment soon turned against the Knights of Labor, although no wrongdoing on its part was proved, and the union began to lose membership. In 1917, it collapsed.

The American Federation of Labor

The American Federation of Labor (AFL) was formed in 1886 under the leadership of Samuel Gompers, who ran the organization until his death in 1924. Gompers believed that the AFL should consist mainly of skilled workers. Membership in the AFL was approximately 2 million in 1904, rising to 5 million in 1920 and then falling to 3 million in 1930. Its activities were almost solely directed to lobbying for better pay and improved working conditions for its members.

◄ The Haymarket riot: What started off as a Knights of Labor demonstration at Haymarket Square in Chicago in 1886, ended up as a riot.

CASE STUDY (continued)

The Courts in the Early Days

In the early days of the labor union movement, the courts had treated unions as illegal conspiracies. Union leaders had regularly been prosecuted and sued for damages. In 1842, in an important case decided by the Supreme Court of Massachusetts, the court ruled that unions were not illegal but that certain union practices were. For example, later, the Sherman Antitrust Act, which was passed by Congress in 1890, began to be applied to labor unions, although many persons said that Congress had only intended it to be applied to businesses. The Sherman Act declared that "every person who shall . . . combine or conspire with any other person or persons, to monopolize any part of the trade or commerce . . . shall be guilty of a misdemeanor."

During this period, injunctions were used against labor unions to prevent strikes and some other activities. (Injunctions are court orders that were originally designed to prevent damage to property when it was thought that other court processes would be too slow.) Owing to the use of injunctions by employers during this period, labor unions found it very difficult to strike.

The Norris-LaGuardia and Wagner Acts

The legal climate in which labor unions operated changed dramatically in 1932 with the passage of the Norris-LaGuardia Act by the U.S. Congress. The main thrust of the act was to restrain the use of injunctions. It declared that workers should be "free from the interference, restraint, or coercion of employers" in choosing their union representatives.

In 1935, Congress passed the Wagner Act, which required employers to bargain in good faith with workers; it also made it illegal for employers to interfere with their employees' rights to organize or join a union. In addition, the act set up the National Labor Relations Board (NLRB) to investigate unfair labor practices. Union membership grew by leaps and bounds as a result of the Norris-LaGuardia and Wagner Acts.

The Congress of Industrial Organizations

Because of the better legal climate for labor unions, a push was made to unionize major industries such as steel and automobiles. This caused some discontent within the AFL. The AFL was largely made up of *craft unions*—unions made up of individuals who practice the same craft or trade (for example, everyone within a particular craft union may be a plumber, or an electrician, or the like). Some people within the AFL wanted to unionize people only into craft unions. Others wanted to extend unions to include everyone in a particular industry, whether or not they all practiced the same craft. For example, people doing many different jobs in the automobile industry would belong to the same union. Such a union is called an *industrial union*. In 1938, John L. Lewis of the United Mine Workers broke with the AFL and formed the Congress of Industrial Organizations (CIO). The CIO successfully unionized the steel, rubber, textile, meat-packing, and automobile industries along industrial union lines.

For a time, both the AFL and the CIO increased their memberships. Then, after World War II, membership in the CIO began to decline. Some persons thought that the bickering between the AFL and the CIO was the cause. In 1955, the AFL, a craft union, and the CIO, an industrial union, merged under the leadership of George Meany into the AFL-CIO.

CASE STUDY (continued)

The Taft-Hartley Act

The congressional sentiment that made the Wagner Act possible in 1935 began to shift after World War II. A few particularly damaging strikes in 1946 set the stage for the Taft-Hartley Act in 1947. This act gave states the right to pass right-to-work laws. As stated earlier, these laws prohibit unions from requiring employers to make union membership a condition of employment.

The Landrum-Griffin Act

Congress passed the Landrum-Griffin Act in 1959 with the intent of policing the internal affairs of labor unions. The act calls for regular union elections and secret ballots and requires union leaders to report on their unions' finances. It also prohibits ex-convicts and communists from holding union office. The Landrum-Griffin Act was passed because during the late 1950s the American public became concerned over reports that some labor union leaders had misappropriated funds and were involved in corruption.

The Growth in Public Employee Unions

A public employee union is a union whose members work for the local, state, or federal government. By far the most important development in the labor movement in the 1960s and 1970s was the sharp growth in public employee union membership. The main issue raised by public employee unions is the right to strike. Public employee unions feel they should be able to exercise this right, but their opponents argue that public sector strikes—by police and fire fighters, for example—could have a crippling effect on society.

▲ Fire fighters are often members of public-employee unions.

1. Do you think it was right for the courts, in the early days of labor unions, to issue injunctions that prevented strikes and other union activities? Why or why not?
2. What did the Norris-LaGuardia Act accomplish?
3. What did the Taft-Hartley Act accomplish?
4. Do you think public employee unions should have the right to strike? Why or why not?

Unions' Effects on Union and Nonunion Wages

On average, do union workers receive higher pay than comparable nonunion labor? (By saying *comparable* nonunion labor, we are comparing union and nonunion workers who do essentially the same work.) One important economics study concluded that over the period of 1920–1979, the *average wage* of union members was 10-to-15 percent higher than that of comparable nonunion labor. That is, for every $100 earned by nonunion labor, comparable union labor earned between $110 and $115.

There is an economic reason for believing these results. We can see this by examining a simple example, illustrated in Exhibit 7-5. Suppose there are 100 persons in the labor force. Currently, 25 of these persons are members of a union, and 75 are

not. We'll assume that each of the 100 persons can work in either the union or the nonunion part of the economy. Furthermore, we assume that each of the 100 persons currently earns a wage rate of $8.

Suppose now that the labor union (of which 25 persons are members) calls a strike and ends up bargaining its way to a wage rate of $9. At $9 per hour, the businesses that currently employ union labor do not wish to employ as many persons as they wished to employ at a wage rate of $8, so a few of the union workers get fired. Let's say that five workers get fired.

The five union workers who have been fired seek jobs in the nonunion part of the economy. As a result, the supply of persons in the nonunion part rises (from 75 to 80). An increase in the supply of labor puts downward pressure on wage rates in the nonunion part of the economy. We'll assume the wage rate moves down from $8 to $7.50.

Most studies support the conclusion that union

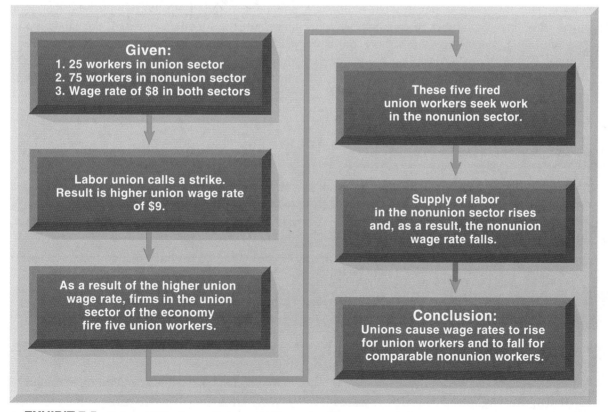

▲ **EXHIBIT 7-5**. Unions' Effects on Union and Nonunion Wages.

labor earns more than comparable nonunion labor. For example, throughout most of the 1980s, weekly earnings were higher for union labor than for comparable nonunion labor in the mining, construction, manufacturing, retail, and services parts of the economy. The dollar differences varied, though. For example, there was a difference of only $4 in mining, whereas there was a difference of approximately $200 in construction.

Two Views of Labor Unions

There are two major views of labor unions' effects on production and efficiency.

The Traditional (or Orthodox) View.   The traditional view holds that labor unions are an obstacle to establishing reasonable work standards. Consequently, they end up making companies that employ union labor less competitive. For example, suppose some members of a plumbers' union work for a manufacturing company. The union may insist that only a plumber in this company (and no one else) can change the washer on a leaky faucet. The critics of labor unions argue that such rigid staffing requirements are unreasonable and that they make these companies less competi-

tive in a world economy. When a company loses its competitive edge, it may end up going out of business.

A New View: The Labor Union as a Collective Voice.   There is evidence that in some industries, union firms have a higher rate of productivity than nonunion firms. Economists explain this by saying that the labor union plays a role as a collective-voice mechanism for its members. Without a labor union, some argue, workers who are disgruntled with their jobs, feel taken advantage of by their employers, or feel unsafe in their work would leave their jobs and seek work elsewhere. This "job exiting" comes at a cost. It raises training costs for the firm, and it results in lengthy job searches during which those searching for jobs are not producing goods. Such costs can be reduced, it is argued, when a labor union acts as a collective voice for its members. Instead of individual employees' having to discuss ticklish employment matters with their employers, the labor union does it for them. Overall, the labor union makes the employees feel more confident, less intimidated, and more secure in their work. Such positive feelings usually mean happier, more productive employees.

 LEARNING CHECK

1. If the demand for computers rises, and you work at a factory producing computers, would you expect the demand for your labor services to increase, decrease, or remain constant?
2. What is a union shop?
3. How do unions affect union wages? How do unions affect nonunion wages?

SECTION 3   THE CHALLENGE FOR LABOR IN FUTURE YEARS

Some economists have recently argued that there are economic forces loose in the world that will greatly affect the workplace in the mid-to-late 1990s. We talk about these forces in this section and consider how the labor market of to-

morrow might be different from the labor market of the early 1990s.

As you read, keep this key question in mind:

■ What are the three major economic forces currently affecting the workplace?

Major Economic Forces Affecting the Workplace

Economists who specialize in the study of labor markets say that there are three major economic forces currently affecting the workplace: global competition, technology, and downsizing.

Global Competition. On March 10, 1993, the *Wall Street Journal* printed a story that mentioned a California worker, Yolanda Navarro, who had lost her job as a vegetable packer at Green Giant, a unit of the Pillsbury Company. She had lost her job because her employer had moved its operation to Mexico. Green Giant argued that it moved its operation because it wanted to be closer to East Coast markets. Yolanda Navarro argued that Green Giant moved its operation because it wanted to reduce its labor costs. Navarro earned $7.71 an hour at the time she lost her job, which was significantly above the hourly wage paid to vegetable packers in Mexico.

The **global competition** that American labor faces from relatively low-wage nations is real, but it is not the only factor to consider. Companies may prefer to pay lower wages rather than higher wages, but they also care about the productivity of the labor they hire. To illustrate, suppose there are two countries, A and B. In Country A, wage rates are $10 an hour, and in Country B, wage rates are $4 an hour. Furthermore, assume that workers in Country A are more productive than workers in Country B. Each worker in Country A can produce 10 units of good X in an hour, whereas each worker in Country B can produce 2 units of this good in an hour. Certainly, wages are lower in Country B than in Country A, but productivity is higher in Country A than in Country B. In fact, it is so much higher that it is cheaper for a company to hire the higher-priced labor than the lower-priced labor. With each $10-an-hour worker the company hires, it receives 10 units of good X an hour, for a cost of $1 per unit per hour ($10 ÷ 10 = $1). With each $4-an-hour worker the company hires, it receives 2 units of good X an hour, for a cost of $2 per unit per hour ($4 ÷ 2 = $2).

▲ Sometimes U.S. companies will locate factories in countries where wages are relatively low. These workers are employed at a Chrysler factory in Mexico.

Let's return to our example of Yolanda Navarro. Suppose she was right that Green Giant moved its operation to Mexico in order to pay lower wages. This would only have made sense if Mexican vegetable packers (1) were more productive than American vegetable packers, (2) were as productive as American vegetable packers, or (3) were less productive than American packers but received wages so much lower that the company still saved money by moving its operation.

In a national economy, a worker competes with other workers in the same nation. For example, a worker in Colorado might compete in terms of wages and productivity with a worker in Arizona. But in a global economy, such as exists today, a

MINI GLOSSARY

Global Competition Competition from all over the world. American business firms and workers today are said to be faced with global competition.

ECONOMICS AND PEOPLE

Francisco Hernandez Juarez

In the early 1990s, Mexico, under the leadership of President Carlos Salinas, was beginning to change its economy. Salinas's objective was to move Mexico from the status of a poor nation to a moderately rich nation. To accomplish this objective, Mexico had to recognize that it had to become part of the global economy, it had to be competitive, and many of its outdated rules and regulations had to be tossed aside.

In this environment, we find Francisco Hernandez Juarez, head of the 50,000-member telephone workers' union. He was a new kind of labor leader for Mexico. Previously, it had been said that labor union leaders would demand higher wages for workers even when the Mexican companies that employed the workers were so hurt by foreign competition that they couldn't afford the wage hikes. Francisco Hernandez Juarez realized that if there is no company, there will be no labor union.

Hernandez Juarez's plan was to try to increase the productivity of the workers and then have the wage hikes follow. In his speeches to workers, he would often remind them that they were now living in a global economy, with increased competition, and that they had to work hard and smart to do well in this new economic environment.[a]

Hernandez Juarez also had the reputation of being extremely watchful over the workers in his union. For example, when the Mexican telephone company first began to replace old switchboards with new computerized workstations, Hernandez Juarez made sure that the equipment was designed to minimize computer-stress injuries. He also insisted that the company retrain any of the workers who would lose their jobs once the computerized system was in place.

Many Mexicans believe that a labor union leader like Hernandez Juarez is essential to the success of Mexico's economy in the late 1990s and beyond. In a global economy, where employers can shop the world over for high-skilled, relatively low-cost workers, it is important to have labor leaders who understand worldwide competition and are willing to stress productivity and cooperation as a way to a better economic life.

1. What labor union did Hernandez Juarez lead?
2. How might an old-time labor union leader be different from Hernandez Juarez when it comes to wage hikes?

---

a. Juanita Darling, "The Battle for Control of Mexico's Unions," *Los Angeles Times*, April 4, 1993, Section D, p. 1.

---

worker in Colorado will be competing not only with a worker in Arizona but also with a worker in Mexico and with workers in many other nations, too.

The story of Yolanda Navarro is instructive. One way to make sure you do not lose your job in

a highly competitive world is to make sure you are more productive than most people. In today's world—and tomorrow's, too—this largely means acquiring an education. The educated have, on average, always earned higher incomes than the less educated; but in recent years, the gap between the two has grown. For example, in 1980, a college-educated worker earned, on average, 33 percent more than a worker with only a high-school diploma. In 1990, a college-educated worker earned over 60 percent more than a worker with only a high-school diploma. Also, in 1992, the *Economic Report of the President* stated that "educational attainment is one of the primary characteristics that distinguishes high-income from low-income workers. . . . The earnings premium for college-educated workers over the last two decades is consistent with a steadily increasing demand in the market for their skills." The report went on to say that "the current wage premium paid to college-educated workers should serve as an incentive for high-school students to go to college." In the 1993 edition of the report, it was stated that "estimates suggest that an additional year of schooling increases wages by about 10 percent, on average."

Technology. Technology has made the automation of routine tasks commonplace. For example, more and more people who work in companies processing orders and tracking inventories are finding that their jobs are becoming computerized. Increasingly, it is becoming important to have the skills to work with, rather than against, technology.

Downsizing. Many of America's biggest companies have been restructuring themselves and getting smaller in the process—they have been **downsizing**. For example, between 1982 and 1992, the nation's 500 largest manufacturing companies eliminated 4 million jobs. This was part of the move to become less costly and more efficient companies in a highly competitive global economy.

▲ These students are learning to work with computers so that they will have the skills necessary to work in today's workplace and in the workplace of tomorrow.

MINI GLOSSARY

Downsizing Restructuring a firm and decreasing its size so that it is a less costly, more productive, more efficient operation.

 LEARNING CHECK

1. Why is it not necessarily the case that companies will end up hiring low-wage workers instead of high-wage workers?
2. According to the 1993 *Economic Report of the President*, by how much, on average, does an additional year of schooling increase one's wages?
3. According to economists who specialize in the study of labor markets, what are the three major economic forces currently affecting the workplace?

We have been discussing people who work at jobs in the labor force. Not everyone who wants to work is working, however. There are some people who are unemployed. We consider the facts and figures of unemployment next.

As you read, keep these key questions in mind:

■ What two categories comprise the civilian labor force?
■ What two major categories comprise the noninstitutional adult civilian population?
■ How do we calculate the unemployment rate?
■ How do we calculate the employment rate?
■ If the unemployment rate is 10 percent, does it follow that the employment rate is 90 percent?

Who Are the Unemployed?

Start with the total population of the United States. Next, divide the population into two broad groups. One group consists of persons who are (1) under 16 years of age, (2) in the armed forces, or (3) in a mental or correctional facility. The other group, which consists of all others in the total population, is called the *noninstitutional adult civilian population*.

Now take the noninstitutional adult civilian population and divide it into two groups. The first group consists of those persons *not in the labor force*. The second group consists of those persons in the *civilian labor force*.

Who are those persons not in the labor force? They are persons who are neither working nor looking for work. For example, retired persons fall into this category, as do persons engaged in housework in their own homes and persons who choose not to work.

Persons in the civilian labor force can be categorized as being either *employed* or *unemployed*. Exhibit 7-6 diagrams the classification scheme.

How Do You Know If You're Employed or Unemployed?

On the surface, the question "How do you know if you're employed or unemployed?" is silly. You

◀ These people, currently unemployed, are seeking information on job opportunities.

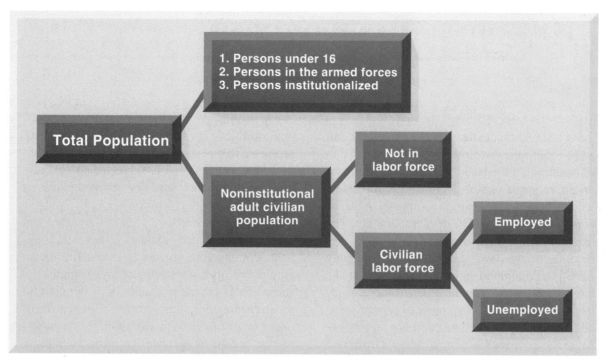

▲ **EXHIBIT 7-6**. **Breakdown of the Total U.S. Population by Employment Status.** In the early to middle 1990s, the noninstitutional adult civilian population was about 190 million persons, and the civilian labor force was about 125 million persons, of whom about 117 million were employed and about 8 million were unemployed.

might say that you know if you're employed or unemployed by simply answering this question: Do you have a job? If the answer is yes, you are employed. If the answer is no, you are unemployed.

Unfortunately, things are not this simple. For example, suppose Frank, age 20, worked 12 hours last week as an "unpaid" worker on his father's farm. Furthermore, Frank is not looking for work. Would you consider him to be employed or unemployed? Some people would say Frank is unemployed because he is not earning a wage, whereas others would say he is employed because he is working at a job.

To clarify the situation, let's turn to the official government definitions of unemployed and employed persons.

A person is employed if he or she:

1. Did at least one hour of work as a paid employee during the past week, or

2. Worked in his or her own business or profession, or

3. Worked at least 15 hours per week as an "unpaid" worker on a family-owned farm or business, or

4. Was temporarily absent from work for reasons of illness, vacation, strike, or bad weather.

A person is unemployed if he or she:

1. Did not work during the past week, actively looked for work within the past four weeks, is currently available for work, or

2. Is waiting to be called back to a job from which he or she has been laid off, or

3. Is waiting to report to a job within 30 days.

Let's return to the case of Frank. Frank worked 12 hours as an unpaid worker on his father's farm. Is he employed? According to our definition of an employed person, Frank would have had to work at least 15 hours as an unpaid worker on his fa-

CONSUMER ECONOMIC DECISIONS

Know Your Employee Protections and Rights

In the United States, both employees and job applicants are protected against discrimination on the basis of race, color, national origin, religion, or sex. To illustrate, suppose a woman applies for a job at Company ABC. A person at Company ABC does not hire her. The reason is simply because she is a woman. According to the law, this person at Company ABC has committed an unlawful act. He or she has discriminated against a person because of her sex. Or suppose an employee is not promoted to a higher position in a company simply because he is a member of a religion different from that of his boss. Again, there is discrimination. The law says that a person cannot be denied a promotion on the basis of religion.

An employee is also protected against sexual harassment. Sexual harassment occurs when opportunities at work, or promotions, are promised to a person in return for sexual favors, or when an employee is subjected to sexually oriented comments, sexually oriented jokes, or physical contact that is offensive.

Female employees are protected by law from being discriminated against if they are pregnant. For example, it would be unlawful for an employer to fire a female employee simply because she is pregnant. Similarly, it is unlawful to discriminate against employees because of age. For example, suppose an employer wants to fire a 54-year-old worker, who is earning $55,000 a year, and replace this person with a 25-year-old worker whom he or she can hire for $36,000. If the employer actually goes through with the firing, he or she has committed an unlawful act.

◄ It is unlawful to discriminate against this employee because of her age.

Making CONSUMER ECONOMIC DECISIONS (continued)

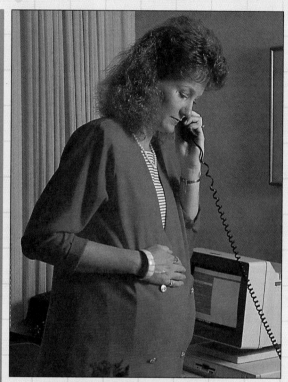

▲ It is unlawful to discriminate against female employees who are pregnant.

Just as an employee is legally entitled to a discrimination-free work environment, he or she is also entitled to a safe and healthful work environment. For example, an employee cannot be fired if she refuses to work in an area where her safety or health is threatened, such as in an area where she may inhale chemicals that can cause sickness or death. An employee is entitled to compensation if he is injured while working at his job.

Also, there are laws that relate to the wage rate an employee must be paid. As we discussed earlier in this chapter, an employee must be paid at least the federally mandated minimum wage. Also, any employee who is paid an hourly wage and who works over 40 hours a week must be paid at least 150 percent of her hourly wage (which amounts to 1.5 times the hourly wage rate). To illustrate, suppose an employee earns $10 an hour. After having worked 40 hours in a given week, she must be paid $15 an hour ($10 × 1.5 = $15) for any additional hours she works.

Finally, while employees have certain protections and rights provided, they have certain responsibilities, too. First, employees should do the jobs they are paid to do, as long as unreasonable demands are not placed upon them. Second, they should never steal any of their employers' property (even if it is a pencil or pen from the work office, or a few pieces of lumber from the lumber yard). Third, employees have the responsibility to watch out for their own safety on the job. Simply because an employer tells them it is safe to do a particular job, it does not necessarily follow that it is. The employees have the responsibility to make sure the job is safe.

---

1. It is unlawful to discriminate against an employee according to race and religion. What else might be an occasion of discrimination?

2. An employee who earns $22 an hour has worked 45 hours this past week. How much did she earn?

3. Do you think it is important to have laws that make it illegal to discriminate against an employee or job applicant on the basis of race, color, national origin, religion, or sex? Explain your answer.

ther's farm to be considered employed. Since he worked only 12 hours, Frank cannot be considered employed. Does this mean, then, that Frank is unemployed? The answer is no, since he does not meet any of the three criteria just given for an unemployed person.

If Frank is neither employed nor unemployed, what is he? Frank is *not in the labor force*. How do we know this? A quick glance at Exhibit 7-6 will help explain. First, we established that Frank is not employed. Next, we established that Frank is not unemployed. Looking at the exhibit, we can see that this means Frank cannot be part of the civilian labor force. If he is not part of the civilian labor force, but is still a part of the noninstitutional adult civilian population (which he is, since he is not under 16, in the armed forces, or institutionalized), then he must fall into the "not in the labor force" category.

The Unemployment and Employment Rates

The **unemployment rate** is the percentage of the civilian labor force that is unemployed. It is equal to the number of persons unemployed divided by the civilian labor force.

$$\text{Unemployment rate} = \frac{\text{Number of persons unemployed}}{\text{Number of persons in the civilian labor force}}$$

For example, if the number of persons unemployed is 1 million, and the labor force is 10 million, then the unemployment rate is 10 percent.

The **employment rate** is the percentage of the noninstitutional adult civilian population that is employed. It is equal to the number of persons employed divided by the number of persons in the noninstitutional population.

$$\text{Employment rate} = \frac{\text{Number of persons employed}}{\text{Number of persons in the noninstitutional adult civilian population}}$$

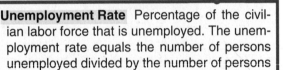

MINI GLOSSARY

Unemployment Rate Percentage of the civilian labor force that is unemployed. The unemployment rate equals the number of persons unemployed divided by the number of persons in the civilian labor force.

Employment Rate Percentage of the noninstitutional adult civilian population that is employed. The employment rate equals the number of persons employed divided by the number of persons in the noninstitutional adult civilian population.

LEARNING CHECK

1. Which of the following persons would be included in the labor force?
   a. A 13-year-old looking for a summer job.
   b. A farmer working 12 hours a day on her own farm.
   c. A full-time college student.
   d. A person working 37 hours a week as a salesclerk in a department store at the local mall.
   e. A person fired from work yesterday.
2. If a person is not employed, does it follow that he or she is necessarily unemployed? Why or why not?

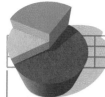

DEVELOPING ECONOMIC SKILLS

The Economics Paper: Doing the Research

In the previous chapter we discussed how to find a topic for your economics paper. We chose the example, "U.S. Businesses and Foreign Competition." What's next? It is time to do the research. One popular dictionary defines research as the "diligent and systematic inquiry into a subject in order to discover or revise facts, theories, etc."[a] Simply put, a researcher is an investigator. Think of a private investigator trying to solve a case. He or she has to pay attention to details, hunt for the facts, decide whether the current explanations make sense, and much more. As a researcher you will have to do many of the same things. Where does a researcher begin?

First, you must define your goal. You probably have a number of questions about the chosen topic. Suppose you want to know the name of the largest corporation in the world, the country with the most large corporations, the country whose corporations most intensely compete with U.S. companies, and so on. You need answers to your questions. Your goal is to learn enough about the topic that you have selected to answer many, if not all, of your questions.

The private investigator has questions also. He asks, Where should I go to get answers to my questions? Who should I talk to? The same holds true for the researcher. The place to begin your research is the library. A key person to speak with is the librarian. You might tell the librarian, "I want to write a paper on U.S. businesses and foreign competition. Here are a few of the questions I would like to answer in my paper. Where would you suggest I begin my research?" Librarians are experts at finding information. They are some of the best investigators around.

The librarian will probably begin by searching the library catalog. All libraries have a catalog that contains information on every book in the library.

The catalog is organized so that you can search for books by author, title, or subject. It will also tell you where in the library a book is located.

Some libraries have card catalogs that list the author, title, and subject information on individual index cards in large filing drawers. Today, many libraries have replaced their card catalogs with computerized catalogs. Using one of these, a person can sit down at a computer terminal in a library and search the library's resources very quickly. The catalog is the researcher's most important tool. If you don't know how to use the catalog, ask a librarian to show you.

To research the particular topic that we have chosen, we would want to search the library catalog using the subject index. To do this we would identify a couple of "key words" that pertain to the topic. We might try using the key words "foreign competition," "U.S. businesses," and "foreign firms in the U.S." The librarian might also suggest some key words to use in our search. The catalog will identify any books in your library on the subjects listed. It usually provides you with the title of the book, the author, and the call number (used to locate the book in the library). Then it is a matter of locating the books and examining them to see if they have information that is relevant to the topic.

A quick way to determine whether the books that you have located are relevant to your research is to check the index at the back of the book. Try looking for listings of the same key words that you used in the subject index of the card catalog. If you find nothing, then a quick glance through the entire index might turn up something useful.

Besides searching for information in books, you can search for information in newspapers and magazines. Many libraries subscribe to database services. A database is a collection of organized, related information in electronic form that can be accessed through a computer. For example, some companies provide a database

---

a. *Random House Webster's College Dictionary* (New York: Random House, Inc., 1992).

DEVELOPING ECONOMIC SKILLS (continued)

service on newspapers. If your school or city library is connected to a newspaper database service, you can sit down at a computer terminal and, as you did before when searching for books, type in key words pertaining to the subject of interest to you. The computer screen will then display a list of articles that contain information on your chosen subject from the newspapers in the database. If you find articles that appear to be relevant, check with the librarian to see if the library carries the newspapers that you need.

Other excellent sources of information are encyclopedias and dictionaries of economics. A widely respected encyclopedia that contains essays on hundreds of economics topics is the *International Encyclopedia of the Social Sciences.* A well-respected economics dictionary is *The Fortune Encyclopedia of Economics*, edited by David R. Henderson. An invaluable resource for researching any subject, not just economics, is the *Reader's Guide to Periodical Literature*.

There are other ways to pursue your investigation. You can talk to people who are likely to be good sources of information. Ask yourself who might know about U.S. businesses and foreign competition; perhaps someone who works at a company in your town or city who has had dealings with foreign competitors. A letter or phone call to such people might yield results.

As you are conducting your research, it is important that you take clear and detailed notes. Each time you find some information that pertains to the topic, write down a summary of what you have found. If you copy passages from any source, be sure to note that it is a quotation so that you can give proper credit in your paper. If you use someone else's words or ideas you must let your reader know that you are doing so. Also note where you find your information. It is a good habit to keep detailed bibliographic references including the name of the source, the author, the publisher, the date of publication, and the page where you found the information. This will help you when it comes time to write the

paper and it will help someone reading your paper who is interested in learning more about your topic in the sources you found.

Finally, keep in mind that research often requires a lot of somewhat tedious work (going to the library, searching for the right books, and so on). Often you will find yourself having spent hours looking for a book that ends up being of little use to you when writing your paper. That's an inevitable part of research. Research is not about finding *the* book, or coming across *the* person who can give you all the answers. It is about making the best use of all the resources available to you. Research requires you to sift through books, newspapers, journals, and other sources to find the pieces of information that will answer your questions. You will need your powers of reasoning, creativity, and determination in this search. Again, the work is similar to that of the private investigator, who spends many hours chasing leads that turn out to be dead ends. Finally, if he is persistent enough, and resourceful enough, he finds what he has been searching for. It is the same for the researcher. Persistence and resourcefulness are key ingredients to becoming a good researcher.

---

1. Choose an economics topic to research. (You may consider one of the topics you chose when working on the "Developing Economic Skills" feature in Chapter 6.) Next, visit either your school or city library (or both) and write a list of five sources (books, articles, magazines, or newspapers) which seem relevant to your topic. If any of your sources are books, identify the pages in the book which you think will be most useful. (You can do this by checking the index.)

2. Learn how to locate information by subject using your school library catalog (either the card catalog or the electronic catalog, depending on your school library). Write an explanation of how this is done at your school library.

CHAPTER 7 REVIEW

CHAPTER SUMMARY

1. The demand curve for labor is downward sloping. This means that employers are willing and able to hire more people at lower wages than at higher wages.

2. The supply curve of labor is upward sloping. This means that more people are willing and able to work at higher wages than at lower wages.

3. The equilibrium wage rate in a competitive labor market setting is the wage rate at which the number of people employers are willing and able to hire is the same as the number of people who are willing and able to be hired.

4. Wage rates may differ because the demand conditions for different types of labor are not the same or because the supply conditions for different types of labor are not the same.

5. The demand for a good and the wage rate of the employees who produce the good increase and decrease together.

6. The minimum wage rate is determined by the Congress of the United States. If the minimum wage rate is higher than the equilibrium wage rate, then employers will hire fewer workers than they would at the equilibrium wage rate.

7. The Taft-Hartley Act of 1947 gave states the right to pass right-to-work laws.

8. A specific objective of a labor union is to obtain increased pay for its members. This means it must direct its activities to increasing the demand for its labor, decreasing the supply of its labor, or both.

9. A closed shop is an organization that hires only union members. Closed shops are illegal today.

10. A union shop is an organization that requires employees to join the union within a certain period after being hired. The union shop is illegal in the 21 states that have right-to-work laws.

11. An economics study concluded that over the period 1920–1979, the average wage of union members was 10 to 15 percent higher than that of comparable nonunion labor.

12. Economists who specialize in the study of labor markets say that there are three major economic forces that will greatly affect the workplace in the mid-to-late 1990s. These forces are global competition, technology, and downsizing.

13. The noninstitutional adult civilian population consists of all people other than persons who are under 16 years of age, or are in the armed services, or are in a mental or correctional facility. This population can be broken down into two groups: (1) persons not in the labor force and (2) the civilian labor force. Persons not in the labor force are persons who are neither working nor looking for work. The civilian labor force consists of those persons either unemployed or employed.

14. The unemployment rate equals the number of persons unemployed divided by the number of persons in the civilian labor force.

15. The employment rate equals the number of persons employed divided by the number of persons in the noninstitutional adult civilian population.

CHAPTER 7 REVIEW

BUILD YOUR ECONOMIC VOCABULARY

Match the word with the correct definition, example, or statement.

1. equilibrium wage rate
2. right-to-work law
3. minimum wage
4. unemployment rate
5. closed shop
6. union shop
7. a retired person
8. a person on strike

a. an example of an employed person
b. an organization that hires only union members
c. the wage rate at which the quantity of labor supplied equals the quantity demanded
d. the number of persons unemployed divided by the number of persons in the civilian labor force
e. law that makes it illegal for employers to require union membership as a condition of employment
f. a wage rate determined by Congress
g. an organization that does not require individuals to be union members in order to be hired but does require them to join the union within a certain period
h. an example of a person not in the labor force

REVIEW QUESTIONS

1. In a competitive labor market, what happens to the wage rate when there is a surplus of labor? when there is a shortage of labor?
2. "John earns a higher wage rate than Wilson. It necessarily follows that the demand for John's labor services is greater than the demand for Wilson's labor services." Do you agree or disagree? Explain your answer.
3. Explain the relationship between the demand for a good and the wage rate of employees who produce the good.
4. "If the minimum wage rate is higher than the equilibrium wage rate, fewer people will end up working at the minimum wage rate than at the equilibrium wage rate." Do you agree or disagree? Explain your answer.
5. Is the state in which you live one of the right-to-work states?
6. Discuss two ways in which a labor union may try to affect the demand for its labor services.

7. What is the difference between a closed shop and a union shop?
8. What are unions' effects on union wages? on nonunion wages? Explain your answers.
9. If the noninstitutional adult civilian population is 190 million and there are 115 million people employed and 9 million unemployed, what does the civilian labor force equal?
10. Given your answer to question 9, calculate the unemployment rate.
11. Given the information in question 9, calculate the employment rate.
12. Economists realize that a change in one thing (such as the wage rate) often brings about a change in something else (such as the number of persons that will be offered jobs). But sometimes, other people say things that would lead us to believe that they do not understand this point. For example, someone might say that we should pay everyone who

REVIEW QUESTIONS (continued)

works as a truck driver 25 percent more than he or she is currently earning because truck drivers do an important job. The economist points out that there will be fewer persons working as truck drivers at higher wages than at lower wages, all other things remaining the same. (This is because the demand curve for workers is downward sloping.) The economist does not argue against paying truck dri-

vers (or anyone else) more. He or she simply tries to get us to recognize what will happen as a result of this change. Write an essay at least one page long in which you explain how a change in any one of the following leads to a change in something else: wage rate received by unionized labor, demand for cars, minimum wage rate.

SHARPEN YOUR CRITICAL THINKING SKILLS

1. There are four resources, or factors of production: land, labor, capital, and entrepreneurship. The payment to land is called *rent*, the payment to labor is called *wages*, the payment to capital is called *interest*, and the payment to entrepreneurship is called *profits*. If we sum the dollar amounts of rent, wages, interest, and profits, we have *total income*. (Total income = rent + wages + interest + profits.) Now, suppose we want to know the fraction of income that goes to labor. We take the payment that

goes to labor—called wages—and divide it by total income. For example, if total income is $100,000 and wages equal $75,000, then we'd say that 75 percent of total income is earned by labor ($75,000 ÷ $100,000 = 0.75). The percentage of total income earned by labor has stayed roughly the same during this century in this country. Does this fact support the hypothesis that labor unions have benefited their members *at the expense of those who earn profits*? Explain your answer.

ACTIVITIES AND PROJECTS

1. List 10 jobs that interest you. For example, you might list teacher, attorney, computer analyst, construction worker, chef, and so on. After each, specifically note what it is about the job

that interests you. Next, visit your school or city library and try to find the average salary of someone who works at each of the 10 jobs you have listed.

ECONOMIC DICTIONARY

Closed Shop (Pg. 178)
Downsizing (Pg. 187)
Employment Rate (Pg. 192)
Global Competition (Pg. 185)

Labor Union (Pg. 178)
Minimum Wage Law (Pg. 177)
Right-to-Work Law (Pg. 179)
Strike (Pg. 179)

Taft-Hartley Act (Pg. 179)
Unemployment Rate (Pg. 192)
Union Shop (Pg. 179)
Wage Rate (Pg. 170)

CHAPTER 8

Government and Business

Adam Smith, the 18th-century economist, was a major advocate of the free-enterprise system. Still, he believed that businesspersons rarely get together without talking about how they can make themselves better off at their customers' expense. His words, cited in Chapter 2, are: "People of the same trade seldom meet together, even for merriment and diversion, but the conversation ends in a conspiracy against the public, or in some contrivance to raise prices."

There are cases in which business firms "conspire against the public" and "contrive to raise prices." Most economists agree that government has a role to play in trying to prevent this and if it has already happened, in punishing the persons responsible.

Still, we have to be careful not to slip into the error of thinking that every time business and government are involved in some matter, it is business that is wrong and government that is right. Also, we should remember that sometimes government and business do things together that end up hurting the public. We consider the many ways in which government and business interact in this chapter.

SECTION 1   ANTITRUST LAW

One of the stated objectives of government is to encourage competition so that monopolists do not have substantial control over the prices they charge. The government tries to meet this objective through its **antitrust laws**, laws meant to control monopoly power and to preserve and promote competition. We examine five of the major antitrust laws in this section.

As you read, keep these key questions in mind:

- What do the antitrust acts deem illegal?
- What are the criticisms of the antitrust acts?

Ford Motor Company agrees to sell cars only in the West, General Motors agrees to sell cars only in the South and East, and Chrysler agrees to sell cars only in the North. Government authorities would likely rule that these companies were conspiring to eliminate competition and that such actions were illegal under the Sherman Antitrust Act. The word *likely* was used in the last sentence because the Sherman Antitrust Act is somewhat vague. For example, the act never explains which specific acts constitute "restraint of trade," although it declares such acts illegal.

The Sherman Act

The Sherman Act was passed in 1890. During these times, there were numerous mergers between companies. A **merger** occurs when one company buys more than half the stock in another company. A merger puts two companies under one top management. At the time of the Sherman Antitrust Act, the organization that companies formed by combining was called a **trust**; this in turn gave us the word *antitrust*.

The Sherman Act contains two major provisions:

1. "Every contract, combination in the form of trust or otherwise, or conspiracy, in restraint of trade or commerce . . . is hereby declared to be illegal."
2. "Every person who shall monopolize, or attempt to monopolize, or combine or conspire with any other person or persons to monopolize any part of the trade or commerce . . . shall be deemed guilty of a misdemeanor."

Together, these two provisions state that either attempting to become a monopolist or trying to restrain trade is illegal. For example, suppose three companies that sell basically the same product get together and promise not to compete with each other in certain regions of the country. Perhaps

The Clayton Act

The Clayton Act of 1914 made certain business practices illegal when their effects "may be to substantially lessen competition or tend to create a monopoly." The following practices were prohibited by the act:

1. *Price discrimination*. Price discrimination occurs when a seller charges different buyers different prices for the same product, and when the price differences are not related to cost differences. For example, if a company charges you $10 for a product and charges your friend $6 for the same product, and there is no cost difference for the company in providing the two of you with this product, then the company is practicing *price discrimination*.

   Now, someone might argue that this goes on every day, sometimes very innocently. For example, suppose 10-year-old Jonathan has a lemonade stand in front of his house. He advertises that he will sell a glass of lemonade for 50 cents. George, a neighbor, comes along and buys a glass for 50 cents. Then Karen, a girl Jonathan likes, comes along, and Jonathan sells her a glass of lemonade for only 5 cents. Is Jonathan price-discriminating? Probably. Does the Clayton Act apply to him? Probably not. Remember, the act says that price discrimination is only illegal when it has the effect of *substantially* lessening competition. It is doubtful that Jonathan's pricing policy in his neighborhood is substantially lessening competition in the lemonade industry.

2. *Tying contracts.* A tying contract is an arrangement whereby the sale of one product depends on the purchase of some other product or products. For example, suppose the owner of a company that sells personal computers and computer supplies agrees to sell computers to a store only if the store owner agrees to buy paper, desk furniture, and some other products, too. This agreement is a tying contract.

3. *The acquisition of competing companies' stock if the acquisition reduces competition.* For example, if Ford Motor Company acquired stock in General Motors, its competitor, the government might rule this acquisition illegal. Again, it is important to note that an acquisition must *substantially* lessen competition before the Clayton Act applies. If Ford owned one share of General Motors, this would hardly substantially lessen competition.

4. *Interlocking directorates.* An interlocking directorate is an arrangement whereby the directors of one company sit on the board of directors of another company in the same industry. For example, such an arrangement would exist if Jones, Brown, and Smith were on the board of directors of Chrysler and were also on the board of directors of Ford.

The Federal Trade Commission Act

The Federal Trade Commission Act, passed in 1914, declared illegal "unfair methods of competition in commerce." In particular, the act was designed to prohibit aggressive price-cutting acts, which sometimes are referred to as *cutthroat pricing*. For example, suppose you own a business that produces and sells tires. A competitor begins to

drastically lower the prices of the tires he sells. From your viewpoint, your competitor may be engaged in cutthroat pricing. From the viewpoint of the consumer, your competitor is simply offering a good deal. The officials who are supposed to enforce the Federal Trade Commission Act will have to decide. If they believe your competitor is cutting his prices so low that you will have to go out of business and that he intends to raise his prices later, when you're gone, they may find that he is violating the act.

Some economists have noted that the Federal Trade Commission Act, like other antitrust acts, contains vague terms. For instance, the act doesn't precisely define what "unfair methods of competition" consist of. Suppose a hotel chain puts up a big, beautiful hotel across the street from an old, tiny, run-down motel, and the old motel ends up going out of business. Was the hotel chain employing "unfair methods of competition" or not?

The Robinson-Patman Act

The Robinson-Patman Act was passed in 1936 in an attempt to decrease the failure rate of small businesses by protecting them from the competition of large and growing chain stores. At this time in our economic history, large chain stores had just begun to appear on the scene. These chain stores were buying goods in large amounts and were sometimes being offered price discounts from their suppliers. The chain stores began to pass on

MINI GLOSSARY

Antitrust Law Legislation passed for the stated purpose of controlling monopoly power and preserving and promoting competition.

Merger A joining of two companies that occurs when one company buys more than half the stock in the other company. As a result, the companies come to act as one.

Trust A combination of firms that come together to act as a monopolist.

the price discounts to their customers. The small businesses that were competing with the chains were not being offered the price discounts. Thus, they found it increasingly difficult to compete with the chain stores. The Robinson-Patman Act prohibited suppliers from offering special discounts to large chains unless they also offered the discounts to everyone else.

Many economists believe that, rather than preserving and strengthening competition, the Robinson-Patman Act limited it. The act seemed more concerned about a certain group of competitors (small businesses) than about the process of competition.

The Wheeler-Lea Act

The Wheeler-Lea Act, passed in 1938, empowered the Federal Trade Commission (FTC), a government agency, to deal with false and deceptive acts or practices by businesses. Major moves by the FTC in this area have involved advertising that the FTC has deemed false and deceptive.

LEARNING CHECK

1. In the context of antitrust law, what is a trust?
2. A company advertises its product in a deceptive manner. Which act would apply to this action?
3. Which act declares illegal "unfair methods of competition in commerce"?
4. Which act is not specific as to what acts constitute "restraint of trade"?

SECTION 2   REGULATION

Government sets up rules, or regulations, that business firms must abide by. Today, regulations are a part of the economic landscape. In the early 1990s, nearly 60,000 persons were employed in 27 regulatory agencies of the United States government. Many others were employed in smaller regulatory agencies in the federal government, and tens of thousands were employed by state and local regulatory agencies. One area in which government regulation is prominent is the area of natural monopoly. We consider this area next.

As you read, keep these key questions in mind:

- What are the two principal ways of regulating a natural monopoly?
- How does the public interest theory of regulation differ from the capture theory of regulation?

Natural Monopoly Regulation

Chapter 6 defined a *natural monopoly* as a firm that has such low average total costs that it can outcompete all other firms in the industry, thus remaining as the sole survivor. Examples of natural monopolies include local gas, water, and electricity firms. In most cities around the country, the local government grants a *public franchise* to a natural monopoly firm to supply natural gas, electricity, or the like. It does so on the stated grounds that permitting, say, a number of gas firms to compete in an area would result in many of the firms going out of business. In the process, scarce resources would have been wasted. Many local gov-

▲ In some cities, there is only one bus company. Often, this one bus company is considered a natural monopoly and, therefore, it is regulated.

ernment officials argue that it is better to permit only one company to provide a particular good or service and then to regulate this one firm. There are two principal ways in which government can and does regulate natural monopolies: price regulation and profit regulation.

Price Regulation.   Instead of allowing the regulated natural monopoly to charge any price it wants, **public utility commissions** or other government groups can set what price the monopoly can charge. These commissions need to be careful. If they set a price that is below costs, the natural monopoly will go out of business. Critics point out, though, that if the price is set slightly above costs, then the monopolist will have no incentive to hold costs down. For example, suppose a government commission rules that a regulated monopolist can charge $1 over costs for every unit sold.

In this case, would the regulated monopolist be concerned if its costs increased? Probably not. According to the government commission's rule, it can charge a higher price if its costs increase.

Profit Regulation. Another way in which government can regulate a natural monopoly is by specifying that it can earn only a certain rate of profit. Again, though, when this is the case, the monopolist may have little incentive to watch costs. If it knows a certain profit rate is guaranteed no matter what, whether costs go up or not may be immaterial to the monopolist.

Social Regulation

When the word regulation is used, different people often think of different things. Some people may think of the price and profit regulation that is part of regulating a natural monopoly, which we just discussed. Others may think of what has been referred to as *social regulation*. Social regulation is concerned with the conditions under which goods and services are produced and the safety of these items for the consumer. For example, the Occupational Safety and Health Administration (OSHA) is a regulatory government agency that is concerned with protecting workers against occupational injuries and illnesses. The Consumer Product Safety Commission (CPSC) specifies minimum standards for potentially unsafe products. For example, a business firm can't simply make any type of toy to sell, but only toys that aren't likely to be harmful when children use them. The Environmental Protection Agency (EPA) regulates business firms as to the amount of pollution they can emit into the air or rivers.

MINI GLOSSARY

Public Utility Commission Government group that regulates public utility companies (such as electric, water, and gas companies).

CONSUMER ECONOMIC DECISIONS

Understanding Your Consumer Rights

As stated earlier in the chapter, the Federal Trade Commission Act was passed in 1914. The act created the Federal Trade Commission (FTC). The powers of the FTC were enlarged in 1938 through the passage of the Wheeler-Lea Act. Today, the FTC is principally involved in bringing court cases against businesses involved in unfair trade practices, monitoring business practices that affect consumers, providing consumers with information, and moving against advertising that is deemed false and deceptive. We look at a few FTC rules in this section.

Door-to-Door Sales

Suppose a door-to-door salesperson comes to your home and urges you to subscribe to some magazines. You tell him that you do not want to subscribe to any magazines. He continues to talk about how much pleasure and knowledge you will gain from the magazines. You still say no. He urges you to subscribe. Finally, tired of his high-pressure tactics, you subscribe to a few magazines. You write him a check for $40, and he tells you the magazines will arrive in approximately two weeks.

The next day you feel awfully bad about having made the purchase. If you had it to do over, you would say no and stick to it. The FTC says that you still have time to undo what you have done. An FTC rule states that consumers have up to three days to cancel most door-to-door sales.[a] Here is what you need to do:

---

a. In some states, the rule does not hold for purchases under $25.

1. Write a letter to the seller stating that you are canceling the purchase. (Make sure to date and sign the letter.) If you are provided with a cancellation form, then sign it.
2. Either mail the letter or form to the seller or hand-deliver it to him or her by midnight of the third business day after agreeing to the purchase.

The seller, upon receipt of your cancellation, must:

1. Cancel the order and return any papers you signed.
2. Refund any money you paid.
3. Inform you whether the merchandise will be picked up, if any merchandise was left at your home.

Receiving Unordered Merchandise by Mail

According to an FTC ruling, if you receive merchandise in the mail that you did not order, it is yours. You have no obligation to return or pay for any merchandise that is sent to you if you did not order it. Also, it is illegal for the sender of the unordered merchandise to try to pressure you to return the merchandise or to pay for it. According to the FTC, there are only two kinds of merchandise that can legally be mailed to you without your ordering them: (1) free samples of merchandise that are clearly marked "free" and (2) merchandise mailed by a charitable organization for contributions. For example, some charitable organizations mail address labels to people and ask in turn for a donation. Although the charitable organization can legally mail these labels, the recipient is under no obligation to make a donation.

Buying Eyeglasses

Let's suppose you go to the eye doctor (optometrist or ophthalmologist) and get your eyes examined. The doctor tells you that you need glasses and that you can buy them from him. He has a complete selection in the main entrance to his office. So far, he has not given you a prescription for your glasses. He simply tells you to pick out the glasses you want to buy and he'll have them made up for you.

According to an FTC ruling, the doctor has trampled on your consumer rights. He is obligated to give you the prescription so that you can go anywhere you want to purchase your glasses. This is called the *eyeglass rule*, and it requires eye doctors to give patients their prescriptions immediately after an eye exam. Before the eyeglass rule was made, some doctors held back the prescription in order to pressure patients into buying eyeglasses from them. This prevented patients from shopping around and finding the best-quality glasses for the best price.

Going to Small Claims Court

Suppose you hire a person to paint your car. He agrees to do this for $200. You agree to his asking price. You pay him in advance and then you leave. When you return at the end of the day, you find your car painted light green instead of dark green. You call the person who painted your car and tell him that his work was not acceptable and that you want your car repainted the "right" color. He says that he believes he painted your car the "right" color and adds that he doesn't plan to do it over again. You ask for your money back, and he refuses to give it to you, having already deposited your check in his bank account. What can you do now?

The first thing you should do is to learn from your mistake. You paid the person before he completed the job, which is not a good practice. It is reasonable to pay a deposit up front for the work to be done (for example, 10 percent of the full payment). It is unreasonable to pay the full amount before the job has been completed and you have had time to inspect the work.

The second thing you can do is to take the person to *small claims court*. Small claims court is a trial court where cases involving claims of less than a certain amount, usually $5,000, are heard before a judge. In small claims court, you are not required to hire a lawyer to represent you. Instead, you state your own case before a judge, as does the other party. You have a right to be heard in small claims court, and it is a right that you may choose to exercise one day.

---

1. If you buy something from a door-to-door salesperson and later regret the decision, how long do you have before you can no longer get your money back?
2. A charitable organization sends you merchandise through the mail. Two days later, someone from the organization calls you and says you need to pay $20 for the merchandise. Are you legally obligated to pay?
3. What is small claims court?

◀ Government regulations require certain safety standards for cars. Critics charge that government regulations often increase the costs of producing cars. Proponents argue that the benefits of producing safer cars outweigh the costs.

As with almost any type of government regulation, not everyone agrees on its worth. Some people argue that the bulk of social regulation is too costly to taxpayers and only indicates an intrusive, meddlesome government. The proponents of social regulation believe that while the costs are high, the benefits are even higher. They say, for example, that highway fatalities would be 40 percent higher in the absence of auto safety features mandated through regulation, that mandated child-proof lids have resulted in 90 percent fewer child deaths caused by accidental swallowing of poisonous substances, and that government regulations on the use of asbestos save between 630 and 2,553 persons from dying of cancer each year.

The proponents of social regulation also argue that government regulation of, and vigilance over, business is important because atrocious things can happen without it. For example, they cite the case of Beech-Nut Nutrition Corporation, a baby food manufacturer, which, in 1987, pleaded guilty to 215 felony counts. (A felony is considered a major crime.) The company had sold millions of containers of sugar water and flavoring that it had labeled "100 percent apple juice." Also, the case of Cordis Corporation is often cited. Cordis Corporation produced and sold thousands of pacemakers that it knew were defective.[1] Many of the pacemakers failed. The company ended up pleading guilty to 25 criminal violations.

Government regulation, whether it has to do with prices and profits, consumer information, working standards, or anything else, continues to be a major topic of debate. In the next section, we hope to explain why.

The Costs and Benefits of Government Regulation

Suppose a business firm is polluting the air with smoke from its factories. The government passes an environmental regulation requiring that this business firm purchase antipollution devices that cut down on the smoke emitted into the air.

What are the benefits of this kind of regulation? First, there is cleaner air. With cleaner air, there may be fewer medical problems in the future. For

---

1. A pacemaker is an electronic device implanted in the body and connected to the wall of the heart. It is designed to provide regular, mild, electric shock that stimulates contraction of the heart muscles and restores a normal heartbeat.

example, in some cities in the nation, the pollution from cars and factories causes people to cough, feel tired, and experience eye discomfort. More importantly, some of these people go on to have continuing medical problems from constantly breathing dirty air. Government regulation that ends up reducing the amount of pollution in the air surely helps these people.

Regulation may also benefit the environment and the people who enjoy a clean environment. For example, some air pollution can harm birds and destroy certain types of plants and trees. With cleaner air, there may be more birds singing and prettier trees to view.

But regulation doesn't come with benefits only. It comes with costs, too. For example, because a business firm has to incur the cost of antipollution devices, its overall costs of production rise. Simply put, it is costlier for this business firm to produce its product than before the regulation was imposed. This may end up causing the business firm to produce fewer units of its product, raising its product price and resulting in some workers losing their jobs.

Now if you are the worker who loses his job, you may view the government's insistence that business install pollution devices differently than if, say, you are a person suffering from weak lungs. If you have weak lungs, less pollution may be the difference between your feeling well and your feeling sick. If you are a worker for the business firm, less pollution may end up costing you your job. Ideally, you may prefer to have a little less pollution in your neighborhood, but not at the cost of losing your job.

Where do economists stand on these issues? Are they for or against government regulation of the type described? The answer is, neither. The job of the economist is continually to make the point that there are both benefits and costs to regulation. To the person who only sees the costs, the economist asks: But what about the benefits? And to the person who only sees the benefits, the economist asks: But what about the costs? Then, the economist goes on to outline the benefits and the costs as best as he or she can.

▲ Pollution—which is often a byproduct of the way many goods are produced—is a problem that many countries are beginning to address.

Some Effects of Regulation Are Unintended

Besides outlining the benefits and costs of regulation, the economist tries to point out the sometimes unintended consequences of regulation. To illustrate, the government often regulates the manufacturers of automobiles by imposing fuel economy standards on cars. For example, the government may state that new cars must get an average of 40 miles per gallon instead of, say, 30 miles per gallon.

Many people will say that this is a good thing. They will reason that if car companies are made to produce cars that get better mileage, people will not need to buy and burn as much gasoline. With less gasoline burned, less pollution will be produced.

It is not guaranteed to work out this way, though. It could work out another way. With car companies producing more fuel-efficient cars, people will have to buy less gasoline to take them from one place to another—say, from home to work. This means that the cost per mile of traveling will fall. As a result of cheaper traveling costs, people might begin to travel more. Leisure driving on Saturday and Sunday might become more common. People might begin to drive farther on car vacations, and so on. If people begin to travel more, then the gasoline saving that resulted from the higher fuel economy standards might be offset or even outweighed. And more gasoline consumption due to more travel will mean more gas will be burned and more pollutants will end up in the air.

In other words, a regulation requiring car companies to produce cars that get better fuel mileage may have an unintended effect. The net result might be not that less gasoline is purchased and burned and thus less air pollution is produced, but that more gasoline is purchased and burned and thus more air pollution is produced.

LEARNING CHECK

1. It has been argued that if a public utility commission sets a certain limit on the profit rate a public utility may earn, the public utility will have little incentive to hold down its costs. Do you agree or disagree? Explain your answer.
2. What is social regulation?
3. "If the government imposes higher fuel economy standards, the amount of pollution produced by automobiles will undoubtedly become less." Do you agree or disagree? Explain your answer.

SECTION 3 EXTERNALITIES

Sometimes, a person's or group's actions produce side effects that are felt by others. In general, these side effects are called **externalities**, because the costs or benefits are *external* to whoever caused them. There are two types of externalities, negative and positive. We consider both types in this section.

As you read, keep these key questions in mind:

- What is a negative externality?
- What is a positive externality?
- What can be done about negative externality problems?

Negative Externalities

Suppose it is 3 A.M. and you are fast asleep. Suddenly, you awaken to the sounds of a radio blasting away. You get up, open the window of your bedroom, and realize that the loud music is coming from your neighbor's house. Your neighbor is taking an action—playing the radio loudly—that has an adverse side effect on you. Economists call this adverse side effect a **negative externality**, or a *negative third-party effect*.

Consider another example of a negative externality. The owner of a house rarely mows his lawn or cuts his shrubbery. The people who live in the houses nearby complain that not only is his property not kept up and therefore difficult to look at, but that his property lowers the value of their own houses. One neighbor, who lives across the street, says: "I need

MINI GLOSSARY
Externality A side effect of an action that affects the well-being of third parties.
Negative Externality An event or action that causes harm (an adverse side effect) to be felt by others.

ANALYZING PRIMARY SOURCES

Why and How Governments Regulate

The president of the United States has a council of economic advisors who advise him on economic matters. Each year, the members of the president's Council of Economic Advisors (CEA) submit an economic report to the president. Here is some of what they had to say in the report submitted in 1992 about why and how governments regulate.

"Regulation, it is commonly argued, is intended to correct market imperfections, or 'market failures.' Imperfections in competition among firms are one type of market failure. For example, in an industry that is a 'natural monopoly,' where a single supplier can most efficiently meet consumer needs, regulation of prices and the number of competitors may be desirable. In a broader set of markets, no economic regulation is generally necessary. In those cases the antitrust laws exist as a check against the possibility of anticompetitive behavior.

A second justification given for regulation is the presence of 'externalities,' or effects on third parties. An externality occurs when people do not account for all the effects of their actions on others. A manufacturer who dumps pollutants into a river, for example, does not consider the effects of those pollutants on fishermen who also use the river. The presence of this type of harmful externality has been the rationale underlying most environmental regulation.

An externality can, however, benefit rather than harm third parties. Information is one important example. Private organizations acquire information about product characteristics, such as the nutritional value of foods, which they then sell to consumers. However, it may be difficult for these organizations to capture all the benefits of supplying the information. Once the information is disclosed, consumers can benefit from the use of the information without compensating the provider for its use. In that event, the incentives to invest in supplying the information are diminished.

In principle, when the benefits to consumers of having the information outweigh the cost of requiring that it be provided, the government may want to supplement the role of the private market in supplying information. The government can provide information directly or require firms to provide it. People can then make more informed choices about which products to buy. Examples of government-required information include food and drug labeling and energy-efficiency labels for household appliances. . . .[a] **"**

---

1. According to this passage, what is the relationship between negative (or harmful) externalities and environmental regulation?
2. Suppose there was a situation where the benefits to consumers of having certain information were less than the costs of requiring firms to provide it. Would you propose that the government require firms to provide it anyway? Explain your answer.

---

a. *Economic Report of the President* (Washington, D.C.: U.S. Government Printing Office, 1992), pp. 161–63.

to sell my house, but I'm going to have a hard time doing it because the man across the street doesn't keep up his property. No one wants to live across from an eyesore. I will probably have to lower the price of my house before anyone will even start to think about buying it." Undoubtedly, the owner of the property which is not kept up is acting in a way that adversely affects his neighbors. The adverse side effect is a negative externality.

Erica Richards is a beekeeper who lives near an apple orchard. Erica's bees occasionally fly over to the orchard and pollinate the blossoms, in the process making the orchard more productive. Thus, Erica takes an action—keeping bees—in which a benefit external to the action is felt by some other person. Because Erica's beekeeping activity results in an externality that benefits someone else, it is referred to as a **positive externality**, or a *positive third-party effect*.

Consider another example of a positive externality. Yolanda visits a physician and is inoculated against polio. Now she can be sure that she will not become sick with polio. But Yolanda's actions also benefit other people. People who come into contact with Yolanda are protected from getting polio from her. Since it is now impossible for her to get polio, it also is impossible for her to pass on polio to anyone else. As far as the community as a whole is concerned, Yolanda's inoculation against polio is a positive externality.

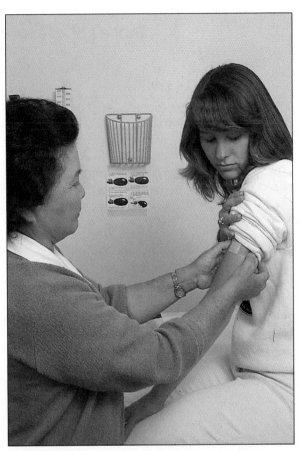

▲ When people are inoculated against contagious diseases, they not only help themselves, but also provide a positive externality for others. They protect others by not being able to infect them.

Government and Positive Externalities

Some people argue that education generates positive externalities. They say that when you attend school, you not only learn things that will directly help you in life and in the workplace but you also become a better citizen and a more informed voter. Becoming a better citizen and a more informed voter ends up benefiting more people than just yourself.

To illustrate, let's take your case. You are in high school taking this economics course. We hope that

because of it you will become more knowledgeable about economic issues than you would have been otherwise. One day, you are listening to two politicians running for the U.S. Senate from your state debating some economic issues on television. One politician is inaccurate on almost all of the issues. The other accurately portrays economic issues. You decide to vote for the politician who is accurate on the issues, because you feel that she will more likely end up promoting economic policies that are good for the United States.

Your informed vote increases (by a tiny percentage) the probability that the politician who understands economics will get elected. If she is elected, whom have you helped? You have helped yourself, no doubt, but you have also helped all the other people who will now benefit by having a person knowledgeable about economics shape government policy instead of an uninformed person. In short, your education has not only helped you, but it has helped others, too. In economic terminology, your education has produced a positive externality.

At this point, some people argue that since your education can help other people, these other people ought to pay something for the benefits they derive from your education. How might they do this? One way is to have the members of society pay taxes to support the schools that you attend. In other words, as this argument goes, since the public benefits from your education and the education of other persons like you, it should pay toward that education. We have the public-school system as a result.

Persons who attend public schools do not directly pay for the education they receive, although they indirectly pay if their parents pay property taxes, since property taxes are largely used to fund public education. Instead, their education is paid for with taxpayer money. That is, the education of public-school students is subsidized. Some people argue that government ought to subsidize those activities—like education—that generate positive externalities for society at large. What do you think?

Government and Negative Externalities

If you are on the receiving end of a negative externality (if you are awakened at 3:00 A.M. by loud music, or the smoke the factory is emitting is getting into your lungs), you will probably feel that negative externalities are bad. But what then?

Some people argue that it is government's duty to minimize the "bad" in society. This translates into a proposal for government to reduce the incidence of negative externalities (get rid of some of the "bad").

How does government reduce the incidence of negative externalities? There are three principal ways: through the court system, through regulation, and through taxation.

THINKING LIKE AN ECONOMIST

The discussion of externalities opens our eyes to the fact that some activities produce negative side effects for third parties. For example, a factory emits smoke into the air and adversely affects the health of those who live nearby. For these people, the smoke is a negative externality.

Many economists argue that the market system is incapable of doing anything about this problem. They go on to say that the market fails whenever it doesn't take into account and adjust for externalities—negative or positive. There is, simply put, market failure.

When markets fail to address externality issues, government may have a role to play. But the economist warns that just because government may have a role to play, it does not follow that anything or everything the government does will make matters better. Just as markets may fail, so may government. For example, government may enact such stringent regulations or high taxes on, say, polluting firms that some firms go out of business and thousands of jobs are lost.

Once again, for the economist, it comes down to a matter of costs and benefits. When there is market failure, there is little doubt that there are potential benefits to be realized through government action. The question remains, though: Will government take the right actions to turn the potential benefits into actual ones, and will the costs of these actions be worth it?

MINI GLOSSARY

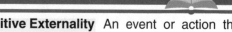

Positive Externality An event or action that causes a benefit (a beneficial side effect) to be felt by others.

The Court System.   It is a fall day. Frank lives in a house with many trees on the grounds. The leaves have fallen, and Frank rakes them up into a pile. Instead of tossing them into a trash can, he decides to burn them. The smoke from the burning leaves drifts over to Richard's house. Richard, it so happens, is allergic to smoke. He walks over to Frank's house and asks Frank to stop burning the leaves. He tells Frank he is allergic to smoke. Frank says that he has a right to burn his leaves on his property. Richard says that he has a right to a smoke-free neighborhood. Frank says again that he has the right to burn his leaves on his property—even if the smoke from the leaves adversely affects someone else.

Richard decides to take Frank to court. The lawyers for the two parties argue the case. In the end, the court has the duty to decide (a) whether the smoke is a negative externality (in fact, it was at the time) and (b) who has the right to do what. Specifically, even if the smoke is a negative externality, does Frank have the right to burn the leaves on his property? Or does Richard have the right to a smoke-free environment in his neighborhood?

Regulation.   Pollution—specifically the pollution emitted from both cars and factory smokestacks—is considered a negative externality. In many cases, government regulates the amount of pollution that can be emitted into the air. For example, most states require car owners to meet pollution standards. Also, in many places, government limits the amount of pollution factories can emit into the air. Government may also deem it illegal to dump chemicals into rivers and lakes.

Taxation.   You may recall from Chapter 3 that some taxes raise the per-unit costs of production and cause a leftward shift in the supply curve. Stated differently, some taxes reduce output and raise prices. (Whenever the supply curve shifts left, and demand is constant, price increases and the quantity of output decreases.) All this is simple supply-and-demand economics, but what does it have to do with negative externalities?

To illustrate, suppose a business firm is producing steel. As a by-product of producing steel, pollutants are discharged into the air through a smokestack. Instead of imposing an environmental regulation on the steel-producing firm, government decides to impose a tax. For every ton of steel produced, the firm has to pay $100 in taxes.

As a result of the tax, the business firm will find that it is now costlier to produce steel. The firm is likely to end up producing less steel. And less steel production ends up meaning fewer pollutants discharged into the air. In other words, the tax on steel has indirectly reduced the amount of negative externality (pollutants in the air) by making the production of steel more costly.

We have to be careful in our analysis, though. As we have already pointed out in this chapter, regulation sometimes comes with unintended consequences. It is the same for taxation, too.

Let's change our example. This time suppose we discuss automobile instead of steel production. In year 1, there are no taxes on the automobile industry. In year 2, government places a tax of $500 per car on the auto industry. In other words, for every new car a firm produces, it must pay the government $500 in taxes. In which year, 1 or 2, do you think the auto industry would produce more cars? The correct answer is year 1, all other things remaining the same. Taxes of the sort described here raise the cost of producing and selling cars; car firms react by producing fewer cars.

At this point, someone might say that because there are fewer cars there will be less pollution. This may overlook something important, though. The fact is, there are fewer *new* cars produced and purchased. People may simply drive their old cars longer. If it is the case that old cars emit more pollution than new cars, then the tax on the production of new cars will reduce the number of new cars on the road relative to the number of old cars and, if miles driven do not change, we can expect more, not less, pollution from cars. Taxation, like regulation, does not always have its intended effect.

✔ LEARNING CHECK

1. What is a negative externality?
2. What is a positive externality?
3. Explain how the court system can be used to deal with negative externalities.
4. Explain how regulation can be used to deal with negative externalities.
5. Explain how taxes can be used to deal with negative externalities.

SECTION 4 — THE BUSINESS OF AGRICULTURE

Although only 2.9 percent of the U.S. work force is employed in agriculture, it is an important industry. The agricultural industry faces unusual problems, however. We examine those problems in this section and consider a few government policies that have been implemented to try to solve them.

As you read, keep these key questions in mind:

■ What does increased productivity do to the supply curve of farm products?
■ What government programs exist to keep the prices of farm products high?

Agriculture and Increased Productivity

At the beginning of this century, one farmer produced enough food to feed 8 people. Today, one farmer produces enough food to feed 35 people. Obviously, farmers have become more productive over the years. Today, U.S. farmers produce enough food to feed the entire U.S. population and export large quantities of food to the rest of the world, too.

Think of what increased productivity means to the supply of a particular farm product, such as wheat. Increased productivity in wheat production means, of course, that farmers can produce more wheat. Thus, the supply curve of wheat shifts to the right, from S_1 to S_2, as shown in Exhibit 8-1.

As a result of this shift, the price of wheat falls from $7 per bushel to $4 per bushel, as shown in the exhibit. Conclusion: When wheat farmers become more productive, the price of wheat falls.

What does this mean in terms of the total revenue received by wheat farmers? As explained in

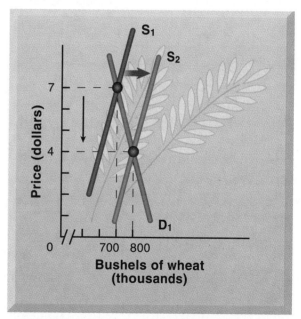

▲ **EXHIBIT 8-1**. **Increased Productivity, Supply, and Price**. Suppose wheat farmers experience increased productivity in wheat production. This shifts the supply curve of wheat to the right, from S_1 to S_2. As a result, the price of wheat (per bushel) falls from $7 to $4.

ECONOMIC FOCUS

In 1992, there were approximately 2.1 million farms in the United States. A farm is defined as any place from which $1,000 worth of agricultural products or more are produced and sold, or normally would have been sold, during the year. In 1992, there were approximately 4.6 million farmers in the United States. Farmers made up 1.9 percent of the total U.S. population.

There are fewer farmers today than in the past. For example, in 1980, there were 6 million farmers in the United States, comprising 2.7 percent of the population. In 1970, there were 9.7 million farmers, comprising 4.7 percent of the population, and in 1960, there were 15.6 million farmers, comprising 8.7 percent of the population.

▼ **EXHIBIT S-8-1**. Crops across the States.

STATE	NUMBER OF FARMS	FOUR PRINCIPAL COMMODITIES
Texas	183,000	cattle, cotton, dairy products, greenhouse
Missouri	107,000	cattle, soybeans, hogs, corn
Iowa	102,000	hogs, corn, cattle, soybeans
Kentucky	91,000	tobacco, cattle, horses, dairy products
Minnesota	88,000	corn, dairy products, soybeans, cattle
Tennessee	88,000	cattle, dairy products, tobacco, cotton
California	81,000	dairy products, greenhouse, cattle, grapes
Illinois	81,000	corn, soybeans, hogs, cattle
Wisconsin	79,000	dairy products, cattle, corn, hogs
Ohio	78,000	soybeans, corn, dairy products, hogs
Oklahoma	71,000	cattle, wheat, greenhouse, broilers
Kansas	67,000	cattle, wheat, corn, hogs
Indiana	65,000	corn, soybeans, hogs, cattle
North Carolina	60,000	tobacco, broilers, hogs, turkeys
Nebraska	56,000	cattle, corn, hogs, soybeans
Michigan	54,000	dairy products, corn, cattle, soybeans
Pennsylvania	52,000	dairy products, cattle, greenhouse, mushrooms
Georgia	46,000	broilers, peanuts, eggs, cattle
Arkansas	46,000	broilers, cattle, soybeans, rice
Alabama	46,000	broilers, cattle, greenhouse, peanuts
Virginia	44,000	cattle, broilers, dairy products, tobacco
Florida	39,000	oranges, greenhouse, tomatoes, sugar
New York	38,000	dairy products, greenhouse, cattle, apples
Mississippi	38,000	cotton, broilers, cattle, soybeans
Washington	38,000	apples, dairy products, cattle, wheat

SOURCE: U.S. Bureau of the Census, *Statistical Abstract of the United States: 1993*, 113th edition.

FARMERS AND CROPS

Why are there fewer farmers today than in the past? One major reason is that the productivity of the average farm has been increasing, so that fewer farmers are needed to produce the same amount of food. For example, the crop production per acre doubled on farms between 1955 and 1991. In the short period from 1980–90, crop production increased 25 percent.

In Exhibit S-8-1, we list the number of farms and the principal crops in each state. The principal crops are listed in order of their importance in generating farm income. For example, the farmers in Minnesota (the fifth state listed in the exhibit) earn more from corn than from dairy products, and they earn more from dairy products than from soybeans, and so on.

▼ **EXHIBIT S-8-1** (continued).

STATE	NUMBER OF FARMS	FOUR PRINCIPAL COMMODITIES
Oregon	38,000	cattle, greenhouse, dairy products, wheat
South Dakota	35,000	cattle, hogs, corn, soybeans
North Dakota	33,000	wheat, cattle, barley, sunflowers
Louisiana	30,000	cotton, cattle, sugar, soybeans
Colorado	26,000	cattle, corn, wheat, dairy products
Montana	25,000	cattle, wheat, barley, hay
South Carolina	25,000	tobacco, cattle, broilers, greenhouse
Idaho	21,000	cattle, potatoes, dairy products, wheat
West Virginia	20,000	cattle, broilers, dairy products, turkeys
Maryland	16,000	broilers, greenhouse, dairy products, soybeans
New Mexico	14,000	cattle, dairy products, hay, chili peppers
Utah	13,000	cattle, dairy products, hay, turkeys
Wyoming	9,000	cattle, sugar beets, hay, barley
New Jersey	9,000	greenhouse, dairy products, eggs, peaches
Arizona	8,000	cattle, cotton, dairy products, lettuce
Vermont	7,000	dairy products, cattle, greenhouse, hay
Massachusetts	7,000	greenhouse, cranberries, dairy products, eggs
Maine	7,000	potatoes, eggs, dairy products, aquaculture
Hawaii	5,000	sugar, pineapples, greenhouse, nuts
Connecticut	4,000	greenhouse, eggs, dairy products, tobacco
New Hampshire	3,000	dairy products, greenhouse, apples, cattle
Nevada	3,000	cattle, hay, dairy products, potatoes
Delaware	3,000	broilers, soybeans, corn, greenhouse
Rhode Island	1,000	greenhouse, dairy products, eggs, potatoes
Alaska	1,000	greenhouse, dairy products, hay, potatoes

U.S. ECONOMIC FOCUS (continued)

The farmers in these 50 states produce a large proportion of the agricultural products of the world. For example, in 1992, they produced 52.7 percent of the soybeans, 45.6 percent of the corn, 18.3 percent of the cotton, and 12.1 percent of the wheat produced in the world. U.S. farmers are also major exporters of their agricultural goods. For example, in 1992, their wheat exports comprised 36 percent of all the wheat exported in the world. Their corn exports comprised approximately 70 percent of all the corn exported in the world, and their soybeans comprised approximately 66 percent of all the soybeans exported in the world.

Turn again to Exhibit S-8-1. Notice that pineapples are a principal crop in Hawaii, but not in, say, Pennsylvania. Isn't it possible to grow pineapples in Pennsylvania? It is possible; but it is much more costly than in Hawaii. In Pennsylvania, you may need a greenhouse to grow pineapples. In Hawaii, you don't. In agriculture, crops tend to be grown where it is relatively cheap to produce them. To understand this fully, consider this example. Suppose there is a farmer in Pennsylvania and one in Hawaii, both of whom can produce soybeans and pineapples. The Pennsylvanian farmer has to pay $7 to produce one pineapple which he will sell for $2, and he has to pay $2 to produce one bushel of soybeans which he will sell for $5. The Hawaiian farmer has to pay 50 cents to produce one pineapple which he will sell for $2, and he has to pay $4 to produce one bushel of soybeans which he will sell for $5. It is likely that the Pennsylvanian farmer will end up producing soybeans (it is unprofitable to produce pineapples) and the Hawaiian farmer will end up producing pineapples (it is profitable to produce both pineapples and soybeans but more profitable to produce pineapples). Our lesson: It is not a matter of whether or not it is possible to produce pineapples in Pennsylvania (it *is* possible); it is a matter of whether or not it is *worth* it.

Does society, as a whole, benefit by having Pennsylvanian farmers produce soybeans and Hawaiian farmers produce pineapples, instead of the other way around? The answer is probably yes. Society usually benefits anytime the person who can produce a good more cheaply ends up producing the good. The reason is that in a world of scarcity, where resources are finite, the person who uses the fewest resources to produce a good (of a given quality) leaves the most resources for others to use to produce other goods. For example, it is probably better for society that the Hawaiian farmer only uses 50 cents worth of resources to produce a pineapple than for the Pennsylvanian farmer to use $7 worth of resources to produce a pineapple.

1. There are only 1,000 farms in Alaska and 183,000 farms in Texas. What does this large difference between the number of farms in these two states imply about the cost of producing agricultural products in the two states? Explain your answer.

Chapter 3, the demand for a product may be inelastic, elastic, or unit elastic. The demand for many farm products is inelastic. That means a decrease in price causes an increase in quantity demanded that is proportionately smaller than the decrease in price. We can turn to Exhibit 8-1 to see what this means to total revenue.

Let's compute the total revenue for wheat at two prices: $7 per bushel, the price *before* increased productivity shifted the supply curve of wheat to the right, and $4 per bushel, the price *after* the shift. Total revenue, as defined in previous chapters, equals the price of a good, times the quantity of the good sold. At $7 per bushel, the quantity sold is 700,000 bushels, so total revenue is $4,900,000 ($7 × 700,000 = $4,900,000). At $4 per bushel, the quantity sold is 800,000 bushels, so total revenue is $3,200,000 ($4 × 800,000 = $3,200,000).

Let's look again at what increased productivity in wheat production does to wheat farmers. First, it lowers the per-bushel price at which they can sell their wheat (from $7 per bushel to $4 per bushel). Second, it lowers their total revenue (from $4,900,000 to $3,200,000). As far as wheat farmers are concerned, increased productivity hurts them. (Of course, as far as consumers of wheat and wheat products are concerned, it is helpful, since they end up paying lower prices.)

Farmers Prefer Selling at High Prices to Selling at Low Prices

Farmers are in a bind. On the one hand, they want to be more productive so that they can sell more of what they produce. On the other hand, if they become more productive, they simply end up lowering the price of what they sell. And since the demand for what they sell is inelastic, this results in a decrease in their total revenue. What's a farmer to do?

What farmers have done is to ask for help from the federal government. The federal government has responded through a host of policies. The ob-

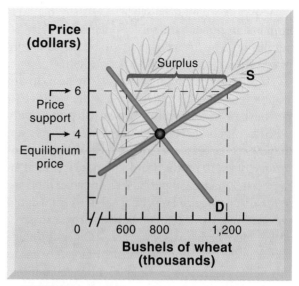

▲ **EXHIBIT 8-2. Effects of an Agricultural Price Support**. At a price support of $6 per bushel, buyers of wheat pay higher prices, and a surplus results. Government buys and stores the surplus (and taxpayers end up paying for it).

jective of each policy is to keep the prices of farm products higher. Let's look at a few of the policies government has used.

Price Support Program. An agricultural **price support** is a government-guaranteed minimum price for an agricultural product. Some of the agricultural products that either have price supports now or have had them in the past include wheat, cotton, feed grains, dairy products, and tobacco. To illustrate the effects of a price support, look at Exhibit 8-2. It shows the demand for and supply of wheat. The equilibrium price of wheat is $4 per bushel. At this price, buyers want to buy 800,000 bushels of wheat.

Farmers, however, may think that $4 per bushel is too low a price and pressure the government to

---

MINI GLOSSARY

Price Support The minimum price, as determined by government, that farmers will receive from buyers for their products. Not all agricultural products have price supports.

place a price support on wheat. Let's say the government responds and sets a price support at $6 per bushel. This means that it will be illegal to buy or sell wheat for less than $6 per bushel.

Now, at $6 per bushel, buyers of wheat do not want to purchase as much wheat as they did at $4 per bushel. In the exhibit, we see that they only wish to purchase 600,000 bushels of wheat, not 800,000 bushels any longer. However, wheat farmers want to produce and sell more wheat at $6 per bushel than at $4 per bushel. In the exhibit we see that at a price of $6 per bushel, farmers want to produce and sell 1,200,000 bushels of wheat.

We have here a case in which farmers produce and want to sell more wheat than buyers want to buy at the current price. Chapter 4 pointed out that this condition is called a surplus. A surplus exists when the quantity supplied of a product is greater than the quantity demanded of the product. In the exhibit, the surplus is 600,000 bushels of wheat—which is the difference between what buyers will buy (600,000 bushels) and what farmers will produce (1,200,000 bushels).

What happens to the surplus of wheat? Under the price support program, the government buys the surplus wheat and stores it.

Let's review the effects of the price support program. First, the buyers of wheat pay higher prices for wheat—$6 per bushel instead of $4 per bushel. Second, buyers buy less wheat—600,000 bushels instead of 800,000 bushels. Third, farmers receive higher prices for their wheat—$6 per bushel instead of $4 per bushel. Fourth, a surplus of wheat results. Fifth, the government buys the surplus, and taxpayers end up paying for it.

Acreage Allotment Program.

There are two ways to get a higher price for an agricultural good. First, you can put a price support on the good, as just described. Second, you can try to get the supply curve of the product to shift to the left, thus raising price. The acreage allotment program is an example of a government policy that tries to reduce the supply of an agricultural good.

The acreage allotment program works by limiting the number of farm acres that can be used to produce a particular crop. Suppose Farmer Perez has a 10,000-acre farm on which he plants wheat. When the acreage allotment program is put into effect, government limits him to planting only 7,500 acres. The idea is that if all wheat farmers reduce the number of acres they plant in wheat, the quantity of wheat brought to market will decrease. In other words, the supply curve of wheat will shift to the left, from S_1 to S_2 in Exhibit 8-3. As a result, price will rise.

Marketing Quota System.

Under a marketing quota system, government does not restrict land usage. Instead, it sets a limit on the quantity of a product that a farmer is allowed to bring to the market. For example, one year in California, a large crop of oranges was harvested, but oranges were under a marketing quota system. Farmers ended up destroying a large part of the orange crop because they could bring only a limited number of oranges to market to sell.

Target Price Program.

Another way in which government tries to aid farmers is by setting a guaranteed price called a **target price**. This is different from a price support in that consumers do not necessarily pay the target price. Also, with a target price, there is no surplus for the government to purchase and store. Exhibit 8-4 shows this.

Suppose government sets the target price for wheat at $8 per bushel. At this price, wheat farmers choose to produce 1,400,000 bushels of wheat. However, buyers will not buy 1,400,000 bushels at a price of $8 per bushel. We see from the exhibit

MINI GLOSSARY

Target Price A guaranteed price set by government. If the market price is below the target price, the farmer receives from the government a deficiency payment equal to the difference between the market price and the target price. For example, if the target price is $8 per unit and the market price is $2, then the farmer receives a $6 deficiency payment per unit.

▶ **EXHIBIT 8-3**. **Effects of an Acreage Allotment Program**. The acreage allotment program seeks to reduce the number of acres a farmer can use to produce a particular crop, such as wheat. If the acreage allotment program is effective, it ends up shifting the supply curve to the left. This results in a higher price.

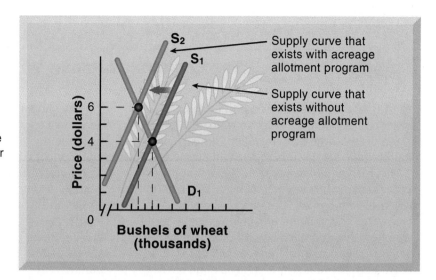

▶ **EXHIBIT 8-4**. **How a Target Price Program Works**. With target prices, the government guarantees farmers a certain price per unit produced. For example, suppose government sets the target price of wheat at $8 per bushel, and farmers produce 1,400,000 bushels. When this wheat is placed on the market, buyers end up paying $2 per bushel. The difference between the target price ($8) and the price buyers pay ($2) is the deficiency payment per bushel ($6) that is paid by the government (taxpayers) to the farmers.

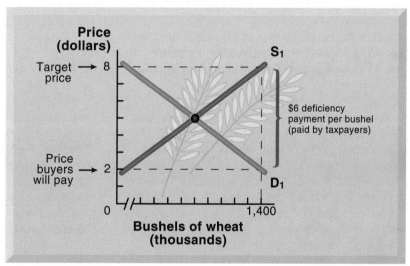

that they are willing to pay only $2 per bushel to buy this amount of wheat. Under the target price program, consumers pay the $2 per bushel. But since government has guaranteed farmers a price of $8 per bushel, government ends up using tax dollars to pay the dollar difference to farmers. In our example, this is $6 per bushel ($8 − $2 = $6). This $6 is called the *deficiency payment*. With the target price program, then, consumers buy cheap wheat, and taxpayers pay.

 LEARNING CHECK

1. What two government agricultural programs try to reduce the supply of an agricultural good?
2. What two government agricultural programs end up costing taxpayers money?
3. What government agricultural program ends up producing a surplus of agricultural goods?

DEVELOPING ECONOMIC SKILLS

The Economics Paper: Writing It

In Chapter 6, we explained how to find an economics topic on which to write. In Chapter 7, we discussed how to research the topic. In this chapter, we discuss how to write the paper.

It is a common mistake to believe that once your research has been completed, it is time to sit down with pen and paper, or in front of a typewriter or computer, and start writing. People who take this approach usually produce poor writing. Before writing, there should be prewriting. Prewriting is a process of generating and organizing ideas that moves the writer from the thinking stage to the writing stage.

One way to prewrite is to brainstorm and write down everything that comes into your head about the topic at hand. Let's continue with our example of U.S. businesses and foreign competition. If this had been a topic that you were going to write about and had researched at the library, you might have found out the answers to some of your questions, such as where the major foreign firms in the U.S. are located, what they produce, and so on. To begin prewriting, the first step would be to take out a piece of paper and simply write down everything that comes to mind about the topic. Prewriting notes do not have to be written in complete sentences, nor does your handwriting have to be neat.

Once you have written down as many statements or ideas as you can, look at them to see if there is any theme that links them all. For example, many of your thoughts about U.S. businesses and foreign competition might have to do with the kinds of products for which they compete to produce and sell. There is no telling what theme might emerge. However, there is a good chance that most of your thoughts will relate to *some* theme. Once you have identified the theme, you will have a good idea of which information from your research to include. It is now time to structure your paper.

How should your paper be structured? Think about this as we tell you a story. A friend says, "I have a story to tell you. It's about a car, a dog, and a banana peel." With such an opening, your friend probably grabs your attention. You may be curious to learn what kind of story includes a car, a dog, and a banana peel. It sounds like an intriguing combination, doesn't it?

Your friend continues, "The dog was a collie. He was about five years old. Oh, wait a minute, perhaps I should first tell you about the car. It was a red car. On second thought, I should tell you about the banana peel first."

What would you think if you heard your friend say this? You might think that he is ruining what, at first, seemed to have the potential to be a good story. Where has your friend gone wrong? Clearly, he hasn't taken the time to identify the best way to present the story. He is thinking about the story, and telling it, at the same time. That isn't the way to tell a story, and it isn't the way to write an essay. This is where structuring comes in. Structuring your paper is "figuring out" the best way to tell your story.

One useful way to organize your thoughts is to use index cards. (If you don't have a supply of index cards, lined paper cut into 3" × 5" rectangles can be used.)

Step 1: Write down each of the main points that you want to make in your paper on a separate index card.

Step 2: Organize the cards into the order in which you want to discuss each point.

Step 3: Using your index cards, pretend you are giving an oral report to your class. You may do this by saying the words out loud, or silently to yourself. The important point is to hear yourself "write" the paper.

Step 4: Consider reordering your main points so that your paper is better organized.

DEVELOPING ECONOMIC SKILLS (continued)

You may want to switch the order of points 6 and 7. This is where the practice of using index cards makes things easy. Now repeat step 3. Continue reordering your main points, and orally presenting your paper, until you are comfortable that you have found the best way to present the information.

Step 5: Using your sequenced index cards as your guide, write the paper. Do not worry about grammar or spelling at this stage of the process.

What have you noticed? This feature was titled "The Economics Paper: Writing It." You may think that very few words have been used to explain how you should write the paper. In step 5 we told you simply to "write the paper." That may not seem like very much direction on how to write an essay. Try looking at things in a new way.

Writing is not simply the physical act of using a pen, typewriter, or word processor to put letters, words, sentences, and paragraphs on paper. Writing requires thinking and preparation: specifically, the free, unconstrained thinking that is used in prewriting and the focused thinking that is used in structuring. Without prewriting and structuring, your essay might turn out like the story of the car, the dog, and the banana peel. Your audience may get confused and wonder, "What is the point of this story?"

Think of writing as a process. The first step in the process is to decide what it is you want to say. The second step is to work your ideas into a logical structure that gets your message across in the best way possible. Only after you have spent time on these first two steps will you be ready to write the paper.

---

1. What is a person trying to accomplish by prewriting?
2. What is a person trying to accomplish through structure?
3. If you were given the assignment in the previous chapter to research a topic, do the following:
   a. On one sheet of paper, write down any ideas or comments that come to mind that relate to the topic.
   b. On a second sheet of paper, write down the theme of your ideas or comments.
   c. On a stack of index cards (or small squares of paper), write down the main points you want to make and then place these in the sequence that you will follow in the paper.
   d. Write the paper.

CHAPTER 8 REVIEW

CHAPTER SUMMARY

1. The stated purpose of the antitrust laws is to preserve and promote competition in the marketplace.

2. Important antitrust legislation includes the Sherman Act, the Clayton Act, the Federal Trade Commission Act, the Robinson-Patman Act, and the Wheeler-Lea Act.

3. The Sherman Act stated that attempting to become a monopolist by trying to restrain trade is illegal. The Clayton Act prohibited price discrimination, tying contracts, the acquisition of competing companies' stock if the acquisition reduces competition, and interlocking directorates. The Federal Trade Commission Act declared illegal "unfair methods of competition in commerce." The Robinson-Patman Act attempted to decrease the failure rate of small businesses by protecting them from the competition of large and growing chain stores. The Wheeler-Lea Act empowered the Federal Trade Commission to deal with false and deceptive acts or practices.

4. In natural monopoly situations, government usually applies either price or profit regulation. In price regulation, government sets the price at which the natural monopoly can sell

its output. In profit regulation, government sets the profit rate the natural monopoly can earn.

5. Social regulation is concerned with the conditions under which goods and services are produced and the safety of those items for the consumer.

6. There are two types of externalities: negative and positive.

7. There are three major ways in which government deals with a negative externality problem: through the court system, through regulation, and through taxation.

8. Increased productivity in the agricultural sector of the economy leads to falling prices for agricultural products.

9. Since the demand for most agricultural products is inelastic, a fall in these products' prices will lead to a fall in the total revenues received by the farmers who produce them.

10. Government agricultural programs seek to keep the prices of agricultural products higher than they would otherwise be. These programs usually end up costing consumers or taxpayers money.

BUILD YOUR ECONOMIC VOCABULARY

Match the word with the correct definition, example, or statement.

1. target price
2. negative externality
3. antitrust laws
4. Clayton Act
5. acreage allotment program
6. positive externality

a. beneficial side effect
b. reduces the number of acres that can be farmed
c. laws to promote and preserve competition
d. outlawed price discrimination and interlocking directorates, among other things
e. adverse side effect
f. government-guaranteed price for agricultural products

REVIEW QUESTIONS

1. What is one criticism of the Sherman Act?
2. Which antitrust act states that "every contract, combination in the form of trust or otherwise, or conspiracy, in restraint of trade or commerce . . . is hereby declared to be illegal"?
3. False or deceptive advertising violates which antitrust act?
4. Some economists have argued that a natural monopoly has little if any incentive to hold down costs if either price or profit regulation is applied to it. Explain why.
5. "Economists are against regulation." Do you agree or disagree? Explain your answer.
6. Explain how taxation may be used to eliminate a negative externality problem.
7. What may be an unintended effect of fuel-efficiency standards?
8. Explain how the court system may be used to eliminate a negative externality problem.
9. Justify the public-school system on positive externality grounds.
10. Explain the difference between how the price support program affects consumers and how the target price program affects consumers.

SHARPEN YOUR CRITICAL THINKING SKILLS

1. Suppose we accept the idea that there are many negative externalities in the world, that government should try to solve some of the many negative externality problems, and that it is more important to try to solve some negative externality problems than others. For example, most people would probably agree that air pollution is a more important negative externality problem than many others, such as a person playing music loudly at 11:00 P.M. How would you decide which negative externality problems are important enough for government to try to solve and which are not?
2. "Negative externalities can exist even on an island with only one inhabitant." What is wrong with this statement?

ACTIVITIES AND PROJECTS

1. Glance through any newspaper or magazine to find a story that deals with one of the topics covered in this chapter. Next, carefully read the story. Finally, write a two-page essay explaining how what you learned in this chapter helped you to understand the story.

ECONOMIC DICTIONARY

Antitrust Laws (Pg. 200)
Externality (Pg. 208)
Merger (Pg. 200)
Negative Externality (Pg. 208)

Positive Externality (Pg. 210)
Price Support (Pg. 217)
Public Utility Commission (Pg. 203)

Target Price (Pg. 218)
Trust (Pg. 200)

CHAPTER
9

Economic Challenges: The Environment, Health Care, and Poverty

Wilson, 68 years old, was taken to the hospital last night after suffering a heart attack. The doctors say he will have to stay in the hospital for four or five days and take some tests.

"This is a nice hospital," Wilson says to his brother, who is visiting him.

"Yeah, I think so, too," says his brother Jack. "How is your doctor?"

"Which one? I have three. There's my family doctor and two specialists."

"I'll bet this is going to cost you a lot of money."

"Don't talk about money," Wilson says, "I don't want another heart attack."

Jenny, who is 25 years old, has three small children. Jenny is poor. Her mother is poor, too, and so is her grandmother. In fact, everyone in Jenny's family is poor. One night, Jenny and her best friend, Marianne, are sitting on the steps of their apartment building watching their children play.

"I wanted to buy Jonathan new shoes today," Jenny says, "but I didn't have enough money."

"I know how hard that can be. Doesn't it just tear you up that you want to do so much for your kids, but just can't?" Marianne asks.

"I think it's what I hate most about being poor," Jenny answers.

This chapter is about the issues that these scenes from everyday life represent: the environment, health care, and poverty.

1. Explain why pollution is more common in some places than others.
2. Discuss and compare the two major methods of reducing pollution: setting standards and selling pollution permits.
3. Explain why, for many people, the benefits of recycling are less than the costs of recycling.
4. Cite some facts on the state of health care in the United States.
5. Utilize a supply-and-demand framework to explain rising health care prices.
6. Explain the difference between absolute and relative definitions of poverty.
7. Understand why people disagree as to the causes of poverty.
8. List some government poverty programs.

KEY TERMS

Guaranteed Income Level

Implicit Marginal Tax Rate

In-Kind Benefit

Medicaid

Medical Malpractice Suit

Medicare

Poverty Line

Third-Party Payer

SECTION 1 THE ENVIRONMENT

The environment became an acknowledged major economic, political, and social issue in the 1980s. Nations of the world met at conferences to discuss environmental issues. Problems of the environment are many and cover such things as acid rain, the greenhouse effect, deforestation (including the destruction of the rain forests), solid waste (garbage) disposal, water pollution, air pollution, and much more. In this section, we focus on air pollution, but much of what is said about it here holds for other types of environmental problems, too.

As you read, keep these key questions in mind:

- Is it better to have some pollution than no pollution?
- Why does pollution exist in some places but not in others?
- Which is a cheaper method of reducing pollution—setting standards or selling pollution permits?

What Is Pollution?

Chapter 8 explained that when a person's or group's actions cause a side effect that is felt by others, this side effect is called an externality; and when this side effect is adverse to others, it is a negative externality. Air pollution is a negative externality.

To illustrate, consider people in cars driving to work in the morning. They drive down interstate highways, city streets, back roads, and so on. Their cars give off some pollution. The people who live in the houses near the interstate highways, city streets, and so on, smell the car fumes. Furthermore, the pollution from the cars affects these people's eyes and lungs. The air pollution is a side effect of driving a car that adversely affects some people. In other words, the air pollution is a negative externality.

Is Some Pollution Better Than No Pollution?

The world would be different without pollution—and not only in terms of having cleaner air, rivers, and oceans. Pollution is a by-product of the production of many goods and services. For example, as the last chapter pointed out, it is unlikely that steel could be produced without some pollution as a by-product. Given the current state of pollution technology, less steel pollution would mean less steel and fewer products made from steel.

Pollution is also a by-product of many of the goods we use daily, including—as we've already seen—our cars. We could certainly end car pollution in a short time, but it would mean that we would have to give up driving cars. Would ending car pollution be worth taking this drastic step? Are there benefits to driving cars? If there are, then perhaps we wouldn't choose zero car pollution. In short, to some people zero car pollution is not preferable to a certain amount of car pollution if we take into account that we'd have to stop driving cars to end car pollution.

Economists don't like pollution any more or less than anyone else. But economists recognize that pollution comes with other things—such as steel production, driving cars, and so on. To get rid of *all* pollution, we might have to get rid of these other things, too.

Why Is There Air Pollution and Water Pollution but Not Front-Yard Pollution?

Think of where you see pollution. Two major places are in the air and in the water. News programs often show the pollution in the air of cities

THINKING LIKE AN ECONOMIST

Chapter 1 explained that economists think in terms of costs and benefits. Thus, as explained in the text, the economist wants to know both the costs and the benefits of polluting. Furthermore, economists do not often think in terms of "either-or" situations. For them, it is not a matter of either *a world that is so polluted that no one can breathe* or *a world of no pollution at all*. These are two radical extremes. Economists think in terms of costs and benefits; and because they do, they realize that there are benefits and costs to reducing pollution.

like Los Angeles and in the water of the Great Lakes, a river, or an ocean. Think now where you rarely see pollution. You rarely see it in a person's front yard. Most people keep their front yards neat. Why do we see air and water pollution but not "front-yard pollution"? Some economists have suggested that it is because no one *owns* the air or most water (for example, oceans) but someone

does own a front yard. In other words, pollution is more likely to exist where ownership rights do not.

The point is a simple one: resources that are not owned have a higher probability of being polluted, trashed, dirtied, and neglected than resources that are owned.

QUESTION: *Should someone own the air and oceans so that air and water pollution could be reduced? If so, who would this person be?*

ANSWER: *It would probably not be practical for people to own the air and the oceans. The problems with deciding who owned what air and what water would be numerous and difficult to solve. For example, would a person own the air above his or her house? If so, for how many miles up? If it were too many miles, then airplanes couldn't fly over anyone's house without getting the owner's permission, and this might create quite a few problems of its own.*

Government has decided to deal with water and air pollution in different ways. One way is through issuing regulations to polluters or setting pollution standards. The other way, which is relatively new, is through selling permits to pollute. We discuss both ways next.

Reprinted with permission.
Wayne Stayskal, *Tampa Tribune.*

CASE STUDY

Why Don't More People Recycle?

ecycling is the process of converting waste products into reusable materials. When people recycle such items as old newspapers, glass bottles, and plastic containers, they often take them to recycling centers instead of throwing them into the garbage. Old newspapers can be turned into new newspapers, old glass bottles can be turned into new glass bottles, and so on. The idea behind recycling is to reduce the amount of resources needed to produce new items and to reduce the amount of garbage (much of which takes a long time to decompose). Supporters of recycling say that it is good for the economy and especially good for the environment. They urge everyone to recycle.

But relatively few people consistently recycle. Why? Let's look at it from an economic point of view. To the person deciding whether to recycle, there are benefits and costs to recycling. The bene-

fits may come in the good feeling that results from helping the environment. The costs may come in the form of having to take recyclable items to a recycling center or having to save them at home instead of throwing them away (and so having a slightly cluttered house). For many people, it is simply much easier to throw a glass bottle or plastic container away after using it than to save it temporarily and then have it recycled. The people who do not recycle perceive the benefits of recycling to be less than the costs. In short, they tell us by their actions that recycling is just not worth it.

For those people who do recycle, this may be difficult to understand. For them, of course, the benefits of recycling are greater than the costs. They can't understand why everyone doesn't recycle. But consider what the situation looks like from the perspective of one person. Alex hears the pleas to recycle, but he thinks to himself that

◀ There are many benefits that can be obtained from recycling for society as a whole. For individuals, doing their part in protecting the environment often leads to feelings of personal satisfaction.

CASE STUDY (continued)

if he recycles, the environment won't be that much better off—after all, he is only one person. It would be different if everyone recycled, but he doesn't have control over anyone but himself, and his recycling wouldn't change the environment by much at all. Alex sees few benefits, if any, for the environment if he recycles. He fully realizes, however, that he will incur some costs if he recycles. Under these conditions, Alex will probably choose not to recycle.

How would an economist go about trying to increase the amount of recycling that people do? She would try to increase the benefits of recycling or reduce its costs. How might we do this? First, we could pay people to recycle. If we paid people for all the old newspapers and empty glass containers they returned, there would certainly be more recycling. Or suppose we fined people for not recycling. If people had to pay a fine for every empty glass or plastic container found in their garbage, we would expect there to be more recycling. Or perhaps we could lower the costs of recycling by having regular home pickups for recyclables. In many states, various programs, including some of those listed, are being tried in an effort to encourage recycling.

The economic point of view informs us that if we want to change behavior—whether with regard to recycling or anything else—we must change the benefits and costs of the behavior. It may not be enough for persons interested in the environment to urge us to recycle. Their words may simply fall on deaf ears. In the end, it may take real economic incentives to do the trick.

---

1. If people came to think that they were "better" people if they recycled, how would this affect the amount of recycling? Explain your answer in terms of the benefits and costs of recycling.
2. Many individuals are unlikely to recycle because they perceive their recycling as doing little, if anything, to change the local environment. This being the case, would people in a town with a population of 7,000 be more or less likely to recycle than people in a town of 2 million? Explain your answer.

Two Methods to Reduce Pollution

One of the biggest movements of the 1990s will surely prove to be *market environmentalism*, the use of market forces to clean up the environment. This was the idea behind the Clean Air Act amendments, which then President George Bush signed in November 1990.

This section shows you how market environmentalism works. First, though, another major method of reducing pollution is discussed: government pollution standards.

Method 1: Government Sets Pollution Standards. Suppose there are three firms, X, Y, and Z, located in the same area. Currently, each firm is spewing three units of pollution, to make up a total of nine pollution units in the area under consideration. The government wants to reduce the total pollution in the area to three units and, to accomplish this objective, sets pollution standards (or regulations) stating that each firm must reduce pollution

Cost of eliminating	Firm X (clothing manufacturer)	Firm Y (clothing manufacturer)	Firm Z (automobile manufacturer)
First unit of pollution	$50	$70	$500
Second unit of pollution	75	85	1,000
Third unit of pollution	100	200	2,000

▲ **EXHIBIT 9-1. The Cost of Reducing Pollution Units for Three Firms.**

by two units. Exhibit 9-1 shows the respective cost of eliminating each unit of pollution for the three firms. For each firm, the costs of eliminating pollution are different; not all kinds of firms can eliminate pollution equally easily. For example, the pollution that an automobile manufacturer produces might be more costly to eliminate than the pollution a clothing manufacturer produces. Stated differently, we assume that the three firms eliminate pollution by installing antipollution devices in their factories, and the cost of the antipollution devices may be much higher for an automobile manufacturer than for a clothing manufacturer.

The cost to Firm X of eliminating its first two units is $125 ($50 + $75 = $125); the cost to Firm Y of eliminating the first two units is $155 ($70 + $85 = $155); and the cost to Firm Z of eliminating its first two units is $1,500 ($500 + $1,000 = $1,500). The total cost of eliminating six units of pollution, and thus bringing the total pollution in the area down to three units, is $1,780 ($125 + $155 + $1,500 = $1,780).

Method 2: Market Environmentalism at Work: Government Allocates Pollution Permits and Allows Them to Be Bought and Sold. Now, still suppose the objective of the government is to reduce the pollution in the area from nine units to three units, but it goes about doing this in a different way. This time the government issues one pollution permit (sometimes these pollution permits are called allowances or credits) to each firm. It tells each firm that it can emit only one unit of pollution for each permit it has in its possession. Furthermore, it allows firms to buy and sell these permits from each other.

Since the government wants to reduce pollution from nine units to three units, it passes out only three pollution permits—one to Firm X, one to Firm Y, and one to Firm Z. Look at things from the perspective of Firm X. One pollution permit is in its possession, so two units of pollution must be eliminated and one unit of pollution can be emitted. But Firm X also has a pollution permit in its possession which can be sold. Might Firm X not be better off eliminating three units of pollution and selling the permit?

The same thing holds for Firm Y. This firm, likewise, has to eliminate two units of pollution since only one permit is in its possession. But Firm Y has to wonder if it might not be better off eliminating three units of pollution and instead selling the permit.

Now look at things from the perspective of Firm Z. Exhibit 9-1 informs us that this firm has to pay $500 to eliminate its first unit of pollution, and $1,000 to eliminate its second unit of pollution. Firm Z has to wonder if it might not be better off buying the two permits in the possession of Firms X and Y and not eliminating any pollution at all.

Suppose the owners of the three firms get together one day and talk about buying and selling the permits they have in their possession. The owner of Firm Z says to the owners of the other firms, "I have to spend $500 to eliminate my first unit of pollution and $1,000 to eliminate my second unit. If either of you is willing to sell me your pollution permit for less than $500, I'd be willing to buy it."

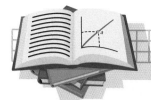

ANALYZING PRIMARY SOURCES

Economics and the Environment

In this feature we present some of the questions often asked about economics and the environment. In presenting our answers, we draw from a number of people's ideas in the hope of presenting you with different points of view.

Do economists place more importance on jobs and earning income than they do on having a clean environment?

Economists don't all think alike when it comes to this subject. Some economists, in their private lives, value a clean environment more than other economists. You may find the words of one economist, James Eggert, instructive here. He says:

"Perhaps it is time we economists begin to rethink our strict adherence to dollar. . . values. We should not, of course, discard our old and valuable skills: of recognizing scarcity, of making efficient choices, and of pointing out trade-offs. But it's time to broaden ourselves, to incorporate ecological thinking and ecological values *along with* market thinking and market values—call it, if you wish, 'Meadowlark Economics.'

I'm ashamed to admit that I took my first elementary class in ecology after teaching economics for more than two decades. I still have a ways to go. I am beginning to read (and appreciate) some of the latter day economists who represent this new thinking: Kenneth Boulding, Hazel Henderson, Herman Daly, Lester Brown, Leopold Kohr, and E.F. Schumacher, to name a few.

In addition, I hope that more and more prominent economists, the Friedmans, Solows, McConnells, the Boskins, Bradys and Greenspans of today—and the future—will feel comfortable not only with traditional market/growth economics, but will also know something of ecology as well [ecology is the branch of biology that deals with the relations and interactions between organisms and their environment]; to value the integrity of the environment along with the 'bottom line'; to promote development, but *also* protect the standard of living of the other organisms with whom they share the planet.

Along with Environmental Impact Statements (EIS), perhaps future economists can devise what might be called GIS or 'Grandchild Impact Statements,' making sure our kids and *their* kids will have sustainable quantities of biological as well as other resources, helping preserve our soils and waters, fisheries and forests, whales and bluebirds—even the tiny toads and butterflies—that these entities too will have their voices represented. **"**[a]

Are there some people who think a clean environment is an extremely high priority?

Yes. Richard Rosen, director of the Energy Group of the Tellus Institute, says that environmentalists do. He says:

"Indeed, some environmental advocates claim that the appropriate level for most, if not all, pollutants is zero. . . . Some environmentalists hold that measuring human lives or ecosystems in dollars is inappropriate and perhaps even morally repugnant, because people have an inherent right to live in a world free of pollution. **"**[b]

a.   James Eggert, *Meadowlark Economics* (Armonk, New York: M.E. Sharpe, Inc., 1992), pp. 6–7. Reprinted with permission of M.E. Sharper, Inc. Armonk, N.Y. 10504.

b.   Richard Rosen, "Reclaiming Economics," *Dollars & Sense*, July/August 1993, p. 12.

ANALYZING PRIMARY SOURCES (continued)

What are some of the costs of reducing pollution?

Here is what Robert Crandall, who is a senior fellow at the Brookings Institution in Washington, D.C., has to say:

"The way that pollution controls are often built into the production process makes any estimation of their cost extremely difficult. In addition, pollution controls often discourage new investment and production, but no one currently calculates such indirect costs as the value of what is not produced. The federal government has, however, estimated a subset of costs, namely direct expenditures on pollution controls. These expenditures cost governments and private entities an estimated $100 billion in 1988. Some $40 billion was spent on air pollution abatement, $40 billion on water pollution controls, and $20 billion for a variety of solid-waste, hazardous-waste, and other programs. **"** [c]

Have government programs that have tried to reduce the amount of air pollution from cars been beneficial?

Some people think so. Gregg Easterbrook, a journalist, writes:

"Rapid progress has been made against carbon monoxide, a . . . pollutant that can cause respiratory distress, partly because a new oxygenated gasoline that reduces carbon-monoxide emissions was adopted last year in many cities. In 1985, New York City had 71 days that were out of compliance with the EPA standard for carbon monoxide; that number declined to two days in 1991 and zero days last year. Nationally, carbon-monoxide levels have been dropping sharply since 1990. **"** [d]

In this chapter we discussed two methods to reduce pollution. Are there times it would be better for the government to set pollution standards than to allocate pollution permits?

Alan Blinder, who is a member of President Bill Clinton's Council of Economic Advisors, is largely in favor of pollution permits. However, there are instances, he says, when he would not favor them over direct regulations. He says:

"I must confess that there are circumstances under which market-based solutions [such as pollution permits] are inappropriate and quantitative standards are better. One obvious instance is the case of a deadly poison. If the socially desirable level of a toxin is zero, there is no point in imposing an emissions fee. An outright ban makes more sense.

Another case is a sudden health emergency. When, for example, a summertime air inversion raises air pollution in Los Angeles or New York to hazardous levels, it makes perfect sense for the mayors of those cities to place legal limits on driving, on industrial discharges, or on both. There is simply no time to install a system of pollution permits.

A final obvious case is when no adequate monitoring device exists, as in the case of runoff from soil pollution. Then a system of emission fees is out of the question. But so also is a system of direct quantitative controls on

c. Robert W. Crandall, "Pollution Controls," *The Fortune Encyclopedia of Economics* (New York: Warner Books, 1993), pp. 453–54.

d. Gregg Easterbrook, "Winning the War on Smog," *Newsweek*, August 23, 1993, p. 29.

ANALYZING PRIMARY SOURCES (continued)

emissions. The only viable way to control such pollution may be to mandate that cleaner technologies be used. **"** [e]

_____

e. Alan Blinder, _Hard Heads, Soft Hearts: Tough-Minded Economics for a Just Society_ (Reading, Massachusetts: Addison-Wesley Publishing Company, Inc., 1987), p. 149.

1. What is James Eggert proposing?

2. According to Robert Crandall, what are some of the indirect costs of pollution controls?

3. According to Alan Blinder, when might pollution permits be inappropriate to use?

The owner of Firm X says to the owner of Firm Z, "If I sell you my permit, I'd have to eliminate three units of pollution instead of only two. The cost to me of eliminating the third unit of pollution is $100. So if you pay me more than $100, I will be willing to sell my permit to you." (The owner of Firm X thinks, "If I can sell my pollution permit for, say, $250, then I can eliminate the third unit of pollution for $100 and have $150 left over.")

The owner of Firm Y says to the owner of Firm Z, "If I sell you my permit, I'd have to eliminate three units of pollution instead of only two. The cost to me of eliminating the third unit of pollution is $200. So if you pay me more than $200, I will be willing to sell my permit to you." (The owner of Firm Y thinks, "If I can sell my pollution permit for, say, $350, then I can eliminate the third unit of pollution for $200 and have $150 left over.")

So far, then, we have concluded this: It appears to be in the best interest of Firm X and Firm Y to sell their permits to Firm Z, and it appears to be in the best interest of Firm Z to buy the permits. Of course, all this depends on whether the price is right. Obviously the owner of Firm Z wants to buy the pollution permits as cheaply as possible, and the owners of Firm X and Firm Y want to sell the pollution permits for as much as possible. The owners of the three firms start to bargain. Let's say that after a few minutes of bargaining, the three parties agree on the price of $330 per permit. (We knew the price had to be somewhat greater than $100, or Firm X wouldn't sell; and it had to be greater than $200, or Firm Y

wouldn't sell. Finally, it couldn't be more than $500 for the first permit, or Firm Z wouldn't buy.)

At a price of $330 for a pollution permit, Firm Z buys one permit from Firm X and one permit from Firm Y. The cost to Firm Z for the permits is $660 ($330 × 2 permits = $660). With three permits in its possession, Firm Z doesn't have to eliminate any pollution; thus, it does not have to pay for any antipollution devices. Firm X, though, has to eliminate three units of pollution because it no longer has a pollution permit. The cost of its eliminating three units of pollution, according to the data in Exhibit 9-1, is $225 ($50 + $75 + $100 = $225). Firm Y also has to eliminate three units of pollution because it no longer has a pollution permit. The cost of its eliminating three units of pollution is $355 ($70 + $85 + $200 = $355).

Ultimately, six units of pollution have been eliminated (three units by Firm X and three units by Firm Y), so that only three units of pollution remain. In other words, the government has met its objective of reducing pollution from nine units to three. In addition, under the method by which permits are allocated by government, and traded by the firms, the cost to all three firms is $1,240 ($225 for Firm X to eliminate three units of pollution + $355 for Firm Y to eliminate three units of pollution + $660 for Firm Z to buy three pollution permits = $1,240). Notice that this is a lower cost than the cost incurred by the three firms when government standards were used, and each firm was simply ordered to eliminate two units of pollution. The cost in that case was $1,780. In both cases, however, the pollution level was brought down from nine to three units. We conclude that it is less costly for firms to eliminate pollution when the government allocates pollution permits that can be traded than when it simply directs each firm to eliminate so many units of pollution.

QUESTION: *It is easy to see that market environmentalism is a cheaper way to eliminate pollution than government's setting standards. But why?*

ANSWER: *Under the method of selling and buying permits, the firms that can clean up pollution for the least cost are the ones that actually do the job. This is not the case under the* method of setting standards. To illustrate, when standards are set, Firm Z ends up eliminating two units of pollution. The problem is that it is much more expensive for Firm Z to eliminate pollution than for Firm X or Firm Y to do so. For example, it costs Firm Z $1,500 to eliminate the first two units of pollution, whereas it only costs Firm X $125 and Firm Y $155.

When government sets standards, every firm has to reduce its pollution—no matter whether it costs the firm a lot or a little to do so. When government allocates pollution permits, and allows firms to buy and sell them amongst themselves, not every firm will end up reducing its pollution. Firms that reduce pollution are the firms that find it least costly to do so.

LEARNING CHECK

1. What do ownership rights have to do with pollution?
2. Why is it cheaper to reduce pollution by using pollution permits than to reduce it by setting standards?

SECTION 2 HEALTH CARE

Bill Clinton made health care a major issue during his campaign for the presidency of the United States. He said that health care was too expensive and that millions of people did not have health insurance. He said that, when he became president, he would do something about the health care mess.

When Clinton became president, in 1993, he set up a task force to discuss the health care crisis in this nation. This task force was established to identify health care problems and to propose possible solutions to these problems. A major problem that the task force identified was one that was on the minds of millions of people: health care was just too expensive.

We examine the price of health care in this section. Specifically, we try to identify some of the reasons why it has become so expensive.

As you read, keep these key questions in mind:

- What are medical malpractice suits, and what do they have to do with the price of health care?
- What do physician-owned outpatient diagnostic and treatment facilities have to do with the price of health care?
- What do increases in income have to do with the price of health care?
- What are third-party payments and what do they have to do with the price of health care?
- What are Medicare and Medicaid?

Why Has the Price of Health Care Been Rising?

In 1991, $751.8 billion was spent in the United States on health care. This was 13.4 percent of the entire U.S. economy. In other words, out of each dollar that was spent in the U.S. economy in 1991, 13.4 cents went for health care.

By international standards, the U.S. is a big spender in this area. For example, while Americans spent $2,868 per person on health care in 1991, Australians spent $1,407 per person, Japanese spent $1,307 per person, and Italians spent $1,408 per person.

In comparison to other prices, health care prices have risen dramatically. For example, between 1980 and 1992, health care prices increased 153 percent. If we break things down, the price of physicians' services increased 136 percent during this time, and the price of a hospital room increased 207 percent. In contrast, the price of nonmedical items did not increase as much. The price of food, for example, increased 59 percent, housing prices increased 69 percent, and new car prices increased 45 percent.

Why has the price of health care been rising so much? Think of the simple supply-and-demand framework developed in Chapters 3 and 4. Within this framework, the price of a good or service rises if either (1) demand rises or (2) supply falls.[1] Exhibit 9-2 shows these two cases. In part *a*, demand for health care increases, and price increases from P_1 to P_2. In part *b*, supply decreases, and price increases from P_1 to P_2.

We now consider a number of factors that have contributed to the rising price of health care in the

---

1. Actually, different combinations of changes in supply and demand can cause price to rise. For example, price may rise if demand rises and supply falls or if demand rises by more than supply rises. In this section, we keep things simple and consider only the case where demand rises and supply stays the same or supply falls and demand stays the same. There is almost nothing we lose in substance by doing this, since health care prices have risen in recent years primarily because of increases in demand.

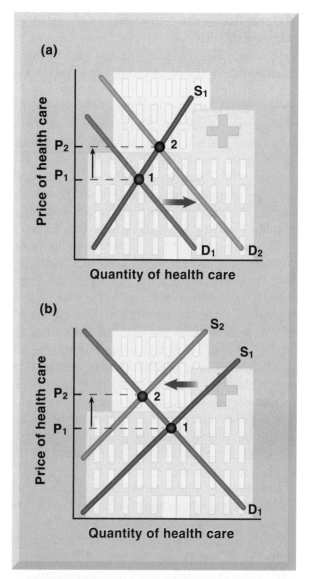

(a)

(b)

▲ **EXHIBIT 9-2. Why Has the Price of Health Care Been Rising?** Using the supply-and-demand framework shown in this exhibit, we realize that the price of health care can rise if either the demand for health care rises as shown in part *a*, or the supply of health care falls as shown in part *b*.

past two decades. In each case, note whether the factor has caused the demand for health care to rise or the supply of health care to fall. You will see that most of the factors that have contributed to the rising price of health care have affected the demand side of the health care market.

Malpractice Suits. In recent years, **medical malpractice suits** have become more common in the United States. When a doctor is sued for malpractice, the insurance company has to pay attorney fees. If the doctor loses the malpractice suit, the insurance company often has to pay large sums of money to the plaintiff. The increase in the number of these costly lawsuits has increased expenses for insurance companies. To cover these expenses, insurance companies have been increasing doctors' liability insurance premiums. For example, between 1982 and 1989, doctors' liability insurance premiums increased at a rate of 15 percent a year.

Two things happened as a result of the increases in malpractice suits and insurance premiums. In the first place, doctors started to perform more tests (X rays, blood tests, and so on) to protect themselves. (It has been estimated that between 20 and 30 percent of all medical tests performed in the United States are unnecessary.) This is called *defensive medicine*, because doctors perform the medical tests so that they can defend themselves against negligence should they be taken to court one day. The practice of defensive medicine by doctors has simply increased the demand for certain kinds of medical tests and pushed up the overall price of health care.

In the second place, physicians in certain specialties, such as obstetrics (the branch of medicine concerned with the care and treatment of women during pregnancy and childbirth), are particularly likely to be defendants in medical malpractice suits. This has caused some physicians to drop out of these specialties, making such specialists hard to find in some communities (supply decreased) and causing rates to rise.

Physician-Owned Outpatient Diagnostic and Treatment Facilities. A growing trend in the late 1980s was for physicians to own the outpatient diagnostic and treatment facilities (such as laboratories) where medical tests were administered. It was not uncommon for a physician to order that a series of tests be done at his or her own lab. This increased the demand for these medical tests as well as the price of health care.

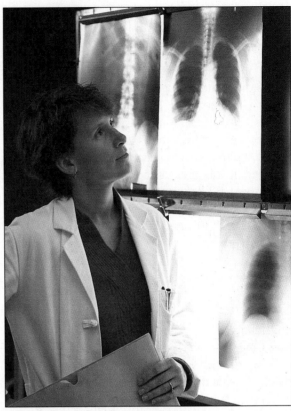

▲ As malpractice suits have become more common, many physicians have begun to practice defensive medicine.

Increases in Income. Chapter 3 said that a *normal good* is a good whose demand rises as people's income rises. Health care is a normal good, and in the past three decades, people's incomes have been rising. As a result, the demand for health care has been rising—and with it the price of health care.

Third-Party Payments. Think of the different ways in which you could pay for health care.

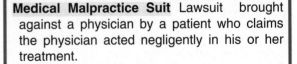

MINI GLOSSARY

Medical Malpractice Suit Lawsuit brought against a physician by a patient who claims the physician acted negligently in his or her treatment.

CONSUMER ECONOMIC DECISIONS

How to Reduce Some Health Care Costs

out of every dollar spent on health care, 6.7 cents goes for dentists' services, 7.1 cents goes for drugs and medical supplies, 8.7 cents goes for nursing-home care, 13.1 cents goes to administration, public health activity, research, and construction, 20.3 cents goes for physicians' services, 41 cents goes for hospital care, and 3.1 cents goes for other personal health care. As you can see, the bulk of each dollar goes for hospital care, and hospital care and physicians' services together account for 61.3 cents of each dollar spent on health care. Are there ways to reduce the cost of health care? There are some, and we consider them here.

1. **Realize that you need not always see a physician; you can sometimes consult other health care personnel instead.** Let's say you need to have your eyes checked. You can go either to an optometrist (who is not a medical doctor) or to an ophthalmologist (a medical doctor who specializes in treating eye diseases). Usually, the optometrist will charge less for a routine eye exam. Of course, if you are concerned about eye disease or an eye injury, it is better to go to an ophthalmologist.

   Suppose you need help for depression, anxiety, or job stress. You may wish to consult a clinical psychologist (who holds a Ph.D. degree and specializes in psychology) or a psychiatrist (who is a medical doctor who specializes in mental illness and can prescribe drugs). Usually, the psychologist is cheaper than the psychiatrist. Here again,

of course, money may not be everything. It may be better to see a psychiatrist than a psychologist for some mental health problems. You should be aware of your options, though. If you have trouble making up your mind, a good person to speak with is your family physician. He or she can advise you of your options in seeking specialist care.

2. **Ask your physician whether he or she will accept your insurance payment as full payment.** Suppose you have health insurance that covers 100 percent of doctors' fees. You would expect that whatever your doctor charged you for a medical visit or treatment would be covered by your insurance. Right? Not necessarily. In terms of insurance coverage, 100 percent really means 100 percent of "usual, customary, and reasonable" doctors' fees. For example, let's say that in your community, most doctors charge $180 to treat a knee injury, but your doctor charges $300. Your insurance company may pay only $180, and you may have to pay the rest. You want to know such things up front. Ask your doctor his or her policy with respect to acceptance of insurance payments.

3. **Generic drugs are cheaper than brand-name drugs.** Generic drugs are chemically equivalent to brand-name drugs but cost less (sometimes generics cost less than half what brand-name drugs cost). You may find it worthwhile to ask your pharmacist for the generic drug instead of the brand-name drug. In a few cases, your physician may re-

Making CONSUMER ECONOMIC DECISIONS (continued)

quire you to purchase the brand-name drug. You have the right to know why. Also, be aware that not all drugs are available in generic form.

4. **Learn how to take your medicine and follow your doctor's orders.** Some medicines don't work when they are taken with certain foods, cold remedies, and so on. Ask your pharmacist or doctor how you should take your medicine. Your medicine may need to be taken at night, or on an empty stomach, or after a meal, or the like. Also, follow your doctor's instructions when it comes to medicine. For example, most doctors trying to rid a patient of a bacterial infection will prescribe that antibiotics be taken for 10 days. Many patients end up feeling much better on the fifth or sixth day, and some stop taking their medications. However, antibiotics must be taken for the full time—even if the patient feels much better. Otherwise, there is a chance the infection will return and the patient will end up buying more medicine.

5. **Get an unbiased second opinion.** Suppose you go to your doctor and she tells you that you need surgery. Do you really? The fact is, you can't be sure, and you may not want to risk the possible complications of surgery and pay the money for an expensive surgery if it is not needed. Get a second opinion, preferably from a doctor who is not connected with your doctor. Many patients are uneasy seeking a second opinion because they feel it might offend the doctor who recommended the surgery. Most doctors understand that it is only natural to ask for a second opinion when it comes to major health care. If your doctor doesn't, or if he or she gets upset with you for suggesting

that you would like a second opinion, then he or she may not be the right doctor for you. Also, to save on costs, be sure to ask your first doctor to send any X rays, lab tests, and so on to your second doctor.

6. **Learn to read and spot errors on hospital bills.** Hospitals sometimes make errors in their bills. If you suspect an error was made in your bill—perhaps you were charged for a hospital room on the day you checked out—then you need to talk to someone in the hospital business office, the patient accounts supervisor, or the patient representative. You may hear a person at the hospital say, "Don't worry, your insurance will cover it." That may or may not be true. The point is that if there is an overcharge, why should you *or* your insurance company pay for it? After you speak with a person at the hospital, inform your insurance company of the overcharges you suspect.

---

1. How much of each dollar spent on health care goes for hospital care and physicians' services together?

2. Why is it often important to get a second opinion when it comes to a medical matter?

3. What are generic drugs? Are they cheaper or more expensive than brand-name drugs?

First, you could pay for the health care yourself, out of your own pocket. Second, you could buy private health care insurance yourself; when you needed health care, the insurance company would pay for it. Third, you could work for a company that provided you with health care insurance. Your employer would buy health care insurance for you, and when you needed health care, the insurance company would pay for it. Fourth, the government could pay for your health care.

We can distinguish between the first way of paying for health care—out-of-pocket—and all others. The others we can put into a group called **third-party payers**. Before we go on, ask yourself whether your behavior in getting health care would be any different if you paid out-of-pocket than it would be if a third party paid. Under which method would you be more likely to monitor your own health and be aware of and alert to differences in medical costs?

Most economists argue that a person who has to pay for each item of health care he or she consumes will be more careful in watching costs. Let's look at an example. Suppose you wake up feeling sick one day. You have a fever, your body aches, and your stomach hurts. You know that if you go to the doctor, you will have to pay for the visit yourself (out-of-pocket) and that if medicine is prescribed or tests ordered, you will pay for them, too. In this setting, you may be more likely to hold off for a few hours or a day to see if you get better on your own. In contrast, if a third party is paying for your health care, you may be more likely to go to the doctor immediately. If the doctor says you need some tests, you may not ask the cost, and you probably won't try to find out how important it is to get them right now. Instead, you may simply go along. After all, someone else is picking up the tab.

You can see that third-party payers end up increasing the demand for health care. And if third-party payers increase the demand for health care, they also increase the price of health care.

Much of the increase in health care costs in the United States in the past three decades is a result of the growth of the third-party payment system in health care. This growth has come from two sources: employer-provided benefits and Medicare and Medicaid.

Employer-Provided Benefits. During World War II, a number of goods and resources were in shortage in the United States. One of the things in shortage was labor. To compete for labor, many business firms began to offer their employees health insurance benefits. Over the years, the percentage of the population whose health coverage was provided by employers grew. Today, approximately 60 percent of the population has employer-provided insurance. Employer-provided health benefits constitute a massive third-party payment scheme. What is the result? As stated before, the result is greater demand for health care, leading to higher health care prices. Over time, the higher health care prices have been taken into account by the insurance companies, and health insurance premiums have risen. Employers have begun to complain about higher health insurance premiums for their employees, because higher premiums have simply raised the cost of doing business for the employers.

Medicare and Medicaid. **Medicare** is a nationwide federal health insurance program that began in 1965. It covers persons over 65 and people of all ages with disabilities. Approximately 11 percent of the population has Medicare coverage. The federal government, through this program, is a third-party payer of health care for persons covered by Medicare.

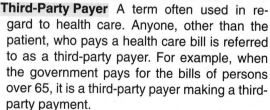

MINI GLOSSARY

Third-Party Payer A term often used in regard to health care. Anyone, other than the patient, who pays a health care bill is referred to as a third-party payer. For example, when the government pays for the bills of persons over 65, it is a third-party payer making a third-party payment.
Medicare A nationwide federal health insurance program for people over 65 and those of all ages with disabilities.

ANALYZING PRIMARY SOURCES

President Clinton Speaks about Health Care

In September 1993, President Bill Clinton presented his health care plan to Congress and to the country. Here is some of what he had to say:

"Tonight I want to talk to you about the principles that I believe must embody our efforts to reform America's health care system—security, simplicity, savings, choice, quality, and responsibility.

First and most important, security. This principle speaks to the human misery, to the costs, to the anxiety we hear about every day—all of us—when people talk about their problems with the present system. Security means that those who do not now have health care coverage will have it; and for those who have it, it will never be taken away. We must achieve that security as soon as possible.

Under our plan, every American would receive a health care security card that will guarantee a comprehensive package of benefits over the course of an entire lifetime, roughly comparable to the benefit package offered by most Fortune 500 companies. . . .

The second principle is simplicity. Our health care system must be simpler for the patients and simpler for those who actually deliver health care—our doctors, our nurses, our other medical professionals. Today we have more than 1,500 insurers, with hundreds and hundreds of different forms. No other nation has a system like this. These forms are time consuming for health care providers, they're expensive for health care consumers, they're exasperating for anyone who's ever tried to sit down around a table and wade through them and figure them out.

The medical care industry is literally drowning in paperwork. In recent years, the number of administrators in our hospitals has grown by four times the rate that the number of doctors has grown. A hospital ought to be a house of healing, not a monument to paperwork and bureaucracy. . . .

Under our proposal there would be one standard insurance form—not hundreds of them. We will simplify also—and we must—the government's rules and regulations, because they are a big part of this problem. . . .

The third principle is savings. Reform must produce savings in this health care system. It has to. We are spending over 14 percent of our income on health care—Canada's at 10; nobody else is over 9. We're competing with all these people for the future. And the other major countries, they cover everybody and they cover them with services as generous as the best company policies here in this country. . . .

So how will we achieve these savings? . . . We believe [the] way to achieve these savings [is] to give groups of consumers and small businesses the same market bargaining power that large corporations and large groups of public employees now have. We want to let market forces enable plans to compete. We

ANALYZING PRIMARY SOURCES (continued)

want to force these plans to compete on the basis of price and quality, not simply to allow them to continue making money by turning people away who are sick or old or performing mountains of unnecessary procedures. But we also believe we should back this system up with limits on how much plans can raise their premiums year in and year out, forcing people, again, to continue to pay more for the same health care, without regard to inflation or the rising population needs. . . .

The fourth principle is choice. Americans believe they ought to be able to choose their own health care plan and keep their own doctors. And I think all of us agree. Under any plan we pass, they ought to have that right. . . .

We propose to give every American a choice among high-quality plans. You can stay with your current doctor, join a network of doctors and hospitals, or join a health maintenance organization. If you don't like your plan, every year you'll have the chance to choose a new one. . . .

The fifth principle is quality. If we reformed everything else in health care, but failed to preserve and enhance the high quality of our medical care, we will have taken a step backward, not forward. Quality is something that we simply can't leave to chance. . . .

Our proposal will create report cards on health plans, so that consumers can choose the highest-quality health care providers and reward them with their business. . . .

The sixth and final principle is responsibility. We need to restore a sense that we're all in this together and that we all have a responsibility to be a part of the solution. Responsibility has to start with those who profit from the current system. Responsibility means insurance companies should no longer be allowed to cast people aside when they get sick. It should apply to laboratories that submit fraudulent bills, to lawyers who abuse malpractice claims, to doctors who order unnecessary procedures. It means drug companies should no longer charge

three times more for prescription drugs made in America here in the United States than they charge for the same drugs overseas. . . .

But let me say this—and I hope every American will listen, because this is not an easy thing to hear—responsibility in our health care system isn't just about them. It's about you, it's about me, it's about each of us.

Too many of us have not taken responsibility for our own health care and for our own relations to the health care system. Many of us who have had fully paid health care plans have used the system whether we needed it or not without thinking what the costs were. Many people who use this system don't pay a penny for their care even though they can afford to. I think those who don't have any health insurance should be responsible for paying a portion of their new coverage. There can't be any something for nothing, and we have to demonstrate that to people. This is not a free system. Even small contributions, as small as a $10 co-payment when you visit a doctor, illustrates that this is something of value. There is a cost to it. It is not free. . . .

Now these, my fellow Americans, are the principles on which I think we should base our efforts: security, simplicity, savings, choice, quality, and responsibility. These are the guiding stars that we should follow on our journey toward health care reform. **"**

---

1. President Clinton says that this country has to have a health care plan that guarantees health coverage to every American. Do you think this is a good idea? Why or why not?
2. President Clinton said, "Many of us who've had fully paid health care plans have used the system whether we needed it or not without thinking what the costs were." Give some examples of what you think he is referring to here.

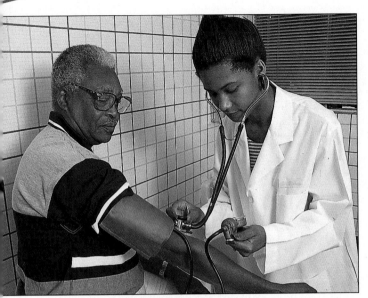

▲ Today, in the United States, 78 percent of the population has third-party health coverage. This includes employer-provided health coverage, Medicare, and Medicaid.

Overall numbers of hospital admissions began to increase, once the Medicare program was in effect, because of an increase in patients admitted through Medicare. For example, between 1967 and 1978, the hospital admission rate for elderly persons increased 33 percent. There is little doubt Medicare has made health care more affordable for the elderly. But the demand for physicians and hospitals stemming from those persons over 65 has resulted in an increase in overall demand. And as the overall demand for physicians and hospitals has increased, so has price.

Medicaid is a federal and state program that provides health care to low-income individuals. Approximately 7 percent of the population has Medicaid coverage. Like Medicare, it has increased the overall demand for health care and led to an increase in price.

If we add the percentage of the population that has employer-provided health coverage (60 percent) to the percentages of the population that have Medicare (11 percent) and Medicaid (7 percent), we see that 78 percent of the population has health care coverage provided by a third-party payer. Some economists agree that this explains much of the high demand for and high price of health care in the United States today.

LEARNING CHECK

1. Explain two ways in which medical malpractice suits can increase the price of health care.
2. What does it mean to say that health care is a normal good?
3. Explain how third-party payments can increase the price of health care.
4. What is Medicare? Medicaid?

SECTION 3 POVERTY

his section presents some facts about poverty and examines its causes and some proposed solutions.

As you read, keep the following key questions in mind:

■ What are the two ways to define poverty?
■ What are in-kind benefits?

■ What are some of the ways proposed to reduce or eliminate poverty?

What is Poverty?

We can define poverty in one of two ways. In the first way, we pick a certain annual income—

such as $10,000—and say that any family of four whose income falls below this level is living in poverty. In the second way, we simply say that any family of four that falls, say, in the bottom 10 percent of income earners is living in poverty. The first way defines poverty in absolute terms, and the second way defines poverty in relative terms.

Which way—the absolute or the relative—is the better way to define poverty? Most people think the absolute way is, since if the relative way is used, poverty will always exist unless every family of four receives exactly the same income. Moreover, if we define poverty in the relative way, then even a family that received a huge income might be considered to live in poverty—which is odd, if not ridiculous. To illustrate, suppose there is a 10-family community where 9 of the 10 families earn $200,000 a year and one earns $100,000 a year. If poverty is defined in relative terms, as including the bottom 10 percent of income earners, then the family that earns $100,000 a year is said to be living in poverty. After all, this family is the poorest family in the 10-family community; it falls in the bottom 10 percent of income earners.

The U.S. government defines poverty in absolute terms. The absolute poverty measurement was developed in 1964 by the Social Security Administration, based on the findings of the Department of Agriculture. The measurement, called the **poverty line**, identifies the income below which people are considered to be living in poverty. Individuals or families with incomes below the poverty line are considered poor. In the early 1990s, approximately 7 million families, or 10 percent of all families, were living below the poverty line.

Money Income and In-Kind Benefits

The poverty statistics just cited—and, sometimes, the poverty statistics quoted on the television news—are based solely on money incomes. But many poor persons receive **in-kind benefits**. These are benefits in the form of specific goods or services, such as food stamps, subsidized housing,

and medical assistance. For example, a family of four with a money income of $11,000 to $12,000 was defined as poor in the late 1980s and early 1990s. However, this family might have received in-kind benefits worth, say, $4,000. If the poverty figures are adjusted for in-kind benefits, the percentage of persons living in poverty drops.

Who Are the Poor?

The poor are made up of persons of all religions, colors, sexes, ages, and ethnic backgrounds. However, some groups are represented much more prominently in the poverty figures than others. For example, there are greater percentages of poor among African Americans and Hispanics than among whites. In 1991, 32.7 percent of African Americans, 28.7 percent of Hispanics, and 11.3 percent of whites lived below the poverty line. The percentage of families headed by females who are poor is greater than that of families headed by males, and families with seven or more persons are much more likely to be poor than are families with fewer than seven persons. Additionally, large percentages of young persons are poor, and the uneducated and poorly educated are more likely to be poor than are the educated.

If we look at things in terms of absolute numbers, instead of percentages, then we see that most poor persons are white. This largely stems from the fact that there are more whites than other

MINI GLOSSARY

Medicaid A federal and state program that provides health care to low-income individuals by making government a third-party payer.

Poverty Line Income level below which people are considered to be living in poverty.

In-Kind Benefit Benefit (usually supplied by government) that takes the form of a specific good or service instead of money. Food stamps, subsidized housing, and medical assistance are examples of in-kind benefits.

◄ In the early 1990s, 10 percent of all families in the United States lived in poverty.

groups in the total population. For example, in 1991, 23.7 million whites, 10.2 million African Americans, and 6.3 million Hispanics lived below the poverty line.

The Causes of Poverty

It would be easy if we could identify one simple reason why people are poor. Of course, there are those who speak as if we could. They may argue that people are poor because they do not want to work. They may argue that people are poor because they are discriminated against in the workplace. Most economists today believe poverty has more than one cause, but they differ as to the importance they assign to the various causes. And sometimes they (along with others) differ as to the cause of poverty in a particular case. Let's examine this latter point through a short fictional story.

Christine is 25 years old; she has only a seventh-grade education; she is a single parent with three small children. She spends her days watching television, taking care of her children, and generally staying around her apartment. Christine and her children live in poverty. Their total income comes from cash and in-kind assistance from government.

Viewing this situation, one person comments that Christine is poor because of her own choosing. She chose not to get an education, she chose to get married and have children at a very young age, and she chose to stay at home instead of work. This person argues that the life Christine is living now—in poverty—is the consequence of decisions that she made years ago.

Another person argues differently. This person says that Christine was unlucky to be born into a family having many problems, and parents who didn't stress the importance of getting an education. This person says that when Christine was young and attending school, she couldn't really do her homework because of the considerable abuse in her family and gang violence in her neighborhood. Additionally, Christine has been discriminated against in the workplace. Besides, with her lack of education, any job she could get would probably pay so little that she would not be able to afford day care for her children. This person concludes that Christine is living in poverty because of bad luck and discrimination.

In broad terms, one person sees choice as the cause of Christine's poverty, and the other sees factors outside her control as the cause. This is not the place to discuss at length which person is closer to the truth or to try to answer the centuries-old question, "Is one's life the result of fate or choice?" The point is simply that there is a great deal of room for disagreement about the specific cause of poverty in a specific case.

Poverty and the Price System

We have seen that most economists believe poverty has more than one cause. Thus, some people may be poor because they cannot work (perhaps they are temporarily disabled), some people may be poor because they don't "want" to work, and some people may be poor because they are discriminated against in the workplace (perhaps few employers want to hire them because of their genders, ethnic origins, or religions).

Some people are poor because what they have to sell commands a very low price. Notice here the effect that price has on poverty. If a person only can sell one thing—whether it is his or her labor services or a good—and the price of this thing is very low, then that person is likely to be poor. Consider John, who has only his unskilled labor services to sell in the market. Because he has very few skills, the demand for his labor services is likely to be very low. Low demand will translate into a low price for what John sells. The low price will, in turn, translate into a low income for John. This is why many persons try to develop skills that are in high demand. Skills in high demand command a high price, which in turn generates high incomes for those who possess and sell them.

Proposed and Existing Ways of Reducing or Eliminating Poverty

We turn now to an examination of three ways in which poverty might be reduced or eliminated: the current welfare system, the negative income tax, and the free-enterprise–oriented program.

The Current Welfare System. The current welfare system largely aids poor people in two ways: by providing cash benefits and by providing in-kind benefits. The major cash payment program is Aid to Families with Dependent Children (AFDC), which helps poor families with children. The major forms of in-kind assistance include food stamps, public housing, and Medicaid.

Some critics of the current welfare system say that too little money is being spent to help get people out of poverty. Other critics comment either that too much money is being spent or that much that is being spent isn't reaching the right people. (For example, in the past, there have been some reports of college students from rich families receiving food stamps.)

Additionally, critics charge that the current welfare system has the unintended result of distorting individuals' incentive to lessen their need. Consider the fictional case of Barbara Sullivan. Barbara receives $496 per month in AFDC payments and $204 per month in food stamps. Barbara is not working, but she is seriously considering trying to find work soon. There is a problem, though. If she works and earns an income, her AFDC payments and food stamps will be cut. On the one hand, she earns income if she works; but on the other hand, she loses money (AFDC) and in-kind benefits (food stamps) if she works. The real question is how much she benefits by working relative to how much she loses. In many instances, the benefit from working over not working is small, or, in fact, nonexistent. In such instances, some individuals choose not to work. Thus, we can reasonably say that welfare assistance acts as a disincentive to work.

The Negative Income Tax. A proposed program called the negative income tax was designed to reduce the disincentive effects of the current welfare system. It would provide cash payments based on income level, as illustrated in Exhibit 9-3. The process of finding a family's negative income tax payment is quite easy. For example, suppose a family earns zero income (column 1). It might receive a negative income tax payment, or cash grant, of $5,000 (column 2). This would

(1) Earned income	(2) Negative income tax payment (cash grant)	(3) Total income = Earned income + Negative income tax payment
$0	$5,000	$5,000
1,000	4,500	5,500
2,000	4,000	6,000
3,000	3,500	6,500
4,000	3,000	7,000
5,000	2,500	7,500
6,000	2,000	8,000

◄ **EXHIBIT 9-3. Negative Income Tax.** The guaranteed income level here is $5,000. A family that earns no income (column 1) receives a negative income tax payment of $5,000 (column 2). If this family earns $1,000, the negative income tax payment falls to $4,500. (The numbers in this exhibit are used for illustrative purposes only.)

make its total income (column 3) $5,000. It follows that no family would be permitted to fall below an income of $5,000. This income would then be the **guaranteed income level**. Exactly what dollar figure would constitute the guaranteed income level would be decided through the political process; $5,000 is simply used here for illustrative purposes.

Suppose now that the family that previously earned no income earns $1,000. How will it be affected? Its cash grant will diminish from $5,000 to $4,500. Notice that the payment falls by less than the earned income increases. For a $1,000 increase in earned income, the negative income tax payment decreases by $500. In other words, the family loses $500 from the government for the $1,000 it earns; this represents a ratio of 50 percent ($500 ÷ $1,000 = 0.5, or 50 percent). This 50 percent is called the **implicit marginal tax rate**. The implicit marginal tax rate is the rate at which the cash grant is reduced as earned income increases. For the family in our example, the implicit marginal tax rate is 50 percent. A person who earns an additional dollar of income loses 50 cents of welfare assistance.

Clearly, the family in the example can make itself substantially better off—as measured by its total income (column 3)—by working and earning income. This system contrasts with many present welfare assistance programs. In these current programs, under certain conditions, a person who earns an additional dollar of income loses a dollar of welfare assistance. As a result, the disincentive to work and earn income is strong, as is the incentive to remain on welfare.

QUESTION: *Wouldn't the cash grant provide people with a disincentive to work if the guaranteed income level were set too high? For example, if the guaranteed income level were set at $20,000, many people currently earning that income might decide to quit their jobs and collect cash grants. Isn't this likely to be the case?*

ANSWER: *Certainly, if the guaranteed income level were set too high, some individuals currently not receiving welfare assistance would have an incentive to put themselves into a position where they would receive it. In this case, the negative income tax program might lead to a situation in which more instead of fewer individuals received welfare assistance. The dollar amount of the guaranteed income is critical to the program's having the desired effect.*

The Free-Enterprise–Oriented Program. In both the current welfare system and the cash grant scheme, government is actively involved in trying to reduce or eliminate poverty. Both use the approach of assisting poor persons directly by giving them cash or goods and services. The free-enterprise–oriented program for reducing poverty does not take the direct assistance approach but rather advocates breaking down the existing legal barriers to employment, thereby indirectly assisting poor persons.

For example, advocates of this approach hold that the minimum wage law actually hurts poor, unskilled persons by pricing them out of the labor market. Due to a young person's lack of work skills, it is not cost effective for a company to hire that person at the minimum wage rate of $4.25 per hour. It would be cost effective to hire and train that person at $3.90 per hour, but that would be illegal. Thus, the person does not get hired. Critics of the minimum wage law argue that it essentially prevents some young, unskilled workers from getting a job and acquiring work skills.

Consider another example. In many major cities, a person must obtain an expensive medallion (license) before operating a taxi business. Advocates of the free-enterprise–oriented approach to reducing poverty argue that such licensing procedures keep some people in poverty. Think about the case of taxis in New York City.

First, ask yourself what requirements a person who wants to operate a taxi business should meet. You may say that the person should prove that he or she is a good driver, has auto insurance, is familiar with the city, is not a criminal, and is in possession of a car that is mechanically safe. Would you think that this person should also have to pay approximately $175,000 for a taxi license? If this amount seems excessive, you may be surprised to hear that it is the amount charged for a license in New York City. Before a person can operate a taxi business, he or she must be licensed. Licensing in-

volves purchasing a taxi medallion, and these medallions are limited in number. In 1993, the price of a medallion was approximately $175,000.

Some economists have argued that the taxi medallion system in New York City prevents poor people from taking advantage of a valuable job opportunity. Certainly, there are poor people in New York City who would be able to scrape together the funds to buy a car and insurance and drive it around town as a taxi but who are prevented from going into the taxi business because they do not have $175,000 for the medallion. These economists argue that the removal of such licensing requirements would promote a more open and free-entry market. They say that the poor would benefit immensely if job opportunities that are currently closed were opened up to them. This group often predicts that if government were to become more involved in opening up the market, instead of working alongside those who wish to close it, poverty would quickly decrease.

MINI GLOSSARY

Guaranteed Income Level With regard to negative income tax, the level below which a person's income is not allowed to fall.

Implicit Marginal Tax Rate The rate at which the negative income tax payment (or any cash grant or subsidy) is reduced as earned income rises. For example, if a person earns an additional $1,000 and his or her negative income tax payment falls by $500, then the implicit marginal tax rate is 50 percent ($500 ÷ $1,000 = 0.50 and 0.50 × 100 = 50 percent).

LEARNING CHECK

1. "Anyone who earns less than $8,000 a year is defined as living in poverty." Does this statement represent an absolute or a relative definition of poverty?
2. "Anyone who falls into the bottom 5 percent of income earners is defined as living in poverty." Does this statement represent an absolute or a relative definition of poverty?
3. In terms of the negative income tax program, to what does *guaranteed income level* refer?

DEVELOPING ECONOMIC SKILLS

The Economics Paper: Rewriting

Author Ernest Hemingway was once approached by a woman who had recently read one of his novels. She praised Hemingway's clear, precise, and engaging writing style. She reminded Hemingway of one sentence he had written that was so beautiful she believed it must have flowed out of him with absolutely no effort. Hemingway had to disappoint her by admitting he had rewritten that one sentence 57 times.

If you remember only one thing about writing, let it be this: good writing is the result of rewriting. When we read a book, a magazine, or a newspaper, we are reading the finished product. We have no idea how many times what we are reading has been reviewed and revised.

You will probably be disappointed if you compare the first draft of something you've written with a published book, story, or article. Keep in mind, however, that your work has not yet been rewritten, whereas the published work has been.

The process of rewriting begins with reading your paper sentence by sentence. After reading each sentence, ask yourself whether you have clearly communicated what you intended. If you haven't, put an X next to the sentence. You will rewrite it later.

As you read, also ask yourself if one sentence proceeds naturally into the next. If not, put a plus sign (+) at the beginning of the sentence that does not flow naturally from the previous one.

Once you have read your paper sentence by sentence, go back and read it paragraph by paragraph. After reading each paragraph, try to identify its main message. Then ask yourself if you have communicated that message clearly. If you didn't, put a minus sign (−) in the margin next to the paragraph.

Go back and rewrite the sentences and paragraphs that need to be rewritten. Try to use as few words as possible to communicate your message. Much of rewriting is getting rid of unnecessary words.

Now, go through the paper again, sentence by sentence, correcting any grammatical and spelling errors.

Finally, read the paper from beginning to end without stopping. Then, ask yourself whether a person picked at random would find it clear, organized, and interesting. If it fails this test, ask yourself why. If it is because your paper is not well organized, improve the organization. If it is because you have left out a step or two in explaining something, fill in the missing steps. If it is because your sentences are too long, awkward, or boring, fix them.

Someone reading the above paragraph might say, "I'm not sure how to fix my writing. Can you give me some rules to follow?" While there are many rules to writing clear and grammatically correct prose, we would like to offer just one rule here. Make your writing clear, simple, and direct. To achieve that goal, avoid the excessive use of adverbs and adjectives. Eliminate long, complex sentences that confuse the point you are trying to make. State things clearly, so no one will mistake your meaning. Use simple words that don't get in the way of your message. Finally, write in a straightforward manner that communicates directly with your reader; it is, after all, for your reader that you have written.

---

1. Why is rewriting so important to good writing?
2. If you were given the assignment in the previous chapter to write an economics paper, rewrite it.

CHAPTER 9 REVIEW

CHAPTER SUMMARY

1. Pollution is a negative externality.

2. Eliminating pollution entirely would mean dramatic changes in our lives. For example, if we wanted to end the air pollution that comes from cars, we would have to stop driving cars.

3. Economists do not often think in terms of "either-or" choices—for example, either an extremely polluted world or a pollution-free world. Economists think in terms of costs and benefits, and because they do, they realize that there are benefits and costs to reducing pollution.

4. Pollution is much more likely to exist where ownership rights do not exist than where such rights do exist.

5. Market environmentalism refers to the use of market forces (such as price) to clean up the environment.

6. Government can reduce pollution by setting standards (or regulations) and by allocating pollution permits (which then can be bought and sold).

7. In recent years, medical malpractice suits have become more common in the United States. As a result, physicians have been practicing defensive medicine by ordering many tests for their patients. This has raised the price of health care. In addition, physicians have been leaving fields of medicine where malpractice suits are especially common, such as obstetrics. This has raised obstetricians' medical fees.

8. Because health care is a normal good, rising income levels have created rising demand for health care, and this has raised its price.

9. People can pay health care bills out-of-pocket or have a third party pay. Third-party payments may come from business or government. For example, employer-provided health insurance, Medicare, and Medicaid are all third-party payment systems. Third-party payers have increased the demand for and the price of health care.

10. There are two ways to define poverty: the absolute way and the relative way.

11. The government defines poverty in absolute terms. It states that anyone who falls below the poverty line is living in poverty.

12. In-kind benefits are benefits given in the form of specific goods or services. For example, food stamps and subsidized housing for the poor are in-kind benefits.

13. In absolute terms, more whites are poor than either African Americans or Hispanics.

14. In relative (or percentage) terms, more African Americans are poor than either whites or Hispanics.

15. Three types of programs are mentioned in discussions of how poverty might be reduced or eliminated. These programs are the current welfare system, the negative income tax, and the free-enterprise–oriented program.

CHAPTER 9 REVIEW
(continued)

BUILD YOUR ECONOMIC VOCABULARY

Match the word with the correct definition, example, or statement.

1. negative externality
2. medical malpractice
3. third-party payment
4. Medicare
5. implicit marginal tax rate
6. in-kind benefit

a. government-provided housing, for example
b. pollution, for example
c. health insurance program for people over 65 and those of all ages with disabilities
d. rate at which the cash grant is reduced as earned income increases
e. blameworthy neglect of a patient by a physician
f. a Medicaid payment, for example

REVIEW QUESTIONS

1. Resources that are not owned are more likely to be polluted, dirtied, or neglected. Why?
2. Economists often say that some air pollution may be better than no air pollution. Hearing this, a person might at first think economists actually like air pollution. Do they? Explain your answer.
3. Using the data that follow, compute (a) the total cost of eliminating six units of pollution if government sets standards whereby each firm must eliminate two units of pollution and (b) the total cost of eliminating six units of pollution if government allocates three pollution permits and they end up selling for $300 per permit.

	Firm X	Firm Y	Firm Z
Cost to eliminate first unit of pollution	$20	$40	$1,000
Cost to eliminate second unit of pollution	40	90	1,500
Cost to eliminate third unit of pollution	60	140	3,000

4. Explain why people in a small town might be more likely to recycle than people in a large city.
5. In 1991, what percentage of each dollar spent in the economy went for health care?
6. How is Medicare different from Medicaid?
7. "Third-party payers end up increasing the demand for health care." Explain why this statement is or is not true.
8. Give an example of defining poverty in (a) a relative way and (b) an absolute way.
9. Explain how the minimum wage law prices some poor, unskilled persons out of the labor market.
10. Define the following terms: *guaranteed income level*, *poverty line*, and *in-kind benefit*.
11. Explain how the negative income tax would work.

SHARPEN YOUR CRITICAL THINKING SKILLS

1. A good welfare system is said to be one that helps the people who may deserve to be helped, but does not distort incentives in such a way that people who may not deserve help can cash in on people's generosity. With this thought in mind, what type of welfare system would you propose, and why?

ACTIVITIES AND PROJECTS

1. In groups of five debate the issue, "Health Care Should Be Provided to Everyone Living in the United States." After the debate, write a paper in which you first (a) state your view and explain why you hold it, and then (b) note and explain what you consider to be the strongest point of the opposing view (assuming there is an opposing view).

ECONOMIC DICTIONARY

Guaranteed Income Level (Pg. 246)
Implicit Marginal Tax Rate (Pg. 246)
In-Kind Benefits (Pg. 243)
Medicaid (Pg. 242)
Medical Malpractice Suit (Pg. 236)
Medicare (Pg. 239)
Poverty Line (Pg. 243)
Third-Party Payers (Pg. 239)

The Economy of the United States

253

CHAPTER 10

Money

When someone mentions the word *money*, you might think of a $20 bill. Money is cold, hard cash to most of us. But there is more to money than that. At one time in the world's history, for example, there was no money. How did money come into existence? And what does money do? You might say that we use it to buy the things that we want. But does it do anything else? Can it be used to pay off a debt? Can it be saved? If it is saved, what is it saved for?

How is the world different with money than it would be without it? Suppose that tomorrow morning you woke up and there was no money in the world. All the money had disappeared. How would the world be different because of this? Would it be a better or a worse place to live? Would people be less greedy, more greedy, or about the same as they were before? Would there be as much production? Would there be as many people working?

These are some of the questions that lie below the surface of a discussion of money. Money is that $20 bill, no doubt. But money is also much more. In this chapter, you'll begin to find out just how much more there is to the story of money.

KEY TERMS

Barter Economy
Currency
Debit Card
Demand Deposit
Double
  Coincidence
  of Wants
Face Value
Federal Reserve
  Note
Fractional Reserve
  Banking

Gresham's Law
Medium of
  Exchange
Money
Money Supply
Near-Money
Savings Account
Store of Value
Unit of Account

SECTION 1 — THE ORIGINS OF MONEY: HOW MONEY CAME TO BE

At one point in the world's history, there was no money. In this section, we describe how things were when there was no money and how money came to be.

As you read, keep these key questions in mind:

- What is a barter economy?
- How did money emerge out of a barter economy?
- What is money?
- What are the functions of money?
- What gives money its value?

A Barter Economy

Many thousands of years ago, there was no money. People traded goods and services for other goods and services. For example, a baker might trade two loaves of bread for a basket of apples. When people consistently trade goods and services for other goods and services, they have a **barter economy**. Money does not exist in a barter economy.

Now imagine yourself in a barter economy, living many thousands of years ago. You are a baker; you bake bread each day. You wake up one morning and realize that you would like some eggs. What do you do? You can't go the store and buy eggs with money, because money doesn't exist. So, instead, you set out to find a person who has eggs.

Let's say you find Jones, who owns many chickens and has numerous eggs. You ask Jones if he would like to trade some bread (which you have) for some eggs (which he has). Jones says that he has all the bread he wants and that he does not want to trade eggs for your bread. Jones says that he wants oranges, not bread, thank you.

In economics, when each of two people has what the other wants, they are said to have a **double coincidence of wants**. In our example, you and Jones *do not* have a double coincidence of wants. Jones has what you want (eggs), but Jones does not want what you have (bread). When people do not have a double coincidence of wants, they do not trade with each other.

So, Jones has turned down your offer of bread for eggs. What do you do now? You continue on your way, hoping to find either (1) a person who has eggs and wants to trade those eggs for your bread or (2) a person who has oranges and wants to trade some oranges for your bread, after which you will return to Jones and trade oranges (which is what Jones wants) for eggs (which is what you want).

In time, you come across Smith, who has oranges. You ask Smith if she would like to trade some of her oranges for some of your bread. Smith says no.

As you can see, your attempt to barter is becoming difficult and time consuming. You set out in the morning to trade some of your bread for some eggs, but things are not working your way. So far, you haven't been successful in meeting your objective.

The point, obviously, is that making trades in a barter economy is not always easy. It can take a lot of time, sometimes all day or longer. For example, who knows for sure how long it will take before you obtain the eggs you want? Compare this with how easy it is to obtain eggs today.

How Did Money Emerge From a Barter Economy?

At one time, there was no money. But today, there is money. This means that money must have emerged, or evolved, out of a barter economy. How did this happen? Did people living in a barter economy go to sleep one night and wake up the next morning to find that there was money? Did the kings and queens of years past issue an order that there should be money?

Here is the economist's explanation of how money came to be. Economists argue that in a barter economy, some goods would naturally have been more readily accepted in exchange than other goods. For example, suppose there are five goods in a barter economy: apples, bananas, cheese, paper, and bricks. On average, bricks are accepted 5 out of every 10 times they are offered in exchange. The other goods are accepted only 2 out of every 10 times. What this means is that if you set out with bricks in your possession, you have a 50 percent chance (5 is 50 percent of 10) of making the exchange you want to make the first time you try to make it.

Now, some people come to realize that bricks are more acceptable in exchange than other goods. They also realize that because this is so, bricks cut down on the time it takes to make an exchange. These individuals start to accept bricks *simply because of their greater acceptability*, even if they have no plans to use the bricks themselves. They do this because they know that with bricks they have a higher probability of getting what they want than with other goods.

The effect snowballs. As more people come to accept bricks because of their greater general acceptability, their relative acceptability becomes still greater. This in turn causes even more people to agree to accept them. For example, let's say you accept bricks because you know they are, on average, accepted 5 out of every 10 times. Because you decide to accept bricks, when previously you did not, the acceptance rate rises from 5 to 6 out of every 10 times. Now John, who did not accept bricks when their acceptance rate was 5 out of every 10 times, chooses bricks because their acceptance rate has risen to 6 out of every 10 times. And because John now accepts bricks, the acceptability of bricks rises even further, and so on. At some point, almost everyone is willing to accept bricks. When a good becomes *widely accepted for purposes of exchange*, it is considered **money**. Historically, goods that have evolved into money include gold, silver, copper, rocks, cattle, and shells, to name a few.

▲ In the past, in outdoor markets such as this one, people would trade goods for goods. Today, people usually trade goods for money.

QUESTION: *Many people think that government first created money. For example, the kings and queens of long ago had their likenesses stamped on gold coins. Isn't this evidence that the kings and queens created money?*

ANSWER: *No. Kings and queens might have stamped their likenesses on money, but neither kings nor queens, nor any government, invented money. Money predates formal government.*

MINI GLOSSARY

Barter Economy An economy in which trades are made in goods and services instead of money.
Double Coincidence of Wants The situation in which each of two parties to an exchange has what the other wants. In a barter economy, it is a requirement that must be met before a trade can be made.
Money A good that is widely accepted for purposes of exchange.

THINKING LIKE AN ECONOMIST

The economist's story of how money evolved out of a barter economy emphasized the spontaneous and unplanned nature of the process. No one had the idea for money and then put the idea into action. Instead, people living in a barter economy were simply trying to reduce the time and effort it took them to make their everyday exchanges; and as a result, money evolved. Money was an unintended consequence *of people's actions.*

Economists, as we have seen, believe that there are many unintended consequences of people's actions. Like money, some of these are beneficial. For example, consider the chemist who wants to become rich. He spends long hours working to develop a medicine that will reduce the pain arthritis sufferers feel. He sets as his objective one thing—becoming rich—and ends up doing something else besides—relieving people's pain.

What Gives Money Its Value?

Is a $10 bill money? To answer the question, you need simply ask yourself whether or not the $10 bill is widely accepted for purposes of exchange. If it is, then it is money; if it isn't, then it is not money. You know, of course, that the $10 bill *is* widely accepted for purposes of exchange, and therefore it is money.

But what is it that gives money (say, the $10 bill) value? Like the bricks in our barter economy, our money has value because of its *general acceptability*. What this means is that money has value to you because you know that you can use it to get what you want. But you can only use it to get what you want because other people will accept it in exchange for what they have.

To illustrate, suppose that tomorrow morning you wake up and begin to walk to school. On the way, you stop by the quick-stop store to buy a doughnut and milk. You try to pay for the doughnut and milk with two $1 bills. The owner of the store says that he no longer accepts dollar bills in exchange for what he has to sell. (What?!) This story repeats itself all day with different store

"Let's face it—man's best friend is money."

Drawing by Bernard Schoenbaum; © 1992. *The New Yorker* Magazine, Inc.

owners. No one is willing to accept dollar bills for what he or she has to sell. Do dollar bills have as much value to you? We would think not. If you can't use dollar bills to get you what you want, then dollar bills are simply paper and ink. They have little value at all.

Here is a historical example to further illustrate the point. Between 1861 and 1865 in the South, Confederate notes (Confederate money) had value. This is because Confederate money was accepted by people in the South for purposes of exchange. Today in the South, Confederate money has little value (except for historical collection purposes), because it is not widely accepted for purposes of exchange. You cannot pay for your gasoline at a station in Alabama with Confederate notes.

Gresham's Law: Good Money, Bad Money

Did you know that money can be good or bad? Here's a story to illustrate.

Silver coins were used as money in the days of King Henry VIII of England. One day, King Henry issued an order to reduce the silver content of coins. Coins that before 1543 had been 92.5 percent pure silver were reduced to 33.3 percent pure silver by 1545, but their **face value** was not reduced. In other words, a 1543 coin had more silver in it than a 1545 coin, but the two coins had the same money denomination. (The same thing happened in the United States in the 1960s. A dime minted before 1965 has a higher silver content than a dime minted after 1965, although both the pre-1965 dime and the post-1965 dime represent 10 cents.)

After King Henry's change in the coins had been made, people began to circulate only the newer, lighter (lower–silver-content) coins and to hoard the older, heavier (higher–silver-content) coins. Why did they do this? Because silver is valuable, and if two coins have the same face value, but one has more silver than the other, it is better to spend the lower–silver-content coin and keep the high-

er–silver-content coin. Suppose you are living during the time of King Henry VIII. You see that the price of bread is one silver shilling. (A shilling is a British coin used during this time.) You have two silver shillings in your pocket. One has a higher silver content than the other. Which shilling will you use to buy the bread? You will probably use the shilling with the lower silver content.

Continuing with our story, King Henry VIII had a daughter, Elizabeth, who later became queen. Queen Elizabeth I wondered why the people in her kingdom were spending one type of silver coin and not the other. A financial adviser to the queen, Sir Thomas Gresham (1519–1579), gave her an explanation similar to the one you have just read. Gresham's explanation is captured in the statement, "Bad money drives good money out of circulation." Today, we say this statement describes **Gresham's law**.

QUESTION: *It was stated earlier that here in the United States, dimes minted before 1965 have a higher silver content than dimes minted after 1965. Does it follow that the pre-1965 dimes are "good money" and the post-1965 dimes are "bad money"? Do "bad dimes" circulate today, and are "good dimes" hoarded?*

ANSWER: *The answer to the first question is yes. The dimes with the higher silver content are considered the good money, and the dimes with the lower silver content are considered the bad money.*

The answer to the second question is also yes. The bad dimes circulate today, and the good

---

MINI GLOSSARY

Face Value The stated denomination on paper money or coins. For example, the face value of a nickel is 5 cents, and the words *five cents* are actually inscribed on a nickel.
Gresham's Law An economic law stating that bad money drives good money out of circulation.

dimes do not. This is a verification of Gresham's law. Look at the dimes you come across. Most, if not all, will be dated after 1965.

FOLLOW-UP QUESTION: *What good is it to hoard dimes with a high silver content?*

ANSWER: *As the price of silver rises, a person can sell the silver in the dimes. To illustrate, suppose a dime has 0.01 ounce of silver in it. Furthermore, suppose silver sells for $7 an ounce. This means one dime has 7 cents worth of silver in it (0.01 × $7.00 = $0.07). Now suppose the price of silver rises to $12 an ounce. This means a dime has 12 cents worth of silver in it (0.01 × $12.00 = $0.12). Given this, it would be better to sell the silver in the dime for 12 cents than to use the dime as 10 cents.*

The Functions of Money

Money has three major functions. It functions as a medium of exchange, a unit of account, and a store of value.

Money As a Medium of Exchange. A **medium of exchange** is anything that is generally acceptable in exchange for goods and services.

Does money function as a medium of exchange? Yes, it does, as we have already seen. This is, in fact, the most basic function of money. Money is present in almost every exchange made.

Money As a Unit of Account. A **unit of account** is a common measurement in which values are expressed. Money functions as a unit of account, since all goods can be expressed in terms of money. For example, we express the value of a house in terms of dollars, say, $120,000; we express the value of a car in terms of dollars, say, $15,000; and we express the value of a computer in terms of dollars, say, $4,000.

Money As a Store of Value. A good functions as a **store of value** by maintaining its value over time. Money serves as a store of value. This means, for example, that you can sell your labor services today, collect money in payment, and wait for a future date to spend the money on goods and services. You do not have to rush to buy goods and services with the money today. Money will store value to be used at a future date.

QUESTION: *Let's say there is only one good in the world, apples, and the price of an apple is $1. John earns $100 on January 1, 1993. If John spends the*

◄ One of the functions of money is to be exchanged for goods and services.

$100 on January 1, 1993, he can buy 100 apples. But suppose instead that he holds the money for one year, until January 1, 1994. Furthermore, suppose the price of apples has doubled to $2. This means that on January 1, 1994, John can buy only 50 apples. Doesn't this mean that money has lost some of its value between 1993 and 1994? If the answer is yes, then how can we say that money acts as a store of value? It appears that if prices rise, the value of money declines.

ANSWER: *This example does illustrate that when prices rise, the value of money declines. Consider this, however. It is possible that even though the value of money may decline, money still can serve as a store of value—but not a constant store of value. In the example, the value of money fell between 1993 and 1994, but it did not disappear altogether. Money was still storing value over the year, even though it did not enter 1994 with all the value it had at the beginning of 1993.*

When economists say that money serves as a store of value, they do not mean to imply that money is a constant store of value or that it always serves as a store of value equally well. Money is better at storing value at some times than at other times. (When is money "bad" at storing value? When prices are rapidly rising.)

LEARNING CHECK

1. Give an example in which two individuals have a double coincidence of wants.
2. Can trade occur without a double coincidence of wants? Explain why or why not.
3. Define *money*.
4. What gives money value?
5. What are the three functions of money?

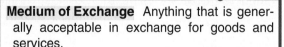

SECTION 2 HOW BANKING DEVELOPED

Just as there was a time when there was no money, so also there was a time when there were no banks. This section discusses the origins of banking. The discussion should help you understand modern banking, a topic in the next chapter.

As you read, keep these key questions in mind:

- Who were the early bankers?
- What are warehouse receipts?
- What is fractional reserve banking?

The Early Bankers

Our money today is easy to carry and transport. But it was not always this way. For example, when money was principally gold coins, carrying it was neither easy nor safe. First, gold is heavy. Second, transporting thousands of gold coins is an activity that can easily draw the attention of thieves. All this led individuals to want to store their gold in a safe place. The person most individuals turned to was the goldsmith, because he was already

MINI GLOSSARY

Medium of Exchange Anything that is generally acceptable in exchange for goods and services.

Unit of Account A common measurement in which values are expressed.

Store of Value Something with the ability to hold value over time.

William Henry Furness III

In economics, William Furness III, an American anthropologist, is known for his discovery of some islanders who used large stone wheels with holes in the center—they looked like giant stone doughnuts—as money. This money, called *fei*, was so large and heavy that the islanders had to carry it by means of a large pole stuck through the center hole with a man at each end of the pole.

One of the things that Furness noted is that the owner of the stone did not have to possess it in order to use it to buy what he or she wanted. Here is what he said about this matter in his book, *The Island of Stone Money*, published in 1910:

My faithful old friend, Fatumak, assured me that there was in the village near-by a family whose wealth was unquestioned—acknowledged by every one—and yet no one, not even the family itself, had ever laid eye or hand on this wealth; it consisted of an enormous fei, wherof the size is known only by tradition; for the past two or three generations it had been, and at that very time it was lying at the bottom of the sea! Many years ago an ancestor of this family, on an expedition after fei, secured this remarkably large and exceedingly valuable stone, which was placed on a raft to be towed homeward. A violent storm arose, and the party, to save their lives, were obliged to cut the raft adrift, and the stone sank out of sight. When they reached home, they all testified that the fei was of magnificent proportions and of extraordinary quality, and that it was lost through no fault of the owner. Thereupon it was universally conceded in their simple faith that the mere accident of its loss overboard was too trifling to mention, and that a few hundred feet of water off shore ought not to affect its marketable value, since it was all chipped out in proper form. The purchasing power of that stone remains, therefore, as valid as if it were leaning against the side of the owner's house.[a]

1. How is the story of stone money, told here by Furness, similar to the story of goldsmiths in the early days of banking?
2. How is paying for something with a check similar to using the stone money?

---

a. William Henry Furness III, *The Island of Stone Money* (Philadelphia and London: J.B. Lippincott Co., 1910), p. 96.

---

equipped with safe storage facilities. Goldsmiths were the first bankers. They took in other people's gold and stored it for them. To acknowledge that they held deposited gold, goldsmiths issued receipts called *warehouse receipts* to their customers. For example, George Adams might have had a receipt from goldsmith Turner stating that he had deposited 400 gold pieces with Turner. (This is much like what happens today when your bank gives you a receipt when you deposit money.)

Before long, people began to circulate the warehouse receipts in place of the gold itself (gold was not only inconvenient for customers to carry, it was also inconvenient for merchants to accept). For instance, if George Adams wanted to buy something for 400 gold pieces, he might give a warehouse receipt to the seller instead of going to the goldsmith, obtaining the gold, and then delivering it to the seller. Using the receipts was easier than dealing with gold itself for both parties. In short, the warehouse receipts circulated as money—that is, they became widely acceptable for purposes of exchange.

At this stage, warehouse receipts were *fully backed* by gold. The receipts simply represented, or stood in place of, the gold in storage. Later, though, goldsmiths began to notice that on an average day, few people came to redeem their receipts for gold. Most individuals were simply trading the receipts for goods.

The goldsmiths of the day sensed opportunity knocking at their doors. Some goldsmiths began to think, "Suppose I lend out some of the gold that people have deposited with me. If I lend it to others, I can charge interest for the loan (great!). And since receipts are circulating in place of the gold, I will probably never be faced with redeeming everyone's receipts for gold at once."

This is exactly what some goldsmiths did. They lent out some of the gold that had been deposited with them and collected the interest on the loans.

The consequence of this lending activity was an increase in the supply of money, measured in terms of gold and paper receipts. Remember, both gold and paper warehouse receipts were widely accepted for purposes of exchange.

The process described here was the beginning of **fractional reserve banking**. Under a fractional reserve system, such as the one that currently operates in the United States, banks (like goldsmiths of years past) create money by holding on reserve only a *fraction* of the money deposited with them and lending the remainder.

QUESTION: *How did the money supply increase when goldsmiths lent out gold?*

ANSWER: *A numerical example can be used to illustrate. Suppose there are only 100 gold coins in the world. We would say that the money supply is represented by 100 gold coins. Now suppose the owners of the gold deposit their coins with the goldsmith. To keep things simple, suppose the goldsmith gives out one paper receipt for each coin deposited. In other words, if Flores deposits three coins with a goldsmith, she receives three warehouse receipts, each representing a coin.*

The warehouse receipts begin to circulate instead of the gold itself, and so the money supply consists of 100 paper receipts, whereas before it consisted of 100 gold coins. But still the number is 100.

Now the goldsmith decides to lend out some of the gold and earn interest on the loans. Suppose Roberts wants to take out a loan for 15 gold coins. The goldsmith grants the loan. Instead of handing over 15 gold coins, though, the goldsmith gives Roberts 15 paper receipts.

What has happened to the money supply? Before the goldsmith went into the lending business, the money supply consisted of 100 paper receipts. Now, though, the money supply has increased to 115 paper receipts. The increase in the money supply (as measured by the number of paper receipts) is a result of the lending activity of the goldsmith.

MINI GLOSSARY

Fractional Reserve Banking A banking arrangement in which banks hold only a fraction of their deposits and lend out the remainder.

 ## LEARNING CHECK

1. Why did people choose to store their gold with goldsmiths instead of holding it themselves?
2. What does it mean to say that the United States has a fractional reserve banking system?
3. Explain how the money supply increased when goldsmiths lent out gold that was deposited with them.

SECTION 3   THE MONEY SUPPLY

In the discussion of early banking, both gold and warehouse receipts were part of the money supply. Both were widely accepted for purposes of exchange. In today's world, people do not circulate warehouse receipts or gold. What does the money supply consist of today? This section answers that question.

As you read, keep these key questions in mind:

- What does the money supply consist of?
- What is a Federal Reserve note?

Components of the Money Supply

The **money supply** in the United States is composed of (1) currency, (2) checking accounts, and (3) traveler's checks. [1]

$$\text{Money supply} = \text{Currency} + \text{Checking accounts} + \text{Traveler's checks}$$

---

1. Actually, this is referred to as the M1 money supply. There are other, broader measures of the money supply, such as M2, which include all of the M1 money supply as well as

1. **Currency**. **Currency** includes coins (such as quarters and dimes) minted by the U.S. Treasury and paper money. About 99 percent of the paper money in circulation is **Federal Reserve notes**. If you look at a dollar bill, you will see at the top the words "Federal Reserve Note." The Federal Reserve system, which is the central bank of the United States (discussed in the next chapter), issues Federal Reserve notes.

2. **Checking Accounts**. Checking accounts are accounts in which funds are deposited and can be withdrawn simply by writing a check. Sometimes checking accounts are referred to as **demand deposits** because the funds can be converted to currency on demand and given to the person to whom the check is made payable. For example, suppose Jim has a checking account at a local bank. The balance in his checking account is $400. He writes a check payable to Tom for $59. Tom presents the check to the bank and $59 in currency is paid to him.

other monies such as small savings accounts, but we do not discuss them in this text.

◄ One of the components of the money supply is currency, which includes coins and paper money. Paper money is mostly Federal Reserve notes, which we see being printed here.

▶ One of the components of the money supply is checking accounts. Here, a woman writes a check to pay for her purchase.

3. Traveler's checks. A traveler's check is a check issued by a bank in any of several denominations ($10, $20, and so on) and sold to a traveler (or to anyone who wishes to buy it), who signs it at the time it is issued by the bank and then again in the presence of the person cashing it.

Of the three major components of the money supply, the checking account component is the largest component. For example, in June 1993, there were $758.9 billion in checking accounts, $306.8 billion in currency, and $8.0 billion in traveler's checks. The money supply was $1,073.7 billion. See Exhibit 10-1.

$8.0 billion
Traveler's
checks

$306.8 billion
Currency

$758.9 billion
Checking accounts

Money supply =
$306.8 billion + $758.9 billion
+ $8.0 billion = $1,073.7 billion

▲ **EXHIBIT 10-1.** **U.S. Money Supply, June 1993.**
Money supply = Currency (coins and paper money) + Checking accounts + Traveler's checks.

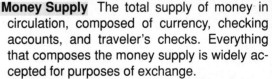

MINI GLOSSARY

Money Supply The total supply of money in circulation, composed of currency, checking accounts, and traveler's checks. Everything that composes the money supply is widely accepted for purposes of exchange.

Currency Coins issued by the U.S. Treasury and paper money (called Federal Reserve notes) issued by the Federal Reserve system.

Federal Reserve Note Paper money issued by the Federal Reserve system.

Demand Deposit A deposit that is withdrawable on demand and transferable by means of a check.

CONSUMER ECONOMIC DECISIONS

Understanding Checking Accounts and Credit Cards

The first commercial experience most persons have with the world of money is the experience of opening a checking account. Usually, the second is getting a credit card. We consider both here.[a]

Checking Accounts

Many people simply open a checking account with a bank that is convenient to where they live, work, or go to school. Certainly, convenience should be a major factor in determining where you open a checking account, but it is not the only factor that should be considered. Here are a few others.

Interest.   Some checking accounts pay interest, and some do not. Two that do not are the *regular checking account* and the *special checking account*. The regular checking account requires a person to hold a certain minimum balance in his or her account; if the balance falls below this minimum level, the bank will charge a fee. There is also usually a fee when a person writes more than the allotted number of checks a month. (By the way, the average person writes 21 checks per month.) The special checking account requires no minimum deposit (or balance) and charges a monthly maintenance fee plus a fee for each check written.

The general name for checking accounts that pay interest is *NOW account* (NOW stands for

negotiable order of withdrawal), but each bank often uses its own "brand name"—such as "High-Interest Checking," or something along these lines. A NOW account requires a person to hold a certain minimum balance in the account or pay a fee.

Minimum Balance.   As noted, some checking accounts require a minimum balance. It is important to know whether the minimum balance is figured on the *average daily balance* or the *lowest daily balance* for the month. The average daily balance for the month is the sum of the funds you have in your account each day of the month divided by the number of days in the month. For simplicity, consider an example that includes only three days. On the first day, you have $600 in your checking account. On the second day, you have $400; and on the third day, you have $200. The average daily balance for these three days is $400 ($600 + $400 + $200 = $1,200, and $1,200 ÷ 3 = $400). The lowest daily balance for the month is simply the lowest dollar balance in the account during the month. In our three-day example, this is $200, the dollar balance in your account on the third day.

For the customer, it is better to have the bank figure the minimum balance on the average daily balance than on the lowest daily balance. Suppose that in our three-day example, the bank has set the minimum balance at $250. If the bank uses the average–daily-balance method, your account does not fall below the minimum balance, since your average daily balance is

---

a. *The Consumer Reports Money Book* Copyright © 1992 by Consumers Union of U.S., Inc., Yonkers, NY 10703-1057. Reprinted by Permission from CONSUMER REPORTS BOOKS, 1992.

$400. But if it uses the lowest–daily-balance method, your account does fall below the minimum balance, since your lowest daily balance is $200; so you will have to pay a fee.

ATM Checking. Automated teller machines (ATMs) are widely used today. It is important to find out how much (if anything) a bank charges for ATM transactions—both at its own branches and at the branches of other banks with which it might be linked. Typically, banks charge less per ATM transaction if you use their machines than if you use some other bank's machines.

Federal Insurance. It is important to make sure the bank you choose is insured by the *Federal Deposit Insurance Corporation (FDIC)*. If you are unsure whether your bank is insured by the FDIC, ask the bank manager. Most banks

that are insured have the FDIC emblem displayed near the entrance. FDIC insurance assures you that any account in the bank is insured up to $100,000.

How the Bank Calculates Interest. It is important to know how a bank calculates interest on its accounts. One method to avoid is called the *low-balance method*. With this method, banks pay interest only on the balance that has been in the account for the entire month. For example, suppose you deposit $100 in your account on September 1 and $600 in the account on September 3. If the bank uses the low-balance method to calculate interest, you earn interest for the month only on the $100, because this is the amount that has been in the account for the entire month. The low-balance method has become less widely used, but still it is important to make sure that your bank doesn't use it.

▶ Many banks are insured by the Federal Deposit Insurance Corporation (FDIC), which insures all accounts up to $100,000.

Returned-Check Fees and Stop-Payment Charges.   If you write a check for more than you have in your account, you may have to pay a returned-check fee. Also, if you write a check and then later decide to stop payment on the check, you will have to pay the bank a stop-payment charge. It is important to know how much each of these fees is.

Canceled Checks.   At one time, it was very common for banks to return customers' *canceled checks* to them. Many people used their canceled checks as legal records of their transactions. Increasingly, though, banks would prefer not to return canceled checks, because it adds to their costs. However, it is a good idea to ask your bank to return your checks, because then you will have a legal record of everything you have purchased by check.

Credit Cards

When you pay for something using a credit card, you are in fact taking out a loan from the bank that issued the card. The two most widely used credit cards are MasterCard and Visa. Let's examine some of the factors to consider in shopping for a credit card.

Interest Rate.   The banks that issue general retail credit cards, such as MasterCard and Visa, charge interest. It is important for you to know what interest rates they charge. Shop around either by calling individual banks or by keeping an eye out for advertisements in newspapers and personal finance publications that may list unusually low interest rates.

Annual Fee.   Some credit card issuers charge annual fees for the use of their cards; others do not. Also, some banks may advertise that their cards have no annual fees but fail to mention that there are other charges. For example, some banks may charge the cardholder a fee for each month in which the card is used. Also, keep in mind that some banks that do not charge annual fees charge higher interest rates than banks that do charge annual fees.

Acceptance.   A credit card is not worth much if few sellers will accept it. MasterCard and Visa are widely accepted in the United States and abroad, while the Discover card is less accepted.

Grace Periods.   Some banks begin charging interest as soon as the charges appear on the cardholder's statement, whereas other banks allow cardholders 25 to 30 days to pay the balance in full before charging interest. Let's say you have a credit card with a bank that extends you a 30-day grace period. On December 1, you buy some clothes that cost $200. You pay for them with your credit card. On December 15, you get your credit card bill and see that the $200 clothing item is listed. Since you have a 30-day grace period, you can pay off your $200 credit bill and not have to pay any interest on the $200 loan.

Cash Advances.   Some banks allow you to use your credit card to get a cash advance at an ATM. If getting a cash advance is important to you, then this is a feature you will want your credit card to have. Many people make the mistake of thinking that the grace period they have

▲ Credit cards are widely used for purchases. Because credit cards make it easier to buy things, it's important to use them in a responsible manner.

for credit card purchases also applies to cash advances. Usually, this is not the case. In most cases, interest is charged from the moment you receive the cash advance. Some banks charge a fee for a cash advance.

Fringe Benefits. Banks compete with each other for credit card customers. Often, this competition takes the form of offering cardholders certain fringe benefits, such as flight insurance for cardholders that charge airline tickets, collision coverage on car rentals, and so on. It is important to know what fringe benefits, if any, a credit card issuer offers its customers.

Be Careful How You Use Your Credit Card. Some people do not use their credit cards in a responsible way. Instead, they use their cards excessively. They often end up buying more than they can pay for in a reasonable period of time, largely because credit cards make it so easy to buy on the spur of the moment. Remember, the use of a credit card provides you with convenience (you don't have to carry around as much cash); and it allows you to buy some things today that you would otherwise have to wait and buy later, after you have saved the money. But it does not make goods and services cheaper, and it only delays your having to pay for the items you buy. Indeed, if you do not pay your credit card bill each month in full, the items you buy on credit will cost you more than the same items purchased with cash. That's because of the interest you will have to pay for using the credit card. It is good to keep these things in mind when deciding whether to make a purchase with a credit card.

---

1. Deposits insured by the FDIC are insured up to what dollar amount?
2. A bank advertises that it does not charge an annual fee to its cardholders. Should you necessarily choose to obtain a credit card from this bank rather than a bank that does charge an annual fee? Why or why not?
3. Is there any way to avoid paying interest on a credit card purchase? Explain your answer.

What about a Savings Account? Is It Money?

A **savings account** is an interest-earning account. For example, if you have $400 in your savings account, and the annual interest rate you are paid is 6 percent, in a year your savings account will increase to $424 ($400 × 0.06 = $24, and $400 + $24 = $424). There are some savings accounts on which you can write checks and some on which you cannot. Those on which you can write checks fall into the category of checking accounts, which we discussed earlier. That leaves only nonchecking savings accounts. For example, a passbook savings account is an example of a nonchecking savings account. With a passbook savings account, you deposit your money into the account, and you are given a small booklet in which deposits, withdrawals, and interest are recorded.

A nonchecking savings account is not considered money because it is not widely accepted for purposes of exchange. You cannot go into a store and show the salesperson the balance in your passbook savings account and buy a $40 sweater. However, nonchecking savings accounts are considered **near-money**. Near-money is anything that can be relatively easily and quickly turned into money. Again consider a nonchecking savings account, such as a passbook savings account. True, you cannot buy a sweater by telling the salesperson that you have so much money in your passbook savings account, but you can go to the bank and request that your nonchecking savings be given to you in currency.

Are Credit Cards Money?

At first sight, a credit card appears to be money. After all, it is often referred to as "plastic money," and most retailers accept credit cards as payment for purchases. But on closer examination, we can see that a credit card is not money.

Consider Tina Quentin, who decides to buy a pair of shoes. She hands the shoe clerk her Visa card and signs for the purchase. Essentially, what the Visa card allows Tina to do is take out a loan from the bank that issued the card. The shoe clerk knows that this bank has, in effect, promised to pay the store for the shoes. At a later date, the bank will send Tina a credit card bill. At that time, Tina will be required to reimburse the bank for the shoe charges, plus interest (if her payment is made after a certain date). Tina is required to discharge her debt to the bank with money, such as currency or a check written on her checking account.

In conclusion, then, a credit card is not money. It is an instrument that makes it easier for the holder to obtain a loan. The use of a credit card places a person in debt, which he or she then has to pay off with money.

Debit Cards

The **debit card** is becoming increasingly popular with people purchasing goods. A debit card allows funds to be withdrawn from automated teller machines, and funds to be transferred from one person's checking account to another's. For example, you have probably seen debit cards used at grocery stores. A customer stands at the checkout stand and runs his or her debit card through a desktop device much like the devices stores currently use to verify credit card purchases. The clerk at the store enters the amount of the food

---

MINI GLOSSARY

Savings Account An interest-earning account.
Near-Money Assets, such as nonchecking savings accounts, that can be easily and quickly turned into money.
Debit Card A card that can be used to withdraw funds at automated teller machines and to pay for purchases by electronically transferring funds from one account to another (where the seller has the appropriate equipment). Debit cards look like credit cards.

purchase, and the customer enters his or her secret personal identification number (PIN). This permits the customer to access his or her checking account. The customer then commands a transfer of funds (equal to the food purchase) from the checking account to the store's account, probably at another bank. As soon as the store has verified that the funds transfer has been completed, the customer leaves with the merchandise. The operation takes a matter of seconds.

✔ LEARNING CHECK

1. What are the components of the money supply?
2. What is another name for a demand deposit?
3. Is a nonchecking savings account considered money? Why or why not?
4. What is a debit card?

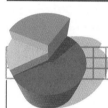

DEVELOPING ECONOMIC SKILLS

Calculating Relative Prices

In this chapter, we said that money serves as a *unit of account*. We remind ourselves that a unit of account is a common measurement in which values are expressed. For example, when we say that a coat is $160, and a telephone is $89, we are using money as a unit of account. We are expressing the value of goods, such as coats and telephones, in terms of money.

Now, in a barter economy there is no money, so the value of all goods has to be expressed in terms of all other goods. For example, let's say there are three goods in a barter economy: apples, paper, and pencils. If we wanted to know the "price" of apples, it would be quoted in terms of both paper and pencils. For example, a person might say that 1 apple has a price of either 10 sheets of paper or 2 pencils. This means that if you have either 10 sheets of paper or 2 pencils you can "buy" 1 apple.

But if 1 apple is priced at 10 sheets of paper, what is the price of 1 sheet of paper in terms of apples? To find the answer to this question, do the following:

1. In a barter economy, think of the good for which you want to find the price as the denominator in a ratio, and any other good as the numerator in a ratio. For example, if we want to find the price of 1 sheet of paper in terms of apples, we would put "paper" in the denominator and "apples" in the numerator.

$$\frac{\text{Apples}}{\text{Paper}}$$

2. Place the quantity of each good alongside the good. Thus we have "1 apple" in the numerator and "10 sheets of paper" in the denominator.

$$\frac{1 \text{ apple}}{10 \text{ sheets of paper}}$$

3. Find the ratio. This is your answer. The ratio is $\frac{1}{10}$. Thus we have our answer: The price of 1 sheet of paper is $\frac{1}{10}$ of an apple.

$$1 \text{ sheet of paper} = \frac{1}{10} \text{ apple}$$

When you are finding the price of one good (say, paper) in terms of another good (say,

DEVELOPING ECONOMIC SKILLS (continued)

apples), you are said to be finding the *relative price* of a good. In our example, the relative price of 1 sheet of paper was ⅒ of an apple.

Even though you live in a money economy and not in a barter economy, it is still important to know how to compute relative prices. In fact, you don't know the cost of anything until you can compute relative prices. To illustrate, suppose one day you buy a book for $15. Later that day, someone asks you the cost of the book. You say $15; but this isn't a complete answer to the question. Remember, according to an economist, the cost of something is what you forfeit, or give up, in order to obtain that something. The opportunity cost of the book is what you would have purchased if you hadn't purchased the book.

Suppose you would have used the money to eat lunch at your favorite restaurant. We'll say that you pay an average of $7.50 for lunch at your favorite restaurant. Now what is the opportunity cost of the book? This is no different from asking, What is the relative price of the book? To compute relative price in a money economy, we do things differently from when we were computing prices in a barter economy. We follow this procedure.

1. **In a money economy, think of the good for which you want to find the relative price as the numerator in a ratio, and any other good as the denominator in a ratio.** We want to know the price of the book, so we put "book" in the numerator and "lunch" in the denominator.

$$\frac{\text{Book}}{\text{Lunch}}$$

2. **Place the dollar amount of each good alongside the good.**

$$\frac{\$15 \text{ book}}{\$7.50 \text{ lunch}}$$

3. **Find the ratio. This is your answer.** The ratio is ⅔, or simply 2 ($15 ÷ $7.50 = 2 ÷ 1 = 2). This means the relative price of the book is 2 lunches at your favorite restaurant.

$$1 \text{ book} = 2 \text{ lunches}$$

This, then, is the opportunity cost of the book.

---

1. One apple trades for 5 marbles. What is the relative price of 1 marble? (In other words, what do you have to pay in terms of apples to buy 1 marble?)
2. One egg trades for 1 orange. What is the relative price of 1 orange?
3. Ten hats trade for 20 shirts. What is the relative price of 1 shirt?
4. Fifty pencils trade for 25 erasers. What is the relative price of 1 pencil?
5. Five paintings by Smith trade for 20 paintings by Jones. What is the relative price of 1 painting by Jones?
6. The price of a lamp is $40; the price of a picture frame is $15. What is the relative price of the picture frame?
7. The price of a table is $123; the price of a computer stand is $78. What is the relative price of the table?
8. If the price of apples rises, and the price of oranges remains the same, what happens to the relative price of apples? Explain your answer with numbers.

CHAPTER 10 REVIEW

CHAPTER SUMMARY

1. A barter economy is one in which trades, or exchanges, are made in terms of goods and services instead of money.

2. When each of two people has what the other wants, they are said to have a double coincidence of wants. A trade will not take place unless people have a double coincidence of wants.

3. Money is said to have emerged, or evolved, out of a barter economy. In a barter economy, people found it difficult and time consuming to make their daily trades. In their attempts to reduce the difficulty and time connected with barter, some people began to accept that good which had greater relative acceptability than all the other goods, even if they had no intention of consuming it. Soon this good was widely accepted for purchases of exchange and hence became money.

4. Money has value to people because they can use it to get what they want. They can do this because money is generally acceptable as a means of payment. In short, money has value because of its general acceptability.

5. Gresham's law says that "bad money drives good money out of circulation."

6. Money functions as a medium of exchange, a unit of account, and a store of value.

7. Under a fractional reserve banking system, such as the one we have in the United States, banks (like goldsmiths of years past) create money by holding on reserve only a fraction of the money deposited with them and lending the remainder.

8. The money supply consists of currency, checking accounts, and traveler's checks.

BUILD YOUR ECONOMIC VOCABULARY

Match the word with the correct definition, example, or statement.

1. double coincidence of wants
2. barter
3. any good widely accepted for purposes of exchange
4. store of value
5. Gresham's law
6. fractional reserve banking
7. currency
8. savings account

a. an apple for an orange
b. "Bad money drives good money out of circulation."
c. a function of money
d. exists when you have what I want and I have what you want
e. coins and paper money
f. earns interest
g. system in which banks lend out a fraction of the money deposited with them
h. money

CHAPTER 10 REVIEW (continued)

REVIEW QUESTIONS

1. Is a double coincidence of wants more likely or less likely to occur in a barter economy than a money economy? Explain your answer.

2. A person goes into a store and buys a pair of shoes with money. Is money principally functioning as a medium of exchange, a store of value, or a unit of account?

3. Jim puts $100 cash in a box in his office and keeps it there for one year. Is money principally functioning as a medium of exchange, a store of value, or a unit of account?

4. Explain how money emerged out of a barter economy.

5. "Governments created money." Do you agree or disagree? Explain your answer.

6. "Money has value if it is backed by gold. If money is not backed by gold, then it has no value." Do you agree or disagree? Explain your answer.

7. Why don't most people use pre-1965 dimes in making purchases today?

8. Explain how goldsmiths increased the money supply. (Note: The money supply consists of gold and warehouse receipts for purposes of this question.)

9. Why is a checking account sometimes called a demand deposit?

10. What is currency?

11. Is a credit card money? Why or why not?

12. Why is a nonchecking savings account considered near-money instead of money?

SHARPEN YOUR CRITICAL THINKING SKILLS

1. A successful painter goes to a small seaside town for a vacation. One day, he is at the grocery store picking up a few items. When he gets to the cashier, he realizes that he doesn't have any money with him. He tells the cashier that he will have to go home and get his money. The cashier, who happens to be the owner of the store, says that there is no need for this. She asks the artist for his autograph on a piece of paper. She tells the painter that his autograph is as good as money. The artist signs his name on a piece of paper, thanks the cashier-owner, and leaves the grocery store.

A week passes. The cashier-owner is at a bookstore. She wants to buy a book but doesn't have any money with her. She goes up to the owner of the store, who is a friend, and says that she will gladly trade the autograph of the famous artist for the book. The owner of the bookstore agrees. A month passes. The owner of the bookstore trades the autograph for an inexpensive watch. Does it appear that the painter's autograph is (or is becoming) money in the small seaside town? Explain your answer.

ACTIVITIES AND PROJECTS

1. Suppose that beginning one minute from now there is no more money in the world. If you want a good or a service, instead of paying money for it, you have to exchange some good or service for what you want. In other words, you live in a barter economy. As a class, discuss what you perceive as both the costs and benefits of living in a barter economy.

ECONOMIC DICTIONARY

Barter Economy (Pg. 256)
Currency (Pg. 264)
Debit Card (Pg. 270)
Demand Deposit (Pg. 264)
Double Coincidence of Wants (Pg. 256)
Face Value (Pg. 259)
Federal Reserve Notes (Pg. 264)
Fractional Reserve Banking (Pg. 263)

Gresham's Law (Pg. 259)
Medium of Exchange (Pg. 260)
Money (Pg. 257)
Money Supply (Pg. 264)
Near-Money (Pg. 270)
Savings Account (Pg. 270)
Store of Value (Pg. 260)
Unit of Account (Pg. 260)

Banking and the Federal Reserve System

INTRODUCTION

You have heard of the Supreme Court. You know that it is an important institution and that the decisions the members of the Court make affect our daily lives.

You have heard of the Congress. You know that it is an important institution and that the decisions the members of Congress make affect our daily lives.

Have you heard of the *Fed*? It, too, is an important institution, and the decisions the members of the Fed's Board of Governors make affect our daily lives. At times, the decisions of these persons affect our lives more than the decisions of the Supreme Court or the Congress. The Fed conducts U.S. monetary policy. It can increase or decrease the money supply with a few simple tools. As you read this chapter, and chapters to come, you will realize just how important and far reaching the effects of changes in the money supply can be.

SECTION 1 THE FEDERAL RESERVE SYSTEM

The **Federal Reserve system**—popularly called the **Fed**—is the central bank of the United States. Other national central banks include the Bank of Sweden, the Bank of England, the Banque de France, and the Bank of Japan. This section outlines the structure of the Federal Reserve system and discusses some of its major responsibilities.

As you read, keep these key questions in mind:

- What is the Federal Reserve system (the Fed)?
- How many persons sit on the Board of Governors of the Federal Reserve system?
- How does the check-clearing process work?

The Structure of the Federal Reserve System

In 1913, the Federal Reserve Act was passed in Congress. This act set up the Federal Reserve system, which began operation in 1914. The principal components of the Federal Reserve system are (1) the Board of Governors, and (2) the 12 Federal Reserve district banks.

Board of Governors. The **Board of Governors of the Federal Reserve System** controls and coordinates the Fed's activities. The board is made up of seven members, each appointed to a 14-year term by the president of the United States with Senate approval. The president also designates one member as chairman of the board for a four-year term. The Board of Governors is located in Washington, D.C.

The 12 Federal Reserve District Banks. The United States is broken up into 12 Federal Reserve districts. The boundaries of these districts are shown in Exhibit 11-1. Each district has a Federal Reserve district bank. (Think of the Federal Reserve district banks as "branch offices" of the Federal Reserve system.) Each of the 12 Federal Reserve district banks has a president.

▼ **EXHIBIT 11-1.** Federal Reserve Districts and Federal Reserve Bank Locations.

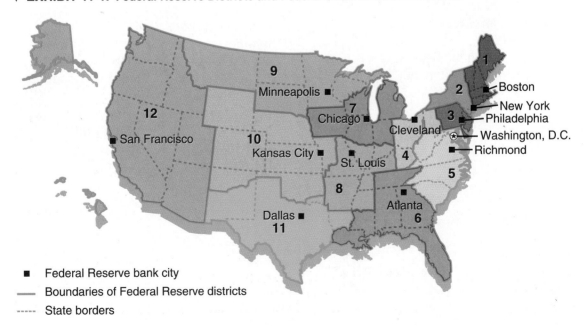

- ■ Federal Reserve bank city
- — Boundaries of Federal Reserve districts
- ----- State borders

▶ A meeting of the Board of Governors of the Federal Reserve system. The Board of Governors controls and coordinates the activities of the Federal Reserve system.

An Important Committee: The FOMC

The major policy-making group within the Fed is the **Federal Open Market Committee (FOMC)**. Later in this chapter, we will consider what the FOMC does. For now, we need only note that the FOMC is made up of 12 members. Seven of the 12 members are the members of the Board of Governors. The remaining five members come from the ranks of the presidents of the Federal Reserve district banks.

Functions of the Federal Reserve System

Let's look briefly at six major responsibilities of the Fed.

1. **Control the money supply.** A full explanation of how the Fed controls the money supply comes later in the chapter.
2. **Supply the economy with paper money (Federal Reserve notes).** As stated in Chapter 10, the pieces of paper money we use are *Federal*

Reserve notes. Federal Reserve notes are printed at the Bureau of Engraving and Printing in Washington, D.C. The notes are issued to the 12 Federal Reserve district banks, which keep the money on hand to meet the demands of the banks and the public. For example, suppose it is the holiday season and people are going to their banks and withdrawing larger-than-usual amounts of $1, $5, and $20 notes. Banks will need to replenish their supplies of these notes, and they will turn to their Federal Reserve district banks to do so. The Federal Reserve district banks will meet this cash need by supplying more paper money. (Remember, the

---

MINI GLOSSARY

Federal Reserve System (the Fed) The central bank of the United States.

Board of Governors of the Federal Reserve System The governing body of the Federal Reserve system.

Federal Open Market Committee (FOMC) The 12-member policy-making group within the Fed. This committee has the authority to conduct open-market operations.

ANALYZING PRIMARY SOURCES

The Federal Reserve Act

The Federal Reserve Act, which set up the Federal Reserve system, was approved on December 23, 1913. Here are the first three points of Section 1 of the act and the first point of Section 2.

FEDERAL RESERVE ACT
Approved December 23, 1913

"**A**n Act to provide for the establishment of Federal reserve banks, to furnish an elastic currency, to afford means of rediscounting commercial paper, to establish a more effective supervision of banking in the United States, and for other purposes.

SECTION 1: SHORT TITLE AND DEFINITIONS

1. Short title
   Be it enacted by the Senate and House of Representatives of the United States of America in Congress assembled, That the short title of this Act shall be the 'Federal Reserve Act.'
2. Definition of 'bank'
   Wherever the word 'bank' is used in this Act, the word shall be held to include State bank, banking association, and trust company, except where national banks or Federal reserve banks are specifically referred to.
3. Definitions of other terms
   The terms 'national bank' and 'national banking association' used in this Act shall be held to be synonymous and interchangeable. The term 'member bank' shall be held to mean any national bank, State bank, or bank or trust company which has become a member of one of the reserve banks created by this Act. The term 'board' shall be held to mean Board of Governors of the Federal Reserve System; the term 'district' shall be held to mean Federal reserve district; the term 'reserve bank' shall be held to mean Federal reserve bank.

SECTION 2: FEDERAL RESERVE DISTRICTS

1. Establishment of reserve cities and districts
   Sec 2. As soon as practicable, the Secretary of the Treasury, the Secretary of Agriculture, and the Comptroller of the Currency, acting as 'The Reserve Bank Organization Committee,' shall designate not less than eight nor more than twelve cities to be known as Federal reserve cities, and shall divide the continental United States, excluding Alaska, into districts, each district to contain only one of such Federal reserve cities. The determination of said organization committee shall not be subject to review except by the Board of Governors of the Federal Reserve System when organized: *Provided* That the districts shall be apportioned with due regard to the convenience and customary course of business and shall not necessarily be coterminous with any State or States. The districts thus created may be readjusted and new districts may from time to time be created by the Board of Governors of the Federal Reserve System, not to exceed twelve in all. Such districts shall be known as Federal reserve districts and may be designated by number. A majority of the organization committee shall constitute a quorum with authority to act. "

1. According to the act, to what does the word *board* refer?
2. According to the act, one of the reasons Federal Reserve banks were established was to provide "elastic currency." Given what you have read in this chapter about the Federal Reserve system, to what do you think "elastic currency" refers?
3. What committee was given the power to designate the Federal Reserve cities?

12 Federal Reserve district banks do not print the paper money; they only supply it.)

3. **Hold bank reserves.** Each commercial bank that is a member of the Federal Reserve system is required to keep a *reserve account* (think of it for now as a checking account) with its Federal Reserve district bank. For example, a bank located in Los Angeles, California, would be located in the 12th Federal Reserve district. This means it deals with the Federal Reserve Bank of San Francisco. The local bank in Los Angeles must have a reserve account, or checking account, with this reserve bank. Soon, we will see what role a bank's reserve account with the Fed plays in increasing and decreasing the money supply.

4. **Provide check-clearing services.** When someone in San Diego writes a check to a person in Los Angeles, what happens to the check? The process by which funds change hands when checks are written is called the check-clearing process. The Fed plays a major role in this process. Here is how it works:

a. Harry Saito writes a $1,000 check on his San Diego bank and sends it to Ursula Pevins in Los Angeles.

b. Ursula takes the check to her local bank, endorses it (signs it on the back), and deposits it into her checking account. The balance in her account rises by $1,000.

c. Ursula's Los Angeles bank sends the check to its Federal Reserve district bank, which is located in San Francisco. The Federal Reserve Bank of San Francisco *increases* the reserve account of the Los Angeles bank by $1,000 and *decreases* the reserve account of the San Diego bank by $1,000.

d. The Federal Reserve Bank of San Francisco sends the check to Harry's bank in San Diego, which then reduces the balance in Harry's checking account by $1,000. Harry's bank in San Diego either keeps the check on record or sends it along to Harry with his monthly bank statement. (See Exhibit 11-2).

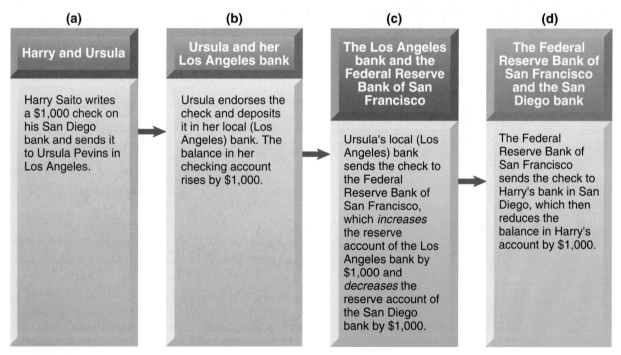

▲ **EXHIBIT 11-2.** The Check-Clearing Process.

5. **Supervise member banks.** Without warning, the Fed can examine the books of member commercial banks to see what kind of loans they have made, whether they have followed bank regulations, how accurate their records are, and so on. If the Fed finds that a bank has not been following established banking standards, it can pressure the bank to do so.

6. **Serve as the lender of last resort.** A tradition-al function of a central bank is to serve as the "lender of last resort" for banks suffering cash management problems. For example, let's say that Bank A has lost millions of dollars and finds it very difficult to borrow from other banks. At this point, the Fed may step in and act as lender of last resort to Bank A. In other words, the Fed may lend Bank A the funds it wants to borrow when no one else will.

 # LEARNING CHECK

1. Explain how a check is cleared.
2. What does it mean to say the Fed is the lender of last resort?
3. What can the Fed do to a bank that is not following bank regulations?
4. In what year did the Fed begin operation?

 **THE MONEY CREATION PROCESS**

You learned in Chapter 10 that the early bankers were goldsmiths. These goldsmiths could increase the money supply (made up of gold and warehouse receipts) by extending loans to people. In this section, we move up in time to the present. Instead of long-ago goldsmiths, we consider modern-day bankers working at desks with computers. You will see, though, that the goldsmiths of yesterday and the bankers of today are not much different when it comes to their ability to change the money supply.

As you read, keep these key questions in mind:

■ What do total reserves equal?
■ What are required reserves? excess reserves?
■ What do banks do with excess reserves?

A Few Preliminary Facts

Before we examine the mechanics of how banks create money, we should consider the following points and definitions.

1. An earlier section mentioned that each member bank has a *reserve account* with the Fed. If we take the dollar amount of a bank's reserve account and add it to the cash the bank has in its vaults (called, simply enough, *vault cash*), we have the bank's **total reserves**.

Total reserves = Deposits in the reserve account at the Fed + Vault cash

For example, if Bank A has $100,000 in its reserve account with the Fed and $200,000 in its vault, then its total reserves equal $300,000 ($100,000 + $200,000 = $300,000).

2. Total reserves can be divided up into required reserves and excess reserves. **Required reserves** are the amount of reserves a bank must hold against its demand deposits (checking accounts) as mandated by the Fed. For example, suppose Bank A holds demand deposits (checkbook money) for its customers totaling $1 million. The Fed requires through its **reserve requirement** that Bank A hold a percentage of

this total amount in the form of reserves—that is, either as deposits in its reserve account at the Fed or as vault cash (since both of these are reserves). Suppose this percentage is 10 percent. This means that Bank A is required to hold 10 percent of $1 million, or $100,000, in the form of reserves ($1,000,000 × .10 = $100,000). This $100,000 is called *required reserves*.

Required reserves = Reserve requirement
× Demand deposits

3. **Excess reserves** are the difference between total reserves and required reserves.

Excess reserves = Total reserves
− Required reserves

For example, if total reserves equal $300,000 and required reserves equal $100,000, then *excess reserves* equal $200,000 ($300,000 − $100,000 = $200,000).

4. Banks can make loans with their excess reserves.

QUESTION: *Suppose Bank B has demand deposits that total $10 million and the Fed sets the reserve requirement at 10 percent. Furthermore, suppose Bank B currently has $800,000 in its reserve account at the Fed and $400,000 in vault cash.*

1. *What do total reserves equal?*
2. *What do required reserves equal?*
3. *How much money is available to Bank B to use for extending loans to people?*

ANSWER: *To find the answer to the first question, we recall that total reserves equal deposits in the reserve account at the Fed plus vault cash. We know that deposits in the reserve account at the Fed equal $800,000 and that vault cash is $400,000. The sum of these two dollar amounts, or total reserves, is $1,200,000.*

To find the answer to the second question, we need to know the reserve requirement, which is 10 percent, and the total dollar deposits at the bank, which equal $10 million. Required reserves equal

"Before we discuss our short-term interest rates, perhaps you could let me know how many hours you'll need the money for."

© 1986 by Sidney Harris, "What's So Funny About Business?" William Kaufmann, Inc.

10 percent of $10 million, or $1 million ($10,000,000 × .10 = $1,000,000).

To find the answer to the third question, we need to know what excess reserves equal, since a bank can extend loans up to the full amount of its

---

MINI GLOSSARY

Total Reserves The sum of a bank's deposits in its reserve account at the Fed and its vault cash.

Required Reserves The minimum amount of reserves a bank must hold against its deposits as mandated by the Fed.

Reserve Requirement A regulation which requires a bank to keep a certain percentage of each dollar deposited in the bank in its reserve account at the Fed or in its vault (as vault cash). In this chapter we have had numerous occasions to note the percentage specified in the reserve requirement. We specify it this way, for example: Reserve requirement = 10 percent.

Excess Reserves Any reserves held beyond the required amount; the difference between total reserves and required reserves.

CASE STUDY

The Fed in the Great Depression

▲ During the Great Depression, bank closures and failures were common.

In the early 1930s, the United States was in economic distress. The period is referred to as the Great Depression. Thousands of businesses went bankrupt, and the unemployment rate went up to a sky-high 25 percent. Also, there were many bank failures—bank after bank had to close its doors. Numerous banks had lost their depositors' money because they had made loans that were not repaid.

Where was the Fed? As noted earlier, one of the major responsibilities of the Fed is to serve as a lender of last resort. In other words, when a bank is in financial trouble and can't find anyone from whom to borrow money, the Fed may choose to step in and lend money to the troubled institution. But the Fed did not do this during the years of the Great Depression. Some people think that, as a result, the economic distress in the United States was made worse. Why didn't the Fed serve as lender of last resort? Here are two reasons that economists have given.

First, some economists say that Fed officials viewed bank failures as the consequence of poor management and believed that poorly managed banks *should* go out of business. Fed officials failed to understand that if they sat back and allowed some banks to fail, these failures would lead to bank panics, which might hurt other banks that were not poorly managed.

It works this way. Suppose there are 100 banks in the country, and 3 fail. The customers of the other 97 banks wonder if their banks might not be next to fail. Scared, the customers of the 97 banks start to ask their banks for their money. The banks cannot repay everyone's money on the spot, though, since they have extended loans with much of their depositors' money. Thus, the bank customers, by suspecting their banks will fail and acting accordingly, actually cause their banks to fail. It is an example of what is called a self-fulfilling prophecy. If individuals *believe* the bank is in financial trouble (when in fact it may not be), and if they *act* as if it is (by withdrawing their money), then their actions will actually bring about what they believed was true all along.

Second, some economists suggest that, at the time of the Great Depression, the Fed sat back and did nothing because it was responding to the wishes of the owners of big banks. Big banks, mainly located in big cities, did not like the competition from small banks, mainly located in small towns and rural areas. In general, the first banks to fail were the small banks. Seeing their competition going out of business, the big banks did not want the Fed to do anything that would save the small banks.

---

1. According to economists, what are two reasons why the Fed did not serve as lender of last resort during the Great Depression?
2. Some people say that during the Great Depression, it was possible for a bank that was managed well to end up failing. Explain how this might have happened.

excess reserves. We have already found that total reserves equal $1.2 million and that required reserves equal $1 million. Excess reserves are the difference between the two, or $200,000 ($1,200,000 − $1,000,000 = $200,000). Bank B can extend loans up to $200,000.

See Exhibit 11-3 for a review of these points.

How Banks Create Demand Deposits and Thus Increase the Money Supply

In Chapter 10 we said that the money supply is the sum of currency (coins and paper money), checking accounts, and traveler's checks. For example, if there is $300 billion in currency, $500 billion

in checking accounts, and $10 billion in traveler's checks, the money supply is $810 billion ($300 billion + $500 billion + $10 billion = $810 billion).

We also said in Chapter 10 that checking accounts are sometimes referred to as demand deposits. This is because a checking account contains funds that can be withdrawn not only by a check, but also on demand.

Now, banks (such as your local bank down the street) are prohibited from printing currency. Your bank cannot legally print a $10 bill, for example. However, banks can create demand deposits. And if they do, this increases the money supply. For example, again suppose the money supply is $810 billion, composed of $300 billion in currency, $500 billion in checking accounts or demand deposits, and $10 billion in traveler's checks. Then, suppose

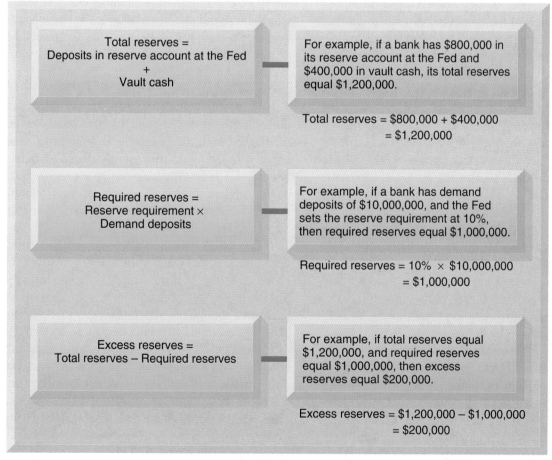

▲ EXHIBIT 11-3. Reserves: Total, Required, and Excess.

banks create an additional $20 billion in demand deposits, raising the total demand deposits from $500 billion to $520 billion. As a result, what happens to the money supply? It increases from $810 billion to $830 billion (since $300 billion currency + $520 billion in checking accounts or demand deposits + $10 billion in traveler's checks = $830 billion).

In this section we want to show you just how banks can create demand deposits and thus increase the money supply. Stated differently, we want to show you how, when banks create demand deposits, there is more money in the economy. But someone might say, "I thought it was said earlier that banks were prohibited from printing money, such as a $10 bill." This is still true, but remember the important point: money is more than simply currency; it is more than coins (like quarters and dimes) and paper money (like $1 and $5 bills). Our definition of the money supply takes into account not only currency, but also checking accounts (demand deposits) and traveler's checks.

We start with a fictional character, Fred (his name rhymes with Fed for a reason you will learn about later). Fred has the magical ability of snapping his fingers and creating, out of thin air, a $1,000 bill.

On Monday morning, at 9 A.M., outside Bank A, Fred snaps his fingers and creates a $1,000 bill. He then immediately walks into the bank and deposits it into a demand deposit (checking) account he opens up. Entry a in Exhibit 11-4 shows this deposit.

Once the bank has the $1,000 bill, it places it into its vault. This means the money has found its way into vault cash. Vault cash, remember, is part of total reserves. (Total reserves equal deposits in the reserve account at the Fed plus vault cash.) This means that if vault cash goes up by $1,000, total reserves rise by the same amount.

Now, in order to keep things simple, let's assume that Bank A had no demand deposits before Fred walked into the bank. Now it has $1,000. Also, let's say that the Fed has set the reserve requirement at 10 percent. What are Bank A's required reserves? We know that required reserves equal the reserve requirement, times demand deposits. Since 10 percent times $1,000 is $100,

Bank A has to keep $100 of its demand deposits in reserve form—either in its reserve account at the Fed or as vault cash. (See Entry b in Exhibit 11-4).

Currently, Bank A has more than $100 in its vault—it has the $1,000 bill Fred handed over to it. What, then, do its excess reserves equal? Since excess reserves equal total reserves minus required reserves, it follows that excess reserves equal $900, the difference between $1,000 (total reserves) and $100 (required reserves). (See Entry c in Exhibit 11-4.)

What Does the Bank Do with Excess Reserves?

What does Bank A do with its $900 in excess reserves? The answer is, it creates new loans with the money. For example, suppose Georgia walks into Bank A and asks for a $900 loan. The loan officer at the bank asks Georgia what she wants the money for. She tells the loan officer that she wants a loan to buy a television set. The loan officer grants Georgia the loan.

Now, at this point some people may think that the loan officer of the bank simply walks over to the bank's vault, takes out $900 in currency, and hands it to Georgia. This usually doesn't happen. Instead, the loan officer opens up a checking account for Georgia at Bank A and informs Georgia that the balance in the account is $900. (Again, see Entry c in Exhibit 11-4.)

Ask yourself what Bank A has done by opening up a checking account (with a $900 balance) for Georgia. It has, in fact, increased the money supply by $900. To understand this, remind yourself again that the money supply consists of currency, checking accounts (demand deposits), and traveler's checks. When Bank A opens up a checking account (with a balance of $900) for Georgia, the dollar amount of currency has not changed, nor has the dollar amount of traveler's checks changed. The only thing that has changed is the dollar amount of demand deposits or checkbook money. It is $900 higher. This means the money supply is $900 higher, too.

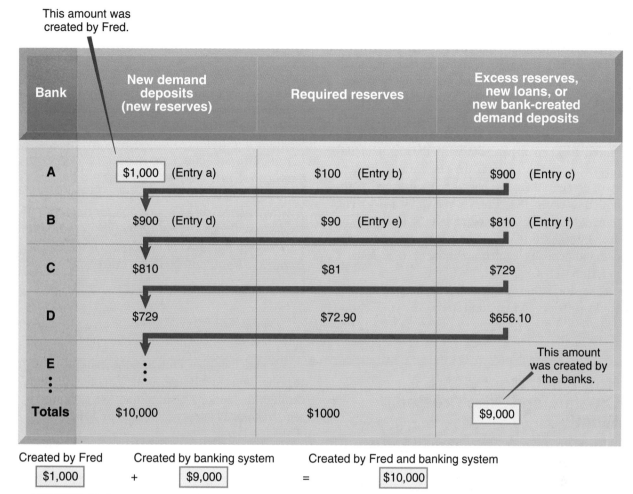

This amount was created by Fred.

Bank	New demand deposits (new reserves)	Required reserves	Excess reserves, new loans, or new bank-created demand deposits
A	$1,000 (Entry a)	$100 (Entry b)	$900 (Entry c)
B	$900 (Entry d)	$90 (Entry e)	$810 (Entry f)
C	$810	$81	$729
D	$729	$72.90	$656.10
E	⋮		This amount was created by the banks.
Totals	$10,000	$1000	$9,000

Created by Fred		Created by banking system		Created by Fred and banking system
$1,000	+	$9,000	=	$10,000

▲ **EXHIBIT 11-4. The Banking System Creates Demand Deposits (Money).** In this exhibit, the reserve requirement is 10 percent. We start with Fred, who has the ability to create money out of thin air. He snaps his fingers and creates $1,000 in currency and then deposits it in Bank A. The $1,000 is new reserves for Bank A and is also a new demand deposit. Required reserves equal $100, and excess reserves equal $900. Excess reserves can be used by the bank to create new loans or demand deposits (new money). The process continues for Banks B, C, D, E, and so on. In the end, we see that the banking system creates $9,000 in new demand deposits (new money) based on Fred's initial deposit of $1,000 of new money.

The Story Continues . . .

So far, Georgia has been granted a loan in the form of a $900 balance in a new checking account. Let's say that Georgia goes to a retail store and buys a $900 television set. She pays for the set by writing out a check for $900 drawn on Bank A. She hands the check to the owner of the store, Roberto Ruiz.

At the end of the business day, Ruiz takes the check to Bank B. As with Bank A, for simplicity's sake, we assume that demand deposits in Bank B equal zero. Ruiz, however, changes this by depositing the $900 into his checking account. (See Entry d in Exhibit 11-4.)

At this point, the check-clearing process (described earlier) kicks in. Bank B sends the check to its Federal Reserve bank, which increases the balance in Bank B's reserve account by $900. At the same time, the Federal Reserve bank decreases the funds in Bank A's reserve account by $900.

Back to Bank B. Once the Federal Reserve bank has increased the balance in Bank B's reserve account, total reserves for Bank B rise by $900. (Why? Because, again, total reserves equal deposits in the reserve account at the Fed plus vault cash.) Again, see Entry *d* in Exhibit 11-4.

And what happens to the demand deposits at Bank B? They rise to $900, too. Bank B is required to keep a percentage of the demand deposits in reserve form. If the reserve requirement is 10 percent, then $90 has to be maintained as required reserves. (See Entry e in Exhibit 11-4.) The remainder, or excess reserves—$810—can be used by Bank B to extend new loans or create new demand deposits (which are money). (See Entry f in Exhibit 11-4.)

The story continues in the same way with other banks—Banks C, D, E, and so on.

How Much Money Was Created, and Who Created What?

So far, Bank A has created $900 in new loans or demand deposits, and Bank B has created $810 in new loans or demand deposits. If we continue by bringing in Banks C, D, E, and so on, we'll find that all banks together—that is, the entire banking system—create $9,000 in new loans or demand deposits (money) as a result of Fred's deposit. You will notice that this dollar amount is boxed in Exhibit 11-4.

This is $9,000 of new money—money that did not exist before Fred snapped his fingers, created $1,000 out of thin air, and then deposited it into a checking account in Bank A.

The facts can be summarized as follows:

1. Fred created $1,000 in new money out of thin air.
2. After Fred deposited the $1,000 in Bank A, the banking system as a whole created $9,000 in additional new money.

THINKING LIKE AN ECONOMIST

The layperson often mistakenly thinks that money is simply currency (coins and paper money). To the economist, money is a generally accepted medium of exchange. In this chapter, we have said that currency, checking accounts (demand deposits), and traveler's checks are all money. You will notice that all three are widely accepted as exchange for payment. Often, you can just as easily buy something by writing a check, or endorsing a traveler's check, as you can by using currency.

We conclude that Fred and the banking system together created $10,000 in new money. In short, through the actions of Fred and the banking system, the money supply increased by $10,000.

A Simple Formula

Here is a simple formula you can use to find the (maximum) change in the money supply ($10,000) brought about in the example:

$$\text{Change in money supply} = \frac{1}{\text{Reserve requirement}} \times \text{Change in reserves of first bank}$$

In the example, the reserve requirement was set at 10 percent (0.10). The reserves of Bank A, the first bank to receive the injection of funds, changed by $1,000. Filling in the data in the formula, we have:

$$\text{Change in money supply} = \frac{1}{0.10} \times \$1,000$$
$$= \$10,000$$

LEARNING CHECK

1. Fred creates $2,000 with the snap of his fingers and deposits it in Bank A. The reserve requirement is 10 percent. By how much does the money supply increase?
2. Fred creates $1,500 with the snap of his fingers and deposits it in Bank A. The reserve requirement is 20 percent. By how much does the money supply increase?
3. Bank B has $20 million in demand deposits. The reserve requirement is 10 percent. How much do required reserves equal?
4. What do banks do with excess reserves?

SECTION 3   FED TOOLS FOR CHANGING THE MONEY SUPPLY

When the Fed changes the money supply, it is said to be conducting **monetary policy**. The Fed can change the money supply in three ways: (1) by changing the reserve requirement, (2) by conducting open-market operations, and (3) by changing the discount rate. We consider these three ways of changing the money supply next.

As you read, keep these key questions in mind:

■ How does a change in the reserve requirement change the money supply?
■ How does an open-market operation change the money supply?
■ How does a change in the discount rate change the money supply?

Changing the Reserve Requirement

Again, consider the formula to find a change in the money supply.

$$\text{Change in money supply} = \frac{1}{\text{Reserve requirement}} \times \text{Change in reserves of first bank}$$

Now consider three cases. In each case, the money supply is initially zero, and $1,000 is created out of thin air. The difference in the three cases is the reserve requirement, which is 5 percent in the first case, 10 percent in the second case, and 20 percent in the third. Let's calculate the change in the money supply in each of the three cases.

Case 1 (Reserve requirement = 5 percent); Change in money supply = $1 \div .05 \times \$1,000 = \$20,000$.

Case 2 (Reserve requirement = 10 percent); Change in money supply = $1 \div .10 \times \$1,000 = \$10,000$.

Case 3 (Reserve requirement = 20 percent); Change in money supply = $1 \div .20 \times \$1,000 = \$5,000$.

From looking at the three cases, in which case is the money supply the largest? It is the largest ($20,000) when the reserve requirement is 5 percent. When is it the smallest? The money supply is the smallest ($5,000) when the reserve requirement is 20 percent.

What happens if the Fed changes the reserve requirement? Again, using the numbers in the three

 MINI GLOSSARY

Monetary Policy The deliberate control of the money supply by the Fed.

CASE STUDY

The Savings and Loan Bailout

avings and loan institutions are like banks: they accept deposits (of money) from some people and lend the funds to other people. For most of its history, the savings and loan industry (1) principally lent funds to people who wanted to buy houses and (2) was prohibited from offering its depositors (the people who put their money in the savings and loan) an interest rate higher than the interest rate mandated by the federal government. This interest rate was commonly between 5¼ and 5½ percent. Also, for much of the industry's history, anyone who deposited his or her money in a savings and loan had that money automatically insured, by the federal government, up to $40,000 per account. The $40,000 insurance per account, called deposit insurance, was important to many depositors. They knew that if they put their money in a savings and loan, and the savings and loan ended up making numerous bad loans (a bad loan is one that is not repaid), and therefore was unable to repay them their money with interest, the federal government would step in and pay them back—up to $40,000.

All went well for a while. Then in the 1970s, some financial institutions began to offer depositors a higher interest rate than that offered by the savings and loan institutions. The deposits in these institutions weren't insured (as they were in the savings and loans), but still for many people the higher interest rate they paid was worth taking their money out of the savings and loan institutions and depositing it elsewhere.

Congress decided to do something to help the savings and loan industry. First, it said that the savings and loan institutions had the right to in-

▲ Historically, one of the primary functions of the savings and loan industry has been to extend credit to people who want to buy homes.

vest in high-risk ventures—ventures quite unlike the low-risk home loans they were making. Second, they were allowed to pay their depositors higher interest rates. Third, deposit insurance per account in a savings and loan was increased from $40,000 to $100,000.

In this new economic environment, some savings and loan institutions began to offer their depositors high interest rates, and then they would

CASE STUDY (continued)

take the money and invest in highly speculative (but potentially high-profit) ventures. On the one hand, the depositors didn't care how the savings and loans were investing, because they knew that if the savings and loan institutions ended up not collecting on their investments, the federal government would pay off the depositors up to $100,000 per account. And on the other hand, some of the savings and loan institutions looked at it this way: If the highly speculative ventures paid off, the payoff would be big, and the profits would be theirs to keep. But if the ventures didn't pay off, the government (taxpayers) would have to repay the depositors.

How did things turn out? Many of the high-risk, high-payoff ventures did not come through, and by the late 1980s, one-third of all the savings and loan institutions in the country were in financial trouble. The federal government had to offer a bailout that will, by some estimates, end up costing American taxpayers between $200 billion and $400 billion.

Some people say the savings and loan crisis was created by greedy savings and loan owners who didn't operate according to sound and conservative banking practices. In short, the bankers were gamblers. Many economists would disagree. They see the crisis as being created by bad economic policies.

Economists don't place as much emphasis on individuals as on policies as the cause of economic events. The economist would ask, Under what conditions or policies is the banker likely to act as a gambler? For example, would the savings and loan owner be more careful with other people's money if he could pass less of the risk on to taxpayers? Would depositors be more watchful of the savings and loans if there were less or no deposit insurance? Policies matter.

▲ Charles Keating, Jr. of Lincoln Savings and Loan, was one of a number of savings and loan executives who invested depositors' money in risky enterprises, paid themselves and their staffs extravagant salaries, and committed unlawful acts.

Economists do not believe that under all policies savings and loan owners are careless, and depositors are asleep—only under some policies. Economists believe that economic crises are not usually caused by "bad" people, but rather by "wrong" policies.

1. Do you think depositors in savings and loan institutions would have been more interested in where their money was invested if there were no deposit insurance? Explain your answer.

2. Suppose there are two financial institutions in which you can deposit your savings and receive an annual interest rate return. In the first institution, your deposits are insured; in the second, they are not. In which institution, the first or the second, would you expect to receive a higher annual interest rate return? Explain your answer.

cases, we can see that if the Fed increases the reserve requirement from 5 percent to 10 percent, then the money supply decreases from $20,000 to $10,000. If the Fed decreases the reserve requirement from 20 percent to 10 percent, the money supply increases from $5,000 to $10,000.

We conclude that the Fed can increase or decrease the money supply by changing the reserve requirement. If it increases the reserve requirement, the money supply decreases; if it decreases the reserve requirement, the money supply increases.

Open-Market Operations

Earlier in this chapter, we mentioned an important committee in the Federal Reserve system—the Federal Open Market Committee, or FOMC. This committee of 12 members conducts **open-market operations**. Before we can discuss these operations in detail, we need to provide some background information that relates to government securities and the U.S. Treasury.

The U.S. Treasury is an agency of the U.S. government. The Treasury's job is to collect the taxes and borrow the money needed to run the government. Now, let's suppose the U.S. Congress de-

cides to spend $1.2 trillion on various federal government programs. The U.S. Treasury has to pay the bills. It notices that it has collected $1.1 trillion in taxes, which is $100 billion less than the Congress wants to spend. It is the Treasury's job to borrow the $100 billion from the public. To borrow this money, the Treasury issues or sells government (or Treasury) securities. A government security is no more than a piece of paper promising to pay a certain dollar amount of money in the future. Think of it as an IOU statement.

These government securities are bought by members of the public. For example, let's say Lynn buys a government security for $9,000 which promises to pay $10,000 in a year. In buying the security, Lynn is, in fact, lending $9,000 to the Treasury, which it promises to pay back the next year with interest.

Now, the Fed (which is different from the Treasury) may buy government securities from any member of the public or sell them. When it buys a government security, it is said to be conducting an *open-market purchase*. When it sells a government security, it is said to be conducting an *open-market sale*. Let's examine the effects of these operations on the money supply.

◀ The United States Treasury in Washington, D.C. The Treasury is the agency that collects taxes and borrows the money needed to operate the government.

Open-Market Purchases. Let's say that you currently own a government security, which the Fed offers to purchase from you for $10,000. You agree to sell your security to the Fed. You hand over the security to the Fed, and in return, you receive a check made out to you for $10,000.

It is important to realize where the Fed gets this $10,000. It gets the money "out of thin air." Recall the story of Fred, who had the ability to snap his fingers and create a $1,000 bill out of thin air. Obviously, no such person has this power. But the Fed does have this power—it can create money out of thin air.

How does the Fed create money out of thin air? Think about the answer in this rough form: You have a checking account, and the Fed has a checking account. There is a balance in each account. The Fed can take a pencil and increase the balance in its account at will—legally. If you do this, however, and then write a check for an amount you don't have in your account, your check bounces. Fed checks don't bounce.

We return to our example of an open-market purchase. Once you have the $10,000 check from the Fed, you take it to your local bank and deposit it in your checking account. Is the total dollar amount of demand deposits in the economy more or less than before the Fed purchased your government security? The answer is "more." Furthermore, no other component of the money supply (not currency or traveler's checks) is less. This means the overall money supply has increased.

In conclusion, when the Fed conducts an open-market purchase, the money supply increases.

Open-Market Sales. Suppose the Fed has a government security that it offers to sell you for $10,000. You agree to buy the security. You write out a check to the Fed for $10,000 and give it to the Fed. The Fed, in return, turns the government security over to you.

Next, the check is cleared, and a sum of $10,000 is removed from your account in your bank and transferred to the Fed. Once this sum is in the Fed's possession, it is removed from the economy altogether. It seems *as if* the $10,000 no longer existed or *as if* it had disappeared from the face of the earth. Is the total dollar amount of demand deposits more or less than before the Fed sold you a government security? The answer is "less." We conclude that an open-market sale reduces the money supply.

QUESTION: *We know that the Fed can change the money supply through open-market operations, but why would it want to change the money supply? Of what benefit to the Fed is an increase or decrease in the money supply?*

ANSWER: *The Fed states that it changes the money supply in order to try to achieve certain economic objectives, such as to keep prices stable and unemployment low. In later chapters, you will learn how changes in the money supply affect the economy.*

Changing the Discount Rate

Suppose Bank A wants to borrow $1 million. It could borrow this dollar amount from another bank, say, Bank B. Or it could borrow this money from the Fed. If Bank A borrows the money from Bank B, Bank B will charge an interest rate for the $1 million loan. The interest rate charged by Bank B is called the **federal funds rate**. If Bank A borrows the money from the Fed, the Fed will charge an interest rate for the $1 million. The interest rate charged by the Fed is called the **discount rate**.

Whether Bank A borrows from Bank B or from the Fed depends on the relation between the federal funds rate and the discount rate. If the federal funds rate is lower than the discount rate, Bank A will bor-

---

MINI GLOSSARY

Open-Market Operations Buying and selling of government securities by the Fed.
Federal Funds Rate The interest rate one bank charges another bank for a loan.
Discount Rate The interest rate the Fed charges a bank for a loan.

Fed monetary tool	Money supply
Open-market operation	
Buys government securities	Increases
Sells government securities	Decreases
Reserve requirement	
Raises reserve requirement	Decreases
Lowers reserve requirement	Increases
Discount rate	
Raises rate (relative to the federal funds rate)	Decreases
Lowers rate (relative to the federal funds rate)	Increases

▲ **EXHIBIT 11-5. Fed Monetary Tools and Their Effects on the Money Supply.** The following Fed actions increase the money supply: purchasing government securities in the open market, lowering the reserve requirement, and lowering the discount rate relative to the federal funds rate. The following Fed actions decrease the money supply: selling government securities on the open market, raising the reserve requirement, and raising the discount rate relative to the federal funds rate.

row from Bank B instead of from the Fed. (Why pay a higher interest rate if you don't have to?) If, however, the discount rate is lower than the federal funds rate, Bank A will probably borrow from the Fed.

Now, is there any difference between borrowing from Bank B and borrowing from the Fed? The answer is yes. If Bank A borrows from Bank B, no new money enters the economy. Bank B simply has $1 million less, and Bank A has $1 million more.

But if Bank A borrows from the Fed, the Fed creates new money in the process of granting the loan. It creates this money out of thin air. We conclude that if the Fed lowers its discount rate relative to the federal funds rate, and if banks then borrow from the Fed, the money supply will increase.

See Exhibit 11-5 for a review of the ways in which the Fed can change the money supply.

QUESTION: *Suppose the Fed raises its discount rate so that it is higher than the federal funds rate. Does it follow that the money supply will decrease?*

ANSWER: *Eventually, the money supply will decrease. Here's why. If the Fed raises its discount rate relative to the federal funds rate, banks will begin to borrow from each other rather than from the Fed. There will come a day, though, when the banks will have to repay the funds they borrowed from the Fed in the past, when the discount rate was lower (say, funds they borrowed many months ago). When the banks repay these loans, money is removed from the economy, and the money supply drops. We conclude that if the Fed raises its discount rate relative to the federal funds rate, the money supply will eventually fall.*

 # LEARNING CHECK

1. The Fed wants to increase the money supply. (a) What can it do to the reserve requirement? (b) What can it do to the discount rate? (c) What type of open-market operation can it conduct?
2. The Fed wants to decrease the money supply. (a) What can it do to the reserve requirement? (b) What can it do to the discount rate? (c) What type of open-market operation can it conduct?

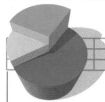

DEVELOPING ECONOMIC SKILLS

Identifying Economic Trends

A *trend* is a general tendency or inclination in a particular direction. To illustrate, suppose Robert is currently a senior in high school. In his freshman year in high school, his grade point average (GPA) was 2.45. In his sophomore year, his GPA was 2.97. In his junior year, his GPA was 3.33. And so far this year, his GPA is 3.56. As we can see, Robert's GPA has been rising during his time in high school. In other words, there is a general tendency, or inclination, for his grades to go up. Here, then, is a trend: an upward trend in Robert's academic performance.

Consider another example. Suppose that this year, in a city in the Midwest, two feet of snow fell in the winter. Last year three feet of snow fell. Three years ago, four feet of snow fell, and four years ago, five feet of snow fell. Is there a trend? Yes; there is a trend toward less snow.

It is important to know the difference between a trend and a one-time change in the direction of some variable. For example, suppose the average daytime temperature in San Diego in January is 63 degrees. One day in January in San Diego, the average temperature happens to be 45 degrees. Is this a trend toward cooler temperatures in San Diego? Not at all. This is simply one day when the temperature fell below average. Before we can say a trend exists, we'd need to see cooler temperatures occurring regularly.

Economists often try to identify trends in economic data. For example, consider the trend in the growth rate of the money supply. In the decade of the 1960s, the average annual growth rate of the money supply was 3.86 percent. This means the money supply was growing by an average of 3.86 percent each year during the '60s. The average annual growth rate was higher in the 1970s, at 6.51 percent. And it was even higher in the 1980s, 7.66 percent. In other words, the trend in the average annual growth rate of the money supply, measured in decades, was up. In later chapters you will learn how an upward trend in the money supply growth rate may affect the prices of goods and services.

Consider a trend in the growth rate of the economy. In the next chapter, you will learn how economists measure the size of the economy. For now, though, we'll keep things simple and consider the economy as a pie. If the pie gets larger, the economy is growing; if the pie gets smaller, the economy is shrinking. Now, what usually happens from one year to the next is that the economic pie (the economy) gets bigger. But sometimes it gets much bigger than at other times. For example, in the 1960s, the average annual growth rate of the economy was 4.07 percent. In other words, the economy in the 1960s was getting larger (expanding) each year by an average of 4.07 percent. In the 1970s, the economy grew, but not by the same average annual growth rate as in the 1960s. In the 1970s, it grew an average of 2.85 percent each year. In the 1980s, the average annual growth rate was slightly lower than in the 1970s; it was 2.48 percent. In other words, there was a downward trend in the growth rate of the economy.

Now consider the unemployment rate. In the 1960s, the average annual unemployment rate—which is the percentage of the civilian labor force that is unemployed—was 4.78 percent. In the 1970s, the average annual unemployment rate was 6.21 percent. And in the 1980s, the average annual unemployment rate had risen to 7.27 percent. In short, there was an upward trend in the unemployment rate.

Finally, consider the inflation rate—which is a measure of the rate at which the prices of goods and services have been rising. In no year during the 1960s did the inflation rate go over 5 percent. But in the 1970s, there was only one year in which the inflation rate was under 5 percent. In other words, there was an upward trend in the inflation rate.

DEVELOPING ECONOMIC SKILLS (continued)

Now that we have identified a few economic trends, ask yourself if you have some idea of what was happening in the economy during the period 1960 through 1989 (the decades of the '60s, '70s, and '80s). You know there was an upward trend in the growth rate of the money supply, a downward trend in the growth rate of the economy, an upward trend in the unemployment rate, and an upward trend (during 1960–79) in the inflation rate. Might we have preferred different economic trends? For example, would we have preferred a downward trend in the unemployment rate instead of an upward trend? Most people will answer yes. Would we have preferred stable prices (no trend) instead of an upward trend in the inflation rate? Most people will answer yes. One of the jobs of economists is to identify trends in economic data and, if the trend is going in the "wrong" direction, try to figure out how to reverse it. For example, try to figure out how to turn an upward trend in the unemployment rate into a downward trend.

1. Global warming is defined as "an increase in the earth's average atmospheric temperature that causes corresponding changes in climate and that may result from the greenhouse effect." Is there anything in the definition of global warming that indicates a trend? If so, what?

2. *The Universal Almanac* states, "Since the 1920 census, more than one half of all Americans have lived in an urban area, which can be loosely defined as a place of 2,500 or more inhabitants. During the 1980s, the population of urban areas grew by 20 million people, from 167.1 million to 187.1 million, an increase of 12%. By 1990, the proportion of the U.S. population living in urban areas reached 75.2%, up from 73.7% in 1980. California had the highest proportion of urban population, at 92.6%. In comparison, the country's rural population grew by 3.6%, from 59.5 million in 1980 to 61.7 million in 1990. Only 11 states had increased percentages of rural population in the 1980s even though 32 states recorded an increase in the number of rural residents."[a]

   Are there any trends identified here? If so, what are the trends?

3. Harry has promised himself that he will exercise three to four times each week. Today was his first day of exercising. Is this a trend? Explain your answer.

---

a. *The Universal Almanac, 1994* (Kansas City: Andrews and McMeel, 1993), p. 280.

CHAPTER 11 REVIEW

CHAPTER SUMMARY

1. The Federal Reserve system is the central bank of the United States. The Federal Reserve Act of 1913 set up the Fed, and the Fed began operation in 1914.

2. The principal components of the Federal Reserve system are (1) the Board of Governors, (2) the 12 Federal Reserve district banks.

3. The major policy-making group within the Fed is the Federal Open Market Committee (FOMC). The FOMC is made up of 12 members. Its job is to conduct open-market operations.

4. The major duties of the Fed include: (1) controlling the money supply, (2) supplying the economy with paper money (Federal Reserve notes), (3) holding bank reserves, (4) providing check-clearing services, (5) supervising member banks, and (6) serving as the lender of last resort.

5. The reserves of banks that are members of the Federal Reserve system are described by the following equations:

Total reserves = Deposits in the reserve account at the Fed + Vault cash

Required reserves = Reserve requirement × Demand deposits

Excess reserves = Total reserves − Required reserves

6. Banks can make loans with their excess reserves. For example, if a bank has $500,000 in excess reserves, it can create loans up to $500,000.

7. Banks cannot print currency, but they can create demand deposits. When banks create demand deposits, they are creating money, since demand deposits are a component of the money supply.

8. The overall change in the money supply brought about by a particular injection of funds is described by the following equation:

$$\text{Change in money supply} = \frac{1}{\text{Reserve requirement}} \times \text{Change in reserves of first bank}$$

9. When the Fed deliberately increases or decreases the money supply—through changing the reserve requirement, changing the discount rate, or conducting open-market operations—it is conducting monetary policy.

10. If the Fed raises the reserve requirement, the money supply falls; if it lowers the reserve requirement, the money supply rises.

11. An open-market operation takes place when the Fed buys or sells government securities. When the Fed buys government securities, it is conducting an open-market purchase. When the Fed sells government securities, it is conducting an open-market sale. An open-market purchase increases the money supply, and an open-market sale decreases the money supply.

12. The federal funds rate is the interest rate one bank charges another bank for a loan. The discount rate is the interest rate the Fed charges a bank for a loan. If the Fed lowers the discount rate relative to the federal funds rate, the money supply increases. If the Fed raises the discount rate relative to the federal funds rate, the money supply (eventually) decreases.

CHAPTER 11 REVIEW (continued)

BUILD YOUR ECONOMIC VOCABULARY

Match the word with the correct definition, example, or statement.

1. Board of Governors
2. FOMC
3. total reserves
4. excess reserves
5. reserve requirement
6. discount rate
7. federal funds rate
8. open-market operation

a. the percentage of demand deposits a bank is required to hold in reserve form
b. total reserves minus required reserves; can be used to extend loans
c. consists of seven persons
d. conducts open-market operations
e. interest rate one bank charges another bank for a loan
f. interest rate the Fed charges a bank for a loan
g. deposits in the reserve account at the Fed plus vault cash
h. buying and selling of government securities by the Fed

REVIEW QUESTIONS

1. Explain how a check clears. Illustrate this process using two banks in the Federal Reserve district in which you live.
2. List the locations of the 12 Federal Reserve district banks.
3. State what each of the following equals: (a) total reserves, (b) required reserves, (c) excess reserves.
4. A bank has $600,000 in demand deposits, and the reserve requirement is 15 percent. What do required reserves equal?
5. A bank has $100,000 in its reserve account at the Fed and $40,000 in vault cash. The reserve requirement is 10 percent. What do total reserves equal?
6. The chapter stated that when a bank creates a demand deposit (by extending a loan), it is in effect *creating money*. What is the rationale for equating a demand deposit with money?
7. The Fed conducts an open-market purchase and increases the reserves of Bank A by $1 million. The reserve requirement is 10 percent. By how much does the money supply increase?
8. The Fed conducts an open-market purchase and increases the reserves of Bank A by $2 million. The reserve requirement is 20 percent. By how much does the money supply increase?
9. What is the relationship between changes in the reserve requirement and changes in the money supply?
10. Explain how an open-market purchase increases the money supply.
11. Explain how an open-market sale decreases the money supply.
12. Suppose the Fed sets the discount rate much higher than the existing federal funds rate. With this action, what signal is the Fed sending banks?

REVIEW QUESTIONS (continued)

13. According to Exhibit 11-1, in what Federal Reserve district are you located?

14. According to Exhibit 11-1, where is the Federal Reserve bank in the ninth district located? the second district? the eleventh district?

SHARPEN YOUR CRITICAL THINKING SKILLS

1. Look at a Federal Reserve note. On the left-hand side of the front, there is an emblem. In small letters in the emblem, the name of the Federal Reserve district bank that issued the note is written. Federal Reserve district banks issue notes to the banks in their districts. For example, the Federal Reserve Bank of Dallas issues notes to banks in Houston. With this in mind, consider the following: There are two towns in two different Federal Reserve districts. One is a tourist town, and the other is not. In which town would you expect to find more Federal Reserve notes issued by Federal Reserve district banks *other than* the one in the district in which the town is located? Explain why.

ACTIVITIES AND PROJECTS

1. Check in your school library to see if you can find information on any of the following topics. (You will need to check encyclopedias, magazines, and books.) Then, write a two- to three-page report on one of the topics.
   a. Federal Reserve system
   b. How the Bureau of Engraving and Printing prints paper money (Federal Reserve notes)
   c. The current chairperson of the Board of Governors of the Federal Reserve system
   d. The history of the savings and loan crisis

ECONOMIC DICTIONARY

Board of Governors of the Federal Reserve System (Pg. 278)
Discount Rate (Pg. 293)
Excess Reserves (Pg. 283)
Federal Funds Rate (Pg. 293)
Federal Open Market Committee (FOMC) (Pg. 279)
Federal Reserve System (the Fed) (Pg. 278)
Monetary Policy (Pg. 289)
Open-Market Operations (Pg. 292)
Required Reserves (Pg. 282)
Reserve Requirement (Pg. 282)
Total Reserves (Pg. 282)

CHAPTER 12

Measuring Economic Performance

INTRODUCTION

Economics can be divided into two branches: microeconomics and macroeconomics. *Microeconomics* is the branch of economics that deals with human behavior and choices as they relate to relatively small units—the individual, the firm, a single market. In Units 1 and 2 of this book, you studied microeconomics. Macroeconomics is discussed in Unit 3.

Macroeconomics is the branch of economics that deals with human behavior and choices as they relate to the entire economy. In this chapter, you begin your study of macroeconomics. The emphasis will be on the "big picture." Instead of the output of a single firm, we examine the output of the entire economy. Instead of the price of a single good (say, apples), we consider the prices of all goods. Instead of analyzing how taxes affect one firm or one industry, we see how taxes affect the economy. It is macroeconomic news that you usually read about in the newspaper and hear about on the radio. Inflation, unemployment, economic growth, and interest rates are all topics for the macroeconomist.

This chapter begins with two of the basics. We first discuss the economy's output and then consider overall prices in the economy.

You are in the car listening to the news on the radio. The newscaster says that, according to a newly released government report, the economy has been growing and prices are rising only slightly. What exactly does it mean when someone says, "The economy has been growing"? Is the economy like a person—can it grow taller or heavier? If not, how does an economy grow? And what about prices? When someone says that prices are rising only slightly, what does this mean? Does it mean all prices are rising slightly, or just some prices? And what is meant by *slightly*?

In this section, we begin our examination of economic measurements. In regard to these measurements, it is perhaps easiest to think of the economy as you would your own body. If you go to the doctor and tell her that you are sick, she will take some measurements—she will take your temperature, run some blood tests, take your blood pressure, and so on. She will try to assign numbers to things. "You are running a fever," she may say, "because your temperature is 100.8 degrees."

Economists try to measure things, too. They measure things for the same reason the doctor measures things—to get some "fix" on how the patient (or the economy) is doing. Two things the doctor usually measures are temperature and blood pressure. Two things an economist usually measures are gross domestic product (GDP) and prices. This section explains what gross domestic product is and how it is measured. Later in the chapter, we consider prices.

As you read, keep these key questions in mind:

- What is GDP?
- Why are only *final* goods and services computed in GDP?
- What is omitted from GDP?

Gross Domestic Product

Gross domestic product (GDP) is the total market value of all final goods and services pro-

duced annually in an economy. For example, suppose there is a tiny economy in which only four goods are produced, in these quantities: 10 computers, 10 cars, 10 watches, and 10 greeting cards. Furthermore, suppose the price of a computer is $4,000, the price of a car is $10,000, the price of a watch is $100, and the price of a greeting card is $1. If we wanted to find the GDP of this small economy—that is, if we wanted to find the total market value of the goods produced during the year—we would multiply the price of each good, times the number of units of the good produced and then sum the dollar amounts. Here are the calculations:

$4,000 \times 10$ computers $= \$40,000$
$10,000 \times 10$ cars $= \$100,000$
100×10 watches $= \$1,000$
1×10 greeting cards $= \$10$
$40,000 + \$100,000 + \$1,000 + \$10 = \$141,010$

This total, $141,010, is the gross domestic product, or GDP, of our tiny economy.

Why Final Goods?

The definition of GDP specified "final goods and services"; GDP is the total market value of all final goods and services produced annually in an economy. Economists often distinguish between a *final good* and an *intermediate good*. A final good is a good sold to its final user. For example, when you buy a hamburger at a fast-food restaurant, the hamburger is a final good. You are the final user. No one uses (eats) the hamburger besides you. We might say that your purchase of the hamburger is at the "end" of the hamburger line.

An intermediate good, in contrast, has not reached its final user. For example, consider the bun that the restaurant buys and on which the hamburger is placed. The bun is an intermediate good at this stage because it is not yet in the hands of the final user—that is, the person who buys the hamburger. It is in the hands of the people who run

▶ The market value of this telescope, along with all other final goods and services, makes up GDP. A final good is a good that is sold to its final user.

the restaurant, who use the bun, along with other goods (lettuce, mustard, hamburger meat, and so on) to produce a hamburger for sale.

When computing GDP, economists only count final goods and services because if they counted final *and* intermediate goods and services, they would be **double-counting**, which is counting a good more than once.

Consider another example. Suppose that a book is a final good and that paper and ink are intermediate goods used to produce the book. In a way, we can say that the book is paper and ink (book = paper + ink). Now, if we were to calculate GDP by adding together the value of the book, the paper, and the ink (book + paper + ink), we would, in effect, be counting the paper and ink *twice*. Since the book is paper and ink, once we count the book, we have automatically counted the paper and the ink. There is no need to count them again.

What GDP Omits

Some exchanges that take place in an economy are omitted from the GDP measurement. We discuss them next.

Illegal Goods and Services. In order for something to count as part of GDP, that something has to be capable of being counted. Illegal trades are not capable of being counted, for obvious reasons. For example, when someone makes an illegal purchase, there is no record of the transaction.

Legal Goods and Services for which There is No Record of a Transaction. Suppose a gardener goes to someone's house and offers to mow the lawn and prune the shrubbery for $25 a week. The person agrees. The gardener then asks that he be paid in cash instead of by check, and that no written record of the transaction be made. In other words, there will be no sales receipt. Again the person agrees. Does the payment for

MINI GLOSSARY
Gross Domestic Product (GDP) The total market value of all final goods and services produced annually in an economy.
Double-Counting Counting a good more than once in computing GDP.

CASE STUDY

GDP Replaces GNP

We have been discussing gross domestic product (GDP) in this chapter. Today, economists, government officials, and laypersons talk about GDP when they want to discuss the overall performance of the economy. For example, they might say, "GDP has been on the rise" or "GDP has been declining a bit." It wasn't always GDP that these individuals talked about, though. Until a few years ago, it was GNP instead—that is, gross *national* product.

What is the difference between gross domestic product (GDP) and gross national product (GNP)? GNP measures the total market value of final goods and services produced by U.S. citizens—*no matter where in the world they reside.* GDP is the total market value of final goods and services produced within the borders of the United States—*whoever produces them.*

For example, suppose a U.S. citizen owns a business in Japan. The value of the output she is producing in Japan is counted in GNP, because she is a U.S citizen. But it is not counted in GDP, because it was not produced within the borders of the United States.

Now, suppose a Canadian citizen is producing goods in the United States. The value of his output is not counted in GNP, because he is not a U.S. citizen, but it is counted in GDP, because it was produced within the borders of the United States.

The shift from GNP to GDP reflects the fact that GDP has become more closely related than GNP to changes in important economic factors, such as employment.

---

1. Is the value of output produced by an American residing in Germany computed in GDP or GNP?
2. Is the value of output produced by a Mexican residing in the U.S. computed in GDP or GNP?

◀ This is a Honda plant in the United States. The market value of the cars produced in this plant is included in GDP.

these gardening services find its way into GDP? No. With cash payment and no sales receipt, there is no evidence that the transaction was ever made. On the other hand, if a check were written, there would be a record of the transaction and it would be counted in GDP.

Some Nonmarket Goods and Services. Some goods and services are traded, but not in an official market setting. For example, let's say that Eileen Montoya cooks, cleans, and takes care of all financial matters in the Montoya household. She is not paid for doing all this; she does not receive a weekly salary from the family. Because she isn't paid, the value of the work she performs is not counted in GDP.

Sales of Used Goods. Suppose you buy a used car tomorrow. Will this purchase be recorded in this year's GDP statistics? No. A used car does not enter into the current year's statistics, because the car was counted when it was originally produced.

Stock Transactions and Other Financial Transactions. Suppose Elizabeth Sullivan buys 500 shares of stock from Keesha Wilson for a price of $100 a share. The total price is $50,000 ($100 × 500 = $50,000). The transaction is not in-cluded in GDP. The reason is that GDP is a record of goods and services *produced* annually in an economy. A person who buys stock is not buying a product but an ownership right in the firm that originally issued the stock. For example, when a person buys IBM stock, she is becoming an owner of the IBM Corporation.

Government Transfer Payments. In every-day life, one person makes a payment to another usually in exchange for a good or service. For ex-ample, Nancy may pay Harriet $140 to buy her used CD player. When the government makes a payment to someone, and does not get a good or service in exchange, the payment is said to be a government transfer payment. For example, the Social Security check that 67-year-old Frank Umchuck receives is a government transfer pay-ment. Frank Umchuck, who is retired, is not current-ly supplying a good or a service to the government in exchange for the Social Security check. Since GDP accounts for only current goods and services produced, and a transfer payment has nothing to do with current goods and services produced, trans-fer payments are properly omitted from GDP sta-tistics. (See Exhibit 12-1 for a review of items omitted from GDP.)

What GDP omits	
Items	**Examples**
Illegal goods and services	An illegal sale takes place.
Legal goods and services for which there is no record of the transaction	A gardener works for cash and no sales receipt exists.
Some nonmarket goods and services	A family member cooks, cleans, and so on.
Sales of used goods	You buy a used car.
Stock transactions and other financial transactions	You buy 100 shares of stock in a company.
Government transfer payments	Frank Umchuck receives a Social Security check.

▲ **EXHIBIT 12-1. What GDP Omits.**

LEARNING CHECK

1. Define *GDP*.
2. In a simple economy, three goods are produced during the year, in these quantities: 10 pens, 20 shirts, and 30 radios. The price of pens is $4 each, the price of shirts is $30 each, and the price of radios is $35 each. What is the GDP for this economy?
3. Why are only final goods and services computed in GDP?
4. Which of the following are included in the calculation of this year's GDP? (a) Twelve-year-old Bobby mowing his family's lawn. (b) Terry Yanemoto buying a used car. (c) Barbara Wilson buying 100 shares of Chrysler Corporation stock. (d) Stephen Ferguson's receipt of a Social Security check. (e) An illegal sale at the corner of Elm and Jefferson.

SECTION 2   MEASURING GDP

We know what GDP is and how to measure it in a small economy (such as one with only three or four goods). But how is the GDP of the giant U.S. economy measured? This section explains how.

As you read, keep these key questions in mind:

- What are the four sectors of the economy?
- How is GDP computed?

How Is GDP Measured?

Economists break the economy into four sectors: the household sector, the business sector, the government sector, and the foreign sector. Next, they state a simple fact. They state that the people in each of these sectors buy goods and services—that is, they make expenditures. Economists give names to the expenditures made by each of the four sectors. The expenditures made by the household sector (or by consumers) are called *consumption*. The expenditures made by the business sector are called *investment*. The expenditures made by the government sector are called *government expenditures*. And the expenditures made by foreigners for American-produced goods are

called *exports*. See Exhibit 12-2 for examples of goods purchased by households, businesses, government, and foreigners.

Now, consider all the goods and services produced in the U.S. economy in a year: houses, tractors, watches, restaurant meals, cars, computers, radios, compact discs, and much, much more. Suppose someone from the household sector—you, for example—buys a compact disc. This purchase falls into the category of *consumption*. Suppose someone from the business sector buys a large machine to install in his or her factory. The purchase of this machine is considered *investment*. If the U.S. government purchases a tank from a company that produces tanks, this purchase is considered a *government expenditure*. And if a foreigner, say, living in Sweden, buys an American-made sweater, this purchase is considered an *export*.

Now, it stands to reason that all goods produced in the economy must be bought by someone in one of the four sectors of the economy. It follows that if economists simply sum the expenditures made by each sector—that is, sum consumption, investment, government expenditures, and exports—they will be *close* to computing GDP.

Sector of the economy	Name of expenditures	Definition	Examples
Household	Consumption	Expenditures made by the household sector on goods for personal use	TV sets, telephones, clothes, lamps, cars
Business	Investment	Expenditures made by the business sector on goods used in producing other goods; also includes business inventories	Tools, machines, factories
Government	Government expenditures	Expenditures made by federal, state, and local governments	Paper, pens, tanks, planes
Foreign	Exports	Expenditures made by foreigners for American-made goods	Cars, wheat, computers
	Imports	Expenditures made by Americans for foreign-made goods	Cars, radios, computers

▲ **EXHIBIT 12-2. The Expenditures Made by the Four Sectors of the Economy.**

They are only *close* because they still need to adjust for American purchases of foreign-produced goods. For example, suppose Roberta, living in Austin, Texas, purchases a Japanese-made television set for $500. Should this $500 TV purchase be included in GDP? The answer is no. GDP is a measure of goods and services produced annually in an economy. Specifically, the U.S. GDP is a measure of goods and services produced annually in the territorial area we know as the United States. The TV was not produced in the United States, so it is not part of the U.S. GDP. Expenditures made by Americans for foreign-made goods are *imports*.

In order to compute the U.S. GDP, then, we need to sum consumption, investment, government expenditures, and exports and then *subtract* imports. In economics, the following symbols are used: C for consumption, I for investment, G for government expenditures, X for exports, and M for imports. We can now write GDP in symbol form:

$$GDP = C + I + G + X - M$$

In 1992, consumption in the United States was $4,139.9 billion, investment was $796.5 billion, government expenditures were $1,131.8 billion, exports were $640.5 billion, and imports were $670.1 billion. Thus, we can calculate 1992 GDP to be $6,038.6 billion. (See Exhibit 12-3.)

QUESTION: *In the equation GDP = C + I + G + X − M, does the G stand for only federal government expenditures?*

ANSWER: *No. G stands for the expenditures made by the federal, state, and local governments. This is government spending at all levels.*

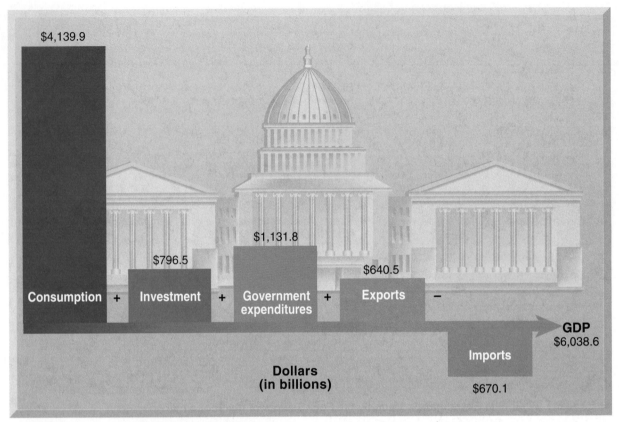

$4,139.9

$796.5

$1,131.8

$640.5

Consumption + Investment + Government expenditures + Exports −

GDP
$6,038.6

Imports

**Dollars
(in billions)**

$670.1

▲ **EXHIBIT 12-3. Computing GDP (1992).**

QUESTION: *This section stated that "it stands to reason that all goods produced in the economy must be bought by someone in one of the four sectors of the economy." Is this really true? It seems that a good can be produced but not sold. For example, General Motors doesn't always sell every car it produces in a year.*

ANSWER: *The way national income accountants do things, every good that is produced is bought by someone. (The national income accountants are the persons who compute GDP.) Here's an example. Suppose IBM produces 10,000 computers this year and sells 9,000 to the public. This means that 1,000 computers that IBM produces this year are not sold to the public. We could say that 1,000 computers are not bought. But national income accountants wouldn't say this. They would say that the 1,000 computers go into IBM's inventory. As far as the national*

income accountants are concerned, the 1,000 computers have been "purchased" by IBM. In other words, whatever the company produces and does not sell to the public is considered (by national income accountants) to be purchased by the company. Looking at things this way, we can say that every good that is produced is purchased by someone.

Large GDP Figures Aren't the Only Thing in Life

In 1991, the U.S. GDP was more than five times larger than the GDP of France. (See Exhibit 12-4.) Does it follow that because Americans live in a country with a higher GDP than the French, Americans are better off than the French? If your answer is yes, then you have made the mistake of

Nation	GDP (Approximate dollar figure, in billions)
1. United States	$5,677
2. Japan	2,370
3. China	1,660
4. Germany	1,250
5. France	1,040
6. India	1,000
7. Italy	980
8. Great Britain	900
9. Brazil	790
10. Mexico	600
11. Canada	520
12. Spain	500

▲ **EXHIBIT 12-4. GDP Selected Nations (1991).**
SOURCE: International Monetary Fund, and *Economic Report of the President, 1993.*

equating a higher GDP with being "better off" or having greater "well-being."

There are many things that go into being better off or possessing greater well-being. Greater production of goods and services is only one of those things.

Look at the issue on an individual basis. Franklin has $1 million in the bank, owns a large home, drives a fast car, and works 70 hours per week. He has little time to enjoy the outdoors or his family. In contrast, Harris has $100 in the bank, owns a small home, drives an old, slow car, and works 30 hours a week. He has much time to enjoy the outdoors and his family.

Who is better off—Franklin or Harris? In terms of expensive goods, there is no doubt that Franklin has more than Harris. In this one respect, Franklin is better off than Harris. In terms of leisure time, though, Harris is better off than Franklin. In overall terms—taking everything into account—we can't say who is better off. We just don't know.

Similarly, we simply can't say whether Americans are better off than the French on the basis of their GDPs. All we can say for sure is that Americans live in a country in which greater production

exists. Being "better off" takes into account much more than simply how much output is produced.

Along similar lines, some economists have been trying to devise an economic measurement that comes closer than GDP to measuring such intangibles as happiness or well-being. For example, economists William Nordhaus and James Tobin have developed what they call *MEW (measures of economic welfare).* MEW adds to GDP many of those things that are presently excluded but nonetheless increase our overall standard of living—for example, the value of leisure time and household pro-

THINKING LIKE AN ECONOMIST

Economists understand that life is full of tradeoffs. More of one thing may mean less of something else. For example, a higher GDP may come at the expense of less leisure.

▼ The value of time spent in leisure activities is not included in GDP.

ECONOMIC FOCUS

Suppose there is a tiny economy in which only 10 units of a good are produced, and each unit is sold for $40. The GDP of this tiny economy would be $400 ($40 × 10 = $400). This $400 can also be considered as *income* for the person who produced and sold the 10 units. In other words, in this tiny economy, GDP = Total income. In a large economy, there is a close correspondence between GDP and income. When people produce and sell goods, they increase GDP; they also generate income for themselves equal to the dollar amount of what they produced and sold.

Sometimes, instead of using GDP to get a "fix" or measurement of the economy, economists will use *total personal income*. Total personal income is the amount of income that individuals receive in an economy. In 1992 in the United States, total personal income was $5,265.1 billion.[a]

One thing we can do is to compare the total personal income for the different states in 1992. We show this in Exhibit S-12-1. There you will see that the total personal income in Alabama that year was $69.6 billion; in Alaska, it was $12.9 billion; and so on. The total personal income figures in the second column of Exhibit S-12-1 can be used to give us an idea of the size of each state's economy relative to another state's economy. For example, the total personal income for California was $673.4 billion in 1992. This was the largest state economy in the United States. New York had the second-largest state economy, at $448.1 billion, and Texas had the third-largest state economy, at $331.5 billion.

---

a. This figure is based on the fourth quarter figures for total personal income, adjusted at an annual rate.

Why do some states have larger economies than other states? One major reason is that some states have a larger population than other states. For example, suppose we took the northern half of California and made it part of the state of Oregon (which lies north of California). What would you predict would happen to the total personal income in Oregon? in California? We would expect the total personal income in Oregon to rise, and the total personal income in California to fall. Why? Because generally a greater population means more people producing and selling goods and services and earning incomes. For example, it is interesting that in terms of population, California, New York, and Texas rank 1, 2, and 3. They also happen to rank 1, 2, and 3 in total personal income.

But then how do we explain that Mississippi, which has a population roughly equal to that of Kansas, has a lower total personal income than does Kansas? The total personal income for Kansas is $51.3 billion; for Mississippi, it is $38 billion. If population were the only thing that mattered in calculating total personal income, we'd expect that states with nearly equal populations would have nearly equal total personal incomes. The fact is that other things besides population matter. This is obvious when we compare nations. For example, the population of China is much larger than the population of the United States, but China has a much lower total personal income than does the United States.

Economists are not all agreed as to what determines total personal income. In other words, they don't all agree as to why the total personal income in the United States is higher than that in China; nor do they all concur as to why the total personal income is higher in California than in New York.

TOTAL PERSONAL INCOME ACROSS THE STATES

We can, however, cite some of the factors that some economists say affect total personal income.

Some economists say the business tax climate of a state affects its total personal income. Their argument goes like this: Wherever state taxes on businesses are low, that is where businesses will

locate. The more businesses that locate in a state, the more jobs will be generated. The more jobs generated, the more income will be earned.

Some economists argue that the level of education of the state residents affects total personal income. Their argument, especially in recent

▼ **EXHIBIT S-12-1.** Total Personal Income, across the States.

STATE	TOTAL PERSONAL INCOME (IN BILLIONS)	% OF TOTAL PERSONAL INCOME IN U.S.	STATE	TOTAL PERSONAL INCOME (IN BILLIONS)	% OF TOTAL PERSONAL INCOME IN U.S.
Alabama	69.6	1.3	Montana	13.9	0.2
Alaska	12.9	0.2	Nebraska	32.2	0.6
Arizona	68.2	1.3	Nevada	28.3	0.5
Arkansas	38.7	0.7	New Hampshire	26.7	0.5
California	673.4	12.8	New Jersey	216.0	4.1
Colorado	72.8	1.4	New Mexico	25.0	0.5
Connecticut	92.5	1.7	New York	448.1	8.5
Delaware	15.2	0.3	North Carolina	126.0	2.4
Florida	273.9	5.2	North Dakota	11.7	0.2
Georgia	127.6	2.4	Ohio	210.7	4.0
Hawaii	25.6	0.5	Oklahoma	53.7	1.0
Idaho	18.0	0.3	Oregon	56.0	1.0
Illinois	261.2	5.0	Pennsylvania	252.4	4.8
Indiana	106.4	2.0	Rhode Island	21.1	0.4
Iowa	53.5	1.0	South Carolina	59.5	1.1
Kansas	51.3	0.9	South Dakota	12.4	0.2
Kentucky	64.5	1.2	Tennessee	91.4	1.7
Louisiana	69.2	1.3	Texas	331.5	6.3
Maine	23.2	0.4	Utah	29.0	0.5
Maryland	116.3	2.2	Vermont	11.1	0.2
Massachusetts	150.2	2.8	Virginia	136.0	2.6
Michigan	192.0	3.6	Washington	109.5	2.1
Minnesota	94.4	1.8	West Virginia	28.1	0.5
Mississippi	38.0	0.7	Wisconsin	98.1	1.9
Missouri	101.6	1.9	Wyoming	8.3	0.1

SOURCE: *Survey of Current Business* (Washington, D.C.: Bureau of Economic Analysis of the U.S. Department of Commerce, July 1993), p. 38. Total personal income figures are for the fourth quarter of 1992, adjusted at an annual rate.

U.S. ECONOMIC FOCUS (continued)

years, goes like this: Increasingly, the major, up-and-coming industries—such as telecommunications, computers, software development, and so on—require an educated work force. Businesses will locate wherever those educated workers are. If the residents of one state are, on average, better educated than the residents of another state, their state is likely to get the businesses that generate the jobs and incomes.

Still other economists argue that infrastructure in a state affects total personal income. Infrastructure relates to the fundamental facilities serving an area, such as transportation and communication systems, power plants, and roads. Their argument goes like this: People produce and sell more goods when they can get them to market. One important way of getting goods to market is by road. A state with numerous good roads is better able to transport goods to market than a state with few good roads. Along these lines, consider the earthquake that hit Los Angeles on January 17, 1994. Many of the major freeway systems in and around Los Angeles were damaged. At the time, some economists speculated that, since trucks (carrying goods) couldn't travel on these damaged freeways, the California economy would likely suffer. People who couldn't get their goods to the Los Angeles markets as a result of the earthquake may not earn the income they would otherwise have earned.

Today, the representatives of many states are hard at work trying to increase the size of their respective states' economies and raise total personal income. One of the ways states go about this is by trying to get companies in other states, and nations, to relocate in their states. They often do this by promising low taxes (at least for a few years), the building of roadways to and from the new site of the business, and other such ameni-

▲ The January 17, 1994, earthquake in Los Angeles destroyed some of the nearby infrastructure.

ties. We can expect this feature of state competition to continue on through the 1990s and most likely into the next century.

1. According to Exhibit S-12-1, what is the total personal income of your state?
2. Find out the population of your state in 1992. (There are probably reference books in your school library that will have this information.) Then use the population figure, along with total personal income for your state, to compute the per-capita personal income in your state.
3. What percentage of total personal income in the United States do the states of California, New York, and Texas together comprise?

duction. It also subtracts from GDP those things that decrease our overall standard of living—for example, pollution costs and "regrettable necessities" such as police protection and national defense.

The MEW measurement is controversial. It assumes a utopian view of society. For one thing, Nordhaus and Tobin exclude defense expenditures. Their assumption is that no reasonable country buys national defense for its own sake. If there were no war or risk of war, there would be no need for national defense and no one would be the worse off. Other economists disagree with the idea of excluding defense expenditures. These economists argue

that the same reasoning could be applied to many of the other components of GDP. For example, it could be said that no one wants a hospital for its own sake. If there were no accidents, or illnesses, there would be no hospitals and no one would be the worse off. But, of course, we need hospitals.

In summary, the construction of MEW is an attempt to measure more closely economic welfare. Whether MEW does a better job at this than GDP is debatable; nevertheless, the search continues for more finely tuned economic measurements.

LEARNING CHECK

1. Why are imports subtracted from the sum of consumption, investment, government expenditures, and exports in computing GDP?
2. T.S. Typewriter Company produces 1,000 typewriters this year and sells 920 units to its customers. According to the national income accountants, though, all 1,000 typewriters have been purchased. How do the accountants reach this conclusion?
3. Suppose consumption is $2,001 billion, investment is $700 billion, state government expenditures are $300 billion, local government expenditures are $200 billion, federal government expenditures are $555 billion, exports are $323 billion, and imports are $455 billion. What does GDP equal?
4. What is the difference between GDP and GNP?

SECTION 3 REAL GDP

In a simple economy with only one good, we compute GDP by multiplying the price of the good, times the quantity of the good sold. For example, suppose the good is watches and the price is $100. If the quantity of watches produced is 54 in a given year, then the GDP is $5,400 ($100 × 54 = $5,400). Now, suppose the next year the quantity of watches stays steady at 54 but the price rises to $200 ($200 × 54 = $10,800). GDP is now $10,800—double what it was last year. Notice that although GDP is higher in the second year than in the first year, *the quantity of watches produced in both years is the same, 54.* Only the price of

watches is different. We conclude that it is possible for GDP to rise from one year to another even if there is no increase in the quantity of goods produced.

Realizing this, economists often adjust GDP for price changes, so that they can separate price changes from output changes. This brings us to the topic of this section, real GDP.

As you read, keep these key questions in mind:

- If GDP is higher in one year than another, do we automatically know why it is higher?
- What is real GDP?

The Two Variables of GDP: P and Q

In the example of computing GDP in a simple, one-good economy, we multiplied two variables to find GDP: price (P) and quantity (Q). Now, if there are two variables that multiplied together give us GDP, this means that if either of the two variables rises, and the other remains constant, GDP will rise.

To illustrate, look at the following chart.

	Price	Quantity	GDP
(1)	$10	2	$20
(2)	$15	2	$30
(3)	$10	3	$30

We start with a price of $10 and a quantity of two. We compute GDP to be $20. Next, we raise price to $15 but hold quantity constant at two. GDP rises to $30. Finally, we keep price constant at $10 and increase the quantity to three. GDP again is $30. Clearly, an increase in either price or quantity will raise GDP.

Now, suppose someone told you simply that GDP was $20 one year and $30 the next year. You would have no way of knowing whether GDP increased because price increased, because quantity of output increased, or because both price and quantity increased.

But suppose there was a way to hold price constant. If price was held constant and GDP increased, would you know what caused the rise in GDP? Of course you would. If price is held constant, then any rise in GDP must be due to a rise in quantity. (What else could it be?)

How can we keep price constant? Economists do it by computing the GDP for each year—1990, 1991, 1992, and so on—*using the prices that existed in one particular year, say, 1987.* When economists do this, they are said to be computing **real GDP**.

To illustrate, again let's assume that we have a simple, one-good economy that produces only watches. Look at Exhibit 12-5. Column 1 of the exhibit lists several years, column 2 gives the price of watches in these years, and column 3 gives the quantity of watches produced in these years. Column 4 shows the GDP for each year. The GDP equals the *current-year price,* times the *current-year quantity* of watches.

Real GDP is shown in column 5. To calculate it, we multiply the *price of watches in 1987,* times the *current-year quantity.* For example, to get the real GDP in 1990, we take the quantity of watches produced in 1990 and multiply it, times the price of watches in 1987.

A quick look at the real GDP figures tells us that since the real GDP in 1991 ($160,000) is higher than that in 1990 ($152,000), the quantity of watches produced in 1991 must have been greater than the quantity of watches produced in 1990. Looking at the quantities in column 3 confirms this. Also, since the real GDP figure for 1992 ($148,400) is lower than that for 1991 ($160,000), the quantity of watches produced in 1992 must have been less than the quantity of watches produced in 1991. Again, looking at the quantities in column 3 confirms this.

The Base Year

In computing real GDP for 1990, 1991, and 1992, we multiplied the quantity of watches produced in each year, times the price of watches in 1987. Economists have a name for the year used to price the output of different years. It is called the **base year**. Thus, another name for real GDP is "GDP in base-year prices"—or if 1987 is the base year, for example, "GDP in 1987 prices."

The Business Cycle

Suppose that real GDP is initially $4,000 billion. During the next eight months, real GDP steadily increases, eventually reaching a peak of $4,500 billion. Then, real GDP begins to turn down over the next few months, generally decreasing until it hits a low of $3,900 billion. Then,

(1) Year	(2) Price of watches	(3) Quantity of watches produced	(4) GDP	(5) Real GDP
1987	$80	—		
.			Price in current year × Quantity in current year	Price in 1987 × Quantity in current year
.				
.				
1990	$120	1,900	$120 × 1,900 = $228,000	$80 × 1,900 = $152,000
1991	$150	2,000	$150 × 2,000 = $300,000	$80 × 2,000 = $160,000
1992	$190	1,855	$190 × 1,855 = $352,450	$80 × 1,855 = $148,400

▲ **EXHIBIT 12-5. Computing GDP and Real GDP in a Simple, One-Good Economy.** In column 4, we compute GDP for a simple, one-good economy. We multiply the price in the current year, times the quantity produced in the current year. In column 5, we compute real GDP by multiplying the price in 1987, times the quantity produced in the current year. Economists prefer working with real GDP to working with GDP because they know that if real GDP in one year is higher than real GDP in another year, output is greater in the year with the higher real GDP.

afterward, it begins to turn up over the next few months, growing to $4,400 billion.

Notice what we have described here. Simply put, we have described a situation where the real GDP first expands (from $4,000 billion), reaches a peak of $4,500 billion, then turns down, reaching a low of $3,900 billion, and then expands again. Stated differently, we have described recurrent swings (up and down) in real GDP. Economists have a name for the recurrent swings (up and down) in real GDP. They call it the **business cycle**.

The business cycle has been a regular part of the U.S. economic landscape for many years. To illustrate, in 1978, real GDP in the United States was $3,703.5 billion. The next year, in 1979, it had risen to $3,796.8 billion. One year later, in 1980, real GDP had fallen to $3,776.3 billion. The next year, in 1981, it had risen to $3,843.1 billion. In

1982, it had gone down again, to $3,760.3 billion. In 1983, one year later, it went up again, to $3,906.6 billion. Up, down, up, down. It is as if real GDP was on a roller coaster: first climbing up

M INI G LOSSARY

Real GDP GDP that has been adjusted for price changes; GDP measured in base-year, or constant, prices.

Base Year In general, a benchmark year; a year chosen as a point of reference for comparison. When real GDP is computed, the output of different years is priced at base-year levels.

Business Cycle Recurrent swings (up and down) in real GDP.

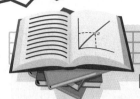

ANALYZING PRIMARY SOURCES

Economists and Others on the Business Cycle

In this chapter we have discussed the business cycle. The business cycle refers to recurrent swings (up and down) in real GDP. In this feature we present many of the most commonly asked questions about business cycles, and give you answers to these questions from a number of different people, representing a variety of viewpoints.

The word "cycle" in business cycle implies that there is a regularity to the business cycle. In other words, it sounds as if real GDP always rises for, say, six months, and then it falls for five months, and so on. Is there this kind of regularity to the business cycle?

Most economists say no. Here is what economist Christina Romer says:

"In many ways the term *business cycle* is misleading. 'Cycle' seems to imply that there is some regularity in the timing and duration of upswings and downswings in economic activity. Most economists, however, believe otherwise. Booms and recessions [a boom refers to an expansion in real GDP; a recession refers to a contraction in real GDP] occur at irregular intervals and last for varying lengths of time. For example, economic activity hit low points in 1975, 1980, and 1982. The 1982 trough [a trough is the low point of real GDP; it is similar to the low point on the roller coaster ride] was then followed by eight years of uninterrupted expansion. For describing the swings in economic activity, therefore, most modern economists prefer the term *economic fluctuations* [to *business cycle*]. **"**[a]

a. "Business Cycles," by Christina Romer, *The Fortune Encyclopedia of Economics*, edited by David Henderson (New York: Warner Books, 1993), p. 173.

How many business cycles have there been in the United States in recent years?

According to economist John Miller, there have been eight since World War II. He writes:

"A [business] cycle runs its course from the trough of a recession to the peak of an expansion and back down into a trough. [What this means is that one business cycle consists of the time it takes for real GDP to go from one low point to another. Think of real GDP on the roller coaster again. It is at the bottom of the ride, then it rises to the top, and goes to the bottom again. That ride—starting at the bottom, rising to the top, and back to the bottom again— is one business cycle.] The NBER (National Bureau of Economic Research) has identified eight such business cycles in the United States since World War II. **"**[b]

Do all economists agree as to what causes the business cycle?

No, they do not. Economist Campbell McConnell writes:

"Historically, economists have suggested a variety of theories to explain fluctuations in business activity. Some theories center upon innovation, contending that major innovations such as the railroad, the automobile, or synthetic fibers have a great impact upon investment and consumption spending and therefore upon output, employment, and the price level. But these major innovations occur irregularly and thus contribute to the variability of economic activity. Other economists have explained the business cycle in terms of political and random effects. . . . Wars, for example, can

b. "When is a Recession Over," by John Miller, *Dollars & Sense*, March 1993, p. 18.

ANALYZING PRIMARY SOURCES (continued)

be economically disruptive. A virtually insatiable demand for war goods during hostilities can generate a period of overfull employment and sharp inflation, frequently followed by an economic slump when peace returns and military spending plummets. Still other economists view the [business] cycle as a purely monetary phenomenon. When government creates too much money, an inflationary boom is generated; a relative paucity of money will precipitate a declining output and unemployment. **"** [c]

In the answer to the preceding question, mention is made of "political and random effects" as causing the business cycle. How might politics be related to the business cycle?

Some economists and political scientists have suggested that politicians will try to enact economic policies that will increase real GDP shortly before they run for reelection, so that they will have a better chance of being reelected to office. Here is what one political scientist has to say:

"The topic of the political business cycle (PBC) has attracted continuous attention in the field of political economy. Analysts have examined whether and how the incumbent president manipulates the macroeconomy in order to maximize his (or her) party's probability of reelection. **"** [d]

In later chapters, you will learn about the two major policies—monetary and fiscal policy—that

---

some economists and political scientists believe are used by politicians to increase their chances of reelection.

In the chapter it is stated that economists try to eliminate or smooth out the business cycle. Have they been successful here?

According to Alfred Malabre, who is a journalist for the Wall Street Journal, *they have not been. Here is some of what he has to say on the business cycle:*

"Textbooks devote countless pages to examining the business cycle: this tendency of the economy to expand, go into recession, and then expand once again—a sort of two-steps-forward and then one-step-backward progression. But my favorite analysis of why the business cycle endures comes from a noneconomist, a *Wall Street Journal* reader named Russell Fowler, who recently retired from a county-government job in upstate New York. Fowler says: 'Maybe the reason the business cycle endures is the economy is solidly based on human nature. When things are going good, some human reactions occur: overconfidence, complacency, poor worksmanship, greed, overexpansion, mistakes; all bad and leading to a downturn [in economic activity]. Then, when things are going bad, there's a tendency to shape up and turn things around. Maybe that's all there is to it.'

Amen. That is as sound an explanation of the why of the cycle as I have encountered. The message is clear: so long as human nature is with us, so will be the business cycle. . . .

Doubtless, most economists will continue to disregard the business cycle as they go about mapping new pathways to utopia. A wonderful family doctor, who actually made house calls every day, used to give some sound advice to his patients. 'Enjoy life,' he would say. 'Have some fun and do everything—but do it in

c. McConnell, Campbell, and Stanley Brue, *Economics, 11th edition,* (New York: McGraw-Hill Publishing Company, 1990) p. 156–57.

d. "Political Business Cycles In The Public Mind," by Motoshi Suzuki, *Political Science Review,* December 1992, p. 989.

ANALYZING PRIMARY SOURCES (continued)

moderation.' That may be good advice, in a different context, for economists.

Have some fun. Continue to issue your forecasts, seeking to make them more accurate. Keep dreaming up ways to make the economy sounder and increase prosperity. But be moderate in what you claim and in what you expect, and remember that the business cycle, like human nature, is here to stay. 🗲 [e]

1. According to Christina Romer, are most business cycles equal in length? Explain your answer.

e. Reprinted by permission of Harvard Business School Press from *Lost Prophets: An Insider's History of Modern Economists* by Alfred Malabre. Boston: 1994, pp. 232–36. Copyright © 1994 by the President and Fellows of Harvard College.

2. How many business cycles have there been in the United States since World War II?
3. According to John Miller, what constitutes the course of a business cycle?
4. According to Campbell McConnell, how can a war generate a business cycle?
5. According to Campbell McConnell, some "economists view the cycle as a purely monetary phenomenon." What do you think it means to view the business cycle as a *purely monetary phenomenon*?
6. Alfred Malabre cites Russell Fowler's explanation for the business cycle. What is Fowler's explanation?

the tracks, then coming down, climbing up again, then falling again.

One of the objectives of the economist is to try to eliminate the business cycle, or at least smooth it out. Ideally, economists would like real GDP to grow year after year; in other words, get on a roller coaster that continues to go up and never turns down. If this can't be done, the next-best choice is to get real GDP on a roller coaster that

doesn't have steep drops. In other words, it's all right for real GDP to go up, but when it turns down, don't let it be a sharp drop down. This is what economists mean when they say they want to smooth out the business cycle.

In later chapters, we will discuss some of the tools economists use to smooth out the business cycle. Mainly, they are called monetary and fiscal policy, which you will learn about in Chapter 14.

LEARNING CHECK

1. GDP is $4.2 billion in one year and $5.5 billion in the next year. Is output necessarily higher in the second year than the first? Explain your answer.
2. Why do economists compute real GDP?
3. When real GDP increases, which variable, P or Q, is increasing?
4. What is a business cycle?

SECTION 4 MEASURING PRICE CHANGES

We have seen that economists measure changes in output from one year to the next by comparing the real GDP for these years. If the real GDP for 1994 is $4,500 billion and the real GDP for 1993 is $4,000 billion, for example, economists know that in 1994 the economy produced $500 billion worth of goods and services over and above what it produced in 1993.

Changes in output are not the only thing economists are interested in. They are also interested in changes in prices. Next, we discuss how economists calculate changes in prices.

As you read, keep these key questions in mind:

■ What is the consumer price index?
■ How is the consumer price index calculated?

Calculating the Change in a Single Price

Suppose that in 1991 a Honda Accord was priced at $15,000 and in 1992 a Honda Accord was $16,500. By what percentage did the price of a Honda Accord increase? Here is the formula we use to find out.

$$\text{Percentage change in price} = \frac{\text{Price in later year} - \text{Price in earlier year}}{\text{Price in earlier year}} \times 100$$

If we fill in the numbers, we have:

$$\text{Percentage change in price} = \frac{\$16,500 - \$15,000}{\$15,000} \times 100$$

$$\text{Percentage change in price} = \frac{\$1,500}{\$15,000} \times 100$$

$$\text{Percentage change in price} = 10\%$$

In this example, we found the percentage increase in a single price from one year to the next.

Economists are much more interested, though, in what has happened to prices in general than in what has happened to a *single* price. Before they can calculate the change in prices from one year to the next, they need to compute a **price index**. The most widely cited price index is the **consumer price index (CPI)**. You might have heard a newscaster say, "Today it was reported in Washington that the consumer price index has risen 4 percent on an annual basis." We now consider how the CPI is computed and what it means.

The Consumer Price Index

The CPI is calculated by the U.S. Bureau of Labor Statistics. The bureau uses a sampling of thousands of households and determines what these consumers have paid for a representative group of goods called the market basket. This is compared with what a typical "consumer unit" paid for the same market basket in 1982–1984. (A consumer unit is a household of related or unrelated individuals who pool their money. In the last survey, the average consumer unit was made up of 2.6 people.)

Calculating the CPI involves this process:

Step 1. Calculating the total dollar expenditure on the market basket in the base year and in the current year.

Step 2. Dividing the total current-year expenditure by the total base-year expenditure and multiplying by 100.

MINI GLOSSARY

Price Index A measure of the price level, or the average level of prices.
Consumer Price Index (CPI) The most widely cited price index.

CONSUMER ECONOMIC DECISIONS

Shopping for a College

Suppose you are about to buy a car or a computer. You are not confined to buying your car from one car dealership, nor are you confined to buying your computer from one store. You can shop around. The same thing holds for a college education. Most students have a number of colleges and universities from which to choose.

How do you shop for a college education? How do you shop for the right college? This section offers some suggestions.

In what Type of College Are You Interested?

Colleges and universities come in all shapes and sizes. You have to decide what type of college interests you. For example, would you prefer to go to a college with a small student body or one with a large student body? If you don't have a preference as to size, then probably you should take some time to consider this matter. Ask your teachers and guidance counselors what colleges they attended. Ask them their ideas on the benefits and drawbacks of small colleges versus those of large colleges.

There are, of course, other things to consider here besides size. Here are a few of the many questions you may want to ask yourself:

- Do I want to attend a college close to home?
- Do I want a college that provides a good social atmosphere, a good social life?
- Do I want a college with a national reputation? a regional reputation? a local reputation? Does reputation matter to me?

- Does the average class size at the college matter to me? Do I want small classes? moderate-sized classes? big classes?
- Does the academic reputation of the professors at the college matter to me? Do I want to attend a college that has a well-known faculty?
- Do I want a college that has many dormitories? many apartments nearby?
- Does the city or town in which the college is located matter to me? Do I want to attend college in a large city or a small town? Does the safety of the town matter to me?

The answers to these questions may not be readily forthcoming. Perhaps, for example, you don't know if you would prefer to attend a college located in a small town or a large city. But, then, perhaps the questions will start you thinking, and you will realize your preference in time.

Set Realistic Goals (and Reach a Little, Too)

Sadly, not all the colleges in which we are interested are interested in us. For example, let's say you're interested in going to College X, a highly selective school, but you do not have good enough grades to be admitted to College X. It is one thing to set your goals high, but it is another to be unrealistic. If the college you want to attend says that it will *only* accept applicants with a Scholastic Assessment Test (SAT) score of 1200 or over and a grade point average (GPA) of 3.5 or over, and you

Making CONSUMER ECONOMIC DECISIONS (continued)

have neither, then it is unlikely that you will be admitted if you apply. You need to focus most of your time and effort on learning about colleges to which you have a good chance of being admitted. This is not to say you shouldn't apply to a few colleges that may be "just beyond your reach." But don't spend the bulk of your time and effort doing this.

How Do I Learn about Various Colleges?

By the time you are a sophomore, junior, or senior in high school, you know the names of several colleges and universities. But there are hundreds of colleges and universities you may not know about. One of those you have not heard of may be the perfect one for you. Many books provide the information you may need. They tell you the locations of colleges, their admission standards, their student populations, the number of dormitories they have, and so on. Most of these books can be purchased at bookstores, and many of them may be in your school library. Your school guidance counselor may also have copies.

What about Money?

Many students need financial assistance to attend college. You can usually obtain information on federal government financial assistance from your school guidance counselor, the local library, the financial aid officer of the college or university you wish to attend, or the federal government's Student Financial Aid Information Center at 1-800-433-3243.

Talk to Your Teachers and Guidance Counselors

You have some of the best sources of college information at your high school. Your teachers and guidance counselors are there to answer many of the questions you might have about college.

College Fairs

Many high schools hold college fairs. At these events, representatives from numerous colleges and universities come to answer questions, pass out literature, and so on. For the high-school student interested in attending college, the college fair is a place to get a great deal of information about numerous colleges in a short time.

Order College Catalogs

Every college and university publishes a college catalog that describes its academic programs, its faculty, its admission requirements, and so on. You can order catalogs directly through the college itself. Alternatively, many school libraries and city libraries have copies of the catalogs, through which you can browse. It is extremely important to read through the catalogs of the colleges or universities you are considering.

I Want to Study ____. Which College Should I Attend?

Many students don't know what college they want to attend, but they are fairly certain of what they want to study. Say a person wants to study music. It is in his or her best interest to

CONSUMER ECONOMIC DECISIONS (continued)

find out what colleges have good music departments. The college in your town—the one you've heard about all your life—may be a great college to attend if you are majoring in business, political science, or psychology. But it may not be very good at all if you want to major in music, economics, or English. To find out if the college you wish to attend actually offers a major in the subject of your choice, consult the *Index of Majors*. There may be a copy in your school or town library. To find the ratings of various colleges, academic departments, and much more, see *Educational Rankings*. Again, a copy may be found in your school or town library. Finally, a particularly good source of college information is the Educational Reference Division of the New York Public Library. The telephone number is 212-340-0849.

Learn to Use the Telephone to Your Advantage

You would be surprised at how many people are willing to give you the information you seek, if you simply ask them for it. This is where the telephone comes in handy. Suppose you have narrowed your choice of colleges down to three: X, Y, and Z. You have also decided to major in English at college. Now you need specific information on the English program at each of the three colleges. Why not call the chairperson of the English department and ask a few questions? (You are best advised to call the secretary of the English department first and set up an appointment time to talk with the chairperson. You can find the telephone number for the academic departments at colleges through Directory Assis-

tance.) If you have trouble asking questions on the spur of the moment, then take some time to write down a few questions before you call. Here are a few sample questions for a person who plans to major in English:

- What courses would I take as an English major?
- How many credits would I need to graduate?
- What is the size of most of the English classes?
- Are there good library facilities?
- Is there an English Club? What do the students in the English Club do?
- What types of job offers have your recent English-major graduates received?

Visit the Colleges If You Can

Once you have narrowed down your choice of colleges, it is a good idea to visit the colleges you are considering. At each college, arrange a meeting with an admissions counselor, if possible. Walk around and look at the classrooms, the student union, the library, and the dormitories and other facilities in which you are interested.

---

1. Whom can you call if you are interested in financial assistance for college?
2. You want to know if College X offers a major in biology. What book can you consult?
3. What is a college fair?
4. Identify some people at your school with whom you can talk about college.

Let's go through an example with the aid of Exhibit 12-6. To simplify things, we'll say that the market basket is made up of only two goods instead of the hundreds of items that it actually contains. Our market basket will contain 10 CDs and 5 T-shirts.

We find the total dollar expenditure on the market basket in the *base year* by multiplying the quantities of goods in the market basket (column 1), times the prices of the goods in the base year (column 2). A look at column 3 shows us that $130 was spent on CDs and $20 was spent on T-shirts for a total dollar expenditure of $150.

We find the total dollar expenditure on the market basket in the *current year* by multiplying the quantities of goods in the market basket (column 1), times the prices of the goods in the current year (column 4). A look at column 5 shows us that $150 was spent on CDs and $30 was spent on T-shirts, for a total dollar expenditure of $180.

Next, we divide the total current-year expenditure, $180, by the total base-year expenditure, $150, and then multiply by 100:

$$\frac{\$180}{\$150} \times 100 = 120$$

The CPI for the current year is 120.

QUESTION: *The CPI is just a number. What does this number tell us?*

ANSWER: *By itself, the number tells us very little. It is when we compare the CPI for one year against the CPI for another year that we learn something. For example, in the United States in 1990, the CPI was 130.7. One year later, in 1991, the CPI was 136.2. We can use the two CPI numbers to figure out the percentage by which prices increased between 1990 and 1991. We do this in the same way we determine the percentage increase for a single price. Here is the formula we use.*

Step 1: Calculate the total dollar expenditure on the market basket in base year and in current year. These amounts are calculated in column 3 ($150) and column 5 ($180) respectively.	(1) Goods in the market basket	(2) Price in base year	(3) Base-year expenditure (1) × (2)	(4) Price in current year	(5) Current-year expenditure (1) × (4)
	10 CDs	$13	10 × $13 = $130	$15	10 × $15 = $150
	5 T-shirts	$4	5 × $4 = $20	$6	5 × $6 = $30
			→ $150		→ $180
			Total dollar expenditure on the market basket in base year		Total dollar expenditure on the market basket in current year

Step 2: Divide the total dollar expenditure on the market basket in current year by the total dollar expenditure on the market basket in base year, and then multiply by 100.

$$CPI_{current\ year} = \frac{\text{Total dollar expenditure on the market basket in current year}}{\text{Total dollar expenditure on the market basket in base year}} \times 100$$

$$= \frac{\$180}{\$150} \times 100$$

$$= 120$$

▲ **EXHIBIT 12-6. Calculating the CPI.**

$$\begin{matrix} \textit{Percentage} \\ \textit{change in} \\ \textit{CPI} \end{matrix} = \frac{\begin{matrix}\textit{CPI in}\\\textit{later year}\end{matrix} - \begin{matrix}\textit{CPI in}\\\textit{earlier year}\end{matrix}}{\textit{CPI in earlier year}} \times 100$$

If we fill in the numbers, we have:

$$\begin{matrix}\textit{Percentage}\\\textit{change in CPI}\end{matrix} = \frac{136.2 - 130.7}{130.7} \times 100$$

$$\begin{matrix}\textit{Percentage}\\\textit{change in CPI}\end{matrix} = \frac{5.5}{130.7} \times 100$$

Percentage change in CPI = 4.2%

The Determination of the Quantity of Goods and Services and the Price Level

Chapter 3 explained that there are two sides to every market—a demand side and a supply side. We represent the demand in a market with a downward-sloping demand curve and the supply in a market with an upward-sloping supply curve. As you may recall, equilibrium price and quantity in a market are determined by the forces of supply and demand.

What holds for a market holds for an economy, too. There is a demand side and a supply side to any economy. The demand side is represented by the **aggregate demand curve**, which shows the quantity of goods and services buyers are willing and able to buy at different price levels. (Sometimes the quantity of goods and services is simply referred to as output.) The supply side is represented by the **aggregate supply curve**, which shows the quantity of goods and services, or output, producers are willing and able to supply at different price levels. The equilibrium price level and equilibrium quantity of goods and services are determined by the forces of aggregate demand and aggregate supply.

Aggregate demand and supply are illustrated in Exhibit 12-7. There you will see an aggregate demand curve (AD) that is downward sloping. This implies that people are willing and able to buy a greater quantity of goods and services (more output) at lower price levels than at higher price levels. For example, when the price level is high, at P_1, we notice that the quantity of goods and services that is demanded is Q_1. But when the price level is lower, at P_2, the quantity of goods and services demanded by people increases to Q_2.

The aggregate supply curve (AS) is upward sloping, indicating that producers are willing and able to produce and offer to sell a greater quantity of goods and services (more output) at higher price levels than at lower price levels. When the price level is low, at P_2, producers will produce and offer to sell Q_1; but when the price level rises to P_1, producers are willing to produce and offer to sell a greater quantity of goods and services, Q_2.

The forces of aggregate demand and supply determine the equilibrium price level and equilibrium quantity of goods and services (equilibrium output) in an economy. The equilibrium price level, which is P_E in Exhibit 12-7, and the equilibrium quantity for goods and services, or output, which is Q_E in the exhibit, come to exist over time. For example, at P_1 the quantity demanded of goods and services (Q_1) is less than the quantity supplied of goods and services (Q_2), and there is a surplus of goods and services. As a result, the price level drops. As a result of a lower price level, people buy more goods and services and producers produce less. The surplus begins to disappear because of these actions on the part of buyers and sellers. (Buyers are helping to eliminate the surplus by buying more, and sellers are helping to eliminate the surplus by producing less.)

MINI GLOSSARY

Aggregate Demand Curve Shows the quantity of goods and services buyers are willing and able to buy at different price levels.

Aggregate Supply Curve Shows the quantity of goods and services producers are willing and able to supply at different price levels.

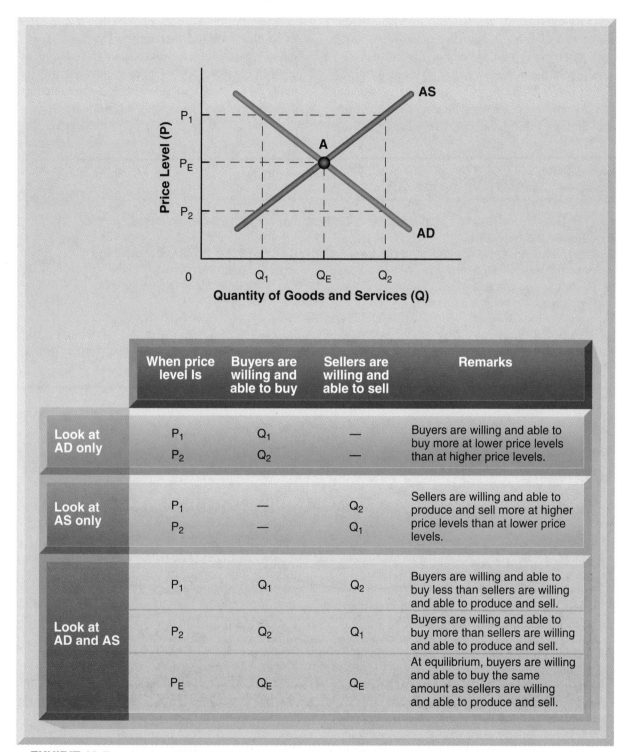

When price level Is	Buyers are willing and able to buy	Sellers are willing and able to sell	Remarks
Look at AD only P_1 P_2	Q_1 Q_2	— —	Buyers are willing and able to buy more at lower price levels than at higher price levels.
Look at AS only P_1 P_2	— —	Q_2 Q_1	Sellers are willing and able to produce and sell more at higher price levels than at lower price levels.
Look at AD and AS P_1	Q_1	Q_2	Buyers are willing and able to buy less than sellers are willing and able to produce and sell.
P_2	Q_2	Q_1	Buyers are willing and able to buy more than sellers are willing and able to produce and sell.
P_E	Q_E	Q_E	At equilibrium, buyers are willing and able to buy the same amount as sellers are willing and able to produce and sell.

▲ **EXHIBIT 12-7. Aggregate Demand and Aggregate Supply.** Equilibrium in an economy comes about through the economic forces of aggregate demand and aggregate supply. The economy is in equilibrium at point A in the exhibit.

At P_2, the quantity demanded of goods and services (Q_2) is greater than the quantity supplied (Q_1), and there is a shortage of goods and services. As a result, the price level rises. As a result of the higher price level, people buy fewer goods and services and producers produce more. The shortage begins to disappear because of these actions on the part of buyers and sellers. (Buyers are helping to eliminate the shortage by buying less, and sellers are helping to eliminate the shortage by producing more.) Only at P_E is the quantity of goods and services supplied equal to the quantity of goods and services demanded. Both are Q_E.

LEARNING CHECK

1. The CPI is 103 in year 1 and 177 in year 2. By what percentage have prices increased between the two years?
2. The market basket is composed of 6 books, 5 shirts, 4 blouses, and 2 pairs of shoes. The price of books is $10 each, the price of shirts is $20 each, the price of blouses is $23 each, and the price of a pair of shoes is $40 each. What is the total dollar expenditure on the market basket?
3. Suppose the CPI was 143 in year 1 and 132 in year 2. Did prices rise or fall between year 1 and year 2?
4. What does an aggregate demand curve show? What does an aggregate supply curve show?

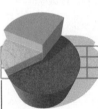

DEVELOPING ECONOMIC SKILLS

Using Percentages to Make Comparisons

During the period 1981–1991, medical care prices rose by 115 percent while food prices increased by 46 percent. Comparing the price change in one thing with the price change in another in this way can be useful. To illustrate, suppose you are a farmer. As a farmer, you produce certain food goods to sell. You also buy certain goods and services in your role as consumer. What might be of interest to you is the percentage change in the price of what you sell (food products) compared with the percentage change in the price of what you buy (all kinds of consumer goods and services).

To compute the change in the prices of what the farmer buys, we can look at the CPI in different years. For example, in 1989, the CPI was 124, and in 1990, it had risen to 130.7. We use the formula that follows (the same one given earlier in the chapter) to compute the percentage change in prices.

$$\text{Percentage change in CPI} = \frac{\text{CPI in later year} - \text{CPI in earlier year}}{\text{CPI in earlier year}} \times 100$$

$$= \frac{130.7 - 124}{124} \times 100$$

$$= \frac{6.7}{124} \times 100$$

$$= 5.40\%$$

DEVELOPING ECONOMIC SKILLS (continued)

In 1989, the price index for food goods that farmers sell was 115.4, and in 1990, it had risen to 118.6. We use the formula that follows to compute the percentage change in prices.

$$
\begin{array}{l}
\text{Percentage} \\
\text{change in} \\
\text{prices of food} \\
\text{goods that} \\
\text{farmers sell}
\end{array}
=
\dfrac{\begin{array}{l}\text{Price} \\ \text{index in} \\ \text{later year}\end{array} - \begin{array}{l}\text{Price} \\ \text{index in} \\ \text{earlier year}\end{array}}{\text{Price index in earlier year}} \times 100
$$

$$
= \frac{118.6 - 115.4}{115.4} \times 100
$$

$$
= \frac{3.2}{115.4} \times 100
$$

$$
= 2.77\%
$$

Having made our computations, we see that the prices of the goods farmers buy increased by more (5.40 percent) than the prices of the goods farmers sell (2.77 percent) during 1989–1990. Most likely, farmers would have preferred the situation reversed.

Consider another example that may be important to you. You take a number of different courses at school and receive grades in each. Let's say two of your courses are economics and English. Suppose you earned a grade of 85 on the first test in economics and a grade of 91 on the first test in English. Then you earn a 95 on your second test in economics and a 97 on your second test in English. We know that you did better in both subjects on the second test than on the first. Still, we want to know in which subject you are improving more. To find out, we need to find the percentage change in your grade between the two tests in each subject. To find the percentage change, we use the following formula:

$$
\begin{array}{l}
\text{Percentage} \\
\text{change in grade}
\end{array}
=
\dfrac{\begin{array}{l}\text{Grade on} \\ \text{later test}\end{array} - \begin{array}{l}\text{Grade on} \\ \text{earlier test}\end{array}}{\text{Grade on earlier test}} \times 100
$$

English:

$$
\begin{array}{l}
\text{Percentage} \\
\text{change in grade}
\end{array}
= \frac{97 - 91}{91} \times 100
$$

$$
= \frac{6}{91} \times 100
$$

$$
= 6.59\%
$$

Economics:

$$
\begin{array}{l}
\text{Percentage} \\
\text{change in grade}
\end{array}
= \frac{95 - 85}{85} \times 100
$$

$$
= \frac{10}{85} \times 100
$$

$$
= 11.76\%
$$

Your second test grade in economics was 11.76% percent higher than your first test grade, while in English, your second test grade was 6.59 percent higher than your first test grade. You improved more in economics than in English.

1. Valerie's objective is to cut back on buying clothes and entertainment in order to save money. Last month, she spent $136 on clothes and $98 on entertainment. This month, she has spent $129 on clothes and $79 on entertainment. Compute the percentage change in spending for each good, and then compare the changes. Is Valerie cutting back more in spending on clothes or in spending on entertainment?

2. Suppose the price index for the goods Juan sells is 132 in year 1 and 145 in year 2. The price index for the goods he buys is 124 in the first year and 135 in the second year. How much have prices increased between the two years for the goods he sells? for the goods he buys?

CHAPTER 12 REVIEW

CHAPTER SUMMARY

1. Gross domestic product (GDP) is the total market value of all final goods and services produced annually in an economy.

2. Economists do not count intermediate goods and services when computing GDP. If they did so, they would be double-counting.

3. GDP omits (1) illegal goods and services, (2) legal goods and services for which there is no record of a transaction, (3) some nonmarket goods and services, (4) sales of used goods, (5) stock transactions and other financial transactions, and (6) government transfer payments.

4. Economists divide the economy into four sectors: the household sector, the business sector, the government sector, and the foreign sector. Expenditures made by the household sector are called consumption (C); expenditures made by the business sector are called investment (I); and expenditures made by the government sector are called government expenditures (G). Expenditures made in the foreign sector are called either exports (X) or imports (M). Exports are expenditures made by foreigners for American-made goods. Imports are expenditures made by Americans for foreign-made goods.

5. GDP = C + I + G + X − M.

6. GDP is measured in current prices. Real GDP, however, is measured in base-year prices, or constant prices.

7. Economists prefer working with real GDP to working with GDP. In short, there is less uncertainty in working with real GDP figures than in working with GDP figures.

8. The business cycle refers to recurrent swings (up and down) in real GDP. Business cycles have been a regular part of U.S. economic history.

9. The most widely cited price index is the consumer price index (CPI). We compute it by: (1) finding the total dollar expenditure on the market basket in the base year and in the current year and (2) dividing the total current-year expenditure by the total base-year expenditure and multiplying by 100.

BUILD YOUR ECONOMIC VOCABULARY

Match the word with the correct definition, example, or statement.

1. GDP
2. intermediate good
3. final good
4. double-counting
5. homemaker's cooking, cleaning, and taking care of family finances
6. consumption
7. CPI

a. a hamburger purchased by a patron at a restaurant
b. happens when intermediate goods are counted in GDP
c. total market value of final goods and services produced annually in an economy
d. an example of a nonmarket service omitted from GDP
e. expenditures made by the household sector
f. a widely cited price index
g. the hamburger meat purchased by a restaurant from a wholesale meat company

REVIEW QUESTIONS

1. Consumption is $2,022 billion, investment is $567 billion, government expenditures are $999 billion, exports are $232 billion, and imports are $354 billion. What does GDP equal?

2. Define and give examples of the following: (a) consumption, (b) investment, (c) government expenditures.

3. What is the difference between a final good and an intermediate good?

4. Why does GDP omit illegal transactions?

5. Why does GDP omit stock transactions?

6. Why does GDP omit government transfer payments?

7. Why does an economist prefer to work with real GDP figures than with GDP figures?

8. If an economist uses 1982 prices in computing GDP for all years, then what is 1982 called?

9. Explain the two-step process for calculating the CPI.

10. Turn to Exhibit 12-6. Change the prices in column 2 to $14 for CDs and $6 for T-shirts, and change the prices in column 4 to $17 for CDs and $8 for T-shirts. Now calculate the CPI.

11. Explain how equilibrium is achieved in the economy.

SHARPEN YOUR CRITICAL THINKING SKILLS

1. The manuscript for this book was typed by the author. Had he hired someone to do the typing, GDP would have been higher than it was. In general, what other things would increase GDP if they were done differently? What things would decrease GDP if they were done differently?

2. "If a firm produces a good that it does not sell, GDP is lower than it would have been if the firm had sold the good." What is wrong with this statement?

ACTIVITIES AND PROJECTS

1. Go to a supermarket once a week for two weeks. In the first week, write down the prices of any 10 food items. The next week, return to the store and write down the prices of the same 10 food items. Then, compute the percentage change in price (if any) for each of the 10 items.

ECONOMIC DICTIONARY

Aggregate Demand Curve (Pg. 324)

Aggregate Supply Curve (Pg. 324)

Base Year (Pg. 314)

Business Cycle (Pg. 315)

Consumer Price Index (CPI) (Pg. 319)

Double-Counting (Pg. 303)

Gross Domestic Product (GDP) (Pg. 302)

Price Index (Pg. 319)

Real GDP (Pg. 314)

CHAPTER 13

Inflation and Unemployment

INTRODUCTION

Ray Fair is an economist who teaches at Yale University. He has developed an economic theory that predicts which candidate will win a presidential election. The theory predicts that the higher the inflation and unemployment rates in the economy during the election months, the higher the probability that the incumbent president will lose the election. To a large degree, Fair's theory predicts correctly. In other words, the last thing a president thinking of running for reelection wants is high inflation, high unemployment, or both. Not only do inflation and unemployment scare sitting presidents, they scare the average person, too. In this chapter, you will learn about both inflation and unemployment.

AFTER YOU STUDY THIS CHAPTER, YOU WILL BE ABLE TO:

1. Explain what inflation is.
2. Identify the general conditions necessary for inflation to occur.
3. Discuss a few specific causes of demand-side and supply-side inflation.
4. Measure the inflation rate.
5. Explain the differences between frictional, structural, natural, and cyclical unemployment.
6. Explain why full employment does not correspond to zero unemployment.
7. Identify the relationship between a fall in aggregate demand and the unemployment rate.

KEY TERMS

Cyclical
  Unemployment
Demand-Side
  Inflation
Frictional
  Unemployment
Full Employment
Hedge
Natural
  Unemployment

Simple Quantity
  Theory of
  Money
Structural
  Unemployment
Supply-Side
  Inflation
Velocity

SECTION 1 INFLATION

This section defines inflation, shows how it is measured, and discusses its causes and its effects.

As you read, keep these key questions in mind:

- What is inflation?
- How is inflation measured?
- What causes inflation?
- What are the effects of inflation?

What Is Inflation?

Because there are many goods in an economy, there are many prices in an economy. There is the price of apples, the price of bread, the price of pencils, and so on. An average of all these prices is called the *price level*. Someone might say, "The price level has increased." This means that the prices of goods produced and sold in the economy are higher, *on average*. It doesn't necessarily mean that every single price is higher, only that on average prices are higher.

You may remember from Chapter 12 that *inflation* is defined as an increase in the price level. Stated a little differently, inflation is an increase in the average level of prices. Our recent economic history is one of inflation. *Deflation* is defined as a decrease in the price level, or the average level of prices. Deflation has not been present during our recent economic history.

How Do We Measure Inflation?

How do you know whether the economy has experienced inflation? You need to know whether the price level has increased. If it has, then there has been inflation; if it hasn't, then there hasn't been inflation.

Chapter 12 explained that the consumer price index (CPI) is used to measure the price level. Suppose the CPI last year was 110 and the CPI this

year is also 110. Has there been inflation between the two years? The answer is no, since the price level (as measured by the CPI) has not increased.

Suppose, though, that the CPI was 110 last year and is 121 this year. Has there been inflation between the two years? Yes, since the CPI has risen.

We can find the *inflation rate* between these two years—that is, the percentage increase in the price level—by using the following simple formula:

$$\text{Inflation rate} = \frac{\text{CPI in later year} - \text{CPI in earlier year}}{\text{CPI in earlier year}} \times 100$$

Filling in the numbers, we get:

$$\text{Inflation rate} = \frac{121 - 110}{110} \times 100 = 10\%$$

The inflation rate is 10 percent.

Inflation Can Originate on the Demand Side or the Supply Side of the Economy

Chapters 3 and 4 discussed supply and demand in a market setting. For example, we saw that when the demand for a good increases and supply remains the same, price increases; and when the supply of a good decreases and demand remains the same, price increases.

Chapter 12 introduced the concept of supply and demand in an economy. The demand side of the economy was represented by aggregate demand, and the supply side of the economy was represented by aggregate supply.

Inflation, which is an increase in the price level, can originate on either the demand side or the supply side of the economy. Consider Exhibit 13-1a. Here we see an aggregate demand curve, AD_1, and an aggregate supply curve, AS_1. The equilibrium price level is P_1. Now, suppose aggregate demand

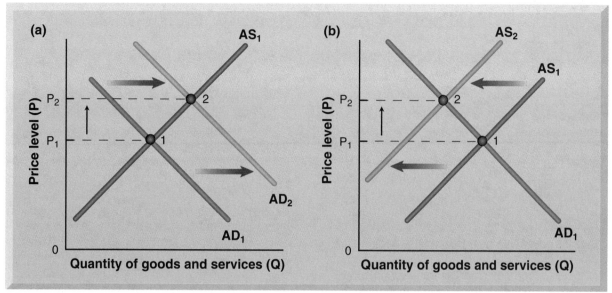

▲ **EXHIBIT 13-1. Inflation.** Inflation is an increase in the price level. An increase in the price level can be caused by an increase in aggregate demand (shown in part *a*) or by a decrease in aggregate supply (shown in part *b*). When an increase in the price level originates on the demand side of the economy, it is called *demand-side inflation*; when it originates on the supply side of the economy, it is called *supply-side inflation*.

increases; the aggregate demand curve shifts rightward from AD_1 to AD_2. Consequently, the price level increases from P_1 to P_2. Since the price level has increased, we have inflation. We conclude that if aggregate demand increases and aggregate supply stays the same, inflation will occur. When an increase in the price level originates on the demand side of the economy, economists call it **demand-side inflation**. One of the things that can cause demand-side inflation is an increase in the money supply. For example, suppose the Fed increases the money supply. As a result, there is more money in the economy, and demand in the economy rises. As a consequence of the increased demand, the price level increases.

Next, consider the decrease in aggregate supply from AS_1 to AS_2 in Exhibit 13-1*b*. As a result of this decrease, the price level increases from P_1 to P_2. Again, since the price level has increased, we have inflation. We conclude that if aggregate supply decreases and aggregate demand stays the same, inflation will occur. When an increase in the price level originates on the supply side of the

economy, economists call it **supply-side inflation**. One of the things that can cause supply-side inflation is a major drought that lowers the output of agricultural goods. As a result, there is a smaller supply of goods in the economy, and the price level increases.

QUESTION: *Is it possible for both aggregate demand and aggregate supply to increase, and there still be inflation?*

ANSWER: *Yes, if aggregate demand increases by more than aggregate supply. For example, look at Exhibit 13-2. Initially, the economy is at point 1,*

MINI GLOSSARY

Demand-Side Inflation An increase in the price level that originates on the demand side of the economy.
Supply-Side Inflation An increase in the price level that originates on the supply side of the economy.

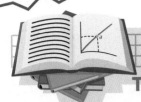

ANALYZING PRIMARY SOURCES

The Cause of Inflation Is Not Always Easy to See

Without a knowledge of economics, it is easy to mistake the cause of inflation. In this passage, the economist Milton Friedman makes this point.

"In your country and in mine, every businessman is persuaded that inflation is produced by labor unions, or by wage pressure, whether or not from trade unions. And that is because of the fallacy of composition. What is true for each individual is often the *opposite* of what is true for everybody together. Any person in this room could get out of that door in two seconds; but if everybody tried at once to get out of that door, you could not do it. In the same way, pressure on an employer to increase his prices comes to him in the form of an increase in wages and costs. It looks to him as if he is being required to increase prices because of that increase in wages and costs. That is true for him by himself. But where did that increase in costs come from? It came because somewhere else in the system somebody was increasing demand, which was tending to draw away the employer's labor or other resources. He was required to bid in the market to keep them.

In *University Economics*, Professors A. A. Alchian and W. R. Allen have an excellent little parable which I think brings this truth home very well. It says, let us suppose in a country in which everything else is fine all of a sudden there is a great craze for increasing the consumption of meat, and all the housewives rush to the butchers to buy meat. The butchers are delighted to sell them the meat. They do not mark up the prices at all, they just sell out all the meat they have, but they place additional orders with the wholesalers. The wholesalers are delighted to sell the meat. They clean out their inventories. They go back to the packing houses. The packing houses ship out their meat. The price is the same but the packing houses send orders to their buyers at the cattle market:

'Buy more beef.' There is only a fixed amount of cattle available. And so the only thing that happens is that in the process of each packer trying to buy more beef he bids up the price. Then a notice goes from the packer to the wholesaler, 'We are very sorry, but due to an increase in our costs we are required to increase the price.' A notice goes from the wholesaler to the retailer. And the retailer finally says to the customer when she comes in to complain that beef has gone up, 'I'm terribly sorry, but my *costs* have gone up.' He's right. But what started the increase in costs all the way up and down the line? It was the housewife rushing in to buy the meat.

In exactly the same way, every businessman has a misconception of the process. From his point of view he is right—the pressure on him to raise his prices derives from increases in costs. If there happen to be unions, he will attribute it to the pressure of the unions. If there are no unions, he will attribute it to some other force which is driving up wages—perhaps the world shortage of sugar or the Arabs. But the truth of the matter is that the ultimate source of inflation is always the increase in *demand* which percolates through to him in this or some other form.[a] "

1. In this passage, does Friedman blame inflation on labor unions? Explain your answer.
2. Explain how an increase in demand can percolate over to appear as an increase in costs.

a. Milton Friedman, "Unemployment vs. Inflation," *Occasional Paper, No. 44* (London: Institute of Economic Affairs, 1975), pp. 34–35.

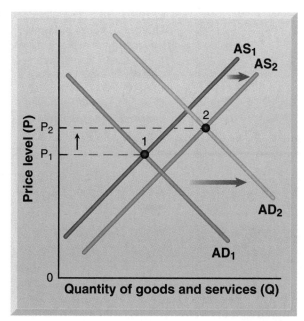

▲ **EXHIBIT 13-2. Aggregate Demand Increases by More Than Aggregate Supply.** When aggregate demand increases by more than aggregate supply, the price level increases; we have inflation.

and the price level is P_1. Then, both the increasing aggregate demand and the increasing aggregate supply curves shift rightward, to AD_2 and AS_2, respectively. Notice, though, that the aggregate demand increases more: the curve shifts rightward by more than the aggregate supply curve shifts rightward. What happens to the price level? It increases from P_1 to P_2; we have inflation.

The Simple Quantity Theory of Money

The simple quantity theory of money presents a clear picture of what causes inflation. Before examining this theory, though, we must know something about **velocity** and the exchange equation.

Velocity. Velocity is the average number of times a dollar is spent to buy final goods and ser-

vices. To illustrate the concept of velocity, we'll consider a tiny economy with only five $1 bills. In January, the first of the $1 bills moves from Maria's hands to Nancy's hands to buy a newspaper. Then, in June, it goes from Nancy's hands to Bob's hands to buy a bagel. And in December, it goes from Bob's hands to André's hands to buy a used paperback book. Over the course of the year, this $1 bill has changed hands three times. The other $1 bills also change hands during the year. The second one changes hands five times; the third, six times; the fourth, three times; and the fifth, three times. Given this information, we can calculate the number of times the average dollar changes hands in purchases. We calculate it by finding the sum of the times each dollar changed hands (3 + 5 + 6 + 3 + 3 = 20 times) and then dividing by the number of dollars (5). The answer is 4. The number 4 is the velocity in this example.

The Exchange Equation. This is the exchange equation:

$$M \times V = P \times Q$$

In the equation, M stands for the money supply, P stands for the price level or average price, Q stands for the quantity of output (quantity of goods and services), and V stands for velocity. Now, M times V *must equal* P times Q. To see why, think of the equation on a personal basis. Suppose you have $40—this is your money supply (M). You spend the $40 one time, so velocity (V) is 1. You spend the $40 on five books, so 5 is the quantity of goods and services you purchase—it is your Q in the exchange equation. Now ask yourself what P must equal, given that M is $40, V is 1, and Q is 5. If you spend $40 on five books, the average price per book must be $8. P must be $8, since $8 times

MINI GLOSSARY		

Velocity The average number of times a dollar is spent to buy final goods and services in a year.

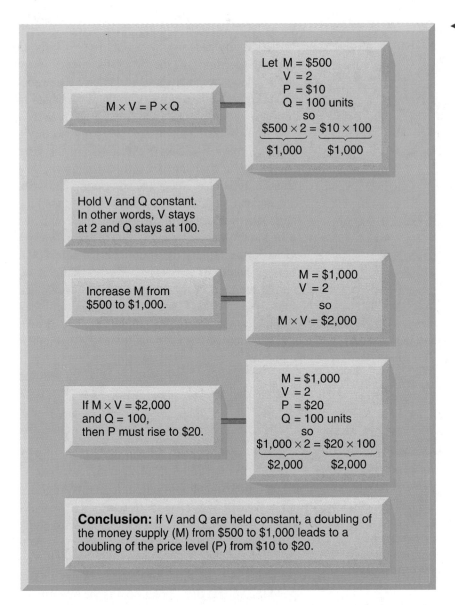

The top of the exhibit outlines the basics of the simple quantity theory of money. Start with M × V = P × Q. Then, if V and Q are held constant, it follows that a change in the money supply (M) will lead to a proportional change in the price level (P). The numbers that we use in the exhibit support this conclusion.

5 books equals $40. Here is how things look for this example.

$$M (\$40) \times V (1) = P (\$8) \times Q (5 \text{ books})$$
$$\$40 = \$40$$

The Simple Quantity Theory of Money. The **simple quantity theory of money** is used to explain inflation. The theory begins by making two assumptions. First, it assumes that velocity (V) is constant; second, it assumes that the quantity of output or goods and services (Q) is constant.

Let's set velocity (V) at 2, and the quantity of output (Q) at 100 units. We will hold these numbers constant throughout our discussion.

Suppose we let the money supply (M) equal $500. If V is 2, and Q is 100 units, then what must the price level (P) equal? According to what we learned about the exchange equation, it must equal $10.

$$M (\$500) \times V (2) = P (\$10) \times Q (100 \text{ units})$$
$$\$1,000 = \$1,000$$

Now, suppose we increase the money supply from $500 to $1,000. This is a doubling of the money supply. As we stated earlier, we will hold velocity and output constant. Velocity (V) is still 2, and output (Q) is still 100 units. What happens to the price level (P)? It increases to $20. (See the equation.)

$$M (\$1,000) \times V (2) = P (\$20) \times Q (100 \text{ units})$$
$$\$2,000 = \$2,000$$

In other words, if the money supply doubles (from $500 to $1,000), the price level doubles (from $10 to $20). See Exhibit 13-3. This is a prediction of the simple quantity theory of money, which generally says that changes in the money supply will bring about strictly proportional changes in the price level. In other words, if the money supply increases by 100 percent, the price level will increase by 100 percent; if the money supply increases by 20 percent, the price level will increase by 20 percent; and so on. More generally, early economic writers used the simple quantity theory of money to explain inflation. It states that inflation—which is an increase in the price level (P)—is caused by an increase in the money supply.

Rates of Growth in the Money Supply and the Inflation Rate

The simple quantity theory of money predicts that changes in the money supply will bring about strictly proportional changes in the price level. When we check the data in the real world, however, we find that this strict proportionality does not usually hold. In other words, an increase in the money supply of, say, 10 percent does not usually bring about an increase of 10 percent in the price level.

But what we do usually find is that the greater the increase in the money supply, the greater the increase in the price level. For example, a nation that increased its money supply by 30 percent would usually have a greater increase in its price level (its

---

THINKING LIKE AN ECONOMIST

*E*conomists do the following. First, they find something they want to explain. Second, they construct a theory to try to explain it. Third, they seek out real-world evidence that will tell them whether the theory is correct. Look at this three-step approach in light of our discussion of inflation.

First, economists wanted to discover what causes inflation. Second, they constructed the simple quantity theory of money to explain it. (The theory held that inflation is caused by increases in the money supply.) Third, they gathered evidence that would either support the theory or disprove it. This approach—find something to explain, construct a theory to explain it, and then gather evidence to see whether the theory is correct—is used by economists in many situations.

---

inflation rate) than a nation that increased its money supply by 20 percent. This finding is, of course, consistent with the "spirit" of the simple quantity theory of money. After all, the theory says that changes in the money supply bring about strictly proportional changes in the price level. It follows that larger changes in the money supply should bring about larger changes in the price level.

The Effects of Inflation

There is a tendency to think that inflation only affects the buyer of goods, as when a person pays

---

MINI GLOSSARY

Simple Quantity Theory of Money A theory that predicts that changes in the price level will be strictly proportional to changes in the money supply.

$60 instead of $50 a week for groceries. In truth, people are affected by inflation in many other ways as well. Here we consider some of the many effects of inflation.

Inflation and Individuals on Fixed Incomes. Suppose Denise has lived on a fixed income for the last 10 years; that is, every year for the past 10 years, her income has been the same. However, each year for the past 10 years, the price level has increased; there has been inflation. What has inflation done to Denise? It has lowered the purchasing power of her money. This means she can buy fewer units of goods with a given amount of money than she could previously buy. In turn, this reduces her material standard of living.

Inflation and Savers. On January 1, Lorenzo puts $2,000 into a savings account that pays 6 percent interest. On December 31 the following year, he removes $2,120 from the account ($2,000, which is the original amount, and $120 in interest; $2,000 × 0.06 = $120). Suppose that during the

▲ Inflation reduces the purchasing power of people's money.

year prices have not increased at all (the inflation rate is zero percent). Saving has made Lorenzo better off, since at the end of the year he can purchase $120 more of goods and services than he could at the beginning of the year.

Now change the situation. Suppose that during the year prices had increased by 10 percent (the inflation rate is 10 percent). Ask yourself this: How much money would Lorenzo need at the end of the year to buy exactly what $2,000 could buy at the beginning of the year? Answer: if prices had increased by 10 percent, he would need 10 percent more money, or a total of $2,200 ($2,000 × 0.10 = $200, and $200 + $2,000 = $2,200). But instead of having $2,200, Lorenzo has only $2,120 from his savings account. In other words, Lorenzo must settle for purchasing $80 less of goods and services than he could at the beginning of the year ($2,200 − $2,120 = $80). What happened? Since the inflation rate (10 percent) was greater than the interest rate (6 percent) Lorenzo earned on his savings, Lorenzo ended up worse off. It is clear that inflation hurts savers.

However, if inflation persists, it is customary for financial institutions to compete for customers by offering an interest rate that has been adjusted upward by the inflation rate. To illustrate, suppose financial institutions would offer a 4 percent interest rate next year if prices were going to stay the same as this year (that is, if there were no inflation). However, they anticipate a 5 percent inflation rate during the year. Many institutions will begin to compete for customers by offering a 9 percent interest rate, which is the sum of the interest rate they would offer if prices did not change. The anticipated inflation rate is 9 percent (4% + 5% = 9%).

Inflation and Past Decisions. Inflation often turns past decisions into mistakes. Consider the contractor who last year signed a contract to build a shopping mall for $30 million. She agreed to this dollar figure based on her estimates of what it would cost to buy the materials and hire the labor to build the mall. She estimated $28 million in costs. All of a sudden, inflation hits. Prices of labor, concrete, nails, tile, roofing, and so forth rise. Now the contractor realizes it will cost her $31 million to build the mall. She looks back on her decision to build the mall for only $30 million as a mistake—a costly mistake for her.

Inflation and Hedging against Inflation. What do individuals in an inflation-prone economy do that individuals in a stable-price economy do not do? They try to **hedge** against inflation. That is, they try to figure out what investments offer the best protection against inflation. Would gold, real estate, or fine art be the best hedge? They travel to distant cities to hear "experts" talk on inflation. They subscribe to numerous newsletters that claim to predict future inflation rates accurately. All this, obviously, requires an expenditure on resources. Resources, we remind ourselves, that are expended in the effort to protect against inflation can no longer be used to build factories or produce houses, shoes, or cars. One effect of inflation is that it causes individuals to try to hedge against it, thereby diverting resources away from being used to produce goods.

 LEARNING CHECK

1. The CPI is 167 in year 1 and 189 in year 2. What is the inflation rate between the two years?
2. "An increase in the money supply is more likely to cause supply-side inflation than demand-side inflation." Do you agree or disagree? Explain your answer.
3. If financial institutions do not compensate savers for inflation, what effect does inflation have on savers?
4. A war breaks out in a country, and factories are destroyed. Is this more likely to cause demand-side or supply-side inflation? Explain your answer.

SECTION 2   UNEMPLOYMENT

Many people seem to think that unemployment is avoidable. If we only implement the "correct" economic policies, some people argue, the unemployment rate (as it is now measured) will drop to zero percent. That thought is pure fantasy. This section explains why. It also discusses four categories of unemployment: frictional, structural, natural, and cyclical.

As you read, keep these key questions in mind:

■ What is frictional unemployment?
■ What is structural unemployment?
■ What is natural unemployment?
■ What is cyclical unemployment?
■ What does aggregate demand have to do with the unemployment rate?

The Unemployment Rate

Chapter 7 shows how the government calculates the unemployment rate. It is shown again here.

$$\text{Unemployment rate} = \frac{\text{Number of persons unemployed}}{\text{Number of persons in the civilian labor force}}$$

MINI GLOSSARY

Hedge To try to avoid or lessen a loss by taking some counterbalancing action.

For example, if the number of persons unemployed is 10 million, and the labor force is 100 million, then the unemployment rate is 10 percent (10 million ÷ 100 million = .10, or 10 percent). It is this unemployment rate that you will read about in a newspaper, or hear mentioned on a news show. Sometimes it is referred to as the official unemployment rate.

Now look again at the numerator of the unemployment rate. It is "number of persons unemployed." Suppose this number is 10 million persons. Not every one of the 10 million unemployed persons is unemployed for the same reason. In economics, there are three different categories of unemployed persons. Persons are said to be frictionally unemployed, structurally unemployed, or cyclically unemployed. Frictional, structural, and cyclical unemployment are discussed next.

Frictional Unemployment

Every day in the United States, millions of buying decisions are being made. Consequently, the demand for some goods is rising, and the demand for other goods is falling. This has an effect on the number of people producing different goods. To illustrate, suppose there are two goods: IBM computers and Apple computers. During, say, April, the demand for Apple computers rises, and the demand for IBM computers falls. As a result, IBM decides to fire some workers, and Apple decides to hire some additional workers.

Suppose you are a worker fired from IBM. In time, you may find work at Apple (doing what you did at IBM), but in the meantime you are said to be *frictionally unemployed*. A person is frictionally unemployed if he or she is unemployed as a result of changing market (demand) conditions and has transferable skills.

Will **frictional unemployment** always exist? The answer is yes, because there will always be changing market conditions; the demand for some goods will increase as the demand for other goods decreases. Frictional unemployment is simply the result of buyers expressing their freedom to buy what they want when they want it. As long as buyers have freedom, some people will be unemployed.

Structural Unemployment

Now consider another example. This time we have Apple, which produces computers, and the

◀ People who are structurally unemployed because of changing market conditions usually have to be retrained in order to qualify for a position in a different industry.

Ford Motor Company, which produces cars. In April, the demand for Apple computers rises, and the demand for Ford cars falls. Apple begins to hire additional workers, and Ford fires some workers. Suppose you are a worker fired by Ford. In time, you may find work at Apple (doing something different from what you did at Ford), but in the meantime you are *structurally unemployed*. A person is structurally unemployed if he or she is unemployed as a result of changing market (demand) conditions and does not currently have the skills necessary to work for a company hiring workers. This person may have to retrain in order to get a new job.

Will **structural unemployment** always exist? The answer is yes, because there will always be changing market conditions, and there will always be people fired who do not currently possess the skills necessary to obtain the available jobs.

QUESTION: *Is the only difference between a person who is frictionally unemployed and one who is structurally unemployed that the one who is frictionally unemployed* does *have transferable skills and the one who is structurally unemployed* does *not?*

ANSWER: *Yes.*

Natural Unemployment

Natural unemployment is the sum of frictional and structural unemployment. For example, if 3 million persons were frictionally unemployed, and 2 million persons were structurally unemployed, we would say that 5 million persons (2 million + 3 million = 5 million) were naturally unemployed.

Now suppose someone wants to know what percentage of the civilian labor force is naturally unemployed. How would we calculate this? We would simply take the number of persons naturally unemployed (5 million) and divide it by the number of persons in the civilian labor force. Suppose the civilian labor force consists of 100 million persons. The natural unemployment rate is then 5 percent (5 million ÷ 100 million = .05, or 5 percent).

$$\text{Natural unemployment rate} = \frac{\text{Number of persons naturally unemployed}}{\text{Number of persons in the civilian labor force}}$$

Economists have estimated the natural unemployment rate for the United States to be between 4.0 and 6.5 percent. Economists go on to say that when the nation's unemployment rate (that is, the official unemployment rate that is computed by the federal government) is equal to the natural unemployment rate, **full employment** exists in the economy. For example, if the natural unemployment rate is, say, 6 percent, and the unemployment rate is 6 percent, the economy is operating at full employment.

You may think it is odd that economists claim the economy is operating at full employment when a 6 percent unemployment rate exists. You may have thought that full employment means that the unemployment rate is zero percent: there are no unemployed persons. This is not, however, what

MINI GLOSSARY

Frictional Unemployment Refers to workers who have lost their jobs because of changing market (demand) conditions and who have transferable skills. Unemployment due to the natural "frictions" of the economy. A person is frictionally unemployed when he or she is unemployed because of changing market conditions and has transferable skills.

Structural Unemployment Refers to workers who have lost their jobs because of changing market (demand) conditions and whose skills do not match the requirements of available jobs. Unemployment that arises when the skills of available workers do not match the requirements of available jobs.

Natural Unemployment Unemployment that is caused by frictional and structural factors in the economy.

Full Employment The situation that exists when the official unemployment rate equals the natural unemployment rate.

ECONOMIC FOCUS

In the United States in 1992, the unemployment rate was 7.4 percent. In some states, the unemployment rate was higher than it was in the nation as a whole. For example, in Alaska the unemployment rate was 9.1 percent, in Mississippi it was 8.1 percent, and in West Virginia it was 11.3 percent. (See Exhibit S-13-1.) In some states, the unemployment rate was lower than it was in the nation as a whole. For example, it was 5.9 percent in Colorado, 3 percent in Nebraska, and 4.5 percent in Hawaii. Why was the unemployment rate higher in some states than in others?

One reason has to do with cutbacks in government defense spending occurring at the time. The January 1993 edition of the *Economic Report of the President* (which was reporting on economic conditions in 1992) states: "New England and California were particularly hard hit by ongoing defense cutbacks."[a] Many of the New England states (such as Massachusetts, Rhode Island, and New York in particular), as well as California, had a large number of firms that produced goods used in national defense. As cutbacks in defense came, these firms lost business. They ended up laying off many of their workers. As a result, the unemployment rate in these states increased, and became higher than the national unemployment rate. For example, the unemployment rate was 8.5 percent in Massachusetts, 8.9 percent in Rhode Island, 8.5 percent in New York, and 9.1 percent in California.

Another reason for different unemployment rates in different states is that during this time there was some restructuring (fundamental changes being made) in the auto industry. The *Economic Report of the President* states that "restructuring in the domestic auto industry hurt Michigan and Illinois."[b] This largely explains why both Michigan and Illinois had higher unemployment rates than the nation as a whole: the rate in Michigan was 8.8 percent, and in Illinois, 7.5 percent.

You will notice a certain theme developing. Unemployment rates tend to be higher in states where major industries are suffering an economic downturn or are undergoing fundamental changes in their structure. The unemployment rate in California was higher than the nation's unemployment rate in 1992 partly because a major industry in California—the defense industry—was not receiving as many orders for goods from the federal government. The unemployment rate was higher in Michigan than the nation's unemployment rate partly because a major industry in Michigan—the auto industry—was in the midst of restructuring.

To illustrate our point with an extreme example, consider the case of Nevada. Major industries in Nevada are entertainment and casino gambling. Each year, millions of people go to cities like Las Vegas and Reno (in Nevada) to be entertained and to gamble. Suppose the demand for Nevada entertainment and gambling decreases. What would we expect would initially happen to the unemployment rate in Nevada? We would expect it to rise. What holds for Nevada holds for other states, too—but not necessarily to the same degree.

We can also look at different unemployment rates across the states in much the same way that we looked at frictional and structural unemploy-

a. *Economic Report of the President* (Washington, D.C.: United States Government Printing Office, 1993), p. 62.

b. Ibid, p. 21.

ment in this chapter. Remember, the cause of both frictional and structural unemployment was changing market (demand) conditions in the economy. With this in mind, suppose there are two states, X and Y. In State X, the production of good X is the major industry. In State Y, the production of good Y is the major industry. Over a certain time period, the preferences of the buying public in the nation change away from good X and toward good Y. In short, people demand less of good X and more of good Y. As a result, what would we expect to happen to the unemployment rate in each state? Under certain conditions (such as firms in State Y hiring workers living in State Y), we would expect the unemployment rate in State Y to decrease, as firms in that state hire

▼ **EXHIBIT S-13-1.** Unemployment Rates in the 50 States.

STATE	UNEMPLOYMENT RATE	STATE	UNEMPLOYMENT RATE
Alabama	7.3%	Montana	6.7
Alaska	9.1	Nebraska	3.0
Arizona	7.4	Nevada	6.6
Arkansas	7.2	New Hampshire	7.5
California	9.1	New Jersey	8.4
Colorado	5.9	New Mexico	6.8
Connecticut	7.5	New York	8.5
Delaware	5.3	North Carolina	5.9
Florida	8.2	North Dakota	4.9
Georgia	6.9	Ohio	7.2
Hawaii	4.5	Oklahoma	5.7
Idaho	6.5	Oregon	7.5
Illinois	7.5	Pennsylvania	7.5
Indiana	6.5	Rhode Island	8.9
Iowa	4.6	South Carolina	6.2
Kansas	4.2	South Dakota	3.1
Kentucky	6.9	Tennessee	6.4
Louisiana	8.1	Texas	7.5
Maine	7.1	Utah	4.9
Maryland	6.6	Vermont	6.6
Massachusetts	8.5	Virginia	6.4
Michigan	8.8	Washington	7.5
Minnesota	5.1	West Virginia	11.3
Mississippi	8.1	Wisconsin	5.1
Missouri	5.7	Wyoming	5.6

SOURCES: U.S. Bureau of the Census, *Statistical Abstract of the United States: 1993*, 113th edition, p. 396.

people to produce more of good Y; and we would expect the unemployment rate in State X to increase, as firms in that state fire some employees because customers are not buying as many units of good X as before. What our example points out is that a state in which there is not much diversification—in short, a state that does not produce a wide variety of goods but principally only one or two—may find its unemployment rate sharply increasing if the demand decreases for the one or two goods it produces and sells.

1. According to Exhibit S-13-1, what was the unemployment rate in your state in 1992?
2. Why is the unemployment rate likely to be higher in some states than in other states?
3. Would you expect a state with a highly diversified economy—one that produced many goods and services—to, on average, have a higher or lower unemployment rate than a state with an undiversified economy? Explain your answer.

full employment means to economists. Remember, according to economists, there will always be some people unemployed due to frictional and structural reasons. There will always be people changing jobs because the demand for goods and services is increasing in one place and decreasing in another. To economists, a zero unemployment rate is unrealistic.

QUESTION: *What's so natural about natural unemployment?*

ANSWER: *Remember, natural unemployment is the sum of frictional and structural unemployment. Changing market conditions cause frictional and structural unemployment, which means here that demand for some goods is increasing while the demand for other goods is decreasing. In short, it is due to people deciding to buy more of some goods and less of other goods. Economists think this is a very natural event—much like breathing. It will go on forever.*

Cyclical Unemployment

Persons who are neither frictionally nor structurally unemployed, but are nonetheless unemployed, are said to be **cyclically unemployed**. For example, suppose there are 10 million unemployed persons in the United States. Three million are frictionally unemployed, and 1 million are structurally unemployed. This leaves 6 million persons who are cyclically unemployed (3 million + 1 million = 4 million, and 10 million − 4 million = 6 million).

Why would a person be cyclically unemployed? Obviously, it can't have anything to do with demand increasing for some goods while at the same time demand is decreasing for other goods. If such were the case, these persons would be either frictionally or structurally unemployed. It has to be something else.

Many economists think that an increase in the number of persons who are cyclically unemployed is due to a decrease in aggregate demand. In other words, it is caused by a decrease in the total demand for goods and services. It is as if, one day, buyers in the economy want to buy $400 billion worth of goods and services, and then, the next day, they decide to buy only $370 billion worth of goods and services.[1] Fewer shoppers are seen in the stores across the nation. We will explain more about this shortly. But before we do this, consider what happens to the unemployment rate (the official unemployment rate calculated by the government) if the ranks of the cyclically unemployed increase. Obviously, the unemployment rate increases. To illustrate, suppose that in 1992 there are 3 million frictionally unemployed persons, 2 million structurally unemployed persons, and 5 million cyclically unemployed persons. In total, there are 10 million unemployed persons (2 million + 3 million + 5 million = 10 million). And if the civilian labor force is 100 million persons, the unemployment rate is 10 percent (10 million ÷ 100 million = .10, or 10 percent). In 1993, there are still 2 million frictionally unemployed persons, and 3 million structurally unemployed persons, but now there are 6 million cyclically unemployed persons. In total, there are 11 million unemployed persons (2 million + 3 million + 6 million = 11 million) and, if the civilian labor force is still 100 million, the unemployment rate is 11 percent (11 million ÷ 100 million = .11, or 11 percent).

The Unemployment Rate and Aggregate Demand

Most economists believe that the unemployment rate will increase if aggregate demand decreases. To explain, we start with an economy operating at full employment. Suppose then the Fed reduces the money supply, which in turn leads to a reduction in aggregate demand in the economy. Translated, this means the Fed's action has reduced the overall amount of spending.

---

1. We are assuming here that there has been no change in prices.

As overall spending drops, some firms begin to sell less. Because they are selling less, they cut back on their production. Consequently, they fire some workers. ("We're not producing as many cars, so some of the workers have to be fired.") Our conclusion: A drop in aggregate demand brings about a rise in unemployment.

QUESTION: *Suppose a company has 1,000 workers and pays each $15 an hour. Then, because of a drop in spending in the economy, the company sells fewer goods. In reaction, it cuts back on production. At this point, we usually expect that because production has dropped, fewer workers will be needed, and so some workers will be fired. But can't all workers keep their jobs if they agree to accept lower wages? For example, instead of paying 1,000 workers $15 an hour, the company could pay 1,000 workers $11 an hour. That way, no one would have to lose his or her job; people would simply work for lower wages.*

ANSWER: *If, as aggregate demand falls, wage rates fall, too, then certainly fewer people will end up losing their jobs. But things don't always work this way, for several reasons.*

First, not all workers will agree to lower wages. Again, suppose there are 1,000 workers at a company. One of these workers is Jim, who has worked for the company for 25 years and has seniority. He knows that if there are cutbacks, or firings, he will be one of the last persons to go. Does he accept lower wages so that some workers don't get fired, or does he keep his higher wages even if it means that some workers will be fired? Because Jim isn't going to be one of the persons fired, he may prefer to keep his old, higher wages

---

MINI GLOSSARY

Cyclical Unemployment The difference between the official unemployment rate and the natural rate of unemployment.

than to accept new, lower wages. In short, workers may resist lower wages.

Oddly enough, managers may also resist lower wages. Consider the manager of a factory. Production is down, and it is her job to either fire some workers or reduce wages for the entire work force. She may believe that if she lowers everyone's wages, worker morale will drop and everyone will dislike her. On the other hand, if she fires some workers and maintains the wages of the remaining workers, only the fired workers will be unhappy. But the fired workers won't be around—they'll be somewhere else looking for a job. Simply put, managers may prefer to fire some workers and keep wages up than to pay all workers a lower wage.

LEARNING CHECK

1. What is the difference between frictional and structural unemployment?
2. "The economy has not achieved full employment until the unemployment rate is zero percent." True or false? Explain your answer.
3. The natural unemployment rate is 6 percent and the officially reported unemployment rate is 7 percent. What does the cyclical unemployment rate equal?
4. Explain why some business managers may prefer to fire some workers than to have lower wages for all workers.

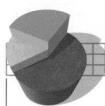

DEVELOPING ECONOMIC SKILLS

Interpreting Editorial Cartoons

"**A** picture is worth a thousand words." This often-repeated saying aptly states the goal of editorial cartoonists. Using the cartoon, a unique medium, cartoonists entertain us and shape our opinions just as others use print, music, or the electronic airwaves. Often, the editorial cartoon consists of a funny picture, but it involves much more than superficial humor: it allows the cartoonist to communicate a message in a direct and powerful manner.

Have you ever looked at an editorial cartoon and not understood what it was the cartoonist was trying to express? If you answered yes, welcome to the club! Some cartoons don't make a point as well as others. Perhaps you don't have the proper background to understand fully what the cartoonist is trying to communicate. Yet, most of the time we do get the point, and, whether we agree or disagree with the cartoonist, we are generally better informed for having seen the cartoon.

Confused Economists

There is an old joke among economists that goes something like this: If you placed all the economists in the world end to end, they would never reach a conclusion. Keep this joke in mind as you examine the cartoon at the top of the next page.

Now that you have studied the cartoon, do you notice confusion, disagreement, and chaos? The birds in the trees certainly do. This cartoon effectively communicates a notion held by many people: economists cannot agree on anything. In reality, economists agree on many things.

Economists often classify issues as either positive or normative. Positive economic issues can be proved true or false. Economists

DEVELOPING ECONOMIC SKILLS (continued)

"What makes you think these guys are economists?

Lee Judge, *The Kansas City Star*

THE FAR SIDE By GARY LARSON

"Well, shoot. I just can't figure it out. I'm movin' over 500 doughnuts a day, but I'm still just barely squeakin' by."

generally agree on positive economic issues. For example, saying the rate of inflation is 3.2% can readily be proved by examining statistics, so we would say this is a positive economic statement. However, normative economic statements are opinions that cannot be proved true or false. Saying the inflation rate should be 2.5% is an opinion; therefore, this is an example of a normative statement. Just as friends may have differences of opinion, so do economists. But remember, their disagreements typically deal with normative issues, not positive ones.

Doughnut Shop

Some cartoons are not intended to editorialize, but they still use economic principles to make a point and have some fun. Inspect the cartoon above and try to identify the economic concepts illustrated in *The Far Side* cartoon.

Probably the first thing you think about is profit. The shop owner is puzzled because his revenues are not high even though he is "movin'" over 500 doughnuts per day. When he states he is barely "sqeakin' by," he is referring to the low profit he is making. To determine profit, subtract total costs from total revenue. Clearly, if his total revenue were higher, he would be making more profit. Another less-obvious concept is that of ethics. An ethical employee would not steal from the company, but it is implied in the picture that the helper has yet to meet a doughnut he did not like.

Economics Lecture

Here is another example of a cartoon making fun of economics. This cartoon introduces the

DEVELOPING ECONOMIC SKILLS (continued)

FRANK & ERNEST® by Bob Thaves

FRANK AND ERNEST reprinted by permission of NEA, Inc.

concept of velocity. Velocity refers to the average number of times a dollar is spent to buy final goods and services during a year. Consider the cartoon above and how it relates to the concept of velocity.

Frank and Ernest are attending a lecture on the topic of velocity. However, the comic strip characters act as if learning this economic concept is no big deal. After all, one spends his paycheck two or three times over before he is even paid. He must have very good credit!

1. Explain how editorial cartoons differ from other methods of expression.

2. Describe the difference between positive and normative economic statements. Give an example of each.

3. Create your own editorial cartoon using one of the themes addressed earlier, or create one of your own.

4. Find an example of an editorial cartoon in a recent paper. Examine it carefully and then write a brief report explaining what the cartoonist is trying to say.

5. In the comic strip section of the newspaper, find cartoons that deal with an economic theme such as scarcity, opportunity cost, demand, supply, or money. Bring them to class and explain the economic concept and how the cartoon illustrates the concept.

CHAPTER 13 REVIEW

CHAPTER SUMMARY

1. Inflation is an increase in the price level; deflation is a decrease in the price level.

2. One way to measure the inflation rate is to compute the percentage change in the CPI from one year to the next.

3. Inflation reduces the purchasing power of money. For example, with a 10 percent inflation rate, each dollar transfers 10 percent fewer goods and services.

4. When an increase in the price level originates on the demand side of the economy, economists call it demand-side inflation. When an increase in the price level originates on the supply side of the economy, economists call it supply-side inflation.

5. The money supply (M) times velocity (V) must equal the price level (P) times the quantity of output (Q). ($M \times V = P \times Q$)

6. Velocity is the average number of times a dollar is spent to buy final goods and services in a year.

7. The simple quantity theory of money assumes that velocity (V) and quantity of output (Q) are constant. It predicts that changes in the money supply will lead to strictly proportional changes in the price level.

8. The simple quantity theory of money is a theory of inflation, since it says that an increase in the price level—which is what inflation is—is brought about by an increase in the money supply.

9. Here are some of the effects of inflation: (a) It lowers the standard of living for persons on fixed incomes. (b) It reduces the gain from saving (unless the interest rate paid for saving has been adequately adjusted for inflation). (c) It sometimes turns past decisions into mistakes. (d) It causes people to hedge against it, thus diverting resources from strictly productive activities.

10. Frictional unemployment is due to the natural "frictions" of the economy. A person who is frictionally unemployed is unemployed as a result of changing market conditions and has transferable skills.

11. Structural unemployment arises when the skills of available workers do not match the requirements of available jobs.

12. Natural unemployment is the sum of frictional and structural unemployment. Most economists estimate the natural unemployment rate to be somewhere between 4.0 and 6.5 percent.

13. If the economy is operating at the natural unemployment rate, full employment is said to exist.

14. Here is how some economists explain why unemployment rises if aggregate demand falls: Suppose the Fed reduces the money supply. This reduces aggregate demand in the economy. Some firms begin to sell fewer goods. These firms cut back their operations; and in the process, some workers get fired.

CHAPTER 13 REVIEW (continued)

BUILD YOUR ECONOMIC VOCABULARY

Match the word with the correct definition, example, or statement.

1. inflation
2. deflation
3. demand-side inflation
4. supply-side inflation
5. frictional unemployment
6. natural unemployment
7. structural unemployment
8. cyclical unemployment rate

a. a person losing her job because of changing market conditions but having transferable skills
b. the difference between the official unemployment rate and the natural unemployment rate
c. a decrease in the price level
d. an increase in the price level that originates on the demand side of the economy
e. an increase in the price level
f. an increase in the price level that originates on the supply side of the economy
g. a person losing his job because of changing market conditions but not having transferable skills
h. the sum of frictional and structural unemployment

REVIEW QUESTIONS

1. The CPI is 145 in year 1 and 154 in year 2. What is the inflation rate between the two years?

2. The CPI is 155 in year 1 and 123 in year 2. What is the deflation rate between the two years?

3. What is the difference between inflation and deflation?

4. Inflation reduces the purchasing power of money. What does this mean? Give an example.

5. What might happen on the supply side of the economy to cause an increase in the price level?

6. What might happen on the demand side of the economy to cause an increase in the price level?

7. What are the assumptions of the simple quantity theory of money? What is its prediction?

8. Explain how inflation affects (a) individuals on fixed incomes and (b) savers.

9. Give an example of a person who is frictionally unemployed.

10. Give an example of a person who is structurally unemployed.

11. "Full employment will not be achieved until the unemployment rate is zero percent." Do you agree or disagree? Explain your answer.

12. Explain why the unemployment rate might rise if aggregate demand falls.

SHARPEN YOUR CRITICAL THINKING SKILLS

1. "Every year between and including 1971 and 1993, consumption spending was higher than in the previous year. Also, in each of these years, there was inflation. It follows that continuous increases in consumption were the direct cause of the supply-side inflation." What is wrong with this statement?

ACTIVITIES AND PROJECTS

1. See if you have a copy of the *Economic Report of the President* in your school or city library. In this book you will find the CPI and the unemployment rate listed for different years. They are usually listed in an appendix. List both the CPI and the unemployment rate for each year beginning in 1985 and going to the most recent year published. Then, calculate the percentage change in CPI between 1985 and the most recent year published.

ECONOMIC DICTIONARY

Cyclical Unemployment (Pg. 344)
Demand-Side Inflation (Pg. 333)
Frictional Unemployment (Pg. 340)
Full Employment (Pg. 341)
Hedge (Pg. 339)

Natural Unemployment (Pg. 341)
Simple Quantity Theory of Money (Pg. 336)
Structural Unemployment (Pg. 341)
Supply-Side Inflation (Pg. 333)
Velocity (Pg. 335)

CHAPTER 14

Government and the Economy: Fiscal and Monetary Policy

INTRODUCTION

In the past in our nation's history, people thought that government had no right to try to manage the economy. Government was simply there to provide goods (such as national defense) that the economy couldn't produce itself.

Today, many people believe that if there is something wrong with the economy, the government should get to work on it. Government should manage the economy.

Specifically, if there is inflation, government should get rid of it; if the level of unemployment is too high, government should lower it; if economic growth is weak, government should give the economy a boost; and so on. The two major policies that government uses in managing the economy are monetary policy and fiscal policy. This chapter discusses both.

SECTION 1   FISCAL POLICY

Fiscal policy refers to changes government makes in spending or taxation (or both) to achieve particular economic goals. Some economists believe that fiscal policy can be used by government to solve the twin problems of inflation and unemployment. We will examine their theories here, as well as what the critics have to say.

As you read, keep these key questions in mind:

■ What is fiscal policy?
■ What type of fiscal policy does government use to try to reduce unemployment?
■ What type of fiscal policy does government use to try to reduce inflation?
■ What are crowding out and crowding in?

Types of Fiscal Policy

Fiscal policy deals with government spending and taxes. If government spending is increased or if taxes are reduced (or both), government is said to be implementing **expansionary fiscal policy**. The objective of this type of policy is directly to increase total spending in the economy and indirectly to reduce the unemployment rate.

If government spending is decreased or if taxes are raised (or both), government is said to be implementing **contractionary fiscal policy**. The objec-

tive is directly to contract total spending in the economy and indirectly to reduce inflation. (See Exhibit 14-1.)

Expansionary Fiscal Policy and Unemployment

Suppose the official unemployment rate is 8 percent and the natural rate is 5 percent. Government sets a goal of reducing the unemployment rate. It hopes to reduce the rate to 5 percent and thus achieve full employment. How might the use of fiscal policy help government meet its goal? Here is what some economists say:

■ A high unemployment rate is the result of people not spending enough money in the economy. In other words, if people spend more money, firms sell more goods, and they have to hire more people to produce the goods.
■ To reduce the unemployment rate, Congress should implement expansionary fiscal policy— that is, it should increase government spending, lower taxes, or both. Let's say that it chooses to increase government spending instead of to lower taxes. Government can choose to spend more on health care, education, national defense, and many other things.

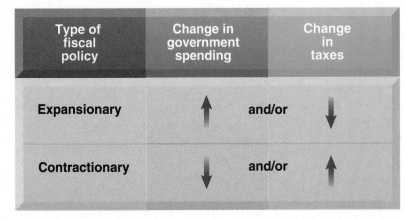

◄ **EXHIBIT 14-1. Two Types of Fiscal Policy.** If government increases its spending or decreases taxes (or both), it is implementing expansionary fiscal policy. If government decreases its spending or raises taxes (or both), it is implementing contractionary fiscal policy.

Type of fiscal policy	Change in government spending		Change in taxes
Expansionary	↑	and/or	↓
Contractionary	↓	and/or	↑

■ As a result of government increasing its spending, there will be more spending in the economy. To illustrate, suppose that at current prices the government is spending $400 billion, business is spending $200 billion (buying factories, machines, and so on), and consumers are spending $800 billion (buying television sets, clothes, computers, and so on). Total spending at current prices is $1,400 billion ($400 billion + $200 billion + $800 billion = $1,400 billion). Government decides to increase its spending to $450 billion. Now total spending increases to $1,450 billion ($450 billion + $200 billion + $800 billion = $1,450 billion).

■ As a result of the increase in total spending, firms sell more goods.

■ When firms start to sell more goods, they have to hire more workers to produce the additional goods. The unemployment rate goes down as a result of more people working.

The Issue of Crowding Out

Some economists don't agree that things will turn out the way they were just presented. They say that when government spends more, total spending in the economy doesn't necessarily rise. They bring up the issue of **crowding out**, which occurs when increases in government spending lead to reductions in private spending. (When we talk about private spending, this refers to spending made in the private sector by consumers and businesses.)

For example, suppose that currently in the economy, $60 million is spent on an average day. We'll say that $45 million is spent by the private sector (households and businesses buying such things as television sets, houses, factories, and so on) and $15 million is spent by government (buying such things as defense, education, and so on). Suppose now that government decides to increase its spending on education, thus raising its average daily spending to $17 million. What is the consequence? Does total spending rise to $62 million ($17 million in public spending plus $45 million in private spending)? Not necessarily, say some economists.

Suppose that because govern＿＿ education, people decide to ＿＿ tion. Specifically, because gove＿＿ on public schools and public-s＿＿ ple decide there is less need fo＿ much on private schools and pri＿ ers. As a result, private spending ＿＿m $45 million to $43 million. Total spending therefore remains at $60 million ($17 million in government spending plus $43 million in private spending).

In this example, where an increase of $2 million in government expenditures causes a $2 million decline in private spending, we have *complete crowding out*; each dollar increase in government expenditures is matched by a dollar decrease in private spending. With complete crowding out, an increase in government expenditures *does not* lead to an increase in total spending in the economy. Thus, it does not affect unemployment.

QUESTION: *Suppose that government spends an extra $2 million and consumers and businesses spend less—but not $2 million less. What then?*

ANSWER: *This is an example of* incomplete crowding out. *Incomplete crowding out occurs when a decrease in private spending only partially offsets an increase in government spending. If this happens, then an increase in government spending does raise the total spending in the economy.*

For example, again suppose that current spending in the economy is $60 million a day— $45 million in private spending and $15 million in

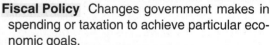

MINI GLOSSARY

Fiscal Policy Changes government makes in spending or taxation to achieve particular economic goals.

Expansionary Fiscal Policy An increase in government spending or a reduction in taxes.

Contractionary Fiscal Policy A decrease in government spending or an increase in taxes.

Crowding Out Situation in which increases in government spending lead to a reduction in private spending.

vernment spending ($45 million + $15 million = $60 million). Government spending increases to $17 million and as a result, private spending falls, but not by $2 million. Let's say it falls by $1 million. Now private spending is $44 million, government spending is $17 million, and total spending is $61 million ($44 million + $17 million = $61 million); so total spending has increased.

THINKING LIKE AN ECONOMIST

Ask an economist a question, and you are likely to get a conditional answer. For example, suppose you ask an economist if expansionary fiscal policy will bring about more spending in the economy. He might say that it will, given the condition *that complete crowding out doesn't occur. In other words, if complete crowding out occurs, then the expansionary fiscal policy* will not *increase spending in the economy; but if complete crowding out doesn't occur, then expansionary fiscal policy* will *increase spending in the economy. Some people, hearing this conditional answer, may think the economist simply can't give a direct answer. But this is not the case at all. The economist is simply specifying the conditions under which expansionary fiscal policy works and the conditions under which it does not work. Consider a similar situation. We might ask a physician if the medicine she is prescribing for us will make us feel better. She might say that if we are not allergic to the medicine and if we take it in the prescribed dosage, then it will make us feel better; but if we are allergic to the medicine or if we do not take it in the prescribed dosage, then it will not make us feel better. She is specifying the conditions under which the medicine will work. The answers to economic questions are similarly conditional.*

Contractory Fiscal Policy and Inflation

Chapter 13 stated that inflation (increases in the price level) can occur when the aggregate demand in the economy grows faster than the aggregate supply in the economy. Stated differently, inflation is the result of too much spending in the economy relative to the quantity of goods and services available for purchase. Some economists have characterized inflation as "too much money chasing too few goods." Many of these economists argue that the way to get prices down in the economy is to reduce spending. This can be done through contractionary fiscal policy, they say. Here are the points they make:

- Inflation is the result of too much spending in the economy. In other words, if people spent less money, firms would initially sell fewer goods. The firms would end up with a surplus of goods in their warehouses. In order to get rid of their goods, they would have to lower prices.
- To get prices down, Congress should implement contractionary fiscal policy by decreasing government spending, raising taxes, or both. Let's suppose that government cuts its spending.
- As a result of the fall in government spending, there will be less spending in the economy. To illustrate, suppose that at current prices the government is spending $400 billion, business is spending $200 billion, and consumers are spending $800 billion. Total spending at current prices is $1,400 billion ($400 billion + $200 billion + $800 billion = $1,400 billion). Government decides to cut its spending to $350 billion. Now total spending decreases to $1,350 billion ($350 billion + $200 billion + $800 billion = $1,350 billion).
- As a result of the decrease in total spending, firms initially sell fewer goods.
- As a result of selling fewer goods, firms have surplus goods on hand. The inventories in their warehouses and factories are rising above a desired level. To get rid of the unwanted inventory—the surplus goods—firms lower prices.

John Maynard Keynes

John Maynard Keynes is considered one of the greatest economists. He was born in Cambridge, England, on June 5, 1883, and died in Sussex, England, on April 21, 1946. Keynes was educated in England at Cambridge University, where he received a degree in mathematics in 1905. At Cambridge, he studied under the economist Alfred Marshall, whom we discussed in Chapter 4. (It was Marshall, you may remember, who talked about supply and demand being like the two blades of a pair of scissors.)

Keynes's major work in economics is called *The General Theory of Employment, Interest, and Money*, which was published in 1936. This book changed the way many economists thought about the economy. In this book, Keynes argued that too little spending in the economy was the cause of high unemployment.[a] Before Keynes, most economists thought it was impossible for insufficient (too little) spending within an economy to cause a high level of unemployment. They said, if people were initially spending too little, firms would simply lower prices, people would see the lower prices, and start buying more goods. For example, if car manufacturers were selling too few cars, they would lower the price of cars and people would end up buying more cars.

Keynes said that things might not work out this way. Specifically, he argued that even if people weren't spending much money, firms might not lower prices. In other words, the car manufacturer sees that he is not selling many cars, yet he does not lower the price of cars so that he can sell more.

_____

a. We are assuming that there is too little spending at a given price level. In other words, total or aggregate demand in the economy is too low to bring about full employment.

But why wouldn't the car manufacturer lower car prices? Keynes hints that it has to do with the wages the car manufacturer pays to his workers. If workers would take a cut in wages, then the car manufacturer would see his costs go down and he would lower car prices. But if wages don't go down, the car manufacturer might not lower prices. In other words, the car manufacturer is waiting for the wage rates he has to pay his workers to decrease before he will lower prices.

So, why aren't wage rates decreasing? For example, you would think that the car manufacturer could go to the workers and say: "I am not selling many cars. There is a way to sell more cars; I can lower prices. But before I can lower prices, I need to lower my costs. Paying your wages is a large part of my costs. If you would accept lower wages, I can lower car prices, and people will end up buying more cars. If not, I might have to lay off some workers. What do you say?"

According to some economists, Keynes said that the workers would initially say no. They would resist wage cuts. They might think that the car manufacturer was simply trying to pay them less because he wanted to earn higher profits, and that business wasn't really that bad and he had no intentions of lowering car prices very much at all. In other words, the story is simply a ploy to get wages down.

What's left to do? If wages aren't coming down quickly, and sellers are not reducing prices, people may actually be laid off from their jobs because consumers aren't spending enough for full employment to exist. At this point, Keynes argued that what had to be done was to raise total spending in the economy. This goes back to our earlier discussion of expansionary fiscal policy. Simply put, it was up to government to either increase its spending, or lower taxes, so that total spending in the economy would increase.

Critics argue that Keynes's proposal to enact expansionary fiscal policy did not take into account crowding out: if government spends more, consumers and businesses will spend less, and therefore there will be little, if any, change in total spending in the economy. Also, say the critics, Keynes opened the door to government involvement in the economy. They argue that once government was given the responsibility of using expansionary fiscal policy to reduce unemployment, it would abuse its newfound power. Instead of only increasing government spending to reduce unemployment, government would also want to increase government spending to "buy" votes at election time—whether or not there was an unemployment problem.

---

1. Before Keynes, economists thought that it was impossible for too little spending within an economy to cause high unemployment. According to these economists, what happens to turn "too little spending" into more spending?

The Issue of Crowding In

As with expansionary fiscal policies, some economists don't agree that things will turn out the way they are supposed to. They say that if government reduces its spending, total spending in the economy will not necessarily decline. They bring up the issue of **crowding in**, which occurs when decreases in government spending lead to increases in private spending. To illustrate, suppose government decreases its spending on public education by $2 million. As a result, people turn to private education, increasing their purchases of it by $2 million. This dollar-for-dollar tradeoff is referred to as *complete crowding in*. For every dollar decrease in government spending on education, there is a dollar increase in private spending on education. Because of complete crowding in, there is no change in total spending in the economy. Thus, if complete crowding in occurs, a decrease in government expenditures will not lead to a decrease in total spending in the economy, and so it will not bring prices down. (See Exhibit 14-2.)

Enterprise Zones: Beyond Fiscal and Monetary Policy

In recent years, *enterprise zones* have been proposed as a way to reduce unemployment. An enterprise zone is an area specified to receive tax and regulatory relief. To illustrate, suppose that the unemployment rate is extremely high in a certain city. Furthermore, suppose the federal government would like to reduce the unemployment rate in that city. The government, therefore, designates the city an enterprise zone. It specifies, for example, that any business firm that locates in the city and hires local workers will not have to pay taxes for, say, five years. Furthermore the firm will not need to abide by certain regulations. The idea behind an enterprise zone is to give businesses an incentive to locate in a certain area and stimulate economic activity in order to alleviate the problem of unemployment and associated problems.

MINI GLOSSARY

Crowding In Situation in which decreases in government spending lead to an increase in private spending.

(a)

Objective	Policy	Condition existing	Does the policy affect total spending in the economy?	Does the policy meet the objective (as stated in the first column)?
Reduce unemployment	Expansionary fiscal policy (as measured by an increase in government spending)	No crowding out	Yes	Yes
Reduce unemployment	Same as above	Complete crowding out	No	No
Reduce unemployment	Same as above	Incomplete crowding out	Yes	Yes

(b)

Objective	Policy	Condition existing	Does the policy affect total spending in the economy?	Does the policy meet the objective (as stated in the first column)?
Reduce inflation	Contractionary fiscal policy (as measured by a decrease in government spending)	No crowding in	Yes	Yes
Reduce inflation	Same as above	Complete crowding in	No	No
Reduce inflation	Same as above	Incomplete crowding in	Yes	Yes

▲ **EXHIBIT 14-2. The Effectiveness of Fiscal Policy.** Part *a:* If crowding out is complete, expansionary fiscal policy is not effective at reducing unemployment. If crowding out doesn't occur or is incomplete, expansionary fiscal policy is effective at reducing unemployment. Part *b:* If crowding in is complete, contractionary fiscal policy is not effective at reducing inflation. If crowding in doesn't occur or is incomplete, contractionary fiscal policy is effective at reducing inflation. (If crowding in is incomplete this means for every dollar decrease in government spending, there is less than a dollar, but more than $0.00, increase in private spending.) The conclusion: Fiscal policy does not work under all conditions; it works only under some.

☑ LEARNING CHECK

1. What is expansionary fiscal policy, and for what purpose is it likely to be implemented?
2. What is contractionary fiscal policy, and for what purpose is it likely to be implemented?
3. Give a numerical example of complete crowding out.
4. Give a numerical example of incomplete crowding out.

SECTION 2   MONETARY POLICY

The preceding section described how government uses fiscal policy to try to reduce unemployment and inflation. This section discusses monetary policy. Remember from Chapter 11 that monetary policy deals with how government changes the money supply. Monetary policy is implemented by the Federal Reserve.

As you read, keep these key questions in mind:

■ What type of monetary policy is used to reduce unemployment?
■ What type of monetary policy is used to reduce inflation?
■ How does monetary policy reduce unemployment and inflation?

Types of Monetary Policy

If the Fed increases the money supply, it is implementing **expansionary monetary policy**. Its objective is to increase total spending in the economy and reduce the unemployment rate. If the Fed decreases the money supply, it is implementing **contractionary monetary policy**. Its objective is to contract total spending in the economy and reduce the price level (reduce inflation).

By MAL, Associated Features, Inc.

Expansionary Monetary Policy and Unemployment

Here is how many economists believe expansionary monetary policy works to lower the unemployment rate:

■ The Fed increases the money supply.
■ A greater money supply is usually associated with greater total spending in the economy. (There is more money to spend.)
■ As a result of increased spending in the economy, firms will begin to sell more products.
■ As firms sell more products, they will hire more workers. This will lower the unemployment rate.

The issue of crowding out does not arise when it comes to monetary policy. Consider why. When the federal government (acting through the U.S. Congress) spends more, it is altogether possible that some other sector of the economy will spend less. This is particularly so if government raises taxes in order to be able to spend more. For example, suppose it increases taxes by $40 million so that it can spend the $40 million. Out of the pockets of some, into the pockets of others. With monetary policy, this need not happen. If the Fed increases the money supply, no one need spend less. There is simply more money to spend.

Since crowding out is not an issue with expansionary monetary policy, many economists argue that an increase in the money supply will increase total spending in the economy and therefore indirectly lower the unemployment rate.

MINI GLOSSARY

Expansionary Monetary Policy An increase in the money supply.
Contractionary Monetary Policy A decrease in the money supply.

ANALYZING PRIMARY SOURCES

Monetary and Fiscal Policies

In this chapter we have discussed both monetary and fiscal policies. All economists do not agree that monetary and fiscal policies are equally effective. For example, some economists believe that expansionary fiscal policy can be effective at lowering unemployment and contractionary fiscal policy can be effective at reducing inflation, whereas other economists do not believe fiscal policy can do either. There are similar differences of opinion when it comes to monetary policy. In this section, we present a few of the diverse views on the effectiveness of monetary and fiscal policies.

James Tobin, Economist

"Monetary policy is the subject of a lively controversy between two schools of economics, monetarist and Keynesian. Although they agree on goals, they disagree sharply on priorities, strategies, targets, and tactics. . . .

Here is the crucial issue: Expansionary monetary policy, all agree, increases aggregate spending on goods and services—by consumers, businesses, governments, and foreigners. Will these new demands raise output and employment? Or will they just raise prices and speed up inflation?

Keynesians say the answers depend on circumstances. Full employment means that everyone (allowing for persons between jobs) who is productive enough to be worth the prevailing real wage and wants a job at that wage is employed. In these circumstances more spending just brings inflation. Frequently, however, qualified, willing workers are involuntarily unemployed; there is no demand for the products they would produce. More spending will put them to work. Competition from firms with excess capacity and from idle workers will keep extra spending from igniting inflation.

Monetarists answer that nature's remedy for excess supply in any market is price reduction. If

wages do not adjust to unemployment, either government and union regulations are keeping them artificially high or the jobless prefer leisure and/or unemployment compensation to work. Either way, the problem is not remediable by monetary policy. Injections of new spending would be futile and inflationary. **"** [a]

Economic Report of the President, 1993

"The Keynesian view [the activist approach], which reached its peak of influence in the 1960s, advocated government spending increases and tax cuts, supported by expansionary monetary policy, to stimulate overall demand whenever output fell below the economy's estimated capacity to produce. More restrictive policies were advocated when inflation became a greater concern. Many economists believed that a stable tradeoff existed between unemployment and inflation rates: Expansionary policies would lower unemployment at the cost of somewhat higher— but not continually rising—inflation. It was believed that 'activist' or 'fine-tuning' policies could increase demand whenever the economy was below capacity, reducing business cycle fluctuations and at the same time increasing the long-term growth in the economy's capacity. Such policies frequently changed course in response to short-term economic developments.

The foundation of the activist approach was discredited by the historical experience of the 1960s and 1970s. Output grew rapidly in the 1960s, but inflation, as measured by the rate of change in the consumer price index, rose from 0.7 percent during 1961 to 6.2 percent during

---

a.   Reprinted by permission of Warner Books, Inc. From *The Fortune Encyclopedia of Economics.* Copyright © 1993 by Time Inc.

ANALYZING PRIMARY SOURCES (continued)

1969. In the 1970s the economy experienced many difficulties, including large simultaneous increases in both inflation and unemployment. This development contradicted the idea that a stable tradeoff existed between inflation and unemployment and led to a rethinking of the efficacy of fine-tuning [continually using fiscal and monetary policy to stabilize the economy]. **"** [b]

Milton Friedman, Economist

"Inflation occurs when the quantity of money rises appreciably more rapidly than output, and the more rapid the rise in the quantity of money per unit of output, the greater the rate of inflation. There is probably no other proposition in economics that is as well established as this one. **"** [c]

Alan Blinder, Economist

"Monetarists accused Keynesians of falsely advertising the efficacy of fiscal policy, keeping insufficient faith in the free market, fostering inflationary expectations, and ignoring the most important economic variable in the world—the money supply. But events in the Reagan years have shown graphically that fiscal policy does indeed work more or less as Keynesian theory says: a strong fiscal stimulus gave the economy a boost. **"** [d]

---

b.   *Economic Report of the President, 1993* (Washington, D.C.: United States Government Printing Office, 1993), pp. 77–78.

c.   Milton Friedman, *Monetary Mischief* (New York: Harcourt Brace Jovanovich, 1992), p. 193.

d.   Alan Blinder, *Hard Heads, Soft Hearts: Tough-Minded Economics for a Just Society* (Reading, Mass.: Addison-Wesley Publishing Company, Inc., 1987), p. 105.

A Federal Reserve Publication

"The basic goal of monetary policy . . . is to ensure that, over time, expansion in money and credit will be adequate for the long-run needs of a growing economy at reasonably stable prices. Over the shorter run, monetary policy is also conducted so as to combat cyclical inflationary or deflationary pressures [high inflation and high unemployment].

Monetary policy is far from the only influence on the economy. Fiscal policy—that is, the policy of the federal government with respect to taxation and spending—has an important impact on demands for goods and services and on credit market conditions. . . . **"** [e]

Jude Wanniski, Journalist, Consultant

"In special circumstances, the government can actually benefit the economy by inflating [increasing] the money supply. But when this occurs, it is invariably by accident rather than by design. The government, remember, has two instruments by which it influences the national economy. By monetary policy, it can increase, decrease, or hold constant the money supply. By fiscal policy, it can increase or decrease the wedge between commercial transactions—making it easier or more difficult for Smith and Jones to trade their labor in the money economy. What effect does a change in the monetary instrument have on fiscal policy? The answer depends on what kinds of taxes the government has levied. **"** [f]

---

e.   *The Federal Reserve System: Purposes and Functions* (Washington, D.C.: Board of Governors of the Federal Reserve System, 1984), p. 13.

f.   Jude Wanniski, *The Way The World Works* (New York: Simon & Schuster, 1978), p.113.

ANALYZING PRIMARY SOURCES (continued)

Charles Freedman, Deputy Governor, The Bank of Canada

"The underlying goal of monetary policy is price stability. **"** [g]

James Q. Wilson, Political Scientist

"The most important part of the economic policy-making machinery, of course, is Congress. It must approve all taxes and almost all expenditures; there can be no wage or price controls without its consent; and it has the ability to alter the policy of the nominally independent Federal Reserve Board by threatening to pass laws that would reduce its powers. And Congress itself is fragmented, with great influence wielded by the members of key committees, especially the House and Senate Budget Committees, the House and Senate Appropriations Committees, the House Ways and Means Committee, and the Senate Finance Committee. **"** [h]

1. According to James Tobin, economists who consider themselves members of the Keynesian school of economics, and economists who consider themselves members of the monetarist school of economics, do not always agree as to the effect of expansionary monetary policy (an

increase in the money supply) on prices. Do you agree or disagree with this statement? Explain your answer.

2. According to the *Economic Report of the President*, what kinds of fiscal and monetary policies do Keynesian economists support when the economy's output is below its potential output (its "estimated capacity to produce")? According to the *Economic Report of the President*, do these Keynesian prescriptions work? Explain your answer.

3. Do you think Alan Blinder would agree with the words in the last sentence of the *Economic Report of the President*? Explain your answer.

4. According to Milton Friedman, expansionary monetary policy could lead to inflation if what condition holds?

5. According to the Federal Reserve publication, is fiscal policy effective in controlling the overall level of spending in an economy? Explain your answer. Is there anything in the words of the Federal Reserve publication that would lead you to believe that crowding out exists? Explain your answer.

6. According to Jude Wanniski, are there always benefits to the economy if the Fed increases the money supply? Explain your answer.

7. Do you think Charles Freedman believes monetary policy should be used to try to increase real GDP and lower interest rates? Explain your answer.

8. According to James Q. Wilson, does the Congress have any influence over the Fed? Explain your answer.

g. Charles Freedman, "Monetary Policy in the 1990s," *Monetary Policy Issues in the 1990s* (Kansas City: Federal Reserve Bank of Kansas City, 1989), p. 39.
h. James Q. Wilson, *American Government* (Lexington, Mass.: D.C. Heath and Company, 1992), p. 461.

Objective	Policy	Does the policy affect total spending in the economy?	Does the policy meet the objective (as stated in the first column)?
Reduce unemployment	Expansionary monetary policy	Yes	Yes
Reduce inflation	Contractionary monetary policy	Yes	Yes

▲ **EXHIBIT 14-3. The Effectiveness of Monetary Policy.** Expansionary monetary policy is used to reduce unemployment; contractionary monetary policy is used to reduce inflation.

Contractionary Monetary Policy and Inflation

Here is how many economists believe contractionary monetary policy works to reduce inflation:

- The Fed decreases the money supply, say, by conducting an open-market sale. (Open-market sales are discussed in Chapter 11.)
- A smaller money supply is usually associated with lower total spending in the economy. (There is less money to spend.)
- As a result of the decrease in spending in the economy, firms begin to sell less.
- As firms sell fewer products, their inventories rise. (If a firm doesn't sell as many goods, the inventory in the warehouse rises.) In order to get rid of surplus goods, firms reduce prices.

See Exhibit 14-3 for a summary of expansionary and contractionary monetary policies.

LEARNING CHECK

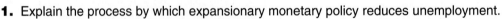

1. Explain the process by which expansionary monetary policy reduces unemployment.
2. Explain the process by which contractionary monetary policy reduces inflation.
3. Which is likely to be more effective at reducing unemployment and inflation, fiscal policy or monetary policy? Explain your answer.
4. Who conducts monetary policy in the United States?

SECTION 3 STAGFLATION: THE TWIN MALADIES APPEAR TOGETHER

So far, we have talked about inflation and unemployment. Always, below the surface of the discussion, was the implicit assumption that the economy experienced *either* inflation *or* high unemployment, but never both at the same time.

Unfortunately, though, real-world economies sometimes do experience inflation and high unemployment at the same time. When they do, they are said to be experiencing **stagflation**. In the late 1970s and early 1980s in this country, stagflation was a major economic problem. We consider stagflation in this section.

As you read, keep these key questions in mind:

- When the money supply rises, why does the output of goods and services rise before prices?
- When the money supply falls, why does the output of goods and services fall before prices?
- What causes stagflation?
- What is the solution to stagflation?

Rising Unemployment and Inflation

For many years, economists believed that the economy would experience either high inflation or high unemployment, but not both at the same time. Moreover, they believed that inflation and unemployment moved in opposite directions. As the inflation rate increased, the unemployment rate decreased; and as the inflation rate decreased, the unemployment rate increased. Inflation and unemployment were on opposite ends of a seesaw.

There was good reason for economists to believe this. Actual, real-world data appeared to support it. For example, for much of the 1960s, inflation and unemployment moved in opposite directions. But then, in the 1970s, the inflation-unemployment tradeoff disappeared for a few years. Instead of moving in opposite directions, inflation and unemployment began to move in the same direction. Specifically, they both began to increase. The economy began to experience high inflation and high unemployment; it began to experience stagflation.

Stagflation was also a concern for other nations, as shown in Exhibit 14-4. For example, in Canada

MINI GLOSSARY

Stagflation The occurrence of inflation and high unemployment at the same time.

Nation	Years	Average annual inflation rate (%)	Average annual unemployment rate (%)
Canada	1963–1973	4.6%	4.8%
Canada	1974–1979	9.2%	7.2%
France	1963–1973	4.7%	2.0%
France	1974–1979	10.7%	4.5%
Italy	1963–1973	4.0%	5.2%
Italy	1974–1979	16.1%	6.6%
Japan	1963–1973	6.2%	1.2%
Japan	1974–1979	10.2%	1.9%
United Kingdom	1963–1973	5.3%	3.0%
United Kingdom	1974–1979	15.7%	5.3%
U. S. A.	1963–1973	3.6%	0.8%
U. S. A.	1974–1979	4.7%	3.2%

▲ **EXHIBIT 14-4. Evidence of Stagflation.** The nations listed in the exhibit experienced stagflation—as evidenced by higher inflation rates *and* higher unemployment rates—in the 1970s. Notice that the inflation rate and the unemployment rate are higher in the later period (1974–1979) than in the earlier period (1963–1973). This is stagflation at work.

▲ Stagflation was a major economic problem for former President Jimmy Carter when both inflation and unemployment rates increased.

during the period 1963–1973, the average annual inflation rate was 4.6 percent and the average annual unemployment rate was 4.8 percent. Then, during the 1974–1979 period, both inflation and unemployment increased. The average annual inflation rate rose to 9.2 percent and the average annual unemployment rate rose to 7.2 percent. The same thing that was happening in Canada and the United States was also happening in France, Italy, Japan, and the United Kingdom.

How Money Changes Affect the Economy: Output First, Prices Second

Some economists believe that stagflation is the result of a stop-and-go, on-and-off monetary policy. Before we examine their position, though, it is important that we look at the sequence of effects monetary policy has on the economy.

Most economists agree that changes in the money supply affect both the output of goods and services and prices, but that output is affected before prices. For example, suppose the Fed increases the money supply. This increases total spending in the economy. As a result, firms sell more goods. Consequently, they begin to hire more laborers and produce more output. It is only later that prices rise.

Why does output rise before prices? Because when firms begin to sell more, they do not know at first whether this increase is a temporary or a permanent state of affairs. Thinking it may be temporary ("It was a good sales week, but next week may not be so good"), they do not yet want to change prices. Why? Because if they raise prices, and later learn that the higher sales were only a quirk, they may become less competitive.

Consider Bill, who owns a pizza restaurant. In an average week, he sells 400 pizzas at an average price of $6. This week, he sells 550 pizzas. Bill doesn't know why he did so well this week. He doesn't know if people are getting tired of hamburgers, or if people are getting tired of eating at home, or if the Fed raised the money supply and increased total spending.

Bill could immediately raise the price of his pizzas from $6 to, say, $8; but suppose his higher-than-average sales don't last. If this week's higher sales represent only a temporary state of affairs, and he raises his price to $8 (while his competitors keep their prices the same), Bill may hurt his business. It is one thing to raise prices when you are sure the demand for your product has increased; it is another thing to raise prices when you are not sure what has happened. Bill is therefore likely to be cautious and take a wait-and-see attitude. If sales continue at 550 a week, then maybe after a few weeks he will raise the price. But if sales drop back to 400 a week, he will keep the price as it is. We conclude that, given an increase in the money supply, output is likely to go up before prices do.

Now, let's consider a decrease in the money supply. Does it follow that output will be affected before price? Again, the answer is yes. To illustrate, suppose that instead of selling his average of 400 pizzas this week, Bill sells only 250 pizzas. He doesn't know why sales are lower than aver-

CONSUMER ECONOMIC DECISIONS

Fiscal and Monetary Policies and Your Employment

This chapter discussed the federal government's use of fiscal and monetary policy to decrease unemployment and inflation. As you might expect, the federal government doesn't simply apply one type of economic policy—such as contractionary fiscal policy—month after month, year after year. Instead, it often moves from one type of economic policy to another, depending on economic circumstances. For example, it might institute expansionary fiscal policy one year and contractionary monetary policy the next. These policies are not without their effects—some of which can touch your life.

To illustrate, suppose Frank is working at a clothing store as a salesman. Currently, the store is busy, and he is earning a reasonable monthly income. On the national economic front, though, the inflation rate is rising rapidly. The Fed decides to reduce the money supply. This is contractionary monetary policy. Time passes. The contractionary monetary policy reduces the amount of money consumers have to buy goods and services. Frank notices that there is not as much customer activity in the clothing store. The manager of the store decides to run a few sales to try to stimulate business. The sales do stimulate buying, but only a little.

Finally, one day the manager comes to Frank and tells him that she is sorry, but she has to let him go. The manager says that business has been so bad recently that she has to lay off some salespersons. She wishes Frank good luck and sends him on his way.

Would Frank have been any better off if he had known about the effects of contractionary monetary policy? Probably not. Knowing about something doesn't guarantee us that we won't be affected by it. What Frank can learn from his current situation, though, is that not all jobs are as responsive to changes in economic policy as his job turned out to be. Some jobs are more unresponsive to economic policy changes, of the fiscal or monetary variety, than others. For example, construction workers are more likely to lose their jobs as a result of contractionary monetary policy—which decreases spending in the economy—than public-school teachers. The reason: With less money in the economy, people might put off buying or remodeling a house, but they don't stop sending their children to school. In short, the demand for construction workers may decrease, but the demand for schoolteachers probably will not.

What does this information say to you? It should say that when you get a full-time job, you may want to make sure your job is not highly sensitive to the sometimes harsh winds of economic change. When interviewing for a job, you may consider asking this question: What percentage of the work force at this company or institution has been laid off in the last 5 to 10 years? The answer will give you some idea of how permanent this job is likely to be.

---

1. List five jobs you think would be highly responsive to contractionary monetary policy. Explain your answer.

2. List five jobs you think would be highly unresponsive to contractionary monetary policy. Explain your answer.

▲ A change in the money supply is likely to affect output (production) before it affects prices.

age; he just knows they are. He reduces his output of pizzas and perhaps cuts back on overtime for his employees. He doesn't immediately reduce the price, though, because he can't be sure if the lower-than-average sales will continue. He doesn't want to lower the price until he is sure that the demand for his good has fallen. We conclude that, given a decrease in the money supply, output is likely to go down before prices do.

What Causes Stagflation?

As we said earlier, some economists believe stagflation is caused by a **stop-and-go, on-and-off monetary policy**. Here is how they describe what happens:

■ The Fed increases the money supply. It pushes the monetary accelerator to the floor. This first raises output and then, later, raises prices.

■ Time passes. The increased money supply has raised the price level—that is, it has caused inflation.

■ At the same time people are dealing with the high inflation, the Fed contracts the money supply. It presses on the monetary brake. As a result, output is affected first; it falls. Since less output is being produced, fewer people are required to work in the factories, and so on. Unemployment rises.

Notice what is occurring in the economy. There is inflation coupled with a cutback in output and an increase in unemployment. The previous monetary policy (money supply up) caused the high inflation, and the current monetary policy (money supply down) caused the high unemployment. The economy is experiencing the effects of *both* monetary policies. It is experiencing *stagflation*.

Not all economists agree that this is the cause, or only cause of stagflation. Some economists maintain that a marked decrease in aggregate supply (perhaps due to a fall in the market supply of a major resource, such as oil) can also cause stagflation.

MINI GLOSSARY
Stop-and-Go, On-and-Off Monetary Policy Erratic monetary policy. The money supply is increased, then decreased, then increased, and so on. It is similar to driving a car by putting the accelerator to the floor, then slamming on the brakes, then putting the accelerator to the floor, then slamming on the brakes again, and so on.

 LEARNING CHECK

1. What is stagflation?
2. When the money supply rises, output rises before prices. Why?
3. What causes stagflation? Explain in detail.

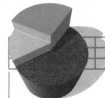

DEVELOPING ECONOMIC SKILLS

Understanding Economists in the News

Economists are sometimes interviewed on news shows. For example, an economist might be asked on a nightly news show whether she thinks the inflation rate will rise, unemployment will go down, or the budget deficit will grow larger or get smaller. Upon completion of this text, you should have a good idea of what economists are talking about when they answer the questions they are asked. However, sometimes economists use key phrases that may be difficult to understand without an explanation. We present a few of these phrases, along with their explanations, in this feature.

■ "After all, there is such a thing as a boom-and-bust cycle." When an economist says this, he is referring to the business cycle, discussed in Chapter 12. As you may remember, the business cycle relates to swings (up and down) in real GDP. The "boom" in the economist's statement refers to an upswing in real GDP. Real GDP is increasing. The "bust" refers to a downswing in real GDP. Real GDP is decreasing.
■ "The money stock increased by 11 percent last year." The money stock is simply a synonym for the money supply.
■ "The bond market likes what is going on in Washington." Washington refers to the president of the United States and the Congress. The phrase "what is going on" refers to what is being done in the area of economic policy. When the bond market "likes" something, there are a lot of people buying bonds. The price of bonds is rising, as a result.
■ "The stock market likes what is going on in Washington." The explanation here is the same as it is for the previous statement concerning bond markets—with the exception

that we are talking about the stock market instead of the bond market.
■ "Fiscal policy is tight." This is a reference to contractionary fiscal policy.
■ "Fiscal policy is loose." This is a reference to expansionary fiscal policy.
■ "Monetary policy is tight." This is a reference to contractionary monetary policy.
■ "Monetary policy is loose." This is a reference to expansionary monetary policy.
■ "The administration is leaning on the Fed." The administration is a reference to the president's administration. It usually consists of the president, his economic advisors, and the Secretary of the Treasury. When the administration is leaning on the Fed, it is trying to get the Fed to increase the money supply—usually at a higher rate. For example, the Fed may have been increasing the money supply at a rate of 3 percent a year. The administration may prefer the money supply to increase by 7 percent. The people on whom the administration usually leans are the Board of Governors, especially the chairperson of that group.
■ "The Fed is pumping the money supply." This means increasing the money supply at a relatively high rate.

---

1. What does it mean if monetary policy is loose?
2. To what does "boom and bust" refer?
3. What does it mean to say the stock market likes what is going on in Washington?
4. What is another term for the money supply?

CHAPTER 14 REVIEW

CHAPTER SUMMARY

1. Fiscal policy refers to changes government makes in spending or taxation to achieve particular economic goals. If government spending is increased or taxes are reduced (or both), government is said to be implementing expansionary fiscal policy. If government spending is decreased or taxes are raised (or both), government is said to be implementing contractionary fiscal policy.

2. If government wants to reduce the unemployment rate, it may implement expansionary fiscal policy. Expansionary fiscal policy will be effective at reducing the unemployment rate if there is no crowding out or if crowding out is incomplete. Expansionary fiscal policy will be ineffective at reducing the unemployment rate if there is complete crowding out.

3. If government wants to reduce inflation, it may implement contractionary fiscal policy. Contractionary fiscal policy will be effective at re-

ducing the inflation rate if there is no crowding in or if crowding in is incomplete.

4. Monetary policy deals with how government changes the money supply to meet particular economic goals. Monetary policy is implemented by the Federal Reserve. If the Fed increases the money supply, it is implementing expansionary monetary policy. If it decreases the money supply, it is implementing contractionary monetary policy.

5. Expansionary monetary policy is used to reduce the unemployment rate; contractionary monetary policy is used to reduce inflation.

6. Most economists agree that changes in the money supply affect both output and prices but that output is affected first.

7. Stagflation is the simultaneous occurrence of inflation and unemployment. Some economists believe stagflation is caused by a stop-and-go, on-and-off monetary policy.

BUILD YOUR ECONOMIC VOCABULARY

1. expansionary fiscal policy
2. contractionary fiscal policy
3. complete crowding out
4. incomplete crowding out
5. complete crowding in
6. incomplete crowding in
7. expansionary monetary policy
8. contractionary monetary policy
9. stagflation

a. government spending increases by $1, and private spending decreases by $1

b. government spending decreases by $1, and private spending increases by $1

c. government spending increases by $1, and private spending decreases by 50 cents

d. government spending decreases by $1, and private spending increases by 50 cents

e. an increase in government spending or a decrease in taxes

f. an increase in the money supply

g. a decrease in the money supply

h. a decrease in government spending or an increase in taxes

i. the simultaneous occurrence of high inflation and high unemployment

REVIEW QUESTIONS

1. "If the official unemployment rate is above the natural unemployment rate, expansionary fiscal policy will always reduce it." Do you agree or disagree? Explain your answer.
2. Describe the process by which expansionary fiscal policy reduces the unemployment rate. (Assume there is no crowding out.)
3. Explain how complete crowding in affects contractionary fiscal policy.
4. Explain the process by which expansionary monetary policy reduces the unemployment rate.
5. Explain the process by which contractionary monetary policy reduces inflation.
6. Explain why expansionary monetary policy is probably not a solution to stagflation.
7. Rosa, who owns a hotel, has rented out a higher-than-average number of rooms this week. Why is she likely to wait awhile before she raises the room rent?
8. In general, what is the cause of stagflation? Specifically, what causes the inflation part of stagflation? What causes the unemployment part of stagflation?

SHARPEN YOUR CRITICAL THINKING SKILLS

1. In this chapter we have described how fiscal policy may affect total spending in the economy. Some economists suggest that fiscal policy may also affect the amount of work people are willing to perform and the quantity of goods they produce. How do you think a reduction in income tax rates (expansionary fiscal policy) would affect people's incentives to work and produce goods?

ACTIVITIES AND PROJECTS

1. Read your local newspaper for one week. Write out the paragraph in which any of the following words are mentioned: monetary policy, fiscal policy, money supply, taxes, government spending (or government expenditures). After each paragraph, explain what is being said in the paragraph.

ECONOMIC DICTIONARY

Contractionary Fiscal Policy (Pg. 354)
Contractionary Monetary Policy (Pg. 360)
Crowding In (Pg. 358)
Crowding Out (Pg. 355)
Expansionary Fiscal Policy (Pg. 354)

Expansionary Monetary Policy (Pg. 360)
Fiscal Policy (Pg. 354)
Stagflation (Pg. 364)
Stop-and-Go, On-and-Off Monetary Policy (Pg. 368)

Taxes, Deficits, and Debt

INTRODUCTION

In recent years, perhaps no economic topics have been discussed as much as the federal budget deficit and the national debt. The budget deficit, you may recall, exists because government expenditures are greater than tax revenues. The government has to borrow money, resulting in a national debt.

Should you be concerned about deficits and debt? It would certainly seem so, since deficits and debt will affect your standard of living in the years to come.

To illustrate, consider this story. Mr. and Mrs. Smith want to buy more things than they can afford. To do this, they obtain a credit card and use it to buy many goods and services. One day, the credit card bill arrives at their house. They notice that they owe a lot

of money, but instead of paying off the entire bill, they decide to make low monthly payments. Eventually, the Smiths die, and you move into their house. You walk out to the mailbox one Saturday morning, and there you find a credit card bill. It has your name on it. You say, "But wait a minute, I didn't buy all these things. There must be a mistake." But there is no mistake. What you owe on the credit card bill was put there by the Smiths years ago. Now they are dead, and you have to pay off the bill that they ran up.

This story describes a situation much like the one that exists today in regard to deficits and debt. The Smiths' spending represents the federal deficit. Their borrowing on credit represents the national debt. Sadly, the bill is headed straight for you.

AFTER YOU STUDY THIS CHAPTER, YOU WILL BE ABLE TO:

1. Explain the difference between the benefits-received principle and the ability-to-pay principle.
2. Discuss how proportional, progressive, and regressive income taxation differ.
3. Explain the budget process.
4. Explain how the national debt relates to future generations.
5. Explain the relationship between budget deficits and the national debt.

KEY TERMS

National Debt

Progressive
   Income Tax

Proportional
   Income Tax

Regressive
   Income Tax

This section discusses taxes in general and the federal income tax in particular. It also discusses two principles of taxation.

As you read, keep these key questions in mind:

■ What types of taxes exist?
■ How do progressive, proportional, and regressive income taxation differ?

Types of Taxes

Taxes come in a wide variety. We briefly consider a few here.

Personal Income Tax. The personal income tax is the tax a person pays on his or her income. There is a federal personal income tax, applied by the federal government, and many (but not all) states have a personal income tax. At the federal government level, the personal income tax raised $476 billion in 1992. This accounted for approximately 44 percent of total federal tax revenue in 1992. In other words, for every one dollar the federal government received in taxes in 1992, 44 cents of that dollar came from the personal income tax. See Exhibit 15-1.

Corporate Income Tax. The tax corporations pay on their profits is the corporate income tax. The federal government applies a corporate income tax and so do many states. At the federal government level, the corporate income tax raised $100 billion in 1992. This was 10 percent of the total federal tax revenue in 1992.

Excise Tax. Excise taxes are taxes placed on the purchase of certain goods. For example, there are excise taxes on tobacco products and gasoline, to name two products. Every time a person buys a gallon of gasoline at the local gas station, he or she pays an excise tax on gasoline. The federal government applies excise taxes, as do many states. At the federal level, excise taxes raised approximately $45 billion in 1992. This was 4.1 percent of the total federal tax revenue in 1992.

Social Security Tax. The Social Security tax is a federal government tax placed on income generated from employment. Half of the tax is placed on the employer, and half is placed on the employee. In 1992, at the federal government level, the Social Security tax raised approximately $413 billion. This was 38 percent of the total federal tax revenue in 1992.

Sales Tax. Whereas excise taxes are applied to the purchase of a few goods, sales taxes are applied to the purchase of a broad range of goods—cars, computers, clothes, books, and so on—when they are purchased. State governments typically raise tax revenue through sales taxes. There is no federal (national) sales tax.

▲ Some people wait until the April 15 deadline before filing their income tax returns.

| Personal income tax | Corporate income tax | Social Security tax | Other taxes |

▲ **EXHIBIT 15-1. Where the Money Comes From.** For each dollar the federal government raises from taxes, 44 percent comes from the personal income tax, 10 percent comes from the corporate income tax, 38 percent comes from the Social Security tax, and 8 percent comes from other federal taxes. (These percentages are for 1992.) SOURCE: *Budget of the U.S. Government FY 1994* (Washington D.C.: Office of Management and Budget), 1993.

Property Tax.   Property tax is a tax on the value of property (such as a home). It is a major revenue raiser for state and local governments.

Taxes and Work

Individuals pay an assortment of taxes, as we have briefly discussed. For example, a few of the taxes they pay include personal income taxes and Social Security taxes to the federal government, sales taxes to the state, and property taxes to the local government. Did you ever wonder how many days each year the average person has to work to pay all his or her taxes? Let's look at the situation for 1993. It was calculated that if a person began work on January 1, 1993, he or she would have to work until May 3, 1993 before earning enough to pay all taxes owed. In 1929, a taxpayer only had to work from January 1 to February 9 to pay all taxes; in 1960, he or she had to work from January 1 to April 16; and in 1970, from January 1 to April 26.

Where Does the Money Go?

In 1992, the federal government collected approximately $1,091 billion through taxes and fees. Approximately 92 percent of this money came from federal income taxes, federal corporate income taxes, and Social Security taxes. In 1992, the federal government spent approximately $1,381 billion. How was this money spent? The federal government breaks down its spending according to categories. We briefly discuss a few of the major categories.

National Defense.   In 1992, the federal government spent $298 billion on national defense. This was 21.6 percent of total federal government spending in that year. In other words, out of every dollar the federal government spent in 1992, 21.6 cents went to national defense. This money largely goes to pay the men and women who are in the armed services and to buy and maintain military weapons.

◄ In 1992, 21.6 percent of total federal government spending went for national defense. In other words, out of every dollar the federal government spent in 1992, 21.6 cents went to national defense.

Income Security. In 1992, the federal government spent $198 billion on income security. This was about 14.3 percent of total federal government spending. Income security refers to government programs such as housing assistance, food and nutrition assistance for the poor, unemployment compensation (for those persons who have lost their jobs), and federal employee retirement and disability payments.

Health. In 1992, the federal government spent $89 billion on health care, exclusive of Medicare (discussed next) and hospital and medical care for veterans. This was 6.4 percent of total federal government spending. Some of this money went for health care research, but the bulk of it went for health care services.

Medicare. In 1992, the federal government spent $119 billion on Medicare, which is hospital and medical insurance for Social Security beneficiaries aged 65 and over. This was 8.6 percent of total federal government spending.

Social Security. In 1992, the federal government spent $287 billion on Social Security pay-

ments, which largely go to retired persons. This was 20.8 percent of total federal government spending.

Education, Training, Employment, and Social Services. In 1992, the federal government spent $45 billion in this category. This was about 3.3 percent of total federal government spending. Most of this money went for elementary, secondary, and higher (college and university) education.

Net Interest on the National Debt. This category requires some explanation. When the government spends more money than it receives in tax revenues, it is said to run a budget deficit. For example, if the government spends $1,200 billion and its tax revenues are $1,000 billion, the budget deficit is $200 billion. It has to borrow the $200 billion, in much the same way that a person would have to borrow money if his expenditures were greater than his income. The federal government has borrowed much money over the years; in 1992, its total debt—referred to as the **national debt**—was $4,002.7 billion. The federal government has to pay interest on this debt, in much the same way that a person would have to make an interest payment on his or her general credit card bill (such as Visa or MasterCard). In 1992, this interest payment the government had to make on the national debt was approximately $200 billion. This was 14.5 percent of total federal government spending. See Exhibit 15-2.

The National Debt in Perspective

In recent years, the high interest payments on the national debt have received much attention. Two hundred billion dollars is an extraordinary amount of money to pay out in interest payments. We get some idea of this by comparing the interest payments on the national debt to the amount of money spent on other things. For example, while in 1992 the federal government spent $200 billion

in interest payments on the debt, it spent $23 billion on education (elementary, secondary, vocational, and higher education), approximately $19 billion on housing assistance for the poor, $32 billion for food and nutrition assistance for the poor, $77 billion on health care services (unrelated to Medicare), and $14 billion on the administration of justice (including the court system, federal law enforcement, and so on).

In fact, one way to look at this is to ask what could have been done with $200 billion if it didn't have to go for interest on the national debt. Consider that in the early 1990s, there were approxi-

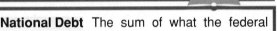

MINI GLOSSARY

National Debt The sum of what the federal government owes its creditors.

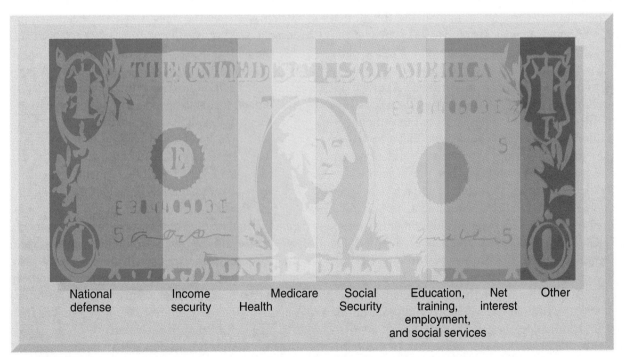

| National defense | Income security | Medicare Health | Social Security | Education, training, employment, and social services | Net interest | Other |

▲ **EXHIBIT 15-2. Where the Money Goes.** For each dollar the federal government spends, 21.6 percent goes for national defense, 14.3 percent for income security, 6.4 percent for health, 8.6 percent for Medicare, 20.8 percent for Social Security benefits, 3.3 percent for education, training, employment, and social services, 14.5 percent for net interest, and 10.5 percent for other things (such as the court system, agricultural programs, transportation, veterans' benefits, and so on).
SOURCE: *Economic Report of the President, 1993* (Washington, D.C.: U.S. Government Printing Office, 1993).

mately 36 million people in the United States who were living in poverty. At that time, a person was said to be living in poverty if he or she had less than approximately $6,300 a year to buy the necessities of life. Now, suppose the interest payment on the debt for 1992 ($200 billion) were added to the federal money going to housing assistance for the poor ($19 billion) and food and nutrition programs for the poor ($32 billion). This would give us a total of $251 billion ($200 billion + $19 billion + $32 billion = $251 billion). And then suppose this $251 billion had been equally divided among the 36 million persons living in poverty. This would mean that each of the 36 million persons living in poverty would end up with $6,972 ($251 billion ÷ 36 million persons = $6,972 per person). This would eliminate (absolute) poverty in the United States, since every individual in the United States would receive an amount of money greater than the federally established poverty level for an individual. (Recall that this amount is approximately $6,300.)

What is even more amazing is that in the early 1990s, the federal government said that a family of four was living in poverty if it had less than approximately $13,000 to use to buy the necessities of life. But by dividing $251 billion among 36 million persons, this would mean that a family of four persons living in poverty would receive $27,888 ($6,972 per person × 4 persons = $27,888). This is an amount of money more than double what the federal government states a family of four has to receive to avoid living in poverty.

Or consider another alternative. Suppose the federal government didn't have to pay $200 billion in interest payments on the national debt in 1992. If the federal government chose not to spend this $200 billion elsewhere (on education, the poor, national defense, and so on), then it is possible that taxes could have been lower by $200 billion. If taxes had been lower, then people would have had more money to spend the way they saw fit. They could have spent more money on houses, cars, computers, clothes, and so on. This would have generated more employment in these industries.

Our point throughout this discussion is an economic one. Economists look at things in terms of opportunity costs. They ask, "What is the opportunity cost of $200 billion in interest payments paid on the national debt?" In other words, if there were no national debt, and thus interest payments did not have to be made, how might things be different? No one knows for sure exactly how things would be different. For example, it is impossible to know if the money would have been used to help the poor, or if taxes would have been lower, or any of a number of other things. We simply are trying to show that certain alternatives are necessarily forfeited because the national debt is as large as it is.

The Budget Process

Just as an individual may have a budget, in which she specifies how she will spend her income—$200 a month for food, $50 a month for clothes, and so on—the federal government has a budget, too. In the federal budget, the federal government specifies how it will spend the money it has. It may decide to spend $250 billion on national defense, $92 billion on health care, and so on.

Preparing a budget and passing it into law is a long process. It begins with the president of the United States, who, with others in the executive branch of government, has the job of preparing the budget. The president's budget, as the federal budget is initially called at this stage, will recommend (to Congress) how much should be spent for such things as national defense, income security programs, education, agricultural programs, and so on. The president has the responsibility of submitting his budget to Congress on, or before, the first Monday in February of each year.

Once the president's budget is in the hands of the Congress, the members of the many congressional committees and subcommittees take a look at it. Within the Congress, the Congressional Budget Office (CBO) advises the members of the committees and subcommittees on any technical details of the president's budget. At this time,

ANALYZING PRIMARY SOURCES

Government and the Economy

Throughout your reading of this text, we have discussed government numerous times. For example, in Chapter 2 we discussed government's role in providing public goods. In Chapter 8 we discussed government in conjunction with antitrust and regulation policy. In Chapter 9, we discussed the role government plays in health care. In Chapter 14, we discussed government's use of monetary and fiscal policy. In this chapter, we have discussed how government spends tax dollars.

When it comes to the proper role for government to play in the economy, there is a wide divergence of opinion. Some people think that government should play a large role in the economy. Others think that government should play only a small role in the economy. Still others place themselves somewhere in between. Here is what some people have to say on the subject of government and the economy.

Alan Blinder, Economist [a]

"**O**ur market economy can usefully be thought of as a game with winners and losers in varying degrees. But the economic game is no more (and no less) fair than a contest between the New York Giants and your local high-school football team. Some players have advantages.

Some of us are born into wealthy families, or with nimble minds that enable us to pursue lucrative and pleasant professions, or with the shrewdness and drive that make for success in business. Some of us are blessed with 'good upbringings' that provide high-quality education and instill 'the right values,' meaning the values that promote success in the economic game.

_____
a. *Hard Heads, Soft Hearts* (pp. 22–24), © 1987 by Alan S. Blinder. Reprinted by permission of Addison-Wesley Publishing Company, Inc.

These are the born (or bred) winners. They can be expected to do well in the economic game year after year without help from the government. Although some will fail, most will fare well under laissez faire. Neither David Rockefeller nor Lee Iacocca needed handouts from the government to achieve personal success—though each got some.

Others are born into poverty, or with less intelligence, or into environments where education and economic success are neither prized nor expected. Some remarkable individuals overcome these disadvantages through sheer determination, skill, and guts, but most lack the ability to accomplish that feat. These are the born (or bred) losers. Without help from someone, they will founder and live in penury.

That all men and women are not created equally equipped to play the economic game is clear. Now comes the hard question, the one that separates the soft-hearted from the hard-hearted. What are we to do about this inequality?

The hard-hearted attitude is that our wonderful market system is so essential, and so fragile, that we must not tamper with it in order to aid the underprivileged, the shortsighted, the indolent, or even the unlucky. Let everyone compete on an equal basis, the argument goes, and let the chips fall where they may. If some of the players are lame or injured, that's a shame. But they must be left to nurse their own wounds, for efforts to assist them would be futile at best and harmful at worst. . . .

The soft-hearted attitude holds that we ought to soften the blows for those who play the economic game and lose, or who cannot play it at all. The objective can be served by making the game less vigorous and risky—which is the rationale for Medicare, Social Security, and unemployment compensation. Or it can be done

ANALYZING PRIMARY SOURCES (continued)

by making the victors share some of the spoils with the vanquished—via welfare benefits, public housing, Medicaid, and progressive taxation. Liberals generally favor such public generosity. But, of course, society as a whole has no Daddy Warbucks. If benefits are to be provided to the underdogs (or losers), the favorites (or winners) must foot the bill. . . .**"**

Charles Wolf, Jr., Analyst, RAND Corporation [b]

"I n 1977, John Kenneth Galbraith [an economist] presented a television series entitled 'The Age of Uncertainty.' Two years later, Milton Friedman [an economist] followed with a series entitled 'Free to Choose,' intended as a rebuttal to the Galbraith series, although, as in some election campaigns, the adversary was not mentioned explicitly. . . .

Age of Uncertainty and Free to Choose dealt with the same subject: the market economy—how it originated and evolved, how it functions, and its strengths and weaknesses. Both books presented the policy implications of this analysis with respect to the cardinal economic choice: that between the market and government as the predominant regulator of economic activity. There the resemblance between the two contestants ended.

While Galbraith, in the tradition of Marx and Schumpeter, fully acknowledged the accomplishments of the market, he identified its evolution and maturation with macroeconomic instability ('uncertainty'), microeconomic inefficiency, and social inequity. . . . To remedy these deficiencies of the market, Galbraith and Age of Uncertainty viewed government policy and intervention as essential to bringing about economic stability, efficiency, and enhanced social equity.

Friedman, in the tradition of Adam Smith's Wealth of Nations, viewed the salient characteristics of the market system very differently from Galbraith. According to Friedman, a freely functioning market economy results in economic and technological progress, efficient utilization of resources, a rising standard of living that, with certain acknowledged exceptions, is distributed with reasonable equity, and a society characterized by social mobility and political freedom. In the view of Friedman and Free to Choose, expansion of government beyond its minimal ('public good') functions (e.g., defense and public order, but not the postal service) impairs efficient resource use, impedes economic progress, and restricts social mobility and ultimately political freedom as well.

What accounts for these two knowledgeable observers' sharply contrasting views of the market and government?

The promarket view, represented by Friedman, is based on an idealized model of a perfectly competitive market, which tends toward full employment equilibrium for the economy as a whole (the macroeconomy), and efficient use of resources by the firm and the individual (the microeconomy). This view draws support from the past century's experience of market economies in the industrialized West and Japan, the 1970s and 1980s experience of the predominantly market economies in the 'newly industrialized countries' of Hong Kong, Malaysia, Singapore, South Korea, and Taiwan, and the more recent growth experience of increased marketization in Thailand and Indonesia.[c] Friedman's stance against government intervention draws additional support from innumerable anecdotes about the propensity of large government organizations, wherever they may be, to mismanage their tasks (e.g., the post office, welfare agencies, defense, and

b. Charles Wolf, Markets or Governments: Choosing between Imperfect Alternatives (Cambridge, Mass.: The MIT Press, Copyright © 1993), pp. 1–3.

c. It is important to note that Hong Kong is not an independent country, but is a British Crown Colony, until 1997 when China will take possession.

ANALYZING PRIMARY SOURCES (continued)

nationalized industries), the persistently disappointing economic records of most Third World countries in which government intervention has been pervasive, and, since the late 1980s, the collapse and dismantling of the centrally planned command economies of the former Soviet Union, East Germany, and Eastern Europe.

On the other hand, the progovernment view represented by Galbraith and *Age of Uncertainty* is based on an idealized model of an informed, efficient, and humane government, able to identify and remedy failures of the market and to achieve national goals arrived at by democratic means, in accord with the precepts of formal welfare economics, as elaborated by I.M.D. Little, Richard Musgrave, and others, and the theory of optimal economic planning developed by Oscar Lange and Abba Lerner. This view draws empirical support from the generally favorable economic performance of the Scandinavian countries and the Netherlands in the post–World War II period (at least until the late 1970s, when their economic trends became less favorable), specific instances of efficient governmental performance such as Europe's national railway systems, and the dramatic record of Japan's sustained postwar economic growth attributed to guidance and targeting by government policy (Japan's experience is cited in support of *both* sides of the argument!). Similarly, the Galbraith stance against the market also draws support from anecdotes about such negative market externalities as atmospheric pollution, airport noise, advertising billboards, and the often low quality of commercial television.**"**

Alexis de Tocqueville, French Statesman and Author

"The major concern of government ought to be to teach the people to gradually do without it. (1831)**"**

H. Craig Petersen, Economist [d]

"At the risk of oversimplification, the test for government involvement in the marketplace can be considered a three-step process. The first step is to determine if there is a serious market failure. The second is to determine if there is action by government that could correct the problem. And the third step is to assess the costs of government action compared with the likely benefits. In making this evaluation, it is important to consider all costs. These must include not only direct expenditures by government but also any indirect compliance costs that may be imposed on the market. Only if the benefits of government action exceed the total costs is there a legitimate case for intervention.**"**

Andrew Schotter, Economist [e]

"The world seems divided between people who see markets as the cure for all our problems and people who see markets as the cause of all problems.**"**

---

1. In your own words, describe both the hard-hearted and soft-hearted attitudes about which Blinder talks.
2. According to Wolf, what are some of the differences between Galbraith and Friedman?
3. In your own words, describe Petersen's three-step process for government involvement in the economy.

---

d.   H. Craig Petersen, *Business and Government* (New York: Harper Collins, 1993), p. 21.
e.   Andrew Schotter, *Free Market Economics: A Critical Appraisal* (New York: St. Martin's Press, 1985),p. v.

THE PRESIDENT'S ECONOMIC PLAN

	ADMINISTRATION	HOUSE	SENATE
$500 Billion in Deficit Reduction	X	X	X
Entitlement Cuts:			
Agriculture	X	X	X
Veterans	X	X	X
Medicare	X	X	X
Medicaid	X	X	X
Social Security	X	X	X
Discretionary Cuts	X	X	X
Energy Tax	X	X	X
Taxes on the Wealthy/ Progressivity	X	X	X
...ients:			
EITC	X	X	X
Hunger Prevention	X	X	
Immunizations	X	X	
Family Preservation	X	X	X
Empowerment Zones	X	X	
Tax Incentives	X	X	X
Deficit Reduction Trust Fund	X	X	X

◀ A member of President Clinton's administration, Leon Panetta, director of the Office of Management and Budget, discusses the president's plans for federal spending and taxation. In 1994 Panetta was named President Clinton's chief of staff and Alice Rivlin assumed the role of director of the Office of Management and Budget.

there may be disagreements between the president and members of Congress relating to how money should be spent (for example, the president may want to spend more money for health care than many members of Congress think should be spent), or how much tax revenue is likely to be raised over the next few months. With respect to this, the president and his staff may have estimated that the federal government will have $1,200 billion in tax revenues to spend, but Congress has estimated tax revenues to be $1,100 billion. The president and the Congress will work to try to resolve their differences. (Both the executive and legislative branches of government have to make estimates of tax revenues because they do not know for certain what economic conditions will be like, and tax revenues depend on the state of the economy. For example, if the economy is sluggish, and many millions of people are out of work, there will be less income earned. If less income is earned, income taxes will be down.)

Between the time when the president first submitted his budget to Congress, and when the Congress actually votes on the budget, many details of the president's budget may have been changed. These changes may reflect compromise between the president and the Congress for any of a number of reasons.

Where are the American people in the budget process? Do they have a role to play? Some political pundits have suggested that once the president submits his budget to Congress (on, or before, the first Monday in February), the people get a chance to hear about it. For example, there are usually numerous newspaper stories and newscasts about what the president is proposing. The American people have a chance to write or call their congresspersons and express their preferences on the president's budget. Also, during this time, special interest groups may lobby congresspersons and express their preferences on the president's budget.

The Congress has the obligation of passing a budget by the beginning of the fiscal, not calendar, year. (A calendar year begins on January 1 and runs through December 31; a fiscal year, under which the federal government operates, begins on October 1 and runs through September 30.) Once the budget is passed by Congress, the details of spending outlined in the budget become law for that fiscal year. And the whole process will begin again in only a few months.

What Is a Fair Share?

Most persons say that it is only right for everyone to pay his or her fair share of taxes. The problem is, how do we decide what a fair share is? If Eloy and Dorothy disagree about the amount of Eloy's fair share, who is to decide which of them is right?

Historically, there are two principles of taxation that touch on this issue: the benefits-received principle and the ability-to-pay principle.

Benefits-Received Principle. The benefits-received principle holds that a person should pay in taxes an amount equal to the benefits he or she receives from government expenditures. For example, if you drive often on government-provided roads and highways, you ought to pay for the upkeep of the roads. This goal is usually met through the excise tax on gasoline. People who drive a lot buy a lot of gas, and thus they pay more in gas taxes than people who drive very little. Since gas tax revenues are used for the upkeep of the roads, the major users of the roads end up paying the bulk of road upkeep costs.

Ability-to-Pay Principle. With some government-provided goods, it is easy to figure out roughly how much someone benefits. For instance, in the roads-and-highways example, we can assume that the more a person drives on the road or highway, the more benefit he or she obtains from it.

With other government-provided goods, it is not as easy to relate benefits received to taxes paid. For example, consider national defense. We could say that almost all Americans benefit from national defense, but we would have a hard time figuring out how much one person benefits relative to another person. Does Jackson, down the street, benefit more than, less than, or the same as Stein, who lives up the street? The benefits-received principle is hard to implement in such cases.

Often, the ability-to-pay principle is used instead. This principle says that people should pay

▲ People who purchase gas for their cars pay a tax that is used for the upkeep of roads. This is an example of the benefits-received principle in action.

taxes according to their abilities to pay. Since a rich person is more able to pay taxes than a poor person, a rich person should pay more taxes than a poor person. For example, the millionaire might pay $330,000 a year in income taxes, whereas the person who earns $30,000 a year might pay $8,000.

Proportional, Progressive, and Regressive Income Taxes

When it comes to the federal income tax, the issue of fairness almost always arises. This is because the income tax can be made proportional, progressive, or regressive. Here is what each means.

CASE STUDY

Federal Income Taxes

In 1993, the U.S. Congress passed, and President Bill Clinton signed, a new tax law. It stipulated that there would be five federal (personal) income tax rates: 15, 28, 31, 36, and 39.6 percent. This means that the United States has a progressive income tax structure. In other words, a person pays taxes at a higher rate as his or her income rises. In Exhibit 15-3, we show the tax rate schedules for two categories of persons: (a) single individuals, and (b) married individuals filing jointly. (When a married couple files jointly, this means they take their separate in-comes, add them, and then pay taxes on the sum. For example, suppose a wife has a taxable income of $30,000 and a husband has a taxable income of $30,000. Their combined income is $60,000. They will pay taxes on the $60,000.)

Take a look at the first column in either part *a* or part *b* of Exhibit 15-3. It reads "Taxable income." A person's taxable income is different from the income he or she earns on a job. It is less than this amount by the dollar amount of al-lowable deductions. Here is how it works: Suppose a person earns an annual income of $40,000

(a)

Taxable income	What a single individual pays
$0.00 – $22,100	15% of sum over $0.00
$22,100 – $53,500	$3,315 + 28% of sum over $22,100
$53,500 – $115,000	$12,107 + 31% of sum over $53,500
$115,000 – $250,000	$31,172 + 36% of sum over $115,000
Over $250,000	$79,772 + 39.6% of sum over $250,000

(b)

Taxable income	What a married couple (filing jointly) pays
$0.00 – $36,900	15% of sum over $0.00
$36,900 – $89,150	$5,535.00 + 28% of sum over $36,900
$89,150 – $140,000	$20,165.00 + 31% of sum over $89,150
$140,000 – $250,000	$35,928.50 + 36% of sum over $140,000
Over $250,000	$75,528.50 + 39.6% of sum over $250,000

◀ **EXHIBIT 15-3. Federal Income Tax Tables.** The U.S. has a progressive income tax structure. The five rates of the federal income tax are 15, 28, 31, 36, and 39.6 percent. Part *a* shows what a single individual with different levels of taxable income will pay in income taxes. Part *b* shows what a married couple (filing jointly) with different levels of taxable income will pay in income taxes. Note: The government changes the taxable income figures annually to adjust for inflation.

SOURCE: Internal Revenue Service, 1993.

CASE STUDY (continued)

working at a job. She won't have to pay income taxes on the entire $40,000 because the government allows her to deduct certain things from her income. For example, she may be able to deduct some medical expenses, moving costs, and a certain dollar amount for a dependent (a person who lives with her who depends on her for his or her food and shelter), among other things. Let's say this person's deductions total $5,000. If we take the person's income ($40,000) and subtract $5,000 in deductions, we are left with a taxable income of $35,000. It is this $35,000 on which the person pays income taxes.

How much does this person pay in income taxes? If we assume this person is single, we get the answer by looking at part *a* of Exhibit 15-3. We see that her $35,000 taxable income falls be-tween $22,100 and $53,500. She will therefore have to pay $3,315 in income taxes plus 28 percent of her taxable income that is over $22,100. The dollar difference between $35,000 and $22,100 is $12,900 ($35,000 − $22,100 = $12,900). Twenty-eight percent of this is $3,612 ($12,900 × 0.28 = $3,612). In total, she pays $6,927 in federal income taxes ($3,315 + $3,612 = $6,927).

---

1. Suppose a married couple (filing jointly) has a taxable income of $77,000. How much does the couple pay in federal income taxes?
2. According to Exhibit 15-3, what is the highest federal income tax rate?

Proportional Income Taxation. With a **proportional income tax**, everyone pays taxes at the same rate, whatever the income level. For example, if Kuan's taxable income is $100,000, she will pay taxes at the same rate as Jones, with a taxable income of $10,000. Suppose this rate is 10 percent. It follows that Kuan pays $10,000 in income taxes and Jones pays $1,000 in income taxes. Notice that Kuan, who earns 10 times as much as Jones, pays 10 times as much in taxes ($10,000 as opposed to $1,000). However, Kuan pays at exactly the same rate—10 percent—as Jones.

Progressive Income Taxation. With a **progressive income tax**, a person pays taxes at a higher rate as his or her income level rises. To illustrate, suppose Davidson pays taxes at the rate of 10 percent on a taxable income of $10,000. When his income doubles to $20,000, he pays at a rate of 12 percent. A progressive income tax is usually capped at some tax rate. This means it rises to some rate, and then stops. For instance, perhaps no one will pay at a rate higher than 36 percent, no matter how high his or her income is.

Regressive Income Taxation. With a **regressive income tax**, a person pays taxes at a lower rate as his or her income level rises. For example, Lowenstein's tax rate is 10 percent when her income is $10,000 and 8 percent when her income rises to $20,000.

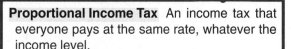

MINI GLOSSARY

Proportional Income Tax An income tax that everyone pays at the same rate, whatever the income level.

Progressive Income Tax An income tax whose rate increases as income level rises. Progressive income tax structures are usually capped at some rate.

Regressive Income Tax An income tax whose rate decreases as income level rises.

LEARNING CHECK

1. Define the benefits-received principle of taxation.
2. Define the ability-to-pay principle of taxation.
3. Describe a regressive income tax structure.
4. Describe a progressive income tax structure.

SECTION 2 — DEFICITS AND DEBT

This section discusses federal budget deficits and the national (or public) debt. It begins with a short historical discussion.

As you read, keep this key question in mind:

■ What is the relationship between federal budget deficits and the national debt?

Budgets: Balanced and in Deficit

Adam Smith, the 18th century economist, said that "what is prudence in the conduct of every private family, can scarce be folly in that of a great kingdom." This means that if it is right and reasonable for a family to do something, it is probably also right and reasonable for a great nation to do the same thing. For example, if it is right for a family to save and to make sure it doesn't stay in debt, then it is right for a nation to do the same. For many years in the United States, this notion, originating with Adam Smith, carried over to the discussions of federal budget policy. Most people believed that the federal budget should be balanced—that is, government expenditures should be equal to tax revenues. Budget deficits, which occur when government expenditures exceed tax revenues, were acceptable—but only during wartime.

Things began to change around the time of the Great Depression, 1929–33, a period of great economic distress in this country. During this time, unemployment skyrocketed, the production of goods and services plummeted, prices fell, banks closed, and companies went bankrupt. Until this time, many people in the United States had thought that the free-enterprise economy was a stable, smooth mechanism and that it was not subject to violent and abrupt downturns. The economic downturn of the Great Depression gave these people cause for doubt. Their old, cherished notion of how an economy worked was upset. Slowly, many previously accepted ideas of budget policy began to be discarded. One notion in particular that fell by the wayside was the idea that the federal budget ought to be balanced. Slowly, people began to accept budget deficits in order to try and reduce unemployment.

What do budget deficits have to do with reducing unemployment? Suppose the federal budget is balanced. Government spending is $1,200 billion, and tax revenues are $1,200 billion. But we notice that there is high unemployment in the economy, say, around 10 percent. The president of the United States, along with the Congress, wants to reduce the unemployment rate by implementing expansionary fiscal policy (increase government spending or decrease taxes). Together, they decide to increase government spending to $1,250 billion. Tax revenues, we'll assume, remain constant at $1,200 billion. In this instance, *expansionary fiscal policy has led to a budget deficit*; government spending ($1,250 billion) is greater than tax revenues ($1,200 billion). The federal budget deficit is $50 billion ($1,250 billion − $1,200 billion = $50 billion).

Now, many people came to see budget deficits as necessary given the high unemployment that plagued the economy. According to them, the choice was simple: (1) Either keep the federal budget balanced and suffer with high unemployment (and the reduced output of goods and services that is a consequence of it), or (2) accept the budget deficit and reduce the unemployment rate. For many people, it was "better to balance the economy than to balance the budget." For a list of budget deficits stretching back to 1970, see Exhibit 15-4.

QUESTION: *Do all economists agree that it is better to have a budget deficit and reduce unemployment than to maintain a balanced budget?*

ANSWER: *No. One reason is that not all economists believe that expansionary fiscal policy, which can sometimes create a budget deficit, is effective at reducing unemployment. Chapter 14 discussed this issue in relation to the topic of crowding out. Some economists believe that complete crowding out will prevent expansionary fiscal policy from being effective at reducing the unemployment rate.*

THINKING LIKE AN ECONOMIST

Suppose the economy is faced with high inflation. Political leaders turn to economists and ask them what should be done. The economists say that contractionary fiscal policy should be put into effect. Specifically, government spending should be cut or taxes raised. The economists say this will reduce inflation. The government officials swallow hard, because they know that, while this may be good economic advice, it is bad political advice. Few politicians win election by proposing to cut people's benefits or raise their taxes.

An economist is aware that what may be the "best medicine" for the economy may turn out to be so bitter tasting that politicians won't want to prescribe it to the electorate. There is sometimes a tension between economics and politics. The economist knows that politics may often be a stronger force than economics.

Year	Condition of federal budget	Year	Condition of federal budget
1970	Deficit ($2.8 billion)	1982	Deficit ($128.0 billion)
1971	Deficit ($23 billion)	1983	Deficit ($207.8 billion)
1972	Deficit ($23.4 billion)	1984	Deficit ($185.4 billion)
1973	Deficit ($14.9 billion)	1985	Deficit ($212.3 billion)
1974	Deficit ($6.1 billion)	1986	Deficit ($221.2 billion)
1975	Deficit ($53.2 billion)	1987	Deficit ($149.8 billion)
1976	Deficit ($73.7 billion)	1988	Deficit ($155.2 billion)
1977	Deficit ($53.7 billion)	1989	Deficit ($152.5 billion)
1978	Deficit ($59.2 billion)	1990	Deficit ($221.4 billion)
1979	Deficit ($40.2 billion)	1991	Deficit ($269.5 billion)
1980	Deficit ($73.8 billion)	1992	Deficit ($290.2 billion)
1981	Deficit ($79.0 billion)	1993	Deficit ($327.3 billion)

◄ **EXHIBIT 15-4. More Than Two Decades of Federal Budget Deficits.** Beginning in 1970, the United States has experienced a continuous string of federal budget deficits. The budget deficit for 1993 is an estimate. Source: *Economic Report of the President* (Washington, D.C.: U.S. Government Printing Office, 1993).

ECONOMIC FOCUS

A s we have said in this chapter, the federal government has an income tax. In 1990, the federal income tax raised approximately $447 billion. A look at Exhibit S-15-1 will tell you where the $447 billion came from. Let's go through the exhibit column by column.

In column 1, we list "Size of Income." The first entry in this column is "$1,000–$2,999." In column 2, we notice that there were 7,379,000 federal income tax returns filed by people who earned between $1,000 and $2,999 in income in 1990. Column 3 tells us the total income of this group of persons. It was $14.6 billion in 1990. Remember, though, that income is not the same as taxable income. According to column 4, this group of persons had a taxable income of $1.1 billion in 1990. How much did they pay in income taxes? Column 5 gives us the answer: $200 million (which is 0.2 of one billion dollars). Column 6 shows us what this group paid in taxes as a percentage of their total income. It was 1.37 percent. This percentage was obtained by dividing the total amount this group paid in taxes ($200 million, or 0.2 of a billion dollars) by the total income of this group ($14.6 billion). In column 7, we see the average income tax paid by a member of this income group, $100.

Let's go to the opposite end of the income spectrum, and look at the taxes paid by millionaires in 1990. The last entry in column 1 is "$1,000,000 or more." According to column 2, there were 61,000 income tax returns filed by people who earned $1 million or more in 1990. From column 3, we learn that the total income of this group amounted to $154.7 billion. In column 4, we see that the taxable income of this group was $134.6 billion. Of this amount, this group of persons paid $37.4 billion in income taxes, ac-

cording to column 5. This was 24.18 percent of the total income of the members of the group, according to column 6. In column 7, we see the average income tax paid by a member of this income group, $616,500. Finally, what percentage of all income taxes did millionaires pay in 1990? Remember, we stated earlier that the federal government raised approximately $447 billion in income taxes in 1990. Millionaires paid $37.4 billion in income taxes, which is 8.37 percent of all income taxes ($37.4 billion ÷ $447 billion = 0.0837, and 0.0837 × 100 = 8.37 percent).

According to the exhibit, the people who earn between $50,000 and $74,999 paid the largest total amount in income taxes in 1990. This was $87.2 billion, as we see by looking in column 5 across from this income group. The major reason this group pays the largest total amount in income taxes is because there are so many people who earn an income in this income group. Notice from column 2 there were 10,944,000 returns filed by this group. (Only in one income group were more income tax returns filed: $30,000–$39,999. Here, there were 12,283,000 income tax returns filed.) Notice also that the group of persons who earn between $50,000 and $74,999 had the largest total income, $657.2 billion.

Numbers such as those shown in Exhibit S-15-1 can be used to make different points and advance different causes. For example, someone might want to point out that middle-income people pay more in taxes than rich people., He may want to do this in order to argue that the rich don't pay their fair share of income taxes. For example, if we let, say, middle-income people be defined as those who earn between $30,000 and $74,999, and rich people as those who earn $500,000 or more, then it is easy to calculate that

INCOME GROUPS AND INCOME TAXES

▼ **EXHIBIT S-15-1.** Taxes: Who Pays What?

(1) SIZE OF INCOME	(2) NUMBER OF TAX RETURNS	(3) TOTAL INCOME (IN BILLIONS OF DOLLARS)	(4) TAXABLE INCOME (IN BILLIONS OF DOLLARS)	(5) TOTAL INCOME TAX (IN BILLIONS OF DOLLARS)	(6) TAXES PAID AS A PERCENTAGE OF TOTAL INCOME	(7) AVERAGE TAX PAID
$1,000-$2,999	7,379,000	$14.6 billion	$1.1 billion	$0.2 billion	1.37%	$100
3,000-4,999	6,317,000	25.2	2.1	0.4	1.59	200
5,000-6,999	6,004,000	36.1	4.9	0.8	2.22	200
7,000-8,999	6,026,000	48.2	10.2	1.6	3.32	400
9,000-10,999	5,891,000	58.9	16.2	2.3	3.90	600
11,000-12,999	5,573,000	66.9	25.3	3.1	4.63	800
13,000-14,999	5,382,000	75.3	31.1	4.1	5.44	1,000
15,000-16,999	4,686,000	74.9	35.8	4.9	6.54	1,200
17,000-18,999	4,656,000	83.9	42.9	6.1	7.27	1,400
19,000-21,999	6,308,000	129.2	71.8	10.6	8.20	1,700
22,000-24,999	5,465,000	128.1	75.9	11.3	8.82	2,100
25,000-29,999	7,838,000	215.3	133.5	20.5	9.52	2,700
30,000-39,999	12,283,000	426.4	280.6	45.3	10.62	3,700
40,000-49,999	8,837,000	394.8	270.5	44.9	11.37	5,100
50,000-74,999	10,944,000	657.2	466.6	87.2	13.27	8,000
75,000-99,999	3,276,000	279.6	205.3	44.3	15.84	13,600
100,000-199,999	2,330,000	305.6	230.4	57.9	18.95	24,900
200,000-499,999	644,000	188.1	152.6	43.5	23.13	67,500
500,000-999,999	130,000	87.1	74.4	20.9	24.00	161,000
1,000,000 or more	61,000	154.7	134.6	37.4	24.18	616,500

SOURCE: U.S. Bureau of the Census, *Statistical Abstract of the United States*: 1993, 113th edition, p. 340.

the middle-income group paid $177.4 billion in income taxes ($45.3 billion + $44.9 billion + $87.2 billion = $177.4 billion) and the rich group paid $58.3 billion in income taxes ($20.9 billion + $37.4 billion = $58.3 billion). Is it the case that the rich didn't pay their fair share? Looking at these numbers alone is misleading. The principal reason the middle-income group paid more in taxes than the rich is that there are so many more people who fall into the middle-income category. For example, there were over 32 million tax returns filed by per-

sons in the middle-income category (12,283,000 + 8,837,000 + 10,944,000 = 32,064,000) and 191,000 tax returns filed by persons in the rich category (130,000 + 61,000 = 191,000).

We could look at things differently and say this: Because people who earned over $500,000 paid a higher percentage of their incomes in income taxes (see column 6) than people who earned between $30,000 and $74,999, the rich paid more than their fair share in income taxes. For example, people earning between $30,000

U.S. ECONOMIC FOCUS (continued)

and $39,999 paid 10.62 percent of their total income in taxes, while people earning between $500,000 and $999,999 paid 24.00 percent of their total income in taxes.

Our point is not to argue whether the rich do not pay their fair share of taxes, or whether they pay more than their fair share. Our point is to inform you that the numbers and percentages shown in Exhibit S-15-1 can be used by people in misleading ways—sometimes knowingly and sometimes unknowingly—to support the points they want to make.

1. In which income group were the largest number of income tax returns filed?
2. What was the average income tax paid by a person who earned between $40,000 and $49,999?
3. What percentage of total income taxes paid in 1990 were paid by person, who earned between $75,000 and $99,999?
4. What percentage of total income taxes paid in 1990 were paid by persons who earned between $25,000 and $29,999?

Budget Deficits Lead to National Debt

The only way an individual can spend more than he or she earns is to borrow the difference and incur a debt. (We are ruling out monetary gifts to this person.) For example, if Harry earns $10,000 a year, and spends $12,000, he would have had to borrow $2,000 ($12,000 − $10,000 = $2,000). This $2,000 is Harry's debt.

What is true for Harry is true for the federal government. If it spends more than it receives in tax revenues, it has to borrow the difference and incur a debt. Of course, another way to say this is that every time the federal government runs a deficit, it has to borrow money and incur a debt. In short, deficits lead to debt. The debt of the federal government is called the national debt.

A look at Exhibit 15-4 tells us that the federal government has been running a budget deficit ever since 1970. We would expect that it has piled up a lot of debt. Earlier in this chapter we stated that the national debt in 1992 was $4,002.7 billion. One year later, in 1993, it had grown to $4,410.5

billion. How much would each person in the United States have to pay in order to eliminate the national debt? At the end of 1993, it was over $17,000. This is sometimes referred to as "your" share of the national debt.

The Link between Budget Deficits Today, the National Debt, and Higher Taxes in the Future

We have learned that when the government spends more than tax revenues, it has to borrow the difference. Deficits lead to debt. But what does debt lead to? Some economists argue that it leads to higher taxes in the future. Look at it this way. When the government borrows the money to pay for the excess of its spending over tax revenues, it has to borrow that money from people. Those people will have to be repaid one day; the debt has to be paid off. (It would be the same if you borrowed some money from a bank. You would have to repay the money one day, with interest. You would have to pay off your debt.) What happens when

*"What's this I hear about you
adults mortgaging my future?"*

From *The Wall Street Journal*—permission, Cartoon Features
Syndicate

the debt has to be paid off? Taxes must be used, so taxes have to be higher than they would have been had the debt not been incurred in the first place. Some economists say that, as far as future taxpayers are concerned, current budget deficits are a form of "taxation without representation."

This brings us to the issue of ethics. Is it ethical for one generation to buy things that another generation ends up partly paying for? Some people say no. But others say it depends on whether what the first generation buys benefits the next generation. For example, suppose the present generation decides to buy an interstate freeway system for $10 billion. The present generation decides to pay $2 billion itself through taxes and borrow $8 bil-

lion. The present generation knows that the future generation will have to pay off the $8 billion (plus interest), but it reasons that the future generation will use the freeway system, so it should pay for some of it. If the current generation had purchased $10 billion of something from which only it could benefit, then the situation would be different.

A Constitutional Amendment to Balance the Budget

As stated earlier, the recent history of the United States has been one of continued budget deficits. This has caused some people to argue for a constitutional amendment that would require the federal government to balance its budget each year unless there were a national emergency.

Of course, we know that there are three ways to balance the budget. For example, suppose government spending is $1,000 billion and tax revenues are $800 billion. The deficit is $200 billion. To balance the budget, we can (1) cut government spending by $200 billion, or (2) raise taxes by $200 billion, or (3) cut spending while raising taxes—for example, cut spending by $100 billion and raise taxes by $100 billion.

Some economists are in favor of a balanced budget amendment while others are not. Even those who favor it do not all agree on to how the budget should be balanced (raise taxes? cut spending? or both?). Some economists who are against a budget amendment say that it will limit the government's use of fiscal policy to lower unemployment, and so on.

The Congress has debated the merits and drawbacks of a balanced budget amendment numerous times.

 LEARNING CHECK

1. Does expansionary fiscal policy always result in a budget deficit? Explain your answer.
2. What was the national debt in December 1993?
3. How are current budget deficits linked to higher taxes in the future?

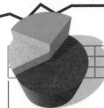

DEVELOPING ECONOMIC SKILLS

Thinking Critically in Economics

There is a right and a wrong way to conduct economic analysis. If you want to do it the right way, you must avoid certain *fallacies*, or errors in thinking. We examine a few of the more common fallacies here.

Association Is not Causation

Suppose you are in school listening to your teacher explain the economic concept of scarcity. You look outside and notice that it has started to rain. Three minutes later, your teacher says, "All right, that is enough about scarcity. Let's get out pencil and paper and take a pop quiz."

Two events occurred: (1) It started to rain, and (2) your teacher announced a pop quiz. Did the two events occur close together in time? Yes. Because they did, we could say that the two events are *associated*.

But did the first event cause the second event? In other words, is the rain the *cause* of the quiz? Is the quiz the *effect* of the rain? Probably not. Most likely, the two events—the rain and the pop quiz—are not related by cause and effect. It was just coincidence that they occurred a few minutes apart.

The point is this: The simple fact that two events are associated in some way does not make one event the cause of the other. In short, *association is not causation*.

QUESTION: *But surely, when two events occur close together in time, the first event sometimes causes the second event.*

ANSWER: *Yes, of course. For example, suppose a bee stings your arm, and your arm begins to swell. The bee sting and the swollen arm occur close together in time. And it so happens that the bee sting causes the swollen arm. The point is simply that there isn't* necessarily *a cause-and-effect relation between two events that occur close together in time.*

The Fallacy of Composition

It is Friday night, and John, who attends George Washington High School, is in the football stadium cheering on his team. Suddenly, John stands up so that he can see better. Does it follow that if everybody stood up, then everybody could see better? No. The principle we deduce from this observation is that what is good for the individual is not necessarily good for the group.

The *fallacy of composition* is the erroneous view that what is good (or true) for the individual is necessarily good (or true) for the group.

Test your knowledge of this important concept. Suppose Mary moves to the suburbs because she dislikes the crowds in the city. Does it follow that if everyone moved from the city to the suburbs because they disliked crowds, then everyone would be better off? If your answer is yes, then you have committed the fallacy of composition. If your answer is no, then you have not committed the fallacy of composition. We know that if Mary, and Mary alone, moves to the suburbs because she dislikes the crowds, she makes herself better off. But if everyone moves to the suburbs for the same reason, not everyone is made better off. Why? Because if everyone moves to the suburbs, the suburbs become as crowded as the cities were.

QUESTION: *Is there any case in which what is good for one person is also good for everyone?*

ANSWER: *Yes. In fact, there are many such cases. For example, if Ramon eats more vegetables and fewer fatty foods, he is better off (he is healthier). If everyone eats more vegetables and fewer fats, then everyone makes*

DEVELOPING ECONOMIC SKILLS (continued)

himself or herself better off in the same way. In this example, what is good (or true) for one is good (or true) for everybody. Again, the point is simply that this isn't necessarily, *or* always, *the way things work. Sometimes, what is good for one person is good for everybody. Sometimes, what is good for one person is not good for everybody.*

Fact and Opinion

There is a difference between fact and opinion. A *fact* is something that is objectively true. For example, it is a fact that George Washington was the first president of the United States; and it is a fact that you are reading this sentence at this moment. There is no room for doubt about either. An *opinion*, on the other hand, is not necessarily objectively true. An opinion expresses a subjective, or personal, judgment, preference, or belief. For example, your friend may say that Jefferson was the most intelligent American president. You may disagree with your friend's statement and feel that some other president had more intelligence.

Both of you may be well informed in history and able to support your statements. However, the matter can never be proved because you are both making subjective evaluations—both you and your friend hold an opinion.

1. Explain what it means to say that association is not causation.
2. Give an example (other than one used in the text or in class) that illustrates the fallacy of composition.
3. "Yesterday, I exercised for the first time in years. Today, I have no appetite. Exercise was the cause of my reduced appetite." Is the person making this statement implying that association is causation or that association is not causation? Explain your answer.
4. List any three facts that you know. Next, list three of your opinions. Finally, identify the essential difference between a fact and an opinion.

CHAPTER 15 REVIEW

CHAPTER SUMMARY

1. The personal income tax is the tax a person pays on his or her taxable income. The corporate income tax is the tax corporations pay on their profits. Sales taxes are taxes applied to the purchase of a broad range of goods. Excise taxes are taxes applied to the purchase of a narrow range of products. The Social Security tax is a tax placed on income generated from employment. The property tax is a tax on the value of property (such as a home).

2. Much of the tax revenue raised by the federal government comes from the personal income tax, the corporate income tax, and the Social Security tax.

3. The benefits-received principle holds that a person should pay in taxes an amount equal to the benefits he or she receives from government expenditures.

4. The ability-to-pay principle holds that people should pay taxes according to their abilities to pay.

5. With a proportional income tax, everyone pays taxes at the same rate, whatever the income level. With a progressive income tax, a person pays taxes at a higher rate as his or her income level rises. With a regressive income tax, a person pays taxes at a lower rate as his or her income level rises.

6. The federal income tax is a progressive tax.

7. The federal budget has been in deficit every year, beginning in 1970.

8. If the federal government spends more than its tax revenues—it runs a budget deficit—it has to borrow the difference. When it borrows money, it incurs a debt, called the national debt.

9. The national debt has to be paid off through taxes. As a result, taxes are higher.

BUILD YOUR ECONOMIC VOCABULARY

Match the word with the correct definition, example, or statement.

1. corporate income tax
2. sales tax
3. personal income tax
4. benefits-received principle
5. ability-to-pay principle
6. progressive income tax
7. proportional income tax
8. budget deficit
9. regressive income tax
10. national debt

a. exists when government spending is greater than tax revenues

b. the sum total of what the federal government owes its creditors

c. a tax paid at the same rate no matter what the income level

d. a tax that is a percentage of taxable income

e. a tax that is paid on the purchases of a broad range of goods and services

f. the idea that a person should pay in taxes an amount equal to the benefits he or she receives from government expenditures

g. the idea that people should pay taxes according to their abilities to pay

h. a tax paid at a lower rate at higher income levels

i. a tax that is a percentage of corporate profits

j. a tax paid at a higher rate at higher income levels

REVIEW QUESTIONS

1. Could rich people pay more taxes than poor people if the benefits-received principle were in effect? Explain your answer.
2. Define the following: (a) proportional income taxation, (b) progressive income taxation, (c) regressive income taxation.
3. What are the ways in which the budget deficit can be reduced or eliminated?
4. What is the national debt, and how is it related to budget deficits?
5. Do all economists agree that it is better to have a budget deficit and reduce unemployment than to maintain a balanced budget? Explain your answer.
6. "Politicians are probably more inclined to follow expansionary fiscal policy than contractionary fiscal policy." Do you agree or disagree? Explain your answer.
7. What does it mean to say deficits are a form of taxation without representation?
8. Is the federal income tax proportional, regressive, or progressive? Explain your answer.

SHARPEN YOUR CRITICAL THINKING SKILLS

1. Most opinion polls taken during the 1970s and 1980s showed that the vast majority of Americans wanted a balanced budget. During this time, most members of Congress also said they wanted a balanced budget. Why, then, was there a budget deficit in every year of this period?
2. "With a proportional income tax, people with higher incomes pay the same amount of taxes as people with lower incomes." What is wrong with this statement?

ACTIVITIES AND PROJECTS

1. As a class, discuss whether you think the federal budget should be balanced. If you favor a balanced budget, state whether you prefer to balance it by (a) cutting government expenditures, (b) raising taxes, or (c) some of both.

ECONOMIC DICTIONARY

National Debt (Pg. 376)
Progressive Income Tax (Pg. 385)
Proportional Income Tax (Pg. 385)
Regressive Income Tax (Pg. 385)

The Global Economy

397

Economic Growth and Development

INTRODUCTION

Economic growth and economic development are major topics of interest to most nations of the world. Economic growth reflects increases in real GDP or per-capita real GDP. It is essentially a numerical measurement. Economic development includes not only economic growth but also other changes that are taken to indicate improvement in the overall standard of living, not just the material standard of living.

Consider a small country that exports only bananas. Its people are poor and can only barely meet the necessities of life. Certainly it is possible for this nation's economy to grow;

it is possible for the country to produce and export more bananas this year than last year. But even if it did this, it would not be economically developed. Economic development implies more than economic growth. In this example, it implies the enhancement of the nation's ability to produce goods other than bananas. In general, it implies better ways to produce goods and services. It implies a higher overall standard of living for the residents of the nation—better transportation networks, better schools, more and higher-quality goods to consume, and so forth.

AFTER YOU STUDY THIS CHAPTER, YOU WILL BE ABLE TO:

1. Explain the difference between real economic growth and per-capita real economic growth.
2. Discuss the factors that affect economic growth.
3. Discuss some of the benefits and costs of economic growth.
4. Discuss some of the obstacles to economic development.

KEY TERMS

Dependency Ratio
Developed
  Country
Less-Developed
  Country (LDC)
Per-Capita Real
  Economic
  Growth
Population Growth
  Rate

Production
  Possibilities
  Frontier (PPF)
Real Economic
  Growth
Status Quo
Vicious Circle of
  Poverty

This section discusses economic growth. As you read, keep these key questions in mind:

- What are real economic growth and per-capita real economic growth?
- How is economic growth portrayed in a production possibilities frontier framework?
- What factors affect economic growth?
- What is the Rule of 72?

What Is Economic Growth?

The term *economic growth* is used to refer to both real economic growth and per-capita real economic growth. **Real economic growth** is an increase from one period to the next in real GDP. For example, if the real GDP of a country is $400 billion in year 1 and $430 billion in year 2, then the country has experienced real economic growth. **Per-capita real economic growth** is an increase from one period to the next in per-capita real GDP, which is real GDP divided by population. (Exhibit 16-1 shows a representation of the world in which each country's size is proportionate to its population.) For example, if the population of a country is 10 million persons and real GDP is $50 billion, then the per-capita real GDP is $5,000 ($50 billion ÷ 10 million persons = $5,000 per person).

Most economists think the per-capita measurement is more useful, since it tells us how much better or worse off the "average" person is in one country or one period compared with another. For example, India has a higher real GDP than Norway. From this, someone might conclude that Indians are better off than Norwegians. But this is not the case, since India has a population 171

▼ Shown are busy streets in Norway (left) and India (right). Although India has a higher real GDP than Norway, Norway has a higher per-capita real GDP, indicating that the average Norwegian is better off in terms of material goods and services.

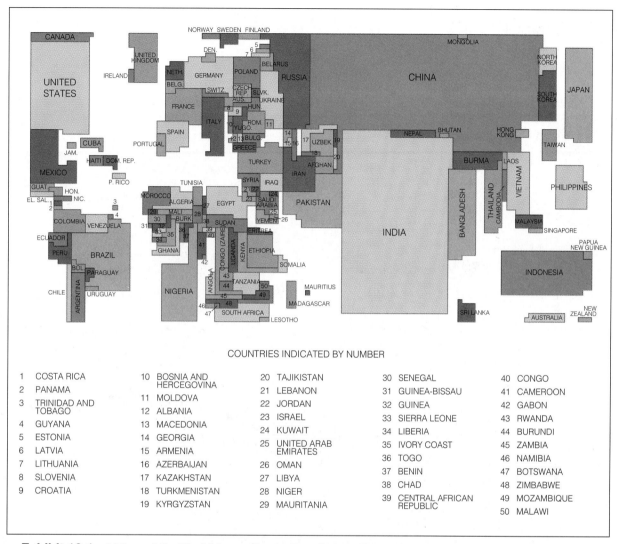

COUNTRIES INDICATED BY NUMBER

1	COSTA RICA	10	BOSNIA AND HERCEGOVINA	20	TAJIKISTAN	30	SENEGAL	40	CONGO
2	PANAMA	11	MOLDOVA	21	LEBANON	31	GUINEA-BISSAU	41	CAMEROON
3	TRINIDAD AND TOBAGO	12	ALBANIA	22	JORDAN	32	GUINEA	42	GABON
4	GUYANA	13	MACEDONIA	23	ISRAEL	33	SIERRA LEONE	43	RWANDA
5	ESTONIA	14	GEORGIA	24	KUWAIT	34	LIBERIA	44	BURUNDI
6	LATVIA	15	ARMENIA	25	UNITED ARAB EMIRATES	35	IVORY COAST	45	ZAMBIA
7	LITHUANIA	16	AZERBAIJAN	26	OMAN	36	TOGO	46	NAMIBIA
8	SLOVENIA	17	KAZAKHSTAN	27	LIBYA	37	BENIN	47	BOTSWANA
9	CROATIA	18	TURKMENISTAN	28	NIGER	38	CHAD	48	ZIMBABWE
		19	KYRGYZSTAN	29	MAURITANIA	39	CENTRAL AFRICAN REPUBLIC	49	MOZAMBIQUE
								50	MALAWI

▲ **Exhibit 16-1. A View of the World According to Population.** This may be a map of the world unlike any you have seen before. This type of map is called a cartogram. Countries are drawn according to their populations: a country with a large population (such as India) is drawn larger than a country with a smaller population (such as Russia)—although, in reality, Russia covers a larger landmass than India.
©Hammond Incorporated, Maplewood, New Jersey.

times that of Norway. It turns out that the per-capita real GDP in Norway is higher than the per-capita GDP in India.

The Production Possibilities Frontier Framework

Before we continue with our discussion of economic growth, we need to discuss one of the key

---

MINI GLOSSARY

Real Economic Growth An increase from one period to the next in real GDP.
Per-Capita Real Economic Growth An increase from one period to the next in per-capita real GDP.

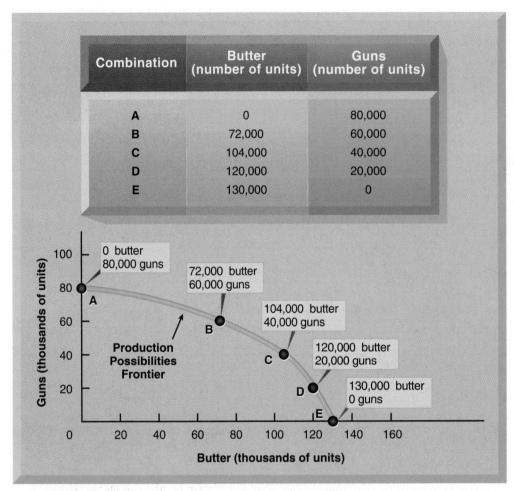

Combination	Butter (number of units)	Guns (number of units)
A	0	80,000
B	72,000	60,000
C	104,000	40,000
D	120,000	20,000
E	130,000	0

▲ **Exhibit 16-2. Deriving a Production Possibilities Frontier.** The economy can produce any of the five combinations, labeled A–E, of the two goods. These combinations are plotted, and the curve that connects points A–E is called the production possibilities frontier (PPF).

concepts in economics: the **production possibilities frontier (PPF)**. To develop it, let us first assume that there are only two goods in the world, guns (usually used to represent military goods, such as tanks and bombs) and butter (used to represent civilian goods, such as television sets and cars). If *all* the resources of the economy are used to produce guns, 80,000 can be produced in a year. If *all* the resources of the economy are used to produce butter, 130,000 units can be produced.

Besides these two maximum amounts of guns and butter, the following combinations of the two goods can be produced in a year: 72,000 units of butter and 60,000 guns; 104,000 units of butter and 40,000 guns; and 120,000 units of butter and 20,000 guns. If we plot the different combinations of the two goods the economy can produce when it uses all its resources, we obtain the production possibilities frontier in Exhibit 16-2. A society can produce any combination of goods on or below its production possibilities frontier. Anything beyond the frontier, though, is currently beyond the society's reach.

Now look at Exhibit 16-3a, which shows a production possibilities frontier shifting to the right. There you will see two production possibilities frontiers, PPF$_1$ and PPF$_2$. The arrows between the two curves—pointing rightward—indicate that

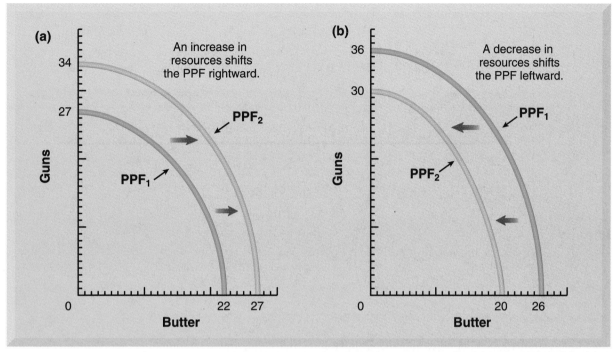

▲ **Exhibit 16-3. A Shifting Production Possibilities Frontier (PPF).** Part *a*: We start with PPF$_1$. Then, resources are added, shifting the production possibilities frontier to position PPF$_2$. With more resources, more guns and butter can be produced. Part *b*: We start with PPF$_1$. Then, resources are subtracted, shifting the production possibilities frontier to position PPF$_2$. With fewer resources, fewer guns and butter can be produced.

PPF$_1$ has moved rightward and now occupies the position of PPF$_2$.

What would need to happen for PPF$_1$ to shift rightward? To answer this question, remember how we derived the production possibilities frontier in Exhibit 16-2. We first specified the different combinations of the two goods, guns and butter, that could be produced in a year if all resources (all labor, capital, and so on) were used in the production of the two goods. We then noted five different combinations of the two goods that could be produced, plotted them, and connected the points.

Suppose additional resources are discovered, so that the society has more labor, more capital, and so on. *Additional* resources make it possible to produce *additional* guns and butter. This makes sense: with more land, labor, and capital, it is possible to produce more goods. We conclude that, before the production possibilities frontier can

shift rightward (indicating greater production possibilities for both goods), it is necessary to have more resources.

What would shift the production possibilities frontier leftward? A decrease in resources (less labor, less capital, and so on). With fewer resources, it would be impossible to produce as many goods. Exhibit 16-3b illustrates a leftward shift in the production possibilities frontier.

MINI GLOSSARY

Production Possibilities Frontier (PPF) All possible combinations of two goods that an economy can produce in a certain period of time, under the conditions of a given state of technology, no unemployed resources, and efficient production.

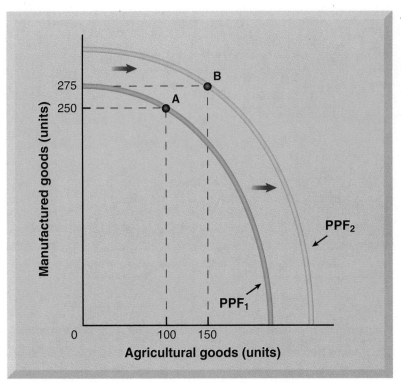

◄ **Exhibit 16-4. Economic Growth in a Production Possibilities Frontier Framework.** Economic growth is represented by a shift rightward in the production possibilities frontier, such as from PPF$_1$ to PPF$_2$.

What Factors Affect Growth?

We can illustrate growth in the framework of a production possibilities frontier, as Exhibit 16-4 shows. The horizontal axis represents agricultural goods, and the vertical axis, manufactured goods. Growth is represented by a shift rightward in the production possibilities frontier, say, from PPF$_1$ to PPF$_2$. With PPF$_2$, it is possible to have more of both goods, as you can see by comparing point A on PPF$_1$ and point B on PPF$_2$.

Why do some countries experience economic growth while others do not? Why do some countries experience fast economic growth while others experience slow economic growth? Not all economists answer these two questions the same way. They agree, however, that four factors affect growth: natural resources, capital formation, technological advances, and the property rights structure.

Natural Resources. People often think that countries with a plentiful supply of natural re-

sources (such as land, iron ore, oil, and so on) experience economic growth, whereas countries that are short on natural resources do not. The facts, though, do not always support this. For example, both Bolivia and Ghana are rich in resources but have not experienced rapid economic growth. In contrast, Singapore, which has few natural resources, has experienced rapid economic growth. In short, nations rich in natural resources are not guaranteed economic growth, whereas nations poor in natural resources may grow. Nevertheless, it is easier and more likely for a nation rich in natural resources to experience economic growth, *all other things being equal*. For example, if Singapore had been blessed with an abundance of natural resources, it probably would have experienced even greater economic growth.

Capital Formation. Chapter 1 pointed out that *capital* represents produced goods that can be used as resources for further production. Such things as factories, machines, and farm tractors are considered capital. Capital increases the ability of an individual to produce.

For example, consider two methods of catching fish. The first method requires a person to try to catch fish with his hands. The second method requires a person to try to catch fish using a net. Most of us would agree that a person using a net would be able to catch more fish than a person using his hands.

What is a net? It is a *capital good*—a produced good that is used to increase production. We can see that with added capital formation comes economic growth. Thus, modern American farmers produce much more food than their great-grandparents largely because they have capital goods, such as tractors, that their great-grandparents didn't have.

Technological Advances. Technological advances make it possible to obtain more output from the same amount of resources. For example, contrast the amount of work that can be done by a business that uses computers with the amount accomplished by a business that does not. The world has witnessed major technological advances in the past 200 years. Consider what your life would have been like if you had lived 200 years ago, around 1790. Most of the major technological achievements we take for granted today—cars, computers, telephones, electricity—did not exist.

Property Rights Structure. The term *property rights structure* refers here to the laws, rules, and regulations that define rights in the use and transfer of resources. Consider two property rights structures. In one, people are allowed to keep 90 cents of every dollar they earn. In the other, people are allowed to keep only 30 cents of every dollar they earn. Many economists would predict that the first property rights structure would stimulate more economic activity than the second, *all other things being equal.* Individuals will invest more, take more risks, and work harder when the property rights structure allows them to keep more of the fruits of their investing, risk taking, and labor.

THINKING LIKE AN ECONOMIST

When discussing economic growth, economists think in terms of tangibles and intangibles. The tangibles include natural resources, capital formation, and technological advances. The intangibles include the property rights structure, which directly affects the incentives individuals have to use the tangibles in the production of goods and services. No amount of resources, capital, and technology can alone produce economic growth. People must be motivated to put them all together; in addition, the degree of motivation affects the result. In a world in which it is easy to think that only things that occupy physical space matter, the economist reminds us to look for intangible factors, too.

▲ Computer technology has forever changed the workplace by increasing productivity and requiring new skills of workers.

CASE STUDY

Economic Growth and Special Interest Groups

Special interest groups are subsets of the general population that hold preferences—usually intense preferences—for or against particular government services, activities, or policies. Labor unions, farmers, and car manufacturers are all examples of special interest groups. Sometimes, special interest groups benefit from public policies that may not be in accord with the interests of the general public. For example, suppose American car manufacturers lobby Congress to place a tariff, or tax, on Japanese cars imported into the country. The tariff will make Japanese cars more expensive for American car buyers and less competitive with the cars U.S. companies produce. Consequently, U.S. consumers will lose, and U.S. car manufacturers will gain.

The economist Mancur Olson has argued that special interest groups often propose policies that end up taking money away from some people to give to themselves. In short, they are more interested in getting a bigger slice of the economic pie than in trying to increase the overall size of the pie through economic growth.

Olson goes on to say that in nations where there is a long period of political stability, special interest groups have an opportunity to grow and achieve political power. In turn, they use this power to push for policies that mainly help them at the expense of others and at the expense of

economic growth. For example, Olson argues that the United States, having experienced a long period of political stability, currently has powerful special interest groups that can accomplish their goals. In comparison, Japan and Germany, when they lost World War II, had their societies turned upside down. In the process, once-powerful special interest groups were dismantled; and as yet, these groups have not had time to reestablish themselves and become as strong as their American counterparts. Olson argues that during much of the time since World War II, the relative weakness of special interest groups in the former West Germany and Japan explains why their economic growth rates have often been higher than the growth rate in the United States.

---

1. What is a special interest group?
2. As time passes, and Germany and Japan experience longer periods of political stability, what would Olson predict will happen to their economic growth rates, and why?

The Rule of 72

The *Rule of 72* is a simple arithmetical rule for compound calculations. We can use it when discussing economic growth rates. For example, suppose a country experiences a 4 percent economic growth rate each year for 20 years. How many years will it take for the country's economy to double in size?

The answer, according to the Rule of 72, is 18 years. We obtain the number 18 by dividing 72 by the specified growth rate, 4 percent ($72 \div 4 = 18$). Formally, the Rule of 72 states that we can calculate the time required for any variable to double by dividing 72 by the percentage growth rate of the variable.

$$\text{Time required for variable to double} = \frac{72}{\text{Percentage growth rate of variable}}$$

We can use the Rule of 72 to calculate other things of interest to us. For example, suppose you put $1,000 into a savings account that pays 6 percent interest a year. How many years will it take for you to double your money (and have $2,000)? The answer is 12 years ($72 \div 6 = 12$).

Or suppose you are working at a job and receive an 8 percent raise each year. How many years will it take for your salary to double? The answer is 9 years ($72 \div 8 = 9$).

Finally, suppose the inflation rate is 9 percent each year. How many years will it take for prices to double? The answer is 8 years ($72 \div 9 = 8$). This means that a house that costs $100,000 today will cost $200,000 in 8 years (assuming that the price of houses rises by the inflation rate).

Future Economic Growth: Is It Good or Bad?

Traditionally, most people have believed that economic growth is a good thing and that faster growth is better than slower growth. But not everyone agrees.

▲ Some people point out that economic growth brings many positive things, such as the ability to support art projects and museums.

Two worries commonly crop up in discussions of economic growth. One concerns the costs of growth. Some individuals argue that more economic growth comes with more pollution, more factories (and thus fewer open spaces), more crowding in cities, more emphasis on material goods and getting ahead, more rushing around, more psychological problems, and so on. They argue for less growth instead of more.

Others maintain there is no evidence that economic growth (or faster as opposed to slower economic growth) causes all or most of these problems. They argue that growth brings many positive things: more wealth, less poverty, a society that is better able to support art projects and museums, less worry in people's lives (not having enough is a huge worry), and so forth.

Another debate surrounds the issue of economic growth and the future availability of resources. Some people believe that continued economic and population growth threaten the very survival of the human race, since such growth will simply shorten the time until the world runs out of resources. No doubt, they say, a time will come when there will be no more natural resources, no more food, no more clean air, no more pure water, and no more land on which people can live comfortably. They urge government to implement social policies that will slow down growth and preserve what we have.

Critics of this position often charge that such "doomsday forecasts," as they have come to be called, are based on unrealistic assumptions, oversights, and flimsy evidence. For example, one economist, Julian Simon, contends that, contrary to the doomsday forecasts, the quantity of land suitable for farming has increased in recent years owing to swamp drainage and land improvement, a larger population does not necessarily mean a poorer population (for example, some countries with dense populations have high per-capita incomes), the incidence of famine is decreasing, and we are not running out of natural resources.

The various debates between those who favor more growth and those who favor less are not simple. Economists have become engaged in them, as have psychologists, biologists, sociologists, and many others. The debates promise to continue for a long time.

✔ LEARNING CHECK

1. Country 1 has a population of 10 million and a real GDP of $40 billion. Country 2 has a population of 50 million and a real GDP of $100 billion. What is the per-capita real GDP for each country?
2. How is capital formation related to economic growth?
3. Country C has an annual growth rate of 2 percent. How many years will it take for Country C's economy to double in size?
4. "Economic growth is good." Do you agree or disagree? Explain your answer.

SECTION 2 ECONOMIC DEVELOPMENT

 Economic development encompasses more than economic growth. It implies a higher standard of living—for example, better transportation networks, better schools, and more and higher-quality goods to consume.

In this section, we consider economic development in terms of the less-developed countries—often simply referred to as LDCs. These countries are also sometimes called developing countries or economies, underdeveloped countries, or third-world countries. Mainly, we will be concerned with the question, "Why are some nations poor?"

As you read, keep these key questions in mind:

■ What is a less-developed country (LDC)?
■ Why are some nations so poor?

The Problem of the LDCs

A **less-developed country (LDC)** is a country with a low per-capita GDP. A **developed country** is a country with a high per-capita GDP. About three-quarters of the world's people live in less-developed countries.

To get some idea what a low per-capita GDP figure is, consider a few nations with high per-capita GDP figures. In 1991, Switzerland had a per-capita GDP of $33,500; the United States, a per-capita GDP of $22,560; and Japan, a per-capita GDP of $26,920. Countries with low per-capita GDP figures include (to name only a few) Afghanistan, Bangladesh, Cambodia, China,

Chad, Ethiopia, India, Nigeria, Pakistan, Somalia, Tanzania, Uganda, and Zambia. For example, in 1991 the per-capita GDP in India was $330; in China, $370; and in Nigeria, $290.

Why has economic development largely bypassed the people of the LDCs? Why are some nations so poor? Here are a few of the obstacles that some economists believe stifle economic development in the LDCs.

Rapid Population Growth. It is commonly noticed that the **population growth rate** is higher in LDCs than in developed nations. For example, the population growth rate has been around 0.5 percent in developed nations (such as the United States and Great Britain), whereas it has been around 2 to 3 percent in LDCs. The population growth rate is equal to the birthrate minus the death rate.

Population growth rate = Birthrate − Death rate

For example, if in Country X the birthrate is 3 percent in a given year and the death rate is 2 percent, then the population growth rate is 1 percent[1] (3% − 2% = 1%).

What has caused the relatively high population growth rate in the LDCs? First, the birthrate tends to be higher than in developed nations. In countries where pensions, Social Security, and the like do not exist, and where the economy revolves around agriculture, children are often seen as essential labor and as security for parents in their old age. In this setting, people tend to have more children.

Second, in the past few decades in the LDCs, the death rate has fallen, largely because of medical advances. The combination of higher birthrates and declining death rates explains why the population grows more rapidly in LDCs than in developed nations.

But is a high population growth rate always an obstacle to economic development? True, today many of the countries of the world that have high population growth rates are poor. But this fact, by itself, does not mean that a country with a high population growth rate cannot become economically developed. For example, many of today's developed nations—such as the United States—had a high population growth rate in the past and still managed to develop.

Nonetheless, some still argue that rapid population growth, though not necessarily a deterrent to economic development, can stifle it. This is be-

---

MINI GLOSSARY

Less-Developed Country (LDC) A country with a low per-capita GDP.
Developed Country A country with a high per-capita GDP.
Population Growth Rate The birthrate minus the death rate.

▼ In some less-developed countries (LDCs) where agriculture is an important part of the economy, children sometimes work along with their parents.

---

1. In many cases, the birth- and death rates are not given in percentage terms but in births or deaths per thousand. For example, the birthrate of Country X might be cited as "30 per thousand." This means that 30 babies were born for every 1,000 persons in the population.

Thomas Malthus

The economist Thomas Malthus has been called a prophet of doom. Malthus, who lived in England from 1766 to 1834, predicted that the population of the world would increase at a faster rate than the food supply, resulting in mass starvation.

Specifically, Malthus said that the population increases at a *geometric rate*. A number that increases at a geometric rate continually multiplies itself by a constant. For example, in the series 1, 2, 4, 8, 16, 32, 64, 128, 256, and so on, each number is multiplied by 2, so the series increases at a geometric rate. In contrast, according to Malthus, the food supply increases at an *arithmetic rate*. When numbers increase by an arithmetic rate, the same number is added at each step—for example, the number 1 in the series 1, 2, 3, 4, 5, 6, 7, 8, 9, and so on.

What does this mean? To see, look at Exhibit 16-5. Column 1 lists the years 1–9; column 2, the population in these years; and column 3, the food supply in these years. Notice that the population increases geometrically (1, 2, 4, 8, . . .) and the food supply increases arithmetically (1, 2, 3, 4, . . .). Now, notice that in year 4, there are 8 persons and 4 baskets of food, so that the average amount of food per person is ½ basket. Five years later, in year 9, there are 256 people and 9 baskets of food, so that the average amount of food per person has decreased to about 0.035 of a basket.

Malthus warned that if something was not done quickly, the world was headed for dismal times. He proposed that couples put off marriage until later years and have fewer children.

The population in many nations did not increase at the high rate that Malthus predicted, nor did the food supply grow as slowly. For one thing, Malthus did not foresee that major technological changes in agriculture would make farmers much more effective in producing food.

Nor did Malthus foresee another change. At earlier times in the world's history, most people had just enough to get by—a subsistence living. With a move away from subsistence living in many parts of the world toward a higher standard of living and increased urbanization, couples naturally chose to have fewer children. (Today, in the poor nations, not the wealthy, the birthrate is relatively high.)

As stated earlier, Malthus predicted that the future would be bleak unless radical changes were made. For this reason, people today who do the same thing are often called Malthusians. What Thomas Malthus did, and what Malthusians today do, is look at what is happening in the present and then *assume* it will continue into the future. For example, suppose that as the population increases, the demand for oil increases. A Malthusian might argue that if the demand for oil continues to grow, one day there will be no more oil. But, in fact, if the demand for oil continues to grow, the price will rise, people will cut back on their purchases of oil, and entrepreneurs will begin to look for substitutes for oil or additional supplies of oil. The Malthusian view is very static and rigid: what is bad today will be worse tomorrow if something isn't done. Some people believe that the evidence, though, does not always support the Malthusian view of things.

---

1. What does it mean to say that the population grows geometrically as the food supply grows arithmetically?

2. Malthus made some predictions that did not come true. Explain why they didn't come true. What did Malthus overlook?

▶ **Exhibit 16-5. The Malthusian View in Numbers.** Thomas Malthus believed that population increases geometrically, while the food supply increases arithmetically. Accordingly, as time passes, there will be, on average, less food per person. The evidence does not support this Malthusian view.

(1) Year	(2) Population (persons)	(3) Food supply (baskets of food)
1	1	1
2	2	2
3	4	3
4	8	4
5	16	5
6	32	6
7	64	7
8	128	8
9	256	9

cause in countries with fast-growing populations, the **dependency ratio** rises. The dependency ratio is the number of children under a certain age plus the number of the elderly (aged 65 and over) divided by the total population. For example, if the number of children and elderly equals 500 and the total population is 1,500, the dependency ratio is 33 percent (500 ÷ 1,500 = 0.33). The high dependency ratio in LDCs like India, Bangladesh, and Egypt puts added burdens on the productive working-age population.

Low Savings Rate. We have seen that a farmer with a tractor (which is a capital good) is likely to be more productive than one without a tractor, all other things being equal. Now, consider a farmer who cannot afford to buy a tractor. This farmer may decide to borrow the money from a bank. But where does the bank get the money to

lend? It gets money from the people who have savings accounts at the bank. Savings, then, are important to economic growth and development. If there is a low savings rate, then there will not be much money to borrow, and capital goods such as tractors (which increase productivity) will not be produced and purchased.

Some economists argue that the LDCs have low savings rates because the people living there are so poor that they can't save. In short, they earn only enough income to buy the necessities of life—

MINI GLOSSARY

Dependency Ratio The number of children under a certain age plus the elderly (aged 65 and over) divided by the total population.

▲ In many poor countries where people often do not have enough money to buy the necessities of life, there is little, if any, money that can be saved.

shelter and food. There is no "extra income" left over to save. This is what is called the **vicious circle of poverty**: LDCs are poor because they can't save and buy capital goods, but they can't save and buy capital goods because they are poor.

Other economists argue, though, that being poor is not a barrier to economic development. They say that many nations that are rich today (such as the United States) were poor in the past but still managed to become economically developed.

Cultural Differences. Do some of the LDCs have cultures that retard economic growth and development? Some people think so. For example, some cultures are reluctant to depart from the **status quo**. The people may think that things ought to stay the way they always have been; they view change as dangerous and risky. In such countries, it is not uncommon for people's upward economic and social mobility to depend on who their parents were rather than on who they are or what they do. Furthermore, in some cultures, the people

are fatalistic by Western standards. That is, they believe that a person's good or bad fortune in life depends more on fate or the spirits than on how hard the person works, or how much he or she learns, or how hard he or she strives to succeed.

Political Instability and Government Seizure of Private Property. Individuals sometimes do not invest in businesses in the LDCs because they are afraid either that the current government leaders will be thrown out of office or that the government will seize their private property. People are not likely to invest their money in places where the risk of losing it is high.

MINI GLOSSARY

Vicious Circle of Poverty The idea that countries are poor because they do not save and buy capital goods, but they cannot save and buy capital goods because they are poor.

Status Quo That which exists now; the existing state of affairs.

✔ LEARNING CHECK

1. What is a less-developed country?
2. What is the dependency ratio?
3. Explain the vicious circle of poverty.

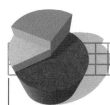

DEVELOPING ECONOMIC SKILLS

Applying the Production Possibilities Frontier

Exhibit 16-6 represents a production possibilities frontier for two types of goods: military goods (tanks, bombs, and so on) and nonmilitary goods (cars, television sets, schools, and so on). Suppose that this production possibilities frontier holds for the United States and that currently the United States is operating at point C. At point C, it is producing a certain amount of military goods and a certain amount of nonmilitary goods.

Some U.S. citizens propose that the United States should produce more military goods and fewer nonmilitary goods—that is, more tanks and bombs and fewer cars, and so on. These people argue that we live in a dangerous world and that we have to protect ourselves to the best of our abilities. They argue that the United States should shift from point C in Exhibit 16-6 to, say, point B. At point B, there are *more military goods* than at point C. What thinking in terms of the production possibilities frontier makes clear, though, is that at point B there are also *fewer nonmilitary goods*.

Now consider some U.S. citizens who argue that the United States should produce more nonmilitary goods and fewer military goods. They say that the United States already has too much military hardware and propose that it move from point C to, say, point D. At point D, there are *more nonmilitary goods* but, of course, *fewer military goods*.

The person who thinks in terms of a production possibilities frontier always remembers a key fact

in life: that for an economy that operates on its production possibilities frontier, more of one good necessarily means less of some other good.

You might say that this is just common sense, and you would be right. But often we fail to use

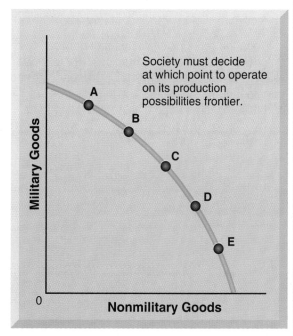

▲ **Exhibit 16-6. Choices and the Production Possibilities Frontier.** We assume this is the production possibilities frontier for the United States. The nation has to operate at some point; it cannot operate at more than one point at a time.

DEVELOPING ECONOMIC SKILLS (continued)

our common sense. Thinking in terms of the production possibilities frontier, though, makes it less likely that we will neglect to use our common sense at important times. For example, in 1993, President Bill Clinton proposed that the health care system in the United States be restructured. At the time, there were millions of persons who did not have health insurance, and some people in this uninsured group were not receiving medical attention. In Clinton's health plan, these persons were to receive health insurance and necessary medical attention.

There is no doubt that the United States has the resources to provide every single person in the country with the medical attention that he or she needs. However, if the United States is operating on its production possibilities frontier, and if the quality of medical attention is not to be lowered, it is impossible to provide more people with health insurance and medical attention without sacrificing some other goods and services.

Does the recognition of this fact dampen our optimism about providing medical care to those who need it but can't afford it? Perhaps for some people it does. We would like to think that we can accomplish one goal without reducing our

ability to accomplish any other goal. Sadly, though, the world doesn't always work this way. An understanding of what is possible—and what isn't—often comes to us through the production possibilities frontier. It may not always be pleasant, but thinking in terms of the production possibilities frontier does keep us grounded in reality—and this is no small accomplishment.

1. There are many things that you can do in a day: work, go to school, study at home, watch TV, hang out with friends, and so on. How is this like an economy that can produce many different goods in a year?

2. There is a saying in economics: "There is no such thing as a free lunch." We might change this to say, "There is no such thing as free medical care for everyone." Would these statements more likely be made by a person who thinks in terms of a production possibilities frontier or a person who does not? Explain your answer.

CHAPTER 16 REVIE

CHAPTER SUMMARY

1. The term *economic growth* is used to refer to both real economic growth and per-capita real economic growth. Real economic growth is an increase in real GDP. Per-capita real economic growth is an increase in per-capita real GDP.

2. Economic growth is represented as a shift rightward in the production possibilities frontier.

3. Economists agree that the following four factors affect economic growth: natural resources, capital formation, technological advances, and property rights structure. There is a direct relationship between each of the first three factors and economic growth. For example, the more natural resources a nation has, the greater its economic growth, *all other things being equal*.

4. The Rule of 72 states that the time required for any variable to double is equal to 72 divided by the percentage growth rate.

5. Greater economic growth comes with both benefits and costs. Given this, we should not say that more growth is *necessarily* a good thing. It depends on whether the benefits are greater than or less than the costs.

6. Economic development includes more than economic growth. Economic development implies a higher standard of living—better transportation networks, better schools, more and higher-quality goods to consume, and so forth.

7. A less-developed country (LDC) is a country with a low per-capita GDP. About three-quarters of the world's people live in LDCs.

8. A few of the obstacles that economists believe stifle economic development are rapid population growth, a low savings rate, certain cultural practices, political instability, and government seizure of private property.

BUILD YOUR ECONOMIC VOCABULARY

Match the word with the correct definition, example, or statement.

1. real economic growth
2. per-capita real GDP
3. capital
4. LDC
5. population growth rate
6. dependency ratio
7. vicious circle of poverty
8. status quo

a. the way things are now
b. real GDP divided by population
c. a country with a low per-capita GDP
d. an increase from one period to the next in real GDP
e. produced goods that can be used as resources for further production
f. birthrate minus death rate
g. number of children below a certain age plus number of elderly people divided by total population
h. idea that LDCs are poor because they can't save and buy capital goods but they can't save and buy capital goods because they are poor

CHAPTER 16 REVIEW (continued)

REVIEW QUESTIONS

1. Which do most economists think is more useful in measuring economic growth, real economic growth or per-capita real economic growth? Explain why.

2. Calculate per-capita real GDP for each of the following:
   a. In Country 1, real GDP is $800 billion, and the population is 250 million.
   b. In Country 2, real GDP is $1,050 billion, and the population is 100 million.
   c. In Country 3, real GDP is $5,000 billion, and the population is 250 million.

3. What would shift the production possibilities frontier leftward? Explain why.

4. Explain how each of the following factors affects economic growth, *assuming all other things are equal*: (a) natural resources, (b) capital formation, and (c) technological advances.

5. Make the following calculations:
   a. You put $4,000 into a savings account that pays interest at a rate of 9 percent a year. In how many years will your money have doubled?
   b. You receive a 6 percent raise each year. In how many years will your salary have doubled?
   c. The inflation rate is 4 percent a year. In how many years will prices have doubled?

6. What is the difference between economic development and economic growth?

7. Why might couples living in less-developed countries have more children than couples living in developed countries?

8. The birthrate in a country is 5 percent, and the death rate is 3 percent. What is the population growth rate?

9. What is the vicious circle of poverty?

10. Explain how a low savings rate can stifle economic growth and development.

SHARPEN YOUR CRITICAL THINKING SKILLS

1. Economic growth comes with benefits and costs. The benefits usually include more goods from which the consumer can choose, more jobs, and higher tax revenues (which may be used for such things as building more and better schools). The costs of economic growth usually include more pollution, more traffic, and perhaps more stress in our daily lives. In a small, pollution-free town where the unemployment rate is high, there is a tendency to believe that the benefits of growth outweigh the costs. In a large city where pollution is a major problem and the unemployment rate is low, there is a tendency to believe that the costs of growth outweigh the benefits. Consider the town or city in which you live. Do you think the benefits of economic growth are currently greater than or less than the costs? Explain your answer.

2. "In Country A, real GDP was $1,000 billion this year. In Country B, real GDP was $3,000 billion this year. It follows that the inhabitants of Country B are better off than the inhabitants of Country A." Identify the economic error in this statement.

ACTIVITIES AND PROJECTS

1. Thomas Malthus has been called a prophet of doom. A prophet of doom is one who predicts bad things for the future unless some things are changed in the present. Sometimes the prophet of doom is correct in his or her predictions and sometimes he or she is wrong. Read through a few newspapers and magazines and see if you can identify someone who would be, for you, a current-day prophet of doom. Explain why you think this person is either correct or incorrect in what he or she is predicting.

ECONOMIC DICTIONARY

Dependency Ratio (Pg. 411)
Developed Country (Pg. 408)
Less-Developed Country (LDC) (Pg. 408)
Per-Capita Real Economic Growth (Pg. 400)
Population Growth Rate (Pg. 409)

Production Possibilities Frontier (PPF) (Pg. 402)
Real Economic Growth (Pg. 400)
Status Quo (Pg. 412)
Vicious Circle of Poverty (Pg. 412)

International Trade

INTRODUCTION

We live in a global economy. Precision ice hockey equipment is designed in Sweden, financed in Canada, and assembled in Cleveland, Ohio. An advertising campaign is conceived in England, and footage for it is shot in Canada, dubbed in England, and edited in New York. A sports car is financed in Japan, designed in Italy, and assembled in Indiana, Mexico, and France. It uses advanced electronic components invented in New Jersey and fabricated in Japan. A jet plane is designed in the state of Washington and in Japan and assembled in Seattle, with tail cones from Canada, special tail sections from China and Italy, and engines from England.[1]

Americans deal more and more with people in other nations. As they do, they may learn things about other people that they either did not know before or did not stop to think about.

In this chapter, we consider an increasingly important activity of people in a global economy: trade.

---

1. All examples are from Robert B. Reich, *The Work of Nations* (New York: A.A. Knopf, 1992).

418

1. Define *balance of trade*.
2. Calculate which country has a comparative advantage in the production of which good.
3. Discuss the effects of tariffs and quotas.
4. State the arguments for and against trade restrictions.
5. Explain the fixed and flexible exchange rate systems.

KEY TERMS

Absolute Advantage	Exchange Rate
Appreciation	Export
Balance of Trade	Fixed Exchange Rate System
Comparative Advantage	Flexible Exchange Rate System
Depreciation	Import
Dumping	Specialize

This section discusses some of the facts and figures of international trade, especially as they relate to the United States. It also introduces the important concept of comparative advantage.

As you read, keep these key questions in mind:

- What goods are major U.S. exports?
- What goods are major U.S. imports?
- What is comparative advantage?

Why Do People in Different Countries Trade with Each Other?

We have international trade for the same reason we have trade at any level. Individuals trade to make themselves better off. Frank and Bob, who live in Detroit, trade because both value something the other has more than they value something of their own. For example, perhaps Frank trades $10 for Bob's book. On an international scale, Elaine in the United States trades with Cho in China because Cho has something that Elaine wants and Elaine has something that Cho wants.

Obviously, different countries have different terrains, climates, resources, and so on. It follows that some countries will be able to produce some goods that other countries cannot produce or can produce only at extremely high cost. For example, Hong Kong has no oil, and Saudi Arabia has a large supply. Bananas do not grow easily in the United States, but they flourish in Honduras. Americans could grow bananas, if they used hothouses, but it is cheaper for Americans to buy bananas from Honduras than to produce bananas themselves.

Imports and Exports

Exports represent the dollar value of products sold to foreign countries, and **imports** represent the dollar value of products brought into a country

◄ Every day in the United States goods arrive from other countries. In 1992, imported goods totaled $615 billion.

U.S. Exports		U.S. Imports	
Products	Value ($ millions)	Products	Value ($ millions)
1. Transportation equipment	$38,613	1. Road vehicles	$74,532
2. Road vehicles	37,946	2. Electric machinery and parts	39,729
3. Electric machinery and parts	37,424	3. Office and ADP machines	36,393
4. Office and ADP machines	30,983	4. Apparel/clothing/accessories	31,242
5. Miscellaneous manufactured articles	23,283	5. Miscellaneous manufactured articles	28,541
6. Industrial machinery and parts	18,876	6. Telecom and sound-reproduction equipment	25,819
7. Power-generating machinery	18,454	7. Power-generating machinery	15,910
8. Special industrial machinery	17,245	8. Industrial machinery and parts	15,522
9. Professional/scientific/control instruments	14,944	9. Special industrial machinery	11,826
10. Telecom and sound-reproduction equipment	12,327	10. Nonmetallic mineral manufactures	10,170

▲ **EXHIBIT 17-1. U.S. Exports and Imports.** Here is a list of the top 10 U.S. exports and imports.
Source: *The Universal Almanac, 1994* (Kansas City, Mo.: Andrews and McMeel, 1993), p. 342. Data are for 1992.
Copyright © 1993 by John W. Wright. Reprinted with permission of Andrews and McMeel. All rights reserved.

from other countries. In 1992, U.S. exports totaled $573 billion, and U.S. imports totaled $615 billion. Major U.S. exports include automobiles, computers, aircraft, corn, wheat, soybeans, scientific instruments, coal, and plastic materials. Major imports include petroleum, automobiles, clothing, iron and steel, office machines, footwear, fish, coffee, and diamonds.

The Balance of Trade

A nation's **balance of trade** is the difference between the value of its exports and the value of its imports.

Balance of trade = Exports − Imports

For example, if a country's exports this year total $300 billion and its imports total $260 billion, then it has a positive balance of trade of $40 billion ($300 billion − $260 billion = $40 billion). If, however, the numbers are reversed, and exports are $260 billion and imports are $300 billion, it

has a negative balance of trade of $40 billion ($260 billion − $300 billion = −$40 billion). A positive balance of trade occurs when exports are greater than imports; a negative balance of trade occurs when exports are less than imports. See Exhibit 17-1 for a list of the top 10 U.S. exports and imports.

Absolute Advantage

Suppose that using the same quantity of resources as Japan, the United States can produce

MINI GLOSSARY

Exports Dollar value of products sold in foreign countries.
Imports Dollar value of products brought into a country from other countries.
Balance of Trade The difference between the value of a nation's exports and the value of its imports.

The United States can produce either	Japan can produce either
Combination A: 150 units of food and 0 units of clothing *or* Combination B: 100 units of food and 25 units of clothing	Combination C: 30 units of food and 120 units of clothing *or* Combination D: 0 units of food and 180 units of clothing
Case 1 **No specialization and no trade**	**Case 2** **Specialization and trade**
The United States produces combination B, 100 units of food and 25 units of clothing. Since it does not trade with Japan, the United States consumes what it produces.	The United States specializes in food production and produces 150 units of food; Japan specializes in clothing production and produces 180 units of clothing.
Japan produces combination C, 30 units of food and 120 units of clothing. Since it does not trade with the United States, Japan consumes what it produces.	The United States and Japan agree to trade 40 units of food for 40 units of clothing.
	The United States ends up with 110 units of food and 40 units of clothing. This is 10 more units of food and 15 more units of clothing than in Case 1.
	Japan ends up with 40 units of food and 140 units of clothing. This is 10 more units of food and 20 more units of clothing than in Case 1.
	There is no doubt about it. Countries are made better off through specialization and trade.

▲ **EXHIBIT 17-2. Specializing and Trading versus Not Specializing and Trading.** Nations are better off—that is, they can consume more—when they specialize and trade than when they do not specialize and trade.

either of two combinations of food and clothing, shown here and in Exhibit 17-2.

The United States can produce either
Combination A: 150 units of food and 0 units of clothing
or
Combination B: 100 units of food and 25 units of clothing

Now, suppose that Japan, using the same quantity of resources as the United States, can produce either of two combinations of food and clothing, also shown here and in Exhibit 17-2.

Japan can produce either
Combination C: 30 units of food and 120 units of clothing
or
Combination D: 0 units of food and 180 units of clothing

When a country can produce more of a good than another country using the same quantity of resources, it is said to have an **absolute advantage** in the production of that good. In our example, the United States has an absolute advantage in producing food, since the maximum amount of food it can produce (150 units) is greater than the maximum amount of food Japan can produce (30 units). Japan, on the other hand, has an absolute advantage in producing clothing, because the maximum amount of clothing it can produce (180 units) is greater than the maximum amount of clothing the United States can produce (25 units).

Comparative Advantage

Suppose that in year 1, Japan and the United States do not trade with each other. Instead, each nation decides to produce some quantity of each good and consume it. The United States produces and consumes combination B (100 units of food and 25 units of clothing); and Japan produces and consumes combination C (30 units of food and 120 units of clothing).

In year 2, things change. Each country decides to **specialize** in the production of one good and then trade some of it for the other good. Which good—clothing or food—should the United States specialize in producing? Which good should Japan specialize in producing?

The general answer to both questions is that the country should specialize in the production of the good in which it has a **comparative advantage**. Simply put, this means each country should specialize in the production of the good it can produce at lower opportunity cost.

How to Determine Opportunity Cost. Recall from Chapter 1 that the opportunity cost of producing a good is what you give up to produce that good. For example, if Jones gives up the opportunity to produce three towels if he produces a blanket, then the opportunity cost of the blanket is three towels.

What is the opportunity cost of producing food for the United States? What is the cost for Japan? First, consider the United States. We know that it can produce either combination A (150 units of food and 0 units of clothing) or combination B (100 units of food and 25 units of clothing). Suppose it is producing combination B. What are the benefits and costs of deciding to produce combination A instead? By producing combination A, the country

will make itself better off by 50 additional units of food, but it will have to give up 25 units of clothing to do so. In other words, for every 1 extra unit of food, it will have to give up ½ unit of clothing. In economic terms, for the United States, the opportunity cost of 1 unit of food is ½ unit of clothing.

The process is similar for Japan. We know that Japan can produce either combination C (30 units of food and 120 units of clothing) or combination D (0 units of food and 180 units of clothing). Suppose it is producing combination D. What are the benefits and costs of deciding to produce combination C instead? By producing combination C, Japan will make itself better off by 30 additional units of food, but it will have to give up 60 units of clothing to do so. In other words, for every 1 extra unit of food, it will have to give up 2 units of clothing. In economic terms, for Japan, the opportunity cost of 1 unit of food is 2 units of clothing.

We have found that the opportunity cost of producing food is ½ unit of clothing for the United States and 2 units of clothing for Japan. We conclude that the United States can produce food more cheaply than Japan. In other words, the United States has a comparative advantage in food production. Food, then, is what the United States should specialize in producing. If we followed this procedure for clothing production, we would find that Japan can produce clothing more cheaply than the United States. Therefore, it has a comparative advantage in clothing production. Clothing, then, is what Japan should specialize in producing.

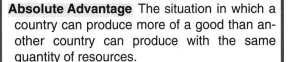

MINI GLOSSARY

Absolute Advantage The situation in which a country can produce more of a good than another country can produce with the same quantity of resources.
Specialize To do only one thing. For example, when a country specializes in the production of a good, it produces only that good.
Comparative Advantage The situation in which a country can produce a good at lower opportunity cost than another country.

The Benefits of Specialization and Trade

Consider two cases, both shown in Exhibit 17-2. In the first, neither Japan nor the United States specializes in the production of either good (thus, both produce some amount of each good), and the two nations do not trade. In this case, the United States produces combination B (100 units of food and 25 units of clothing), and Japan produces combination C (30 units of food and 120 units of clothing).

In the second case, each country specializes in the production of the good in which it has a comparative advantage, and then it trades some of that good for the other good. The United States produces combination A (150 units of food and 0 units of clothing), and Japan produces combination D (0 units of food and 180 units of clothing). The countries decide that the United States will trade 40 units of food to Japan in return for 40 units of clothing. After trade, then, the United States ends up with 110 units of food and 40 units of clothing. Japan, in turn, ends up with 40 units of food and 140 units of clothing.

In which case are Japan and the United States better off? The answer is the second case, where there is specialization and trade. In the first case, the United States ended up with 100 units of food and 25 units of clothing; whereas in the second, it ended up with 110 units of food and 40 units of clothing. In other words, through specialization and trade, the United States ended up with more of both food and clothing. The same holds for Japan. In the first case, it ended up with 30 units of food and 120 units of clothing; whereas in the second, it ended up with 40 units of food and 140 units of clothing. Through specialization and trade, Japan ended up with more of both food and clothing.

The lesson is this: If nations specialize in the production of the goods in which they have a comparative advantage and then trade these goods for other goods, they can make themselves better off.

 LEARNING CHECK

1. Suppose the United States can produce either 90 apples and 20 oranges or 80 apples and 30 oranges. What is the opportunity cost of producing 1 apple?
2. Suppose Japan can produce either 100 cars and 30 television sets or 80 cars and 60 television sets. What is the opportunity cost of producing 1 television set?
3. What does it mean to say that Country A has a comparative advantage in the production of computers?

SECTION 2 **TRADE RESTRICTIONS**

The preceding section showed that countries benefit by specializing in the production of goods in which they have a comparative advantage and trading these goods for other goods. In the real world, though, there are numerous trade restrictions. This leads us to ask, "If countries gain from free international trade, why are there restrictions on trade?" This section answers that question.

As you read, keep these key questions in mind:

■ What is a tariff?
■ What is a quota?
■ How do tariffs and quotas affect price?
■ What are the arguments for and against trade restrictions?

Trade Restrictions: Tariffs and Quotas

There are two major types of trade restrictions: tariffs and quotas. A *tariff* is a tax on imports. For example, currently some Americans buy cars made in Japan. These Japanese cars are considered imports. Let's say each car sells for $18,000. Now suppose the U.S. government places a $1,000 tariff on each car. The tariff raises the price of a Japanese car from $18,000 to $19,000. As a result, Americans will buy fewer Japanese cars. (Remember the law of demand: As price rises, quantity demanded falls.)

A *quota* is a legal limit on the amount of a good that may be imported. To illustrate, suppose Japan is sending 300,000 cars into the United States each year. The U.S. government decides to set a quota on Japanese cars. It sets the legal limit—the quota—at 200,000 cars per year. In short, the U.S. government says it is legal for Japan to send 200,000 cars each year to the United States, but not one car more.

What is the effect of the quota? It is to raise the price of Japanese cars. With a smaller supply of Japanese cars, and with demand for Japanese cars constant, the price of Japanese cars will rise. (Recall that when the supply of a good falls and the demand for the good remains the same, the price of the good rises.)

In effect, then, both tariffs and quotas raise the price of the imported good to the American consumer.

The U.S. Government and Producer Interests

If tariffs and quotas result in higher prices for American consumers, why does the government impose them? The answer is that government is sometimes more responsive to producer interests than consumer interests. To see why, suppose there are 100 U.S. producers of good X and 20 million U.S. consumers of good X. The producers

From *Herblock At Large* (Pantheon Books, 1987).

want to protect themselves from foreign competition, so they lobby for, and receive, tariffs on foreign goods that compete with what they sell. As a result, consumers end up paying higher prices. We'll say that consumers end up paying $40 million more, and producers end up receiving $40 million more, for good X than they would have if the tariffs had not been imposed. If we equally divide the additional $40 million received among the 100 producers, we find that each producer receives $400,000 more as a result of tariffs ($40 million ÷ 100 producers = $400,000 per producer). If we equally divide the additional $40 million paid among the 20 million consumers, we find that each customer pays $2 more as a result of tariffs ($40 million ÷ 20 million consumers = $2 per consumer). A producer is likely to think, "I should lobby for tariffs, because if I am effective, I will receive $400,000 more." A consumer is likely to think, "Why should I lobby against tariffs? If I am effective, I will only save myself $2. It isn't worth my lobbying to save $2."

CONSUMER ECONOMIC DECISIONS

Making $

When Your Consuming Interest Is at Odds with Your Producing Interest

When you are acting as a consumer, tariffs and quotas are clearly not in your best interest, since they raise the prices you pay for goods and services. When you are acting as a producer, though, tariffs and quotas may work in your favor. For example, suppose you are an accountant, lawyer, or factory worker for an American car manufacturing company. Foreign car companies are doing better in the market than your company. The executives in your company lobby the members of Congress and get a tariff placed on imported cars. The result will be that foreign car prices are generally higher and fewer foreign cars are sold in the United States. As a person who may want to buy a foreign car, you may not like this. But as a person who works for an American car company, you may favor anything that helps you to hang on to your job. Here, then, your consuming interest is pitted against your producing interest. Which will you favor?

Usually, individuals favor their producing interests over their consuming interests, because they realize they won't be able to consume much if they're not producing (working). This is part of the explanation for why we see more producer interests than consumer interests lobbying in Washington. The autoworker who is also a consumer usually is quicker to argue against anything that will adversely af-

fect his or her job than to argue against anything that will adversely affect the prices of some of the goods he or she buys. The farmer who is also a consumer is quicker to argue against anything that will adversely affect his or her income than to argue against anything that will adversely affect the prices of some of the goods he or she buys.

The problem, though, is that if almost everybody is advancing his or her producer interests and not doing anything about his or her consumer interests, we will naturally see producer interests being weighted more heavily than consumer interests in our state and national legislatures.

---

1. "A person only produces one thing (such as economics lectures), but she consumes many things (cars, houses, clothes, and so on). It seems, then, that she would be more interested in advancing her consumer interests than her producer interests." Do you agree or disagree with this statement? Explain your answer.

2. Which would you expect to be more likely: (a) the case in which a person always speaks against tariffs and quotas or (b) the case in which a person selectively speaks against tariffs and quotas? Explain your answer.

In short, the benefits of tariffs are concentrated on relatively few producers, and the costs of tariffs are spread out over relatively many consumers. This makes each producer's gain relatively large compared with each consumer's loss. We predict that producers will lobby government to obtain the relatively large gains from tariffs but that consumers will not lobby government in order to save themselves from paying the small additional payment due to tariffs. Politicians are put in the awkward position of hearing from those people who want the tariffs but not hearing from those people who are against them. It is likely they will respond to the vocal interests. Politicians may mistakenly assume that consumers' silence means that the consumers accept the tariff policy, when in fact they may not. They may simply not find it worthwhile to do anything to fight the policy.

QUESTION: *Is this the only reason that there are tariffs and quotas—that government is sometimes more responsive to producer interests than consumer interests?*

ANSWER: *No. This is a rather general reason for trade restrictions. The next section presents some specific arguments for trade restrictions (that is, tariffs and quotas).*

Arguments for Trade Restrictions

Here are some of the arguments for trade restrictions (tariffs and quotas). In each case, we first consider the argument and then see how the critics have responded to it.

The National-Defense Argument. It is often argued that certain industries—such as aircraft, petroleum, chemicals, and weapons—are necessary to the national defense and therefore deserve to be protected from foreign competition. For example, suppose the United States has a comparative advantage in the production of wheat and China has a comparative advantage in the production of weapons. Should the United States special-

THINKING LIKE AN ECONOMIST

Section 1 showed that free trade between two nations can make both nations better off. But economists understand that just because free trade produces a net gain overall, it does not necessarily follow that every single person benefits more from free trade than restricted trade. For example, a U.S. producer might be put out of work by a foreign producer if the foreign producer outcompetes him. In the end, the persons who are temporarily hurt by free trade may have more influence on government decision makers than the persons who are helped by free trade. In short, economists realize that the position one takes on the issue of free trade may have more to do with the answer to the question, "How does it affect me*?" than with "How does it affect* us*?"*

ize in the production of wheat and then trade wheat to China in exchange for weapons? Many Americans would answer no. It is too dangerous, they maintain, to leave weapons production to another country—whether that country is China, or England, or Canada.

The national-defense argument may have some validity. But even valid arguments may be overused or abused. Industries that are not necessary to the national defense may still argue for trade restrictions placed on imported goods. For example, in the past, the national-defense argument has been used by some firms in the following industries: pens, pottery, peanuts, candles, thumbtacks, tuna fishing, and pencils. It is hard to believe that these goods are necessary to the national defense.

The Infant-Industry Argument. Alexander Hamilton, the first U.S. secretary of the treasury, argued that "infant," or new, industries often need to be protected from older, more established foreign competitors until they are mature enough to compete on an equal basis. Today, some persons voice the same argument. The infant-industry argument is clearly an argument for temporary protection from foreign producers. Critics charge, however, that once an industry is protected from foreign competition, removing the protection is almost impossible. The once-infant industry will continue to argue that it isn't old enough to go it alone.

The Antidumping Argument. **Dumping** is selling goods in foreign countries at prices below their costs and below the prices charged in the domestic market. For example, if Japan sells a Japanese-made television set in the United States for a price below the cost to produce the TV set, and at a price below what it sells the TV set for in Japan, then Japan is said to be *dumping* TV sets in the United States. Critics of dumping say that dumpers (in our example, Japan) seek only to get into a market, drive out American competitors, and then raise prices. However, some economists point out that such a strategy is not likely to work. Why? Because once the dumpers have driven out their competition and raised prices, their competition is likely to return. The dumpers, in turn,

would have obtained only a string of losses (because they have been selling below cost) for their efforts. Second, opponents of the antidumping argument point out that U.S. consumers benefit from dumping. They end up paying lower prices.

The Low-Foreign-Wages Argument. It is sometimes argued that American producers can't compete with foreign producers because American producers pay high wages to their workers and foreign producers pay low wages to their workers. The American producers insist that free trade must be restricted, or they will be ruined. What the argument overlooks is the reason American wages are high and foreign wages are low. The reason is productivity. High wages and high productivity usually go together, as do low wages and low pro-

---

MINI GLOSSARY

Dumping The sale of goods abroad at prices below their costs and below the price charged in domestic (home) markets.

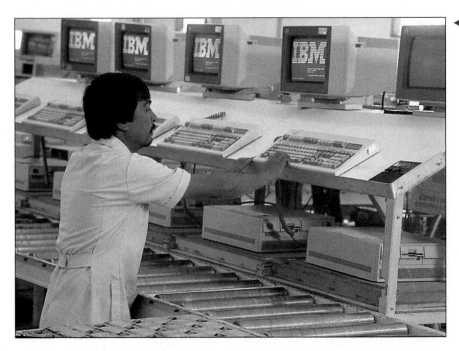

◄ Business firms are not only concerned about wages but also productivity. IBM has chosen to locate this plant in Mexico.

ANALYZING PRIMARY SOURCES

Free Trade

In recent years there has been much talk about free (international) trade. Both the proponents and critics of free trade have been vocal. Here is what a few people have to say about free trade.

Paul Krugman, Economist[a]

"Economists have a notorious, only partly deserved reputation for disagreeing about everything. One thing that almost all economists have almost always agreed about, however, is the desirability of free trade. . . .

Let me be clear from the outset that economists are basically right . . . about international trade. Those who criticize the professional wisdom rarely do so because they have a serious alternative. Usually what their objections amount to is simply a failure to understand the idea of opportunity cost. And it is certainly disturbing when rewards are lavished on economists or self-described political economists who seem to pander to popular misconceptions. . . .

The broad argument for free trade, to which many economists implicitly subscribe, is essentially political: free trade is a pretty good if not perfect policy, while an effort to deviate from it in a sophisticated way will probably end up doing more harm than good.**"**

Aaron Bernstein, Walecia Konrad, and Lois Therrien, Journalists[b]

"You'll have to excuse the McAmis family of Greenville, Tenn., if they cringe at talk of free trade. After 12 years of assembling Magnavox TVs at North America Phillips Corp.

plant, Allen McAmis was laid off in February and his $13-an-hour job moved to Juarez, Mexico, where it pays $2 an hour. He was recalled in June to fill in for workers on sick leave. But Allen and his wife, Sherry, who also works at the plant, fear that Phillips will move more jobs south. The couple have cut out birthday gifts and allowances for their children, Christina and Brian, and survey the future with dread. If Allen loses his job again and 'I get laid off, too, we'll be a welfare family,' Sherry says.

"Ever since the British economist David Ricardo advanced the theory of comparative advantage in 1817, conventional economic wisdom has held that the benefits of dropping trade barriers—lower prices and higher growth—outweigh the loss of jobs and pay that some workers suffer in the process. Most analysts have held to this view as global competition soared in the 1980s . . . But now, a flurry of studies by disparate economists— everyone from middle-of-the-road academics to ardent defenders of Reaganomics—are finding that the tradeoff isn't nearly that simple.**"**

Art Hilgart, Writer[c]

"Of course, the economists give lofty reasons for supporting NAFTA. But the arguments are all based on the eighteenth-century principle that if goods are produced where relative costs are lowest, prices everywhere will be at a minimum relative to wages and everyone will produce and consume more. This holds true, roughly, if prices are set by free markets of many buyers and many sellers. It does not hold true if sellers control prices through cartels like OPEC, DeBeers, and Sunkist. It does not hold true if prices are set unilaterally by owners of copyrights and patents.

a. "The Narrow and Broad Arguments for Free Trade," *American Economic Review*, Vol. 83, No. 2, May 1993, pp. 362–63. Reprinted by permission of Paul Krugman.
b. Reprinted from the August 10, 1992 issue of *Business Week* by permission. Copyright © 1992 by McGraw-Hill Inc.

c. "Unfree Trade," by Art Hilgart, November 22, 1993. This article is reprinted from *The Nation* magazine. © The Nation Company, Inc.

ANALYZING PRIMARY SOURCES (continued)

It does not hold true for natural monopolies like utility rates and airline fares when there is only one supplier.**"**

Everett Carll Ladd, Political Scientist[d]

"The best available data for international comparison, from the Organization for International Cooperation and Development (OICD), show that the U.S. today has the highest real income in the world and has maintained a large lead on its closest competitors. Our rate of job creation since 1980 has far exceeded that of any other advanced industrial nation. The evidence is clear that no informed American should want for a moment to swap his country's economic position for that of any other.

Nonetheless, Americans have been told incessantly that their economy is in deep trouble and is about to be overwhelmed by Japan's. This gross misrepresentation has several different sources, including at times the interest of the 'outs' in making the case that the policies of those in power have failed, and a media world where Cassandra seems constantly in vogue.

This has taken its toll: Many people, without ready means of assessing a global economy, have been made unnecessarily fearful.

On top of this, the U.S. once again has been passing through a vast economic transformation which, like its predecessors, has carried with it hardship as well as gain. Consider the first great economic shift, which saw the American work force shift *en masse* from farms and the countryside to factories and cities. In retrospect it seems both inevitable and, overall, beneficial, but it brought hardships to many.

Today's transformations won't be stopped or ameliorated by turning from free trade to protectionism; quite the opposite. But too many Americans haven't been shown clearly why this is so. This failure, too, has its price.**"**

Alan Blinder, Economist[e]

"Americans should appreciate the free trade more than most people. We inhabit the greatest free trade zone in the world. Michigan manufactures cars; New York provides banking; Texas pumps oil and gas. The fifty states trade freely with one another, which helps all enjoy great prosperity. Indeed, one reason why the United States did so much better economically than Europe for two centuries is that we have free trade movement of goods and services, while the European countries 'protected' themselves from their neighbors. To appreciate the magnitude of what is involved, try to imagine how much your personal standard of living would suffer if you were not allowed to buy any goods or services that originated outside of your home state.**"**

1. According to Krugman, what is the argument for free trade?
2. Bernstein, Konrad, and Therrien point out that Allen McAmis lost his job due to free trade. Can some people become unemployed due to free trade? If so, why?
3. What is Hilgart's position on free trade?
4. What is the essence of what Ladd says?
5. According to Blinder, why should Americans favor free trade?

---

d. "Better Education on NAFTA Would Have Aided Its Passage," *Christian Science Monitor*, November 19, 1993, p. 22. Permission granted by Everett Carll Ladd.

e. Reprinted by permission of Warner Books Inc. From *The Fortune Encyclopedia of Economics*. Copyright © 1993 by Time Inc.

▶ **EXHIBIT 17-3. Hourly Compensation for Production Workers, Selected Countries.** Here we show the hourly compensation for production workers in different countries in 1992. Hourly compensation includes wages, premiums, bonuses, vacation, holidays and other leave, insurance, and benefit plans.

Country	Hourly compensation for production workers (in dollars)	Country	Hourly compensation for production workers (in dollars)
Australia	$12.94	Mexico	$2.35
Austria	19.65	Netherlands	20.72
Belgium	22.01	New Zealand	7.91
Canada	17.02	Norway	23.20
Denmark	20.02	Portugal	5.01
Finland	18.69	Singapore	5.00
France	16.88	Spain	13.39
Germany	25.94	Sweden	24.23
Ireland	13.32	Switzerland	23.26
Italy	19.41	Taiwan	5.19
Japan	16.16	United Kingdom	14.69
Korea, South	4.93	United States	16.17

SOURCE: *The Universal Almanac, 1994* (Kansas City, Mo.: Andrews and McMeel, 1993), p. 350. Copyright © 1993 by John W. Wright. Reprinted with permission of Andrews and McMeel. All rights reserved.

ductivity. Suppose an American worker who receives $20 per hour produces 100 units of good X per hour. The cost per unit is 20 cents ($20 ÷ 100 units = 20 cents per unit). Now, suppose a foreign worker who receives $2 per hour produces 5 units of good X per hour. The cost per unit is 40 cents ($2 ÷ 5 units = 40 cents per unit)—twice as high as for the American worker. In short, a country's high-wage disadvantage may be offset by its productivity advantage. (See Exhibit 17-3 for the hourly compensation paid to production workers in different countries.)

The Tit-for-Tat Argument. Some people argue that if a foreign country uses tariffs or quotas against American goods, then the United States ought to apply equal tariffs and quotas against that foreign country, in the hope that the foreign country will lower or eliminate its trade restrictions. This is the tit-for-tat argument. We do to them as they do to us. Critics of this type of policy argue that tit-for-tat has the potential to escalate into a full-blown trade war. For example, suppose Japan

places a tariff on American-made radios. The United States retaliates by placing a tariff on Japanese-made radios. But then Japan reacts to this by placing a tariff on American-made computers. And then the United States retaliates by placing a tariff on Japanese-made computers. And so on, and so on. At some point, it might be difficult to figure out who started what.

International Economic Integration

One of the hallmarks of a global economy is economic integration. Economic integration occurs when nations combine to form either a common market or a free-trade area. In a common market, the member nations trade, without restrictions, and all share the same trade barriers with the outside world. For example, suppose Nations A, B, C, D, E, and F form a common market. They would do away with all trade barriers among themselves (free trade would exist), but they would have common trade barriers with all other nations. Thus, if tariffs were placed on Country Z's goods, the tariffs would apply in all member nations.

A major common market is the European Community (EC), which is more recently referred to as the European Union (EU). The EU consists of 12 European nations—France, Germany, the Netherlands, Belgium, Luxembourg, Italy, Denmark, Ireland, the United Kingdom, Portugal, Spain, and Greece. Other nations want to join the EU. For example, at the end of 1993, Austria, Finland, Norway, and Sweden were negotiating to become part of the EU by 1995. Members of the European Union have eliminated trade barriers among themselves.

They are also seeking a monetary union among themselves that would result in a single EU money, instead of different monies for the different member nations, and a European Central Bank (much like the Federal Reserve system in the United States). This is a novel and bold move which is not always proceeding smoothly. Nations are commonly slow to give up their own currencies and to

forfeit individual control over their own money supplies. For example, the United Kingdom has consistently argued against giving up its national currency, the pound.

The movement toward a single European currency, and a European Central Bank, will be completed, if all goes as planned, by 1997 or 1999. One of the benefits of a single European currency is that people in different member nations of the EU wouldn't have to pay the costs of exchanging their national currencies. (For example, currently a person with British pounds has to exchange his pounds for French francs if he wants to buy something in a shop in France.) It has been estimated that this will result in a savings of between $18 billion and $26 billion a year.

In a free-trade area, trade barriers among the member nations are eliminated and each nation is allowed to set its own trade rules with the rest of the world. For example, suppose nations G, H, I, and J form a free-trade area. They would get rid of trade barriers among themselves, but each nation could decide on its trade relationship with all other

▲ In late 1993, there was much debate surrounding the advantages and disadvantages of NAFTA. A free-trade area was created by NAFTA for Canada, Mexico, and the United States.

nations of the world. Country G might place tariffs on Country Z's goods, for instance, but Country J might decide not to do this.

A major free-trade area has been created by the North American Free Trade Agreement (NAFTA). This free-trade area includes Canada, Mexico, and the United States. The goal of NAFTA is to eliminate all trade barriers between the three nations over a period of time. The United States and Canada signed an agreement to this effect in 1988, but the real debate over the merits of NAFTA was heard in the United States in mid-to-late 1993. This was when the proposed agreement between the United States and Mexico was under consideration. At the time, some people in the United States said that if the U.S. Congress voted in favor of NAFTA, many U.S. companies would locate in Mexico and hire relatively low-cost Mexican labor to produce goods. Then, these companies would ship the goods into the United States to be sold. According to this point of view, NAFTA simply meant fewer jobs for U.S. workers.

Other people argued that this was unlikely to happen. They said that while wages were lower in Mexico than in the United States, companies would consider other factors, too—such as the productivity of the workers in the two nations. They were referring to the amount of output that could be produced (in, say, an hour) by workers in the two nations. To illustrate, suppose that in the United States a worker can produce 10 units of good X an hour, and he or she is paid $10 an hour. In Mexico, a worker can produce 5 units of good X an hour, and he or she is paid $2 an hour. It follows that the labor cost per unit is $1 in the United States (10 units per hour ÷ $10 per hour = $1 per unit) and it is $2.50 in Mexico (5 units per hour ÷ $2 per hour = $2.50 per unit). We conclude that, using these numbers, although wages are lower in Mexico than in the United States, it is cheaper to use U.S. workers rather than Mexican workers to produce good X.

The real question becomes: Is U.S. worker productivity high enough to compensate for lower wages in Mexico? So far, in many industries the answer is yes. This is largely a reflection of the United States being a relatively developed and highly industrialized nation compared to Mexico. In time, economists expect that Mexico's economy will grow and that its labor force will become increasingly more productive.

The proponents of NAFTA, which was signed into law by President Bill Clinton in 1993, argue that the agreement will be good for all three nations involved. They say that free trade allows consumers to buy the highest-quality products at the lowest price, and places pressure on the producers in each country to stay competitive. Finally, it moves nations toward producing those products for which they have a comparative advantage, which, as we have shown earlier in this chapter, brings benefits.

Are common markets and free-trade areas likely to be the way nations will proceed in the near future? Many economists think so. Already, there are numerous such trade agreements, as a quick look at Exhibit 17-4 shows. Increasingly, nations of the world are finding that it is in their best interests to lower trade barriers between themselves and their neighbors. Along these lines, it is important to mention the General Agreement on Trade and Tariffs, or GATT. (There is currently a discussion of dropping the name GATT and replacing it with WTO, for World Trade Organization.) This is an organization, composed of 117 member nations, that seeks to remove barriers to world trade in goods, services, and ideas. The articles of agreement in GATT provide principles of behavior and a general set of rules which govern trade among nations. Individual nations with trade disputes can use GATT to negotiate a settlement between themselves. Periodically, the members of GATT meet to negotiate tariff reductions. The latest round of negotiations was called the Uruguay Round, which successfully ended in December 1993. This round of negotiations ended by obligating its 117 members to an average reduction in tariffs of about 33 percent; agricultural tariffs would fall by 36 percent in some nations and by 24 percent in others. Also, most quotas on manufacturing imports would be eliminated, although some could be replaced with tariffs.

Group	Members	Combined Population
Andean Group	Bolivia, Colombia, Ecuador, Peru, Venezuela	92 million
ASEAN (Association of Southeast Asian Nations)	Brunei, Indonesia, Malaysia, Philippines, Singapore, Thailand	333 million
EC* (European Community)	Belgium, Denmark, France, Germany, Greece, Ireland, Italy, Luxembourg, Netherlands, Portugal, Spain, Great Britain	345 million
ECO (Economic Cooperation Organization)	Azerbaijan, Iran, Kyrgyzstan, Pakistan, Tajikistan, Turkey, Turkmenistan, Uzbekistan	250 million
ECOWAS (Economic Community of West African States)	Benin, Burkina Faso, Cape Verde, Gambia, Ghana, Guinea, Guinea-Bissau, Ivory Coast, Liberia, Mali, Mauritania, Niger, Nigeria, Senegal, Sierra Leone, Togo	206 million
GCC (Gulf Cooperation Council)	Bahrain, Kuwait, Oman, Qatar, Saudi Arabia, United Arab Emirates	23 million
LAFTA (Latin American Free Trade Association)	Argentina, Bolivia, Brazil, Chile, Colombia, Ecuador, Mexico, Paraguay, Peru, Uruguay, Venezuela	380 million
NAFTA (North American Free Trade Agreement)	Canada, Mexico, United States	365 million

*European Community (EC) is now referred to as European Union (EU).

▲ **EXHIBIT 17-4. Selected Common Markets and Free-Trade Areas.** SOURCE: *Los Angeles Times*, March 22, 1992.

Other International Organizations

Besides GATT, there are other international organizations. Two in particular are the World Bank and the International Monetary Fund (IMF). These two institutions are located across the street from each other in Washington, D.C. The World Bank, which is officially known as the International Bank for Reconstruction and Development (IBRD), is the biggest development bank in the world. Its primary function is to lend money to the world's poor and less-developed nations. The money for lending comes from rich member nations, such as the United States, and from selling bonds (and lending the money raised through bond sales). Usually it makes loans for economic development projects that are expected to produce a return sufficient to pay back the loan. When the World Bank was first formed, in 1944, it channeled funds from the United States and other nations into rebuilding Europe after World War II.

There are other development banks, but most of these are regional. That is, they mostly lend to nations in a certain regional area. For example, the Inter-American Development Bank (IADB) is a development bank that provides loans for projects in the underdeveloped nations of Latin America.

The African Development Bank provides loans for the poorest regions of Africa.

The IMF is an international organization that, among other things, provides economic advice and temporary funds for nations with economic difficulties. It has been referred to as "a doctor called in at the last minute." When a nation is in economic difficulty, the IMF might submit a list of economic reforms for it to follow (such as cutting its excessive government spending in order to reduce its budget deficits, decreasing the growth rate in its money supply so that it can reduce inflation, and so on). Often the funds the IMF lends to a nation in economic trouble are given on the condition that its economic advice is followed. For example, in December 1993, the IMF promised Russia, which was going through difficult economic times, that aid to the nation would be increased if it stopped subsidizing inefficient state (government) industries, started spending more on the poor, and moved toward establishing a style of banking closer to that of the West.

Usually, a nation's acceptance of IMF reforms is a signal to other international organizations, such as the World Bank, that it is serious about getting its economic house in order. This can lead to long-term funding by the World Bank and other sources.

Finally, an important administrative agency is the International Development Cooperation Agency (IDCA), established in 1979 to oversee all forms of U.S. assistance to less-developed countries, including foreign aid grants, food aid, and personnel transfer (for example, the Peace Corps). Probably the most important suborganization which is part of the IDCA is the Agency for International Development (AID), which is responsible for the implementation of almost all aid programs.

✔ LEARNING CHECK

1. What is a tariff, and what effect does it have on the price of imported goods?
2. What is a quota, and what effect does it have on the price of imported goods?
3. First state, and then criticize, the low-foreign-wages argument for trade restrictions.
4. First state, and then criticize, the infant-industry argument for trade restrictions.
5. First state, and then criticize, the tit-for-tat argument for trade restrictions.

SECTION 3 THE EXCHANGE RATE

People in different countries have different monies. For example, Americans use dollars, Greeks use drachmas, and Indians use rupees. This brings us to a discussion of the exchange rate. This section discusses the exchange rate.

As you read, keep these key questions in mind:

■ What is an exchange rate?
■ What does it mean to say a currency appreciates in value?
■ What does it mean to say a currency depreciates in value?

What Is the Exchange Rate?

The **exchange rate** is the price of one nation's currency in terms of another nation's currency. For example, suppose that you take a trip to England.

MINI GLOSSARY

Exchange Rate The price of one nation's currency in terms of another nation's currency.

CASE STUDY

Dollar Appreciation and Its Effects on People

Here we consider how dollar appreciation may affect a number of people.

The Farmer

Suppose George is an American farmer selling wheat to foreigners. Let's say that currently $1 equals 2 German marks and that George's wheat sells for 12 marks in Germany. This means he receives $6 for every bushel of wheat he sells in Germany (12 marks ÷ 2 marks per dollar = $6). Now, suppose the dollar appreciates from 2 to 3 marks. After the dollar has appreciated, if George's wheat still sells for 12 marks, he will receive only $4 for every bushel (12 marks ÷ 3 marks per dollar = $4). Currency appreciation lowers George's income.

The Loan Officer

Suppose Michelle is a loan officer in a bank. One day, months ago, George went to Michelle and asked for a $500,000 loan to modernize his farm. She granted him the loan because his current business looked good. But this was before the dollar appreciated and his income dropped. Frankly, his income has dropped so much that he can't pay off the loan. Michelle's boss, Francine, now comes to Michelle and wonders why she gave George the loan in the first place. To

▲ The value of foreign currencies in relation to the United States dollar can have wide-ranging effects on businesses and individuals.

Francine, it looks as if Michelle has made one too many loans.

The Owner of a Small Shop

Suppose Jerry owns a small shop in a town where many of the inhabitants produce goods that are sold in foreign countries. As a result of the dollar appreciation, the firms which employ the inhabitants lose business; consequently, they don't need as many workers, so they fire some. These fired workers have less money, so they buy fewer goods in Jerry's shop. Jerry's business ends up hurting.

The Shop Owner's Family

Jerry has a family. Because his business is doing poorly, he earns less income. His family, in turn, has less money for going to the movies, buying clothes, perhaps going to college, and so on.

---

1. Explain why an American traveling to a foreign nation to buy goods would prefer the dollar to appreciate in value, but an American selling goods to a foreign nation would prefer the dollar to depreciate in value.

In order to buy goods and services in England, you will need to have British currency. The basic unit of British currency is the pound (£). Therefore, you will need to exchange the dollars you have for pounds.

Suppose you want to exchange $200 for pounds. How many pounds will you get for $200? This depends on the exchange rate, which may be determined in two ways. It is determined by the forces of supply and demand under a **flexible exchange rate system**, and it is determined by government under a **fixed exchange rate system**. Let's suppose the exchange rate is currently £1 for $2. This means for every $2 you have, you will get £1 in exchange. So you will receive £100 in exchange for $200. (Exhibit 17-5 shows the value of the U.S. dollar in terms of 10 foreign currencies.)

Country	Currency	Currency units per U. S. dollar
China	yuan	5.52
Finland	markka	4.49
Germany	deutsche-mark	1.56
Greece	drachma	190.81
India	rupee	28.16
Italy	lira	1,232.17
Japan	yen	126.78
Portugal	escudo	135.07
Spain	peseta	102.38
Thailand	baht	25.14

▲ **EXHIBIT 17-5. Exchange Rates.** Here we show the value of the U.S. dollar in terms of 10 foreign currencies. For example, it takes 5.52 yuan (China) to buy $1, 4.49 markka (Finland) to buy $1, and so on. SOURCE: *The Universal Almanac, 1994* (Kansas City, Mo.: Andrews and McMeel, 1993), p. 342. Data are for 1992. Copyright © 1993 by John W. Wright. Reprinted with permission of Andrews and McMeel. All rights reserved.

Appreciation and Depreciation

Suppose that on Tuesday the exchange rate between pounds and dollars is £1 for $1.60. By Saturday, the exchange rate has changed to £1 for $1.80. On Saturday, then, a pound fetches more dollars and cents than it did on Tuesday. When this happens, economists say that the pound has *appreciated* relative to the dollar. **Appreciation** is an increase in the value of one currency relative to other currencies. **Depreciation** is the opposite; it is a decrease in the value of one currency relative to other currencies. A currency has depreciated if it fetches less of another currency. For example, if the exchange rate is £1 for $1.60 on Tuesday and £1 for $1.40 on Saturday, the pound has *depreciated* relative to the dollar.

MINI GLOSSARY

Flexible Exchange Rate System The system whereby currency exchange rates are determined by the forces of supply and demand.
Fixed Exchange Rate System The system whereby currency exchange rates are fixed, or pegged, by nations' governments.
Appreciation An increase in the value of one currency relative to other currencies.
Depreciation A decrease in the value of one currency relative to other currencies.

 ## LEARNING CHECK

1. If the exchange rate is £1 for $2, how many pounds does it take to buy a good priced at $1,000?
2. Which exchange rate would American producers of exported goods prefer: £1 for $2 or £1 for $3? Explain your answer.

DEVELOPING ECONOMIC SKILLS

Converting Currency from One Nation's to Another's

Different nations, of course, have different currencies. In the United States, we have dollars. England has pounds, France has francs, Japan has yen, and so on. It is important to know how to convert from one currency to another. For example, suppose you are in England and see that a sweater has a price tag of £20. How much is this in U.S. dollars? To answer this question, you need to know the exchange rate between dollars and pounds. You can get this information by looking at the business section of many newspapers, or you can get it by calling up almost any bank. Let's say the exchange rate is $2 for £1. To find out what the English sweater costs in U.S. dollars, we simply use this formula:

Price of sweater in dollars = Price of sweater in foreign currency × Number of dollars needed to buy 1 unit of foreign currency

For example, let's find the price in dollars of the sweater priced at £20, given an exchange rate of $2 for £1.

Price of sweater in dollars = £20 × $2 (per £1)
= $40

Our answer is $40.

Suppose you knew the price of the sweater in dollars and you wanted to find out its price in some other currency. You could use this formula:

Price of sweater in foreign currency = Price of sweater in dollars ÷ Number of dollars needed to buy 1 unit of foreign currency

Let's find the price in pounds of the $40 sweater, given an exchange rate of $2 for £1.

Price of sweater in foreign currency = $40 ÷ $2 (per £1)
= £20

The answer is £20.

---

1. The price for a German car is 30,000 marks, and the exchange rate is 1 mark = $0.33. What does the German car cost in dollars?
2. The price for a French perfume is 215 francs, and the exchange rate is 1 franc = $0.20. What does the French perfume cost in dollars?
3. Suppose you are working in Mexico and you earn 2,000 pesos a week. The exchange rate is 1 peso = $0.25. What is your weekly pay in dollars?

CHAPTER 17 REVIEW

CHAPTER SUMMARY

1. A nation's balance of trade is the difference between the value of its exports and the value of its imports. If exports are greater than imports, the nation has a positive balance of trade. If exports are less than imports, the nation has a negative balance of trade.

2. A country has a comparative advantage in the production of a good if it can produce the good at lower opportunity cost than another country.

3. Countries can make themselves better off (in terms of being able to consume more) if they specialize in the production of the good in which they have a comparative advantage and then trade some of the good for other goods.

4. There are two major types of trade restrictions: tariffs and quotas. A tariff is a tax on imports. A quota is a legal limit on the amount of a good that may be imported. Both tariffs and quotas raise the price of imported goods to the American consumer.

5. The national-defense argument for trade restrictions holds that certain goods are necessary to the national defense and therefore should be produced domestically whether the country has a comparative advantage in their production or not.

6. The infant-industry argument states that "infant," or new, industries should be protected from older, more established foreign competitors until they have had time to develop and compete on an even or equal basis.

7. The antidumping argument states that domestic producers should not have to compete with foreign producers that sell products below cost and below the prices they charge in their domestic, or home, markets.

8. The low-foreign-wages argument states that domestic producers that pay high wages to their employees cannot compete with foreign producers that pay low wages to their employees. In order that high-paying domestic firms may survive, limits on free trade are proposed.

9. The tit-for-tat argument states that if a foreign country uses tariffs or quotas against American goods, the United States ought to apply equal tariffs and quotas against that foreign country, in the hope that the foreign country will lower or eliminate its trade restrictions.

10. The arguments for trade restrictions are not accepted as valid by everyone. Critics often maintain that the arguments can be and are abused and, in most cases, are motivated by self-interest.

11. The exchange rate is the price of one currency in terms of another currency.

12. A currency has appreciated in value if it fetches more of another currency. It has depreciated in value if it fetches less of another currency.

CHAPTER 17 REVIEW (continued)

BUILD YOUR ECONOMIC VOCABULARY

Match the word with the correct definition, example, or statement.

1. positive balance of trade
2. negative balance of trade
3. comparative advantage
4. tariff
5. quota
6. infant-industry argument
7. dumping
8. appreciation

a. exports greater than imports
b. a legal limit on the amount of a good that may be imported
c. exports less than imports
d. a tax on imported goods
e. selling below cost and below the price domestic residents are asked to pay
f. idea that new industries have to be given time to develop
g. occurs when a nation's currency fetches more of some other nation's currency
h. producing at lower opportunity cost

REVIEW QUESTIONS

1. What is the balance of trade?
2. The United States can produce either combination A, 100 units of food and 0 units of clothing, or combination B, 80 units of food and 20 units of clothing. Japan can produce either combination C, 80 units of food and 0 units of clothing, or combination D, 75 units of food and 10 units of clothing. Which country has a comparative advantage in the production of food? Which country has a comparative advantage in the production of clothing?
3. What does it mean to say that the United States has a comparative advantage in the production of computers?
4. Define both *tariff* and *quota*.
5. After a tariff is imposed on imported cars, would you expect consumers to buy more or fewer imported cars, all other things remaining the same? Explain your answer.

6. State the national-defense argument for trade restrictions.
7. State the infant-industry argument for trade restrictions.
8. State the low-foreign-wages argument for trade restrictions.
9. What do the critics of the national-defense argument say?
10. What do the critics of the infant-industry argument say?
11. What do the critics of the low-foreign-wages argument say?

SHARPEN YOUR CRITICAL THINKING SKILLS

1. Consider two U.S. cities, Houston and Dallas. Some goods that are produced in Houston are sold in Dallas, and some goods produced in Dallas are sold in Houston. Suppose the people in Houston buy more goods from the people in Dallas than the people in Dallas buy from the people in Houston. This means Houston has a negative balance of trade with Dallas and Dallas has a positive balance of trade with Houston. It is not news when one city has a negative balance of trade with another city in the same country, but it is big news when one country has a negative balance of trade with another country. For example, when the United States has a negative balance of trade with Japan, it is front-page news. Why do you think that the city-to-city trade balance is not news but the country-to-country trade balance is?

ACTIVITIES AND PROJECTS

1. Check your local newspaper to see if it lists the exchange rates of different currencies. If it does not, consult the *Wall Street Journal,* which does print daily exchange rates. Next, state the value of the U.S. dollar in terms of any three foreign currencies.

ECONOMIC DICTIONARY

Absolute Advantage (Pg. 422)
Appreciation (Pg. 436)
Balance of Trade (Pg. 421)
Comparative Advantage (Pg. 423)
Depreciation (Pg. 436)
Dumping (Pg. 428)
Exchange Rate (Pg. 435)
Exports (Pg. 420)
Fixed Exchange Rate System (Pg. 436)
Flexible Exchange Rate System (Pg. 436)
Imports (Pg. 420)
Specialize (Pg. 423)

CHAPTER 18

Comparative Economic Systems: Past, Present, and Future

INTRODUCTION

Chapter 2 discussed the free-enterprise economic system in detail. In addition, throughout this book, we have been discussing the U.S. economy, which is considered a free-enterprise economy. You should have by now a fairly good understanding of how a free-enterprise economic system works.

But there are types of economic systems in the world other than free enterprise. This chapter discusses the major alternative to the free-enterprise system—socialism. It also discusses two other topics: first, the transition from socialism to free enterprise occurring in some countries, and then prospects for the U.S. economic system in the years ahead.

AFTER YOU STUDY THIS CHAPTER, YOU WILL BE ABLE TO:

1. Discuss the details of both the capitalist vision and the socialist vision.
2. Outline the major differences between the free-enterprise and socialist economic systems.
3. Give some details of how command-economy socialism worked in the former Soviet Union.
4. Discuss some of the problems a nation has when it changes from a socialist economic system to a free-enterprise economic system.

KEY TERMS

Command-Economy
Socialism
Gosplan

Industrial Policy
Infrastructure
Vision

TWO VISIONS SHAPE TWO ECONOMIC SYSTEMS

In this section, we examine the two major economic systems—free enterprise and socialism. Each is based on a certain vision of the way the world works, and we consider those visions, too.

As you read, keep these key questions in mind:

- What is an economic system?
- What are the details of the capitalist vision?
- What are the details of the socialist vision?

Economic Systems: How Have They Been Defined and How Many Are There?

Chapter 1 said that a society's economic system is the way the society goes about answering the three economic questions: What will be produced? How will the goods be produced? For whom will the goods be produced?

There are hundreds of nations with differing economic systems. Some live in what is called the traditional economy, one which is based on customs and beliefs that have been handed down from one generation to the next. Most people who live in traditional economies live at a subsistence level and often use primitive tools. However, there are two dominant modern economic systems in the world: free enterprise and socialism.

The free-enterprise (or capitalist or market) economic system and the socialist economic system form the two major ways of answering the three economic questions. Some nations' economies fall naturally into one category or the other, but many nations have chosen "ingredients" from both economic systems. These latter nations have economies that are neither purely free enterprise nor purely socialist; instead, they are some mixture of both. They are called *mixed economies*.

As noted in Chapter 1, then, it is best to look at the two radically different economic systems—free enterprise and socialism—as occupying opposite ends of an economic spectrum, as illustrated in Exhibit 1-4 in Chapter 1. Nations' economies lie along the economic spectrum, some closer to the free-enterprise end and some closer to the socialist end.

Different Visions Shape the Different Economic Systems

The reason there are principally two major and radically different economic systems is that there are principally two major and radically different visions, or views, of the world. After all, socialism did not fall from the sky, full blown and complete, for people to pick up off the ground and put into operation. Nor did free enterprise come about in this way. Both are the products of a certain way of looking at, understanding, and explaining the world. Both are the products of certain visions.

The economist Thomas Sowell defines **vision** as "our sense of how the world works." For example, suppose Michael's vision of the world, as it relates to government, is that our elected officials are endlessly trying to solve society's problems in a way that is good for the general public. Maria's vision may be quite different. She may believe that our elected officials respond to narrowly focused special interest groups at the expense of the general public. Their different visions of how government works will determine what policies Michael and Maria will support. For example, Michael will be much more willing than Maria to argue that government should play a major role in solving society's problems. He does this because, in a real sense, he *envisions* government doing the right thing much more often than Maria does.

What Shall We Call the Two Different Visions?

For simplicity's sake, we shall call the vision that produces socialism the socialist vision, and the vision that produces free enterprise, or capitalism, the capitalist vision. It is important not to fall into the trap of thinking one vision is better or worse than the other because of what it is called. For example, it may be your inclination to think that socialism is "bad" and that capitalism is "good," or vice versa. If so, you may believe the vision that gives rise to your preferred economic system is a better vision than the other. But resist the temptation to prejudge. It is not our purpose here to label either of the two visions, or either of the two major economic systems, as "good" or "bad." Our purpose is to understand each vision and then to understand how these visions could give birth to different economic systems. At this stage, we must place our emphasis on *understanding* instead of *judging*.

The Two Visions as They Relate to the Market

The proponents of the two visions—we can call them socialist thinkers and capitalist thinkers—have different views on a host of topics. This section discusses their views on several market phenomena.

Price.   When we buy something in a market—whether it is a car, a house, or a loaf of bread—we pay a price. Price is a common market phenomenon. The capitalist thinker sees price as doing a job. Price (1) rations goods and services, (2) conveys information, and (3) serves as an incentive for buyers and sellers to respond to information.

We considered the rationing role of price in Chapter 4. Price rations goods and services in that people who are willing and able to pay the price of a good obtain the good. Persons who are not willing and able to pay the price do not obtain the good. For capitalist thinkers, because we live in a world of scarcity, we must have some rationing device—whether it is price; first-come, first-served; brute force; or some other device. There must be some way of determining who gets what of the available resources, goods, and services. Price serves this purpose.

A socialist thinker views price in a very different light. For example, the rationing function of price is largely invisible to or ignored by the so-

MINI GLOSSARY

Vision   One's sense of how the world works.

▶ Goods are bought and sold in the market for a price. Many economists argue that price plays an important role in an economy.

CASE STUDY

Traditional Economies

Before capitalism or free enterprise, and before socialism, there was the traditional economy. A traditional economy is an economic system in which the answers to the three economic questions (What will be produced? How will the goods be produced? For whom will the goods be produced?) are based on customs, traditions, and cultural beliefs.

In a traditional economy, skills and beliefs are passed on from one generation to the next. An example of a traditional economy would be the feudal system in Western Europe. Under the feudal system, all land was owned by a king. Land was granted to nobles who, in turn, granted small plots of land to peasants to farm. They kept part of what they produced. The remainder went to the nobles and, ultimately, to the king.

There are many traditional economies still in existence today. They are found all over the world and are very different from each other, according to their respective customs and traditions. Most people who live in traditional economies live at a subsistence level, working with tools which are relatively primitive compared to those used in countries with modern technology.

One type of traditional economy is the hunting and gathering society. As the name implies, the hunters and gatherers sustain themselves by pursuing game and collecting wild fruits and vegetables. Because they do not cultivate crops, they must travel to find their food supplies. Often, they follow the migratory routes of animals. As nomads, hunters and gatherers do not have the same concept of ownership of land as people in more modern societies. For example, the Hadza of Tanzania and the Inuit of the North American tundra have no concept of trespassing. All members of these societies are free to collect food wherever they can find it.

Some traditional economies discourage the accumulation of personal wealth by redistributing goods from those who have to those who do not. This is often accomplished by way of a tribute paid to a tribal chief, in much the same way that taxes are paid. The chief then gives to those who are in need. In other traditional economies, the redistribution of goods is entirely voluntary, and those who give away their surplus goods attain higher status.

While the 1980s and 1990s have seen many countries in Eastern Europe make the transition from socialist to capitalist economies, there are still traditional economies in many parts of the world that are resistant to change and continue to maintain economic relationships going back hundreds of years. The customs and beliefs that sustain these traditional economies continue to be passed from generation to generation, despite the encroachment of the technological world. It remains to be seen whether traditional economies can continue to survive into the 21st century and, if so, what form they will take.

---

1. What is a traditional economy?
2. Why is it common in a traditional economy to share goods?

cialist thinker. Whereas the capitalist thinker views price as being determined by the impersonal forces of supply and demand, the socialist thinker views price in a free enterprise economy as being set by businesses with vast economic power.

Perhaps because of this, the socialist thinker, unlike the capitalist thinker, is ready to "control" price. The socialist is willing to have a law passed stating that "it is unlawful to charge more than a certain price for gasoline or rental homes" or "it is unlawful to pay less than a certain wage to workers." By passing laws that make it unlawful to charge more than a certain price, the socialist thinker seeks to reduce some of the economic power that he or she believes sellers have over consumers. By passing laws that make it illegal to pay less than a certain wage, the socialist seeks to reduce some of the economic power that he or she believes the owners of businesses have over workers.

Competition. A capitalist thinker believes that competition is intense under free enterprise. The capitalist believes that the competition between producers will force them to offer the highest-quality product to consumers for the lowest price. In contrast, the socialist thinker sees little competition between producers. In the socialist view, the marketplace is controlled by big business interests dictating to people (through advertising) what they will buy and at what price.

Private Property. The capitalist thinker places high value on private property. This thinker agrees with the Greek philosopher Aristotle that "what is common to many is taken least care of, for all men have greater regard for what is their own than for what they possess in common with others." In other words, capitalists believe that if you own something yourself—if, say, your house is your private property—you are more likely to take care of it than if it was owned communally by you and others or was owned by the government.

The capitalist thinker also believes that having private property encourages individuals to use their resources in a way that benefits others. For example, suppose Johnson owns a factory that is

▲ As a result of the intensity of competition under free enterprise, customers have a wide variety of choices.

his private property. If Johnson wants to maximize his income, he will have to use his factory to produce goods that people are willing and able to buy. If he did otherwise, and produced something that people were unwilling and unable to buy, he would not benefit the people or earn an income.

The socialist vision of property is very different. The socialist thinker believes that those who own property will end up having more political power than those who do not own it. Furthermore, they will use their greater political power to their advantage and to the disadvantage of others. For the socialist thinker, it would be better for government to own most of the nonlabor property in the economy (such things as factories, raw materials, and machinery). Government would be more likely than private individuals to make sure this property was used to benefit the many instead of the few.

Exchange. Consider an ordinary, everyday exchange of $100 for some clothes. The capitalist thinker believes that both the buyer and the seller of the clothes benefit from the exchange, or else they would not have entered into it. The socialist thinker often (but not always) believes that one person in an exchange is made better off at the expense of the other person. In our example, perhaps the clothes seller took advantage of the buyer by charging too much money for the clothes.

QUESTION: *Is one vision of how the world works correct and the other incorrect?*

ANSWER: *As mentioned earlier, our purpose in this section has not been to determine if one vision is correct and the other incorrect. It has been to understand that the capitalist vision of the way the world works—right or wrong—has given birth to the free-enterprise economic system and the socialist vision—right or wrong—has given birth to the socialist economic system. Consider an analogy. Suppose your vision of the world is that it is frightening and dangerous because everyone is trying to hurt everyone else. As a consequence, you rarely leave your home. Your vision of the world—right or wrong—has caused you to take a certain action: stay home. If someone wants to know something about why you choose to stay at home, it is important that this person should know your vision. Similarly, if we want to know something about an economic system, we need to understand the vision of the world that is contained within it.*

The Two Visions as They Relate to Government

Capitalist and socialist thinkers have different visions of government. The socialist thinker believes government decision makers promote what is in the best interest of society as a whole. The capitalist thinker sees this as a naive and mistaken view of how government operates. The capitalist thinks government decision makers respond to well-organized special interest groups and not to the unorganized members of the general public. For example, government is more likely to respond to

▲ Both producer and consumer interests lobby government. Some people believe producer interests are better organized and, because of this, are more effective at meeting their objectives.

the farmers who lobby for higher crop prices than to the consumers who will end up paying higher food prices in the grocery stores. It is more likely to respond to car producers than car consumers.

The socialist thinker sees the goal of government decision makers as doing the right thing. The capitalist thinker sees the goal of government decision makers as getting elected and reelected to office. The socialist thinker believes that when government decision makers make a mistake, it is because they did not have all the facts. Give them the facts, and they will do the right thing. The capitalist thinker believes that when government decision makers make a mistake, it is likely that the mistake was politically motivated. Give them the facts, and they may still do what is in the best interest of well-organized special interest groups at the expense of the general public.

THINKING LIKE AN ECONOMIST

Many people think that businesses will advance the capitalist vision, but this is not necessarily correct. Businesses often lobby government for legislation that could end up hampering the free-enterprise system. For example, some business firms in the United States lobby government to enact tariffs and quotas on foreign products that compete with the products they produce and sell. As we saw in Chapter 17, U.S. tariffs and quotas end up helping American producers (by reducing the competition they face from foreign producers) and hurting American consumers (because tariffs and quotas end up raising the prices consumers pay). Although it is perhaps natural to connect business firms with capitalism, and thus to believe that all business firms promote the capitalist vision, in reality this turns out not to be true. In reality, narrow business interests are not always best served by free enterprise, which emphasizes competition, determination of prices by supply and demand, and free and voluntary exchange (trade). There is sometimes a difference between being pro-business and pro-free enterprise. In fact, the benefits of free enterprise often fall more to consumers than to producers.

The Two Visions as They Relate to Unintended Consequences and Deliberate Actions

According to the capitalist thinker, the unintended consequences of individuals' actions sometimes produce good things. For example, consider the equilibrium price in a market. As described in Chapter 4, at equilibrium price, the quantity of the good that buyers are willing and able to buy equals the quantity of the good that sellers are willing and able to sell. In other words, both buyers and sellers are *content* at equilibrium price. Buyers don't want to buy more or less, and sellers don't want to sell more or less.

The important point for our discussion is that this balance between buyers and sellers came about naturally. There was no blueprint that buyers and sellers followed to get equilibrium price. There was no government committee that identified equilibrium price and then directed buyers and sellers to trade at it. Equilibrium price simply emerged as an unintended consequence of buying and selling goods. To a capitalist thinker, things that naturally emerge—like equilibrium price in a market—are often desirable. It is desirable, for example, that both buyers and sellers are content at equilibrium price.

In contrast to the capitalist, the socialist rarely thinks that unintended consequences of individuals' actions are desirable. The attention of the socialist thinker is placed elsewhere. It is focused on things deliberately created to serve some purpose. For example, the socialist thinker may focus on such things as government programs deliberately created and designed to reduce poverty. Here is something tangible, in the socialist's view. A problem exists (poverty), and a program has been created and designed to deal with it.

Of course, this difference between capitalist and socialist visions has consequences. The capitalist thinker emphasizes that we should not disturb the natural (and often invisible) processes at work in society that bring about desirable outcomes. For example, the capitalist would argue that government should not interfere with the market forces of supply and demand. To do so would reduce the likelihood that equilibrium price would emerge. To the socialist thinker, this sounds like fantasy, since the socialist is unaware of how equilibrium came to exist in the first place and what special and desirable properties it possesses. The socialist sees no good reason for government to keep "hands off" the forces of supply and demand.

QUESTION: *How commonly do we find desirable things that no one directly set out to create? Are there other examples besides equilibrium price?*

ANSWER: *You may recall one example from Chapter 10, which discussed money. That discussion started by focusing on a barter economy. In a barter economy, where there is no money, people trade goods for other goods. But making trades is time consuming in a barter economy. For example, suppose you have apples and you want bread. You locate someone with bread, but she says that she doesn't want to trade her bread for apples; she prefers oranges. You set out to find someone else who has bread, hoping that this person is willing to trade bread for your apples, or to find someone with oranges who wants to trade oranges for your apples, so you can go to the person with bread and trade oranges for bread.*

Individuals in a barter economy wanted to make trade less time consuming and thus easier. They noticed that some goods were more widely accepted in trade than others. For example, suppose bricks were more widely accepted for trade than any other goods in a barter economy. A person in this economy would know that if she had bricks, she could make her trades in less time than if she had, say, apples, which were not as widely accepted. More and more people would come to accept bricks in exchange for what they had to trade.

In conclusion, money—any good that is widely accepted in trade—emerged as an unintended consequence of the attempts of people in a barter economy to make their everyday trades less time consuming and easier.

The Two Visions in a Nutshell

We have discussed some details of the capitalist and socialist visions as they relate to (1) the market, (2) government, and (3) unintended consequences and deliberate actions. Let us bring the material together and summarize.

The capitalist vision holds that market phenomena—such as prices determined by supply and demand, competition, private property, and exchange—together make up a marvelous system. Within this system, goods are rationed, information conveyed, high-quality goods are produced at the lowest prices, and people are induced to use their resources in a way that will benefit others and generally raise the standard of living. The socialist vision holds that in the marketplace, some people exploit others—for example, by charging high prices, paying low wages, and manipulating people's preferences through such things as advertising.

The socialist vision holds that government is made up of people who want to, and in most cases will, do the right thing by the general public. The capitalist vision sees government as being made up of people who respond more readily to well-organized special interest groups than to the general public. Socialist thinkers have a higher degree of trust in the intentions and actions of government decision makers than do capitalist thinkers.

Finally, the capitalist vision focuses on the desirable qualities of things that were not deliberately created but that naturally emerged as the unintended consequences of people's actions. The socialist vision focuses on things that were deliberately created to serve a purpose.

 LEARNING CHECK

1. What is a vision, as defined in this chapter?
2. What is the difference between the capitalist vision and the socialist vision as they relate to the following topics: prices, private property, and government?
3. Money was described as an unintended consequence of the attempts of people in a barter economy to make their everyday trades less time consuming and easier. Explain what this means.

AN EXAMPLE OF SOCIALISM IN THE 20TH CENTURY

During the 20th century, many nations have experimented with socialism. A list of these nations includes the former Soviet Union, China, Poland, Sweden, the former Yugoslavia, and Cuba. This section discusses one 20th century variety of socialism: the command-economy socialism that was practiced in the former Soviet Union.

As you read, keep these key questions in mind:

■ What is central economic planning, and what is the case against it?

■ How were prices set in the former Soviet Union?

Command-Economy Socialism in the Former Soviet Union

What today makes up the Commonwealth of Independent States used to be the Union of Soviet Socialist Republics (USSR)—commonly called the Soviet Union. Between approximately 1917 and 1991, the Soviet economy was described as **command-economy socialism**. This is as extreme a version of socialism as can be found: government is involved in almost every aspect of the economy. That is to say, government owns all the nonlabor resources (such as land and capital), it decides what will be produced and in what quantities, it sets prices and wages, and much more. Here are a few of the particulars of the command-economy socialism that was practiced in the former Soviet Union.

Gosplan. In the former Soviet Union, under command-economy socialism, **Gosplan** was the central planning agency. It had the responsibility of drafting the economic plan for the Soviet economy. Gosplan did not, however, draft the economic plan without receiving input from high government officials in the Politburo (parliament).

Gosplan constructed two types of plans: five-year (long-range) plans and one-year (short-range) plans. The five-year plans allocated the nation's resources. They determined how much would go into producing investment goods (such as factories

MINI GLOSSARY

Command-Economy Socialism An economic system characterized by government ownership of the nonlabor factors of production, government allocation of resources, and centralized decision making. Most economic activities take place in the public sector, and government plays a very large role in the economy.

Gosplan Under Soviet command-economy socialism, the planning agency that had the responsibility of drafting the economic plan for the nation.

▲ The Kremlin, in Moscow, where central economic planning activities were conducted in the former Soviet Union.

and machinery), how much would go into producing military goods (such as bombers and tanks), and how much would go into producing consumption goods (such as television sets and washing machines). The one-year plans were much more detailed than the five-year plans. They outlined what each of the more than 200,000 Soviet enterprises under Gosplan's supervision were to produce, the amounts of labor and raw materials each would be allocated, the amount and type of machinery that would be installed, and so on.

To get a sense of how this process worked, let's translate it to the American scene. If there were an American Gosplan, it would probably be located in Washington, D.C. The American Gosplan would issue orders to Pepsi-Cola, Apple Computers, Ford Motor Company, and other companies stating what each was to produce. For example, it might direct Ford Motor Company to produce 300,000 cars. Then, it would direct the companies supplying Ford to send so much steel, so much plastic, and so many tires to the company. It would also tell Ford whether it could expect to have its factories updated, what type of new capital goods would be arriving, and other crucial information.

The Case against Central Economic Planning. In a nation that practices command-economy socialism, central economic planning—planning done by the government—is commonplace. The critics of central economic planning say that the economic planners cannot take into account as much relevant information as a market does. Therefore, economic plans cannot coordinate economic activity or satisfy consumer demand as well as market forces.

Consider an economic planning board, composed of 30 or 40 persons, that must decide how many houses, apartment buildings, buses, cars, and pizza restaurants should be built within the next year. Where would the planners start? Would they know about people's changing demands for houses, apartment buildings, and the rest? The critics of economic planning argue that they would not. At best, the planners would be making a guess about what goods and services consumers would demand and how much they would buy at different prices. If they guessed wrong, resources would be wasted, and demands would go unfulfilled.

Private individuals, guided by rising and falling prices and by the desire to earn profits, are better

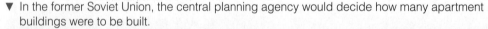

▼ In the former Soviet Union, the central planning agency would decide how many apartment buildings were to be built.

at satisfying consumer demand. Economic planners risk little themselves when they draw up economic plans for others to follow (they don't put *their* money on the line). Therefore, they aren't as likely to avoid costly economic mistakes as are the risk-taking entrepreneurs in a free market.

QUESTION: *Everybody makes plans. A person makes plans for his or her life. A business may draw up a plan for the next five years. If individuals and firms plan, why not let government plan for the economy? What do the critics of central planning say to this?*

ANSWER: *There are two major distinctions to be made between the plan an individual or business firm makes and an economic plan for all of society. First, if an individual or a firm makes a plan that fails, only the individual or the firm suffers. For the most part, the rest of society is unaffected. This is not the case if a central economic plan fails. One mistake here can have major consequences for many people.*

Second, if one person makes a personal plan, others can still make and follow their own plans. In contrast, an economic plan that encompasses all of society might prohibit people from following their own plans.

Setting Prices.   As we have seen, a planning agency determines the total quantity of goods produced in a command economy—that is, how many radios, television sets, cars, refrigerators, toasters, and so forth will be produced. This is the supply side of the market. As we know, there is also a demand side to every market, and supply and demand determine price.

Under command-economy socialism in the former Soviet Union, besides determining the supply of a particular good, the economic planners also set its price. For example, they might decide to sell 11 million toasters for a price of 25 rubles each. Unless 25 rubles happened to be the equilibrium price, though, this would result in either a surplus or a shortage of toasters.

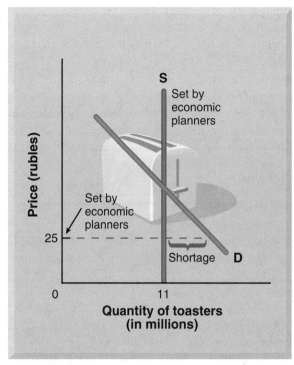

▲ **EXHIBIT 18-1. Prices in a Command-Economy Socialist Nation.** Planners set the ruble price for toasters too low. A government-mandated maximum price, above which legal trades cannot be made, is referred to as a *price ceiling*. One consequence of a price ceiling is a shortage. Toasters will be rationed by some combination of ruble price and waiting in line.

In Exhibit 18-1, economic planners have set the price of toasters at 25 rubles. This is an example of a *price ceiling*. A price ceiling is a government-mandated maximum price above which legal trades cannot be made. For example, it would be illegal to buy or sell toasters at a price higher than 25 rubles (the price ceiling). As we can see from the exhibit, the price ceiling of 25 rubles does not equate supply with demand. There are consequences of this, as the exhibit shows. A major consequence is that there will be a shortage of toasters. At this point in a free-enterprise economic system, the price of toasters would be bid up to the equilibrium price, where the quantity demanded of toasters would equal the quantity supplied. But in the former Soviet Union under command-economy socialism, it was illegal to bid up the ruble price of a good. Instead, toasters were rationed by some combination of ruble price and waiting in line. (That is, the rationing device was first-come, first-served.)

Western travelers to the former Soviet Union observed long lines of people in front of some stores—the result of shortages. But they also observed no people at all in front of other stores.

What accounted for this? Just as some prices were set below the equilibrium price, producing shortages and long lines of people, some prices were set above the equilibrium price, producing surpluses and relatively empty stores. As long as price is centrally imposed, shortages or surpluses are the likely result. It would be most unusual if the planners could correctly guess the equilibrium price.

LEARNING CHECK

1. What was Gosplan?
2. State the case against central economic planning.
3. How were prices determined in the former Soviet Union under command-economy socialism?

SECTION 3 **MOVING FROM SOCIALISM TO FREE ENTERPRISE**

In the early 1990s, many formerly socialist nations began trying to throw off their socialist economic ways and move toward a free-enterprise economic system. This was most notable in the nations of Eastern Europe and the Commonwealth of Independent States, the former Soviet Union. This section discusses some of the problems of moving from socialism to free enterprise.

As you read, keep these key questions in mind:

- In the move from socialism to free enterprise, what is likely to happen at first to prices and jobs?
- What is infrastructure?

The Rise in Prices

Remember that prices are set by government officials in a nation that practices command-economy socialism. When a nation moves away from command-economy socialism to free enterprise, prices are no longer set by government. Instead, buyers and sellers together—through demand and supply—determine prices. If many prices were previously set at levels below the equilibrium price, then

we can clearly expect prices to rise as the economy moves from socialism to free enterprise.

This is exactly what happened in Russia (one of the republics in the Commonwealth of Independent States), Poland, the former Yugoslavia, Czechoslovakia, Hungary, and other countries in the early 1990s as they moved from socialism toward free enterprise. Unfortunately, it takes time for the benefits of free enterprise to be seen. What the peoples of these formerly socialist nations were experiencing was pain caused by the economic mistakes of the past. Government officials had controlled prices—or, stated differently, had prevented supply and demand from working—for too long. The higher prices caused a lot of discontent in these nations, because people expected free enterprise to make their lives easier, not harder.

The Elimination of Certain Firms and Jobs

In a free-enterprise economic system, consumers have a large say-so as to which firms survive and which firms fail. For example, suppose we consider two firms: A, which produces goods consumers are willing and able to buy, and B, which produces goods that consumers do not want to buy. In a free-enterprise economic system, Firm A will survive, and Firm B will go out of business.

Not so under command-economy socialism. Here, a firm will go out of business only if the government economic planners say that it will go out of business. Consumers have little power in this regard.

As we might expect under command-economy socialism, there will be a number of firms that consumers care little about and buy little from. In the transition from socialism to free enterprise, these firms will go out of business, and the workers will lose their jobs.

In time, the resources used by these firms will be bought by surviving firms, and the workers who lost their jobs will end up finding new jobs. But in the meantime, we would expect output production to go down and the unemployment rate to rise. Here, then, are two additional reasons for people to get upset.

Private Property

In a free-enterprise economic system, business firms compete with each other. For example, General Motors, Ford, and Chrysler, along with other car companies, compete with each other for consumers' car dollars. Competition is a necessary part of free enterprise.

But in order to have competition, we must have private property. If individuals are not allowed to own businesses, land, capital, and so on, then they can't compete with each other. Clearly, if we want to move away from socialism, where the government owns the nonlabor resources, to free enterprise, then we must make it possible for people to have private property. Thus, a socialist nation that wants to move toward free enterprise must have a way of turning government property into private property.

Consider the case of the former Soviet Union. When it operated under command-economy so-

▲ The move toward free enterprise has not been a smooth one in Russia. Here people are demonstrating because they believe they were better off under command-economy socialism.

cialism, the government owned the stores, factories, apartment buildings, and more. How are these things going to become private property? Is the government simply going to give the stores away to the first persons who ask for them? Is the government going to sell them? These are questions that have to be answered, and the answer put into effect, before free enterprise can get started.

Infrastructure

Infrastructure refers to the basic structures and facilities on which the continuance and

---

MINI GLOSSARY

Infrastructure The basic structures and facilities on which the continuance and growth of a community depend. Interstate highways, bridges, and communication networks are some of the things that make up a nation's infrastructure.

CASE STUDY

China and Free Enterprise

The Commonwealth of Independent States and many of the Eastern European nations aren't the only nations making a move away from socialism and toward free enterprise. China is, too. China, once a staunch command-economy nation, is beginning to change. This was obvious in November 1993 when there was a meeting of communist party officials in Beijing, China. They met for the express purpose of discussing the Chinese economy. At this meeting, they wrote a 16,000-word document titled "Decision on Issues Concerning the Establishment of a Socialist Market Economic Structure." In this document, the communist officials indicated that they intended China to continue its move toward a free-market economy.

Of course, China is not making a move toward free enterprise overnight. For example, the government will continue to be the majority owner of a few large state-owned enterprises. Many of the smaller state-owned enterprises will likely be sold to private parties in the future.

Currently in China, 90 percent of the prices in goods markets are set by market forces; that is, by supply and demand. An economic document, written by communist party officials, states that the forces of supply and demand will now extend to such things as labor (workers), property, and financial markets. For example, interest rates will be determined by supply and demand. Also, the rents on housing, which were controlled, will be raised so that they are closer to their equilibrium levels.

In macroeconomic affairs, China is attempting to move away from central planning, where high government officials simply issue economic orders; specifying, for example, how much of certain goods may be produced. It plans to move

◀ Free enterprise is playing a larger role in the Chinese economy today than it did in the recent past. Here a Chinese couple shops for new electronic goods.

CASE STUDY (continued)

toward using monetary and fiscal policy, much as the United States does.

The move toward free enterprise has brought substantial economic growth to China. Its real GDP grew approximately 13 percent in 1992. This is a phenomenal growth rate, especially when compared to the 2 to 3 percent growth rates of many nations, such as the United States. Many economists expect high growth rates to continue in China for the near future. The relatively high growth rate is largely a reflection of China moving away from being a less-developed country (LDC) toward becoming a developed one. Once the economy of China has developed, economists expect its growth rate will decrease. (It is common for nations to grow rapidly once they start to develop; it is much like a person growing rapidly between birth and the age of 16. After a certain stage is reached, though, growth is much slower.)

Many businesses around the world are looking favorably on China. Specifically, they see it as a vast consumer market. Already, businesspersons and national leaders are traveling to China to transact business. For example, on November 16,

1993, Helmut Kohl, the chancellor of Germany, was in China for the signing of 20 contracts, worth $2.8 billion, enabling German firms to supply Chinese buyers.

What does the future hold for China? So far, it has moved toward free enterprise in its economic life, but its political life is still strongly communist. Will this change in the future? It is difficult to say at this time. Many economists believe that once people begin to experience economic freedom, they will demand political freedom, too. China should be an interesting nation to watch in the years to come.

---

1. What did the document, "Decision on Issues Concerning the Establishment of a Socialist Market Economic Structure," propose for China?
2. Do you think the new economic freedoms in China will prompt the Chinese to demand political freedom, too? Explain your answer.

---

growth of a community depend. Interstate highways, bridges, and communication networks are some of the things that make up a nation's infrastructure.

Many of the nations attempting to move from socialism to free enterprise lack infrastructure, which makes the move difficult. For example, the former Soviet Union had a low-quality telephone system compared with that in the United States. Of course, in the former Soviet Union, where the managers of firms were simply given orders as to what to produce, where to ship it, and so on, telephones were not as important. In a free-enterprise system, though, telephones are very important.

Materials have to be bought and sold daily, for example, and the owners and managers of firms need to find out who has the materials, their prices, and so on. Currently, many of the Eastern European nations and the independent countries of the Commonwealth of Independent States lack the infrastructure necessary for full-blown free enterprise.

Attitude

If you were raised in the United States, you were raised in a country that has a free-enterprise economic system. As a result, you have probably developed certain attitudes. For example, you probably believe that it is worthwhile for people to start their own businesses, work hard, and save in order to get ahead. People who have lived their lives in a free-enterprise economic system more readily accept the ideas that you have to take some risk to succeed, that you have to produce goods that people want to buy, and that government isn't there to take care of you.

This is not the attitude of people who have lived much of their lives under socialism. For example, they are not accustomed to taking business risks, since government has not let them start their own businesses. They are not used to the idea of having to produce goods that people want to buy. Instead, many of them have been used to simply producing whatever goods the government told them to produce. They feel that government should take care of them. In short, when we compare the person who has lived under free enterprise with the person who has lived under socialism, we notice a difference in attitudes.

For free enterprise to get started, a certain attitude must exist. Some people have to be willing to take business risks, accept that they may lose their jobs if they don't produce what consumers want to buy, and so on. It is sometimes reported that the people of the formerly socialist nations lack initiative, that they don't want to take risks, and that they are used to having government take care of them. This attitude has grown up over years of living under socialism, and it will not be easy to change overnight.

LEARNING CHECK

1. When nations move away from socialism toward free enterprise, some people lose their jobs. Why?
2. Why did the former Soviet Union under command-economy socialism have less need of a sophisticated telephone system than it did when it attempted to move away from socialism?
3. How might the attitudes toward work and risk taking of a person who has spent his or her life in a free-enterprise nation differ from the attitudes of a person who has spent his or her life in a socialist nation?

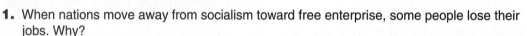

SECTION 4 WHAT'S AHEAD FOR THE UNITED STATES?

In many ways, the polarity between the two major economic systems of the 20th century—free enterprise and socialism—is over. It ended when the nations of Eastern Europe and the former Soviet Union decided to move away from socialism toward free enterprise.

In the years ahead, struggles are likely to emerge between different varieties of free enterprise. In particular, people will debate the role government should play in free-enterprise eco-nomic systems. This debate will involve free-enterprise nations all over the world, nations such as Japan, Great Britain, Germany, and the United States. This section discusses some of the arguments made in the debate, especially as they relate to the U.S. economy.

As you read, keep these key questions in mind:

■ What is industrial policy?
■ What role does MITI play in Japan?

- What are the arguments for and against industrial planning?
- What are the arguments for and against the government's playing a role in training workers?
- What are the arguments for and against lifetime employment for workers?

Industrial Policy, or Not?

In recent years, there has been talk of **industrial policy** in some free-enterprise nations. Industrial policy is a deliberate governmental policy of "watering the green spots," or aiding those industries that are most likely to be successful in the world marketplace. Many people say that one of the free-enterprise nations that uses industrial policy is Japan.

In Japan, the Ministry of International Trade and Industry (referred to as MITI) is the organization that implements most industrial policy. The idea behind MITI "is that the private sector alone has insufficient vision, coordination, resources, and risk-bearing ability to conduct its affairs in an optimal manner. To alleviate bottlenecks, to avert overproduction, to anticipate market shifts, to develop and deploy unchartered technology, the government is needed to assist in the sharing of information, pooling of resources, and overall collaboration of efforts. As a result of the successful implementation of this approach, MITI has referred to the Japanese [economic] system as a *plan-oriented market economy.*"[1]

MITI's powers to aid and guide certain industries are numerous. They include (1) designating certain regions as industrial parks and providing an infrastructure for the parks, (2) imposing trade barriers to protect Japanese firms from foreign competition, and (3) coordinating research efforts among firms in an industry.

People disagree about how much MITI has aided Japanese economic growth. While there have been economic success stories, some economists argue that MITI sometimes gets in the way of good ideas. For example, it mistakenly tried to discourage Japanese car manufacturers from competing in the world automobile market in the 1960s.

The proponents of industrial policy—and they exist in almost every free-enterprise nation, including the United States—argue that government needs to work with business firms in the private sector to help them compete in the world marketplace. In particular, they argue that government needs to identify the industries of the future—such as microelectronics, biotechnology, telecommunications, robotics, and computers and software—and help these industries to grow and develop now.

The critics of industrial policy state that such a policy—however good its intentions—does not always turn out the way its proponents would like. First, the critics argue that if government decides which industries to help, it may simply end up favoring the industries with the most political influence, not the industries that it makes economic sense to help. They argue that elected government officials are not beyond rewarding people who have helped them win election. Thus, industrial policy may turn out to be more a way to reward friends and injure enemies than a good economic policy.

Second, the critics of industrial policy argue that the government officials who design and implement industrial policy aren't really smart enough to know which industries will be the industries of the future. They shouldn't try to impose their uninformed guesses about the future on society.

Finally, the critics of industrial policy argue that government officials who design and implement industrial policy are likely to hamper free trade by

1. Andrew Zimbalist, Howard J. Sherman, and Stuart Brown, *Comparing Economic Systems: A Political-Economic Approach* (San Diego: Harcourt Brace Jovanovich, 1989), p. 52.

MINI GLOSSARY

Industrial Policy A deliberate policy by which government "waters the green spots," or aids those industries that are most likely to be successful in the world marketplace.

protecting industries that they have chosen to help. For example, suppose there is an industrial policy in the United States. U.S. government officials have decided that the American computer industry needs to be protected from foreign competition. In their attempt to aid the computer industry, they impose tariffs and quotas on foreign computers. This might prompt foreign nations to retaliate by placing tariffs and quotas on American computers. In the end, we might simply have less free trade in the world. This would hurt consumers, because they would end up paying higher prices. And it would hurt the people who work for companies that do a lot of exporting. Many of them would lose their jobs.

Social Responsibility for Training Workers, or Not?

In the United States, developing work skills is largely the responsibility of the individual. A person decides what he or she wants to do in the work force and then goes about acquiring the knowledge and skills to do it. Some people say that the gov-

ernment should play a role here. Specifically, it should train and retrain people in the work force. For example, Germany has a government-financed apprenticeship system that serves this purpose. As you might expect, some people are against the government's getting into the business of training workers, and other people are in favor of it.

The critics of government training argue that worker training is not a free good; someone has to pay for it, and this someone will be the taxpayer. It may be true that good training for workers will help the economy. But increasing taxes to pay for this training will hurt the economy, since the more government taxes people, the less they have to spend in the private sector. On balance, the economy might be hurt more than it is helped.

The proponents of government training of workers argue that business firms will not adequately train workers. The firms know that once the workers are trained, they may decide to work for other firms. If they do, much of the firms' investments in worker training will be lost. In this situation, someone else must train workers. This "someone else" is government, according to proponents of government training programs.

◀ Germany has apprenticeship programs that serve to train and retrain workers. Here apprentices learn a new trade.

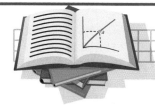

ANALYZING PRIMARY SOURCES

Economists' Differing Views

There is a joke that some people tell. A person asks: If you have five economists in a room, how many opinions will you get? Six.

In fact, there are many things that economists agree upon. But there are a few things that they do not agree upon, and it is usually the things that they don't agree upon that the public hears about. Furthermore, many of the things that economists do not agree upon are weighty matters. For example, one discussion revolves around how much and to what degree government should become involved in the economy.

Among themselves, economists refer to different economic schools of thought. For example, an economist may say he follows Keynesian economic thought, or monetarist economic thought, or supply-side economic thought. An introductory text like this one is not the place to go into the details—some are philosophical and others technical—that separate economists. However, you should know that not all economists are of like mind on some important issues. To give you a flavor of some of the debate that rages within the economics profession, read the following.

Stuart Eizenstat, former Assistant to the President for Domestic Affairs and Policy, and Adjunct Lecturer at the Kennedy School of Government, Harvard University

"When we had to decide on the [Carter] Administration's position on the advisability of raising the minimum wage in 1977 we could expect widely differing economic estimates from the Departments of Labor and Commerce on the impact of a rise in the minimum wage, because each saw the world differently, and their economic assumptions reflected these differences. Similar conflicts of recommendations occurred whether the issue was agriculture, import restraints, or the cost of new regulations. . . .**"**[a]

Lee Hamilton, Congressman from Indiana

"Believe it or not, I've actually come to like and respect most of the economists I've dealt with. Often, they provide a valuable check on the natural problem-solving exuberance of policy-makers. The economist's main message, that resources are scarce and choices must be made, is an important one. Equally important is the message that the economic system is complicated, with unintended consequences lurking everywhere. An economist who wants to contribute to the policy-making process needs to be a good salesman—but not a snake-oil salesman.**"**[b]

Campbell McConnell and Stanley Brue, Economists, on Keynesian Economics

"Keynesians believe that capitalism and, more particularly, the free-market system suffer from inherent shortcomings. Most important . . . is the Keynesian contention that capitalism contains no mechanism to guarantee macroeconomic stability.**"**[c]

David Prychitko, Economist, on Marxism

"Marx condemned capitalism as a system that alienates the masses. His

---

a.   Stuart Eizenstat, "Economists and White House Decisions," *Journal of Economic Perspectives,* Volume 6, Number 3, Summer 1992, p. 66.

b.   Lee Hamilton, "Economists as Public Policy Advisors," *Journal of Economic Perspectives,* Volume 6, Number 3, Summer 1992, p. 63.

c.   Campbell McConnell, and Stanley Brue, *Economics,* 11th ed. (New York: McGraw-Hill, 1990), p. 347.

ANALYZING PRIMARY SOURCES (continued)

reasoning was as follows: Although workers produce things for the market, market forces control things; workers do not. People are required to work for capitalists who have full control over the means of production and maintain power in the workplace. Work, he said, becomes degrading, monotonous, and suitable for machines rather than free, creative people."[d]

Allan Meltzer, Economist, on Monetarism

"To know when and how to adjust [fiscal and monetary] policies, Keynesians developed forecasting models. Some had hundreds of equations . . . . Monetarists have always been critical of these models and their use in policy. They favor stable policy rules that reduce variability and uncertainty for private decision makers. They argue that government serves the economy best by enhancing stability and acting predictably, not by trying to engineer carefully timed changes in policy actions. Monetarists saw such efforts as frequently destabilizing (that is, doing the opposite of what they were supposed to do)."[e]

E. Roy Weintraub, Economist, on Neoclassical Economics

"The framework of neoclassical economics is easily summarized. Buyers attempt to maximize their gains from getting goods, and they do this by increasing their purchases of a good until what they gain from an extra unit is just balanced by what they have to give up to obtain it. In this way they maximize 'utility'—the satisfaction associated with the consumption of goods and services."[f]

Robert King, Economist, on New Classical Macroeconomics

"The NCM [New Classical Macroeconomics] view questions whether typical policy instruments can be manipulated to accomplish specific policy objectives."[g]

N. Gregory Mankiw, Economist, on New Keynesian Economics

"The primary disagreement between new classical and new Keynesian economists is over how quickly wages and prices adjust. New classical economists build their macroeconomic theories on the assumption that wages and prices are flexible . . . new Keynesian theories rely on [the] the stickiness of wages and prices . . ."[h]

Jane S. Shaw, Economist, on Public Choice Economics

"In the past many economists have argued that the way to rein in 'market failures' such as monopolies is to introduce government action. But public choice economists point out that there also is such a thing as 'government failure.' That is, there are reasons why

d.   David Prychitko, "Marxism," *The Fortune Encyclopedia of Economics* (New York: Warner Books, 1993), p. 125.
e.   Allen Meltzer, "Monetarism," *The Fortune Encyclopedia of Economics* (New York: Warner Books, 1993), p. 131.
f.   E. Roy Weintraub, "Neoclassical Economics," *The Fortune Encyclopedia of Economics* (New York: Warner Books, 1993), p. 135.
g.   Robert King, "New Classical Macroeconomics," *The Fortune Encyclopedia of Economics* (New York: Warner Books, 1993), p. 140.
h.   N. Gregory Mankiw, "New Keynesian Economics," *The Fortune Encyclopedia of Economics* (New York: Warner Books, 1993), p. 145.

ANALYZING PRIMARY SOURCES (continued)

government intervention does not achieve the desired effect.**"** [i]

James D. Gwartney, Economist, on Supply-Side Economics

"Supply-side economics stresses the impact of tax rates on the incentives for people to produce and use resources efficiently.**"** [j]

---

1. According to Eizenstat, why did economic estimates from the Departments of Labor and Commerce differ?
2. Hamilton's words imply that economists agree to their main message. What is that message?

---

i.   Jane S. Shaw, "Public Choice Theory," *The Fortune Encyclopedia of Economics*, (New York: Warner Books, 1993), p. 150.

j.   James D. Gwartney, "Supply-Side Economics," *The Fortune Encyclopedia of Economics* (New York: Warner Books, 1993), p. 165.

3. According to McConnell and Brue, what do Keynesian economists believe?
4. Do you think Marxist economists would view the market system the same way that a neoclassical economist would? (Compare the words of Prychitko with those of Weintraub.) Explain your answer.
5. Do you think an economist who followed monetarism would argue in favor of government officials trying to time changes in fiscal policy carefully in order to reduce unemployment? Explain your answer.
6. Do new classical macroeconomists sound like monetarists? Explain your answer.
7. According to Mankiw, what is a difference between New Keynesian economists and New Classical economists?
8. According to Shaw, what might we infer is the major contribution of public choice economics?
9. What do supply-side economists stress?

Lifetime Employment, or Not?

Lifetime employment refers to the institutional arrangement by which a person is guaranteed a job with a specific company until retirement. This policy exists in Japan. Although it does not cover all workers there, it still is a major feature of the Japanese economy.

There are some advantages to lifetime employment. For example, there is lower worker turnover (which results in lower job-training expenses), less worker resistance to technological change, and greater enhancement of worker loyalty to the firm. One of the chief disadvantages to lifetime employment is felt by the company during an economic downturn. To illustrate, suppose the demand for a company's product has decreased. In turn, it sells fewer units of its product and its total revenue is less. Usually, a firm in this situation would want to reduce some of its costs, by laying off some workers, for example. If it has guaranteed its workers lifetime employment, though, it may be difficult to do this. It may not be able to cut its costs by enough to stay economically alive through bad economic times. If the firm goes out of business, this hurts not only the owners of the firm, but also the employees.

Free Trade and Movement, or Not?

The U.S. economy is increasingly a global economy. International trade has become a large part of the U.S. gross domestic product (GDP). Americans can invest their money anywhere in the world, and they can set up businesses in places like Japan, Mexico, and Germany. The same holds for other nations. For example, Japan has set up some factories in the United States.

In the years to come, Americans may become concerned when some U.S. businesses choose to "set up shop" in foreign nations instead of in the United States. Suppose an American business firm chooses to open up a plant in Mexico City instead of Los Angeles. The American workers who would have worked in the plant in Los Angeles may feel slighted and angry. They may express their discontent to their elected representatives, and their representatives may, in turn, try to enact legislation to prevent the U.S. company from "shifting jobs to Mexico."

In a global economy, though, business firms will naturally try to locate where they find it in their best interests to locate. Furthermore, in a global economy, investors will naturally try to put their money where they believe they will receive the highest return. If it is in Germany instead of the United States, then so be it. In a global economy, workers will end up working for the firms that pay them the most and offer them the best working conditions. If an American worker can be paid more and have a better job with a Japanese firm located in the United States than with an American firm located in the United States, then the worker will probably choose to work for the Japanese firm. Finally, in a global economy, American consumers will buy the products made by the firms that offer them the highest quality for the lowest price—whether the firm is Japanese, American, or Mexican.

With all these different groups—business firms, investors, workers, and consumers—looking out for what is in their best interests, the global economic scene is likely to change from day to day. For example, today American consumers may decide to buy from Japanese firms instead of U.S. firms. This will cause U.S. firms to become disgruntled. In their disgruntlement, they may lobby the U.S. Congress to put tariffs and quotas on foreign imports. Tomorrow, U.S. firms may decide to send some of their operations to Mexico or Japan. This will cause U.S. workers to get angry. In their anger, they may lobby Congress to pass laws making it impossible for this to happen.

These are the forces that will likely be present in a global economy. How will Congress respond? Will it prevent American companies from locating where they want to locate—say, in Tokyo, Japan, or Bonn, Germany, or Mexico City, Mexico? Will it place tariffs on foreign imports? If so, to what degree will it do these things? And will foreign legislatures do the same?

We do not know the answers to these questions. Very likely, some restrictions will be placed on movement and free trade, both by the United States and by many other nations of the world. But how much restriction? It's anyone's guess.

LEARNING CHECK

1. "Industrial policy may end up satisfying politically powerful industries and doing little to help the economy." Do you agree or disagree? Explain your answer.
2. What are the advantages and disadvantages of lifetime employment?

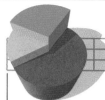

DEVELOPING ECONOMIC SKILLS

Comparing International Statistics

Let's start off with a basic question: Why would we want to compare the data of one country with the data of another country? The answer is, to put things in relative terms. But then someone might ask, Why would we want to put things in relative terms? The answer is, to get some idea, or perspective, as to where a particular country (the United States, for example) stands in relation to others.

Let's consider a simple example to illustrate our point. In Chapter 12, we learned that the gross domestic product (GDP) in the United States in 1992 was slightly over $6 trillion. Perhaps when you first read that number you wonder whether it is large, as these things go, or small, or somewhere in between. In short, if someone tells you the GDP of the United States and you do not have the GDP of any other countries with which to compare it, you don't have a good idea of whether that GDP figure is large, small, or somewhere in between. But once you are shown the GDP figures for other countries, you realize that the GDP for the United States is very large; in fact, you realize that the U.S. has the largest GDP of any country in the world. Our point is that you would not have known this without making a comparison. In short, through comparisons we learn things that we cannot learn in any other way.

Suppose someone tells you that the United States had a trade deficit of $50,002 million with Japan in 1992.[a] Before we go on to look at the trade situation the United States has with Japan, in comparison to that with other countries, let's be sure that we understand what this trade deficit means. A trade deficit occurs when the value of imports is more than the value of exports. In this case, the value of goods

imported by the United States from Japan was worth $50,002 million more than the goods exported to Japan. Now let's ask, Is this a large trade deficit that the United States has with Japan? In order to answer this question, we would need to look at the trade deficit that the United States has with some other countries. This information is shown in Exhibit 18-2. For example, we see that the United States ran a trade deficit of $10,301 million with Canada in 1992. Certainly, this is much smaller than the trade deficit with Japan of the same year. Also, we notice that, in the same year, the United

(1)	(2)
Country	U. S. trade balance (millions of dollars)
Australia	$5,065
Brazil	− 1,874
Canada	− 10,301
China	− 18,249
Germany	− 8,402
Italy	− 3,632
Japan	− 50,002
Mexico	4,881
Singapore	− 1,790
South Korea	− 2,798
Taiwan	− 10,129
United Kingdom	2,410

▲ **EXHIBIT 18-2. The U.S. Trade Balance, Selected Countries, 1992.** A minus (−) sign represents a trade deficit. If a number does not have a sign in front of it, it represents a trade surplus.

SOURCE: *The Universal Almanac, 1994* (Kansas City, Missouri: Andrews and McMeel, 1993), p. 341. Copyright © 1993 by John W. Wright. Reprinted with permission of Andrews and McMeel. All rights reserved.

---

a. No minus (−) sign is inserted in front of $50,002 million in text, as in the exhibit. Why? It is customary to leave off the minus sign if it is clear that the reference is to a trade deficit. When dollar amounts stand alone, however, the minus sign must be present to designate a trade deficit.

DEVELOPING ECONOMIC SKILLS (continued)

States ran a trade deficit of goods and services of $2,798 million with South Korea. Again, this is much smaller than the trade deficit with Japan. By comparing the trade deficit the United States had with Japan with the trade deficit the United States had with Canada and South Korea, we see that the trade deficit it had with Japan is much larger. Again, we learn something by making comparisons.

Now, suppose someone tells you that the inflation rate in the United States for the period 1991–92 was 3 percent. Is this a high or a low inflation rate? We would think, if most other countries in the world had an inflation rate of, say, 1 percent that in comparison, an inflation rate of 3 percent would be high. However, if most countries in the world had an inflation rate much higher than 3 percent, we would conclude that the 3 percent inflation rate was low. Look at Exhibit 18-3. Here, we have shown the inflation rate for selected countries in the period 1991–92. Argentina had an inflation rate of 24.9 percent and Mexico had an inflation rate of 15.5 percent. Turkey, on the other hand, had an extremely high inflation rate of 70.1 percent. Given the countries we have chosen to list, the U.S. inflation rate is relatively low.

There is another point to consider when looking at international statistics: even if, say, the dollar amounts of a particular economic variable are the same in two countries, it does not necessarily mean that the two countries are alike. For example, suppose two countries had nearly the same GDP in a year. Would this mean that the two countries were alike in terms of the composition of the goods and services they produced? Not at all. One country could be producing houses, cars, bookshelves, and desks, whereas another country might be producing oranges, apples, carpets, and computers. Our point is that it is important to use numbers accurately and to read in them only what they tell us and no more.

In terms of our GDP example, we know that two countries that have the same GDP have identical total market value for the goods and services they produced in a year. But this says

(1) Country	(2) Inflation rate 1991-1992 (percent)
Argentina	24.9%
Belgium	2.4
Canada	1.5
Colombia	27.0
Egypt	13.6
India	11.8
Israel	11.9
Japan	1.7
Mexico	15.5
South Korea	6.2
Sweden	2.3
Turkey	70.1
United States	3.0

▲ **EXHIBIT 18-3. Inflation Rate, Selected Countries, 1991–92.**
SOURCE: U.S. Bureau of the Census, *Statistical Abstract of the United States:* 1993, 113th Edition, p. 858.

nothing about other considerations. We cannot make a comparison as to the quality of the goods the two countries produced, the types of goods they produced, and so on. Making the mistake of thinking that two countries with an identical GDP are alike in other respects is similar to assuming that, if two people are both 5'7" tall, their weights are also identical. We know that this is not necessarily the case.

1. Country X has a GDP of $3,000 billion. Given no other information, would you know if Country X's GDP was relatively large or small? Explain your answer.
2. In an earlier chapter, we stated that in 1991 the United States spent 13.4 cents of every dollar on health care. How would you go about determining whether this was a relatively large percentage of each dollar spent?

CHAPTER 18 REVIEW

CHAPTER SUMMARY

1. There are two major economic systems: free enterprise and socialism. Nations' economies lie along a spectrum, some closer to the free-enterprise end and some closer to the socialist end.

2. A vision is a sense of how the world works. Free enterprise is an outgrowth of the capitalist vision; socialism is an outgrowth of the socialist vision.

3. The capitalist vision holds that market phenomena—such as prices determined by supply and demand, competition, private property, and exchange—together make up a marvelous system for rationing goods, conveying information, producing high-quality goods at the lowest prices, getting people to use their resources in a way that will benefit others, and generally raising people's standard of living. The socialist vision holds that in the marketplace, some people exploit others—for example, by charging high prices, paying low wages, and manipulating people's preferences through such things as advertising.

4. The socialist vision holds that government is made up of people who want to and usually will do the right thing by the general public. The capitalist vision sees government as being made up of people who respond more readily to well-organized special interest groups than to the general public.

5. The capitalist vision focuses on the desirable qualities of things that were not deliberately created but that naturally emerged as unintended consequences of people's actions. The socialist vision focuses on things that were deliberately created to serve a purpose.

6. Under command-economy socialism, government is involved in almost every aspect of the economy. Government owns all the nonlabor resources (such as land and capital), it decides what will be produced and in what quantities, it sets prices and wages, and much more.

7. In the former Soviet Union, Gosplan was the central planning agency. It had the responsibility of drafting the economic plan for the Soviet economy.

8. The critics of central economic planning say that economic planners cannot coordinate economic activity or satisfy consumer demand as well as market forces can.

9. In the former Soviet Union, the prices for goods and services were set by government. Usually, these prices were set too low or too high, leading to shortages or surpluses.

10. In the late 1980s and early 1990s, many Eastern European nations and the republics that had made up the former Soviet Union (such as Russia) began to move away from socialism toward free enterprise. Initially, these nations' economies witnessed a sharp increase in prices, the shutdown of certain factories and businesses, and the loss of certain jobs.

11. In many ways, the polarity between the two major economic systems of the 20th century—free enterprise and socialism—is over. In the years ahead, struggles are likely to emerge between different varieties of free enterprise. In particular, people will debate the role government should play in free-enterprise economic systems. The issues that will be debated include: (1) industrial policy, (2) government's role in training and retraining workers, (3) lifetime employment, and (4) free trade and movement.

CHAPTER 18 REVIEW (continued)

BUILD YOUR ECONOMIC VOCABULARY

Match the word with the correct definition, example, or statement.

1. economic system
2. vision
3. command-economy socialism
4. infrastructure
5. Gosplan
6. MITI
7. money
8. "watering the green spots"

a. central planning agency in the former Soviet Union

b. economic system of the former Soviet Union

c. the way in which a society goes about answering the three economic questions: What will be produced? How will the goods be produced? For whom will the goods be produced?

d. unintended consequence of the efforts of individuals in a barter economy to make trades less time consuming and easier

e. one's sense of how the world works

f. industrial policy

g. basic structures and facilities on which the continuance and growth of a community depend

h. implements most industrial policy in Japan

REVIEW QUESTIONS

1. What does the capitalist thinker say about (a) prices, (b) competition, (c) private property, and (d) exchange?
2. What does the socialist thinker say about (a) prices, (b) competition, (c) private property, and (d) exchange?
3. A capitalist thinker would be much less likely to support controls on prices than would a socialist thinker. Why?
4. Explain the case against central planning.
5. Why would we expect to see numerous shortages and surpluses in an economy that is centrally planned and sets prices by government edict?
6. We would expect to see an initial sharp rise in prices in economies moving from socialism to free enterprise. Why?
7. Explain the difference between the capitalist vision and the socialist vision as they relate to government and unintended consequences.
8. What are the arguments in favor of and against industrial policy?

SHARPEN YOUR CRITICAL THINKING SKILLS

1. Some people have suggested that industrial policy is a form of socialism. Do you agree or disagree? Explain your answer.
2. This chapter discussed some of the problems in moving an economy from socialism to capitalism. Which of the problems identified in the chapter seems to you the most difficult to overcome, and why?

ACTIVITIES AND PROJECTS

1. Check with your school or city library to see if it has a recent copy of the *Statistical Abstract of the United States*. Usually, the last section of this book includes comparative international statistics. Show how the U.S. compares to 10 other countries in terms of any five criteria reported in this section of this book.

ECONOMIC DICTIONARY

Command-Economy Socialism (Pg. 451)
Gosplan (Pg. 451)
Industrial Policy (Pg. 459)

Infrastructure (Pg. 455)
Vision (Pg. 444)

UNIT 5

Consumer Economics

You, the Consumer

INTRODUCTION

As a consumer, you will buy many products in your life. Some of those products will be relatively inexpensive, such as clothes and food. Some will be relatively expensive, such as a car, a house, and an education. This chapter discusses some of the everyday purchases you will make. It also discusses some of the major purchases you will make only a few times in your life.

SECTION 1 BUYING CLOTHES

In this section, we consider some of the things you should keep in mind when you buy clothes. As you read, keep these key questions in mind:

- What are some of the tradeoffs involved in buying clothes?
- Can a person shop too long for clothes?

Be Aware of Tradeoffs

When you buy clothes, it is important to be aware of dollar price and durability. *Durability* refers to how long the clothing item will last in good condition. Sometimes, the more durable an item is, the higher its price. If you don't know this, you may make a decision that you would not have otherwise made. For example, suppose you want to buy a shirt. You see two shirts that appeal to you. One is priced at $20 and the other at $30. If you buy the $20 shirt, you may not get the durability that you could get with the $30 shirt. For example, the $30 shirt may be made of a stronger, more durable cloth than the $20 shirt. The point is that the person buying clothes ought to think about more than simply price. Durability is important, and so are other qualities. In short, there are tradeoffs to be considered.

Different Places to Shop

Today, there are many places a person can buy clothes. These places differ in terms of selection, price, quality, and service. For example, consider both the upscale department store and the manufacturer's outlet. In the upscale department store, you will likely find high-quality clothing items at relatively high prices with good-to-excellent service. At the manufacturer's outlet, you will likely find many items of the same quality at lower prices with very little service. You have to be aware of the price you pay for the service and decide whether the service is worth this price.

▲ When shopping for clothes, there are many things to consider: quality, price, durability, style, and more.

Suppose the same shirt can be purchased in an upscale department store and in a manufacturer's outlet. At the department store, it is priced at $40, and at the manufacturer's outlet, at $32. You need to decide whether buying the shirt in the upscale department store with the good service (and fashionable displays, a generally nice atmosphere, and close proximity to other stores and places to eat) is worth $8 to you. Maybe it is. But this is for you to decide once you know how much you pay for the extras.

Can a Person Shop Too Long?

An economist would never advise you to shop for clothes for as long as it takes to find exactly what you want at the lowest possible price. The reason is that it may be too costly for you—costly in terms of what else you could be doing. Some comparison shopping is good, but too much can be costly for you. To illustrate, suppose it is Monday afternoon and you want to do two things before Tuesday morning: buy a pair of shoes and study for your English test. Currently, you are shopping for the shoes. You go from store to store to find the "perfect" shoes. You look at your watch. It is get-

ting late, but you haven't yet found the perfect shoes. You continue to search. Finally, hours after you had hoped, you find the perfect shoes. You purchase them and rush home to study. However, you don't end up studying for as long as you need-ed. As a result, you get a lower grade than you would have if you had studied longer. Was getting the lower grade worth getting the perfect shoes? Or would an average pair of shoes and a higher grade have been better?

 ## LEARNING CHECK

1. "It is always better to buy a cheaper shirt than a more expensive one." Do you agree or disagree? Explain your answer.
2. "You should always shop until you find exactly what you are looking for at the lowest possible price." Do you agree or disagree? Explain your answer.

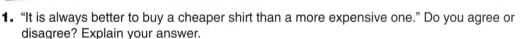

SECTION 2 FOOD

There are a number of things to consider when you buy food. We look at a few of these things in this section.

As you read, keep these key questions in mind:

- From what types of stores do people buy food?
- What is impulse buying and how can people guard against it?
- How is unit price computed?
- What is the difference between national brands, private brands, and generic brands?

Where to Shop

Principally, people buy food from three different types of stores: supermarkets, discount warehouse food stores, and convenience stores.

Supermarket (Grocery Store). The supermarket, or grocery store, is where most people buy their food. Supermarkets often run "specials" on

certain products. For example, there may be a special on a particular soft drink this week and a special on tomatoes next week. Supermarkets in an area can differ in the prices they charge for specific items. A loaf of Brand X bread may be $1.25 at one supermarket and $1.55 at the supermarket down the road. It is a good idea to make a list of the food items you buy on a regular weekly basis and check the prices at different supermarkets to find out which gives you the lowest weekly total for the same quality of service and convenience.

Discount Warehouse Food Store. Discount warehouse food stores don't usually carry as large a variety of foods as supermarkets, but they do sell most items for less. Also, they tend to sell things in large quantities. For example, whereas you can buy a 1 lb. jar of peanut butter at a supermarket, you can buy a 10 lb. jar of peanut butter at a discount warehouse food store at a lower price per pound. Of course, the 10 lb. jar may not be your

◄ Purchasing large quantities of a good usually results in a lower price per ounce for the buyer.

best buy if you normally only use a small amount of this product. It might become stale or rancid and thus be a waste of money.

Convenience Store. Convenience stores, such as 7-Eleven and Quik-Stop, are a prominent part of the American landscape. Most are open 24 hours a day. They charge more than supermarkets, and they do not carry as large a selection. But for some people, what they lack in selection and price, they make up for in convenience. Do you need to pick up a few food items in a hurry? The nearest convenience store could be your best bet.

What to Consider While You're Shopping

There are a number of things to think about while you are shopping at the supermarket. We consider these next.

Know the Pitfalls of Shopping without a List and Shopping When You're Hungry. You are walking down a supermarket aisle when you notice a brand of cookies that was recently advertised on television. You say, "They look good," and toss them into your basket. Going food shopping without a written list of things to buy often leads to this sort of **impulse buying**. It takes time and thought to write out a list, but it can cut down on impulse buying and thus help you get some control over your food budget. It can also help you if you're trying to cut down on buying "junk food." You're more likely to buy junk food when you don't make and follow a list.

It is also a good idea to do your food shopping on a full stomach. If you are hungry, many foods will look good to you, and you may end up buying more than you should.

Unit Price. You come across two sizes of the same laundry detergent—one small (40 ounces) and the other large (120 ounces). The small one is priced at $1.97, and the large one is priced at $5.45. To compute the **unit price**—the price per ounce, in this case—you need to divide the price of each by its weight. In this case, the small size costs 4.9 cents per ounce ($1.97 ÷ 40 ounces = 4.9 cents per ounce), while the large size costs 4.5

cents per ounce ($5.45 ÷ 120 ounces = 4.5 cents per ounce). Many supermarkets list the unit price of a product, along with the total price for the product. If, by chance, your supermarket does not, you may choose to carry a hand calculator along to compute unit prices.

Coupons. Food coupons often appear in newspapers, magazines, and shopping circulars. Using them can lower your grocery bill. Keep in mind, though, that a time cost is involved in clipping the coupons out of the newspaper, and so on. You have to decide whether having a lower grocery bill is worth spending this time.

National Brands, Private Brands, and Generic Brands. Products in food stores may carry national brand names, private brand names, or generic brand names. A **national brand** is owned by the maker of the products. Many national brands are known across the country, such as Kellogg's and Coca-Cola. A **private brand** is often produced for a specific supermarket chain and includes the name of that chain. A **generic brand** simply identifies the product (for example, "Corn Flakes"). National brands are more expensive than private brands, and private brands are more expensive than generic brands.

Should you try a private-brand product or a generic-brand product? This is a matter of choice, of course, but many people think these brands are worth a try. National-brand products have instant name recognition, usually because they have been widely advertised on TV. But often they are no better in quality and taste than the private-brand or generic-brand products.

Quickly Review Your Food Selections before You Enter the Checkout Line. It is a good idea to quickly look over the food selections in your cart before you enter the checkout line. A quick review will tell you about your eating habits. Nutritionists say that to maintain a good diet we should regularly eat lots of grains, fruits, and vegetables. If you find that most of the items in your grocery cart are snacks, you may decide that for your health you should exchange potato chips for fresh fruit.

MINI GLOSSARY

Impulse Buying Buying goods that you did not intend to buy. The impulse to buy something strikes you quickly, and you react by buying.

Unit Price The total price of an item divided by its weight.

National Brand A brand that is owned by the maker of the product. Many national brands are known across the country, such as Kellogg's and Coca-Cola.

Private Brand A brand owned by a seller rather than by the maker of the product. For example, products are often produced for a specific supermarket chain and carry the name of that chain on the label.

Generic Brand A brand that does not carry the name of any company, only the product name.

✔ LEARNING CHECK

1. You are deciding whether to buy food from a discount warehouse food store or a supermarket. What is the tradeoff in terms of price and variety?
2. How can you cut down on impulse buying?
3. The large size of Brand X detergent is priced at $6.25 and contains 150 ounces. The small size is priced at $1.50 and contains 30 ounces. What is the unit price for each size?
4. "Coupons may lower the dollar price of food but increase the time cost of shopping for food." Do you agree or disagree? Explain your answer.

SECTION 3 — BUYING SOMETHING OVER THE PHONE: TELEMARKETING AT WORK[1]

Each day in this country, thousands of telephone calls are made in attempts to sell something over the phone. This is called **telemarketing**. Some of the offers are legitimate, and others are not. It is important to be able to separate the two. This section discusses the ins and outs of telemarketing.

As you read, keep these key questions in mind:

- What are the signs of telemarketing fraud?
- What are the signs that a telemarketing salesperson is trying to swindle you?

Five Things You Should Know about Telemarketing Fraud

Telemarketing refers to selling over the telephone. Here are some things you should know about telemarketing fraud.

1. **Phone swindlers are likely to know more about you than you know about them.** You have to ask yourself where the phone caller got your name and number. It could be from the telephone book, in which case the phone caller may not know much about you. But it could be from a company that sells its mailing lists. In that case, the caller may know your age, income, occupation, and so on. The phone caller may tailor his comments to what he knows about you in an attempt to hold your interest and perhaps gain your trust.

2. **Phone swindlers will say anything to get a sale.** A phone swindler will "say anything" to make a sale. She is always ready with an answer. Don't assume that every telephone salesperson is as honest as you are. Phone swindlers are often coached to misrepresent the truth in order to make a sale. Furthermore, they are often coached to sound believable.

3. **Phone swindlers often sound as if they work for legitimate businesses.** The good phone swindler doesn't sound like a phone swindler. He sounds polished, he tells you about his company, he tells you how many employees work for the company, and so on. In fact, he may tell you so many details about the company that you are convinced that he couldn't be making it up. But he could be. He might have told the same lies a hundred times before he called you. If he sounds believable, it might be because he's had a lot of practice.

4. **Phone swindlers will often advertise in reputable magazines.** You may read an advertisement for some product in a magazine. Attached is a postcard you can use to request "additional information." You return the card. Days later, you receive a telephone call. Don't assume that because you requested the information, the person calling is representing a legitimate business. Many phone swindlers will imitate the marketing practices of legitimate businesses by advertising in reputable publications.

5. **Victims of phone fraud rarely get their money back.** You may realize that you have been swindled and try to get your money back, but usually your efforts will be of little use. Even if regulatory bodies and law enforcement agencies get involved, you aren't likely to get your money back, since the phone swindlers are likely to have spent the money.

---

1. This section is based on the publication "Swindlers Are Calling," published by the Alliance against Fraud in Telemarketing. This publication can be ordered from the Consumer Information Center, Pueblo, Colorado 81002.

MINI GLOSSARY

Telemarketing Direct sales of products by telephone.

CONSUMER ECONOMIC DECISIONS

Beware of Attempts to Cheat Consumers

Living in a free-enterprise economy does not guarantee that an unscrupulous seller will not try to take advantage of you. Consumers must always look out for themselves. Sometimes what looks all right is not. Take the real-world case of Alice Lakeland. (All names have been changed.)

One week, Alice Lakeland received a letter from Jay Questin, a financial advisor who owned his own company. The letter said that Questin had an excellent record of predicting whether the price of gold would go up or down. In the letter to Lakeland, he predicted that by week's end, the price of gold would have risen. The end of the week came, and sure enough the price of gold had risen.

The next week, Lakeland received another letter from Questin. He informed her that he had been right—that the price of gold had risen the previous week. He went on to say that by week's end, the price of gold would rise again. It did.

The following week, Lakeland received another letter from Questin, again informing her that his prediction had been right. As in the previous letter, he went on to make another prediction. He said that by week's end, the price of gold would fall. It did.

Alice Lakeland had so far received three consecutive correct predictions by Jay Questin. Did he have some special ability to "see" which way the price of gold was headed? Lakeland was beginning to think that he did. And when he correctly predicted the direction of the price of gold for the next three weeks—for six consecutive correct predictions—she was even more impressed.

On the seventh week, Lakeland received another letter from Questin, but this time there was no prediction. He wrote that he had proved he could correctly predict the direction of the price of gold. Then he said that for $500, he would send her his financial newsletter each week for the next 30 months. In his newsletter, he would weekly predict the direction for the price of gold. He told Lakeland that she would soon become rich by buying gold before its price rose and then selling it before its price fell. Buy low, sell high—that is the way to make tremendous profits, he said.

Lakeland sent Jay Questin a check for $500. She wondered how she could lose. The man is always right. She would simply read the newsletter, and if it said the price of gold was going to rise, she would buy gold. Then, after the price had risen, she would sell the gold and take her profits. Easy, right?

Well, not exactly. Jay Questin was running a scam (a scam is a fraudulent scheme). In the first week, he sent out letters to 5,000 persons. In 2,500 of the 5,000 letters, he predicted that the price of gold would rise; and in the remaining 2,500 letters, he predicted that the price of gold would fall. He knew that the price would either rise or fall—rarely does the price of gold remain exactly the same from one week to the next. At the end of the first week, when Jay learned that the price of gold had risen, he took the names of the 2,500 persons whom he had told that the price would rise and sent them an-

Making CONSUMER ECONOMIC DECISIONS (continued)

other letter. To all 2,500 persons, he stated that his first prediction had been correct. To 1,250 of them, he again predicted that the price of gold would rise. To the remaining 1,250, he predicted that the price would fall.

The price of gold had risen by week's end. Again, Questin repeated his procedure. He wrote to all 1,250 persons telling them that he had predicted correctly. Then he told half of the group, 625 persons, that the price of gold would rise; and he told the other half that the price would fall. By week's end the price had fallen.

Questin repeated the procedure for three more weeks. Alice Lakeland happened to be one of the persons who received a correct "prediction" from Jay Questin for six consecutive weeks. The only problem, of course, was that Questin wasn't really predicting.

Consumer beware: What looks like an unbelievable ability to predict the future may be some-thing quite different. Looks can be deceiving.

Finally, think about this. Consumers may want to believe things that seem too good to be true. In our story, Alice Lakeland might have wanted to believe that Jay Questin had some special talent or gift for predicting the direction of the price of gold. If he did, perhaps she could have become rich—and she might have wanted that very badly. Con artists know that a person's wish to become rich, or beautiful, or smart often works to their advantage. It is when you want something badly that you are most vulnerable to the words and actions of others.

---

1. An astrologer writes, "In March, someone you know will bring you happiness." How is this like or unlike the scam that Jay Questin was running?

Beware of Telephone Tactics

Not every person involved in telemarketing sales is a crook. There are some telltale signs of the crook, however. Here are some things to look for:

1. **High-pressure sales tactics.** The call may begin politely enough, but if the caller senses that things are not going his way he may try to pressure you into buying. Legitimate salespersons, on the other hand, respect your right to be uninterested in what they have to sell.

2. **Insistence on an immediate decision.** Sometimes telemarketers will say "there are only a few left" in order to get you to make a fast decision. Be wary of this. Phone swindlers don't want you to have time to think through what they have told you or to check it out with others.

3. **The offer sounds too good to be true.** If the offer sounds too good to be true, you have to wonder why someone has to call you on the phone to sell it. Be careful, though. Many phone swindlers are getting more sophisticated. Instead of making their offers sound "too good to be true," they are making the offers sound more realistic.

4. **Unwillingness to provide written information or references (such as the names of satisfied customers in your area) for you to contact.** Phone swindlers usually have a list of reasons why they cannot provide you with written information or references. They may say, "The written material hasn't been published yet," or "Giving out the names of satisfied customers is unethical," or something along these lines.

5. **A request for your credit card number.** Phone swindlers will often ask you for your credit card number for identification or verification purposes. Be wary of giving out your credit card number over the phone, especially if you are not dealing with a company you know about. If you do give out the number, you can have the charge removed from your credit card bill if you do not receive the goods or services or if your order was obtained through misrepresentation or fraud. You must notify the credit card company in writing, at its billing inquiries/disputes address, within 60 days after the charge first appears on your bill.

LEARNING CHECK

1. What is telemarketing?
2. What are two tip-offs that a telemarketing caller may be trying to swindle you?
3. How should you go about having a charge that was made through misrepresentation or fraud removed from your credit card bill?

SECTION 4 — HOUSING

This section discusses housing. As you read, keep the following key questions in mind:

- What is a security deposit?
- How does a person find out the crime rate in the area in which he or she is planning to live?
- What kinds of things are involved in buying and financing a house?
- When a person takes out a loan to buy a house, she may end up paying points. What are points?
- What is the difference between a fixed-rate loan and an adjustable-rate loan?

Different Types of Housing

Different types of housing are available to people: apartments, manufactured homes (or mobile homes), condominiums, and single-family homes.

Apartments. An apartment is a room or suite of rooms in which to live. A number of apartments together make up an apartment building or apartment house. Most people who live in apartments rent them on a six-month or one-year basis, although it is sometimes possible to rent from month to month. A person who rents an apartment is usually required to pay his or her first and last month's rent up front and put down a **security deposit** before actually taking up residence in the apartment.

Manufactured Homes. Many people call manufactured homes "mobile homes." A mobile home is a movable dwelling with no permanent

MINI GLOSSARY

Security Deposit An amount of money a renter pays a landlord before moving into an apartment (or other rental property). The money is to be returned when the renter moves out, but the landlord may keep a part or all of it to make repairs or compensate for rent not paid.

foundation, but it is connected to utility lines and set more or less permanently at a location. Today it is more nearly accurate to call these dwellings manufactured homes because most of them are never moved. Manufactured homes are built in a factory, in sections, towed to the home site, and then assembled.

Condominiums. A condominium is a single unit in a multiunit building or complex. Condominiums may either be built on each other (going up), or side by side (going to the left and right). Those built side by side often have front and back yards. A condominium owner holds full title to the unit and also owns a proportionate share in common areas, such as recreational facilities and grounds.

Single-Family Homes. A single-family home is a dwelling that is separate from dwellings around it and is located on a lot that surrounds the dwelling on all sides.

Renting an Apartment

Many people in their early adult years rent apartments. Here are some things to consider if you are thinking of renting an apartment now or in the near future.

Location. Most people consider it important to rent an apartment near their workplaces or schools, because doing this cuts down on their transportation costs.

Neighbors. As a renter of an apartment, you will likely have a common wall with neighbors on both sides of your apartment. Also, if you live in a multistory apartment complex, your ceiling may be someone else's floor, and your floor may be someone else's ceiling. In many cases, the noises made by your close neighbors will be heard by you. For example, you may hear someone in the apartment above you playing his CD player loudly when you are trying to sleep. For this reason, it is important to know something about the people

▲ When renting an apartment, it is important to consider location, size, price, neighborhood, safety features, and more.

who will be your close neighbors before you move into an apartment. Sometimes simply asking the apartment manager to tell you about them will provide information. If quiet is particularly important to you, you should tell the apartment manager so. Knowing this, she may be more likely to rent you an apartment among some of the quieter tenants.

Safety Features. Before you rent an apartment, make sure the apartment complex has fire escapes, smoke detectors, safe stairs, good lighting outside, good locks on the doors and windows, no large shrubbery near windows where people can hide, and so on.

Crime in the Area. Your may want to know the amount and nature of crime in the area where an apartment is located. The local police department will usually provide this information.

Common Areas. Most apartment complexes have common areas. These are areas that are shared by the tenants—such things as a common TV area, recreational facilities, and meeting rooms. Check the condition of common areas. You may not want to live in an apartment complex that doesn't keep up these areas.

The Lease. A **lease** is a contract that specifies the terms under which property is rented. The lease sets the rent for a period of time. You will be asked to sign a lease by your apartment owner or manager. Read it carefully—every word. Leases often contain formal language that you might find difficult to understand if you have not read many leases before. If you do not understand the terms of the lease, you should ask the apartment owner or manager to carefully explain it to you. If you do not believe the apartment manager will correctly explain the lease, seek out a friend, relative, or attorney.

All leases should indicate the following:

1. The amount of monthly rent and the date it is due.
2. The amount of the late fee (penalty) for turning in your rent after it is due.
3. The amount of the security deposit and the conditions under which it will be returned.
4. Who pays for utilities (electricity and water), repairs, insurance, and so on.
5. Conditions under which a tenant may be evicted, or legally forced to leave. (Perhaps, for example, tenants can be evicted for making too much noise or **subleasing** the apartment—that is, renting the apartment to someone else.)
6. Conditions under which the lease can be renewed. (For example, will it be renewed at the same rent, or will the rate be renegotiated?)

The Condition of the Apartment. Before you accept an apartment and begin paying rent, carefully inspect the premises with the owner or manager. If things need to be fixed (such as a shower rod or stove), urge the owner or manager to fix them promptly. Ask him to state in the lease that the repair will be made by a specified date. It is also a good idea to take a few pictures of the in-

side of the apartment before you move in (as well as after you move out). Get the pictures developed by a company that prints the date on photos. Pictures can be important if, after you move out, you and the apartment owner or manager disagree on the state of the apartment when you received it and when you turned it back to him or her. Without pictures, you may find that you get back less of your security deposit than you think you should.

Buying a Single-Family Home

Let's suppose you are thinking about buying a single-family home in the future. This will probably be the largest single purchase you ever make. Here are some things to do and know.

The Real-Estate Broker. Most home buyers seek out a real-estate broker to help them locate a suitable house. The broker will ask you the type of house you want to buy (number of bedrooms, size of lot, and so on), your price range, and other information. He or she will then take you around to look at the houses for sale that may suit you. As the buyer of a house, you do not pay the real-estate broker a fee. The fee is paid by the seller of the house. The broker's fee amounts to 3 to 6 percent of the price of the home. For example, if you buy a house for \$110,000, and the broker's fee is 6 percent, then the broker receives \$6,600 (\$110,000 $\times$ 0.06 = \$6,600).

House Inspection. If you are like most people, when you enter a house, you might notice the size of the rooms, the color of the carpets, the number of windows, and so on. The house may have a par-

MINI GLOSSARY

Lease A contract that conveys property (such as an apartment) for a specific time period for a fee.
Subleasing Renting from a renter rather than from the owner.

ticularly attractive staircase that you marvel about or extralarge windows that allow in plenty of sunlight. Outside, you might notice such things as how big the backyard is and what the neighborhood is like. But you may not have the expertise to determine such things as whether the house has termites or is solidly built.

Many house buyers like to hire a house inspector to check the house they are thinking about buying. Suppose you do this and learn that the house you want to buy has a plumbing problem. You may wish to offer to buy the house only on the condition that the seller correct this problem. Your real-estate broker will inform the seller of this condition.

The Down Payment. The **down payment** is the amount of money a person pays at the time of purchase toward the price of a house. The difference between the down payment and the purchase price is the amount the person needs to borrow to purchase the house. For example, suppose the price of the house is $110,000 and the down payment is $20,000. The loan amount is $90,000 ($110,000 − $20,000 = $90,000). In return for the loan, the borrower signs a **mortgage note**—a written agreement to repay the loan. Each month the borrower makes a mortgage payment to the lender.

Costs to Consider When Buying a House. The down payment isn't the only cost of buying a house. Some of the additional costs are as follows:

1. **Closing Costs**—Closing costs are costs incurred in transferring property (the house and lot) from one person to another. They include such things as a fee for a title search (to make sure the property really belongs to the person who is selling it), a fee for house inspection, and a loan application fee. A major component of the closing costs are "points," which we consider next.

2. **Points**—When a person takes out a loan to buy a house, the lender usually charges **points**. For example, a loan for $90,000 may come with 2 points. Each point amounts to 1 percent of the loan. So 2 points on a $90,000 loan equal $1,800 ($90,000 × 0.02 = $1,800). The borrower pays this amount to the lender. Lenders charge points when they believe the interest rate they are charging for the loan may turn out to be too low to allow them to make a profit. It is typical for lenders these days to charge between 1 and 4 points.

3. **Real-Estate (or Property) Taxes**—Homeowners have to pay real-estate (or property) taxes each year on their homes. Much of the tax money goes to finance public education. Different localities set different real-estate tax rates. For example, a locality may charge 1 percent of the market price of the house. If the market price is $200,000, the real-estate taxes are $2,000 each year ($200,000 × .01 = $2,000).

4. **Homeowner's Insurance**—A person who owns a home will want to insure it against theft and fire and—depending on where the home is located—hurricanes, tornadoes, or earthquakes.

5. **Mortgage Insurance**—Often, the lender will require the borrower to buy mortgage insurance—especially if the down payment is less than 20 percent of the purchase price of the home. This insures the lender against a loss if the borrower does not pay back the loan.

6. **Mortgage Life Insurance**—Some home buyers purchase mortgage life insurance so that if they die, their mortgage loans will be paid off. For example, suppose a husband and wife borrow $90,000 to buy a house. The wife is working, and the husband is attending school. Each month, the wife meets the monthly mortgage payment out of her salary. The couple decides to buy mortgage life insurance so that if the wife dies, the insurance company will pay the full amount of the loan.

7. **Utilities**—A homeowner must pay for electricity, water, garbage pickup, and heat and air conditioning.

8. **Miscellaneous Costs**—Most first-time home buyers do not have everything they will need to make the house livable—such things as furniture, curtains, and a refrigerator.

▶ This home suffered major damage from the January 1994 earthquake in Los Angeles, California. In addition to fire and theft insurance, insurance against natural disasters such as hurricanes, earthquakes, tornadoes, and floods where appropriate might be prudent.

Interest Rates

A lender that lends money to a borrower charges an interest rate. For example, suppose Jim takes out a simple loan for one year. The loan amount is $1,000. The interest rate charged for the loan is 10 percent. Jim's interest payment (the amount he must pay back in addition to the $1,000) is $100. The interest payment is computed by multiplying the amount Jim borrows, times the interest rate ($1,000 × .10 = $100).

Obviously, the higher the interest rate, the higher the interest payments Jim will have to make. It is the same with a person who borrows money to buy a house. This person would, of course, rather pay an annual interest rate of 8 percent than 10 percent on a $90,000 loan. For this reason, potential home buyers are interested not only in the price of houses but also in the interest rates. Often, when interest rates are dropping, home sales pick up; and when interest rates are rising, home sales slow down or drop. Why? When interest rates are dropping, people realize that they will have to pay less to borrow the money to buy a house. Thus, they are more likely to want to buy a house. But

when interest rates are rising, they realize that they will have to pay more to borrow the money to buy a house. Thus, they are less likely to want to buy a house.

Two Things to Consider When Taking out a Loan to Buy a House

Suppose a home buyer takes out a $90,000 loan at an annual interest rate of 9 percent. There are two things for the home buyer to consider. First,

MINI GLOSSARY

Down Payment Cash paid at the time of a purchase, with the rest of the purchase price to be paid later.

Mortgage Note Written agreement by which a buyer of property agrees to repay a loan taken out to purchase the property. If the loan is not repaid, the lender can take the property.

Point One percentage point of a loan amount. Points are paid by the borrower to the lender.

▲ This couple is applying for a mortgage loan. Basically, there are two types of loans: a fixed-rate loan, and an adjustable-rate loan. Choosing the best loan is one of the most important personal economic decisions they will ever make.

how long a time does she have to pay off the loan? Second, will the interest rate change during this time? We consider these issues next.

Time Period.   Lenders usually allow borrowers 15 or 30 years to pay off their mortgage loans. Most borrowers choose 30 years.

Interest Rate Change.   There are two types of mortgage loans: fixed-rate loans and adjustable-rate loans. On a fixed-rate loan, the interest rate stays the same over the entire period of the loan. For example, you might hear of a "9 percent, fixed-rate, 30-year loan." This means the interest rate on the loan is fixed at 9 percent for all 30

years. On an adjustable-rate loan, the interest may change but can only go up to some ceiling level. For example, a person may have an adjustable-rate loan starting at an interest rate of "6 percent, with a ceiling cap of 12 percent, for 30 years." Here, the borrower begins paying off the loan at an interest rate of 6 percent. The interest rate may rise as high as 12 percent, but no higher, during the 30-year period. (Adjustments in the interest rate may be made after a period of months or years, depending on the specification of the lender and the acceptance of the borrower.)

Lenders who offer adjustable-rate loans cannot simply choose any interest rate they wish. Rates are ultimately governed by a particular economic index. For example, a lender may tie the interest rate to the interest rate the federal government pays people who buy U.S. Treasury bonds. If the interest rate on U.S. Treasury bonds rises, so does the interest rate on the loan.

QUESTION: *Is it better to get a loan with a fixed interest rate or an adjustable interest rate?*

ANSWER: *That depends on the individual. A fixed rate offers more certainty, since the person knows exactly what the interest payments will be for the duration of the loan. An adjustable-rate loan, however, usually comes with a lower initial interest rate. For example, suppose you want to borrow $90,000 for 30 years. The lender may offer you (1) a fixed-rate loan at 9 percent or (2) an adjustable-rate loan starting at 5 percent with a cap of 12 percent. You may find it worthwhile to choose the adjustable-rate loan if you cannot currently afford the payments at a 9 percent interest rate. Understand, though, that your adjustable rate may rise from 5 percent and make it difficult for you to make your payments.*

 LEARNING CHECK

1. Name five safety features you should check before renting an apartment.
2. How would you go about learning the crime rate in the area in which you plan to rent an apartment?
3. What does it mean to sublease an apartment?

4. The broker's fee is between ___ and ___ percent of the sales price of the home.

5. Joan takes out a simple loan for one year. The loan amount is $5,000. The interest rate charged for the loan is 5 percent. How much is her interest payment?

6. What is the difference between a fixed-rate loan and an adjustable-rate loan?

SECTION 5   BUYING A CAR

There are 571 cars per every 1,000 persons in the United States—1 car for every 1.75 persons. Americans, it would seem, are in love with their cars. This section discusses the ins and outs of buying a car.

As you read, keep these key questions in mind:

- What is lowballing? highballing?
- Where can a person buy a car other than from a car dealership?
- Where can you find out the value of a used car?
- What is the difference between a warranty and a service contract?

The Ins and Outs of Buying a Car

Here are some things to consider before you buy a car.

Think about the Type of Car You Want before You Go Shopping. It is a good idea to think about the type of car you want before you set out to shop for one. If you don't, it may be too easy for a salesperson to sell you a car that doesn't really meet your needs—perhaps one that costs too much, is not fuel efficient, or doesn't have the safety features you want. If you're the type of person who likes to window-shop for cars before you start talking to a salesperson, then tell the salesperson this, and you can walk around the lot viewing cars at your leisure. Also, check the publication *Consumer Reports* before setting out to shop for a car. The car edition of *Consumer Reports* comes out in April. It is full of details about new cars—details that relate to safety, maintenance, fuel economy, and so on. Some people find it worthwhile to take their April editions of *Consumer Reports* with them to car dealerships so that car salespersons will know that they have done their homework and are serious about getting a good car at a reasonable price.

Check Out the Competition. Suppose you have decided that you want to buy a Ford. If there are two Ford dealerships in your town, then you may want to visit both of them instead of only one. This will give you a way to get the two dealerships to compete for your business, perhaps by offering you a better price or more features on the car.

Watch Out for Certain Sales Tactics. Some salespersons practice what is known as lowballing. The salesperson quotes an unusually low price for a car to get you interested. Later, when you sit down to do business, the salesperson says she made a "mistake" and forgot to include some costs, or her manager won't let her sell the car for that low a price, or something of the sort. Lowballing is most often used by a salesperson who thinks you're only shopping around right now and are going to look around at other car dealerships. She wants you to remember her "low price" as you shop around and hopes that the price she quoted will bring you back—as it often does.

Also watch out for highballing. Here, the salesperson promises you an unusually high price for a trade-in (the used car you give in partial payment for the car you are buying). Later, she says that the

◀ It is important to take a car you are thinking about buying for a test drive.

car has been checked out and isn't really worth as much as she thought.

Salespersons often try to find out what a person does for a living. For example, if a salesperson learns that a customer is a physician, he may be less likely to bargain on price, because he likely thinks physicians are rich. If you are a teenager looking for a car, the salesperson might ask you what your parents do for a living in an attempt to get this kind of information. Salespersons may also try to find out where you live. If you live nearby, they may be less likely to offer you a lower price than if you live farther away. Why? Because the farther away you live, the less likely it is that you will return after shopping around.

Finally, if you are a teenager seeking to buy a car, watch out for intimidating sales tactics. A salesperson may think that he can take advantage of you because he is older than you and because this is the first time you have ever bought a car. Remember, though, you are the customer, and you are in the driver's seat. He wants your business. Don't act intimidated (even if you feel that way). And don't be afraid to walk out of the car dealership at any time. There are other places you can buy a car.

Your Attitude Matters. When you are talking to a salesperson about a car, your attitude matters. If you act thrilled at seeing "exactly" the car you've always wanted, the salesperson isn't very likely to lower the price of the car. If you act as if you could take the car or leave it, you are in a better position. So don't give the impression that there is only one car in the world for you. Let the salesperson know that you are shopping around, maybe that you're not quite sure you're going to buy a car right now. You want your attitude to say to the salesperson, "If you want my business, you're going to have to give me a fair deal."

Find Out the Wholesale Price (Dealer Cost) of the Car You Want to Buy. Some newsstands carry publications that list the wholesale price, or dealer cost, of most makes of cars. Find out what the wholesale price is for the car you want to buy. If you do not find the information, you can make a reasonable guess by discounting the sticker price of the car by 10 to 15 percent. Knowing the wholesale price of a car lets you know how much room you and the dealer have to negotiate within.

Know the Worth of a Trade-in. You may have an old car that you want to trade in when you buy your new car. Find out its value. You will find it listed in the *Kelley Blue Book Market Report*. Car dealerships have this information, but they won't let you have it. Banks, credit unions, and libraries usually carry the *Blue Book* and will let you see it. Also, it is advisable to make the best deal you can on a new car before discussing the possibility of making a trade-in.

Drive the Car. Make sure to drive the car you are thinking about buying. Drive it without the radio or air conditioner on. Radios and air conditioners can sometimes mask certain car sounds of which you need to be aware. Salespersons will often go with you on the ride and talk to you while you're driving. If you want to drive in silence, so that you can hear the car, tell them so.

The Warranty. New cars, and some used cars, come with warranties. A **warranty** is a guarantee or an assurance given by a seller stating that a product is in good working order. It may also state that the seller will provide certain types of service for a period of time. For example, a car seller may provide

a warranty specifying that if anything goes wrong with the engine in the next five years, the seller will fix it free of charge. It is important to know what the warranty says. Make sure to ask about it and to read it carefully. If you have any problems in getting the car seller to live by the words of the warranty, you may have to call the manufacturer's representative in your area. The phone number should be in your car manual. If you are still unsatisfied, call company headquarters and talk with someone in customer service.

Service Contracts. Service contracts, which you may buy with a new car, provide for the repair of certain parts or problems. Service contracts are usually offered by car manufacturers or car dealerships. Remember, you already have a warranty with the new car, so you need to find out what the

---

MINI GLOSSARY

Warranty A guarantee or an assurance given by a seller stating that a product is in good working order and that the seller will provide certain types of service for a period of time.

▶ It is important for the car buyer to understand the differences between a warranty and a service contract and to know what questions to ask.

service contract provides that the warranty does not. Here are some questions to keep in mind when considering whether to buy a service contract:

1. What is the difference between the coverage under the warranty and the coverage under the service contract?
2. What repairs are covered?
3. Who pays for the labor? the parts?
4. Who performs the repairs?
5. How long does the service contract last?
6. What is the policy on cancellation and refund?

Financing a Car. If you decide to borrow money to finance a new-car purchase, be sure to compare the interest rate the car dealership offers you with those offered by banks, credit unions, and savings and loan institutions. Interest rates on car loans vary. Shop around for the best rate. Keep in mind that car dealerships sometimes offer very low interest rates on specific cars or models but may not be willing to negotiate on the price of these cars. Also, to qualify for the low interest rate, you may be required to make a large down payment. You may find that it is cheaper to pay the higher financing charges on a car that is lower in price or to purchase a car that requires a smaller down payment.

Car-Buying Services and Automobile Brokers. You are not limited to buying a car from a car dealership. You can go to a car-buying service or an automobile broker. For a fee—usually a reasonable one—you can buy a new car from a car-buying service or an automobile broker at factory cost and save perhaps hundreds to thousands of dollars.[2] You may have to wait a month or two for your new car, but the wait may be worth the dollar savings. To find out about car-buying

services and automobile brokers, consult the yellow pages of the telephone book or a credit union. In addition, the American Automobile Association (AAA), an automobile club, can help you contact a car-buying service or an automobile broker.

Buying a Used Car

A new car loses about 25 percent of its value the first year. This makes used cars much less expensive than new cars, and for this reason, the used-car market is quite large. But there is always some risk in buying a used car. Usually, you do not know why the original owner sold or traded in the car. Was it because she wanted to buy a new car? Or was it because the car was always giving her trouble? You need to be especially careful if you are planning to buy a used car. Here are some things to keep in mind.

1. Don't buy a used car that is no longer in production. It will be hard to get parts for the car.
2. Don't buy a used car without taking it for a test drive.
3. Watch out for used cars that are loaded with options, such as power windows, power seats, and so on. Such things need replacing as a car gets older.
4. Find out if the used car you want to buy has been recalled. A manufacturer will recall a car model if it finds out something is wrong with it. The owners of the cars are notified of the recall and asked to bring their cars in to be fixed (at no charge). Almost half the owners do not respond to the recall, however. This means the used car you want to buy might have been recalled but never fixed. To learn about recalls and other safety information, call the Auto Safety Hotline at 1-800-424-9393.
5. Have an auto mechanic inspect the used car you are thinking about buying. This is particularly important. A $50 inspection fee may save you hundreds of dollars and endless hassles later on. In addition, it may put your mind at ease.

---

2. It is typical for an automobile broker to charge as his or her fee either a percentage of the sales price or a flat fee, whichever is higher. For example, an automobile broker might charge 2.5 percent of the sales price of the car or a flat fee of $250, whichever is higher. If you bought a car for $18,000 from this broker, the broker's fee would be $450 ($18,000 × 0.025 = $450).

6. Look for the Buyer's Guide sticker on the window of the used car. The Buyer's Guide sticker is required by the Federal Trade Commission. It gives you important information on the car, such as whether the car comes with a warranty and what major problems may occur in any used car.

7. Be alert to those things on the car that you can check. (Are the tires slick, with very little tread? Are there oil spots under the car?)

LEARNING CHECK

1. Why might a car salesperson try to find out what a potential buyer does for a living?
2. How do you find out the value of a car you want to trade in?
3. Explain how your attitude can help or hinder you in getting a good price when shopping for a car.
4. What is the difference between a service contract and a warranty?
5. How can you find out whether the used-car model you are thinking about buying has been recalled by the manufacturer?

SECTION 6 — THE RIGHTS AND RESPONSIBILITIES OF CONSUMERS

Chapter 8 outlined some of your specific rights as a consumer, such as the right to go to small claims court and the right to keep merchandise you receive through the mail but did not request. Chapter 4 outlined a few of the government agencies that you can go to if you have a consumer complaint. This section discusses some of your general rights and responsibilities as a consumer. The information here will be particularly important to you, since you will make thousands of consumer purchases in your lifetime.

As you read, keep these key questions in mind:

■ What are the rights of a consumer?
■ What are the responsibilities of a consumer?

Consumer Rights

In general, a consumer has four rights: the right to be informed, the right to be safe, the right to choose, and the right to be heard.

The Right to Be Informed. You have the right to have the information you need to make a good consumer decision. For example, suppose you walk into a grocery store and pick up a box of cookies. You turn to the back of the box and read the ingredients. But the label is inaccurate. There is more of one ingredient than is listed, and one ingredient is not listed at all. Your right to have the information you need to make a good consumer decision has been violated. Or suppose you are shopping for a car and the salesperson tells you that the car you are looking at has six cylinders when it only has four cylinders. You have been misled by the car salesperson; you have been given inaccurate information. Again, your right to accurate information has been violated.

The Right to Be Safe. A consumer has the right to a safe product, one that will not harm his or her health or life. For example, a consumer has the right to a safe car (one without, say, defective brakes), a safe home (say, one that is not built on a

◄ Consumers have the right to safe products for themselves and their children.

toxic waste dump), and safe toys (ones that will not harm children).

The Right to Choose. A consumer has the right to choose among a variety of products offered at competitive prices. Choice is not usually present if competition is prohibited. Thus, this right means that firms cannot legally band together to prevent consumers from paying a lower price for a good. For example, suppose American manufacturers of cars got together and decided to not compete on price. Instead, they would sell cars for a certain agreed-on price. If that happened, the consumer's right to choose would have been violated. Or suppose grocery stores got together and tried to prevent any new grocery stores from entering the market. This act would violate the consumer's right to choose and thus would be illegal. Finally, suppose a store chose to sell products only to men and not to women. This would violate women consumers' right to choose and would be illegal.

The Right to Be Heard. A consumer who has a complaint has the right to be heard. He or she can address complaints to various government and private agencies that deal with consumer affairs, or go to small claims court.

Consumer Responsibilities

Just as consumers have rights, they have responsibilities. We consider them next.

The Responsibility to Get Information Yourself. If you are going to buy a car, or a pair of shoes, or anything else, you have to ask questions to get the information you need. You cannot simply wait for the seller to tell you everything there is to know about the subject. For example, if you are worried about a car's safety, you need to ask the salesperson about the safety features of the car, find out about its safety from Consumers Union or *Consumer Reports*, and so on. If you are at a restaurant and you need to know how much salt is in the food you are eating, you need to ask that question. You also have the responsibility to pursue something until you get a satisfactory answer. For example, if a waiter at the restaurant tells you that he doesn't know about the salt content of the food, ask that he check with the cook.

CASE STUDY

Consumers Union and Product Testing

onsumers Union is a highly respected non-profit organization that provides information to consumers on a host of goods and services. A large part of what Consumers Union does involves testing products and reporting the results to the public.

The organization that is known today as Consumers Union got its start in 1929 in Frederick J. Schlink's garage, where he and others tested products. Schlink called his organization Consumers Research. Four years later, Schlink was joined by Arthur Kallet, a graduate of the Massachusetts Institute of Technology. Kallet had written *100 Million Guinea Pigs*. In this book, Kallet said that the American public had unknowingly become the "test animals in a gigantic experiment with poisons conducted by food, drug, and cosmetic manufacturers."

After some internal troubles, Consumers Research was dissolved. A new organization was formed in 1936 by Kallet and 30 former Consumers Research staffers. It was called Consumers Union of United States.

A few months later, the magazine *Consumers Union Reports* (later to become *Consumer Reports*) was published. In the magazine, Consumers Union reported on the tests it had carried out on a wide variety of products, such as shampoos, cars, electric hair dryers, room air conditioners, and much more.

Products are tested scientifically at Consumers Union. When the organization doesn't have a machine to test a product, it will design and build one. For example, Consumers Union wanted to test mattresses' durability. It designed a device called "the basher." The basher would deliver 100,000 controlled strokes to the center of a mattress, this being the place where a sleeper's weight is concentrated. Next, the basher de-

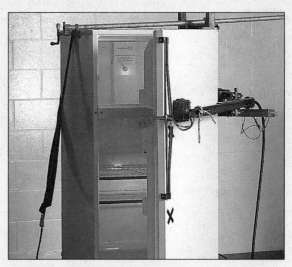

▲ Many products are tested by Consumers Union and other organizations for their overall quality and safety.

livered 25,000 bashes near the edge of the mattress, where a person might sit. Finally, the testers cut open the mattress and assessed the internal damage. In one set of tests, conducted in March 1986, only 6 of 32 mattresses survived without any structural damage or significant change in firmness.

---

1. What was the theme of Arthur Kallet's book *100 Million Guinea Pigs*?
2. In testing mattresses, Consumers Union set the basher on the same number of "hits" for each of the mattresses it tested. Why is it important to have the quality and quantity of the hits the same when conducting a scientific test?

Also, when you are planning to make a purchase, especially a large one, it is your responsibility to call the Better Business Bureau (discussed in Chapter 4) and ask whether it has received any complaints about the seller from whom you are planning to buy. For example, you may be thinking about getting the trees in your yard trimmed by Frank's Tree Service. It's a good idea to call the Better Business Bureau and ask whether Frank's Tree Service is a reputable company and whether any consumers have complained about it.

The Responsibility to Learn How to Assemble or Use the Products You Buy. Some consumer goods come with instructions. In particular, most items that can be used incorrectly come with instructions telling you what to watch out for, how to use the product safely, and so on. Read the instructions carefully and learn how to assemble or use the product. For example, let's say you buy a microwave oven for your kitchen. You do not read the instructions that came with the oven, so you do not learn what can safely be cooked in the oven. One day, you put something in the oven that should not be there. If you had read the instructions, you wouldn't have made this mistake.

The Responsibility to Make Fair Complaints and to Be Honest. Consumers feel they have a right to expect honesty from sellers. In turn, sellers feel they have a right to expect honesty from consumers. For example, suppose you purchase a CD player from a store but drop it on the way into your house. Because you dropped it,

it doesn't play as well as it would have. You could, of course, go back to the store and tell the seller that the CD player you bought does not work properly—without mentioning the fact that you dropped it. But that would be dishonest. You have a responsibility, when making consumer complaints, to provide the seller, or any government agency or court that gets involved, with the whole truth as you know it. This is a consumer responsibility that should not be taken lightly.

The Responsibility to Act Courteously. A consumer has the responsibility to be courteous. You have probably seen people in restaurants who treat waiters and waitresses rudely, order them about, and complain when their every request is not instantly fulfilled. Don't be like these people. Don't take the attitude that a store employee is there to be put down, to be argued with unnecessarily, or to do your full bidding. Remember that a seller is simply there to sell you a product.

The Responsibility to Seek Action through Government Organizations That Deal with Consumer Complaints. If you have a complaint that you cannot settle with the seller, you have a responsibility to report this fact to the appropriate government agency. A number of these agencies were listed in Chapter 4. Don't hesitate to report a seller to a government agency if you feel that you have been wronged. Remember, as a consumer, you have that right, and you also have a responsibility to exercise it.

 ## LEARNING CHECK

1. "Choice is not usually present where competition is prohibited." Explain.
2. List the responsibilities of a consumer.
3. Look at the list of consumer responsibilities. Which of these do you think is most important? Why?

SECTION 7 PAYING FOR A COLLEGE EDUCATION[3]

If you plan to attend college but do not have the resources to pay for it, then you may be interested in applying for some sort of financial aid. Federal grants, college work-study programs, and student loans are described in this section.

As you read, keep these key questions in mind:

■ What is the difference between a grant, a loan, and a work-study arrangement?
■ How does a person obtain information on financial aid for college?
■ In terms of federal financial aid, what is the significance of a college's default rate?

Grants, Loans, and Work Study

The U.S. Department of Education offers the following major student financial aid programs:

(1) Pell Grants, (2) Supplemental Education Opportunity Grants (SEOG), (3) College Work Study (CWS), (4) Perkins Loans, formerly called National Direct Student Loans or NDSL, (5) Stafford Loans, formerly called Guaranteed Student Loans (GSL), and (6) PLUS Loans/Supplemental Loans for Students (SLS).

These six programs fall into three categories: grants, loans, and work study. A grant is financial aid that you do not have to pay back. For example, if you receive a Pell Grant for $2,400 to attend college for a year, you do not have to pay back any of the money. A loan is borrowed money that you must pay back with interest. A work-study program gives you the chance to work and earn money to help you pay for your college education.

Pell Grants.   A Pell Grant is an award to help first-time undergraduates pay for their education after high school. A first-time undergraduate is

3. This section is based on the U.S. Department of Education publication *The Student Guide*. This free publication can be ordered from: Consumer Information Center–2C, P.O. Box 100, Pueblo, Colorado 81002. Any student interested in obtaining accurate information on student financial aid programs is strongly advised to read this publication.

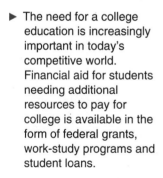

▶ The need for a college education is increasingly important in today's competitive world. Financial aid for students needing additional resources to pay for college is available in the form of federal grants, work-study programs and student loans.

one who has not earned a bachelor's or first professional degree. (Professional degrees include degrees in such fields as pharmacy and dentistry.) To obtain a Pell Grant, a person must show financial need and must be attending school at least half-time, which, for most colleges, means being registered for at least six semester hours. Applications for Pell Grants can be obtained from financial aid offices of colleges and universities and sometimes from high-school guidance counselors' offices.

The amount of the Pell Grant award depends on the degree of financial need and the cost of the school. For example, given two people with equal financial need, the Pell Grant award would be greater for the person attending the more expensive college. There were 3.4 million recipients of Pell Grants in 1991.

Supplemental Educational Opportunity Grants (SEOG). This grant is an award to help first-time undergraduates with exceptional financial need, as determined by the school. Like a Pell Grant, an SEOG does not have to be paid back. However, there is no guarantee that every eligible student will be able to receive an SEOG.

College Work Study (CWS). The work-study program provides jobs for first-time undergraduates; it lets students earn money to help pay for their education. The student's job may be on or off campus, and the student receives at least the federal minimum wage. Students cannot set their work schedules or choose the number of hours they work. These are determined by the school.

Perkins Loans. Perkins Loans are low-interest loans for first-time undergraduates with exceptional financial need, as determined by the school. The student must repay this loan but may be allowed up to 10 years to repay it.

Stafford Loans. Stafford Loans are low-interest loans to students attending school at least half-time. These loans must be repaid.

PLUS Loans/Supplemental Loans for Students (SLS). PLUS Loans (Parent Loans for

"Congratulations, and thanks for the $86,000 . . . Congratulations, and thanks for the $86,000 . . ."

© 1991 by Sidney Harris, *"Can't You Guys Read?" Cartoons on Academia*, Rutgers University Press.

Undergraduate Students) are for parents who want to borrow to help pay for their children's education. Supplemental Loans for Students are for student borrowers. Both types of loans must be repaid.

THINKING LIKE AN ECONOMIST

As you know, an economist looks at things in terms of costs and benefits. For example, when it comes to obtaining financial aid information on college, there are costs and benefits. The costs are a toll-free telephone call, or a visit to the guidance counselor at your school. The benefits could be attending a college you might otherwise not have been able to attend.

▶ A college financial aid office, or a high-school guidance counselor's office, would be an excellent place to obtain information about financial aid for college.

Getting Needed Information

The federal government has a toll-free number to call with questions about financial aid. The number is 1-800-4-FEDAID. Hearing-impaired individuals can call 1-800-730-8913. It is a good idea to call this number and inquire about the **default rate** of the college you are thinking about attending. In many cases, there may be restrictions on borrowing money to attend a college with a default rate of 30 percent or more.

Other places to obtain information on financial aid are the financial aid office of the college you want to attend and the guidance counselor's office at your high school.

M INI G LOSSARY

Default Rate Percentage of loans that are not repaid.

LEARNING CHECK

1. What are the major student financial aid programs offered by the U.S. Department of Education?
2. What is the difference between a student grant and a student loan?
3. On what two factors does the amount of a Pell Grant award depend?

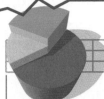

DEVELOPING ECONOMIC SKILLS

Figuring Your Monthly Car Payments

Suppose you buy a car for $12,000. You make a down payment of $3,000 and take out a $9,000 loan at an annual interest rate of 9 percent for three years. What are your monthly payments? It is easy to find out with the help of Exhibit 19-1.

This table shows (1) the dollar amount a person pays each month for a $1,000 loan, (2) at different interest rates, (3) over different time periods from three years to five years. Our example involved a $9,000 loan, at an annual interest rate of 9 percent, for three years. The dollar amount in the 9 percent row and the three-year column is $31.80. This means that, under these conditions, for every $1,000 a person borrows, he or she will pay back $31.80 a month. Since our loan is for $9,000, we must multiply $31.80 by 9 to find the monthly payment. This turns out to be $286.20 per month ($31.80 × 9 = $286.20).

Here's the procedure in step-by-step form:

Step 1: Write down your loan amount.

Step 2: Write down the annual interest rate for the loan.

Step 3: Write down the length of the loan in years.

Step 4: Consult the table to find the monthly payment for every $1,000 borrowed. Write down this amount.

Step 5: Divide your loan amount (from step 1) by 1,000. Write down this number.

Step 6: Multiply the dollar amount in step 4 by the number in step 5. This gives the monthly payment.

For example, suppose you want to borrow $10,500 at an annual interest rate of 10 percent for five years. Here's how you would figure your monthly payments:

Step 1: The loan amount is $10,500.

Step 2: The annual interest rate is 10 percent.

Step 3: The loan is for 5 years.

Annual interest rate (%)	Length of the loan		
	3 years	4 years	5 years
5%	$29.98	$23.03	$18.88
6	30.43	23.49	19.34
7	30.88	23.95	19.81
8	31.34	24.42	20.28
9	31.80	24.89	20.76
10	32.27	25.37	21.25
11	32.74	25.85	21.75
12	33.22	26.34	22.25
13	33.70	26.83	22.76
14	34.18	27.33	23.27
15	34.67	27.84	23.79

▲ **EXHIBIT 19-1.** Calculating Monthly Payments on Loans.

Step 4: The table says that the dollar amount that corresponds to 10 percent for 5 years is $21.25.

Step 5: Divide the loan amount in step 1 ($10,500) by 1,000. This gives 10.5.

Step 6: Multiply the dollar amount in step 4 ($21.25) by the number in step 5 (10.5). This gives $223.13, which is the monthly payment.

1. Victor borrows $11,000 at an annual interest rate of 8 percent for five years. What are his monthly payments?
2. Keesha borrows $8,000 at an annual interest rate of 9 percent for four years. What are her monthly payments?
3. Marcos borrows $10,000 at an annual interest rate of 7 percent for three years. What are his monthly payments?

CHAPTER 19 REVIEW

CHAPTER SUMMARY

1. Clothing purchases involve tradeoffs. For example, a more expensive shirt may be more durable than a less-expensive shirt.

2. It is not always in your best interest to shop until you have found the perfect item of clothing at the lowest price. The reason is that shopping takes time, and you could be using that time to do other things.

3. Food may be purchased from a supermarket (grocery store), a discount warehouse food store, or a convenience store.

4. It is a good idea to do your food shopping on a full stomach. If you are hungry, many foods will look good to you, and you may end up buying more than you should.

5. To find the unit price of a food item, divide its price by its weight.

6. Using coupons to purchase food may reduce your total food bill, but it will cost you time in looking for and clipping the coupons.

7. When renting an apartment, it is important to consider the following factors: location, neighbors, safety features, crime in the area where the apartment is located, the apartment's common areas, the lease, and the condition of the apartment.

8. The seller, not the buyer, pays the real-estate broker's fee.

9. The down payment is the amount of money a person pays at the time of purchase toward the price of a house.

10. The difference between the purchase price of a house and the down payment is the amount a person needs to borrow to purchase the house.

11. Often, when interest rates are dropping, home sales pick up; and when interest rates are rising, home sales slow down or drop.

12. There are two things for the home buyer to consider when taking out a loan to purchase a house: (a) how long it will take to pay off the loan, and (b) whether the interest rate on the loan is fixed or adjustable.

13. You can find out the value of a car you are trading in by checking the *Kelley Blue Book Market Report*.

14. A warranty is a guarantee or an assurance given by a seller stating that a product is in good working order and that the seller will provide certain types of service for a period of time.

15. The U.S. Department of Education offers the following major student financial aid programs: (1) Pell Grants, (2) Supplemental Education Opportunity Grants (SEOG), (3) College Work Study (CWS), (4) Perkins Loans, formerly called National Direct Student Loans or NDSL, (5) Stafford Loans, formerly called Guaranteed Student Loans (GSL), and (6) PLUS Loans/Supplemental Loans for Students (SLS).

CHAPTER 19 REVIEW
(continued)

BUILD YOUR ECONOMIC VOCABULARY

Match the word with the correct definition, example, or statement.

1. unit price
2. impulse buying
3. generic brand
4. telemarketing
5. subleasing
6. point
7. adjustable-rate loan

a. phone sales
b. no company name, only product name
c. total price divided by weight
d. "I just have to have those cookies."
e. "I pay $500 rent a month, but you pay me only $450 rent a month for my apartment while I am out of town on business for the next three months."
f. 6 percent today, but could be 9 percent tomorrow
g. 1 percent of the loan amount

REVIEW QUESTIONS

1. Why wouldn't an economist advise a consumer to shop until he or she found the perfect item at the best price?
2. What makes it possible for convenience stores to charge higher prices than supermarkets for the same items?
3. Calculate the unit price for each of the following items:
   a. Total price = $3.33; size = 11 oz.
   b. Total price = $5.22; size = 1 lb. 3 oz.
   c. Total price = $2.29; size = 1 lb. 1 oz.
4. "Coupons lower the dollar price of buying groceries but increase the time cost." What does this statement mean?
5. What should all apartment leases indicate?
6. What does it mean to sublease an apartment?
7. Compute the real-estate broker's commission for each of the following sales:
   a. Commission fee = 4 percent; sales price = $169,000
   b. Commission fee = 6 percent; sales price = $321,000
   c. Commission fee = 6 percent; sales price = $248,500

8. Compute the amount paid in points on each of the following loans:
   a. Points = 2; loan amount = $90,000
   b. Points = 1.75; loan amount = $144,000
   c. Points = 0.5; loan amount = $249,000
9. Define the following terms: (a) closing costs, (b) mortgage note, (c) adjustable-rate loan, (d) mortgage life insurance.
10. Why would a car salesperson want to lowball?
11. What are the questions to keep in mind when considering whether to buy a service contract from a car dealership?
12. Calculate the monthly payment for each of the following car loans:
   a. Loan amount = $13,200; annual interest rate = 7 percent; length of loan = 4 years
   b. Loan amount = $9,900; annual interest rate = 6 percent; length of loan = 3 years
   c. Loan amount = $8,000; annual interest rate = 9 percent; length of loan = 5 years
13. What is the difference between a grant and a student loan? What is the difference between a college work-study arrangement and a student loan?

SHARPEN YOUR CRITICAL THINKING SKILLS

1. Why would a new-car salesperson ask the following questions?
   a. What are you driving now?
   b. Where do you attend high school?
   c. Do you have a part-time job?
   d. Is there a work phone number where we could reach one of your parents?

2. Is it true that with an adjustable-rate loan starting at 7 percent you will pay less in interest than with a fixed-rate loan at 9 percent? Explain your answer.

ACTIVITIES AND PROJECTS

1. Work in small groups to create informational posters designed to help people avoid being victimized by telemarketing fraud.
2. As a class, create a bulletin board display that outlines the resources available to those students at your school who want to go to college. Be sure to include all available types of financial aid in your display.

ECONOMIC DICTIONARY

Default Rate (Pg. 497)
Down Payment (Pg. 484)
Generic Brand (Pg. 477)
Impulse Buying (Pg. 476)
Lease (Pg. 483)
Mortgage Note (Pg. 484)
National Brand (Pg. 477)

Point (Pg. 484)
Private Brand (Pg. 477)
Security Deposit (Pg. 481)
Subleasing (Pg. 483)
Telemarketing (Pg. 478)
Unit Price (Pg. 476)
Warranty (Pg. 489)

CHAPTER 20

Developing Personal Economic Skills

INTRODUCTION

Life is easier if you know how to do certain things. For example, if you didn't know how to do such things as write out a budget, save, invest, write a job résumé, and buy insurance, you could find life to be difficult indeed. This chapter discusses some of the things you ought to know to make your current and future personal economic life more comfortable and rewarding.

AFTER YOU STUDY THIS CHAPTER, YOU WILL BE ABLE TO:

1. Write out a budget.
2. Explain the benefits of saving.
3. Discuss what the Federal Deposit Insurance Corporation does.
4. Determine the capital ratio of a bank.
5. Discuss the important factors that relate to personal investing.
6. Discuss the ins and outs of joining the work force.
7. Write a job résumé.
8. Discuss in detail the different types of insurance, such as health, auto, and life.

KEY TERMS

Asset	Liability
Beneficiary	Mutual Fund
Budget	Net Worth (Equity,
Capital Ratio	Capital)
Insolvent	Résumé

SECTION 1 BUDGETING

Most people do not take the time to draw up a budget. Perhaps this is because they think budgeting is burdensome and complex. In fact, it is neither. Writing out and following a budget can be of immense value to you. We consider budgets in this section.

As you read, keep these key questions in mind:

■ What is a budget?
■ How do you make a budget?
■ When you save, what do you "buy"?

▲ It is easier to determine your income and expenditures if you keep good financial records.

What Is a Budget?

A **budget** is an organized plan for spending and saving money. Years ago, many people used a budget that worked this way: On payday, they would cash their checks. Then they would take the cash and divide it up among different envelopes. Written on each envelope was a description. On one might be written "House Payments," on another "Food," and on another "Eating Out at Restaurants." This was a way of controlling expenditures. For example, once the proper amount of money had been put into the envelope marked "House Payments," it was difficult to use this money to go to the movies or buy clothes.

The Steps to Take in Making a Budget

Let's consider a five-step process for making a budget.

Step 1. Determine your income and expenditures over the past year. You want dollar amounts for both your income and your expenditures over a year. To find your annual income, you may want to check your pay stubs. Let's suppose Marion, 17 years old, has been working part-time at a department store for the past year. She checks her pay stubs and learns that she earned $2,125 last year.

To figure out your expenditures, you need to keep a list of what you spend for a month or two. An easy way to do this is simply to ask for receipts for everything you buy. Another way is to record your expenditures in a journal each night. You might want to break your expenditures down into four or five categories, such as: (1) school costs, (2) clothes, (3) entertainment, including movies, CD purchases, eating out, and so on, (4) transportation, and (5) miscellaneous. Each day, you register the dollar amount you spent in each category. After you have done this for a month, you compute the dollar amounts you spent.

▶ **EXHIBIT 20-1.**
Marion's Income and Estimated Expenditures for the Year.

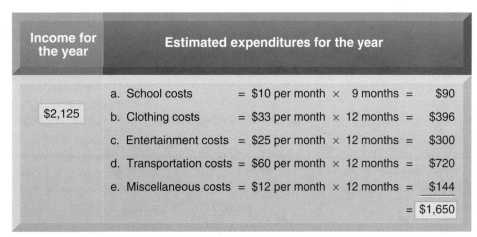

Income for the year	Estimated expenditures for the year			
$2,125	a. School costs	= $10 per month	× 9 months =	$90
	b. Clothing costs	= $33 per month	× 12 months =	$396
	c. Entertainment costs	= $25 per month	× 12 months =	$300
	d. Transportation costs	= $60 per month	× 12 months =	$720
	e. Miscellaneous costs	= $12 per month	× 12 months =	$144
			=	$1,650

Next, you need to decide whether your expenses for the month you have recorded are typical. For example, suppose Marion spent $20 in school costs and $30 for clothes in the month of November. She has to ask herself if $20 is a typical monthly cost for school and if $30 is a typical monthly cost for clothes. If it is not a typical month, then adjust accordingly. For example, if Marion believes she usually spends less than $20 each month on school-related items and more each month for clothing, then she needs to adjust the figures for this fact. Let's say she thinks that $10 is closer to her typical monthly school cost and that $33 is closer to her typical monthly cost for clothes.

Once you have found your typical monthly cost in each category, multiply by 12 to find your yearly cost in each category. For example, Marion's typical monthly cost for clothes is $33. If she multiplies $33 by 12, she finds that her cost for clothes for a year is $396. Marion does this for each spending category and then sums the figures. This gives her estimated dollar expenditures for the year. (See Exhibit 20-1.)

Computing your income and estimated expenditures on an annual basis gives you an idea of (1) how much money is coming in and (2) how much money is going out. In addition, it tells you *how* you spend the money. For example, Marion can see from Exhibit 20-1 that she spent $396 for clothing.

Step 2. Determine how much you are saving. It is important to know whether you are saving or not and, if you are, how much you are saving. This relates to your future goals. For example, think about Marion. We know that she earned $2,125 from her part-time job last year and that she spent approximately $1,650 (see Exhibit 20-1). This leaves a difference of $475, which she saved.

This may not be enough for Marion to save—it all depends on her future plans. For example, Marion may intend to go to college or take a vacation. To do any of these things, she may need to save more than $475 a year, or $39.58 a month ($475 ÷ 12 months = $39.58 a month).

Step 3. View your income, expenditures, and savings, and decide if you want to make any adjustments. Keep in mind that your savings relate to your future goals. At this point, you have dollar amounts for three categories: income, expenditures, and savings. In a way, you have condensed your "money life" into three dollar amounts. As mentioned, Marion's

MINI GLOSSARY

Budget An organized plan for spending and saving money.

three dollar amounts are $2,125 for income, $1,650 for expenditures, and $475 for savings.

Once we see things on paper, it is easier to figure out if we want to make changes or continue the same way. For example, Marion may decide to increase her savings and decrease her expenditures. She may do this because she plans to go to college. To do so, she will need more money.

Step 4. Change the way you view saving. Think of it as a regular "expenditure" item; think of what you "buy" with it. Many people simply save what is left over at the end of the month if they haven't spent their entire paychecks. This attitude relegates saving to a less important position than purchasing goods and services. ("If I have any money left over after I've purchased everything I need, I'll save it.")

Some economists think that many Americans need to change the way they view saving. Instead of seeing it as something "left over"—as something less important than buying—they need to see it as the equal of buying. In fact, when we save, we do buy something—both in the present and in the future.

What we buy in the present is security. When Antonio saves 10 percent of his paycheck each month, he "buys" the comfortable feeling of knowing that if an emergency arises tomorrow, he can meet it. If his car breaks down and he needs to get it repaired, or if he needs to take an emergency trip across the country, he can do it. He sleeps easier each night knowing that he will be better equipped to handle any surprises that arise.

Furthermore, when Sally saves 8 percent of her paycheck each month, she is "buying" the ability to purchase something in the future that she would not have been able to buy if she hadn't saved. Saving today makes it easier for her to buy certain things tomorrow. (Is saving, then, simply consumption postponed? Yes.)

You would do well to develop the habit of saving early in life and to view it as equal in importance to buying. Think of savings as an expenditure item, much as you would think about school costs or transportation costs. What do you buy each month? Let it be food, clothing, books, entertainment—and savings.

Step 5. Write out a monthly budget. Exhibit 20-2 shows the main elements of a monthly budget. Column 1 lists expenditure categories. This column can contain as many or as few categories as you want. Often, one's stage of life determines the number of categories in this column. For example, a high-school student may have

(1) Expenditure	(2) Budgeted	(3) Actual	(4) Difference
School	$10	$15	+$5
Clothing	$33	$37	+$4
Entertainment	$25	$30	+$5
Transportation	$60	$62	+$2
Savings	$37	$20	−$17
Miscellaneous	$12	$13	+$1
TOTAL	**$177**	**$177**	**$0**

◀ **EXHIBIT 20-2. The Main Elements of a Monthly Budget.** This budget shows a person (1) her expenditure categories (school, clothing, and so on), (2) how much she has budgeted in each category, (3) how much she has actually spent in each category, and (4) whether she is spending more, less, or the budgeted amount in each category.

fewer expenditure items than a woman in her thirties who is employed. The woman may have such expenditures as health insurance, mortgage insurance, and so on that the high-school student does not have. Notice that "Savings" is listed in this column. In our budget, it is an expenditure item.

Column 2 lists the dollar amounts we plan to spend in each expenditure category. These are our budgeted amounts. Column 3 lists the actual dollar amounts we end up spending in each category. Column 4 records the difference between the budgeted and actual expenditures. To get this difference, we subtract the dollar amount in column 2 from the dollar amount in column 3. A plus sign before the dollar amount means we spent more in this category than we planned. A minus sign means we spent less.

A quick look at Exhibit 20-2 shows that we spent more than we planned in five categories (school, clothing, entertainment, transportation, and miscellaneous). We spent less money than the budgeted amount in one category (savings).

What a Budget Can and Can't Do

What we do with the information in Exhibit 20-2 is up to us. No one can force us to spend less on, say, clothing and entertainment and more on savings if we do not want to do so. Writing out a budget is not a cure-all for your money problems. By itself, it has no power. It is simply an organized way of looking at your expenditures and your goals and at what you are doing about them. Your budget records your efforts, successes, and failures, much as a thermometer records your body temperature.

If you write out a budget and do not at first follow it successfully—if you do not save as much as you wanted to, perhaps—do not despair. Few people immediately succeed at following a budget. Like practicing good study habits, following a budget takes will power. Only you can decide whether your goals are important enough for you to exercise the will power necessary to achieve

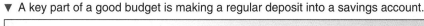

▼ A key part of a good budget is making a regular deposit into a savings account.

CONSUMER ECONOMIC DECISIONS

Making $

Purchasing Major Appliances

An appliance is a device or machine that is customarily used in the home to carry out a specific function. For example, a washing machine, dryer, refrigerator, microwave oven, room air conditioner, dishwasher, computer, and television are all considered appliances. For most people, an appliance can be a major purchase. There are two reasons for this. First, most appliances are relatively expensive (when compared to many other consumer purchases.) A refrigerator may be $700, a microwave oven may be $300, and a computer may be $1,500. These are not small sums of money for most people. Second, people expect to use their ap-

▲ The purchase of a major appliance requires good product research and careful comparison shopping.

pliances for a long time. For example, a person who buys a refrigerator may expect to use the refrigerator for the next 10 years. This is why people usually want to make sure they buy the right refrigerator for their purposes. Or consider buying a computer. A person who buys a computer today plans to use it for the next five to eight years or more. She wants to make sure it is the right computer for her.

Because most appliances are relatively expensive, and because you expect to keep an appliance for a long time, it is important to take time to make sure you buy the right appliance for you. There are some things to consider when buying appliances. They include comparison shopping, price, the daily costs of operating the appliance, the performance or quality of the appliance, and warranties and service contracts. We discuss each of these in turn.

Comparison Shopping

Comparison shopping is especially important when it comes to buying appliances. For example, if you are thinking about buying a television set, you want to get some idea of the quality and price of different brands. One of the ways to comparison shop is to visit different appliance stores. Go in the stores with the idea that you are there simply to get some information. Buying is for another day. Learn about the different brands, write down the prices, and talk to the salespersons about quality and performance of the product. (Keep in mind that salespersons who sell appliances often work on commission—that is, they receive a percentage of the sales price—and therefore they may

CONSUMER ECONOMIC DECISIONS (continued)

have an incentive for directing you toward more expensive brands of refrigerators, washers and dryers, and so on.)

Another way you can comparison shop (especially with respect to price) is by reading advertisements in the newspaper, and by consulting magazine publications such as *Consumer Reports*, which will usually rate major appliances according to performance and price.

Price

The price of a major appliance may sometimes vary by $100 or more, depending on where you purchase it. For example, sometimes stores (such as department stores) that carry hundreds of different items post higher prices on their appliances than stores that carry only appliances. One of the best things to do to find a good price is to call different stores, once you have identified the specific item you would like to buy. For example, let's say you have decided to purchase a particular brand and size of television set. Use the yellow pages of the telephone directory to call different stores and ask (1) whether they carry the particular item and, if so, (2) the price.

Once you are in the store, you may want to bargain with the salesperson. In some stores, and especially for some major appliances, it is not unusual to bargain on price. You may simply ask the salesperson if he or she would be willing to take $50 or so off the price. Or, you can start things off by asking if the price quoted is the "final" price.

Daily Costs of Operating the Appliance

For most appliances, once they are home, there is a certain cost to operating them. For ex-

ample, a refrigerator requires electricity to run. Some refrigerators use less electricity than others and therefore are cheaper to operate. However, you may pay for this feature in the purchase price. Often, on such items as washers, dryers, and refrigerators, you will find some information either posted on the appliance, or in a pamphlet that comes along with the appliance, stating the operating costs per year.

Performance, or Quality

Performance, or quality, is one of the most important considerations when purchasing an appliance. You want to make sure that the television set, refrigerator, or microwave oven you are buying works well. As stated earlier, *Consumer Reports* is a well-respected publication that rates major appliances according to performance. This is an excellent publication to consult. You may also want to call up a repair shop that works on the type of appliance you are considering buying. For example, call a TV repair shop before you buy a TV set and ask the proprietor which he or she thinks are the better brands. Usually, the people who service major appliances have a good idea of what is or is not a good brand of appliance to purchase.

Warranties and Service Contracts

A *warranty* is a guarantee or an assurance given by the seller stating that the product is in good working order and that he or she will perform certain tasks (should any problems arise) for a period of time, free of charge. For example, a new refrigerator may come with a warranty for a year, stating that if there are any problems with the appliance during this time,

CONSUMER ECONOMIC DECISIONS (continued)

the manufacturer will fix the problems. Service contracts are usually applicable after a warranty has run out. In a way, they simply extend the warranty, guaranteeing to repair and service the appliance for a period of time should any problems arise. The purchaser usually pays a flat fee for a service contract.

Before you buy a major appliance, find out what the warranty says. Is it a warranty for six months, a year, two years, or more? Find out what it provides for. For example, does it provide for all service and parts should a problem arise, or does it just provide for service? (It is customary for a warranty to provide for service and parts, but you need to make sure your warranty does this.) When it comes to a service contract, it is important to consider price, time period, and probability of maintenance problems for the appliance you are purchasing. For

example, a salesperson may offer to sell you a service contract for a period of three years; but the appliance you are purchasing may typically not have any problems in three years. The question then becomes how much you are willing to pay to protect yourself from an unlikely event occurring.

---

1. What is an appliance?
2. What publication regularly furnishes information on the performance and price of major appliances?
3. In some stores, salespersons who sell appliances may direct you toward purchasing the more expensive items. Why?
4. What is the difference between a warranty and a service contract?

them. All the economist can do is point out the opportunity costs and the tradeoffs involved. For example, what is the cost to Marion if she buys too many clothes now and doesn't save enough for her college career tomorrow? What is the cost to Antonio of buying an expensive car now and not being able to make the down payment on a house tomorrow?

These are questions that must be raised and answered by the individual. But as a student of economics, you may have a better understanding than others of what current actions mean. They mean that tradeoffs have been made and opportunity costs incurred.

LEARNING CHECK

1. Explain how a person can determine what his or her income and expenditures were over the past year.
2. What might a person "buy" when he or she saves?
3. "Writing out a budget does not guarantee that you will be successful at solving your money problems." Do you agree or disagree? Explain your answer.

SECTION 2 · SAVINGS AND BANKS

For many people, saving means opening up a savings account at a bank. There is more to it, though, as this section shows.

As you read, keep these key questions in mind:

- How can I start the habit of saving?
- What is the Federal Deposit Insurance Corporation?
- What makes a bank safe or unsafe?

How to Get in the Habit of Saving

It is difficult for many people to get in the habit of saving, because it is just too easy to spend money. There are advertisements for things to buy everywhere: television, billboards, magazines, newspapers, and so on. Hundreds of people tell you where you can spend your money. ("Buy it from us. We're at the corner of Park and Main Street!") In contrast, few people argue the benefits of saving some of your money. It is no wonder that spending comes so much easier than saving.

One way to get in the habit of saving is simply to pretend that you earn less than you do. For example, consider a married couple with children. Both the husband and the wife work, and their combined income is approximately $50,000 a year.

If they wanted, these people could simply pretend that their combined income was $45,000 and save the remaining $5,000. That is, instead of consuming like a family earning $50,000 a year, they could consume like a family earning $45,000 a year.

There is little doubt that this is a "trick" you play on yourself, and it isn't likely that the trick will be so convincing that you will not remember your actual income. But that is not the point. The point is to get in the habit of thinking and acting *as if* you earned less income than you do. "Pretending" may make the going easier in the beginning.

Then, once the saving habit is established, you may have no further need for the trick.

Not All Banks Are Alike

Many people place their savings in a bank. Between 1985 and 1990, a period of only five years, 1,016 banks failed in the United States. This is 218 more banks than had failed in the previous 50 years. All kinds of banks failed—big, small, and all sizes in between.

What does it mean for a bank to fail? To understand, we need to look at the banking business more closely. A bank makes most of its income from loans. For example, suppose a person puts $4,000 into a savings account in a bank, and the bank turns around and lends a large percentage of

▲ When banks fail, they can be ordered by government agencies to close their doors. When putting your money in a bank, it is a good idea to seek information concerning the financial integrity of the institution.

the $4,000 (say, $3,600) to someone. The borrower has to pay interest for the $3,600 loan, and the interest payments constitute income for the bank.

Now suppose a bank makes many loans that borrowers cannot repay. Suppose, for example, that the person who borrowed the $3,600 needed the money to start a new business. The business ends up doing poorly, and the owner cannot pay the interest on the $3,600 loan or the loan amount itself.

As far as the bank is concerned, the $3,600 it lent to this person was a "bad" loan. (Loans are "bad" when they are not repaid.) If the bank has many other bad loans, it may not be able to survive. After all, banks are only successful when they get back the loan money plus interest. If they are consistently unable to do so, they fail and go out of business.

Now, if you are the original depositer of the $4,000 in this example, you are probably asking, "What about my money? If the bank has lost my money, what am I going to do?"

Your money is insured through the Federal Deposit Insurance Corporation (FDIC), which was set up by Congress in 1933 to insure bank deposits. There is little doubt that you will get your money back, but you may not get it back as soon as you would like. In the early 1990s, there was much talk about the failure of numerous savings and loan associations. We discussed this in Chapter 11. The deposits in the savings and loan associations were insured, but some depositors who got back their money had to wait several weeks for it. Having to wait may or may not be a problem for a depositor. If a depositor needs his or her money right away in order to pay some unexpected bills, waiting could be a problem. If a depositor has no pressing cash needs, waiting isn't a problem.

Here are some things to keep in mind in attempting to keep your savings safe:

1. **Never place over $100,000 in an account at any one bank.** The reason is that the government only insures accounts up to $100,000. Of course, most persons will say, "Don't worry; placing more than $100,000 in an account is not a problem I'm likely to have." It is true that a savings account containing over $100,000 is rare; but, for brief periods, middle-income families may have over $100,000 in an ac-

Copyright © Levin 1994.

"Yes, I'm thinking of opening an account at this bank, but first I'd like to see some of your references."

CASE STUDY

Savings, Credit, and the Economy

Most of us probably do not think much about the social aspects of saving, or about how our saving affects the economy. Mostly, we simply think about how it affects us. For example, Bobby may simply think that saving $100 each month will make it possible for him to make a down payment on a car in 18 months.

Saving affects us, the savers, but it also affects the economy. To illustrate, suppose we have two people, Tammy and Catalina. Catalina works as a physician. Each month, she saves approximately $1,000. Currently, she has $54,000 in a savings account. Until recently, Tammy was working as a cook in a restaurant. Recently, she decided to open up a restaurant of her own. The problem is that building and running a restaurant take money, and Tammy doesn't have all the money that is needed. She needs a loan.

One day, she goes to a bank to ask for a loan to start her new restaurant. The loan officer asks her how much money she needs, how she plans to spend it, where she wants to locate the restaurant, how many customers she thinks she will have each day, and other questions related to the business. After receiving Tammy's answers and doing some further checking, the loan officer grants Tammy a loan. Where does the loan offi-

▲ To get started in business, people need to borrow money—money which comes from other people's savings in a bank.

cer get the money to lend to Tammy? From the savings of people who have savings accounts at the bank—from people like Catalina. In other words, the bank has channeled some of Catalina's saved funds to Tammy in the form of a loan, so that she can start a new business.

Consider the picture of Catalina going to work one day. She is stopped at a light at the corner of the street where Tammy's new restaurant is being built. She looks over and observes the construction for a few seconds and thinks to herself that there are a lot of new businesses starting up in town. Then the light turns green, and she proceeds on her way. What we, as students of economics, need to know is that Catalina's savings have much to do with these new businesses. The dollars she saves end up as credit for people like Tammy who want to start new businesses.

---

1. "New commercial construction in town (the building of new shops, restaurants, etc.) is related to people's saving." Do you agree or disagree? Explain your answer.

count. For example, a family may sell its home and place the proceeds in a bank for a period of a month or more.

Note that if a person does have over $100,000 to put into a savings account, and he or she opens up an account at two different branches of the same bank, the savings are still insured only for $100,000. For example, suppose a person places $70,000 in an account at one branch of Bank A, and $50,000 in an account at another branch of Bank A. He or she may think that both accounts are insured by the FDIC since neither account contains over $100,000. But, in fact, in the eyes of the FDIC, this person has deposited $120,000 in Bank A; he or she has $20,000 that is not insured at all. It is better for this person to open up accounts at different banks.

2. **Check the capital ratio of the bank.** The **assets** of the bank are those things that the bank owns that have value. The **liabilities** of the bank are its debts. If we subtract the liabilities from the assets, we are left with **net worth**, or **equity**, or **capital**. This is the value of the bank to its owners. For example, let's suppose Bank C's assets total $130 million, and its liabilities total $120 million. The $10 million difference is the equity of the bank—the value of the bank to its owners.

Now, if we take the equity of the bank and divide it by the assets of the bank, we have the **capital ratio**. For example, for Bank C—which has equity of $10 million and assets of $130 million—the capital ratio is 7.7 percent. The average capital ratio for all banks is roughly 6.5 percent. It is generally thought that a bank must have a capital ratio of at least 5 percent to be considered a healthy bank. To be considered a strong bank, a bank should have a capital ratio of between 6 and 7.5 percent. To be considered exceptionally strong, it should have a ratio higher than 7.5 percent. A bank with a ratio below 5 percent is considered weak, and a bank with a ratio below 3 percent is very weak. In addition, if you subtract liabilities from assets and get a negative number, this means that the bank has no equity—that it is **insolvent.**

It is relatively easy to find out a bank's assets and equity if shares of the bank's stock are traded on the stock exchange. A stockbroker, for example, would have this information. Once you know the bank's assets and equity, you can simply do the division yourself to calculate the capital ratio.

LEARNING CHECK

1. How many banks failed between 1985 and 1990?
2. What does it mean to say that a bank has made a "bad" loan?
3. Jones has $40,523 in an account with Branch 1 of Bank A and $64,213 in an account with Branch 2 of Bank A. How much of her money is not insured?
4. Calculate the net worth in each of the following:
   a. Assets = $1.2 million; liabilities = $800,000
   b. Assets = $44 million; liabilities = $39 million
   c. Assets = $10.45 million; liabilities = $8.45 million
5. You are searching for an exceptionally strong bank in which to place your money. For what capital ratio will you look?
6. What does it mean to say that a bank is insolvent?

SECTION 3 INVESTING

As noted in an earlier chapter, the words *invest* and *investment* mean something different to economists than to many others. When an economist talks about investing, she is talking about what a business firm does when it buys new machinery for its factories or increases the size of its present factory. For example, she might say, "Business firms in the United States have invested heavily in the last year. They have built new factories and purchased new machinery in record amounts." When the layperson talks about investing, he is usually talking about buying stocks and bonds, real estate, and so on. For example, a person might say, "My investments in real estate and the stock market are really paying off." This section uses the words *invest* and *investment* in the way the layperson uses the words.

As you read, keep this key question in mind:

- What are some of the incorrect things people say and believe about buying stocks?

Separating Fact from Fiction When It Comes to Buying Stocks

For many people, buying stocks in the stock market has an exciting appeal. Buying stocks may seem far more exciting than buying bonds or putting money in a passbook savings account, for example.

If you are one of the people who think you might find stock market investing exciting, fun, and adventurous, here's one thing you should realize. Excitement is one thing, and profit is another. Sometimes they go together. Sometimes they don't.

Perhaps because the stock market does hold fascination for so many people, a number of things are said about it that aren't true. Here are some of those statements.

1. **"The stock has gone down so much already that it can't possibly go down any more."** People often say this about the stock of a well-known and respectable company. But the stock of such a company can go down, down, down. In a period of one year, the stock price of Polaroid went from $143 to $14. No doubt, when the stock's price was $100, and $50, and $25, some people were saying, "The stock has gone down so much already, it can't possibly go down any more." They were wrong.

2. **"The stock has gone up so far that it can't possibly go higher."** This is, of course, the opposite of the "it can't go any lower" assumption. There are plenty of stocks that continued to go higher even as people were saying that it couldn't happen. McDonald's, Stop & Shop, Subaru, and Philip Morris are examples.

3. **"It's only a dollar a share. How can I lose?"** Look at the stock listings in a newspaper, and you will find different prices for different stocks. Some prices are relatively low. It may be natural to think that you can't lose your money if you only pay $1 per share of stock. However, even a stock that sells for $1 a share can go down in price.

4. **"The stock has gone down in price, but eventually it will come back up."** There is an inclination to think that if a stock goes down in price, it will eventually move back up. But it doesn't always happen this way. There are

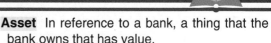

MINI GLOSSARY

Asset In reference to a bank, a thing that the bank owns that has value.
Liability In reference to a bank, its debt.
Net Worth (Equity, Capital) The difference between assets and liabilities.
Capital Ratio Equity divided by assets.
Insolvent Having more liabilities than assets.

companies whose stock has gone down in price and never come back up. In fact, the companies went out of business.

5. **"I can't sell now—the price has gone down."** Suppose a person buys a stock at $20 a share. Afterward, the stock's price falls to $10 a share. The person says, "I can't sell the stock now, because I'd take a loss. I have to wait until the price goes back up to at least $20 a share." This person obviously thinks that a stock will eventually rebound to whatever price he paid for it. Unfortunately, it doesn't necessarily work that way. Remember, there is nothing to prevent a stock's price from continuing to fall.

6. **"I've had this stock for a very long time and nothing has happened. Nothing will ever happen. I'm selling it."** There are a number of companies whose stock hardly moved in price for 5 to 10 years and then moved sharply upward. A few examples include Merck, GAF Corporation, and Lukens. The fact that a stock is quiet today doesn't mean it will be quiet tomorrow.

THINKING LIKE AN ECONOMIST

The economist believes that what people do in the present can influence their future but that what they do in the present can never change their past. For this reason, the economist would not say, "I can't sell my stock now, because the price has gone down." This present action (choosing not to sell the stock) cannot change the past (the fall in the stock's price). However, the present action of not selling the stock may affect the future. The stockholder may take a bigger loss if he waits than if he sells the stock now. Again, you can affect the future through your present actions, but you cannot change the past. Thinking otherwise will only lead you to make mistakes that you could have avoided.

Mutual Funds

Many people today invest their money in mutual funds. A **mutual fund** is a financial organization that pools people's money and invests it in various ways. Suppose you invested in a *stock mutual fund*, for example. You would buy shares in this fund, and the fund manager would invest your money, along with the money of other people, in various stocks. She might invest the money in 20 to 30 stocks. Alternatively, you could put your money in a *bond mutual fund*. This fund invests in different bonds, such as corporate and government bonds. Finally, you could put the money in a *money market fund*. This fund invests in short-term government or U.S. Treasury securities. Putting your money in a money market fund that invests in short-term U.S. Treasury securities is an extremely safe investment. The reason is that there is little doubt that the U.S. government is going to pay what it owes on those securities.

How to Choose a Mutual Fund Company

There are many mutual fund companies. The companies regularly advertise in business publications. Also, many business publications report on how well certain mutual fund companies are doing. It is important to order and read the prospectus of any fund company in which you are interested. In the prospectus, the company outlines its investment philosophy and its results over the past 5 to 10 years. Be sure to check whether the same management team that produced the described results is managing the fund today. A mutual fund company may have invested well a few years ago, but if a different management team is making investments for the company today, past results may not be meaningful.

It is also important to check the fees of the mutual fund company. Usually, the fee is a small percentage of the total amount of funds you invest. Fees can change periodically, so keep in touch with your mutual fund company.

Look for Prompt, Courteous Service

Suppose Julie turns over $10,000 to the XYZ Mutual Fund Company in Boston. She has $5,000 placed in a stock fund, $3,000 in a bond fund, and $2,000 in a money market fund. In all, then, she has her money in three funds (stock, bond, money market) at XYZ Mutual Fund Company.

One of the options XYZ Mutual Fund Company offers is the ability to switch money from one fund to another. Suppose Julie thinks that over the next two months, the value of most stocks is going to fall and the value of most bonds is going to rise.

She may want to switch some of her money from the stock fund to the bond fund. Perhaps she decides to move $4,000 from the stock fund to the bond fund.

Julie calls the mutual fund company to issue this order. The person she talks to on the phone should offer prompt, courteous service. If the person doesn't do so, Julie might want to consider putting her money elsewhere. An investor needs to be able to switch money between funds easily when economic conditions change. Anything that gets in the way—such as discourteous employees—should be a signal that the mutual fund company isn't all the investor might want it to be.

LEARNING CHECK

1. Nancy owns 100 shares of stock which she purchased for $32 a share. Currently, the stock is selling for $23 a share. Nancy says that she can't sell the stock now because she would take too big a loss. Is Nancy exhibiting sensible behavior? Explain your answer.
2. What is a mutual fund?
3. What type of information will you find in a mutual fund company's prospectus?

SECTION 4 · JOINING THE WORK FORCE

This section discusses some important topics that relate to the work world. As you will probably be involved in the world of work for a large portion of your life, this section should be of interest and assistance.

As you read, keep these key questions in mind:

■ How does the education level of today's work force compare with that of the work force several decades ago?

■ Is the dollar difference between a college graduate's income and a high-school graduate's income becoming greater or less over time?

■ What are the things to watch out for when filling out a job application, writing a résumé, and being interviewed for a job?

Education, Income, and Unemployment

As you have probably already been told, education and income are related. The 1992 edition of the *Economic Report of the President* says, "Educational attainment is one of the primary characteristics that distinguishes high-income from

MINI GLOSSARY

Mutual Fund Financial organization that pools people's money and invests it.

low-income workers."[1] In other words, high-income workers generally have more education than low-income workers. Specifically, high-school dropouts earn less than high-school graduates, and high-school graduates earn less than college graduates, and so on. For example, in 1991, the average annual income of a man (25 years and older) with less than a 9th grade education was $19,632.[2] For a man with between a 9th and a 12th grade education (but without a high-school diploma), it was $23,765. For a man with a high-school diploma, it was $28,230. A man who had some college, but did not have a college degree, earned an average of $33,758. A man with a two-year college degree earned an average of $35,500. And a man with a four-year college degree (or more) earned an average of $50,747.

The data for women show the same upward trend as the data for men, but the dollar figures are lower. For example, in 1991, the average annual income of a woman (25 years and older) with less than a 9th grade education was $12,570. For a woman with between a 9th grade and a 12th grade education (but without a high-school diploma), it was $15,352. For a woman with a high-school diploma, it was $19,336. A woman who had some college, but did not have a college degree, earned an average of $22,833. A woman with a two-year college degree earned an average of $25,554. And a woman with a four-year college degree (or more) earned an average of $33,144.

Not only is it likely that income will rise with further education, but also chances of becoming unemployed become less. For example, in 1991, the unemployment rate for high-school dropouts was 11 percent; the unemployment rate for persons with a high-school diploma was 5.9 percent; the unemployment rate for persons with one to three years of college was 4.8 percent; and the unemployment rate for persons with four years of college or more was 2.8 percent.

In summary, the story the data tell is this: If you want to increase your chances of earning a high income, and of not being unemployed, one of the surest ways is to get an education.

---

1. *Economic Report of the President, 1992* (Washington, D.C.: United States Government Printing Office, 1992), p.100.
2. All the average annual income figures to which we refer are for full-time workers who are aged 25 years or older.

◄ Income tends to rise with level of education. These students will earn more, on average, than if they had chosen not to attend college.

The Match between Your Abilities, Your Educational Interests, and a Job

Ideally, a person would like to work at a job (1) that is interesting, (2) that he or she is able to do, and (3) that pays relatively well. For example, let's say Brenda has a natural ability to do mathematics and that she works hard in school to learn as much about mathematics as possible. She goes on to get a college degree in mathematics and ends up working for a company that pays her extremely well. For Brenda, everything has come together. She does something that she likes, that she is good at, and that earns her a relatively good income.

It may not work this way for everyone. John, for example, may be a natural when it comes to music. He may go on to study music at college. But when he graduates, he may learn that as a musician he can't earn the income that he would like to earn. This does not mean that John should not have been a music major in college. John's love of, and ability in, music may give him so much pleasure that he is willing to earn less as a musician than he would as, say, an accountant or a chemist. After all, there are other things in life than earning more money.

Protecting your future requires you to be aware of many things. When it comes to getting a job, it means considering what you are good at doing, what you are interested in, and what pays an income with which you can be comfortable. You do not protect your future when you focus only on what you are interested in and ignore what you are good at doing, and so on. You may end up not being able to do what you are interested in—for example, not everyone who is interested in being a ballet dancer can become a ballet dancer—and earning very little income.

The Job and Earnings Outlook

How do you know if what you are interested in will be in demand and pay well when it is time for

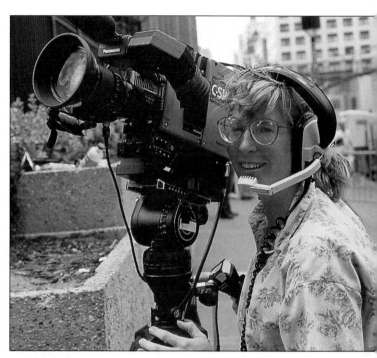

▲ A job is more rewarding if it is something an individual enjoys doing.

you to go job hunting? For example, you may be thinking of becoming an accountant, actor, teacher, or advertiser, but you may be unsure whether there will be a job for you when the time comes, or how much that job will pay.

In a quickly changing economy, such as the U.S. economy, it is impossible to know exactly what skills and talents will be in demand in future years or what they will be worth. However, the U.S. Department of Labor makes an attempt to predict the job and earnings outlook for the future. Two sources of career guidance are the *Occupational Outlook Handbook* (which is found in 9 out of 10 high schools) and *Occupational Projections and Training Data*. The *Handbook* contains detailed information on the outlook for hundreds of occupations, as well as information about the nature of the work, qualifications, average earnings, and so on. *Occupational Projections and Training Data* is a statistical supplement to the *Handbook*. It contains current and projected employment estimates for about 500 occupations. These publications are available from the Bureau of Labor

Statistics Publication Sales Center, P.O. Box 2145, Chicago, Illinois 60690, and the Superintendent of Documents, U.S. Government Printing Office, Washington, D.C. 20402. The price of the publications can be obtained from the U.S. Government Printing Office at 202-783-3238.

Additional information can be obtained from state job service centers (which can be found in the telephone book in the state government section). These centers provide information on local job markets. It is important to get this information, since the outlook for any occupation may vary considerably among local job markets. For example, sections of the country where population growth is slow have less need for elementary-school teachers than regions experiencing growth.

Application Forms, Résumés, and Interviews

When you apply for a job, you will have to fill out an application form or submit a **résumé**, or both. You will also be interviewed. This section discusses these things.

The Application Form. Here are some things to consider when filling out an application form.

1. **Before you start to fill in the application form, photocopy it.** Most people make mistakes when filling in application forms. Then they must erase them, scratch through them with pen, or cover them over with Liquid Paper and type over them. Often, the finished application comes out looking ragged and dirty. A neat, clean application is what you want. Fill in the photocopy of the application first, check it for mistakes, rewrite where necessary, and then use it as a guide to fill in the application form that you will submit to the employer.

2. **Be neat, and type the form if possible.** Suppose an employer reviews two application forms. One is neatly typed. The other is filled in with pencil or pen. There are a few scribbles and a few dark eraser marks. Generally, the ap-

plication form looks rather shabby. The often-subtle message that an employer receives from an application form like this is that the applicant is messy, impatient, and unlikely to take the time to do a job correctly.

3. **Be prepared to fill in an application form when you visit the employer's premises.** Suppose you visit a local company to ask if it is hiring. The personnel manager says yes and hands you an application form to fill in immediately. Keep in mind that you may need some information about yourself. For example, you may need (1) the names, addresses, and telephone numbers of former employers, (2) your Social Security number, and (3) previous home addresses. Keep this information with you when you visit an employer.

4. **Don't leave anything blank. If something does not apply to you, simply write "n/a," which stands for "not applicable."** If you leave some lines of an application form blank, the person reading the form won't know if you missed something or not. If something does not apply to you, then simply write "n/a."

5. **If there is a place on the application form to write down comments, do so.** Many application forms end with a space for you to make some comments if you choose. For example, a form might read: "In the space below, please provide any information about yourself that you feel is relevant to your doing this job."

Don't view this as a stumbling block to finishing up your application form in under five minutes. Instead, look at it as an opportunity to present yourself to this employer. See it as a way to separate yourself from the many others who may be applying for the same job. Tell your potential employer why you think you are right for the job.

The Résumé. A résumé should contain the following information : (1) your name, address, and telephone number; (2) the job you are seeking or your career goal; (3) your education; (4) your work experience; (5) honors you have received; (6) any other information relevant to your ability

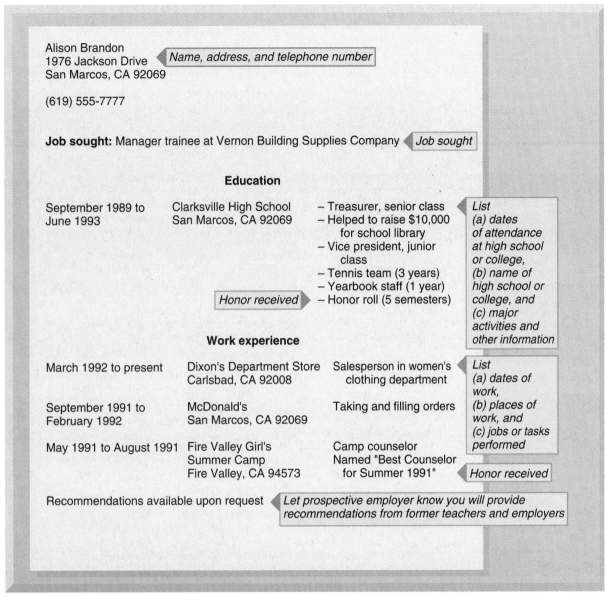

Alison Brandon
1976 Jackson Drive — *Name, address, and telephone number*
San Marcos, CA 92069

(619) 555-7777

Job sought: Manager trainee at Vernon Building Supplies Company — *Job sought*

Education

| September 1989 to June 1993 | Clarksville High School San Marcos, CA 92069 | – Treasurer, senior class
– Helped to raise $10,000 for school library
– Vice president, junior class
– Tennis team (3 years)
– Yearbook staff (1 year)
Honor received – Honor roll (5 semesters) | *List (a) dates of attendance at high school or college, (b) name of high school or college, and (c) major activities and other information* |

Work experience

March 1992 to present	Dixon's Department Store Carlsbad, CA 92008	Salesperson in women's clothing department	*List (a) dates of work, (b) places of work, and (c) jobs or tasks performed*
September 1991 to February 1992	McDonald's San Marcos, CA 92069	Taking and filling orders	
May 1991 to August 1991	Fire Valley Girl's Summer Camp Fire Valley, CA 94573	Camp counselor Named "Best Counselor for Summer 1991"	*Honor received*

Recommendations available upon request — *Let prospective employer know you will provide recommendations from former teachers and employers*

▲ **EXHIBIT 20-3. Résumé A.** This résumé emphasizes education and work experience. See Exhibit 20-4 for a résumé with a different emphasis.

to do the job you are seeking. A résumé should be well organized, easy to read, and no longer than two pages.

Exhibit 20-3 shows a standard way to organize a résumé. The two major parts identify the person's education and work experience in a matter-of-fact way.

Some persons prepare résumés somewhat differently. For example, instead of simply listing their former workplaces and stating what jobs they held, they discuss the talents they exhibited and the skills they acquired working at previous jobs. See Exhibit 20-4 for a résumé of this kind.

MINI GLOSSARY

Résumé A statement of a job applicant's previous employment, education, and so on.

Alison Brandon
1976 Jackson Drive
San Marcos, CA 92069

(619) 555-7777

Job sought: Manager trainee at Vernon Building Supplies Company

Skills, education, and experience

Working with people: Both in high school and in my jobs, I have worked well with people. As treasurer of the senior class, and as vice president of the junior class, I worked on school projects that required me to argue my positions convincingly, listen to the arguments advanced by others, and find suitable compromise positions. I realize that I cannot always get my way, but I continue to state what I believe, accept that people may disagree with me, and move on to see if we can work together.

In my work experience I have enjoyed dealing with the public. I have learned to be patient, listen attentively, and recognize that if people get "hot under the collar," I should try to work things out in a cordial way.

Effective communication: In high school, I played a leadership role in my junior and senior classes. I learned that a part of good leadership is being able to communicate your views and opinions to others in a cordial way. I have developed this skill, which I believe will help me throughout my life.

Hard work and attention to detail: In my school courses, activities, and jobs, I have learned the need to work hard and attentively. I have learned that it is better to do something right the first time than have to re-do it.

Chronology

September 1989 to June 1993	Attended Clarksville High School in San Marcos, California. I was treasurer of the senior class and vice president of the junior class, played on the tennis team for 3 years, worked as a member of the yearbook staff for 1 year, helped to raise $10,000 for the school library, and was on the honor roll for 5 semesters.
March 1992 to present	I worked as a salesperson in the women's clothing department at Dixon's Department Store in Carlsbad, California.
September 1991 to February 1992	I worked taking and filling orders at McDonald's in San Marcos, California.
May 1991 to August 1991	I was camp counselor at Fire Valley Girl's Summer Camp in Fire Valley, California. I was voted "Best Counselor for Summer 1991."

Recommendations available upon request

▲ **EXHIBIT 20-4. Résumé B.** This résumé emphasizes talents and skills. Contrast it with the résumé in Exhibit 20-3.

The Interview.   The job interview is your best opportunity to present yourself in a favorable light to an employer. Keep in mind that you represent a risk to the employer. He or she doesn't know what type of employee you are going to turn out to be. Are you going to be consistently late to work or on time? Are you going to be a good worker or not? Are other employees going to get along with you?

To be equipped for an interview, keep these things in mind:

1. **Learn about the employer before the interview.** Suppose you have an interview with the AAA Company on Monday. Before the interview, you should learn something about that company—what it produces, how long it has been in business, how many employees it has, and so on. The information need not be detailed, but you don't want to walk into an interview knowing nothing about the company you hope to work for. Suppose an interviewer asks, "Do you know what it is we do here at our company?" You want to be able to give a knowledgeable answer.

   You can usually obtain general information on a company at the local library or from persons who work for the company. You can also obtain the information by calling up the company before the interview and asking a few questions.

2. **Rehearse the interview.** One of the best ways to prepare for an interview is to rehearse the interview with a friend or two. Let your friend be the interviewer, and you be the interviewee. Before you start the rehearsal, write down a list of questions the real interviewer is likely to ask you. Here is a possible list:

   - Why did you apply for this job?
   - What do you know about this job or company?
   - Why should I hire you?
   - What are your strengths and weaknesses?
   - What would you like to tell me about yourself?
   - What accomplishment has given you the greatest satisfaction?

   - What courses did you like best in school?
   - What courses did you like least in school?
   - Why did you leave your last job?
   - What do you hope to be doing in three to five years?
   - What are your hobbies?
   - What would you change about yourself?
   - How do your education and work experience relate to this job?
   - What salary do you expect?

3. **Arrive for the interview on time.** Arriving early or late makes a bad impression. When you arrive early, you may interrupt the person who expected you later. When you arrive late, you signal that you are not dependable.

4. **Don't brag, but don't ignore your strong points.** Sometime during the interview, tell the interviewer why you think you would be a good person to hire. The interviewer may give you this chance by simply asking, "Why do *you* think you are right for this job?" If not, then somehow you should work it into the conversation. You might say, "I believe you are looking for a person who is hard working and conscientious and works well with people. I believe I am all these things. Let me give you a few examples. . . ." Then you could describe how, in past jobs or at school, you have shown the characteristics the interviewer is looking for.

   But here you have to be careful. It is one thing to state the truth and tell someone that you are a good person for the job. It is another thing to brag. No one wants to hire a bragger. Almost everyone, though, wants to hire someone who is confident about himself or herself and knows how to tell others of his or her strengths in a positive, polite manner.

5. **Ask questions when you have a chance.** At the end of an interview, the interviewer will often ask if you have any questions. Here are some suggestions:

   - What would a day on this job be like?
   - To whom would I report?
   - Would I supervise anyone?
   - Why did the last person leave this job?

- What is that person doing now?
- What is the greatest challenge of this job?
- Is this company growing?

6. Listen carefully. Many people get nervous in interviews. They wonder if they look right, if they are smiling enough, if they should not have said what they just said, if the interviewer likes them, and so on. This is natural. But try your best to put such concerns aside and listen to what the interviewer is saying and asking. If you don't listen carefully—and if you don't re-spond directly and specifically—the interview-er may get the feeling that your mind is some-where else and that perhaps you really don't want the job.

7. Write a thank-you letter. Soon after the inter-view, send a letter to the interviewer express-ing your appreciation for the interview. If you need to follow up on something you said dur-ing the interview, do it now.

LEARNING CHECK

1. Why is it important to arrive on time to a job interview?
2. List five questions you may be asked in an interview.
3. Name the two government publications that attempt to predict the job and earnings outlook for the future.
4. Why shouldn't you leave anything blank on a job application?

SECTION 5 — HEALTH INSURANCE

Insurance is an important consumer economics topic. This section discusses health insurance. As you read, keep these key questions in mind:

- What does basic health insurance cover?
- What is a health maintenance organization (HMO)?

Basic Health Insurance

Basic health insurance is composed of three different types of insurance: hospital-expense in-surance, surgical-expense insurance, and physi-cian-expense insurance.

Hospital-Expense Insurance. Daily hospital room and board and routine nursing care are cov-ered by hospital-expense insurance. It also pro-vides for laboratory tests, X rays, use of an operating room, drugs and medication, anesthesia, and so on. The insurance policy usually limits the number of hospital days covered and the daily costs. For example, a policy may state that a per-son's hospital stay is covered for up to 180 days at a rate of up to $250 a day.

Surgical-Expense Insurance. The fees of the surgeon are covered by surgical-expense insur-ance. There is a limit to what is covered and how much is paid out. For example, cosmetic surgery (say, a face-lift) is not covered, and usually there is a set fee for specific procedures (say, $600 for gallstone removal).

Physician-Expense Insurance. Doctors' fees for nonsurgical care in the hospital, the home, or the office are covered by physician-expense insurance.

▶ When considering health insurance, it is important to ask key questions regarding the extent of coverage.

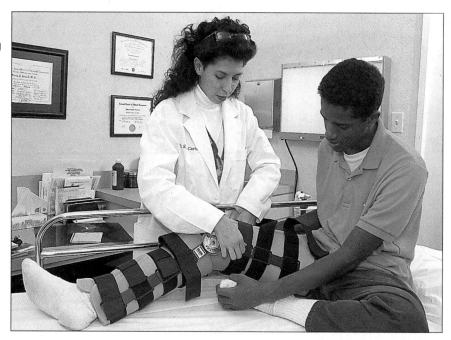

Major Medical Insurance

Major medical insurance is designed to pick up where basic health insurance leaves off. It covers large, catastrophic, and unpredictable medical expenses. Major medical insurance usually comes with a *deductible* and a *co-payment*. The deductible is the amount of a bill that you must pay before you are eligible for benefits. For example, suppose there is a $200 deductible on your policy. This means that if you go into the hospital and the bill comes to, say, $12,000, you have to pay the first $200. You may also have to pay a percentage of the remainder as your co-payment. For example, you may have an 80/20 co-payment plan. If so, the insurance company pays 80 percent of everything after you have met the deductible, and you pay 20 percent. Finally, some major medical insurance policies place limits on what will be paid per illness (say, $300,000 for cancer) or over the lifetime of the insured person (say, $1 million over the person's lifetime).

If a person has both basic health insurance and major medical insurance, he or she is said to have *comprehensive health insurance*.

Health Maintenance Organizations

A *health maintenance organization (HMO)* is a health care plan that offers its members comprehensive medical care for a monthly or yearly fee. It works like this.

First, members pay a monthly or yearly fee no matter how much medical attention they receive. When they go to a doctor or a hospital, there are no deductibles, no co-payments, and no insurance forms to fill out.

Second, members usually receive medical attention from a selected group of doctors and hospitals. In other words, if you are a member of an HMO, you must choose your doctor and hospital from the ones offered by the HMO. You cannot be treated by just any doctor or at just any hospital if you want your HMO to pay for the services you receive. In contrast, when you buy health care insurance, you go to any doctor you wish.

The growth in HMOs has been explosive. In 1971, there were 41 HMOs in the United States. In 1990, there were 556. This growth has been caused by the lower costs of HMOs. It has been estimated that these costs are 10 to 40 percent lower than the costs of regular health care plans. Of course, we need to remember that there are no free lunches. Lower health care costs may come with less flexibility in choosing a doctor, and possibly longer waits to see the doctor. Still, many millions of people are deciding the tradeoff is worthwhile.

What should you look for in an HMO? First, you want to be sure the HMO has a variety of doc-

tors and specialists. Second, you want to make sure the HMO-affiliated hospital has up-to-date facilities and technology. Third, you want to find out how long it takes, on average, to see a doctor for a nonemergency. There are reports of "six weeks to two months" in some HMOs and "right away" in others.

LEARNING CHECK

1. What does basic health insurance cover?
2. What does major medical insurance cover?
3. What does it mean to say that a person has comprehensive health insurance?
4. "When you join an HMO, you can choose any doctor you want." State whether this statement is true or false, and explain your answer.

SECTION 6 LIFE INSURANCE

This section discusses life insurance. If you are like most people, you have seen advertisements for life insurance on television and in newspapers and magazines.

As you read, keep these key questions in mind:

■ What is the difference between term life insurance and whole life insurance?
■ What is universal life insurance?
■ What is variable life insurance?

Two Major Types of Life Insurance

Life insurance guarantees payment if a person dies or reaches a certain age (depending on the type of life insurance policy the person has). There are two major types of life insurance: term and whole life.

Term Life Insurance. With term life insurance, you pay premiums to the insurance company, and in turn your **beneficiaries** are paid a certain sum of money if you die during a specific period. When the specific period ends, your coverage ends. For example, you may buy a five-year term policy for $250,000 worth of coverage for an annual premium of $430. If you die within the five-year period, and if your premiums are paid up, your beneficiaries will receive $250,000.

The price of term insurance varies according to how much coverage you want and your age and health. For example, the premiums are higher for a 30-year-old than for a 25-year-old. Thus, your premiums will be raised if you renew your policy. For example, your premiums will be higher when you renew your policy at age 30 than when you took out the policy at age 25.

Typically, a young married couple with a new house and children purchases term life insurance.

The husband and wife may want to protect themselves against each other's deaths. If one dies, the insurance payment will help the other with house payments, everyday expenses, college costs for the children in future years, and so on. They may simply want term life insurance for 10 to 15 years while the children are growing up.

Whole Life Insurance.   As the name implies, whole life insurance covers a person for his or her whole life, until death. The premiums under whole life insurance stay the same as long as the policy is in effect. (Recall that with term life insurance, the monthly or yearly premiums rise as one gets older.) One important feature of whole life insurance is its cash value. This is the amount of money you would receive if you decided to redeem, or cash in, your policy. Some people see the cash value that is accumulated in a whole life policy as a form of savings to be drawn on in later years. When you make a withdrawal from the cash value in your insurance account, however, you give up insurance protection. A withdrawal, either partial or total, ends the whole life policy. Alternatively, you can take out a loan against the cash value of your policy. For example, suppose you have a cash value of $10,000 and you want to borrow $5,000. The insurance company will give you this loan at an interest rate that is usually low.

Whole life insurance is often costly. For example, a 35-year-old nonsmoking man might pay $2,000 annually for a $200,000 whole life policy, whereas he would pay about $300 annually (until renewal) for a $200,000 term policy. Of course, the term policy premium would increase with each renewal period, whereas the whole life premium would stay the same. Only after many years would the term premium be greater than the whole life premium.

QUESTION: *It seems that with term insurance, you are simply buying insurance. With whole life insurance, you are buying insurance, and you have a savings plan. Is this correct?*

ANSWER: *Yes, it is. With term insurance, there is no cash value to borrow against or withdraw.*

▲ As people grow older, get married, and have children, they often realize it is important to have life insurance.

With whole life, there is. For example, suppose you take out a whole life policy at age 25. When you are 45, you decide to take your cash value and end your insurance protection. The amount of money that you withdraw was, in effect, saved by you.

Other Types of Life Insurance

Two other types of life insurance are universal life and variable life.

Universal Life Insurance.   Universal life insurance is similar to whole life insurance in that it allows you to build up a cash value for the policy. It is also like whole life in that you can borrow

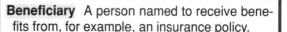

MINI GLOSSARY

Beneficiary A person named to receive benefits from, for example, an insurance policy.

against the cash value or completely withdraw it. It is different, though, in that you may withdraw part of the cash value without ending your insurance protection. However, if you do withdraw part of the cash value, your death benefit is reduced.

Variable Life Insurance. Variable life insurance is similar to universal life insurance, with one exception. With universal life insurance, the money in your cash value account is invested by the insurance company. Under a variable life insurance policy, you decide how your money is invested. You may choose to invest in stocks, bonds, money market funds, or a combination.

LEARNING CHECK

1. "With term life insurance, premiums change over time. With whole life insurance, premiums stay the same over time." True or false?
2. What is the "cash value" of a whole life insurance policy?
3. What is a major difference between whole life insurance and universal life insurance?
4. What is a major difference between universal life insurance and variable life insurance?

SECTION 7 — HOMEOWNER'S AND RENTER'S INSURANCE

This section discusses homeowner's and renter's insurance. Homes represent major investments. Protecting those investments is the purpose of homeowner's insurance.

As you read, keep these key questions in mind:

- What should every homeowner's insurance policy cover?
- In buying homeowner's insurance, why is it a mistake to insure only up to the value of the mortgage?
- How does inflation affect the replacement cost of a house?

What to Consider When You Buy Homeowner's Insurance

There are many things to consider when you purchase homeowner's insurance. Here are a few.

1. **Make certain your homeowner's insurance policy covers (a) damage to the house,** **(b) personal property, (c) personal liability, and (d) loss of use.** Homeowners rarely think of all the things that need to be covered by insurance. What they do think of is coverage for any damage done to the house itself—for example, damage caused by a fire or by a car crashing into the house. But other things need to be considered, too. For example, you need to make sure that your personal property is covered—such things as clothes, jewelry, and computers. You also need to make sure that if a friend falls down your porch stairs, his or her medical expenses are covered. Thus, you need to make sure your homeowner's insurance includes personal liability insurance. Finally, you need to make sure that if your house is damaged and you have to live elsewhere while the damage is being repaired, your homeowner's insurance will pay you for the "loss of use" of your house.

2. **Keep sales slips, and photograph your personal belongings.** Suppose you come home

one night to find that your home has been burglarized. A number of things are missing. You report the missing items to your insurance agent. He or she asks for evidence that you actually owned these items. The best way to show proof of ownership is to show the agent either a sales slip for the item or an actual photograph of the item in your home.

3. **Don't make the mistake of insuring only up to the value of your mortgage.** Suppose your house cost you $150,000. You made a $50,000 down payment and took out a mortgage loan of $100,000. Don't make the mistake of simply insuring your house for the mortgage amount ($100,000). You need to insure the house for its replacement cost—that is, the amount of money that you would need to replace the house if it was destroyed.

4. **Consider inflation when you estimate the replacement cost of your house.** Let's suppose that in 1993, you insured your house for its replacement cost. Say you found out that if your house was completely destroyed, it would cost you $135,000 to rebuild it, so you insured your house for $135,000. A few years passed. It is now 1998. Between 1993 and 1998, building supplies and labor became more expensive because of inflation. You must ask yourself, "Can I still replace my home for $135,000 if it is destroyed?" Because of inflation, the answer is probably no. The best thing to do, then, is to increase insurance coverage to adjust for the inflation that has made rebuilding your home more costly.

5. **Be aware that most insurance companies will reduce your insurance premiums if you install certain safeguards in your home.** Most insurance companies will reduce your insurance premiums if you install a smoke detector, dead bolts on the doors, a security system, and so on. Make sure you tell your insurance agent about what you have done to reduce the chance of crime or fire in your home.

6. **Be aware of what your policy does not cover.** You may assume that your policy covers flood damage done to your house. However, if you

live in an area prone to floods, it may not. When it comes to homeowner's insurance, don't assume anything. Ask questions. You may need to buy some supplemental insurance to protect yourself against floods and other natural disasters.

7. **Be aware that the higher the deductible, the less expensive the policy.** The deductible is the amount of money you must pay for losses before the insurance company begins to pay. The more you are willing to pay before the insurance company has to pay—that is, the higher your deductible—the lower your premiums will be. If your insurance agent tells you that your premium will be, say, $500 a year with a deductible of $200, ask what the premium would be if the deductible were $500 or $1,000. You may prefer to pay a higher deductible and lower premiums. At least you should be aware of this tradeoff.

8. **Consider the financial stability of the insurance company.** In recent years, some insurance companies have had financial problems. You want to make sure your insurance company is financially stable. The Consumers Union, which publishes *Consumer Reports*, advises that you buy insurance only from firms that have an A+ or A rating from *Best's Insurance Reports*, a publication of the Best Company, an independent rating organization. Check with a library for the publication, or ask your insurance agent if he or she can provide you with written documentation of the insurance company's rating.

Renter's Insurance

If you rent an apartment, the landlord probably has insurance on the apartment building itself. But the landlord's insurance will probably not cover you if, say, you are robbed or if a friend comes over to your apartment and slips and hurts herself on the stairs going from the first floor of your apartment to the second floor. Renters often mistakenly think that since they pay monthly rent, they do not have to worry about such things as insurance against loss of personal possessions or personal liability. But renters need insurance, too.

Renter's insurance is widely available and usually quite modest in cost. If you rent an apartment, you should strongly consider having it.

LEARNING CHECK

1. Against what does personal liability insurance (as a part of homeowner's insurance) protect you?
2. Why is it important to photograph the personal belongings in your house?
3. What does inflation do to the replacement cost of a house?
4. What happens to your insurance premiums as the deductible rises? falls?

SECTION 8 AUTOMOBILE INSURANCE[3]

This section discusses automobile insurance. As you will learn, automobile insurance protects more than just the money invested in the automobile.

As you read, keep these key questions in mind:

- What does bodily injury liability insurance pay for?
- What does property damage liability insurance pay for?
- What is the purpose of buying uninsured motorist protection insurance?
- What is no-fault insurance?
- What should you do if you have an automobile accident?

The Automobile Insurance Policy

The automobile insurance policy is a package of several types of coverage, each with its own premium. The sum of these premiums is what you

pay for the policy. We examine a few of the most important types of coverage in this section.

Bodily Injury Liability Insurance. Bodily injury liability insurance pays for losses due to death or injury in a car accident that is the *insured driver's fault*. It covers people both inside and outside the car. Injured persons can make a claim against this coverage to pay for medical bills, lost wages, and damages due to pain and suffering.

Many bodily injury liability policies are referred to as *split-limit policies*. These policies contain provisions that set (1) the maximum dollar amount paid per injured person and (2) the maximum dollar amount paid per accident. For example, a typical split-limit policy might read "25/50." This means that the policy pays a maximum of $25,000 per injured person and not more than $50,000 per accident. For example, if one person was injured in an accident and had damages of $30,000, the policy would pay $25,000 to this person. Most experts recommend carrying bodily injury liability insurance of "100/300." This is a maximum of $100,000 per person and $300,000 per accident.

Property Damage Liability Insurance. Property damage liability insurance covers dam-

3. *The Consumer Reports Money Book* Copyright © 1992 by Consumer Union of U.S. Inc., Yonkers, NY. Reprinted by permission from CONSUMER REPORTS BOOKS, 1992.

▶ Automobile insurance is important to have for many reasons: for car repairs in the case of an accident, medical expenses which may result from an accident, property damage, and more.

age done to another person's car, buildings, fences, and so on. Experts recommend coverage of between $25,000 and $50,000. Keep in mind that sometimes only a small increase in your premium can dramatically increase the coverage.

Medical Payments Insurance. Medical payments insurance pays for medical expenses resulting from a car accident *no matter who is at fault.* Some people do not purchase medical payments insurance because their health insurance pays for injuries sustained in an accident. However, health insurance does not usually pay funeral benefits, whereas medical payments insurance usually does.

Uninsured Motorist Protection Insurance. Some people drive their cars without having any automobile insurance. If one of these persons hits you with his car, and you or your car suffers damages, you may not be able to collect any money from him. To guard against this, you may choose to purchase uninsured motorist coverage. This insurance would cover you if you were in an accident with an uninsured motorist. It would also protect you if you were harmed by a hit-and-run driver.

Collision Insurance. Collision insurance pays for the damage to your car if it is in an accident, no matter who is responsible for the accident. Your coverage is limited by the amount of the deductible, which usually ranges from $100 to $250. As always, the higher the deductible, the lower the premiums.

Comprehensive Insurance. Comprehensive insurance is the companion of collision insurance. While collision insurance covers damage to your car if it is in an accident, comprehensive insurance covers just about everything else that can happen to a car. For example, it covers the damage if the car is stolen, is vandalized, or catches fire. As with collision insurance, the coverage is limited by the deductible.

No-Fault Insurance

No-fault insurance, which began to be adopted in some states in the early 1970s, was designed to eliminate the need to sue the other driver to gain compensation for injuries suffered in a car accident. Instead, a person's own insurance company would pay him or her for injuries suffered, no matter who was at fault. Currently, 26 states, the District of Columbia, and Puerto Rico have adopted some form of no-fault insurance. Usually, no-fault insurance covers you and the passengers in your car, as well as pedestrians hit by your car.

How Are Automobile Insurance Premiums Determined?

People pay different premiums for their automobile insurance. Here are some of the factors that determine how much you will pay.

Your Age.   In most, but not all, states a person's age affects his or her automobile insurance premium. Statistics show that drivers under the age of 25 have a higher accident rate than drivers between the ages of 25 and 35. For this reason, their premiums are higher.

Where You Live.   If you live in a densely populated area, where vandalism and car theft are common, you will pay a higher premium than if you live in a sparsely populated area where vandalism and car theft are relatively uncommon.

Your Driving Record.   If you have a history of car accidents and speeding tickets, your premium is likely to be higher than if you do not have such a history.

The Car You Drive.   If you drive a new, expensive car that is difficult and costly to repair, you will pay a higher premium than if you drive an older car that is easy and inexpensive to repair.

How Much You Drive.   If you drive only a few miles a week, you are likely to pay a lower premium than a person who drives many miles a week.

Whether or Not You Have Had a Driver Education Course.   Many insurance companies will give you a discount on your premium if you have taken a driver education course. The discount is usually 5 to 10 percent.

Whether or Not You Have Air Bags in Your Car.   Some insurance companies will give you a discount on the medical insurance part of your automobile insurance coverage if you have full front air bags in your car.

Whether or Not You Have Antitheft Devices in Your Car.   Many insurance companies will give you a discount on the comprehensive part of your automobile insurance coverage if you have installed antitheft devices in your car.

What to Do if You Are in an Automobile Accident

There are a number of important steps to take if you have a car accident. They are listed here.

1. **Check to see if anyone is injured. Next, call the police.** When you call the police, state where the accident occurred (what are the nearest cross streets?). If someone has been injured, ask that an ambulance or rescue squad be sent immediately.
2. **Don't move injured persons.** If you move injured persons, you could harm them. Cover the injured person with a blanket if one is handy.
3. **When police officers arrive, cooperate fully. State only what you know to be the facts.** You want to be sure to answer police officers' questions honestly, but only state what you know to be the facts. There is no reason to jump to the conclusion that you were the cause of the accident. It is natural to be shaken up after an accident; and some people, in this condition, quickly conclude that they must have been at fault. When it comes to accidents, state the facts—not your guesses, assumptions, or beliefs.
4. **Ask a police officer where you can obtain a copy of the police report.** You may need a

copy of the police report for insurance purposes or for a court case. Ask a police officer on the scene where you should go to obtain a copy.

5. **Make sure you obtain the following information: the names and addresses of all drivers and passengers in the accident; the license plate numbers, makes, and models of the cars involved; other drivers' license identification numbers; insurance identification numbers; the names, addresses, and phone numbers of any witnesses to the accident; and the names of the police officers at the scene.** This information may come in handy later, and your insurance agent may ask for it. Get into the habit of carrying a pencil or pen and paper in the glove compartment of your car so that you are always ready to write down the information you may need.

6. **If you have a camera in the car, take pictures of the accident scene.** Take a picture of the damage done to the cars, skid marks if there are any, and so on. If you don't have a camera, make a rough sketch of the accident. You may need it later to refresh your memory.

7. **If you run into an unattended car, leave your name and telephone number on the car's windshield so that the owner can get in touch with you.**

8. **Get in touch with your insurance company as soon as possible.** Make sure you tell your insurance agent exactly what happened and let him or her advise you as to what to do next. The insurance company will probably want to have an insurance adjuster inspect your car before you get it repaired. It is a good idea to keep the name of your insurance agent and his or her phone number in the glove compartment of your car. That way, if you are out of town and have an accident, you can easily and quickly get in touch.

9. **Keep a record of your expenses.** Make sure to keep a record of all the expenses you incur as a result of the accident. This might include lost wages, the cost of a rental car, and so on.

10. **Keep copies of all your paperwork.** There is a good chance that you will have to refer to certain papers later.

These are general guidelines. It is important to know the laws of your own state in dealing with motor vehicle accidents.

 # LEARNING CHECK

1. What does a split-limit policy that reads "100/300" mean?
2. How much property damage liability coverage do experts recommend that people have?
3. When it comes to medical expenses incurred in an automobile accident, what is the difference between bodily injury liability insurance and medical payments insurance?
4. Which of the following are covered by collision insurance? comprehensive insurance?
   a. Your car is vandalized.
   b. The driver of a Honda Accord runs into and damages your Ford Escort.
   c. Your car is stolen.
   d. You accidentally drive your car off the road and into a wall, causing damage.

DEVELOPING ECONOMIC SKILLS

Building Your Decision-Making Skills

Making decisions is a daily activity. In your life as a consumer, as a citizen, and as a voter, you will make many economic decisions. Just as you have improved your economic knowledge through this course, you can improve your decision-making ability. Decision making, after all, is a skill. Like other skills it can be improved through practice. One of the best ways to improve your decision-making skills is by learning and using a decision-making model. As you will learn, almost all decisions require the same steps. By learning these steps, you will improve your skill as a decision maker. You may find that sometimes the steps in the decision-making process overlap, or that you need to spend more time on one step than on another. After you have learned all the steps in the decision-making process, you can adjust them as necessary for each decision you make.

Steps in the decision-making model are as follows:

1. Define your need or want.
2. Analyze your resources.
3. Identify your choices.
4. Compare the choices.
5. Choose the best alternative.
6. Make a plan to get started.
7. Evaluate your decision.

Learning these seven steps can greatly enhance your abilities as a decision maker. To study these steps individually, let's apply this model to the hypothetical example of choosing a major for college.

Step 1: Define Your Need or Want.

The first step in the decision-making process is to define the need or want that requires a decision. When working through this step, it is important to be as specific as possible. For our example, let's say that you define your need or want as follows: I want to choose a major that I will enjoy and that will help me to fulfill my long-range goal of a happy, productive career.

Step 2: Analyze Your Resources.

Your resources will vary according to the decision you have to make. In this case, your resources might include your parents, who can share their thoughts on education and their experiences in the world of work, and guidance counselors, who can help you to understand the types of things you will be learning in various majors. Additionally, many guidance counselors can provide you with an interest inventory that can help you to determine your main areas of interest. Interest inventories are questionnaires that indicate where your strongest interests lie. If you have never taken an interest inventory, ask your school guidance counselor about them. Interest inventories can be fun, and there is no need to study since there are no right or wrong answers. Another resource is the *Occupational Outlook Handbook*. This handbook describes over 250 occupations and includes information about such things as job duties, working conditions, education and training requirements, job trends, and average earnings for each occupation listed. You might also want to talk with college representatives, or any friends or family members that are attending college. Remember that you will be able to make better decisions if you make the best possible use of the resources that are available to you.

Step 3: Identify Your Choices.

The very fact that a decision needs to be made implies that choices exist. Remember, even deciding not to make a decision *is* a decision, although it is almost never the best decision.

DEVELOPING ECONOMIC SKILLS (continued)

Let's continue with our example of selecting a college major. Suppose that after thinking about your interests, talking with your parents, and completing an interest inventory, you determine that you are most interested in art, art history, and history. Based on this, you narrow your choices for a major to art, art history, and history.

Step 4: Compare the Choices.

At this point, you need to determine which choice is the best possible choice. To do this, you need to make use of your available resources to gather information about each choice.

Returning to our example, let's say that you go back to see your guidance counselor to discuss the options you have to choose from. She tells you that you should look at the career opportunities that each major allows and to research programs at any colleges you are interested in. Then, based on the information you have available, try to imagine as clearly as possible what the outcome of each possible choice would be.

Step 5: Choose the Best Alternative.

After you have compared your choices, or alternatives, it is time to choose the *best* alternative. This can be difficult, since no one alternative may stand out as overwhelmingly the best. Suppose that, for our example, all three majors have basically the same appeal. You finally choose art history because it seems to combine your two interests, and because it might lead to a career as a museum curator, which sounds exciting and rewarding. Supporting your decision are the facts that your favorite college, the University of Texas at Austin, offers an art history degree, and job prospects for museum curators are reasonably good, according to the *Occupational Outlook Handbook*.

Step 6: Make a Plan to Get Started.

Just deciding on a choice will not satisfy your need or want. You must make a plan of action. For our example, your plan of action might include obtaining the college catalog from the University of Texas at Austin, obtaining and completing an application, and writing a letter to the department of art and art history at the university. Remember that even the best decisions can be fouled up by poor planning and execution.

Step 7: Evaluating Your Decision.

Just because you have made a decision does not mean that you cannot change your mind. In fact, evaluating your decision is an important part of the decision-making process. When you evaluate your decision, you judge its worth and its quality. Once your plan is put into action, you will begin to see if your decision was the best one. Look at the results of your decision. If the outcome of your decision is not what you had hoped it would be, perhaps it is time to start over with step 1.

Look back at the decision-making model presented here. As you do, note that it contains words like *choices, wants,* and *resources.* Where else have you recently come in contact with those words? In your study of economics, of course. As you have learned, economics is built around the concept that scarcity exists and that, as a result of scarcity, choices have to be made. Decision making is part of economics, and using the decision-making model is a good example of thinking like an economist.

---

1. Identify the seven steps in the decision-making model.

CHAPTER 20 REVIEW

CHAPTER SUMMARY

1. A budget is an organized plan for spending and saving money.

2. To make a budget, you need to:

   - Determine your income and expenditures over the past year.
   - Determine how much you are saving.
   - View your income, expenditures, and savings, and decide if you want to make any adjustments. Keep in mind that your savings relate to your future goals.
   - Change the way you view saving. Think of it as a regular "expenditure" item; think of what you "buy" with it.
   - Write out a monthly budget (as in Exhibit 20-2).

3. Writing out a budget is not a cure-all for your money problems. By itself, it has no power. It is simply an organized way of looking at your expenditures and your goals and at what you are doing about them.

4. One way to get into the habit of saving is to pretend that you earn less than you do.

5. Here are some things you should do if you want to keep your savings safe:

   - Never place over $100,000 in an account at any one bank, since accounts are only insured up to this amount.
   - Check the capital ratio of the bank (the equity divided by the assets). The average capital ratio of all banks is roughly 6.5 percent. A strong bank has a capital ratio between 6 and 7.5 percent. An exceptionally strong bank has a capital ratio higher than 7.5 percent. A weak bank has a ratio below 5 percent.

6. Some beliefs that guide stock market investing simply are not true. Here are a few examples:

   - "The stock has gone down so much already that it can't possibly go down any more."
   - "The stock has gone up so far that it can't possibly go higher."
   - "It's only a dollar a share. How can I lose?"
   - "The stock has gone down in price, but eventually it will come back up."
   - "I can't sell now—the price has gone down."
   - "I've had this stock for a very long time and nothing has happened. Nothing will ever happen. I'm selling it."

7. A mutual fund is a financial organization that pools people's money and invests it. The three most common types of mutual funds are stock mutual funds, bond mutual funds, and money market funds.

8. Here are some things to consider when filling out a job application form:

   - Before you start to fill in the application form, photocopy it.
   - Be neat, and type the form if possible.
   - Be prepared to fill in an application form if you visit the employer's premises.
   - Don't leave anything blank. If something does not apply to you, simply write "n/a," which stands for "not applicable."
   - If there is a place on the application form to write down comments, do so.

9. A résumé should contain the following information: (a) your name, address, and telephone number; (b) the job you are seeking or career goal; (c) your education; (d) your work experience; (e) honors you have received; and (f) any other information relevant to your ability to do the job you are seeking.

CHAPTER SUMMARY (continued)

10. To be equipped for a job interview, keep these things in mind:

- Learn about the employer before the interview.
- Rehearse the interview.
- Arrive for the interview on time.
- Don't brag, but don't ignore your strong points.
- Ask questions when you have a chance.
- Listen carefully.
- Write a thank-you letter.

11. Basic health insurance covers the cost of hospital care, surgery, and physicians' care.

12. Major medical insurance is designed to pick up where basic insurance leaves off. It covers large, catastrophic, and unpredictable medical expenses.

13. If a person has both basic health insurance and major medical insurance, he or she is said to have comprehensive health insurance.

14. A health maintenance organization (HMO) is a health care plan that offers its members comprehensive medical care for a monthly or yearly fee.

15. Life insurance guarantees payment if a person dies or reaches a certain age (depending on the type of life insurance policy the person has). There are two major types of life insurance: term and life. Term life insurance covers a person for a specific period. When the period ends, the coverage ends. Whole life insurance covers a person for his or her whole life, until death. The premiums under whole life insurance stay the same as long as the policy is in effect, while the premiums under term life insurance increase with the age of the person buying the policy.

16. Here are some things to consider when you purchase homeowner's insurance:

- Make certain your homeowner's insurance policy covers damage to the house, personal property, personal liability, and loss of use.
- Keep sales slips, and photograph your personal belongings.
- Don't make the mistake of insuring only up to the value of your mortgage.
- Consider inflation when you estimate the replacement cost of your house.
- Be aware that most insurance companies will reduce your insurance premiums if you install certain safeguards in your home.
- Be aware of what your policy does not cover.
- Be aware that the higher the deductible, the less expensive the policy.
- Consider the financial stability of the insurance company.

17. The automobile insurance policy is a package of several types of coverage, each with its own premium. The more important types of coverage include: (a) bodily injury liability insurance, (b) property damage liability insurance, (c) medical payments insurance, (d) uninsured motorist protection insurance, (e) collision insurance, and (f) comprehensive insurance.

18. No-fault insurance was designed to eliminate the need to sue the other driver to gain compensation for injuries suffered in a car accident. Instead, a person's own insurance company would pay him or her for injuries suffered, no matter who was at fault.

CHAPTER 20 REVIEW
(continued)

BUILD YOUR ECONOMIC VOCABULARY

Match the word with the correct definition, example, or statement.

1. résumé
2. beneficiary
3. n/a
4. HMO
5. term
6. uninsured motorist protection
7. budget
8. FDIC
9. capital ratio

a. not applicable
b. a statement of a job applicant's previous employment, education, and so on
c. organized plan for spending and saving money
d. a type of life insurance whose premiums change over time
e. insures bank deposits
f. equity divided by assets
g. protects you if you have a car accident involving a person who doesn't have insurance
h. comprehensive medical care for a monthly or yearly fee
i. a person named to receive benefits from an insurance policy

REVIEW QUESTIONS

1. What three things do you learn from computing your income and estimated expenditures on an annual basis?
2. "It is possible to 'buy' something in both the present and the future when we save." Explain this statement.
3. Calculate net worth in the following cases:
   a. Assets = $49.68 million; liabilities = $37.65 million
   b. Assets = $21.54 million; liabilities = $19.54 million
   c. Assets = $10.69 million; liabilities = $11.34 million
4. Calculate the capital ratio in the following cases:
   a. Assets = $50 million; liabilities = $47 million
   b. Assets = $43 million; liabilities = $38 million
   c. Assets = $32 million; liabilities = $29 million
5. What capital ratio indicates that a bank is weak? exceptionally strong?
6. What is a mutual fund?
7. According to the 1992 edition of the *Economic Report of the President*, what is one of the primary characteristics that distinguishes high-income from low-income workers?
8. Why is it important not to leave anything blank when filling out a job application?
9. What are six questions you are likely to be asked in a job interview?
10. Explain what an HMO is and how it works.
11. What is the difference between term life insurance and whole life insurance? between whole life insurance and universal life insurance?

REVIEW QUESTIONS (continued)

12. Installing certain safeguards in your home will lead to lower homeowner's insurance premiums. What are these safeguards?

13. What is no-fault insurance?

14. What are the factors that determine how much a person will pay for his or her automobile insurance?

SHARPEN YOUR CRITICAL THINKING SKILLS

1. You make a down payment of $30,000 on a house that costs $135,000. Your mortgage is the difference between the purchase price ($135,000) and your down payment ($30,000)—which is $105,000. If the house is destroyed in a fire, you will need $105,000 to pay off your mortgage loan, so you decide to insure your house for $105,000. What is wrong with doing this?

ACTIVITIES AND PROJECTS

1. Using either Exhibit 20-3 or 20-4 as a guide, write out a job résumé, seeking the job of your choice. Then, in groups of four or five, exchange your résumé with other people in your group. Offer constructive comments on how each résumé you look at could be made better.

ECONOMIC DICTIONARY

Asset (Pg. 514)
Beneficiary (Pg. 526)
Budget (Pg. 504)
Capital Ratio (Pg. 514)
Insolvent (Pg. 514)

Liability (Pg. 514)
Mutual Fund (Pg. 516)
Net Worth (Equity, Capital) (Pg. 514)
Résumé (Pg. 520)

RESOURCE CENTER

CONTENTS

UNITED STATES
ECONOMIC INFORMATION

▼ **EXHIBIT R-1.** Map of the United States.

▶ **EXHIBIT R-2. U.S. Real GDP**. U.S. Real GDP for each year, beginning in 1980 and ending in 1991 is shown. Think of real GDP as representing an economic pie. The data show that the economic pie in the United States has been getting larger. However, note that it doesn't always grow larger from one year to the next. For example look what happened between 1981 and 1982.

Year	Real GDP (In billions of dollars)
1980	$3,776.3
1981	3,843.1
1982	3,760.3
1983	3,906.6
1984	4,148.5
1985	4,279.8
1986	4,404.5
1987	4,539.9
1988	4,718.6
1989	4,838.0
1990	4,877.5
1991	4,821.0

SOURCE: *Economic Report of the President* (Washington, D.C.: U.S. Government Printing OFfice, 1993), p. 350.

▶ **EXHIBIT R-3. U.S. Real GDP Per Capita, Selected Years.** Real GDP divided by population shows real GDP per capita. The real GDP per capita in the United States is high when compared to that of most other countries.

Year	Real GDP per capita
1980	$16,584
1981	16,710
1982	16,194
1983	16,672
1984	17,549
1985	17,944
1986	18,299
1987	18,694
1988	19,252
1989	19,556
1990	19,513
1991	19,077
1992	19,272

SOURCE: U.S. Bureau of the Census, *Statistical Abstract of the United States*: 1993, 113th Edition, p. 445.

Year	Money Supply (in billions of dollars)
1980	$408.8
1981	436.5
1982	474.6
1983	521.4
1984	552.5
1985	620.2
1986	724.6
1987	750.0
1988	786.9
1989	794.1
1990	826.1
1991	898.1

◀ **EXHIBIT R-4. U.S. Money Supply, 1980–1991.** The money supply in the United States has been growing.

SOURCE: *Economic Report of the President* (Washington, D.C.: U.S. Government Printing OFfice, 1993), p. 423.

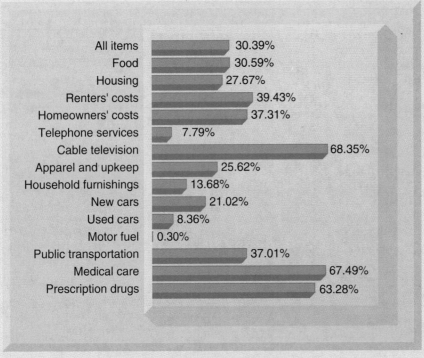

All items	30.39%
Food	30.59%
Housing	27.67%
Renters' costs	39.43%
Homeowners' costs	37.31%
Telephone services	7.79%
Cable television	68.35%
Apparel and upkeep	25.62%
Household furnishings	13.68%
New cars	21.02%
Used cars	8.36%
Motor fuel	0.30%
Public transportation	37.01%
Medical care	67.49%
Prescription drugs	63.28%

◀ **EXHIBIT R-5. Percentage Change in Prices of Selected Goods and Services, 1985–1992.** The prices of some goods and services change by a greater percentage than those of other goods and services. For example, the prices of prescription drugs have changed more than the prices of housing.

SOURCE: Figures for calculations came from the U.S. Bureau of the Census, *Statistical Abstract of the United States*: 1993, 113th Edition, p. 483. Calculations done by Roger Arnold.

▼ **EXHIBIT R-6. Corporate Profits Before and After Taxes, by Industry, 1991.** Corporations that earn profits have to pay taxes on those profits. Notice that profits are significantly less after taxes have been paid.

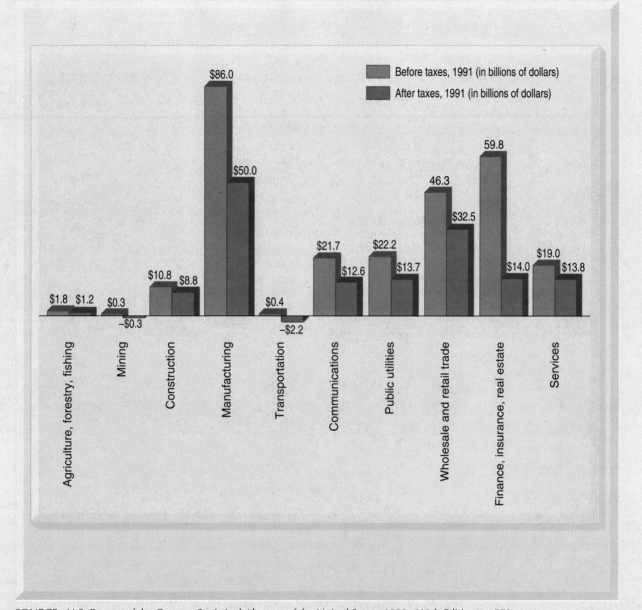

SOURCE: U.S. Bureau of the Census, *Statistical Abstract of the United States*: 1993, 113th Edition, p. 552.

Year	Condition of federal budget	Year	Condition of federal budget
1970	Deficit ($2.8 billion)	1982	Deficit ($128.0 billion)
1971	Deficit ($23 billion)	1983	Deficit ($207.8 billion)
1972	Deficit ($23.4 billion)	1984	Deficit ($185.4 billion)
1973	Deficit ($14.9 billion)	1985	Deficit ($212.3 billion)
1974	Deficit ($6.1 billion)	1986	Deficit ($221.2 billion)
1975	Deficit ($53.2 billion)	1987	Deficit ($149.8 billion)
1976	Deficit ($73.7 billion)	1988	Deficit ($155.2 billion)
1977	Deficit ($53.7 billion)	1989	Deficit ($152.5 billion)
1978	Deficit ($59.2 billion)	1990	Deficit ($221.4 billion)
1979	Deficit ($40.2 billion)	1991	Deficit ($269.5 billion)
1980	Deficit ($73.8 billion)	1992	Deficit ($290.2 billion)
1981	Deficit ($79.0 billion)	1993	Deficit ($327.3 billion)

◄ **EXHIBIT R-7a. Federal Budget Deficit, Selected Years.** More than two decades of Federal Budget Deficits. Beginning in 1970, the United States has experienced a continuous string of federal budget deficits. The budget deficit for 1993 is an estimate.

SOURCE: *Economic Report of the President* (Washington, D.C.: U.S. Government Printing Office, 1993).

▼ **EXHIBIT R-7b. National Debt, Selected Years.** The size of the national debt has been big news in recent years.

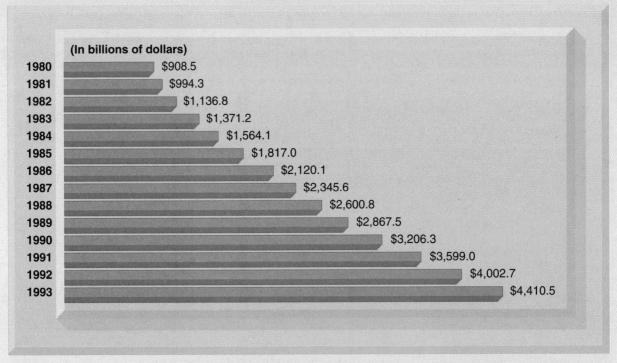

(In billions of dollars)

1980	$908.5
1981	$994.3
1982	$1,136.8
1983	$1,371.2
1984	$1,564.1
1985	$1,817.0
1986	$2,120.1
1987	$2,345.6
1988	$2,600.8
1989	$2,867.5
1990	$3,206.3
1991	$3,599.0
1992	$4,002.7
1993	$4,410.5

SOURCE: U.S. Bureau of the Census, *Statistical Abstract of the United States*: 1993, 113th Edition, p. 328.

▼ **EXHIBIT R-8.** **U.S. Balance of Trade.** The United States exports goods to other countries, and it imports goods from other countries. Here the trade balance for the United States in different years is shown. Notice that in most years the United States has run a trade deficit: its imports were greater than its exports.

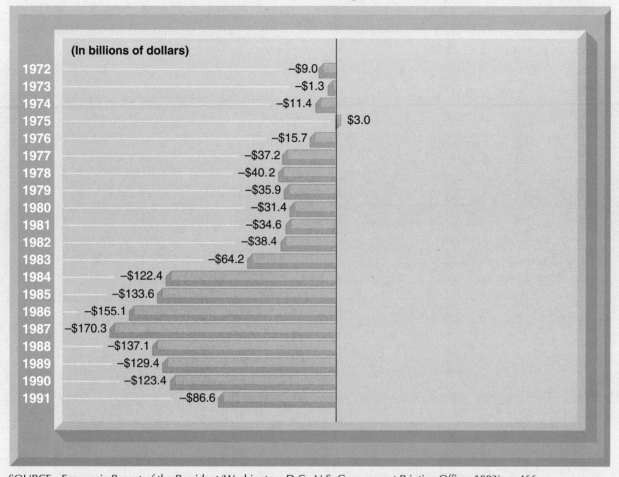

(In billions of dollars)

Year	Balance
1972	−$9.0
1973	−$1.3
1974	−$11.4
1975	$3.0
1976	−$15.7
1977	−$37.2
1978	−$40.2
1979	−$35.9
1980	−$31.4
1981	−$34.6
1982	−$38.4
1983	−$64.2
1984	−$122.4
1985	−$133.6
1986	−$155.1
1987	−$170.3
1988	−$137.1
1989	−$129.4
1990	−$123.4
1991	−$86.6

SOURCE: *Economic Report of the President* (Washington, D.C.: U.S. Government Printing Office, 1993), p. 466.

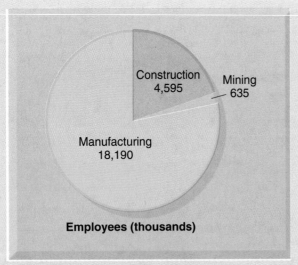

▲ **EXHIBIT R-9a. Number of Employees in Goods-Producing Business Firms, 1992.**

SOURCE: U.S. Bureau of the Census, *Statistical Abstract of the United States*: 1993, 113th Edition, p. 417.

▲ **EXHIBIT R-9b. Number of Employees in Service-Producing Business Firms, 1992.**

SOURCE: U.S. Bureau of the Census, *Statistical Abstract of the United States*: 1993, 113th Edition, p. 417.

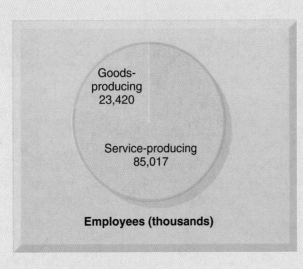

◄ **EXHIBIT R-9c. Number of Employees in Service-Producing and Goods-Producing Business Firms, 1992.** Workers are employed in producing either goods or services. As seen here, most people are employed in producing services.

SOURCE: U.S. Bureau of the Census, *Statistical Abstract of the United States*: 1993, 113th Edition, p. 417.

▶ **EXHIBIT R-10. Job Creation by Firm Size, 1988–1990.** As indicated here, small firms created the jobs during the period 1988–1990.

SOURCE: U.S. Bureau of the Census, *Statistical Abstract of the United States*: 1993, 113th Edition, p. 541.

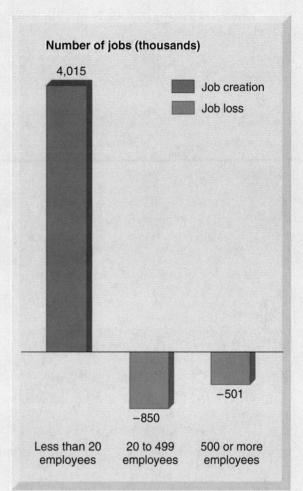

Number of jobs (thousands)

4,015

- ■ Job creation
- ■ Job loss

−850

−501

Less than 20 employees   20 to 499 employees   500 or more employees

▼ **EXHIBIT R-11. Money Income of Households–Percent Distribution, by Income Level, in Constant (1991) Dollars, by group, 1991.** As shown here, 14.9 percent of all households earned under $10,000 in 1991, whereas 10.4 percent of all households earned over $75,000.

Group	Number of households (thousands)	Percent distribution, by income level							Median income (dollars)
		Under $10,000	$10,000– $14,999	$15,000– $24,999	$25,000– $34,999	$35,000– $49,999	$50,000– $74,999	$75,000– and over	
All households[1]	95,669	14.9	9.4	17.4	15.2	17.3	15.4	10.4	30,126
White	81,675	12.8	9.1	17.3	15.4	17.9	16.3	11.2	31,569
Black	11,083	30.8	11.6	18.2	13.8	13.4	8.4	3.7	18,807
Hispanic[2]	6,379	20.7	12.1	21.6	15.8	14.8	10.0	5.0	22,691

1. Includes other races not shown separately. 2. Persons of Hispanic origin may be of any race.
SOURCE: U.S. Bureau of the Census, *Statistical Abstract of the United States*: 1993, 113th Edition, p. 457.

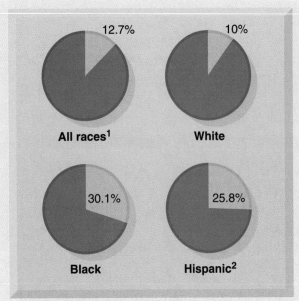

All races[1]   **White**

Black   **Hispanic[2]**

12.7%   10%

30.1%   25.8%

◄ **EXHIBIT R-12. Percentage of U.S. Population Living in Poverty, 1991.** One of the things shown here is that 12.7 percent of the U.S. population lived in poverty in 1991.

1. Includes other races not shown separately.
2. Persons of Hispanic origin may be of any race.
SOURCE: U.S. Bureau of the Census, *Statistical Abstract of the United States*: 1993, 113th Edition, p. 474.

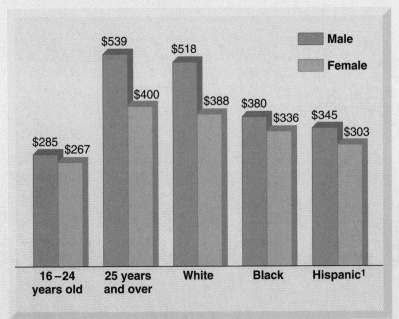

| 16–24 years old | 25 years and over | White | Black | Hispanic[1] |
| $285 $267 | $539 $400 | $518 $388 | $380 $336 | $345 $303 |

■ Male
■ Female

◄ **EXHIBIT R-13. Median Weekly Earnings, Selected Categories, 1992.** The median weekly earnings for different categories of persons.

1. Persons of Hispanic origin may be of any race.
SOURCE: U.S. Bureau of the Census, *Statistical Abstract of the United States*: 1993, 113th Edition, p. 426.

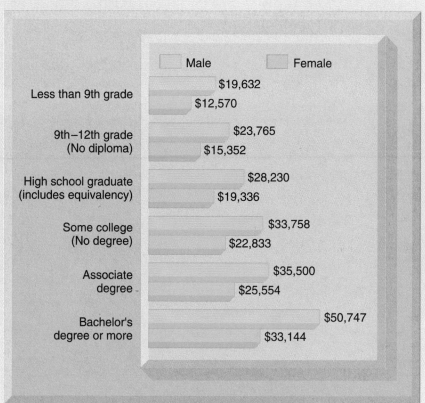

◀ **EXHIBIT R-14.** Average
Annual Earnings of Persons,
by Education and Sex, 1991.
Average income earned tends
to rise with education.

SOURCE: U.S. Bureau of the Census,
*Statistical Abstract of the United
States*: 1993, 113th Edition, p. 467.

Male   Female

Less than 9th grade	$19,632
	$12,570
9th–12th grade (No diploma)	$23,765
	$15,352
High school graduate (includes equivalency)	$28,230
	$19,336
Some college (No degree)	$33,758
	$22,833
Associate degree	$35,500
	$25,554
Bachelor's degree or more	$50,747
	$33,144

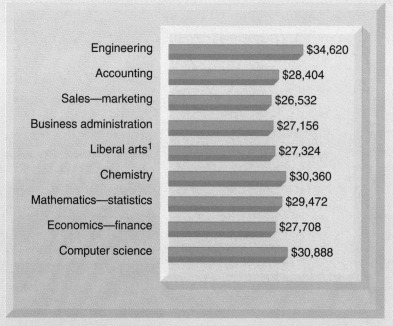

◀ **EXHIBIT R-15.** Average Annual
Starting Salaries of College
Graduates, Selected Fields, 1992.
Notice the difference in starting
salaries between the different fields.

SOURCE: U.S. Bureau of the Census,
Statistical Abstract of the United States: 1993,
113th Edition, p. 161.

Engineering	$34,620
Accounting	$28,404
Sales—marketing	$26,532
Business administration	$27,156
Liberal arts[1]	$27,324
Chemistry	$30,360
Mathematics—statistics	$29,472
Economics—finance	$27,708
Computer science	$30,888

1. Excludes Chemistry, Mathematics, Economics, and Computer Science.

▼ **EXHIBIT R-16a.** Health Expenditures, Per Capita, Selected Years.

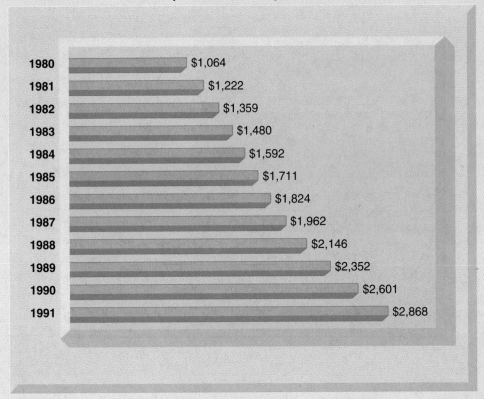

1980	$1,064
1981	$1,222
1982	$1,359
1983	$1,480
1984	$1,592
1985	$1,711
1986	$1,824
1987	$1,962
1988	$2,146
1989	$2,352
1990	$2,601
1991	$2,868

SOURCE: U.S. Bureau of the Census, *Statistical Abstract of the United States*: 1993, 113th Edition, p. 107.

▼ **EXHIBIT R-16b.** Health Expenditures, Total, Selected Years (in billions of dollars).

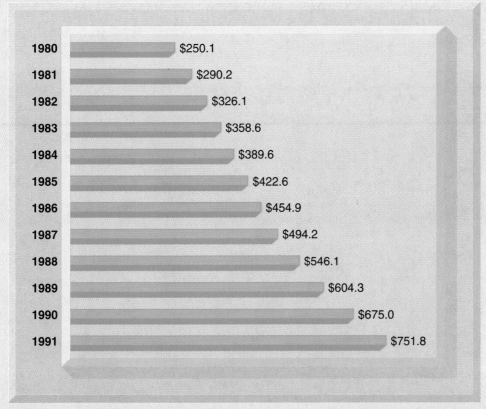

1980	$250.1
1981	$290.2
1982	$326.1
1983	$358.6
1984	$389.6
1985	$422.6
1986	$454.9
1987	$494.2
1988	$546.1
1989	$604.3
1990	$675.0
1991	$751.8

SOURCE: U.S. Bureau of the Census, *Statistical Abstract of the United States*: 1993, 113th Edition, p. 107.

▼ **EXHIBIT R-17. Annual Average Work Week of Production Workers on Manufacturing Payrolls in 1992.**
The national average is 41.00 hours per week.

RANK	STATE	HOURS	RANK	STATE	HOURS
1	Alaska	45.50	26	Arizona	40.80
2	Louisiana	42.60	26	Delaware	40.80
3	Texas	42.50	26	Maryland	40.80
4	Ohio	42.30	26	Minnesota	40.80
5	Indiana	41.90	30	Nevada	40.70
6	Michigan	41.80	30	North Carolina	40.70
6	Wisconsin	41.80	30	West Virginia	40.70
8	Connecticut	41.70	33	Missouri	40.60
8	South Carolina	41.70	34	Colorado	40.50
10	New Hampshire	41.60	35	North Dakota	40.40
11	Georgia	41.50	36	Kentucky	40.30
11	New Jersey	41.50	36	Mississippi	40.30
13	Arkansas	41.40	36	Tennessee	40.30
14	Iowa	41.30	39	Utah	40.20
14	Oklahoma	41.30	40	Rhode Island	40.10
16	Alabama	41.20	41	Hawaii	40.00
16	South Dakota	41.20	41	New Mexico	40.00
18	Illinois	41.00	41	New York	40.00
18	Massachusetts	41.00	41	Washington	40.00
18	Nebraska	41.00	45	Oregon	39.60
18	Vermont	41.00	46	Idaho	39.20
18	Virginia	41.00	47	Montana	38.90
23	Florida	40.90	48	Wyoming	38.60
23	Kansas	40.90	—	California*	N/A
23	Pennsylvania	40.90	—	Maine*	N/A

*Not available.
SOURCE: *State Rankings 1993 A Statistical View of the 50 States* (Lawrence, KS: Morgan Quitno Corporation, 1993), p. 149.
Original Source: *U.S. Department of Labor, Bureau of Labor Statistics unpublished data (March 2, 1993).*

▼ **EXHIBIT R-18. Resident State Population in 1992.** The national total equals 255,082,000*.

RANK	STATE	POPULATION	%	RANK	STATE	POPULATION	%
1	California	30,867,000	12.10%	26	Colorado	3,470,000	1.36%
2	New York	18,119,000	7.10%	27	Connecticut	3,281,000	1.29%
3	Texas	17,656,000	6.92%	28	Oklahoma	3,212,000	1.26%
4	Florida	13,488,000	5.29%	29	Oregon	2,977,000	1.17%
5	Pennsylvania	12,009,000	4.71%	30	Iowa	2,812,000	1.10%
6	Illinois	11,631,000	4.56%	31	Mississippi	2,614,000	1.02%
7	Ohio	11,016,000	4.32%	32	Kansas	2,523,000	0.99%
8	Michigan	9,437,000	3.70%	33	Arkansas	2,399,000	0.94%
9	New Jersey	7,789,000	3.05%	34	Utah	1,813,000	0.71%
10	North Carolina	6,843,000	2.68%	35	West Virginia	1,812,000	0.71%
11	Georgia	6,751,000	2.65%	36	Nebraska	1,606,000	0.63%
12	Virginia	6,377,000	2.50%	37	New Mexico	1,581,000	0.62%
13	Massachusetts	5,998,000	2.35%	38	Nevada	1,327,000	0.52%
14	Indiana	5,662,000	2.22%	39	Maine	1,235,000	0.48%
15	Missouri	5,193,000	2.04%	40	Hawaii	1,160,000	0.45%
16	Washington	5,136,000	2.01%	41	New Hampshire	1,111,000	0.44%
17	Tennessee	5,024,000	1.97%	42	Idaho	1,067,000	0.42%
18	Wisconsin	5,007,000	1.96%	43	Rhode Island	1,005,000	0.39%
19	Maryland	4,908,000	1.92%	44	Montana	824,000	0.32%
20	Minnesota	4,480,000	1.76%	45	South Dakota	711,000	0.28%
21	Louisiana	4,287,000	1.68%	46	Delaware	689,000	0.27%
22	Alabama	4,136,000	1.62%	47	North Dakota	636,000	0.25%
23	Arizona	3,832,000	1.50%	48	Alaska	587,000	0.23%
24	Kentucky	3,755,000	1.47%	49	Vermont	570,000	0.22%
25	South Carolina	3,603,000	1.41%	50	Wyoming	466,000	0.18%
					District of Columbia	589,000	0.23%

*Estimate as of July 1, 1992.
SOURCE: *State Rankings 1993 A Statistical View of the 50 States* (Lawrence, KS: Morgan Quitno Corporation, 1993), p. 380.
Original Source: *U.S. Bureau of the Census Press Release C892-276 (December 30, 1992).*

▼ **EXHIBIT R-19. Percent of Population Urban in 1990.** 75.2% of the population is urban*.

RANK	STATE	PERCENT	RANK	STATE	PERCENT
1	California	92.6	26	Missouri	68.7
2	New Jersey	89.4	27	Louisiana	68.1
3	Hawaii	89.0	28	Oklahoma	67.7
4	Nevada	88.3	29	Alaska	67.5
5	Arizona	87.5	30	Nebraska	66.1
6	Utah	87.0	31	Wisconsin	65.7
7	Rhode Island	86.0	32	Wyoming	65.0
8	Florida	84.8	33	Indiana	64.9
9	Illinois	84.6	34	Georgia	63.2
10	Massachusetts	84.3	35	Tennessee	60.9
10	New York	84.3	36	Iowa	60.6
12	Colorado	82.4	37	Alabama	60.4
13	Maryland	81.3	38	Idaho	57.4
14	Texas	80.3	39	South Carolina	54.6
15	Connecticut	79.1	40	Arkansas	53.5
16	Washington	76.4	41	North Dakota	53.3
17	Ohio	74.1	42	Montana	52.5
18	Delaware	73.0	43	Kentucky	51.8
18	New Mexico	73.0	44	New Hampshire	51.0
20	Michigan	70.5	45	North Carolina	50.4
20	Oregon	70.5	46	South Dakota	50.0
22	Minnesota	69.9	47	Mississippi	47.1
23	Virginia	69.4	48	Maine	44.6
24	Kansas	69.1	49	West Virginia	36.1
25	Pennsylvania	68.9	50	Vermont	32.2
				District of Columbia	100.0

*Urban population is composed of persons living in densely populated areas and in places of 2,500 or more outside urbanized areas.

SOURCE: *State Rankings 1993 A Statistical View of the 50 States* (Lawrence, KS: Morgan Quitno Corporation, 1993), p. 405. Original source: U.S. Bureau of the Census.

▼ **EXHIBIT R-20. State Tax Revenue in 1991.** The national total equals $317,348,543,000*.

RANK	STATE	STATE TAXES	%	RANK	STATE	STATE TAXES	%
1	California	$45,182,854,000	14.24%	26	Iowa	$3,535,715,000	1.11%
2	New York	30,175,285,000	9.51%	27	Colorado	3,305,258,000	1.04%
3	Texas	15,977,447,000	5.03%	28	Oregon	3,163,199,000	1.00%
4	Pennsylvania	14,467,454,000	4.56%	29	Kansas	2,924,463,000	0.92%
5	Florida	13,776,490,000	4.34%	30	Hawaii	2,671,176,000	0.84%
6	Illinois	13,397,893,000	4.22%	31	Arkansas	2,489,815,000	0.78%
7	New Jersey	12,261,691,000	3.86%	32	Mississippi	2,487,769,000	0.78%
8	Ohio	11,773,693,000	3.71%	33	West Virginia	2,328,891,000	0.73%
9	Michigan	11,154,887,000	3.52%	34	New Mexico	2,129,008,000	0.67%
10	Massachusetts	9,681,076,000	3.05%	35	Nebraska	1,840,384,000	0.58%
11	North Carolina	8,203,209,000	2.58%	36	Utah	1,804,118,000	0.57%
12	Washington	8,125,517,000	2.56%	37	Maine	1,563,134,000	0.49%
13	Wisconsin	7,140,946,000	2.25%	38	Nevada	1,442,448,000	0.45%
14	Georgia	7,106,608,000	2.24%	39	Rhode Island	1,276,130,000	0.40%
15	Minnesota	7,069,254,000	2.23%	40	Idaho	1,260,079,000	0.40%
16	Virginia	6,924,312,000	2.18%	41	Delaware	1,196,810,000	0.38%
17	Maryland	6,556,114,000	2.07%	42	Montana	888,534,000	0.28%
18	Indiana	6,229,509,000	1.96%	43	Vermont	726,802,000	0.23%
19	Connecticut	5,599,822,000	1.76%	44	North Dakota	714,231,000	0.23%
20	Missouri	5,058,062,000	1.59%	45	Wyoming	637,892,000	0.20%
21	Arizona	4,882,877,000	1.54%	46	South Dakota	523,220,000	0.16%
22	Louisiana	4,439,372,000	1.40%	—	Alaska**	N/A	N/A
23	Tennessee	4,292,178,000	1.35%	—	Kentucky**	N/A	N/A
24	Alabama	3,970,723,000	1.25%	—	New Hampshire**	N/A	N/A
25	Oklahoma	3,922,040,000	1.24%	—	South Carolina**	N/A	N/A
					District of Columbia***	2,404,434,000	0.76%

*For year ending December 31, 1991. Total includes amounts not shown separately.
**Not available. ***DC is not included in national total but is shown for comparison purposes.
SOURCE: *State Rankings 1993 A Statistical View of the 50 States* (Lawrence, KS: Morgan Quitno Corporation, 1993), p. 255.
Original Source: U.S. Bureau of the Census Quarterly Summary of Federal, State, and Local Tax Revenue (GT-91-Q4, July 1992).

▼ **EXHIBIT R-21. State Individual Income Tax Revenue in 1991.** The national total equals $102,150,059,000*.

RANK	STATE	INCOME TAX	%	RANK	STATE	INCOME TAX	%
1	California	$17,028,180,000	16.67%	26	Louisiana	$831,618,000	0.81%
2	New York	14,677,289,000	14.37%	27	Arkansas	828,710,000	0.81%
3	Massachusetts	5,275,205,000	5.16%	28	Utah	656,664,000	0.64%
4	Illinois	4,540,965,000	4.45%	29	Nebraska	636,848,000	0.62%
5	Ohio	4,322,972,000	4.23%	30	West Virginia	622,038,000	0.61%
6	New Jersey	3,926,087,000	3.84%	31	Maine	598,423,000	0.59%
7	Michigan	3,879,322,000	3.80%	32	Mississippi	478,744,000	0.47%
8	Pennsylvania	3,810,165,000	3.73%	33	Delaware	472,360,000	0.46%
9	North Carolina	3,613,942,000	3.54%	34	Rhode Island	469,933,000	0.46%
10	Virginia	3,317,058,000	3.25%	35	Idaho	463,085,000	0.45%
11	Wisconsin	3,056,370,000	2.99%	36	New Mexico	432,931,000	0.42%
12	Georgia	3,007,469,000	2.94%	37	Montana	284,291,000	0.28%
13	Maryland	2,990,138,000	2.93%	38	Vermont	266,112,000	0.26%
14	Minnesota	2,875,682,000	2.82%	39	North Dakota	120,259,000	0.12%
15	Indiana	2,219,485,000	2.17%	40	Tennessee	93,293,000	0.09%
16	Oregon	2,083,127,000	2.04%	41	Alaska	0	0.00%
17	Missouri	1,843,670,000	1.80%	41	Florida	0	0.00%
18	Colorado	1,527,325,000	1.50%	41	Nevada	0	0.00%
19	Iowa	1,404,301,000	1.37%	41	South Dakota	0	0.00%
20	Arizona	1,352,256,000	1.32%	41	Texas	0	0.00%
21	Oklahoma	1,253,905,000	1.23%	41	Washington	0	0.00%
22	Alabama	1,192,698,000	1.17%	41	Wyoming	0	0.00%
23	Connecticut	932,989,000	0.91%	—	Kentucky**	N/A	N/A
24	Kansas	920,309,000	0.90%	—	New Hampshire**	N/A	N/A
25	Hawaii	900,864,000	0.88%	—	South Carolina	N/A	N/A
					District of Columbia***	616,246,000	0.60%

*For year ending December 31, 1991. Total includes amounts not shown separately.
**Not available. ***DC is not included in national total but is shown for comparison purposes.
SOURCE: *State Rankings 1993 A Statistical View of the 50 States* (Lawrence, KS: Morgan Quitno Corporation, 1993), p. 257.
Original Source: U.S. Bureau of the Census "Quarterly Summary of Federal, State, and Local Tax Revenue" (GT-91-Q4, July 1992).

▼ **EXHIBIT R-22. State Sales Tax Revenue in 1991.** The national total equals $104,306,257,000*.

RANK	STATE	SALES TAX	%	RANK	STATE	SALES TAX	%
1	California	$14,445,224,000	13.85%	26	Alabama	$1,072,991,000	1.03%
2	Texas	8,342,455,000	8.00%	27	Iowa	988,894,000	0.95%
3	Florida	8,122,393,000	7.79%	28	Oklahoma	972,801,000	0.93%
4	New York	6,034,002,000	5.78%	29	Arkansas	955,432,000	0.92%
5	Washington	4,845,312,000	4.65%	30	Kansas	945,704,000	0.91%
6	Illinois	4,232,837,000	4.06%	31	New Mexico	935,018,000	0.90%
7	Pennsylvania	4,229,795,000	4.06%	32	Colorado	867,897,000	0.83%
8	New Jersey	4,025,790,000	3.86%	33	West Virginia	772,891,000	0.74%
9	Ohio	3,611,193,000	3.46%	34	Utah	739,955,000	0.71%
10	Michigan	3,140,930,000	3.01%	35	Nevada	717,599,000	0.69%
11	Georgia	2,633,152,000	2.52%	36	Nebraska	646,262,000	0.62%
12	Connecticut	2,516,728,000	2.41%	37	Maine	526,342,000	0.50%
13	Indiana	2,467,402,000	2.37%	38	Idaho	416,957,000	0.40%
14	Tennessee	2,405,592,000	2.31%	39	Rhode Island	411,175,000	0.39%
15	Wisconsin	2,054,897,000	1.97%	40	South Dakota	250,513,000	0.24%
16	Minnesota	2,054,235,000	1.97%	41	North Dakota	245,108,000	0.23%
17	Arizona	2,036,300,000	1.95%	42	Wyoming	186,633,000	0.18%
18	Massachusetts	1,939,410,000	1.86%	43	Vermont	140,562,000	0.13%
19	Missouri	1,883,589,000	1.81%	44	Alaska	0	0.00%
20	North Carolina	1,877,678,000	1.80%	44	Delaware	0	0.00%
21	Maryland	1,577,000,000	1.51%	44	Montana	0	0.00%
22	Virginia	1,536,959,000	1.47%	44	New Hampshire	0	0.00%
23	Louisiana	1,494,755,000	1.43%	44	Oregon	0	0.00%
24	Hawaii	1,287,819,000	1.23%	—	Kentucky**	N/A	N/A
25	Mississippi	1,124,852,000	1.08%	—	South Carolina**	N/A	N/A
					District of Columbia***	462,425,000	0.44%

*For year ending December 31, 1991. Total includes amounts not shown separately.
**Not available. ***DC is not included in national total but is shown for comparison purposes.
SOURCE: *State Rankings 1993 A Statistical View of the 50 States* (Lawrence, KS: Morgan Quitno Corporation, 1993), p. 261.
Original Source: U.S. Bureau of the Census"Quarterly Summary of Federal, State, and Local Tax Revenue" (GT-91-Q4, July 1992).

▼ **EXHIBIT R-23. Persons Not Covered by Health insurance in 1991.** The national total equals 35,445,000 uninsured persons.

RANK	STATE	UNINSURED	%	RANK	STATE	UNINSURED	%
1	California	5,750,000	16.22%	26	Oregon	422,000	1.19%
2	Texas	3,755,000	10.59%	27	Minnesota	406,000	1.15%
3	Florida	2,496,000	7.04%	28	Wisconsin	396,000	1.12%
4	New York	2,206,000	6.22%	29	Arkansas	385,000	1.09%
5	Illinois	1,361,000	3.84%	30	New Mexico	335,000	0.95%
6	Ohio	1,147,000	3.24%	31	Colorado	334,000	0.94%
7	Virginia	1,002,000	2.83%	32	Kansas	295,000	0.83%
8	North Carolina	990,000	2.79%	33	West Virginia	287,000	0.81%
9	Pennsylvania	954,000	2.69%	34	Connecticut	249,000	0.70%
10	Georgia	885,000	2.50%	34	Iowa	249,000	0.70%
11	Louisiana	869,000	2.45%	36	Utah	238,000	0.67%
12	New Jersey	838,000	2.36%	37	Nevada	232,000	0.65%
13	Michigan	835,000	2.36%	38	Idaho	184,000	0.52%
14	Alabama	749,000	2.11%	39	Nebraska	137,000	0.39%
15	Indiana	721,000	2.03%	40	Maine	135,000	0.38%
16	Tennessee	644,000	1.82%	41	New Hampshire	112,000	0.32%
17	Massachusetts	633,000	1.79%	42	Montana	104,000	0.29%
18	Maryland	625,000	1.76%	43	Rhode Island	96,000	0.27%
19	Missouri	611,000	1.72%	44	Delaware	94,000	0.27%
20	Arizona	607,000	1.71%	45	Hawaii	82,000	0.23%
21	Oklahoma	579,000	1.63%	46	Vermont	74,000	0.21%
22	Washington	518,000	1.46%	47	Alaska	69,000	0.19%
23	Mississippi	507,000	1.43%	48	South Dakota	68,000	0.19%
24	Kentucky	476,000	1.34%	49	Wyoming	53,000	0.15%
25	South Carolina	465,000	1.31%	50	North Dakota	48,000	0.14%
					District of Columbia	136,000	0.38%

SOURCE: *State Rankings 1993 A Statistical View of the 50 States* (Lawrence, KS: Morgan Quitno Corporation, 1993), p. 297. Original Source: U.S. Bureau of the Census unpublished data.

▼ **EXHIBIT R-24. Poverty Rate in 1991.** The national poverty rate equals 14.2% of Population in Poverty*.

RANK	STATE	PERCENT	RANK	STATE	PERCENT
1	Mississippi	23.80	26	Maine	12.50
2	Louisiana	22.00	27	Colorado	12.10
3	New Mexico	20.90	28	Minnesota	12.00
4	Alabama	19.00	29	Ohio	11.80
5	Arkansas	18.40	30	Oregon	11.30
6	Kentucky	17.40	31	Alaska	11.20
7	West Virginia	17.20	32	Kansas	11.10
8	Tennessee	16.90	33	Nebraska	10.90
9	Texas	16.80	34	Pennsylvania	10.80
10	South Carolina	16.50	35	Nevada	10.70
11	Georgia	16.00	36	Virginia	10.60
12	Montana	15.80	36	Wyoming	10.60
12	Oklahoma	15.80	38	Vermont	10.50
14	Arizona	14.20	39	Massachusetts	10.20
14	California	14.20	40	Iowa	10.10
16	Florida	14.10	41	Hawaii	10.00
16	Indiana	14.10	42	Utah	9.80
16	New York	14.10	43	Maryland	9.30
19	Michigan	13.90	43	Washington	9.30
20	Idaho	13.70	45	Wisconsin	9.20
21	Missouri	13.60	46	New Jersey	9.00
22	North Dakota	13.50	47	Rhode Island	8.20
22	South Dakota	13.50	48	Delaware	8.10
24	Illinois	13.30	49	New Hampshire	7.10
25	North Carolina	13.20	50	Connecticut	5.80
				District of Columbia	19.20

*Estimates based on a three-year average (1989-1991). Census Bureau cautions against heavy reliance on state estimates because of relatively larger standard errors due to smaller sample sizes.
SOURCE: *State Rankings 1993 A Statistical View of the 50 States* (Lawrence, KS: Morgan Quitno Corporation, 1993), p. 95.
Original Source: U.S. Bureau of the Census "Poverty in the United States: 1991".

WORLD ECONOMIC INFORMATION

▼ **EXHIBIT R-25** Map of the World.

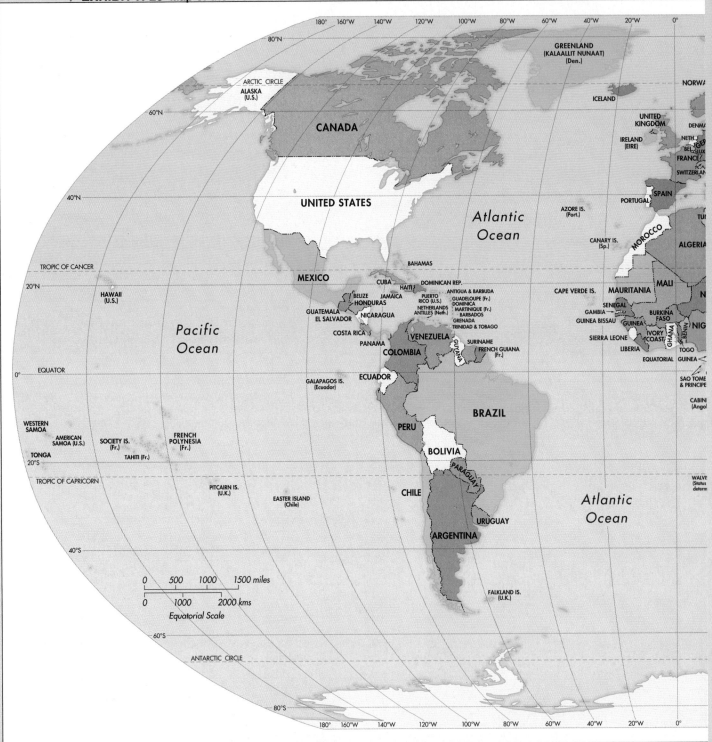

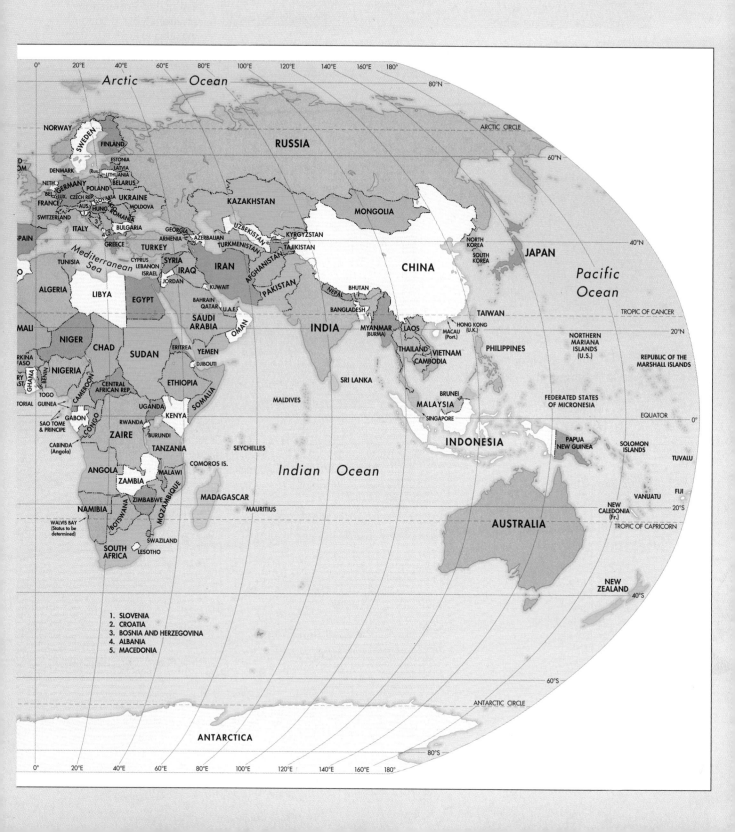

Arctic Ocean

80°N

NORWAY
SWEDEN
FINLAND

ARCTIC CIRCLE

RUSSIA

60°N

ESTONIA
DENMARK [Rus.] LATVIA
LITHUANIA
NETH. GERMANY BELARUS
BEL. LUX. POLAND
FRANCE CZECH REP. UKRAINE
AUS. SLOVAKIA
SWITZERLAND 3 HUNG. ROMANIA
MOLDOVA
ITALY BULGARIA

KAZAKHSTAN

MONGOLIA

NORTH KOREA
SOUTH KOREA

40°N

SPAIN
4
GREECE TURKEY GEORGIA
ARMENIA AZERBAIJAN
UZBEKISTAN KYRGYZSTAN
TURKMENISTAN TAJIKISTAN

CHINA

JAPAN

Pacific Ocean

CYPRUS
LEBANON SYRIA
ISRAEL IRAQ
TUNISIA
JORDAN
IRAN
AFGHANISTAN

Mediterranean Sea

ALGERIA LIBYA EGYPT
KUWAIT
PAKISTAN
BAHRAIN
QATAR
U.A.E.

NEPAL BHUTAN

TROPIC OF CANCER

TAIWAN

MALI
NIGER CHAD SUDAN
SAUDI ARABIA
OMAN

BANGLADESH
INDIA MYANMAR (BURMA) LAOS
HONG KONG (U.K.)
MACAU (Port.)
20°N

NORTHERN MARIANA ISLANDS (U.S.)

REPUBLIC OF THE MARSHALL ISLANDS

BURKINA FASO
ERITREA
NIGERIA
BENIN
YEMEN
THAILAND VIETNAM
CAMBODIA

PHILIPPINES

GHANA
TOGO
DJIBOUTI

CENTRAL AFRICAN REP.
CAMEROON
ETHIOPIA
SRI LANKA

TORIAL GUINEA
UGANDA
SOMALIA
MALDIVES

FEDERATED STATES OF MICRONESIA

SAO TOME & PRINCIPE
GABON CONGO
RWANDA
KENYA
BRUNEI
MALAYSIA
SINGAPORE
EQUATOR 0°

CABINDA (Angola)
ZAIRE
BURUNDI
TANZANIA
SEYCHELLES

INDONESIA
PAPUA NEW GUINEA
SOLOMON ISLANDS

ANGOLA
ZAMBIA
MALAWI
COMOROS IS.

Indian Ocean

TUVALU

NAMIBIA
ZIMBABWE
MOZAMBIQUE
BOTSWANA
MADAGASCAR
MAURITIUS

VANUATU
FIJI

WALVIS BAY (Status to be determined)
SWAZILAND
20°S

NEW CALEDONIA (Fr.)

SOUTH AFRICA
LESOTHO

AUSTRALIA
TROPIC OF CAPRICORN

1. SLOVENIA
2. CROATIA
3. BOSNIA AND HERZEGOVINA
4. ALBANIA
5. MACEDONIA

NEW ZEALAND
40°S

60°S

ANTARCTIC CIRCLE

80°S

ANTARCTICA

0° 20°E 40°E 60°E 80°E 100°E 120°E 140°E 160°E 180°

Urban area	Country	Population (millions)			
		1950	1970	1990	2000[1]
1. Mexico City	Mexico	3.1	9.4	20.2	25.6
2. Tokyo	Japan	6.7	14.9	18.1	19.0
3. São Paulo	Brazil	2.4	8.1	17.4	22.1
4. New York	United States	12.3	16.2	16.2	16.8
5. Shanghai	China	5.3	11.2	13.4	17.0
6. Los Angeles	United States	4.0	8.4	11.9	13.9
7. Calcutta	India	4.4	6.9	11.8	15.7
8. Buenos Aires	Argentina	5.0	8.4	11.5	12.9
9. Bombay	India	2.9	5.8	11.2	15.4
10. Seoul	South Korea	1.0	5.3	11.0	12.7
11. Beijing	China	3.9	8.1	10.8	14.0
12. Rio de Janeiro	Brazil	2.9	7.0	10.7	12.5
13. Tranjin	China	2.4	5.2	9.4	12.7
14. Jakarta	Indonesia	2.0	3.9	9.3	13.7
15. Cairo	Egypt	2.4	5.3	9.0	11.8
16. Moscow	Russia	4.8	7.1	8.8	9.0
17. Delhi	India	1.4	3.5	8.8	13.2
18. Metro Manila	Philippines	1.5	3.5	8.5	11.8
19. Osaka	Japan	3.8	7.6	8.5	8.6
20. Paris	France	5.4	8.3	8.5	8.6
21. Karachi	Pakistan	1.0	3.1	7.7	11.7
22. Lagos	Nigeria	0.3	2.0	7.7	12.9
23. London	United Kingdom	8.7	8.6	7.4	13.9
24. Bangkok	Thailand	1.4	3.1	7.2	10.3
25. Chicago	United States	4.9	6.7	7.0	7.3

1. Projected figures.

◄ **EXHIBIT R-26 The World's Largest Urban Areas Ranked by 1990 Estimated Population (millions).** An urban area includes at least one large central city and the surrounding area with population exceeding 1,000 persons per acre. In 1990, the most densely populated urban area in the world was Mexico City, Mexico.

SOURCE: *The Universal Almanac,* Copyright © 1992 by John W. Wright. Reprinted with permission of Andrews and McMeel. All rights reserved.

Nation	GDP (Approximate dollar figure, in billions)
1. United States	$5,677
2. Japan	2,370
3. China	1,660
4. Germany	1,250
5. France	1,040
6. India	1,000
7. Italy	980
8. Great Britain	900
9. Brazil	790
10. Mexico	600
11. Canada	520
12. Spain	500

◄ **EXHIBIT R-27. GDP, Selected Nations, 1991.** The GDP for selected nations in 1991. Notice that the GDP for Japan is more than double the GDP for France.

SOURCE: *Economic Report of the President,* 1993.

► **EXHIBIT R-28. Tax Revenues as a Percentage of GDP, Selected Nations, 1990.**
Tax revenues are shown as a percentage of GDP. For example, if tax revenues are $100 billion, and GDP is $1,000 billion, then tax revenues comprise 10 percent of GDP (100/1,000=0.1, and 0.1x100=10 percent). Notice that tax revenues comprise a smaller percentage of GDP in the United States than in most countries.

SOURCE: U.S. Bureau of the Census, *Statistical Abstract of the United States*: 1993, 113th Edition, p. 857.

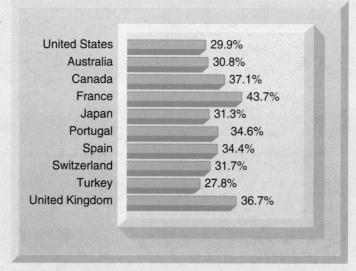

Country	Tax Revenue % of GDP
United States	29.9%
Australia	30.8%
Canada	37.1%
France	43.7%
Japan	31.3%
Portugal	34.6%
Spain	34.4%
Switzerland	31.7%
Turkey	27.8%
United Kingdom	36.7%

► **EXHIBIT R-29. Health Expenditures as a Percentage of GDP, Selected Nations, 1991.**
What percentage of a country's GDP goes for health care? The answer for selected countries is shown here. In 1991, the United States spent 13.4 percent of its GDP on health care.

SOURCE: U.S. Bureau of the Census, *Statistical Abstract of the United States*: 1993, 113th Edition, p. 849.

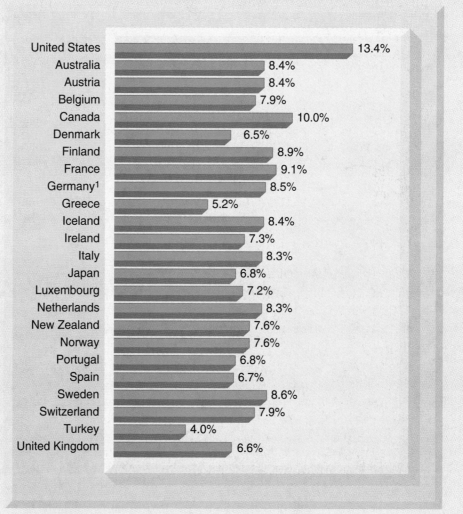

Country	Health Expenditure % of GDP
United States	13.4%
Australia	8.4%
Austria	8.4%
Belgium	7.9%
Canada	10.0%
Denmark	6.5%
Finland	8.9%
France	9.1%
Germany[1]	8.5%
Greece	5.2%
Iceland	8.4%
Ireland	7.3%
Italy	8.3%
Japan	6.8%
Luxembourg	7.2%
Netherlands	8.3%
New Zealand	7.6%
Norway	7.6%
Portugal	6.8%
Spain	6.7%
Sweden	8.6%
Switzerland	7.9%
Turkey	4.0%
United Kingdom	6.6%

1. Former West Germany (prior to unification).

▼ **EXHIBIT R-30. Leading Exporters and Importers in World Merchandise Trade 1990.** Notice that Germany was the leading exporter in 1990, while the United States was the leading importer in 1990.

Exporters		Importers	
Rank/country	1990 share	Rank/country	1990 share
1. Germany[1]	12.1%	1. United States	14.3%
2. United States	11.3	2. Germany[1]	9.9
3. Japan	8.3	3. Japan	6.5
4. France	6.2	4. France	6.5
5. United Kingdom	5.3	5. United Kingdom	6.2
6. Italy	4.9	6. Italy	5.0
7. Netherlands	3.8	7. Netherlands	3.5
8. Canada	3.8	8. Canada	3.4
9. Belgium-Luxembourg	3.4	9. USSR[2]	3.3
10. USSR[2]	3.0	10. Belgium-Luxembourg	3.3
11. Hong Kong[3]	2.4	11. Spain	2.4
12. Taiwan	1.9	12. Hong Kong[6]	2.3
13. South Korea	1.9	13. Switzerland	1.9
14. Switzerland	1.8	14. South Korea	1.9
15. China	1.8	15. Singapore[6]	1.7
16. Sweden	1.7	16. Taiwan	1.5
17. Spain	1.6	17. Sweden	1.5
18. Singapore[4]	1.5	18. China	1.5
19. Saudi Arabia	1.3	19. Austria	1.4
20. Austria	1.2	20. Australia	1.2
21. Mexico[5]	1.2	21. Mexico[5]	1.2
22. Australia	1.1	22. Thailand	0.9
23. Denmark	1.0	23. Denmark	0.9

N.A. = not applicable. 1. Combined trade values for the former Federal Republic of Germany and the former German Democratic Republic. 2. Because of difficulties involved in converting data expressed in the national currency into dollars, the figures are at best rough estimates. 3. Includes reexports. In 1990, they amounted to $53.0 billion, compared to $44.3 billion in 1989. 4. Includes reexports. In 1990, they amounted to $18.0 billion compared to $16.4 billion in 1989. 5. Includes trade flows through processing zones. 6. Includes substantial imports for reexport.
SOURCE: *The Universal Almanac*, Copyright © 1992 by John W. Wright. Reprinted with permission of Andrews and McMeel. All rights reserved.

▶ **EXHIBIT R-31. U.S. Trade Balance, Selected Trade Partners, 1992 (in millions of dollars).** In this exhibit, we show the trade balance the United States had with selected countries in 1992. A minus (−) sign in front of a dollar amount indicates a trade deficit. For example, the U.S. trade deficit with Japan was $50,002 million. If there is no operational sign (no minus or plus sign) in front of a number, this means the U.S. had a trade surplus and no deficit. Note: the dollar amount at the bottom of the exhibit, −$96,275 million, includes the trade balance that the United States currently had with countries in addition to the ones shown in the exhibit. Thus, this exhibit shows in 1992, the United States had a trade deficit with the rest of the world.

SOURCE: *The Universal Almanac,* Copyright © 1992 by John W. Wright. Reprinted with permission of Andrews and McMeel. All rights reserved.

Country	Trade balance
Australia	$5,065
Belgium and Luxembourg	5,267
Brazil	−1,874
Canada	−10,301
China	−18,249
France	−79
Germany	−8,402
Hong Kong	−773
Italy	−3,632
Japan	−50,002
Mexico	4,881
Netherlands	7,698
Singapore	−1,790
South Korea	−2,798
Taiwan	−10,129
United Kingdom	2,410
Venezuela	−2,864
Total[1]	−$96,275

Note: Preliminary data. 1. Includes other countries not shown separately.

▶ **EXHIBIT R-32. Where the World's 500 Largest Corporations are Located, Selected Nations, 1991.** The location of many of the world's 500 largest corporations is shown. The United States is the home of more of the world's 500 largest corporations than any other country.

SOURCE: U.S. Bureau of the Census, *Statistical Abstract of the United States:* 1993, 113th Edition, p. 861.

Country	Number of Companies
Australia	9
Canada	9
Finland	5
France	32
Germany	33
India	6
Italy	7
Japan	119
Netherlands	7
South Korea	13
Sweden	14
Switzerland	10
United Kingdom	45
United States	157

▼ **EXHIBIT R-33. Hourly Compensation for Production Workers, Selected Countries.** Here we show the hourly compensation for production workers in different countries in 1992. Hourly compensation includes wages, premiums, bonuses, vacation, holidays and other leave, insurance, and benefit plans.

Country	Hourly compensation for production workers (in dollars)	Country	Hourly compensation for production workers (in dollars)
Australia	$12.94	Mexico	$2.35
Austria	19.65	Netherlands	20.72
Belgium	22.01	New Zealand	7.91
Canada	17.02	Norway	23.20
Denmark	20.02	Portugal	5.01
Finland	18.69	Singapore	5.00
France	16.88	Spain	13.39
Germany	25.94	Sweden	24.23
Ireland	13.32	Switzerland	23.26
Italy	19.41	Taiwan	5.19
Japan	16.16	United Kingdom	14.69
Korea, South	4.93	United States	16.17

SOURCE: *The Universal Almanac,* Copyright © 1992 by John W. Wright. Reprinted with permission of Andrews and McMeel. All rights reserved.

(1) Country	(2) Inflation rate 1991-1992 (percent)
Argentina	24.9%
Belgium	2.4
Canada	1.5
Colombia	27.0
Egypt	13.6
India	11.8
Israel	11.9
Japan	1.7
Mexico	15.5
South Korea	6.2
Sweden	2.3
Turkey	70.1
United States	3.0

◀ **EXHIBIT R-34. Inflation Rate, Selected Countries.** The United States had a relatively low inflation rate in 1991–1992.

SOURCE: U.S. Bureau of the Census, *Statistical Abstract of the United States*: 1993, 113th Edition, p. 858.

A SURVEY OF CAREERS

There is a high probability that you will be working with a business after high school or college. But what will you be doing? Most high-school students aren't yet certain of their career objectives. It is a good idea, though, to start to obtain some information about different jobs so that you can knowledgeably choose your work instead of just falling into it.

This section provides some information on various jobs. All the information was obtained from the book *Jobs*, written by Robert and Anne Snelling. This book is published by Simon & Schuster and may be purchased at most bookstores. It is an excellent and detailed guide to the job market that is useful for anyone who is not sure what he or she wants to do in the work world. It gives detailed information on approximately 250 occupations. One of the key assets of the book is that it provides the addresses of organizations to which you can write to get more information about particular jobs.

You may also order an inexpensive 10-page booklet from the Consumer Information Center titled *Matching Yourself with the World of Work*. This booklet states the requirements, prospects, and earnings for 200 occupations. Write or call the Consumer Information Center in Pueblo, Colorado 81009. The phone number is 719-948-3334.

Careers in Advertising and Sales Promotion

Careers in advertising and sales promotion include: advertising account executive, advertising copywriter, broadcast technician, graphic designer (commercial artist), market research analyst, media planner or buyer, and production assistant. Here are additional details on two careers in this area.

Advertising Copywriter. Advertising copywriters write slogans and sales materials, produce print ads and brochures, and prepare scripts for radio and television. Requirements include creativity, self-discipline, and a feeling for "what sells." A person in this field should have a bachelor's degree with a major in English or liberal arts. Many copywriters are employed by advertising agencies, public relations firms, and within the marketing departments of major companies.

Market Research Analyst. Market research analysts study and report on things that can affect what products firms will produce, how goods will be packaged, how goods will be marketed, what consumers like and dislike, and so on. They report their findings to top management. Most analysts are employed by manufacturing companies, advertising agencies, and independent research organizations. Requirements include the ability to solve research problems, the ability to formulate new ways to obtain needed information, effective communication (talking and writing) skills, and a bachelor's degree.

Careers in Agribusiness

Careers in agribusiness include: agricultural scientist, biological scientist, agricultural engineer, animal trainer/handler, farm operator or manager, food technologist, range manager, veterinarian, and veterinary technician or assistant. Here are additional details on a few careers in this area.

Agricultural Engineer. Agricultural engineers often apply the theories of the sciences to problems of food and agriculture. For example, they may design agricultural machinery and develop methods to improve the production of agricultural foodstuffs. They also design systems to improve the conservation and management of energy, soil, and water resources. Requirements include an analytical mind, an interest in science and mathematics, and at least a bachelor's degree in engineering. A master's degree is usually necessary for promotion in this field.

Farm Operator.   Farm operators may be farm owners or renters (tenant farmers). On crop farms, they plant, fertilize, cultivate, spray, and harvest crops. They may also package, load, and store crops. On livestock, dairy, and poultry farms, they feed and take care of the animals. Requirements include physical stamina and high-school training, especially courses in sciences. Since modern farming requires a knowledge of many areas, a college degree is highly recommended. All states have land-grant universities that include a college of agriculture.

Veterinarian.   Veterinarians diagnose, treat, and control animal diseases and injuries. Requirements include a love of animals, sensitivity, and the willingness to work hard. To obtain the license required to become a veterinarian, a person must have a doctor of veterinary medicine (D.V.M. or V.M.D.) degree from an accredited college of veterinary medicine and must pass written and oral examinations.

chains, and others work for builders who do a great deal of building or renovation. Requirements include artistic talent, color sense, and an eye for design. Most employers look for people who have professional training. Training is available in three-year certificate programs in professional schools of interior design and in four-year college or university programs offering the specialty.

Urban or Regional Planner.   Urban and regional planners help solve the social, economic, and environmental problems of cities, suburbs, and rural areas. Most planners work for city, county, or regional planning agencies. Some of them are employed by state or federal agencies dealing with housing, transportation, or environmental protection. Requirements include creativity, innovativeness, and an ability to think in terms of spatial relationships. Most urban and regional planners have a master's degree in urban or regional planning.

Architect.   Architects design a wide variety of building structures, including houses, factories, shopping malls, hotels, and airports. Most architects work for architectural firms, real estate firms, or builders. Requirements include a bachelor's or master's degree in architecture.

Careers in Architecture and Design

Careers in architecture and design include: architect, civil engineer, college or campus planner, drafter, industrial designer, interior designer, landscape architect, surveyor, and urban or regional planner. Here are additional details on a few careers in this area.

Interior Designer.   Interior designers plan the interiors of homes, restaurants, business offices, hospitals, libraries, and other structures to make them pleasurable and comfortable. Interior designers usually arrange every detail of an interior and its furnishings. Most designers work for design firms. Others work for large hotel and restaurant

Careers in Computers

Careers in computers include: computer engineer, computer operator, computer service technician, mathematician, programmer, statistician, and systems analyst. Here are additional details on a few careers in this area.

Computer Engineer.   Computer engineers design computers and study how they can be used in various fields. Computer application engineers specialize in how computers can be applied in various situations. Computer engineers are employed throughout government and in many businesses, such as banks and telecommunication companies. Requirements include mathematical ability, an analytical mind, and a degree in mathematics, electrical engineering, mechanical engineering, or electronic engineering.

Computer Service Technician. Computer service technicians (sometimes called field engineers or customer engineers) maintain and repair computers and often help to install new computer equipment. Most technicians are employed by firms that provide maintenance services for a fee. Some technicians work for organizations that have large computer systems. Requirements include mechanical aptitude, patience, and analytical ability. Most employers require applicants to have one or two years of post-high-school training in basic electronics or electrical engineering. This training is usually available in vocational schools, the armed forces, colleges, and junior colleges.

Programmer. Programmers write detailed programs that enable the computer to do what it does. Most programmers are employed by manufacturing firms, data-processing-service organizations, and government agencies. Requirements include the ability to think logically and to perform exacting analytical work. Most programmers are college graduates.

Careers in Construction

Careers in construction include construction worker and construction manager. Here are additional details on both jobs.

Construction Manager. Construction managers direct, supervise, and coordinate all the activities on a construction project. In their work, they regularly review engineering and architectural drawings. Requirements include the ability to be decisive, work well under pressure, and get along with many different people. Most construction managers have substantial experience as construction workers, and many have attended training and educational programs sponsored by industry associations. Others have also attended construction science programs at two-year colleges. The completion of a bachelor's degree pro-

gram in construction science can enhance one's opportunities in this occupation.

Construction Worker. There are many different types of construction workers. They include bricklayers and stonemasons, electricians, carpenters, glaziers, drywall workers, millwrights, painters, plasterers, plumbers, pipefitters, sheet-metal workers, and structural ironworkers. Construction workers build houses, hospitals, shopping malls, schools, restaurants, and so on. Training may be obtained through a vocational school, but most construction workers start out working for someone with experience. In many of the more highly skilled occupations, a formal apprenticeship, combining on-the-job training with classroom instruction, is preferred.

Careers in Education

Careers in education include: secondary school teacher, teacher's aide, elementary school teacher, college and university faculty, college administrator, librarian, and elementary or secondary school administrator. Here are additional details on two careers in this area.

Secondary School Teacher. Secondary school teachers help to educate many young women and men. There are approximately 1.2 million secondary school teachers in the nation. Secondary school teachers usually have subject specialties, such as a foreign language, mathematics, social studies, or science. Some teach vocational-educational classes, such as business skills, welding, or auto mechanics. In addition to their regular classes, secondary school teachers supervise study halls and homerooms, advise student groups, and attend meetings with parents and school personnel. Teachers also participate in college classes to keep up-to-date in their specialty. Requirements include the ability to work well with young people and to inspire enthusiasm for learning. Teachers need a bachelor's degree—although many have a master's degree, too—and they have completed teaching training programs and taken a number of education courses.

Librarian. Today's librarian is an "information specialist" who helps individuals find information on computers, in reference books, and so on. In small libraries, the librarian may handle everything from buying books and other materials to publicizing library services. In contrast, in large libraries, which are usually headed by a chief librarian, staff librarians are usually specialized and oversee major departments. Requirements include a love of books and information, organizational skills, and the ability to do detailed work. A master's degree in library science (M.L.S.) is necessary to obtain an entry-level professional position in most libraries.

Careers in Federal and Municipal Government

Careers in federal and municipal government include: air-traffic controller, city or county manager or assistant, construction inspector, fire fighter, health inspector, recreation worker, and regulatory inspector. Here are additional details on two careers in this area.

Fire Fighter. Fire fighters help protect the public against the danger of fires. They perform many specific duties, such as connecting hose lines to hydrants, positioning ladders, rescuing victims, administering medical aid, ventilating smoke-filled areas, operating equipment, and so on. Requirements include mental alertness, courage, endurance, a sense of public service, and mechanical aptitude. Municipal fire fighters usually have to pass a written test and a medical examination and be able to attain certain standards of strength, agility, and physical stamina. Most cities require the applicant to have a high-school education or the equivalent.

City Manager. The job of city manager involves the administration and coordination of the daily operations of a city. City managers are responsible for overseeing departments involved in tax collection, law enforcement, and public works, among other things. They study and try to correct existing housing problems, traffic congestion, crime problems, pollution problems, and so on. Requirements include administrative ability, sound judgment, and the ability to work well under stress. A master's degree, preferably in public administration or business administration, is an asset in this job.

Careers in Finance

Careers in finance include: financial analyst, commodity trader, securities broker, bank clerk, bank officer, bank teller, economist, insurance actuary, insurance claim representative, accountant, bookkeeper, credit clerk, credit manager, business manager, financial planner, and income-tax preparer. Here are additional details on two careers in this area.

Securities Broker. Securities brokers buy and sell stocks, bonds, shares in mutual funds, and other financial products. They may trade for individuals with a few hundred dollars or for large institutions with millions of dollars to invest. In the beginning, brokers spend much of their time looking for clients. They may develop clients through business or social contacts. Securities brokers are employed by brokerage firms, investment bankers, and mutual fund companies. Requirements include a competitive spirit and an interest in business and finance. Increasingly, a college education is important.

Actuary. Actuaries calculate the costs associated with insuring different risks. They calculate the probabilities of death, sickness, injury, disability, unemployment, retirement, and property loss for all the various kinds of insurance. An actuary would, for example, calculate how likely it is that a person living in Charleston, South Carolina, will be burglarized. Actuaries must keep informed about general economic and social trends and legislative, health, and other developments that may affect insurance policies. Requirements include a strong background in mathematics and statistics. A bachelor's degree in actuarial science is the best academic background to have, but a bachelor's degree in mathematics or statistics is also very helpful.

Careers in Health Services

Careers in health services include dietitian, hospital administrator, medical office assistant, nurse, nurse's aide or psychiatric aide, occupational therapist, physical therapist, speech pathologist, audiologist, and recreational therapist. Here are additional details on one career in this area.

Nurse. Nurses are responsible for the daily care of the physically and mentally ill. While the work can be routine at times (much like any work), it is challenging, too, and it can make the difference between life and death. Nurses fall into one of two categories, depending on their background and training: licensed practical nurse (L.P.N.) and registered nurse (R.N.). An L.P.N. works under the direction of physicians and registered nurses and provides nursing that requires technical knowledge but not the professional education and training of an R.N. Registered nurses usually work with a group of patients who require similar care, such as children, postoperative patients, or surgery patients. Requirements include a desire to help others, good judgment, initiative, and the ability to follow instructions precisely. Both the L.P.N. and the R.N. must be licensed. An L.P.N. must complete a state-approved practical nursing course and pass a written exam. Courses generally last a year and are available through trade, technical, or vocational schools or through community colleges, hospitals, or health agencies. Most schools prefer high-school graduates. An R.N. must graduate from a state-approved school of nursing and pass a state board examination to qualify for a license. A two-year associate degree, a three-year diploma, or a four-year bachelor's degree will satisfy basic licensing requirements for an R.N. A bachelor's degree is usually necessary for supervisory or administrative positions.

Careers in Health Technology

Careers in health technology include: dental assistant or hygienist, electrocardiograph technician, diagnostic medical sonographer, emergency medical technician, nuclear medicine technologist, radiologic (X-ray) technologist, and medical laboratory technologist. Here are additional details on two careers in this area.

Diagnostic Medical Sonographer. Sonography is an important diagnostic tool. It involves using ultrasound (sound-wave frequencies hundreds of times higher than those the ear can hear) and a device that converts electrical energy into sound waves and directs the sound waves into the body. As the sound waves come into contact with body organs, they produce echoes, which are received by the device and then electronically displayed on a screen. This picture of the internal organs allows a physician to recognize tumors, cysts, and other abnormalities. A sonographer is a person who works this diagnostic tool to aid the physician and patient. Requirements include a high degree of technical skill, a knowledge of physiology and anatomy, and a high-school education, plus one or two years of college or technical school.

Medical Laboratory Technologist. Perhaps you have gone to a doctor who has sent you to the lab to get a blood test. The medical laboratory technologists perform the test and then send the results back to the doctor. Requirements include four years of college and the completion of a specialized medical technology training program. For those persons who wish to specialize, advanced degrees are necessary, usually requiring an additional year of training.

Careers in Law and Law Enforcement

Careers in law and law enforcement include: lawyer, legal assistant, shorthand reporter, correction officer, federal agent, and police officer. Here are additional details on two careers in this area.

Lawyer.   Lawyers usually work as either advocates or advisers. As advocates, they represent opposing parties in courtroom trials by presenting arguments that support their side. As advisers, they counsel their clients as to their legal rights and obligations and suggest particular courses of action. Lawyers often specialize in a certain type of law, such as contract law, business law, or family law. Requirements include the ability to speak well, think quickly and logically, and analyze. Education includes a college degree and a law degree.

Federal Agent.   Federal agents do many things: gather information, track down kidnappers, stop counterfeiting, and prevent illegal drugs from entering the country. Most federal agents work either for the Federal Bureau of Investigation (FBI) or for the Central Intelligence Agency (CIA). The work of a federal agent can end in personal injury. Requirements include the ability to pay close attention to detail, perseverance, excellent health, and, in some cases, the ability to handle firearms. Educational requirements vary greatly depending on the job. The minimum is usually a college degree.

Careers in Management and Office Administration

Careers in management and office administration include: administrative assistant, distribution manager, management consultant, purchasing agent, security manager, telecommunications specialist, business-machine repairer, file clerk, receptionist, secretary, telephone operator, and word-processor operator. Here are additional details on two careers in this area.

Telecommunications Specialist.   Telecommunications specialists work with systems involving telephones and data communication equipment, computerized mail (electronic mailboxes), videoconferencing, telegrams, telexes, and facsimiles (faxes) in order to provide businesses with the most efficient communication networks for them. Telecommunications specialists are employed by large companies, particularly in the areas of insurance, banking, investment, communications, and sales and manufacturing. They are also employed by government. Requirements include a college degree (preferably in business, or in telecommunications, which is a field of study only recently available). Computer courses are also helpful.

Purchasing Agent.   Purchasing agents usually work for business firms purchasing lumber, cars, trucks, office supplies, and so on. Their goal is to buy top-quality goods and services at the lowest possible prices. Requirements include the ability to work independently and feel comfortable in a decision-making role. Graduates of two year degree programs are usually hired.

Careers in Medicine

Careers in medicine include: pharmacologist, physiologist, chiropractor, dentist, optometrist, pharmacist, physician, podiatrist, and psychiatrist. Here are additional details on two careers in this area.

Physician.   Physicians are the persons we turn to when something goes wrong with our bodies. Many physicians work long and irregular hours, but exact working conditions depend on the physician's specialty. For example, an obstetrician (who delivers babies) has more irregular hours than a dermatologist (who treats skin disorders). Requirements include emotional stability, the ability to make decisions in emergencies, a willingness to study both in school and later on to keep up with medical advances, and a desire to help others. Educational requirements include a four-year college degree, a four-year medical degree, and a residency period of three to four years. Competition for entrance into medical school is extremely stiff.

Psychiatrist. Psychiatrists are medical doctors who specialize in helping solve patients' mental and emotional problems. Approximately 11 percent of all medical doctors specialize in the field of psychiatry. The educational requirements are the same as for physicians. Other requirements include emotional stability, sensitivity, and the ability to counsel others.

Careers in the Military

Careers in the military include: administrative support, medical technician, dental technician, service and supply handler, combat operations (gun crews, infantry, and so on), and officer training. Here are additional details on two careers in this area.

Administrative Support. Both enlisted persons and officers may be administrative support personnel. Positions for enlisted persons include accounting clerk, personnel assistant, clerk, typist, computer programmer or operator, and storekeeper. Officers in this category work as directors, executives, administrators, personnel training managers, accountants, public affairs specialists, systems analysts, chaplains, attorneys, and so on. The skills needed by persons who provide administrative support in the military are the same as those needed by persons with similar jobs in private business. Educational requirements vary depending on the job.

Officer Training. To obtain a commission as an officer, a person must receive training provided through the service academies, which include the U.S. Naval Academy, the U.S. Military Academy, the U.S. Air Force Academy, and the U.S. Coast Guard Academy. The service academies offer a four-year college program leading to the Bachelor of Science degree paid for by the government. Graduates of the service academies must spend five years in active military duty, or longer if they are entering flight training.

Careers in the Performing Arts

Careers in the performing arts include: actor, dancer, director, producer, musician, television director, television producer, and theater, film, and television support. Here are additional details on two careers in this area.

Musician. Musicians perform various kinds of music, such as classical, jazz, rock, or gospel. Requirements include extensive training in the particular kind of music the musician performs. This may include college training, professional music training, and so on. Most musicians start their musical training at an early age.

Television Director. Television directors are involved in planning the television action, arranging camera locations for the best shots, choosing background music when appropriate, working with actors on their interpretations of the script, and so on. Requirements include creativity, organizational and communication skills, and the ability to work well with many people from different branches of the entertainment business. There are no specific educational requirements, but most people who become directors have had some college education. Work experience is a must. Most directors start as production assistants, associate directors, and so on.

SPANISH EQUIVALENTS FOR IMPORTANT ECONOMIC TERMS IN ENGLISH

A
Ability to trade: Habilidad de intercambiar.
Aggregate demand: Demanda agregada.
Aggregate demand curve: Curva de la demanda agregada.
Aggregate supply: Oferta agregada.
Aggregate supply curve: Curva de la oferta agregada.
Agricultural price supports: Precio sostenido de productos agricolas.
Alternatives: Alternativas.
Appreciation: Appreciatión.
Asset: Activo.
Asset: Partida de activo.
Average fixed cost: Promedio del costo fijo.
Average (total) cost: Promedio del costo (total).
Average variable cost: Promedio del costo variable.

B
Balance of trade: Balanza comercial.
Balance of trade deficit: Déficit en la balanza comercial.
Balance of trade surplus: Superávit en la balanza comercial.
Bank run: Pánico Bancario.
Barrier to entry (or exit): Barrera de entrada (o de salida).
Board of Governors (Federal Reserve): Junta de Gobernadores (Reserva Federal).
Bond price: Valor del bono.
Budget deficit: Déficit presupuestario.
Budget surplus: Excedencia presupuestaria.
Business cycle: Ciclo económico.
Business sector: sector de negocios o sector empresarial.

C
Capital: Capital.

Change in demand: Cambio de la demanda.
Change in quantity demand: Cambio en la cantidad que se demanda.
Change in quantity supplied: Cambio de la cantidad que se ofrece.
Change in supply: Cambio en la oferta.
Circular flow of economic activity: El flujo circular de la actividad economica.
Comparative advantage: Ventaja comparativa.
Complements: Complementos.
Consumer price index: Indice de precios al consumidor (IPC).
Consumers: Consumidores.
Contractionary monetary policy: Política monetaria de contracción.
Corporation: Sóciedad autónoma.
Crowding out effect: Efecto-expulsión.
Currency: Moneda.
Cyclical unemployment: Desempleo cíclico.

D
Deficit: Déficit.
Demand: Demanda.
Depreciation (Currency): Depreciación. (Divisas).
Developed countries: Países desarrollados.
Discount rate: Rata de descuento.
Discount rate: Tasa de descuento.
Dividends: Dividendos de accinones.

E
Economic system: Sistema economíco.
Economics: Economía.
Elasticity of demand: Elasticidad de demanda.
Elasticity of supply: Elasticidad de oferta.
Employed: Ocupados.
Entrepreneurs: Empresarios.
Equality of opportunity: Ingualdad de oportunidad.

Equilibrium: Equilibrio.
Exchange rate: Tasa de cambio.
Expansionary monetary policy: Política monetaria expansionista.
Expansionary policy: Política expansionista.
Exports: Exportaciones.

F
Face value (bond): Valor nominal (bono).
Factors of production: Factores de producción.
Federal Deposit Insurance Corporation (FDIC): (Corporación Federal de Seguros de Depósitos.
Federal Funds rate: Tasa de Fondos Federales.
Federal Open Market Committee: Comité Federal de Operaciones de Mercado Abierto.
Federal Reserve Banking System: El Sistema de Reserva Federal.
Federal Reserve Note: Billete de la Reserva Federal.
Fiscal policy: Política fiscal.
Fixed cost: Costo fijo.
Fixed exchange rate: Tipo de cambio fijo.
Flexible exchange rate: Tipo de cambio variable.
Free-rider: Consumidor que no paga.
Frictional unemployment: Desempleo friccional.
Full employment: Empleo completo.

G
GATT (General Agreement on Tariffs and Trade): Acuerdo General de Aranceles y Comercio (AGAC).
Government bond: Bono del estado.
Government sector: Sector gubernamental.
Gross domestic product (GDP): Producto interno bruto.
Gross national product (GNP): Producto nacional bruto.

H
Household sector: Sector del hogar.

I
Imports: Imortaciones.
Industry: Industria.

Inferior good: Bien inferior.
Inflation: Inflación.
Innovation: Innovación.
Innovators: Innovadores.
Insolvent: Insolvencia.
Intangible: Intangible.
Intermediate good: Bien intermedio.
International Monetary Fund (IMF): Fondo Monetario Internacional (FMI).
Invention: Invención.
Investment: Inversión.

L
Labor: Mano de obra.
Labor force: Fuerza laboral.
Labor productivity: Productividad laboral.
Land: Tierra.
Law of demand: Ley de demanda.
Law of diminishing marginal utility: Ley de la utilidad marginal de consumo decreciente.
Law of diminishing returns: Ley del rendimiento decreciente.
Law of supply: Ley de oferta.
Liability: Obligación.

M
Macroeconomics: Macroeconomía.
Marginal cost: Costo marginal.
Marginal revenue: Ingresos marginales.
Market: Mercado.
Median income: Ingreso mediano.
Medium of exchange: Medio de Cambio.
Microeconomic: Microeconomía.
Minimum wage: Salario mínimo.
Monetary policy: Politica monetaria.
Money: Moneda.
Monopolistic competition: Competencia monopolista.

N
Natural monopoly: Monopolio natural.
Natural rate of unemployment: Tasa natural de desempleo.
Net worth: Valor neto.

O
Oligopoly: Oligopolio.

Open Market Operation: Operación de mercado libre.
Opportunity cost: El Costo de Oportunidad.

P
Partnership: Sociedad colectiva.
Perfect competition: Competencia perfecta.
Producers: Productores.
Production possibilities frontier: La frontera de posibilidades de producción.
Profit: Utilidades o beneficios.
Progressive tax: Impuestos progresivos.
Proportional tax: Impuestos proporcionales.
Pure market capitalism: Capitalismo puro del mercado.
Pure monopoly: Monopolio puro.

R
Regressive tax: Impuestos regresivos.
Rent control: Control del precio de alquiler.
Required reserves: Reservas requeridas.
Reserve requirement: Requisito en reservas.

S
Sales tax: Impuesto de venta.
Services: Servicios.

Single proprietorship: Própiedad singular.
Socialism: Socialismo.
Specialization: Especializacion.
Stagflation: Estancamiento-inflación.
Store of value: Depósito de valor.
Structural unemployment: Desempleo estructural.
Supply: Oferta.
Surplus: Superávit.

T
Taxable income: Ingreso gravable.
Third World Countries: Países del Tercer Mundo.
Treasury bill (T-Bill): Bono de tesorería.

U
Unemployed: Desempleados.
Unemployment rate: Tasa de desempleo.
Union shop: Taller agremiado.
Unit of account: Unidad de cuenta.
Utility: Utilidad de consumo o beneficio de consumo.

V
Variable cost: Costo variable.

GLOSSARY

A

Absolute Advantage The situation in which a country can produce more of a good than another country can produce with the same quantity of resources.

Advancement in Technology The ability to produce more output with a fixed amount of resources.

Aggregate Supply Curve Shows the quantity of goods and services producers are willing and able to supply at different price levels.

Aggregate Demand Curve Shows the quantity of goods and services buyers are willing and able to buy at different price levels.

Antitrust Law Legislation passed for the stated purpose of controlling monopoly power and preserving and promoting competition.

Appreciation An increase in the value of one currency relative to other currencies.

Asset Anything of value to which the firm has legal claim. In reference to a bank, a thing that the bank owns that has value.

Average Fixed Cost Fixed cost divided by quantity of output.

Average Total Cost Total cost divided by quantity of output.

Average Variable Cost Variable cost divided by quantity of output.

B

Balance of Trade The difference between the value of a nation's exports and the value of its imports.

Barriers to Entry Anything that prohibits a firm from entering a market.

Barter Economy An economy in which trades are made in goods and services instead of money.

Base Year In general, a benchmark year; a year chosen as a point of reference for comparison. When real GDP is computed, the output of different years is priced at base-year levels.

Beneficiary A person named to receive benefits from an insurance policy.

Biomedicine Medical science combined with research in biology.

Biotechnology The use of living organisms in the manufacture of goods, such as drugs and other products.

Board of Governors of the Federal Reserve System The governing body of the Federal Reserve system.

Board of Directors An important decision-making body in a corporation. It decides corporate policies and goals, among other things.

Bond A statement of debt issued by a corporation. The corporation promises to pay a certain sum of money at maturity and also to pay periodic fixed sums until that date.

Budget An organized plan for spending and saving money.

Business Cycle Recurrent swings (up and down) in real GDP.

Business Firm An organization that uses resources to produce goods and services, which are sold to consumers, other firms, or the government.

Bylaws Internal rules of the corporation.

C

Capital Ratio Equity divided by assets.

Capital Produced goods that can be used as resources for further production. Such things as factories, machines, and farm tractors are capital.

Circular Flow of Economic Activity Shows the economic relationships that exist between different economic groups in the economy.

Closed Shop An organization that hires only union members.

Command-Economy Socialism An economic system characterized by government ownership of the nonlabor factors of production, government allocation of resources, and centralized decision making. Most economic activities take place in the public sector, and government plays a very large role in the economy.

Comparative Advantage The situation in which a country can produce a good at lower opportunity cost than another country.

Complements Goods that are consumed jointly. With complements, the price of one and the demand for the other move in opposite directions.

Consumer Price Index (CPI) The most widely cited price index.

Contract An agreement between two or more people to do something.

Contractionary Fiscal Policy A decrease in government spending or an increase in taxes.

Contractionary Monetary Policy A decrease in the money supply.

Cooperative A business that provides services to its members and is not run for profit. Usually, a cooperative is formed when a group of persons (the members) want to pool their resources to gain some benefit that they, as individuals, could not otherwise obtain.

Corporate Income Tax A tax paid on a corporation's profits.

Corporation A legal entity that can conduct business in its own name in the same way that an individual does. Ownership of the corporation resides with the stockholders.

Coupon Rate A percentage of the face value of a bond that is paid out regularly (usually quarterly or annually) to the holder of the bond.

Crowding In Situation in which decreases in government spending lead to an increase in private spending.

Crowding Out Situation in which increases in government spending lead to a reduction in private spending.

Currency Coins issued by the U.S. Treasury and paper money (called Federal Reserve notes) issued by the Federal Reserve system.

Cyclical Unemployment The difference between the official unemployment rate and the natural rate of unemployment.

D

Debit Card A card that can be used to withdraw funds at automated teller machines and to pay for purchases by electronically transferring funds from one account to another (where the seller has the appropriate equipment). Debit cards look like credit cards.

Default Rate Percentage of loans that are not repaid.

Demand The willingness and ability of buyers to purchase a good or service.

Demand Curve The graphical representation of the law of demand. It is a graph showing the amount of a good buyers are willing and able to buy at various prices.

Demand Deposit A deposit that is withdrawable on demand and transferable by means of a check.

Demand Schedule A table showing quantities of a good demanded at varying prices.

Demand-Side Inflation An increase in the price level that originates on the demand side of the economy.

Dependency Ratio The number of children under a certain age plus the elderly (aged 65 and over) divided by the total population.

Depreciation A decrease in the value of one currency relative to other currencies.

Developed Country A country with a high per-capita GDP.

Direct Relationship A relationship between two factors in which the factors move in the same direction. For example, as one rises, the other rises, too.

Discount Rate The interest rate the Fed charges a member bank for a loan.

Diversified Economy An economy that has many different types of products and services it produces.

Dividend A share of the profits of a corporation distributed to stockholders.

Double Coincidence of Wants The situation in which each of two parties to an exchange has what the other wants. In a barter economy, it is a requirement that must be met before a trade can be made.

Double-Counting Counting a good more than once in computing GDP.

Down Payment Cash paid at the time of a purchase, with the rest of the purchase price to be paid later.

Downsizing Restructuring a firm and decreasing its size so that it is a less costly, more productive, more efficient operation.

Dumping The sale of goods abroad at prices below their costs and below the price charged in domestic (home) markets.

E

Economic Plan A government program specifying economic activities, such as what goods are to be produced and what prices will be charged.

Economic System The way in which a society decides what goods to produce, how to produce them, and for whom goods will be produced.

Economics The science that studies the choices of people trying to satisfy their wants in a world of scarcity.

Elastic Demand When demand is elastic, the percentage change in quantity demanded is greater than the percentage change in price.

Elastic Supply When supply is elastic, the percentage change in quantity supplied is greater than the percentage change in price.

Elasticity of Demand The relationship between the percentage change in quantity demanded and the percentage change in price.

Elasticity of Supply The relationship between the percentage change in quantity supplied and the percentage change in price.

Employment Rate Percentage of the noninstitutional adult civilian population that is employed. The employment rate equals the number of persons employed divided by the number of persons in the noninstitutional adult civilian population.

Entrepreneur A person who has that special talent for searching out and taking advantage of new business opportunities, and developing new products and new ways of doing things.

Entrepreneurship The special talent that some people have for searching out and taking advantage of new business opportunities and for developing new products and new ways of doing things.

Equilibrium The condition of being at rest or balanced. Equilibrium in a market exists when the quantity of a good that buyers are willing and able to buy is equal to the quantity of the good that sellers are willing and able to produce and offer for sale (that is, quantity demanded equals quantity supplied). Graphically, equilibrium in a market is shown as the intersection point of the supply and demand curves.

Equilibrium Price The price at which a good is bought and sold in a market that is in equilibrium.

Equilibrium Quantity The quantity of a good that is bought and sold in a market that is in equilibrium.

Ethics Relates to principles of right and wrong, morality and immorality, good and bad.

Ethylene A colorless, flammable gas.

Excess Reserves Any reserves held beyond the required amount; the difference between total reserves and required reserves.

Exchange Rate The price of one nation's currency in terms of another nation's currency.

Expansionary Fiscal Policy An increase in government spending or a reduction in taxes.

Expansionary Monetary Policy An increase in the money supply.

Exports Dollar value of products sold in foreign countries.

Externality A side effect of an action that affects the well-being of third parties.

F

Face Value (Par Value) Dollar amount specified on a bond.

Face Value The stated denomination on paper money or coins. For example, the face value of a nickel is 5 cents, and the words *five cents* are actually inscribed on a nickel.

Federal Reserve Note Paper money issued by the Federal Reserve system.

Federal Reserve System (the Fed) The central bank of the United States.

Federal Open Market Committee (FOMC) The 12-member policy-making group within the Fed. This committee has the authority to conduct open-market operations.

Federal Funds Rate The interest rate one bank charges another bank for a loan.

Fiscal Policy Changes government makes in spending or taxation to achieve particular economic goals.

Fixed Cost Cost, or expense, that is the same no matter how many units of a good are produced.

Fixed Exchange Rate System The system whereby currency exchange rates are fixed, or pegged, by nations' governments.

Flexible Exchange Rate System The system whereby currency exchange rates are determined by the forces of supply and demand.

Fractional Reserve Banking A banking arrangement in which banks hold only a fraction of their deposits and lend out the remainder.

Franchise A contract by which a firm (usually a corporation) lets a person or group use its name and sell its goods in exchange for certain payments being made and certain requirements being met.

Franchisee The person or group that buys a franchise.

Franchiser The entity that offers a franchise.

Free Enterprise An economic system in which individuals (not government) own most, if not all, the resources and control their use. Government plays a very small role in the economy.

Free Rider A person who receives the benefits of a good without paying for it.

Frictional Unemployment Refers to workers who have lost their jobs because of changing market (demand) conditions and who have transferable skills. Unemployment due to the natural "frictions" of the economy. A person is frictionally unemployed when he or she is unemployed because of changing market conditions and has transferable skills.

Full Employment The situation that exists when the official unemployment rate equals the natural unemployment rate.

G

General Partner In a limited partnership, a partner who is responsible for the management of the firm and who has unlimited liability.

Generic Brand A brand that does not carry the name of any company, only the product name.

Global Competition Competition from all over the world. American business firms and workers today are said to be faced with global competition.

Global Economy An economy in which economic actions taken anywhere in the world may affect your standard of living.

Good A tangible item that gives a person utility or satisfaction. A *Good* is sometimes referred to as a *product*.

Gosplan Under Soviet command-economy socialism, the planning agency that had the responsibility of drafting the economic plan for the nation.

Gresham's Law An economic law stating that bad money drives good money out of circulation.

Gross Domestic Product (GDP) The total market value of all final goods and services produced annually in an economy.

Guaranteed Income Level With regard to negative income tax, the level below which a person's income is not allowed to fall.

H

Hedge To try to avoid or lessen a loss by taking some counterbalancing action.

High-Tech A shortened version of high technology. High technology is technology that uses highly sophisticated, complex, and advanced engineering techniques.

Household An economic unit of one person or more that sells resources and buys goods and services.

I

Implicit Marginal Tax Rate The rate at which the negative income tax payment (or any cash grant or subsidy) is reduced as earned income rises. For example, if a person earns an additional $1,000 and his or her negative income tax payment falls by $500, then the implicit marginal tax rate is 50 percent ($500 ÷ $1,000 = 0.50 and 0.50 × 100 = 50 percent).

Imports Dollar value of products brought into a country from other countries.

Impulse Buying Buying goods that you did not intend to buy. The impulse to buy something strikes you quickly, and you react by buying.

In-Kind Benefit Benefit (usually supplied by government) that takes the form of a specific good or service instead of money. Food stamps, subsidized housing, and medical assistance are examples of in-kind benefits.

Incentive Something that encourages or motivates a person toward an action.

Income Distribution The way all the income earned in a country is divided among different groups of income earners.

Industrial Policy A deliberate policy by which government "waters the green spots," or aids those industries that are most likely to be successful in the world marketplace.

Inelastic Demand When demand is inelastic, the percentage change in quantity demanded is less than the percentage change in price.

Inelastic Supply When supply is inelastic, the percentage change in quantity supplied is less than the percentage change in price.

Inferior Good A good the demand for which falls as income rises and rises as income falls.

Infrastructure The basic structures and facilities on which the continuance and growth of a community depend. Interstate highways, bridges, and communication networks are some of the things that make up a nation's infrastructure.

Insolvent Having more liabilities than assets.

Intangible Not able to be felt by touch. For example, an economics lecture is intangible.

Inventory The stock of goods that a business or store has on hand.

Inverse Relationship A relationship between two factors in which the factors move in opposite directions. For example, as the *price* of a good increases, the *quantity* demanded of a good decreases.

L

Labor Union An organization that seeks to increase the wages and improve the working conditions of its members.

Labor The physical and mental talents that people contribute to the production of goods and services.

Land All the natural resources found in nature. An acre of land, mineral deposits, and water in a stream are all considered land.

Law of Demand Law stating that as the price of a good increases, the quantity demanded of the good decreases, and as the price of a good decreases, the quantity demanded of the good increases.

Law of Diminishing Marginal Utility Law stating that as a person consumes additional units of a good, eventually the utility gained from each additional unit of the good decreases.

Law of Diminishing Returns States that if we add additional units of a resource (such as labor) to a resource (such as capital) that is fixed in supply, eventually the additional output produced (as a result of hiring an additional worker) will decrease.

Law of Supply Law stating that as the price of a good increases, the quantity supplied of the good increases, and as the price of a good decreases, the quantity supplied of the good decreases.

Lease A contract that conveys property (such as an apartment) for a specific time period for a fee.

Less-Developed Country (LDC) A country with a low per-capita GDP.

Liability In reference to a bank, its debt.

Limited Partner In a limited partnership, a partner who cannot participate in the management of the firm and who has limited liability.

Limited Partnership A partnership made up of general partners and limited partners. The general partners manage the business and have unlimited liability; the limited partners do not manage the business and have limited liability.

Limited Liability A condition in which an owner of a business firm can only lose the amount invested (in the firm) by him or her. Stockholders of a corporation have limited liability.

Loss The amount of money by which total cost exceeds total revenue.

M

Macroeconomics The branch of economics that deals with human behavior and choices as they relate to the entire economy.

Maquiladoras A factory run by a U.S. company in Mexico.

Marginal Cost The change in total cost that results from producing an additional unit of output.

Marginal Revenue The change in total revenue that results from selling an additional unit of output.

Market Any place where people come together to buy and sell goods or services.

Medicaid A federal and state program that provides health care to low-income individuals by making government a third-party payer.

Medical Malpractice Suit Lawsuit brought against a physician by a patient who claims the physician acted negligently in his or her treatment.

Medicare A nationwide federal health insurance program for people over 65 and those of all ages with disabilities.

Medium of Exchange Anything that is generally acceptable in exchange for goods and services.

Merger A joining of two companies that occurs when one company buys more than half the stock in the other company. As a result, the companies come to act as one.

Microeconomics The branch of economics that deals with human behavior and choices as they relate to relatively small units—the individual, the business firm, a single market.

Minimum Wage Law A federal law that specifies the lowest hourly wage rate that can be paid to workers.

Mixed Economy An economy that has features of both free enterprise and socialism.

Monetary Policy The deliberate control of the money supply by the Fed.

Money A good that is widely accepted for purposes of exchange.

Money Supply The total supply of money in circulation, composed of currency, checking accounts, and traveler's checks. Everything that composes the money supply is widely accepted for purposes of exchange.

Monopolistic Competition A market structure in which (1) there are many buyers and many sellers, (2) sellers produce and sell slightly differentiated products, and (3) there is easy entry into and easy exit from the market.

Monopoly A market structure in which (1) there is a single seller, (2) the seller sells a product for which there are no close substitutes, and (3) there are extremely high barriers to entry.

Mortgage Note Written agreement by which a buyer of property agrees to repay a loan taken out to purchase the property. If the loan is not repaid, the lender can take the property.

Mutual Fund Financial organization that pools people's money and invests it.

N

National Brand A brand that is owned by the maker of the product. Many national brands are known across the country, such as Kellogg's and Coca-Cola.

National Debt The sum total of what the federal government owes its creditors.

Natural Monopoly The condition in which one firm has such a low average total cost (per-unit cost) that only it can survive in the market.

Natural Unemployment Unemployment that is caused by frictional and structural factors in the economy.

Near-Money Assets, such as nonchecking savings accounts, that can be easily and quickly turned into money.

Negative Externality An event or action that causes harm (an adverse side effect) to be felt by others.

Net Worth (Equity, Capital) The difference between assets and liabilities.

Neutral Good A good the demand for which remains unchanged as income rises or falls.

Normal Good A good the demand for which rises as income rises and falls as income falls.

O

Oligopoly A market structure in which (1) there are few sellers, (2) sellers produce and sell either identical or slightly differentiated products, and (3) there are significant barriers to entry.

Open-Market Operations Buying and selling of government securities by the Fed.

Opportunity Cost The most highly valued opportunity or alternative forfeited or given up when a choice is made.

P

Partnership A business that is owned by two or more co-owners called partners who share any profits the business earns and are legally responsible for any debts incurred by the firm.

Per-Capita Real Economic Growth An increase from one period to the next in per-capita GDP.

Per-Unit Cost The average cost of a good. For example, if $400,000 is spent to produce 100 cars, the average, or per-unit, cost is $4,000 ($400,000 ÷ 100 = $4,000).

Perfect Competition A market structure in which (1) there are many buyers and many sellers, (2) all firms sell identical goods, (3) buyers and sellers have all relevant information about buying and selling activities, and (4) there is easy entry into the market and easy exit out of the market.

Personal Income Tax A tax paid on a person's income.

Petrochemical A chemical substance obtained from petroleum or natural gas.

Point One percentage point of a loan amount. Points are paid by the borrower to the lender.

Population Growth Rate The birthrate minus the death rate.

Positive Externality An event or action that causes a benefit (a beneficial side effect) to be felt by others.

Poverty Line Income level below which people are considered to be living in poverty.

Price Index A measure of the price level, or the average level of prices.

Price Support The minimum price, as determined by government, that farmers will receive from buyers for their products. Not all agricultural products have price supports.

Private Brand A brand owned by a seller rather than by the maker of the product. For example, products are often produced for a specific supermarket chain and carry the name of that chain on the label.

Private Property Any good that is owned by an individual or a business. For example, suppose John, an individual living in Anywhere, USA, owns his own car. It follows that his car is his private property.

Private Good A good or product whose benefits can be denied to a person other than the owner. A car is a private good.

Production Possibilities Frontier (PPF) All possible combinations of two goods that an economy can produce in a certain period of time, under the conditions of a given state of technology, no unemployed resources, and efficient production.

Profit The amount of money left over after all the costs of production have been paid. Profit exists whenever total revenue is greater than total cost.

Progressive Income Tax An income tax whose rate increases as income level rises. Progressive income tax structures are usually capped at some rate.

Proportional Income Tax An income tax that everyone pays at the same rate, whatever the income level.

Public Franchise A right granted to a firm by government that permits the firm to provide a particular good or service and excludes all others from doing so.

Public Good A good or product whose benefits cannot be denied to anyone. National defense is a public good.

Public Property Any good that is owned by government.

Public Utility Commission Government group that regulates public utility companies (such as electric, water, and gas companies).

Q

Quantity Demanded The number of units of a good purchased at a specific price.

Quantity Supplied The number of units of a good produced and offered for sale at a specific price.

Quota A legal limit on the number of units of a foreign-produced good (or import) that can enter a country.

R

Rationing Device A means for deciding who gets what of available goods and resources.

Real Economic Growth An increase from one period to the next in real GDP.

Real GDP GDP that has been adjusted for price changes; GDP measured in base-year, or constant, prices.

Recession Part of the business cycle where real GDP contracts.

Regressive Income Tax An income tax whose rate decreases as income level rises.

Required Reserves The minimum amount of reserves a bank must hold against its deposits as mandated by the Fed.

Reserve Requirement A regulation which requires a bank to keep a certain percentage of each dollar deposited in the bank in its reserve account at the Fed or in its vault (as vault cash). In this chapter we have had numerous occasions to specify the percentage specified in the reserve requirement. We specify it this way, for example: Reserve requirement = 10 percent.

Resources Anything that is used to produce goods or services. For example, a person's labor may

be used to produce computers, TV sets, and much more, and therefore a person's labor is a resource. Resources fall into four categories: land, labor, capital, and entrepreneurship.

Résumé A statement of a job applicant's previous employment, education, and so on.

Right-to-Work Law A state law that prohibits the practice of requiring employees to join a union in order to work.

S

Savings Account An interest-earning account.

Scarcity The condition in which our wants are greater than the resources available to satisfy all those wants. Everyone, and every society, faces the basic problem of scarcity. There is scarcity in the United States, Russia, France, Argentina, and every other country in the world.

Security Deposit An amount of money a renter pays a landlord before moving into an apartment (or other rental property). The money is to be returned when the renter moves out, but the landlord may keep a part or all of it to make repairs or compensate for rent not paid.

Service An intangible item that gives a person utility or satisfaction.

Shortage The condition in which quantity demanded is greater than quantity supplied. Shortages occur only at prices below equilibrium price.

Simple Quantity Theory of Money A theory that predicts that changes in the price level will be strictly proportional to changes in the money supply.

Small Claims Court A trial court where cases involving claims of less than a certain amount, usually $2,500, are heard before a judge.

Socialism An economic system in which government owns and controls many of the resources. Government plays a major role in the economy.

Sole Proprietorship A business that is owned by one individual who makes all business decisions, receives all the profits or takes all the losses of the firm, and is legally responsible for the debts of the firm.

Specialize To do only one thing. For example, when a country specializes in the production of a good, it produces only that good.

Stagflation The occurrence of inflation and high unemployment at the same time.

Status Quo That which exists now; the existing state of affairs.

Stock A claim on the assets of a corporation that gives the purchaser a share of the ownership of the corporation.

Stockholder A person who owns shares of stock in a corporation. The stockholders of a corporation are the owners of the corporation.

Stop-and-Go, On-and-Off Monetary Policy Erratic monetary policy. The money supply is increased, then decreased, then increased, and so on. It is similar to driving a car by putting the accelerator to the floor, then slamming on the brakes, then putting the accelerator to the floor, then slamming on the brakes again, and so on.

Store of Value Something with the ability to hold value over time.

Strike A work stoppage called by members of a union to place pressure on an employer.

Structural Unemployment Refers to workers who have lost their jobs because of changing market (demand) conditions and whose skills do not match the requirements of available jobs. Unemployment that arises when the skills of available workers do not match the requirements of available jobs.

Subleasing Renting from a renter rather than from the owner.

Substitutes Similar goods. With substitutes, the price of one and the demand for the other move in the same directions.

Supply The willingness and ability of sellers to produce and offer to sell a good or service.

Supply Curve A graph showing the amount of a good sellers are willing and able to sell at various prices. Only the upward-sloping supply curve is a graphical representation of the law of supply.

Supply Schedule A numerical chart that illustrates the law of supply.

Supply-Side Inflation An increase in the price level that originates on the supply side of the economy.

Surplus The condition in which quantity supplied is greater than quantity demanded. Surpluses occur only at prices above equilibrium price.

T

Taft-Hartley Act An act, passed in 1947 by the U.S. Congress, which gave states the right to pass right-to-work laws. These right-to-work laws prohibit employers from establishing union membership as a condition of employment.

Tangible Able to be felt by touch. For example, a book is tangible: you can touch and feel it.

Target Price A guaranteed price set by government. If the market price is below the target price, the farmer receives from the government a deficiency payment equal to the difference between the market price and the target price. For example, if the target price is $8 per unit and the market price is $2, then the farmer receives a $6 deficiency payment per unit.

Technology The body of skills and knowledge concerning the use of resources in production.

Telemarketing Direct sales of products by telephone.

Third-Party Payer A term often used in regard to health care. Anyone, other than the patient, who pays a health care bill is referred to as a third-party payer. For example, when the government pays for the bills of persons over 65, it is a third-party payer making a third-party payment.

Total Cost The sum of fixed costs plus variable costs. Average cost (or expense) of a good, times the number of units of the good sold.

Total Reserves The sum of a bank's deposits in its reserve account at the Fed and its vault cash.

Total Revenue Price of a good, times the number of units of the good sold.

Trust A combination of firms that come together to act as a monopolist.

U

Unemployment Rate Percentage of the civilian labor force that is unemployed. The unemployment rate equals the number of persons unemployed divided by the number of persons in the civilian labor force.

Union Shop An organization that requires employees to join the union within a certain period after being hired.

Unit of Account A common measurement in which values are expressed.

Unit Price The total price of an item divided by its weight.

Unit-Elastic Demand When demand is unit elastic, the percentage change in quantity demanded is the same as the percentage change in price.

Unit-Elastic Supply When supply is unit elastic, the percentage change in quantity supplied is the same as the percentage change in price.

Unlimited Liability The legal responsibility of a sole proprietor of a business or a partner in a business to pay any money owed by the business. The proprietor's or partner's personal assets may be used to pay these debts.

Utility A synonym for this word is satisfaction.

V

Variable Cost Cost, or expense, that changes with the number of units of a good produced.

Velocity The average number of times a dollar is spent to buy final goods and services in a year.

Vicious Circle of Poverty The idea that countries are poor because they do not save and buy capital goods, but they cannot save and buy capital goods because they are poor.

Vision One's sense of how the world works.

W

Wage Rate The price of labor.

Wants Things that we desire to have.

Warranty A guarantee or an assurance given by a seller stating that a product is in good working order and that the seller will provide certain types of service for a period of time.

INDEX